THE TIMES
Guide to the House of Commons February 1974

Times Newspapers Limited

First published in Great Britain in 1974 by
Times Newspapers Ltd, Printing House Square, London EC4P 4DE

Copyright © Times Newspapers Limited 1974

ISBN 0 7230 0115 4

Designed by John Lucioni

Printed in Great Britain by Tonbridge Printers Limited

CONTENTS

General Election Map

Her Majesty's Government

The Cabinet

Prime Minister and First Lord of the Treasury
Mr Harold Wilson

Lord President of the Council and Leader of the House of Commons
Mr Edward Short

Secretary of State for Foreign and Commonwealth Affairs
Mr James Callaghan

Lord Chancellor
Lord Elwyn-Jones (formerly Sir Elwyn Jones)

Secretary of State for the Home Department
Mr Roy Jenkins

Chancellor of the Exchequer
Mr Denis Healey

Secretary of State for Employment
Mr Michael Foot

Secretary of State for Energy
Mr Eric Varley

Secretary of State for Social Services
Mrs Barbara Castle

Secretary of State for Industry
Mr Anthony Wedgwood Benn

Secretary of State for the Environment
Mr Anthony Crosland

Secretary of State for Scotland
Mr William Ross

Chancellor of the Duchy of Lancaster
Mr Harold Lever

Secretary of State for Trade
Mr Peter Shore

Secretary of State for Prices and Consumer Protection
Mrs Shirley Williams

Minister of Agriculture, Fisheries and Food
Mr Frederick Peart

Secretary of State for Defence
Mr Roy Mason

Secretary of State for Northern Ireland
Mr Merlyn Rees

Secretary of State for Wales
Mr John Morris

Secretary of State for Education and Science
Mr Reginald Prentice

Lord Privy Seal and Leader of the House of Lords
Lord Shepherd

Ministers not in the Cabinet

Minister of Overseas Development
Mrs Judith Hart

Paymaster General
Mr Edmund Dell

Parliamentary Secretary to the Treasury and Government Chief Whip in the House of Commons
Mr Robert Mellish

Attorney General
Mr Samuel Silkin

Solicitor General
Mr Peter Archer

Minister of State for Energy
Lord Balogh

Minister for Transport
Mr Frederick Mulley

Minister for Planning and Local Government
Mr John Silkin

Minister for Housing and Construction
Mr Reginald Freeson

Minister of State for Urban Affairs, Department of the Environment
Mr Charles Morris

Minister of State for Sport, Department of the Environment
Mr Denis Howell

Minister of State for Foreign and Commonwealth Affairs
Mr David Ennals

Minister of State for Foreign and Commonwealth Affairs
Mr Roy Hattersley

Minister of State for Industry
Mr Eric Heffer

Minister of State for Northern Ireland
Mr Stanley Orme

Chief Secretary to the Treasury
Mr Joel Barnett

Financial Secretary to the Treasury
Mr John Gilbert

Minister of State for Agriculture, Fisheries and Food
Mr Norman Buchan

Minister of State for Defence
Mr William Rodgers

Minister of State for Education and Science
Mr Gerald Fowler

Minister of State for Employment
Mr Albert Booth

Minister of State for Health and Social Security
Mr Brian O'Malley

Minister of State, Home Office
Mr Alexander Lyon

Minister of State, Home Office
Lord Harris of Greenwich
(formerly Mr John Harris)

Minister of State for Prices and Consumer Protection
Mr Alan Williams

Minister of State, Scottish Office
Mr Bruce Millan

Minister of State, Scottish Office
Lord Hughes

Lord Advocate
Mr Ronald King Murray

Minister of State for Civil Service
Mr Robert Sheldon

Minister of State for Industry and Deputy Leader of the House of Lords
Lord Beswick

Solicitor General for Scotland
Mr John McCluskey

Departments of State and Ministers

AGRICULTURE, FISHERIES AND FOOD

Minister
Mr Frederick Peart

Minister of State
Mr Norman Buchan

Parliamentary Secretary
Mr Roland Moyle

CIVIL SERVICE

Minister
The Prime Minister

Lord President of the Council (responsible for day-to-day administration)
Mr Edward Short

Minister of State
Mr Robert Sheldon

Parliamentary Secretary
Mr John Grant

DEFENCE

Secretary of State
Mr Roy Mason

Minister of State
Mr William Rodgers

Under Secretary for the Royal Navy
Mr Frank Judd

Under Secretary for the Army
Lord Brayley

Under Secretary for the RAF
Mr Brynmor John

DUCHY OF LANCASTER

Chancellor
Mr Harold Lever

EDUCATION AND SCIENCE

Secretary of State
Mr Reginald Prentice

Minister of State (with responsibilities for higher education)
Mr Gerald Fowler

Under Secretary (with responsibilities for the arts)
Mr Hugh Jenkins

Under Secretary
Mr Ernest Armstrong

EMPLOYMENT

Secretary of State
Mr Michael Foot

Minister of State
Mr Albert Booth

Under Secretary
Mr John Fraser

Under Secretary
Mr Harold Walker

5

ENERGY

Secretary of State
Mr Eric Varley

Minister of State
Lord Balogh

Under Secretary for Oil
Mr Gavin Strang

Under Secretary for Coal
Mr Alexander Eadie

ENVIRONMENT

Secretary of State
Mr Anthony Crosland

**Minister for Planning and Local
Government**
Mr John Silkin

Minister for Transport
Mr Frederick Mulley

Minister for Housing and Construction
Mr Reginald Freeson

Minister of State for Urban Affairs
Mr Charles Morris

Minister of State for Sport
Mr Denis Howell

Under Secretary
Mr Neil Carmichael

Under Secretary
Mr Gerald Kaufman

Under Secretary
Mr Gordon Oakes

FOREIGN AND COMMONWEALTH OFFICE

Secretary of State
Mr James Callaghan

Minister of State
Mr David Ennals

Minister of State
Mr Roy Hattersley

Under Secretary
Lord Goronwy-Roberts
  (formerly Mr Goronwy Roberts)

Under Secretary
Miss Joan Lestor

HEALTH AND SOCIAL SECURITY

Secretary of State for Social Services
Mrs Barbara Castle

Minister of State
Mr Brian O'Malley

Under Secretary for Health
Dr David Owen

Under Secretary for Social Security
Mr Robert Brown

**Under Secretary (with responsibilities
  for the disabled)**
Mr Alfred Morris

HOME OFFICE

Home Secretary
Mr Roy Jenkins

Minister of State
Mr Alexander Lyon

Minister of State
Lord Harris of Greenwich
  (formerly Mr John Harris)

Under Secretary
Dr Shirley Summerskill

INDUSTRY

Secretary of State
Mr Anthony Wedgwood Benn

Minister of State
Mr Eric Heffer

Minister of State
Lord Beswick

Under Secretary
Mr Gregor Mackenzie

Under Secretary
Mr Michael Meacher

LAW OFFICERS

Attorney General
Mr Samuel Silkin

Solicitor General
Mr Peter Archer

Lord Advocate
Mr Ronald King Murray

Solicitor General for Scotland
Mr John McCluskey

LORD CHANCELLOR
Lord Elwyn Jones
  (formerly Sir Elwyn Jones)

LORD PRESIDENT OF THE COUNCIL and Leader of the House of Commons
Mr Edward Short

LORD PRIVY SEAL and Leader of the House of Lords
Lord Shepherd

NORTHERN IRELAND OFFICE

Secretary of State
Mr Merlyn Rees

Minister of State
Mr Stanley Orme

Under Secretary
Lord Donaldson of Kingsbridge

OVERSEAS DEVELOPMENT

Minister
Mrs Judith Hart

Parliamentary Secretary
Mr William Price

PAYMASTER GENERAL

(attached to the Treasury)
Mr Edmund Dell

*POSTS AND TELECOMMUNICATIONS

Minister
Mr Anthony Wedgwood Benn

PRICES AND CONSUMER PROTECTION

Secretary of State
Mrs Shirley Williams

Minister of State
Mr Alan Williams

Under Secretary
Mr Robert MacLennan

SCOTTISH OFFICE

Secretary of State
Mr William Ross

Minister of State
Mr Bruce Millan

Minister of State
Lord Hughes

Under Secretary
Mr Robert Hughes

TRADE

Secretary of State
Mr Peter Shore

Under Secretary
Mr Eric Deakin

Under Secretary
Mr Stanley Clinton Davis

---

*Ministry to be abolished. Responsibility for Post Office Corporation transferred to Secretary of State for Industry and responsibility for broadcasting policy transferred to Home Secretary. Transfer of Functions Order approved in April 1974.

TREASURY

Prime Minister and First Lord of the Treasury
Mr Harold Wilson

Chancellor of the Exchequer
Mr Denis Healey

Paymaster General
Mr Edmund Dell

Chief Secretary
Mr Joel Barnett

Parliamentary Secretary and Government Chief Whip in the House of Commons
Mr Robert Mellish

Financial Secretary
Mr John Gilbert

Lords Commissioners (Government Whips)
Mr Donald Coleman
Mr James Dunn
Mr John Golding
Mr James Hamilton
Mr Thomas Pendry

Assistant Whips
Mr Michael Cocks
Mr Thomas Cox
Mr Ernest Perry
Mr Laurence Pavitt
Mr John Dormand

WALES

Secretary of State
Mr John Morris

Under Secretary
Mr Edward Rowlands

Under Secretary
Mr Barry Jones

HER MAJESTY'S HOUSEHOLD

Treasurer (Government Deputy Chief Whip)
Mr Walter Harrison

Comptroller
Mr Joseph Harper

Vice-Chamberlain
Mr John Concannon

Captain, Gentlemen at Arms (Government Chief Whip in the House of Lords)
Lady Llewelyn-Davies of Hastoe

Captain, Yeomen of the Guard
Lord Strabolgi

Lords-in-Waiting
Lord Jacques
Lord Garnsworthy
Lady Birk
Lord Wells-Pestell

The House of Commons

In this list of members returned to the House of Commons at the General Election on February 28, 1974, a † denotes new members. The abbreviations used to designate political parties include the following: Lab — Labour; Lab and Co-op — Labour and Co-operative; C — Conservative; L — Liberal; UUUC — United Ulster Unionist Coalition; Scot Nat — Scottish National; Pl Cymru — Plaid Cymru; SDLP —Social Democratic and Labour Party; Soc Dem—Campaign for Social Democracy.

A

ABSE, Leopold: *Pontypool*	Lab
ALISON, Michael: *Barkston, Ash*	C
ADLEY, Robert: *Christchurch and Lymington*	C
†AITKEN, Jonathan: *Thanet, East*	C
ALLASON, James: *Hemel Hempstead*	C
ALLAUN, Frank: *Salford, East*	Lab
AMERY, Julian: *Brighton, Pavilion*	C
†ANCRAM, Michael: *Berwick and East Lothian*	C
ANDERSON, Miss Harvie: *Renfrewshire, East*	C
ARCHER, Jeffrey: *Louth*	C
ARCHER, Peter: *Warley, West*	Lab
ARMSTRONG, Ernest: *Durham, North-West*	Lab
ASHLEY, Jack: *Stoke-on-Trent, South*	Lab
ASHTON, Joseph: *Bassetlaw*	Lab
ATKINS,Humphrey: *Spelthorne*	C
†ATKINS, Ronald: *Preston, North*	Lab
ATKINSON, Norman: *Haringey, Tottenham*	Lab
AWDRY, Daniel: *Chippenham*	C

B

BAGIER, Gordon: *Sunderland, South*	Lab
BAKER, Kenneth: *Cities of London and Westminster, St Marylebone*	C
BALNIEL, Lord: *Welwyn and Hatfield*	C
†BANKS, Robert: *Harrogate*	C
BARBER, Anthony: *Altrincham and Sale*	C
BARNETT, Guy: *Greenwich*	Lab
BARNETT, Joel: *Heywood and Royton*	Lab

†BATES, Alfred: *Bebington and Ellesmere Port* — Lab
BAXTER, William: *Stirlingshire, West* — Lab
BELL, Ronald: *Beaconsfield* — C
BENN, Anthony Wedgwood: *Bristol, South East* — Lab
†BENNETT, Andrew: *Stockport, North* — Lab
BENNETT, Sir Frederic: *Torbay* — C
BENNETT, Dr Reginald: *Fareham* — C
BENYON, William: *Buckingham* — C
BERRY, Anthony: *Enfield, Southgate* — C
BEITH, Alan: *Berwick upon Tweed* — L
BIDWELL, Sydney: *Ealing, Southall* — Lab
BIFFEN, John: *Oswestry* — C
BIGGS-DAVISON, John: *Epping Forest* — C
BISHOP, Edward: *Newark* — Lab
BLAKER, Peter: *Blackpool, South* — C
BLENKINSOP, Arthur: *South Shields* — Lab
BOARDMAN, Harold: *Leigh* — Lab
BOARDMAN, Tom: *Leicester, South* — C
BODY, Richard: *Holland with Boston* — C
BOOTH, Albert: *Barrow-in-Furness* — Lab
BOOTHROYD, Miss Betty: *West Bromwich, West* — Lab
BOSCAWEN, Robert: *Wells* — C
BOTTOMLEY, Arthur: *Teesside, Middlesbrough* — Lab
BOWDEN, Andrew: *Brighton, Kemptown* — C
BOYDON, James: *Bishop Auckland* — Lab
†BOYSON, Rhodes: *Brent, North* — C
†BRADFORD, Rev. Robert: *Belfast, South* — UUUC
BRADLEY, Tom: *Leicester, East* — Lab
BRAINE, Sir Bernard: *Essex, South-East* — C
BRAY, Ronald: *Rossendale* — C
BREWIS, John: *Galloway* — C
†BRITTAN, Leon: *Cleveland and Whitby* — C
BROCKLEBANK-FOWLER, Christopher: *Norfolk, North-West* — C
BROUGHTON, Sir Alfred: *Batley and Morley* — Lab
BROWN, Sir Edward: *Bath* — C
BROWN, Hugh: *Glasgow, Provan* — Lab
BROWN, Robert: *Newcastle upon Tyne, West* — Lab
BROWN, Ronald: *Hackney, South and Shoreditch* — Lab
BRUCE-GARDYNE, John: *Angus, South* — C
BRYAN, Sir Paul: *Howden* — C
BUCK, Anthony: *Colchester* — C
BUCHAN, Norman: *Renfrewshire, West* — Lab
BUCHANAN, Richard: *Glasgow, Springburn* — Lab
BUCHANAN-SMITH, Alick: *Angus, North and Mearns* — C
†BUDGEN, Nicholas: *Wolverhampton, South-West* — C
†BULMER, Esmond: *Kidderminster* — C
BURDEN, Frederick: *Gillingham* — C

BUTLER, Adam: *Bosworth*	C
BUTLER, Mrs Joyce: *Haringey, Wood Green*	Lab & Co-op

C

CALLAGHAN, James: *Cardiff, South-East*	Lab
†CALLAGHAN, James: *Middleton and Prestwich*	Lab
CAMPBELL, Ian: *Dunbartonshire, West*	Lab
CANT, Robert: *Stoke-on-Trent, Central*	Lab
CARLISLE, Mark: *Runcorn*	C
CARMICHAEL, Neil: *Glasgow, Kelvingrove*	Lab
CARR, Robert: *Sutton, Carshalton*	C
†CARSON, John: *Belfast, North*	UUUC
CARTER, Raymond: *Birmingham, Northfield*	Lab
CARTER-JONES, Lewis: *Eccles*	Lab
CASTLE, Mrs Barbara: *Blackburn*	Lab
†CHALKER, Mrs Lynda: *Wallasey*	C
CHANNON, Paul: *Southend, West*	C
CHATAWAY, Christopher: *Chichester*	C
CHURCHILL, Winston: *Stretford*	C
†CLARK, Alan: *Plymouth, Sutton*	C
CLARK, William: *Croydon, South*	C
CLARKE, Kenneth: *Rushcliffe*	C
CLEGG, Walter: *North Fylde*	C
†CLEMITSON, Ivor: *Luton, East*	Lab
†COCKROFT, John: *Nantwich*	C
COCKS, Michael: *Bristol, South*	Lab
COHEN, Stanley: *Leeds, South-East*	Lab
COLEMAN, Donald: *Neath*	Lab
†COLQUHOUN, Mrs Maureen: *Northampton, North*	Lab
CONCANNON, Dennis: *Mansfield*	Lab
CONLAN, Bernard: *Gateshead, East*	Lab
†COOK, Robin: *Edinburgh, Central*	Lab
COOKE, Robert: *Bristol, West*	C
†COPE, John: *Gloucestershire, South*	C
CORDLE, John: *Bournemouth, East*	C
CORMACK, Patrick: *Staffordshire, South-West*	C
†CORRIE, John: *Ayrshire, North and Bute*	C
COSTAIN, Albert: *Folkestone and Hythe*	C
COX, Thomas: *Wandsworth, Tooting*	Lab
†CRAIG, William: *Belfast, East*	UUUC
CRAWSHAW, Richard: *Liverpool, Toxeth*	Lab
†CRAIGEN, James: *Glasgow, Maryhill*	Lab
CRITCHLEY, Julian: *Aldershot*	C
CRONIN, John: *Loughborough*	Lab
CROSLAND, Anthony: *Grimsby*	Lab
CROUCH, David: *Canterbury*	C

CROWDER, Petre: *Hillingdon, Ruislip-Northwood*	C
†CRYER, Robert: *Keighley*	Lab
CUNNINGHAM, George: *Islington, South and Finsbury*	Lab
CUNNINGHAM, John: *Whitehaven*	Lab

D

DALYELL, Tam: *West Lothian*	Lab
DAVIDSON, Arthur: *Accrington*	Lab
†DAVIES, Bryan: *Enfield, North*	Lab
DAVIES, Denzil: *Llanelli*	Lab
DAVIES, Ifor: *Gower*	Lab
DAVIES, John: *Knutsford*	C
D'AVIGDOR-GOLDSMID, Maj-Gen James: *Lichfield and Tamworth*	C
DAVIS, Clinton: *Hackney, Central*	Lab
DEAKINS, Eric: *Waltham Forest, Walthamstow*	Lab
†DEAN, Joseph: *Leeds, West*	Lab
DEAN, Paul: *Somerset, North*	C
DEEDES, William: *Ashford*	C
DE FREITAS, Sir Geoffrey: *Kettering*	Lab
DELARGY, Hugh: *Thurrock*	Lab
DELL, Edmund: *Birkenhead*	Lab
DEMPSEY, James: *Coatbridge and Airdrie*	Lab
DIXON, Piers: *Truro*	C
DODDS-PARKER, Sir Douglas: *Cheltenham*	C
†DODSWORTH, Geoffrey: *Hertfordshire, South-West*	C
DOIG, Peter: *Dundee, West*	Lab
DORMAND, John: *Easington*	Lab
DOUGLAS-HOME, Sir Alec: *Kinross and West Perthshire*	C
DOUGLAS-MANN, Bruce: *Merton, Mitcham and Morden*	Lab
DRAYSON, Burnaby: *Skipton*	C
DU CANN, Edward: *Taunton*	C
DUFFY, Patrick: *Sheffield, Attercliffe*	Lab
†DUNLOP, John (*Ulster, Mid*)	UUUC
DUNN, James: *Liverpool, Kirkdale*	Lab
DUNNETT, Jack: *Nottingham, East*	Lab
†DUNWOODY, Mrs Gwyneth: *Crewe*	Lab
†DURANT, Anthony: *Reading, North*	C
DYKES, Hugh: *Harrow, East*	C

E

EADIE, Alexander: *Midlothian*	Lab
EDELMAN, Maurice: *Coventry, North-West*	Lab

EDEN, Sir John: *Bournemouth, West* — C
†EDGE, Geoffrey: *Aldridge-Brownhills* — Lab
EDWARDS, Nicholas: *Pembroke* — C
EDWARDS, Robert: *Wolverhampton, South-East* — Lab & Co-op
ELLIOTT, R. W.: *Newcastle upon Tyne, North* — C
†ELLIS, John: *Brigg and Scunthorpe* — Lab
ELLIS, Thomas: *Wrexham* — Lab
EMERY, Peter: *Honiton* — C
ENGLISH, Michael: *Nottingham, West* — Lab
†ENNALS, David: *Norwich, North* — Lab
EVANS, Alfred: *Caerphilly* — Lab
†EVANS, Ioan: *Aberdare* — Lab & Co-op
†EVANS, John: *Newton* — Lab
EWING, Harry: *Stirling, Falkirk and Grangemouth* — Lab
†EWING, Mrs Winifred: *Moray and Nairn* — Scot Nat
EYRE, Reginald: *Birmingham, Hall Green* — C

F

†FAIRGRIEVE, Russell: *Aberdeenshire, West* — C
FARR, John: *Harborough* — C
FAULDS, Andrew: *Warley, East* — Lab
FELL, Anthony: *Yarmouth* — C
FENNER, Mrs Peggy: *Rochester and Chatham* — C
FERNYHOUGH, Eric: *Jarrow* — Lab
FIDLER, Michael: *Bury and Radcliffe* — C
FINSBERG, Geoffrey: *Camden, Hampstead* — C
FISHER, Sir Nigel: *Kingston upon Thames, Surbiton* — C
FITCH, Alan: *Wigan* — Lab
FITT, Gerard: *Belfast, West* — SDLP
†FLANNERY, Martin: *Sheffield, Hillsborough* — Lab
FLETCHER, Alex: *Edinburgh, North* — C
FLETCHER, Edward: *Darlington* — Lab
FLETCHER, Raymond: *Ilkeston* — Lab
FLETCHER-COOKE, Charles: *Darwen* — C
FOOKES, Miss Janet: *Plymouth, Drake* — C
FOOT, Michael: *Ebbw Vale* — Lab
FORD, Benjamin: *Bradford, North* — Lab
FORRESTER, John: *Stoke-on-Trent, North* — Lab
†FOWLER, Gerald: *Wrekin, The* — Lab
FOWLER, Norman: *Sutton Coldfield* — C
FOX, Marcus: *Shipley* — C
FRASER, Hugh: *Stafford and Stone* — C
FRASER, John: *Lambeth, Norwood* — Lab
FREESON, Reginald: *Brent, East* — Lab
FREUD, Clement: *Isle of Ely* — L
FRY, Peter: *Wellingborough* — C

G

GALBRAITH, Thomas: *Glasgow, Hillhead*	C
GALPERN, Sir Myer: *Glasgow, Shettleston*	Lab
†GARDINER, George: *Reigate*	C
GARDNER, Edward: *South Fylde*	C
†GARRETT, John: *Norwich, South*	Lab
GARRETT, Edward: *Wallsend*	Lab
†GEORGE, Bruce: *Walsall, South*	Lab
GIBSON-WATT, David: *Hereford*	C
GILBERT, John: *Dudley, East*	Lab
GILMOUR, Ian: *Chesham and Amersham*	C
GILMOUR, Sir John: *Fife, East*	C
GINSBURG, David: *Dewsbury*	Lab
GLYN, Dr Alan: *Windsor and Maidenhead*	C
GODBER, Joseph: *Grantham*	C
GOLDING, John: *Newcastle-under-Lyme*	Lab
GOODHART, Philip: *Bromley, Beckenham*	C
GOODHEW, Victor: *St Albans*	C
†GOODLAD, Alistair: *Northwich*	C
GORST, John: *Barnet, Hendon, North*	C
GOURLAY, Harry: *Kirkcaldy*	Lab
†GOW, Ian: *Eastbourne*	C
GOWER, Sir Raymond: *Barry*	C
†GRAHAM, Edward: *Enfield, Edmonton*	Lab
GRANT, Anthony: *Harrow, Central*	C
GRANT, George: *Morpeth*	Lab
GRANT, John: *Islington, Central*	Lab
GRAY, Hamish: *Ross and Cromarty*	C
GRIEVE, Percy: *Solihull*	C
GRIFFITHS, Edward: *Sheffield, Brightside*	Lab
GRIFFITHS, Eldon: *Bury St Edmunds*	C
GRIMOND, Jo: *Orkney and Shetland*	L
†GRIST, Ian: *Cardiff, North*	C
GRYLLS, Michael: *Surrey, North-West*	C
GURDEN, Harold: *Birmingham, Selly Oak*	C

H

HALL, Sir John: *Wycombe*	C
HALL-DAVIS, Alfred: *Morecambe and Lonsdale*	C
HAMILTON, James: *Bothwell*	Lab
HAMILTON, Michael: *Salisbury*	C
HAMILTON, William: *Fife, Central*	Lab
HAMLING, William: *Greenwich, Woolwich, West*	Lab
†HAMPSON, Keith: *Ripon*	C

13

HANNAM, John: *Exeter*	C
HARDY, Peter: *Rother Valley*	Lab
HARPER, Joseph: *Pontefract and Castleford*	Lab
HARRISON, Sir Harwood: *Eye*	C
HARRISON, Walter: *Wakefield*	Lab
HART, Mrs Judith: *Lanark*	Lab
HASTINGS, Stephen: *Bedfordshire, Mid*	C
HATTERSLEY, Roy: *Birmingham, Sparkbrook*	Lab
HATTON, Frank: *Manchester, Moss Side*	Lab
HAVERS, Sir Michael: *Merton, Wimbledon*	C
HAWKINS, Paul: *Norfolk, South-West*	C
HAYHOE, Barney: *Hounslow, Brentford and Isleworth*	C
HEALEY, Denis: *Leeds, East*	Lab
HEATH, Edward: *Bexley, Sidcup*	C
HEFFER, Eric: *Liverpool, Walton*	Lab
†HENDERSON, Barry: *Dunbartonshire, East*	C
†HENDERSON, Douglas: *Aberdeenshire, East*	Scot Nat
HESELTINE, Michael: *Henley*	C
HIGGINS, Terence: *Worthing*	C
HILL, James: *Southampton, Test*	C
HOLLAND, Philip: *Carlton*	C
HOOLEY, Frank: *Sheffield, Heeley*	Lab
HOOSON, Emlyn: *Montgomeryshire*	L
HORAM, John: *Gateshead, West*	Lab
HORDERN, Peter: *Horsham and Crawley*	C
HOWE, Sir Geoffrey: *Surrey, East*	C
HOWELL, David: *Guildford*	C
HOWELL, Denis: *Birmingham, Small Heath*	Lab
HOWELL, Ralph: *Norfolk, North*	C
†HOWELLS, Geraint: *Cardigan*	L
HUCKFIELD, Leslie: *Nuneaton*	Lab
HUGHES, Cledwyn: *Anglesey*	Lab
HUGHES, Mark: *Durham*	Lab
HUGHES, Robert: *Aberdeen, North*	Lab
HUGHES, Roy: *Newport*	Lab
HUNT, John: *Bromley, Ravensbourne*	C
HUNTER, Adam: *Dunfermline*	Lab
†HURD, Douglas: *Oxon, Mid*	C
HUTCHISON, Michael Clark: *Edinburgh, South*	C

I

IREMONGER, Thomas: *Redbridge, Ilford, North*	C
IRVINE, Sir Arthur: *Liverpool, Edge Hill*	Lab
IRVINE, Godman: *Rye*	C
†IRVING, Sydney: *Dartford*	Lab

J

†JACKSON, Colin: *Brighouse and Spenborough*	Lab
JAMES, David: *Dorset, North*	C
JANNER, Greville: *Leicester, West*	Lab
JAY, Douglas: *Wandsworth, Battersea, North*	Lab
JEGER, Mrs Lena: *Camden, Holborn and St Pancras, South*	Lab
JENKIN, Patrick: *Redbridge, Wanstead and Woodford*	C
JENKINS, Hugh: *Wandsworth, Putney*	Lab
JENKINS, Roy: *Birmingham, Stechford*	Lab
JESSEL, Toby: *Richmond upon Thames, Twickenham*	C
JOHN, Brynmor: *Pontypridd*	Lab
JOHNSON, James: *Kingston upon Hull, West*	Lab
JOHNSON, Walter: *Derby, South*	Lab
JOHNSON-SMITH, Geoffrey: *East Grinstead*	C
JOHNSTON, Russell: *Inverness*	L
JONES, Alec: *Rhondda*	Lab
JONES, Arthur: *Daventry*	C
JONES, Barry: *Flint, East*	Lab & Co-op
JONES, Daniel: *Burnley*	Lab
*JONES, Sir Elwyn: *Newham, South*	Lab
JONES, Gwynoro: *Carmarthen*	Lab
JOPLING, Michael: *Westmorland*	C
JOSEPH, Sir Keith: *Leeds, North-East*	C
JUDD, Frank: *Portsmouth, North*	Lab

*Made life peer

K

KABERRY, Sir Donald: *Leeds, North-West*	C
KAUFMAN, Gerald: *Manchester, Ardwick*	Lab
KELLETT-BOWMAN, Mrs Elaine: *Lancaster*	C
KELLEY, Richard: *Don Valley*	Lab
KERR, Russell: *Hounslow, Feltham and Heston*	Lab
KERSHAW, Anthony: *Stroud*	C
KILFEDDER, James: *Down, North*	UUUC
†KILROY-SILK, Robert: *Ormskirk*	Lab
KIMBALL, Marcus: *Gainsborough*	C
KING, Evelyn: *Dorset, South*	C
KING, Tom: *Bridgwater*	C
KINNOCK, Neil: *Bedwellty*	Lab
KIRK, Peter: *Saffron Walden*	C
KITSON, Timothy: *Richmond, Yorks*	C
KNIGHT, Mrs Jill: *Birmingham, Edgbaston*	C
KNOX, David: *Leek*	C

L

Lambie, David: *Ayrshire, Central*	Lab
Lamborn, Harry: *Southwark, Peckham*	Lab
Lamond, James: *Oldham, East*	Lab
Lamont, Norman: *Kingston upon Thames*	C
Lane, David: *Cambridge*	C
Langford-Holt, Sir John: *Shrewsbury*	C
Latham, Arthur: *City of Westminster, Paddington*	Lab
†Latham, Michael: *Melton*	C
†Lawrence, Ivan: *Burton*	C
Lawson, George: *Motherwell and Wishaw*	Lab
†Lawson, Nigel: *Blaby*	C
Le Marchant, Spencer: *High Peak*	C
Leadbitter, Edward: *Hartlepool*	Lab
†Lee, John: *Birmingham, Handsworth*	Lab
†Lester, James: *Beeston*	C
Lestor, Miss Joan: *Eton and Slough*	Lab
Lever, Harold: *Manchester, Central*	Lab
Lewis, Arthur: *Newham, North-West*	Lab
Lewis, Kenneth: *Rutland and Stamford*	C
Lewis, Ronald: *Carlisle*	Lab
Lipton, Marcus: *Lambeth, Central*	Lab
Lloyd, Ian: *Havant and Waterloo*	C
Lloyd, Selwyn: *Wirral*	The Speaker
Lomas, Kenneth: *Huddersfield, West*	Lab
Loveridge, John: *Havering, Upminster*	C
Loughlin, Charles: *Gloucestershire, West*	Lab
†Loyden, Edward: *Liverpool, Garston*	Lab
Luce, Richard: *Shoreham*	C
Lyon, Alexander: *York*	Lab
Lyons, Edward: *Bradford, West*	Lab

M

Mabon, Dr Dickson: *Greenock and Port Glasgow*	Lab & Co-op
MacArthur, Ian: *Perth and East Perthshire*	C
MacCormick, Iain: *Argyll*	Scot Nat
†MacFarquhar, Roderick: *Belper*	Lab
†MacGregor, John: *Norfolk, South*	C
Mackenzie, Gregor: *Rutherglen*	Lab
MacLennan, Robert: *Caithness and Sutherland*	Lab
Macmillan, Maurice: *Farnham*	C
McNair-Wilson, Michael: *Newbury*	C
McNair-Wilson, Patrick: *New Forest*	C
McAdden, Sir Stephen: *Southend, East*	C
McBride, Neil: *Swansea, East*	Lab

McCartney, Hugh: *Dunbartonshire, Central*	Lab
McCrindle, Robert: *Brentwood and Ongar*	C
†McCusker, James: *Armagh*	UUUC
McElhone, Frank: *Glasgow, Queen's Park*	Lab
†Macfarlane, Neil: *Sutton and Cheam*	C
McGuire, Michael: *Ince*	Lab
McLaren, Martin: *Bristol, North-West*	C
McMillan, Thomas: *Glasgow, Central*	Lab
McNamara, Kevin: *Kingston upon Hull, Central*	Lab
†Madden, Max: *Sowerby*	Lab
Madel, David: *Bedfordshire, South*	C
†Magee, Bryan: *Waltham Forest, Leyton*	Lab
Mahon, Simon: *Bootle*	Lab
Mallalieu, J. P. W.: *Huddersfield, East*	Lab
Marks, Kenneth: *Manchester, Gorton*	Lab
Marquand, David: *Ashfield*	Lab
Marshall, Edmund: *Goole*	Lab
†Marshall, Michael: *Arundel*	C
Marten, Neil: *Banbury*	C
Mason, Roy: *Barnsley*	Lab
Mather, Carol: *Esher*	C
Maude, Angus: *Stratford-on-Avon*	C
Maudling, Reginald: *Barnet, Chipping Barnet*	C
Mawby, Ray: *Totnes*	C
Maxwell-Hyslop, Robin: *Tiverton*	C
Mayhew, Christopher: *Greenwich, Woolwich, East*	Lab
†Mayhew, Patrick: *Royal Tunbridge Wells*	C
Meacher, Michael: *Oldham, West*	Lab
Mellish, Robert: *Southwark, Bermondsey*	Lab
Mendelson, John: *Penistone*	Lab
Meyer, Sir Anthony: *Flint, West*	C
Mikardo, Ian: *Tower Hamlets, Bethnal Green and Bow*	Lab
Millan, Bruce: *Glasgow, Craigton*	Lab
†Miller, Hilary: *Bromsgrove and Redditch*	C
Miller, Dr Maurice: *East Kilbride*	Lab
Mills, Peter: *Devon, West*	C
Milne, Edward: *Blyth*	Ind Lab
Miscampbell, Norman: *Blackpool, North*	C
Mitchell, David: *Basingstoke*	C
Mitchell, Richard: *Southampton, Itchen*	Lab
Moate, Roger: *Faversham*	C
Molloy, William: *Ealing, North*	Lab
Molyneaux, James: *Antrim, South*	UUUC
Money, Ernle: *Ipswich*	C
Monro, Hector: *Dumfries*	C
†Moonman, Eric: *Basildon*	Lab
†Moore, John: *Croydon, Central*	C

MORE, Jasper: *Ludlow*	C
MORGAN, Geraint: *Denbigh*	C
MORGAN-Giles, Rear Adm M C: *Winchester*	C
MORRIS, Alfred: *Manchester, Wythenshawe*	Lab & Co-op
MORRIS, Charles: *Manchester, Openshaw*	Lab
MORRIS, John: *Aberavon*	Lab
†MORRIS, Michael: *Northampton, South*	C
MORRISON, Charles: *Devizes*	C
†MORRISON, Peter: *Chester, City of*	C
MOYLE, Roland: *Lewisham, East*	Lab
MUDD, David: *Falmouth and Camborne*	C
MULLEY, Frederick: *Sheffield, Park*	Lab
MURRAY, Ronald King: *Edinburgh, Leith*	Lab
MURTON, Oscar: *Poole*	C

N

NEAVE, Airey: *Abingdon*	C
†NEUBERT, Michael: *Havering, Romford*	C
†NEWENS, Stanley: *Harlow*	Lab & Co-op
†NEWTON, Anthony: *Braintree*	C
NICHOLLS, Sir Harmar: *Peterborough*	C
NORMANTON, Tom: *Cheadle*	C
NOTT, John: *St Ives*	C

O

OAKES, Gordon: *Widnes*	Lab
OGDEN, Eric: *Liverpool, West Derby*	Lab
O'HALLORAN, Michael: *Islington, North*	Lab
O'MALLEY, Brian: *Rotherham*	Lab
ONSLOW, Cranley: *Woking*	C
OPPENHEIM, Mrs Sally: *Gloucester*	C
ORBACH, Maurice: *Stockport, South*	Lab
ORME, Stanley: *Salford, West*	Lab
ORR, Capt. Laurence: *Down, South*	UUUC
OSBORN, John: *Sheffield, Hallam*	C
†OVENDEN, John: *Gravesend*	Lab
OWEN, Dr David: *Plymouth, Devonport*	Lab

P

PADLEY, Walter: *Ogmore*	Lab
PAGE, Graham: *Crosby*	C
PAGE, John: *Harrow, West*	C
PAISLEY, Rev. Ian: *Antrim, North*	UUUC

PALMER, Arthur: *Bristol, North-East*	Lab & Co-op
PARDOE, John: *Cornwall, North*	L
†PARK, George: *Coventry, North-East*	Lab
PARKER, John: *Barking, Dagenham*	Lab
PARKINSON, Cecil: *Hertfordshire, South*	C
PARRY, Robert: *Liverpool, Scotland Exchange*	Lab
†PATTIE, Geoffrey: *Chertsey and Walton*	C
PAVITT, Laurence: *Brent, South*	Lab & Co-op
PEART, Frederick: *Workington*	Lab
PENDRY, Thomas: *Stalybridge and Hyde*	Lab
PERCIVAL, Ian: *Southport*	C
PERRY, Ernest: *Wandsworth, Battersea, South*	Lab
PEYTON, John: *Yeovil*	C
†PHIPPS, Colin: *Dudley, West*	Lab
PINK, Bonner: *Portsmouth, South*	C
PRENTICE, Reginald: *Newham, North-East*	Lab
PRESCOTT, John: *Kingston upon Hull, East*	Lab
†PRICE, Christopher: *Lewisham, West*	Lab
PRICE, David: *Eastleigh*	C
PRICE, William: *Rugby*	Lab
PRIOR, James: *Lowestoft*	C
PYM, Francis: *Cambridgeshire*	C

Q

QUENNELL, Miss Joan: *Petersfield*	C

R

RADICE, Giles: *Chester-le-Street*	Lab
RAISON, Timothy: *Aylesbury*	C
†RATHBONE, John: *Lewes*	C
RAWLINSON, Sir Peter: *Epsom and Ewell*	C
REDMOND, Robert: *Bolton, West*	C
REES, Merlyn: *Leeds, South*	Lab
REES, Peter: *Dover and Deal*	C
REES-DAVIES, William: *Thanet, West*	C
†REID, George: *Stirlingshire, East and Clackmannan*	Scot Nat
RENTON, Sir David: *Huntingdonshire*	C
†RENTON, Timothy: *Sussex, Mid*	C
RHODES, Geoffrey: *Newcastle upon Tyne, East*	Lab & Co-op
RHYS-WILLIAMS, Sir Brandon: *Kensington and Chelsea, Kensington*	C
†RICHARDSON, Miss Josephine: *Barking*	Lab
RIDLEY, Nicholas: *Cirencester and Tewkesbury*	C
RIDSDALE, Julian: *Harwich*	C

19

†RIFKIND, Malcolm: *Edinburgh, Pentlands* — C
RIPPON, Geoffrey: *Hexham* — C
ROBERTS, Albert: *Normanton* — Lab
†ROBERTS, Gwilym: *Cannock* — Lab
ROBERTS, Michael: *Cardiff, North-West* — C
ROBERTS, Wyn: *Conway* — C
ROBERTSON, John: *Paisley* — Lab
RODERICK, Caerwyn: *Brecon and Radnor* — Lab
†RODGERS, George: *Chorley* — Lab
RODGERS, Sir John: *Sevenoaks* — C
RODGERS, William: *Teesside, Stockton* — Lab
†ROOKER, Jeffrey: *Birmingham, Perry Barr* — Lab
ROPER, John: *Farnworth* — Lab & Co-op
ROSE, Paul: *Manchester, Blackley* — Lab
†ROSS, Stephen: *Isle of Wight* — L
ROSS, William: *Kilmarnock* — Lab
†ROSS, William: *Londonderry* — UUUC
ROSSI, Hugh: *Haringey, Hornsey* — C
ROST, Peter: *Derbyshire, South-East* — C
ROWLANDS, Edward: *Merthyr Tydfil* — Lab
ROYLE, Anthony: *Richmond upon Thames, Richmond* — C

S

SAINSBURY, Timothy: *Hove* — C
ST JOHN-STEVAS, Norman: *Chelmsford* — C
SANDELSON, Neville: *Hillingdon, Hayes and Harlington* — Lab
SCOTT-HOPKINS, James: *Derbyshire, West* — C
†SEDGEMORE, Brian: *Luton, West* — Lab
†SELBY, Harry: *Glasgow, Govan* — Lab
†SHAW, Arnold: *Redbridge, Ilford, South* — Lab
†SHAW, Giles: *Pudsey* — C
SHAW, Michael: *Scarborough* — C
SHELDON, Robert: *Ashton-under-Lyne* — Lab
SHELTON, William: *Lambeth, Streatham* — C
SHERSBY, Michael: *Hillingdon, Uxbridge* — C
SHORE, Peter: *Tower Hamlets, Stepney and Poplar* — Lab
SHORT, Edward: *Newcastle upon Tyne, Central* — Lab
SHORT, Mrs Renee: *Wolverhampton, North-East* — Lab
SILKIN, John: *Lewisham, Deptford* — Lab
SILKIN, Samuel: *Southwark, Dulwich* — Lab
SILLARS, James: *Ayrshire, South* — Lab
SILVERMAN, Julian: *Birmingham, Erdington* — Lab
†SILVESTER, Frederick: *Manchester, Withington* — C
SINCLAIR, Sir George: *Dorking* — C

†Sims, Roger: *Bromley, Chislehurst*	C
Skeet, Trevor: *Bedford*	C
Skinner, Dennis: *Bolsover*	Lab
Small, William: *Glasgow, Garscadden*	Lab
Smith, Cyril: *Rochdale*	L
Smith, Dudley: *Warwick and Leamington*	C
Smith, John: *Lanarkshire, North*	Lab
†Snape, Peter: *West Bromwich, East*	Lab
†Spence, John: *Thirsk and Malton*	C
†Spicer, James: *Dorset, West*	C
†Spicer, Michael: *Worcestershire, South*	C
Spriggs, Leslie: *St Helens*	Lab
Sproat, Iain: *Aberdeen, South*	C
Stainton, Keith: *Sudbury and Woodbridge*	C
Stallard, Albert: *Camden, St Pancras North*	Lab
Stanbrook, Ivor: *Bromley, Orpington*	C
†Stanley, John: *Tonbridge and Malling*	C
Steel, David: *Roxburgh, Selkirk and Peebles*	L
†Steen, Anthony: *Liverpool, Wavertree*	C
Stewart, Donald: *Western Isles*	Scot Nat
†Stewart, Ian: *Hitchin*	C
Stewart, Michael: *Hammersmith, Fulham*	Lab
Stodart, Anthony: *Edinburgh, West*	C
Stoddart, David: *Swindon*	Lab
Stokes, John: *Halesowen and Stourbridge*	C
Stonehouse, John: *Walsall, North*	Lab & Co-op
Stott, Roger: *Westhoughton*	Lab
Stradling Thomas, J: *Monmouth*	C
Strang, Gavin: *Edinburgh, East*	Lab
Strauss, George: *Lambeth, Vauxhall*	Lab
Summerskill, Dr Shirley: *Halifax*	Lab
Swain, Thomas: *Derbyshire, North-East*	Lab

T

Tapsell, Peter: *Horncastle*	C
Taverne, Dick: *Lincoln*	Soc Dem
Taylor, Edward: *Glasgow, Cathcart*	C
Taylor, Robert: *Croydon, North-West*	C
Tebbit, Norman: *Waltham Forest, Chingford*	C
†Temple-Morris, Peter: *Leominster*	C
Thatcher, Mrs Margaret: *Barnet, Finchley*	C
†Thomas, Dafydd: *Merioneth*	Pl Cymru
Thomas, George: *Cardiff, West*	Lab
Thomas, Jeffrey: *Abertillery*	Lab
Thomas, Peter: *Barnet, Hendon, South*	C
†Thorne, Stanley: *Preston, South*	Lab

THORPE, Jeremy: *Devon, North*	L
†TIERNEY, Sydney: *Birmingham, Yardley*	Lab
TINN, James: *Teesside, Redcar*	Lab
†TOMLINSON, John: *Meriden*	Lab
TOMNEY, Frank: *Hammersmith, North*	Lab
TORNEY, Thomas: *Bradford, South*	Lab
†TOWNSEND, Cyril: *Bexley, Bexleyheath*	C
†TROTTER, Neville: *Tynemouth*	C
TUCK, Raphael: *Watford*	Lab
TUGENDHAT, Christopher: *City of London and Westminster, South*	C
†TYLER, Paul: *Bodmin*	L

U

URWIN, Thomas: *Houghton-le-Spring*	Lab

V

VARLEY, Eric: *Chesterfield*	Lab
VAUGHAN, Dr Gerard: *Reading, South*	C
†VIGGERS, Peter: *Gosport*	C
Van STRAUBENZEE, William: *Wokingham*	C

W

WADDINGTON, David: *Nelson and Colne*	C
WAINWRIGHT, Edwin: *Dearne Valley*	Lab
†WAINWRIGHT, Richard: *Colne Valley*	L
†WAKEHAM, John: *Maldon*	C
WALDEN, Brian: *Birmingham, Ladywood*	Lab
WALDER, David: *Clitheroe*	C
WALKER, Harold: *Doncaster*	Lab
WALKER, Peter: *Worcester*	C
†WALKER, Terence: *Kingswood*	Lab
WALKER-SMITH, Sir Derek: *Hertfordshire, East*	C
WALL, Patrick: *Haltemprice*	C
WALTERS, Dennis: *Westbury*	C
WARREN, Kenneth: *Hastings*	C
WATKINS, David: *Consett*	Lab
†WATT, Hamish: *Banffshire*	Scot Nat
WEATHERILL, Bernard: *Croydon, North-East*	C
WEITZMAN, David: *Hackney, North and Stoke Newington*	Lab

WELLBELOVED, James: *Bexley, Erith and Crayford*	Lab
WELLS, John: *Maidstone*	C
†WEST, Harry: *Fermanagh and South Tyrone*	UUUC
WHITE, James: *Glasgow, Pollok*	Lab
WHITEHEAD, Phillip: *Derby, North*	Lab
WHITELAW, William: *Penrith and the Border*	C
WHITLOCK, William: *Nottingham, North*	Lab
WIGGIN, Jerry: *Weston-super-Mare*	C
†WIGLEY, Dafydd: *Caernarvon*	Pl Cymru
WILLEY, Frederick: *Sunderland, North*	Lab
WILLIAM, Alan: *Swansea, West*	Lab
†WILLIAMS, Alan Lee: *Havering, Hornchurch*	Lab
WILLIAMS, Mrs Shirley: *Hertford and Stevenage*	Lab
WILLIAMS, Thomas: *Warrington*	Lab & Co-op
WILSON, Alexander: *Hamilton*	Lab
†WILSON, Gordon: *Dundee, East*	Scot Nat
WILSON, Harold: *Huyton*	Lab
WILSON, William: *Coventry, South-East*	Lab
†WINSTANLEY, Dr Michael: *Hazel Grove*	L
WINTERTON, Nicholas: *Macclesfield*	C
†WISE, Mrs Audrey: *Coventry, South-West*	Lab
WOOD, Richard: *Bridlington*	C
†WOODALL, Alec: *Hemsworth*	Lab
WOODHOUSE, Christopher: *Oxford*	C
WOOF, Robert: *Blaydon*	Lab
WORSLEY, Sir Marcus (*Kensington and Chelsea, Chelsea*	C
†WRIGGLESWORTH, Ian: *Teesside, Thornaby*	Lab & Co-op

Y

†YOUNG, David: *Bolton, East*	Lab
†YOUNG, Sir George: *Ealing, Acton*	C
YOUNG, George: *Ayr*	C

The General Election of February 1974

Mr Harold Wilson, Leader of the Labour Party and Prime Minister from 1964 to 1970, was asked to form a Government on the evening of Monday March 4, three days after it had become clear that no party would have an overall majority in the Commons. Mr Edward Heath resigned as Prime Minister two hours before Mr Wilson was called to Buckingham Palace. Labour had been in Opposition since June 19, 1970. The new Cabinet was announced on March 5.

The state of the parties compared with the composition of the Commons at dissolution and at the General Election of 1970 was:

	General Election 1974	Dissolution 1974	General Election 1970
Labour	301	287	287
Conservative	296	322	330
Liberal	14	11	6
The Speaker	1	1	1
Others	23*	8	6
Vacant	—	1	—

*United Ulster Unionist Coalition, 11; Scottish National Party, 7; Plaid Cymru, 2; Social Democratic and Labour Party, 1; Social Democracy, 1; Independent Labour, 1.

Details of the seats which changed hands:-

From Conservative to Labour — Bolton, East; Brighouse and Spenborough; Chorley; Gravesend; Keighley; Liverpool, Garston; Middleton and Prestwich; Preston, North; Preston, South; Redbridge, Ilford, South; Stockport; North.

From Labour to Conservative — Berwick and East Lothian.

From Liberal to Conservative — Ripon; Sutton, Sutton and Cheam.

From Conservative to Liberal — Isle of Wight.

From Labour to Liberal — Cardigan; Colne Valley.

From Labour to Plaid Cymru — Caernarvon; Merioneth.

From Labour to Scottish National Party — Dundee, East; Stirlingshire, East and Clackmannan.

From Conservative to Scottish National Party — Aberdeenshire, East; Argyll; Banff-shire; Moray and Nairn.

From Labour to Independent Labour — Blyth.

From Ulster Unionist to United Ulster Unionist Coalition — Armagh; Down, South; Londonderry.

From Ind Unity to UUUC — Ulster, Mid.

From Unity to UUUC — Fermanagh and South Tyrone.

There were 2,135 candidates nominated for the February 1974 General Election. Labour (including Northern Ireland Labour Party) contested 627 seats; Conservatives and pro-Assembly Unionists 630; Liberal 517; Scottish National 70; Plaid Cymru 36; National Front 54; Communists 44; Others (including the Speaker) 157. This is the highest number of candidates since the war.

The 'Inevitable' Election

by George Clark
Political Correspondent of *The Times*

The general election of February 28, 1974, was the first since 1931 to be fought in a period of acute economic crisis. This had been brought on by the decision of the National Union of Mineworkers first, to ban overtime working and, later, to strike, with drastic effects on electricity supplies and industrial activity. The situation was made worse by the decision of the Arab oil-producing states to reduce the production of oil and to increase its price fourfold.

That was an aftermath of the Middle East war which had begun on October 6, 1973, with simultaneous attacks on Israel by Egypt and Syria, and was ended on October 22. The Arab States used the oil weapon for the first time in an attempt to persuade Western nations to support the Arab cause and cease military aid to Israel.

First rumbles of discontent in the mines came on July 3, 1973, when the NUM formally rejected the Government's wage restraint policy and submitted a package claim for increases which would have put over £100m. on to the National Coal Board's wages and pensions bill.

On November 12 Britain's 270,000 miners began an overtime ban in support of their claim. Immediately, the Government reacted. A State of Emergency was declared with effect from midnight on November 13 and restrictions were imposed on the use of electricity. The 'Switch Off Something' (SOS) campaign was begun to persuade people to reduce electricity consumption in the home.

The NUM rejected on November 21 an offer which, with a productivity bonus that was still subject to approval by the Pay Board, would have given an average wage increase of 13 per cent or £44m., against the miners' claim for 31 per cent or £105m. The Government brought in the Fuel and Electricity (Control) Bill giving new powers to control the production, supply and use of petrol and petroleum products.

Mr Harold Wilson, the Leader of the Opposition, appearing in a television programme, called on the Government to allow 'elasticities' in Stage 3 of the prices and incomes policy to get a settlement with the miners. Next day, November 23, Mr Heath accused Mr Wilson of having encouraged the miners to refuse the offer made by the NCB within the limits of Stage 3.

Queues began to form at petrol stations in London and the south-east; motorists were 'topping up' their tanks in anticipation of rationing. On November 26 it was announced that petrol ration coupons were to be issued from November 29 as a precaution. (It was never necessary to enforce rationing.)

Mr Heath continued his efforts to persuade the miners to call off their industrial action and accept the settlement offered within the criteria of Stage 3. They refused and turned down a request that there should be a ballot on the issue (November 28). Government changes were announced on December 2. Mr William Whitelaw, who had obtained agreement on the future constitution of Ulster as Secretary of State for Northern Ireland, was made Secretary of State for Employment and there were high hopes that his skill as a negotiator would bring a settlement with the miners.

The State of Emergency was renewed on December 12, and it was announced that electricity supplies to industry would have to be cut, necessitating the introduction of a three-day week from January 1, 1974. Exemptions were made for key industries and for food manufacturers and farmers.

The Labour Party, led by Mr Anthony Wedgwood Benn, the shadow minister for industry, challenged the need for a three-day week, referring to the level of stocks of fuel at the power stations. Meanwhile, on December 12, the train drivers belonging to ASLEF had begun a ban on overtime and Sunday working in support of a claim for a new wage structure on British Rail. Their industrial action caused widespread disruption of services in the London area.

Mr Heath began the New Year with a letter to Mr Benn saying that the electricity cuts were necessary in order to conserve fuel, and pointed out that 'To give way to wage demands which go beyond what the nation can afford and beyond the Stage 3 code would lead to a situation in which the economy would be damaged infinitely more [than by the three-day week]'.

Opposition leaders condemned the ASLEF action and urged them to use the established arbitration procedure.

Parliament resumed on January 9 for a two-day emergency debate on the economic and industrial crisis. Hints had been dropped by ministers since mid-December that the Government would go to the country on the 'Who governs Britain?' issue. The dispute with the miners had reached deadlock. The NUM went ahead with a ballot of members on strike action. Mr Heath later condemned the way the question was put: it was a test of loyalty to the leadership rather than a ballot on the exact terms offered by the NCB.

The ballot papers stated: 'The national executive committee has rejected as unsatisfactory the Board's offer to increase wages and fringe benefits within the Government's formula (details of the offer have been widely circulated) and recommend members to give the Committee permission to call a national strike in support of our efforts to obtain a satisfactory response to our claim on behalf of all our members. Are you in favour of the National Executive being given authority to call a national strike?'

On February 4 it was announced that 86 per cent of the NUM members had voted, and 81 per cent of those voting backed the national executive call for a strike. On the same day at 10 Downing Street Mr Heath and other senior Ministers saw representatives of the TUC over the role which the Relativities Report from the Pay Board could play in getting a settlement with the miners, but the meeting broke down without agreement.

Brushing aside a last-minute peace plea from Mr Whitelaw, the miners' executive decided on February 5 to call a national strike from February 10. The challenge to the Government was clear and final. Mr Mick McGahey, the Communist vice-chairman of the NUM, and Mr Laurence Daly, general secretary, had made it clear in speeches in November that the industrial action was designed to bring the Conservative Government down.

The Government's argument for an election on the 'Who governs Britain?' issue was held by Mr Heath and his colleagues to have been further demonstrated when Mr McGahey, in a speech in Scotland, said the miners would appeal to the troops for help if they were called in to move coal during the strike. On January 29, Mr Wilson and five leading Labour MPs tabled a Commons motion repudiating Mr McGahey's suggested intention to appeal to the troops and to use the miners' strike to effect a change of government. On January 30, Mr McGahey issued a satement saying that he would not advise troops to disobey orders because it was an industrial dispute which did not concern them; it would be wrong for them to disobey orders. The Commons motion was eventually signed by 114 Labour MPs.

In January there had still been a few members of the Cabinet resisting the pressure from the Conservative Central Office and the constituencies for an election, but after the miners' strike decision there was agreement that an appeal to the country had become 'inevitable' or 'unavoidable'. The alternative, it was argued, would be to wreck the prices and incomes policy by giving in to the miners, thus opening the way for a series of leapfrogging wage claims.

Mr Jim Prior, Lord President of the Council and Leader of the Commons, a close confidante of the Prime Minister, told political reporters at the Parliamentary Press Gallery lunch on February 6 that the Government had gone 'as far as we possibly can to reach an agreement.'

Next day, at 12.45 p.m., Mr Heath announced from 10 Downing Street that he had called a general election for February 28, that Parliament would be dissolved on February 8 and the new Parliament open on March 12. Mr Enoch Powell, Conservative MP for Wolverhampton, South-West, promptly announced that he would not stand in 'an essentially fraudulent election'.

Mr Heath accompanied his announcement with letters to Mr Wilson, Mr Jeremy Thorpe, the Liberal leader, and Mr Joseph Gormley, president of the NUM. He appealed to the NUM executive, in the national interest, to consider suspending the national coal strike during the period of the election campaign.

Mr Heath appealed to both Mr Wilson and Mr Thorpe to support this request. Mr Thorpe did so, but Mr Wilson replied by making a counter-attack on the Government for their handling of the dispute. In a speech on February 8 he expressed regret that the NUM executive had not agreed with Mr Gormley that the pits strike should be called off during the election. 'I am sorry it was not called off, but the fact is that Mr Heath had delayed too long—for three months—the prospect of meaningful negotiations.' The miners were still demanding 'cash on the table.'

Mr Heath commented: 'It is a sad and shameful thing that the Leader of the Labour Party gave no reply and took no action. He knew what it would mean in terms of hardship for the millions of ordinary people who have to go about their daily business in their homes and at work.'

The battle lines for the election were now being drawn. For Mr Heath and the Conservatives it was an appeal to the nation for support in 'Firm Action for a Fair Britain', meaning support for the decision of Parliament on measures to fight inflation against a challenge from 'militants' and 'extremists' in the trade unions who were out to wreck it; indeed, he said they wanted an end to parliamentary democracy itself.

But the Conservative leaders were still being criticised, even by loyal backbenchers, for calling an election when they had an overall majority of 15 and still eighteen months to run in office. If firm and fair government held the secret of success, why should Mr Heath and his colleagues not soldier on, striving for a solution of the miners' dispute?

Mr Heath, in his broadcast on February 7, admitted that people were asking: 'What will an election prove?' He gave the answer: 'An election gives you, the people, the chance to say to the miners and to everyone else who wields similar power in Britain, "Times are hard. We are all in the same boat, and if you sink us now, we will all drown".

"Once you have said that, then the Government you elect will be in a far stronger position to reach a settlement with the miners which safeguards your interests as well as theirs".

'There are some people involved in the mining dispute who have made it clear that what they want is to bring down the elected government—not just this Government but any government. You have seen them on television, and I have seen them at first hand. The great majority of you are fed up to the teeth with them and with the disruption that they cause.'

As Parliament dissolved on February 8, the miners' executive rebuffed Mr Heath's truce appeal and voted 20 to 6 in favour of going ahead with the strike on February 10.

On the same day, the Labour Party launched its manifesto under the slogan: 'Let us work together: Labour's way out of the Crisis.' Later this became: 'Get Britain back to work—Vote Labour.' The party leaders gave a pledge that a future Labour government would not impose a statutory incomes policy; in place of confrontation there would be conciliation.

As the campaign advanced, Mr Wilson spoke of the 'social contarct' agreed with the TUC which would resolve industrial disputes and beat inflation. It meant, said Mr Wilson, that a bargain would be struck involving fairer taxation, better housing, a fairer system of education and a better health service. In return, the unions would co-operate by voluntary wage restraint.

Two days later (February 19) Mr Heath claimed that something said on television byMr Hugh Scanlon, President of the engineers' union, nad shown that this 'social contract' between Labour and the TUC did not exist. Mr Wilson retorted that he had been refer- ring to the document agreed between the party and the TUC on February 18, 1973, later published under the title *Economic policy and the cost of living*.

Mr Hugh Scanlon, at a meeting in Romford on February 22, said he was fully aware that attempts would be made to capitalise on his statement and added: 'Let me emphatically confirm that there is a social contract.' It was the document drawn up jointly by the TUC, the Parliamentary Labour Party and the Labour national executive. This referred to action which would be taken in the first parliamentary session of a Labour government which would allow the unions, on a voluntary basis and under free collective bargaining, to recognise in their wage claims the contribution which these measures made in living standards. The unions would abide by their pledge, said Mr Scanlon, but to call it an agreed incomes policy, with all it conjured up to working people, would create misunderstandings which should be avoided.

In London and on his swift visits to key marginal constituencies in England, Scotland and Wales, Mr Heath was stern and unbending; he spoke of the extremists and wreckers within the unions who had challenged the Government's attempt to lay down a fair prices and incomes policy. He got loud cheers from his supporters when he said that the unions should be asked to bear the costs of strike action and not the rest of the community through social security payments to strikers' families.

His attack on Labour was curt. The last Labour government had shown that it was 'a pushover' when strong unions opposed it on industrial relations and on its prices and incomes policy. It had 'abjectly surrendered,' and would do so again. Mr Heath appealed everywhere for a strong majority for a Government which would carry out a fair and firm incomes policy; given that majority, the moderates would be strengthened and the militants would see that the nation had rejected them.

The Liberal Party's manifesto, *You can Change the Face of Britain*, published on February 12, proposed a penal tax on inflationary wage settlements, to be imposed on both employers and employees. The Conservatives said that the system proposed would be an 'administrative nightmare' and would cause prices to rise even faster.

Mr Thorpe, the Liberal leader, also called for a settlement of the miners' dispute on honourable terms and gave his backing when, on February 14, Mr Wilson proposed a summit meeting of political and industrial leaders to try for a solution. But Mr Heath, speaking at Birmingham later the same day, rejected the idea since the Government had already referred the miners' case to the Pay Board for further consideration in the light of the Relativities Report. Mr Heath continued to rebuke Mr Wilson for not joining in the appeal to the miners to call off their strike.

A reported offer of £2·5m. from some anonymous industrialists to increase miners' pay caused a flurry on February 12, but it came to nothing. Mr Wilson turned his attack on to rising prices and criticised that element in price increases caused by the Government's own actions.

In this context Britain's membership of the European Economic Community was blamed for some price increases and Mr Callaghan, the shadow Foreign Secretary, pledged that Britain would refuse to implement tariff changes due to take effect on April 1 under the transitional arrangements.

The mineworkers put their case to the relativities inquiry and on February 21 the Government was embarrassed by the discovery that some figures given at earlier investigations had not accurately shown the relative position of the miners. Mr Wilson promptly weighed in with an accusation that the Prime Minister had given wrong figures in the Commons. He cited this as further evidence that Mr Heath had never wanted to settle with the miners, that he had needed the miners' strike to stage the election.

Next day Mr Heath was furious. He said there had been no error. For twenty years or more, the Coal Board and the miners' union had dealt with wage claims on a certain basis. All that had happened was that the NUM had now proposed a completely new basis. It had always been open for the NUM to have proposed this in the past if they had wanted it.

By the end of the second week of the campaign the public opinion polls were showing Conservatives ahead of Labour by margins varying from 0·5 to 6·5 per cent, with Liberals increasing their support to between 16·5 per cent and 23·5 per cent.

This prompted both Mr Heath and Mr Wilson to pay more attention to the middle ground of politics. Mr Heath, in Exeter, talked of the 'wobbling voters' who believed there was some easy way out of the present difficulties, and appealed to them to throw their weight behind the fair policies propounded by the Tories. The Government needed to be returned with a strong majority, he said. Mr Wilson thought the Liberals' increased support was coming from the former Conservative ranks and he was not unduly worried. But he made it clear: 'So long as I lead the party there will be no coalition with the Liberals, the Conservatives, or anybody else.'

On February 23, having decided not to fight the election, Mr Enoch Powell made a speech at Birmingham in which he explained that the supreme issue for him was the way Britain had been 'hi-jacked' into the Common Market without the opportunity of choosing. He implied that people who, like him, opposed entry, should vote for the only party which offered a choice to the people, following a renegotiation of the terms: the Labour Party.

For Mr Heath it was another blow when on February 25 it was announced that the gap on visible trade in January was £383m., the biggest monthly deficit in history. Mr Heath said it emphasised the gravity of the situation and justified his call for a new mandate to govern through the crisis months ahead.

Another shock caused dismay in the Conservative camp when on February 26 Mr Campbell Adamson, director-general of the Confederation of British Industry, who had been closely involved in the Downing Street talks over the miners' dispute, called for the repeal of the Industrial Relations Act which, he said, had sullied every relationship between employers and unions at national level.

First reaction from Mr Heath was to emphasise that Mr Campbell Adamson was expressing a personal view and not the official verdict of the CBI. In the Downing Street talks they had never expressed that view. When the election was over, Mr Heath confessed that this intervention did have a bad effect on the Conservative election campaign.

The election was for 635 seats in the House of Commons, compared with 630 in the last Parliament, and polling produced a virtual deadlock between the two main parties. It was largely due to the bigger impact of the Liberals, and the swirling cross-currents produced in Northern Ireland by the Ulster Unionists (now divided on the Conservative Government's proposals), and in Scotland and Wales by the nationalists.

The result: Labour 301, Conservatives 297, Liberals 14 (a poor return for the 6m. votes cast for them), Scottish Nationalists 7, Welsh Nationalists 2, United Ulster Unionists 11, others 3. After a Cabinet meeting on March 1, Mr Heath went from Downing Street to Buckingham Palace to report to the Queen; he did not resign but began negotiations with Mr Jeremy Thorpe, the Liberal leader, for a coalition. The 14 Liberals met in a basement interview room at the House of Commons on March 4 to consider a letter from Mr Heath to Mr Thorpe setting out the possible basis for coalition.

By the time the Liberal MPs met, many Liberals in the country had expressed firm opposition to the party entering into a coalition; they argued that it would lead to the death of the party. Both the Cabinet at 10 Downing Street, and the Shadow Cabinet in Mr Wilson's room at the House of Commons, were in session when the Liberal answer came. Coalition was rejected. Instead, they submitted: 'We believe that the only way in which the maximum degree of national co-operation can be achieved is for a Government of national unity to be formed to include members of all Parties to carry out a limited programme on those matters of overriding priority. This would have our enthusiastic support.'

At the Cabinet meeting, the second of that day, the Liberal proposal was turned down, and at 6.20 p.m. Mr Heath left for the Palace to resign.

The Queen sent for Mr Wilson, and at 8.25 p.m. he and Mrs Wilson arrived at 10 Downing Street. Mr Wilson said on the doorstep: 'We have a job to do. We can only do that job as one people, and I am going right in to start that job now.' The Liberal idea of a government of national unity had been peremptorily dismissed by the Shadow Cabinet.

After the Relativities Report had been studied, new negotiations were begun between the NUM and the NCB. On March 6, the NCB put forward a revised offer to the NUM which gave surface workers £30 a week, underground men £35, and face workers £44.50. This represented an increase of about 29 per cent (or £103m.) on the NCB's wage bill, and the miners' leaders promptly decided to recommend acceptance to their members. The miners agreed and returned to full working on March 11, the day before the new Parliament was opened by the Queen.

The Voting Surveyed

by Professor Richard Rose
University of Strathclyde

The outcome of the February 1974 General Election showed how tenuous is the assertion that Britain has a two-party system. The proposition has never been true as a statement about the number of candidates contesting the Election. In 1974, the total number of candidates rose to a record number of 2,135, an average of 3·4 candidates per constituency, and 293 more than fought the 1970 election. The 517 Liberal candidates were the largest number the party had put forward since the General Election of 1906.

Given such an opportunity to support someone other than a Conservative or Labour candidate, voters did so in numbers unprecedented since the 1920s. In 1929, the Conservative and Labour parties together polled 75·2 per cent of the total vote. In 1974, they polled 75·4 per cent of the vote. By contrast, in 1970, the two largest parties had taken 89·4 per cent of the total vote, and in 1951, 96·8 per cent.

The move away from two party alternatives was pronounced in England as well as other parts of the United Kingdom. In 1970, the Conservative and Labour parties collectively took 91·5 per cent of the English vote; in 1974, their share fell to 77·8 per cent. In Wales, the two Major parties took 72·7 per cent of the vote, and in Scotland, 69·5 per cent. Northern Ireland electors decisively rejected British parties, casting only 15·2 per cent of their vote for candidates supporting the Conservative or Labour parties in the Westminster House of Commons.

The move away from the two major parties was sufficiently great to prevent the electoral system from manufacturing a House of Commons majority for one party. At no Election since 1935 has any party won more than half the popular vote. But at every Election since then, one party has had sufficient votes to ensure that its over-representation in terms of parliamentary seats gave it an absolute majority in the House of Commons. This did not occur in 1974.

The Labour Party won 47 per cent of the seats in the House of Commons with 37·2 per cent of the vote. The Conservatives won 46·6 per cent of the seats with 1·0 per cent more votes than Labour. Among the two major parties, the Conservatives thus suffered the greater disadvantage, since for the first time since 1951 the party winning more votes won fewer seats in the Commons. But Labour's leadership was frustrated by the result, for it left the party 17 seats short of a parliamentary majority.

The electoral system worked true to form in awarding far more seats in proportion to votes to the various Nationalist parties that clustered their support in a limited number of constituencies than to the Liberals, the only lesser party to contest seats throughout Britain. The Liberals won one seat for every 433,000 votes, as against the Scottish National Party's record of winning one seat for every 90,000 votes, and Plaid Cymru's achievement in taking one seat for every 85,000 votes.

The disparities of seats in relation to votes are almost as striking between Nationalists and Liberals, as between the Liberals and the two major parties. With 19·3 per cent of the United Kingdom vote, the Liberals won 14 seats. With 5·4 per cent of the United Kingdom vote, a variety of Nationalist and other candidates won 24 seats. The Liberals thus took 0·7 seats for each per cent of the vote won, whereas 'fourth force' candidates took 4·4 seats for each per cent of the United Kingdom vote taken. The Conservatives won 7·7 seats for each per cent of the vote, and Labour, 8·1 seats.

Had seats in the House of Commons been awarded strictly in proportion to votes, then the Conservatives would have emerged the largest party, with 242 seats, and Labour second with 236 seats, both far short of an overall parliamentary majority. The Liberals would have won 123 seats, and Nationalists and other candidates 34.

The swing away from both major parties was evidenced by the fact that the Conservative share of the vote dropped by 8·2 per cent, and Labour's share by 5·8 per cent. Because the Labour share dropped less, it thus benefited from a swing of 1·2 per cent. But the swing at the 1974 Election, unlike previous swings, did not so much reflect a transfer of votes from one major party to another, but rather a differential success in holding core support against losses to lesser parties.

The redistribution of parliamentary constituencies further complicates any calculation of swing, for in more than 300 seats there is no proper basis for comparing votes at the 1970 and 1974 elections.

Analysis of the seats where Liberals intervened in 1974 showed that their presence hurt the Conservatives, for estimated swings in such seats were one per cent above the national figure. In seats fought by Liberals in both Elections, there was no swing to Labour. In part this was because many were safe Conservative seats, in which the Liberal rise drew votes from electors who were otherwise faced with the prospect of 'wasting' a vote on a weak Labour candidate. The 'dumping' of weaker candidates thus resulted in 28 Labour candidates losing their deposits, the largest total for the party since 1929.

The complexities of redistribution and the differential impact of Liberal intervention make regional comparisons difficult. The swing to Labour appeared less in the South of England (except for Greater London) and above the national average in the Midlands, where the Liberals were at their weakest. In Scotland and Wales the rise in Nationalist votes had as its by-product a nominal swing to the Conservatives, because Labour lost more to the Nationalists.

Both parties succeeded in mobilising their traditional supporters, estimated by students of voting behaviour at between 35 and 40 per cent of the national vote. Such success was illustrated by the above-average swing to Labour in the cities, and the above average performance of the Conservatives in suburban and rural areas. The price of mobilising traditional support was that both major parties drove away floating voters.

In voting against the two major parties, the electorate carefully discriminated between candidates of established lesser parties, and extremist or independent candidates. All 54 of the National Front candidates lost their deposits, notwithstanding their efforts at running a professional election campaign. All but one of the 44 Communist candidates (Jimmy Reid, in Central Dunbartonshire) lost their deposits. Everywhere independents ran badly. Dick Taverne succeeded in Lincoln and Edward Milne at Blyth because each had had an established position, as the local Labour MP, prior to breaking away to stand as an independent Socialist candidate.

The conventional definition of swing is of little meaning in assessing the rise in vote for the lesser parties, because swing is defined as a net movement of votes between the Conservative and Labour parties. It is necessary to take swing apart, and examine the variations in support for individual parties.

The Liberals showed the greatest rises in popular support, increasing their total share of the national vote by 11·8 per cent from 7·5 per cent in 1970. Four per cent of the rise in total Liberal vote can be attributed to the fact that the number of Liberal candidates increased by more than half. The bulk of the increase reflects a real rise in Liberal support among the electorate. The increase in Liberal strength is shown by the fact that the party lost the smallest proportion of deposits in relation to its number of candidates since the 1927 Election.

The Scottish National Party showed a significant gain in votes, too. In 1970, 65 SNP candidates took 11·4 per cent of the Scottish vote. In 1974, the SNP fought all but one of the 71 Scottish constituencies, and polled 21·9 per cent of the Scottish vote. Of this increase in votes, nearly all (9·4 per cent) was accounted for by greater popular support. The distinctive appeal of the SNP showed most clearly on the East Coast of Scotland, the region most affected by the North Sea oil boom. The SNP won four seats from Dundee to Aberdeenshire East, campaigning aggressively on the oil issue. The Liberals, by contrast, failed to win three neighbouring seats where they had been strong: Aberdeenshire West, Ross and Cromarty, and Caithness and Sutherland.

Plaid Cymru's share of the vote in Wales dropped from 11·5 per cent in 1970 to 10·7 per cent in 1974, even though it once again contested all Welsh constituencies. The Plaid succeeded in winning its first two General Election victories, at Merioneth and Caernarvon, and its President, Gwynfor Evans, lost Carmathen by three votes. The Liberals showed a resurgence of strength in Wales, fighting 31 seats, against 19 in 1970; and their total share of the Welsh vote rose from 6·8 per cent to 16·0 per cent. In addition, the Liberals won Cardigan as their second Welsh seat.

In Ulster, party lines were drawn differently from the rest of the United Kingdom. The Northern Ireland Labour Party nominated four candidates for the Province's twelve seats, and three lost their deposits. The Unionists who had accepted the British Conservative policy for an Ulster Assembly and a Council of Ireland contested seven seats, winning none and losing two deposits. Eleven of the twelve seats were won by various Loyalist spokesmen opposed to the policies of government settled on the Province by the United Kingdom Parliament a year ago. Anti-Council of Ireland candidates took an unambiguous majority of the total vote; the Loyalists won 51·1 per cent and various pro-Republican candidates, 7·8 per cent. Of the vote supporting pro-Assembly, pro-Council of Ireland candidates, 22·4 per cent was cast for candidates of the predominantly Catholic Social Democratic and Labour Party, and 18·7 for various Unionist and non-sectarian candidates.

The turnout of voters rose surprisingly little from the post-war low of 72·0 per cent recorded in 1970. The fact that the electoral register was four months newer than in June 1970 accounted for at least three per cent of the additional vote. The widespread press advertising of the postal vote should also have increased the number voting. The turnout of 78·7 per cent thus indicated that the electoral outcome did not reflect a panic decision by millions of apathetic voters stimulated by fears of a political crisis. It was a normal turnout that produced the abnormal result.

Table of the Polls

First and last poll results published during election campaign

Poll	Con	Lab	Lib	Date of Fieldwork
ORC	42 39·7	40 36·7	16 21·2	Feb. 8–10 Feb. 27
NOP	43·4 39·5	37·8 35·5	16·9 22	Feb. 14–17 Feb. 23–27
Louis Harris ..	46 40·2	35 35·2	18 22	Feb. 12–13 Feb. 26–27
Marplan ..	45 36·5	39 34·5	12 25	Feb. 8–9 Feb. 27
Gallup ..	44·5 39·5	43 37·5	11 20·5	Feb. 8–11 Feb. 26–27
Business Decisions ..	44·9 36	37·2 37·5	11·9 23	Feb. 7 Feb. 21
Actual Result	38·2	37·2	19·3	Feb. 28

House of Commons
Elected in February, 1974

Abbreviations used to designate the principal political parties include the following: C—Conservative; Lab—Labour; Co-op—Co-operative; L—Liberal; Scot Nat—Scottish National; Pl Cymru—Plaid Cymru; Comm—Communist; Nat Front—National Front; UUUC—United Ulster Unionist Council; UU Pro-Assembly—Ulster Unionist Pro-Assembly; Soc Dem—Campaign for Social Democracy; SDLP—Social Democratic and Labour Party; NI Lab—Northern Ireland Labour; WRP—Workers' Revolutionary Party. A * denotes a member of the last Parliament.

The percentages of the votes cast for each candidate and of the majority, in relation to the total poll in each constituency, and the swing figures (+ to Conservative) are calculated to the nearest decimal place, as well as the turnout of the electorate. Following upon the boundary changes, constituencies marked 'major' are those where there was a major revision of boundaries, 'minor' those with minor revisions, and 'same' those where there was been no change.

ABERAVON   minor

Electorate 64,164. 1970: 62,481

*Morris, J. (Lab)	31,656
Hubbard-Miles, P. C. (C)	10,968
Foster, The Rev D. G. (Pl Cymru)	5,898
Lab majority	20,688

No change

	1970		1974	
Total vote	46,747		48,522	
Turnout	74·8%		75·6%	
Lab	31,314	67·0%		65·2%
C	10,419	22·3%		22·6%
Pl Cymru	3,912	8·4%		12·1%
Comm	1,102	2·3%		—
Lab maj	20,895	44·7%		42·6%
Swing		+4·9%		+1·0%

Mr John Morris, QC, an Opposition spokesman on defence 1970-74; Minister of Defence for Equipment, 1968 - 70; Parliamentary Secretary, Ministry of Power, 1964-66. Elected in 1959. Barrister (Gray's Inn, 1954). B November, 1931; ed University College of Wales Aberystwyth, Gonville and

Caius College, Cambridge, and the Academy of International Law, The Hague. Chairman, **PLP** defence group, 1971-74; Welsh Labour group 1970-71, and Welsh parliamentary party 1972-73. *Appointed Secretary of State for Wales, March 1974.*

Mr Peter Hubbard-Miles, businessman, was elected to Glamorgan County Council in 1967, and to Porthcawl UDC in 1970. B 1927; ed Lewis Grammar School, Pengam. Elected, Mid-Glamorgan County Council 1973.

The Rev D. G. Foster, aged 29; ed Hornchurch Grammar School, Essex, King's College, London and Chichester Theological College. Member, Mid-Glamorgan County Council.

ABERDARE   same

Electorate 48,025. 1970: 48,771

Evans, I. L. (Lab & Co-op)	23,805
Owen, G. (Pl Cymru)	11,973
Niblock, M. J. (C)	3,169
Wilson, Dr A. T. M. (Comm)	1,038
Lab majority	11,832

No change

	1970		1974
Total Vote	38,049		39,985
Turnout	78·0%		83·2%
Lab and Co-op			59·5%
Lab	22,817	60·0%	
Pl Cymru	11,431	30·0%	29·9%
C	2,484	6·5%	7·9%
Comm	1,317	3·5%	2·6%
Lab and Co-op maj			29·6%
Lab maj	11,386	29·9%	
Swing		+4·0%	+0·9%

Mr Ioan Evans was Comptroller of the Household (whip), 1968-70; an assistant Government whip, 1966-68. He was MP for Birmingham, Yardley, 1964 - 70. Director of the International Defence and

Aid Fund. B July, 1927; ed Llanelli Grammar School and Swansea University College. Party agent in the Birmingham, Small Heath, elections, 1955 and 1959. Former chairman of the West Midlands group of Labour MPs.

Mr Glyn Owen is Plaid Cymru's full-time regional director for East Glamorgan. B 1932. Member, Mid-Glamorgan County Council and Aberdare District Council.

Mr Michael Niblock, head of foreign affairs section of the Conservative Research Department. B 1941; ed Leighton Park School and LSE. Lecturer in political science at Bristol University, 1959-62.

Dr Alistair Wilson, medical practitioner, contested the seat 1970, 1966 and 1950. B 1913; ed Downing College, Cambridge,

University College, Exeter, Welsh National School of Medicine. Chairman, Welsh branch Medical Practitioners' Union.

ABERDEEN North   minor

Electorate 64,349.   1970: 63,833

*Hughes, R. (Lab)	23,193
McGugan, J. (Scot Nat)	11,337
Dunnett, G. (C)	8,115
McCallum, F. (L)	6,001
Lab majority	11,856

No change

	1970		1974
Total Vote	44,626		48,646
Turnout	69·9%		75·6%
Lab	27,707	62·1%	47·7%
C	9,807	22·0%	16·7%
Scot Nat	3,756	8·4%	23·3%
L	2,835	6·3%	12·3%
Comm	521	1·2%	—
Lab maj	17,900	40·1%	24·4%
Swing		+3·4%	+4·5%

Mr Robert Hughes, draughtsman. Elected in 1970. B. January, 1932; ed Benoni High School, Transvaal and Pietermaritzburg Technical College, Natal. Contested North Angus and Mearns, 1959. Member, Aberdeen Town Council 1962 to 1970. Chairman, Aberdeen City Labour Party, 1963-69. Sponsored by AUEW, engineering section. *Appointed Under Secretary, Scottish Office, March 1974.*

Mr James McGugan contested North Angus and Mearns, 1970. Agricultural seedsman. B July, 1937; ed Doune School, Letham, Angus and Forfar Academy. Arbroath councillor, 1968-71.

Dr Gavin Dunnett. B August, 1949; ed Edinburgh Academy and Wellington College. Studied medicine at Aberdeen University.

Mr Forbes McCallum contested the seat in 1970. Personnel manager. B June 10, 1947. ed Aberdeen Grammar School, Aberdeen University and Robert Gordon's Institute of Technology. General Secretary, Scottish League of Young Liberals 1968-69. Member, Scottish Liberal Party Executive.

ABERDEEN South   minor

Electorate 67,379.   1970: 68,020

*Sproat, I. M. (C)	21,938
Middleton, R. (Lab)	18,380
Stronach, A. (Scot Nat)	7,599
Robbie, A. (L)	7,447
C majority	3,558

No change

	1970		1974
Total Vote	52,509		55,364
Turnout	77·2%		82·2%
C	23,843	45·4%	39·6%
Lab	22,754	43·3%	33·2%
L	3,135	6·0%	13·4%
Scot Nat	2,777	5·3%	13·7%
C maj	1,089	2·1%	6·4%
Swing		+2·8%	+2·1%

Mr Iain Sproat runs his own group of companies. Won the seat for the Conservatives in 1970; contested Rutherglen in by-election and general election, 1964. B November, 1938; ed Winchester; Magdalen College, Oxford. Former *Sunday Telegraph* columnist. Chairman, Conservative foreign affairs committee, East Europe group. Treasurer, Anglo-Soviet Group.

Mr Robert Middleton, assistant executive engineer, Post Office telephones. B July, 1932; ed Holburn Primary School, Aberdeen and Aberdeen Grammar School. Contested Banffshire, 1966. Member, Aberdeen Town Council, 1961-68; chairman education committee 1966-68, and external member since 1969.

Mr Alexander Stronach, lecturer. B June, 1937; ed Inverurie Academy and Robert Gordon's Institute of Technology. Chairman, Bucksburn and District Branch SNP.

Mr Angus Robbie is a careers officer at Aberdeen University. B May 28, 1937; ed Robert Gordon's College, Aberdeen and Aberdeen University. Former Liberal agent, Sutton Coldfield and Aberdeen.

ABERDEENSHIRE East   same

Electorate 47,147.   1970: 45,711

Henderson, D. (Scot Nat)	18,333
*Wolrige-Gordon, P. (C)	12,634
Cruickshank, W. (L)	2,727
Sissons, Mrs S. B. (Lab)	2,416
Scot Nat majority	5,699

Scot Nat gain

	1970		1974
Total Vote	31,447		36,110
Turnout	68·8%		76·6%
C	12,866	40·9%	35·0%
Scot Nat	9,377	29·8%	50·8%
Lab	5,656	18·0%	6·7%
L	3,548	11·3%	7·5%
C maj	3,489	11·1%	—
Scot Nat maj			15·8%
Swing		+1·7%	

Mr Douglas Henderson, management consultant. B July, 1935; ed Royal High School and Edinburgh University, Senior vice-chairman, SNP, until 1972. Appointed Whip to SNP parliamentary party, and spokesman on finance, trade and industry March 1974.

Mr Patrick Wolrige-Gordon was returned at a by-election in November, 1958, when still an undergraduate. B August, 1935; ed Eton and New College, Oxford. Secretary, Conservative Parliamentary fisheries committee 1964-74.

Mr William Cruickshank, farmer. B September 1923; ed Longside Secondary School, Aberdeenshire. Member Aberdeen County Council.

Mrs Beverley Sissons, aged 35, formerly teacher of English and social studies at Falkirk Technical College, now teaches English at Peterhead Prison in prisoners' rehabilitation programme.

ABERDEENSHIRE West   minor

Electorate 54,704. 1970: 52,108

Fairgrieve, R. (C)	17,256
Gracie, D. C. P. (L)	15,616
Suttar, M. (Scot Nat)	6,827
Ellis, C. W. (Lab)	4,661
C majority	1,640

No change

	1970		1974
Total Vote	39,496		44,360
Turnout	75·8%		81·1%
C	18,396	46·6%	38·9%
L	12,847	32·5%	35·2%
Lab	6,141	15·5%	10·5%
Scot Nat	2,112	5·3%	15·4%
C maj	5,549	14·0%	3·7%
Swing		+4·2%	−1·3%

Mr Russell Fairgrieve has been vice-chairman of the Conservative Party in Scotland since 1972. A management consultant. B May, 1924; ed St Mary's School, Melrose, and Sedbergh School, Yorkshire. Manager, Border Counties Trustee Savings Bank and governor, Scottish College of Textiles and St Mary's School, Melrose. President, Scottish Conservative Association, 1965-66.

Mr David Gracie, computer consultant. B October, 1934; ed Edinburgh Academy and University College, Oxford. Contested Canterbury, 1970.

Mr Mathew Suttar, technical representative. B December, 1942; ed Peterhead Academy, Vice-chairman, East Aberdeen SNP Constituency Association.

Mr William Ellis, senior lecturer at Robert Gordon's Institute of Technology. B November, 1921; ed Oxted County School and University College, London. Member, Aberdeen City Council.

ABERTILLERY   same

Electorate 36,810. 1970: 37,350

*Thomas, J. (Lab)	20,068
Richards, A. (Pl Cymru)	3,119
Hamilton, N. (C)	2,730
Clark, H. (L)	2,632
Lab majority	16,949

No change

	1970		1974
Total Vote	28,048		28,549
Turnout	75·1%		77·5%
Lab	22,819	81·4%	70·3%
C	3,478	12·4%	9·6%
Pl Cymru	1,751	6·2%	10·9%
L			−9·2%
Lab maj	19,341	68·9%	59·4%
Swing		+3·6%	+4·1%

Mr Jeffrey Thomas, a barrister (Gray's Inn). Elected in 1970; contested Barry in 1957 and 1966. B November, 1933; ed Abertillery Grammar School, King's College, London. President, London University Union, 1955-56. Member, Council, British Caribbean Association. Deputy Assistant Director, Army Legal Services 1960.

Mr Aneurin Richards, senior mining engineer. Ed University College, Cardiff. Qualified chartered engineer; Fellow of Institute of Work Study Practitioners. Islwyn district councillor; vice-president, Newbridge Rugby Club.

Mr Neil Hamilton is an economist and teacher. B 1950.

Mr Hugh Clark, clerk. B March, 1935; ed Gwent College. Newport Councillor.

ABINGDON   minor

Electorate 89,252. 1970: 85,838

*Neave, A. M. S. (C)	34,771
Moriarty, D. E. H. (Lab)	21,028
Fogarty, M. (L)	18,458
C majority	13,743

No change

	1970	1974
Total Vote	66,543	74,257
Turnout	77·5%	83·2%
C	36,209 54·4%	46·8%
Lab	23,136 34·8%	28·3%
L	7,198 10·8%	24·8%
C maj	13,073 19·6%	18·5%
Swing	+7·0%	−0·5%

	1970	1974
Total Vote	41,062	42,259
Turnout	80·2%	83·8%
Lab	20,828 50·7%	47·4%
C	20,234 49·3%	35·5%
L	—	17·0%
Lab maj	594 1·4%	11·9%
Swing	+7·7%	−5·2%

Mr Airey Neave, chairman, Select Committee Science and Technology since 1970; was Under-Secretary for Air, January to October, 1959, after being Parliamentary Secretary, Ministry of Transport and Civil Aviation from January, 1957. Director, Clarke Chapman, Ltd, a company in the Clarke Chapman—John Thompson Group, power station engineers. Returned at a by-election, June, 1953; contested Thurrock 1950 and Ealing, North 1951. B January 1916; ed Eton and Merton College, Oxford. Barrister (Middle Temple, 1943) and author. Escaped from Colditz in 1942 and reached United Kingdom via Switzerland and Gibraltar. Commanded operation to rescue allied pilots from behind enemy lines. Took part in Nuremburg trials and was Commissioner for Criminal Organizations. Chairman, standing conference of British organization for aid to refugees; UK delegate to UN high commission for refugees since 1970. Member, executive, 1922 Committee from March 1974.

Mr Denis Moriarty, television director. B July, 1935; ed Reading School and St John's College, Oxford. Member, Henley-on-Thames Borough Council since 1968. ABS, and ACTT.

Mr Michael Fogarty contested Devizes in 1966, and at the by-election and general election in 1964. B October, 1916; ed Ampleforth College and Christ Church, Oxford. Social scientist. Senior Fellow, Centre for Studies in Social Policy, London; Professor of Industrial Relations, Administrative Staff College, Henley.

ACCRINGTON same

Electorate 50,396. 1970: 51,193

*Davidson, A. (Lab)	20,050
Fearn, A. d'A. (C)	15,018
Cooper, W. I. (L)	7,191
Lab majority	5,032

No change

Mr Arthur Davidson, chairman, Labour parliamentary Home Office group since 1971, was elected in 1966; contested Preston, North, 1959, and Blackpool, South, 1955. Barrister (Middle Temple, 1953). B November, 1928; ed Liverpool College, King George V School, Southport, and Trinity College, Cambridge. Hon legal adviser, Southport Trades Council. NUGMW. On council of Consumer Association.

Mr Alan Fearn contested Ashton-under-Lyne in 1970. Dental surgeon. B July, 1924; ed Bury Grammar School, Shrewsbury School, and Guy's Hospital. Member, Rochdale Borough Council, 1955-60.

Mr William Cooper, deputy headmaster. B February, 1933; ed Preston Grammar School and City of Leeds Training College. Contested Haltemprice in 1959. Member, Haslingden Borough Council 1967-74.

ALDERSHOT major

Electorate 79,839

*Critchley, J. M. G. (C)	29,401
Floyd, G. (L)	18,743
Card, W. L. J. T. (Lab)	15,492
Greenslade, T. (Nat Front)	1,148
C majority	10,658

	1974		1974
Total Vote	64,784	Lab	23·9%
Turnout	81·1%	Nat Front	1·8%
C	45·4%	C maj	16·4%
L	28·9%		

Mr Julian Critchley, an author and journalist, was elected in 1970. MP for Rochester and Chatham, 1959-64; contested seat in 1966. Vice-chairman, Conservative backbench broadcasting and communications committee. B December, 1930; ed Shrewsbury School, Sorbonne, and Pembroke College, Oxford. Chairman of Bow Group and of Crossbow, 1966-67; president, Atlantic Association of Young Political Leaders, 1968;

chairman, Blue Ribbon Club; author of a number of Bow Group pamphlets.

Mr Gareth Floyd is a freelance book illustrator. B December, 1940; ed Sir John Leman Grammar School, Beccles, Lowestoft School of Art, Guildford School of Art and Brighton College of Art. Guildford borough councillor, 1971-74, Surrey county councillor from 1973.

Mr John Card, accountant. B August, 1939; ed Mellow Lane Comprehensive, Hillingdon. Member, Farnborough UDC 1966-68, 1971-74, and Rushmoor District Council since 1973.. TSSA and ASTMS.

Mr Tony Greenslade, businessman, aged 29.

ALDRIDGE-BROWNHILLS major

Electorate 61,051

Edge, G. (Lab)	19,642
*Hornsby-Smith, Dame P. (C)	19,276
Crofton, J. A. (L)	11,883
Lab majority	366

	1974		1974
Total vote	50,801	C	37·9%
Turnout	83·2%	L	23·4%
Lab	38·7%	Lab maj	0·7%

Mr Geoffrey Edge, university lecturer at the Open University. B May, 1943; ed grammar school, London School of Economics and Birmingham University. Member, Bletchley Urban District Council; Milton Keynes District Council.

Dame Patricia Hornsby-Smith represented Chislehurst, 1970-74 and 1950-66. Parliamentary Secretary, Ministry of Pensions and National Insurance, 1959-61; Parliamentary Secretary, Ministry of Health, 1951-57, and Under-Secretary, Home Office, 1957-59. Director, Sutton Harbour Improvement Co, and Abern Associates Ltd. B March, 1914; ed Richmond Grammar School. Council member, Investors' and Shareholders' Association; chairman, appeal committee, Arthritis and Rheumatism Council. Member, London Housing Society; Barnes Borough Council, 1945-49; Commons Services Committee and catering committee.

Mr John Crofton, a chartered engineer, is technical adviser to Southern Universities and part time lecturer, Open University.

B December, 1915; ed College of Technology, Rotherham; College of Aeronautical Engineering, London; University of Edinburgh; College of Advanced Technology; University of Manchester and University of Caen and Paris. Contested Birmingham, Sparkbrook, 1970. Member, Marple UDC and Stockport District Council since 1973.

ALTRINCHAM AND SALE same

Electorate 72,676. 1970: 70,703

*Barber, A. P. L. (C)	26,434
Blackburn, D. (L)	17,738
Rutherford, D. (Lab)	15,550
C majority	8,696

No change

	1970		1974
Total Vote	52,450		59,722
Turnout	74·2%		82·2%
C	27,904	53·2%	44·3%
Lab	16,671	31·8%	26·0%
L	7,875	15·0%	29·7%
C maj	11,233	21·4%	14·6%
Swing		+4·0%	−1·5%

Mr Anthony Barber, Chancellor of the Exchequer, 1970-74. Chancellor of the Duchy of Lancaster, June-July, 1970, with responsibility for EEC negotiations. Chairman of the Conservative Party Organisation, 1967-70; was Opposition spokesman on trade, industry and steel. Minister of Health, 1963-64; Financial Secretary to the Treasury, 1962-63; Economic Secretary, 1959-62. Returned at by-election, February, 1965; represented Doncaster, 1951-64; contested Doncaster, 1950. A Lord Commissioner of the Treasury, 1957-58. B July, 1920; ed Oriel College, Oxford. While prisoner of war took a law degree with first-class honours. Called to the Bar (Inner Temple) 1948. Former chairman, Redfearn National Glass Ltd, and former director, Chartered Bank and British Ropes Ltd. Appointed to Shadow Cabinet March 1974.

Mr Desmond Blackburn, managing director of Sutcliffe Catering Company (Northern) Ltd. B June, 1920; ed Shrewsbury School.

Mr Derek Rutherford, director of the National Council on Alcoholism. B August, 1939; ed Easington Secondary Modern School, Ryhope Grammar School, Sunderland, Leeds University and London University. APEX.

ANGLESEY same

Electorate 43,676.   1970: 41,334

*Hughes, C. (Lab)	14,652
Lewis, T. V. (C)	8,898
Iwan, D. (Pl Cymru)	7,610
Jones, E. (L)	3,882
Lab majority	**5,754**

No change

	1970		1974
Total Vote	32,339		35,042
Turnout	78·2%		80·2%
Lab	13,966	43·2%	41·8%
C	9,220	28·5%	25·4%
Pl Cymru	7,140	22·1%	21·7%
L	2,013	6·2%	11·1%
Lab maj	4,746	14·7%	16·4%
Swing		+2·4%	−0·8%

Mr Cledwyn Hughes, Opposition spokesman on Agriculture, 1970-71. Minister of Agriculture, Fisheries and Food, 1968-70; Secretary of State for Wales, 1966-68; Minister of State for Commonwealth Relations, 1964-66. Elected in  1951; contested Anglesey, 1945 and 1950. Solicitor. B September, 1916; ed Holyhead Grammar School and University College, Aberystwyth. Former town clerk of Holyhead. Member, Anglesey County Council, 1946-52; Public Accounts Committee, 1957-64; chairman, Welsh Parliamentary Party, 1953-54; chairman, Welsh Labour group, 1955-56.

Mr Thomas Lewis, solicitor. B October 1930; ed Friars School, Bangor, and Liverpool University. Member, Bangor City Council 1953-74 (Mayor of Bangor, 1970-72); Caernarvonshire County Council, 1965-74.

Mr Dafydd Iwan, professional Welsh folk singer and director of record company. B August, 1943; ed Brynanman CP, Aman Valley Grammar School, Ysgol ty tan Domen (Y Bala) University College of Wales, Aberystwyth and Welsh School of Architecture. Equity.

Mr Edwin Jones, legal executive. B October, 1917; ed Froncysyllte Junior School, and Rhodes University, Grahamstown, South Africa.

ANGUS NORTH & MEARNS minor

Electorate 37,233.   1970: 37,058

*Buchanan-Smith, A. L. (C)	14,288
Rankin, H. (Scot Nat)	6,837
Hall, J. C. (L)	4,412
Stanley, A. A. C. (Lab)	3,745
C majority	**7,451**

No change

	1970		1974
Total Vote	27,668		29,282
Turnout	74·6%		78·6%
C	14,687	53·1%	48·8%
Lab	5,092	18·4%	12·8%
Scot Nat	4,677	16·9%	23·2%
L	3,212	11·6%	15·1%
C maj	9,595	34·7%	25·4%
Swing		+2·2%	+0·6%

Mr Alick Buchanan-Smith, was Under-Secretary for Home Affairs and Agriculture, Scottish Office, 1970-74. Opposition spokesman on Scottish affairs. Was elected in 1964; con-  tested West Fife in 1959. Farmer. B April, 1932; ed Edinburgh Academy, Glenalmond, Pembroke College, Cambridge, and Edinburgh University. Member, Select Committee on Agriculture, 1968-69, Vice-Chairman, Conservative agricultural committee 1965-66. Secretary, Scottish Unionist MPs 1965-66; vice-chairman 1966-67. Appointed Opposition spokesman for Scotland, March 1974.

Mr Harry Rankin, accountant and lecturer, contested Lanark, 1966 and 1970. B October, 1932; ed Hamilton Academy, Glasgow University, and Institute of Chartered Accountants of Scotland.

Mr John Hall, writer and lecturer. B June, 1925; ed King's School, Bruton and Queen's College, Oxford. Contested Worcestershire South, 1970, and Chippenham, 1959.

Mr Alexander Stanley, schoolteacher. B April, 1945; ed Wolverhampton Grammar School and St Andrews University. Regional Secretary, Scottish Secondary Teachers' Association.

ANGUS South minor

Electorate 51,876.   1970: 49,293

*Bruce-Gardyne, J. (C)	20,522
Slesser, C. G. M. (Scot Nat)	15,179
Perks, R. W. (Lab)	5,721
C majority	**5,343**

No change

	1970		1974
Total Vote	36,405		41,422
Turnout	73·8%		79·8%
C	20,439	56·1%	49·5%
Scot Nat	8,409	23·1%	36·6%
Lab	7,557	20·7%	13·8%
C maj	12,030	33·0%	12·9%
Swing		−2·7%	+0·1%

Mr John Bruce-Gardyne, a journalist, was elected in 1964. Secretary of Scottish Conservative MPs' group, 1967-72; joint vice-chairman, Conservative parliamentary finance committee since 1972. B April, 1930; ed Winchester College and Magdalen College,

Oxford. Was six years in the Foreign Service before joining the *Financial Times.* Member of council of Bow Group, 1962-64.

Mr Malcolm Slesser, a senior lecturer in chemical engineering at Strathclyde University and author. B October, 1925; ed Edinburgh University. Fought seat in 1970.

Mr Robert Perks, lecturer in accountancy, Dundee College of Technology. B July, 1944; ed Chipping Sodbury Grammar School and Reading University. Member ASTMS.

ANTRIM North   major

Electorate 104,168

*Paisley, The Rev I. (Dem U)	41,282
Utley, T. E. (UU Pro Assembly)	13,651
McAllister, Miss M. (SDLP)	10,056
Dem U maj	27,631

	1974		1974
Total Vote	64,989	UU Pro Assem	21·0%
Turnout	62·4%	SDLP	15·5%
Dem U	63·5%	Dem U maj	42·5%

The Rev Ian Paisley, leader of the Democratic Unionist Party, won the seat in 1970. Founder of the Protestant Unionist Party and of the Free Presbyterian Church. He stood against Lord O'Neill of the Maine in the Northern Ireland general election

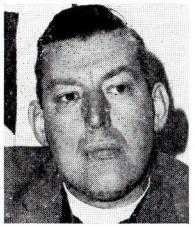

of 1969; won the seat for Bannside in the by-election caused by Lord O'Neill's resignation in 1970. Member, Ulster Assembly since 1973. B April, 1926; ed Model School, Ballymena and Ballymena Technical College.

Mr T. E. Utley is leader writer on the staff of the *Daily Telegraph.* He has been blind since the age of nine.

Miss Mary McAllister was the only woman in the 12-strong SDLP team. Aged 30. Hotel manageress.

ANTRIM South   major

Electorate 118,483

*Molyneaux, J. H. (UUUC)	48,203
Kinahan, C. (Alliance)	12,559
Rowan, P. (SDLP)	8,769
Kidd, R. (Ind NI Lab)	1,801
UUUC majority	35,644

	1974		1974
Total Vote	71,332	SDLP	12·3%
Turnout	60·2%	Ind NILP	2·5%
Alliance	17·6%	UUUC maj	50·0%
UUUC	67·6%		

Mr James Molyneaux, elected in 1970, is a partner in the family firm of letterpress printers. B 1921. Member, Antrim County Council since 1964; chairman, Antrim Unionist Association; Deputy County Grand Master, Orange Order, and Deputy Grand Master

of Ireland. Sovereign Grand Master of British Commonwealth Royal Black Institution.

Mr Charles Kinahan is a farmer. Member, Belfast Harbour Commissioners and Senate of Queen's University. Director of a Belfast brewery. Former member, North-East Area Health and Social Services Board. Member, Antrim and Ballymena Development Commission since its inception.

Mr Patrick Rowan, a teacher, has helped to bring about the existence of two nonsectarian schemes in Lisburn, a credit union project and an enterprise to promote local projects. He is in his early fifties.

Mr Robert Kidd is a member of Newtownabbey District Council. He has been closely involved with community relations work in his area and is identified with social justice campaigns in Northern Ireland.

ARGYLL   same

Electorate 41,444.   1970: 40,825

MacCormick, I. (Scot Nat)	15,646
Hutchison, P. C. (C)	12,358
Macgregor, M. J. N. (Lab)	4,027
Scot Nat majority	3,288

Scot Nat gain

	1970		1974
Total Vote	30,193		32,031
Turnout	73·9%		77·3%
Scot Nat	9,039	29·9%	48·8%
C	13,521	44·8%	38·6%
Lab	7,633	25·3%	12·6%
C maj	4,482	14·8%	
Scot Nat maj			10·3%
Swing		+3·2%	+3·2%

Mr Iain MacCormick, senior history master, Oban High School. B 1939; ed Glasgow High School and Glasgow University. President, Oban branch, SNP. Contested seat in 1970. Appointed SNP spokesman on education, highland affairs and transport, March 1974.

Mr Peter Hutchison, insurance broker and chairman of Ailsa Shipbuilding Co, Troon. B June, 1935; ed Eton and Magdalene College, Cambridge. Contested Glasgow, Craigton 1964, 1966 and Rutherglen 1970.

Mr Malcolm MacGregor, farmer. B January, 1928; ed Oban High School. Chairman West Highland Crofters and Farmers Ltd (Livestock); vice-chairman, West Highland Crofters and Farmers Ltd. Council member NFU Scotland.

ARMAGH   same

Electorate 91,521   1970: 86,847

McCusker, J. H. (UUUC)	33,194
O'Hanlon, P. (SDLP)	18,090
Glendinning, R. (Alliance)	4,983
Moore, T. (Repub Clubs)	4,129
Lewis, H. (Unity)	1,364
UUUC majority	15,104

UUUC gain

	1970		1974
Total Vote	68,144		61,760
Turnout	78·5%		67·5%
UU	37,667	55·3%	—
Nat Unity	21,696	31·8%	—
NI Lab	8,781	12·9%	—
UUUC	—	—	53·7%
SDLP	—	—	29·3%
Alliance	—	—	8·1%
Repub Clubs	—	—	6·7%
Unity	—	—	2·2%
UU maj	15,971	23·5%	—
UUUC maj	—	—	24·4%

Mr James McCusker, a former teacher, has been a member of the Ulster Unionist Council since 1970. Now a personnel officer in Craigavon, aged 34.

Mr Patrick O'Hanlon, Chief Whip of the SDLP in the Assembly, was Independent member for South Armagh in Stormont. Aged 29. Teacher. One of the founders of SDLP. Member, South-East Ulster Development Association.

Mr Robin Glendinning, a teacher, is a fulltime organizer of the Alliance Party.

Mr Thomas Moore is a factory worker. Aged 28. Secretary of the South Armagh Republican Clubs executive. Member, Amalgamated Transport and General Workers Union. He was interned from August, 1971, until April, 1972.

Mr Harry Lewis contested the seat in 1970. He is a schoolteacher.

ARUNDEL   major

Electorate 83,027

Marshall, R. M. (C)	37,655
Kingsbury, J. R. (L)	17,712
Pimlott, B. J. (Lab)	10,597
C majority	19,943

	1974		1974
Total Vote	65,964	L	26·8%
Turnout	79·4%	Lab	16·1%
C	57·1%	C maj	30·2%

Mr Michael Marshall contested The Hartlepools in 1970. Management consultant. B June, 1930; ed Bradfield College and Stanford and Harvard Universities. Vice-chairman, Business Graduates Association. Joint chairman, West Sussex Disabled Living Foundation. Former BBC cricket commentator.

Mr John Kingsbury contested Wembley, North in 1970. Teacher and charity director. B May, 1935; ed Chichester High School and Bognor Regis College of Education. Member, Bognor Regis UDC, 1964-67.

Mr Ben Pimlott is a University lecturer. B 1946; ed Marlborough and Worcester College, Oxford. Member, national executive of Young Fabian group since 1971. Co-opted member, Newcastle upon Tyne art galleries committee.

ASHFIELD   major

Electorate 74,064

*Marquand, D. I. (Lab)	35,994
Kemm, R. N. (C)	14,206
Flint, H. (L)	10,534
Lab majority	21,788

	1974		1974
Total Vote	60,734	C	23·4%
Turnout	82·0%	L	17·3%
Lab	59·3%	Lab maj	35·9%

Mr David Marquand was elected in 1966; Contested Barry in 1964. Journalist and university lecturer. B September, 1934; ed Emanuel School, London, and Magdalen and St Anthony's Colleges, Oxford. Chairman, University Labour Club, 1957. Member, Estimates Committee, 1966-68, Select Committee on Procedure since 1968, executive of Fabian Society since 1963, and PEP executive since 1966. Member, Medical Research Council, 1968-69.

Mr Richard Kemm contested the seat in 1970. Accountant. B November, 1940; ed Hill Brow School, Somerset, and Blundell's School, Tiverton. Member, Bow Group.

Mr Hampton Flint, fruiterer and philatelic dealer. B August, 1926. President, National Market Traders' Federation. Past President, Mansfield Chamber of Trade and Commerce.

ASHFORD   major

Electorate 57,878

*Deedes, W. F. (C)	21,773
Dennis, C. G. (L)	13,314
Jackson, M. B. (Lab)	12,077
C majority	8,459

	1974		1974
Total Vote	47,164	L	28·2%
Turnout	81·5%	Lab	25·6%
C	46·2%	C maj	17·9%

Mr William Deedes has been chairman of the Select Committee on Race Relations and Immigration since 1970, and a member of it since 1966. Minister without Portfolio, 1962-64, with a seat in the Cabinet, and responsible for the co-ordination of Government informa-

tion services at home. Parliamentary Secretary, Ministry of Housing and Local Government, 1954-55; Under Secretary, Home Office, 1955-57. Elected 1950. Journalist. B June, 1913; ed Wellington House, Westgate, and Harrow. Member, Advisory Committee on Drug Dependence since 1966. Chairman, Conservative parliamentary committee on Northern Ireland since 1972, and vice-chairman, home affairs committee, since 1972.

Mr Clive Dennis, a solicitor, former town clerk, including town clerk for the London Borough of Bexley 1964-71. Member, Ashford District Council, since 1973. B June, 1915; ed William Hulme's Grammar School, Manchester, and Manchester University, Nalgo

Mr Martin Jackson, journalist and television critic. B May, 1934; ed Kilburn Polytechnic. Member, Kent County Council. Member, NUJ.

ASHTON-UNDER-LYNE   same

Electorate 59,179   1970: 61,402

*Sheldon, R. E. (Lab)	23,019
Aitken, T. (C)	14,718
Jones, J. G. (L)	9,837
Lab majority	8,301

No change

	1970		1974
Total Vote	43,900		47,574
Turnout	71·4%		80·4%
Lab	23,927	54·5%	48·4%
C	19,973	45·4%	30·9%
L	—		20·7%
Lab maj	3,954	9·0%	17·4%
Swing		+4·2%	−4·2%

Mr Robert Sheldon, Opposition spokesman on the Civil Service and machinery of government, has been chairman, general subcommittee of the Commons committee on expenditure since 1972. Elected in 1964; contested Manchester, Withington, 1959. Company director. B

September, 1923; ed grammar school and technical colleges, external graduate, London University. Member, Public Accounts Committee. Chairman, north-west group of Labour MPs. Member, Fulton Committee on the Civil Service, 1966-68; Parliamentary Labour Party economic and finance committee. TGWU. *Appointed Minister of State, Civil Service Department, March, 1974.*

Mr Timothy Aitken, journalist and company director. B 1944; ed Repton, the Sorbonne and McGill University, Montreal. Member, London committee of PEST, 1971-72.

Mr Trevor T. Jones, teacher. B July, 1932; ed Stockport School and Cheshire County Training College, Alsager. Contested Stockport South, 1970.

AYLESBURY   major

Electorate 67,071

	1974		1974
*Raison, T. H. F. (C)			25,764
Cook, M. J. (L)			14,581
Groves, R. (Lab)			14,463
C majority			11,183

	1974		1974
Total Vote	54,808	L	26·6%
Turnout	81·7%	Lab	26·4%
C	47·0%	C maj	20·4%

Mr Timothy Raison was Under Secretary for Education and Science 1973-74. Journalist and magazine publisher. Elected in 1970. B November, 1929; ed Dragon School, Oxford, Eton, and Christ Church, Oxford. M e m b e r, R i c h m o n d upon Thames Borough Council, 1967-71, and Inner London Education Authority education committee (co-opted), 1967-70. Fought Bedford during 1964 election on behalf of Mr Christopher Soames who was injured. Member, Plowden Council on primary schools, and advisory committee of drug dependence. An Opposition spokesman on social services from March 1974.

Mr Michael Cook, director of family retail motor business. B April, 1927; ed Lord Williams Grammar School, Thame. Member, Aylesbury Vale District Council.

Mr Robin Groves, clerical officer. B November, 1939; ed Chesham Germans Secondary Modern and Chesham Technical Institute. Member Chiltern District Council since 1973. TGWU and CPSA.

AYR   minor

Electorate 51,546   1970: 51,691

*Younger, G. K. H. (C)			21,626
McFadden, Mrs J. A. (Lab)			16,528
Calman, C. D. (Scot Nat)			4,706
C majority			5,098

No change

	1970			1974
Total Vote	42,176			42,860
Turnout	81·5%			83·1%
C	22,220	52·7%		50·4%
Lab & Co-op	17,770	42·1%		—
Lab	—			38·6%
Scot Nat	2,186	5·2%		11·0%
C maj	4,450	10·5%		1 ·9%
Swing		+4·7%		+0·6%

Mr George Younger was Minister of State for Defence January to February 1974; Under Secretary for Development Scottish Office, 1970-74. Elected in 1964; contested Lanarkshire, North, 1959. Scottish Conservative whip, 1965-67. Eldest son of Viscount Younger of

Leckie. Formerly director of George Younger and Sons Ltd, the brewers. B September, 1931; ed Cargilfield School, Edinburgh, Winchester College, and New College, Oxford. Governor, Royal Scottish Academy. In 1968 raised a petition of more than one million signatures to save the Argyll and Sutherland Highlanders, his former regiment, from disbandment. An Opposition spokesman on defence from March 1974.

Mrs Jean McFadden, teacher. B November, 1941; ed Hyndland School and University of Glasgow. Member Glasgow Corporation since 1971 and a magistrate since 1972. EIS and GMWU.

Mr Charles Calman, teacher. Aged 45; ed Robert Douglas Memorial School, Scone and Craigie College of Education.

AYRSHIRE Central   major

Electorate 58,795

*Lambie, D. (Lab)			23,639
Gavin, R. (C)			17,362
Anderson, L. (Scot Nat)			7,255
Lab majority			6,277

	1974		1974
Total Vote	48,256	C	36·0%
Turnout	82·1%	Scot Nat	15·0%
Lab	49·0%	Lab maj	13·0%

Mr David Lambie was elected in 1970; contested Ayrshire, North and Bute in 1966, 1964, 1959, and 1959. Teacher. B July, 1925; ed Ardrossan Academy, Glasgow, and Glasgow and Geneva Universities. Executive member, Educational Institute for Scotland; chairman, Scottish Labour Party, 1965-66.

Mr Robert Gavin, building contractor and surveyor. Contested Glasgow, Bridgeton, 1970. B August, 1944; ed Glasgow Hillhead High School, Glasgow college of business and Paisley Technical College. Member, Glasgow City Council, 1969-72. Member, Federation of Building Trade Employers.

Mr **Leslie Anderson**, advertising executive. contested Ayr in 1970. Aged 37; joined SNP, 1966.

AYRSHIRE North and Bute   same

Electorate 48,720   1970: 47,786

Corrie, J. A. (C)	17,166
Donnelly, R. D. (Lab)	10,436
Murphy, J. A. (Scot Nat)	6,104
Stevenson, R. (L)	3,832
C majority	6,730

No change

	1970		1974	
Total Vote	35,164		37,538	
Turnout	73·6%		77·0%	
C	18,853	53·6%		45·7%
Lab	12,459	35·4%		27·8%
Scot Nat	3,852	10·9%		16·3%
L	—			10·2%
C maj	6,394	18·2%		17·9%
Swing		+5·0%		−0·1%

Mr **John Corrie**, farmer. B July, 1935; ed George Watson's College, Edinburgh and Lincoln Agricultural College, New Zealand. Contested Ayrshire, Central, 1966 and Lanark, North, 1964. Past President, Scottish Young Conservatives and Kirkcudbright Unionist Association. Nuffield Agricultural Scholar, 1972-73. Lecturer with British Wool Board and Agricultural Training Board. District Officer of Rotary International.

Mr **Raymond Donnelly** contested Dumfriesshire in 1970. Teacher. B September, 1947; ed Bearsden Academy, Co-operative College, and Strathclyde and Glasgow Universities. Member, Educational Institute of Scotland.

Mr **John Murphy**, education manager. B June, 1934; ed Glasgow day school; councillor of burgh of Largs since 1969.

Mr **Robert Stevenson** is a food technologist. B December 26, 1928; educated in Paisley. Member, Stevenston Town Council.

AYRSHIRE South   minor

Electorate 50,784   1970: 50,324

*Sillars, J. (Lab)	23,093
Colquhoun, R. (C)	10,643
Mullin, R. (Scot Nat)	6,612
Lab majority	12,450

No change

	1970		1974	
Total Vote	38,688		40,348	
Turnout	76·7%		79·4%	
Lab	23,910	61·8%		5ı·2%
C	11,675	30·2%		26·4%
Scot Nat	3,103	8·0%		16·4%
Lab maj	12,235	31·6%		30·8%
Swing		+1·4%		+0·4%

Mr **James Sillars**, a trade union official, was returned at the by-election in March, 1970. Full-time Labour Party agent 1964 and 1966 elections. B October, 1937; ed Newton Park School, Ayr, and Ayr Academy. Former official Fire Brigades Union and head of Scottish TUC organization department. Former member, Ayr Town Council and Ayr County Council Education Committee.

Mr **Robert Colquhoun** is an information manager of a Scotch whisky company. B January, 1942; ed Renfrew High School, Camphill Senior Secondary, Paisley. Member, Renfrew town council, Renfrew county council, 1967-70. Member, NUJ.

Mr **Roger Mullin**, student of politics. 25; ed Carrick Academy, Maybole, Ayr, and Kilmarnock Technical College, Glasgow College of Science and Technology and the Pon University.

BANBURY   major

Electorate 66,642

*Marten, H. N. (C)	25,167
Booth, A. C. (Lab)	18,289
Fisher, G. J. (L)	11,947
C majority	6,878

	1974		1974
Total Vote	55,403	Lab	33·0%
Turnout	83·1%	L	21·6%
C	45·4%	C maj	12·4%

Mr **Neil Marten**, elected in 1959, was Parliamentary Secretary, Ministry of Aviation, 1962-64. Director, shipping company. B December, 1916; ed Rossall School, and Law Society. Vice-chairman, Conservative Parliamentary foreign and Commonwealth affairs centre, 1968-70; chairman, space committee since 1965. Member, Estimates Committee since 1965, and executive of the 1922 Committee. Chairman, all-Party Disabled Drivers Committee since 1968; Anglo-Norwegian Parliamentary Group since 1962, and Education and Arts Sub-committee of Commons Public Expenditure Committee since 1971. Leading opponent of EEC.

Mr Anthony Booth contested the seat in 1970. Leather manufacturer. B September, 1941; ed Dragon School, Oxford and Stowe School, Buckingham.

Mr Geoffrey Fisher, teacher. B May, 1936; ed Banbury Grammar School and Oxford College of Technology. Contested Banbury, 1970. Former member, Banbury Borough Council, 1965-66. Chairman, South Midlands Public Transport Action Group.

BANFFSHIRE same

Electorate 31,624   1970: 31,705

Watt, H. (Scot Nat)	11,037
*Baker, W. H. K. (C)	8,252
Fraser, T. R. L. (L)	3,121
Dool, R. (Lab)	1,528
Scot Nat majority	2,785

Scot Nat gain

	1970		1974
Total Vote	21,847		23,938
Turnout	68·9%		75·7%
C	8,457	38·7%	34·5%
Scot Nat	5,006	22·9%	46·1%
L	4,589	21·0%	13·0%
Lab	3,795	17·4%	6·4%
C maj	3,451	15·8%	—
Scot Nat maj		—	11·6%
Swing		+2·1%	

Mr Hamish Watt contested the constituency in 1970 and Caithness and Sutherland in 1966 (as a Conservative). Dairy and sheep farmer and company director. B December, 1925; ed Keith Grammar School and St Andrew's University. Appointed SNP County councillor. spokesman for agriculture, forestry and fisheries, March 1974.

Mr Wilfred Baker was elected in 1964. Farmer. B January, 1920; ed Hardye's School and Nottingham, Edinburgh and Cornell Universities. Factor of estates in Scotland, 1949-53, farms at Rothiemay. Was constituency political education officer. Vice-chairman, fisheries sub-committee of Conservative agriculture, fisheries and food committee since 1973.

Mr Ronald Fraser contested Glasgow, Govan, 1950, West Aberdeenshire, 1955, Banffshire, 1970. Writer and broadcaster. B February, 1929; ed McLaren High School, Callander, Strathallan School, Forgandenny, and Glasgow University. Scottish Liberal spokesman on EEC and fisheries.

Mr Robert Dool is a postman, previously an engineer. B June, 1930; ed Possil Senior Secondary School, Glasgow. Member, Aberdeen Town Council since 1971. UPOW.

BARKING Barking major

Electorate 49,616

Richardson, Miss J. (Lab)	22,846
Taylor, M. (L)	8,012
Forth, E. (C)	7,154
Lab majority	14,834

	1974		1974
Total Vote	38,012	L	21·1%
Turnout	76·6%	C	18·8%
Lab	60·1%	Lab maj	39·0%

Miss Josephine Richardson contested Harrow, East, 1964, Hornchurch, 1959, and Monmouth, 1955 and 1951. Export manager. B August, 1923; ed Southend High School for Girls. APEX and ASTMS.

Mr Martin Taylor, administrative officer. B September, 1945; ed Fairclop Secondary Modern School, Beal Grammar School and the University of Essex. Employed by ILEA.

Mr Eric Forth, systems development officer. B September, 1944; ed Jordanhill College School, Glasgow, and Glasgow University. Member, Brentwood Urban Council, 1968-72.

BARKING Dagenham major

Electorate 69,290

*Parker, J. (Lab)	35,765
Hamilton, A. J. (C)	12,275
Wake, G. (Comm)	1,169
Lab majority	23,490

	1974		1974
Total Vote	49,209	C	24·9%
Turnout	71·0%	Comm	2·4%
Lab	72·7%	Lab maj	47·7%

Mr John Parker, a writer and former publisher, was Under-Secretary, Dominions Office, 1945-46. Elected in 1945. Contested Holland with Boston, 1931, and was MP for Romford, 1935-45. B July, 1906; ed Marlborough and St John's College, Oxford. Former secretary, Fabian Society and T & GWU since 1933. Chairman, PLP forestry group; vice-chairman, arts and amenities group. Member, Select Committee on Procedure and of Speaker's Conference. Member, council of National Trust.

Mr Archie Hamilton, company director. B December, 1941. Ed Eton, Mons Officer Cadet School. Member, Kensington and Chelsea council, 1968-71.

BARKSTON ASH same

Electorate 83,139   1970: 78,047

*Alison, M. J. H. (C)		33,979
Muir, J. (Lab)		20,782
Sykes, M (L)		14,618
C majority		13,197

No change

	1970		1974
Total Vote	59,059		69,379
Turnout	75·7%		85·5%
C	35,198	59·6%	49·0%
Lab	23,861	40·4%	29·9%
L	—	—	21·1%
C maj	11,337	19·2%	19·0%
Swing		+3·3%	+0·0%

Mr Michael Alison, Under-Secretary for Health and Social Security 1970 to 1974, was elected in 1964. B June, 1926; ed Eton, Wadham College, Oxford and Ridley Hall, Cambridge. Member, Kensington Borough Council, 1956-59. Research officer, foreign affairs section of Conservative Research Department, 1958-64. Former secretary, Conservative parliamentary power committee and finance committee. Church of England lay reader.

Mr John Muir, barrister. Aged 32; ed Strathclyde University and London University. Former chairman and secretary, Wetherby Labour Party.

Mr Martin Sykes, lecturer in law and director of a brewery. B August, 46; ed Mill Hill School and Pembroke College, Oxford. Barrister. ATTI.

BARNET Chipping Barnet major

Electorate 55,962

*Maudling, R. (C)		22,094
Mills, J. A. D. (Lab)		12,183
Wyn Ellis, Miss N. (L)		11,714
C majority		9,911

	1974		1974
Total Vote	45,991	Lab	26·5%
Turnout	82·2%	L	25·5%
C	48·0%	C maj	21·5%

Mr Reginald Maudling, MP for Barnet, 1950-74, was Home Secretary from 1970-72; Deputy Leader of Conservative Party, 1965-72; Chancellor of the Exchequer, 1962-64; Secretary of State for the Colonies, 1961-62; President of the Board of Trade, 1959-61; Paymaster-General, 1957-59; Minister of Supply, 1955-57; Economic Secretary to the Treasury, 1953-55; Parliamentary Secretary, Ministry of Civil Aviation, 1952. Contested Heston and Isleworth in 1945. Barrister (Middle Temple, 1940) and company director. B March, 1917; ed Merchant Taylors' School and Merton College, Oxford.

Mr John Mills runs his own plastics manufacturing firm. B May, 1938. Ed Trinity College, Glenalmond, and Merton College, Oxford. Member, Camden council 1971-74, chairman housing committee. Member, ASTMS.

Miss Nesta Wyn Ellis, writer and journalist. B November 1940; ed Llanrwst Grammar School and Liverpool University. Contested Spelthorne, 1966, and Brighton, Pavilion, 1969 by-election.

BARNET Finchley major

Electorate 53,550

*Thatcher, Mrs M. H. (C)		18,180
O'Connor, M. J. (Lab)		12,202
Brass, L. (L)		11,221
C majority		5,978

	1974		1974
Total Vote	41,603	Lab	29·3%
Turnout	77·7%	L	27·0%
C	43·7%	C maj	14·4%

Mrs Margaret Thatcher, Secretary of State for Education and Science 1970-74, was chief Opposition spokesman on education, 1969-70. Previously spokesman on transport, power, treasury matters, housing, and pensions. Joined the Shadow Cabinet in October, 1967. Returned for Finchley in 1959. Parliamentary Secretary, Ministry of Pensions and National Insurance, 1961-64. Contested Dartford, 1950 and 1951. Sponsored an Act to open council meetings to the Press. Barrister (Lincoln's Inn, 1954). B October, 1925; ed Grantham High School and Somerville College, Oxford, where she was treasurer and president of the University Conservative Association. Appointed Shadow Cabinet as Opposition spokesman on the environment, March 1974.

Mr Laurence Brass, solicitor. B July, 1947; ed Clifton College, Bristol and University College, London. Contested Hornsey, 1970. Member, Hertsmere District Council since 1973. Member, Association of Liberal Lawyers and the Liberal Friends of Israel.

BARNET Hendon North — major

Electorate 50,142

*Gorst, J. (C)		17,285
Champion, J. S. (Lab)		14,673
Edwards, D. (L)		8,585
C majority		2,612

	1974		1974
Total Vote	40,543	Lab	36·2%
Turnout	80·8%	L	21·2%
C	42·6%	C maj	6·4%

Mr John Gorst, a public relations consultant, was elected in 1970; contested Bodmin in 1966 and Chester-le-Street in 1964. B June, 1928; ed Ardingly College and Corpus Christi College, Cambridge. Vice-chairman, Conservative parliamentary consumer protection committee. Chairman all-party films committee; secretary, Middle East Committee; Director, Cassius Film Production. Founder and secretary of the Telephone Users' Association and of the Local Radio Association, 1946-70.

Mr John Champion, railway clerk. Member, Hendon Borough Council, 1955-64; London Borough of Barnet since 1964. B July, 1925; ed Barsfield Secondary School. TSSA.

Mr David Edwards, an investment analyst. B July, 1945; ed Stowe.

BARNET Hendon South — major

Electorate 51,474

*Thomas, P. J. M. (Con)		17,795
Colne, M. D. (L)		11,198
Hadley, R. M. (Lab)		11,088
C majority		6,597

	1974		1974
Total Vote	40,081	L	27·9%
Turnout	77·9%	Lab	27·7%
C	44·4%	C maj	16·4%

Mr Peter Thomas, QC, Secretary of State for Wales 1970-74, was chairman of the Conservative Organization, 1970-72; Minister of State, Foreign Affairs, 1963-64; Under-Secretary, Foreign Office, 1961-63; Parliamentary Secretary, Ministry of Labour, 1959-61. Elected for Hendon South, 1970. Barrister (Middle Temple, 1947), QC, 1965. B July, 1920; ed Epworth College, Rhyl, and Jesus College, Oxford. MP for Conway, 1951-66. Appointed to Shadow Cabinet as Opposition spokesman on Wales, March 1974.

Mr Michael Colne contested Harrow, East, 1966 and 1970. Company director and executive. B May, 1930; ed Highgate School and Columbia University. Liberal leader on Hertfordshire County Council; member, Hertsmere District Council.

Mr Richard Hadley, barrister. B October, 1946; ed University College School and Oxford University. ASTMS.

BARNSLEY — same

Electorate 75,855   1970: 75,678

*Mason, R. (Lab)		40,595
England, G. (C)		15,969
Labour majority		24,626

No change

	1970	1974
Total Vote	53,953	56,564
Turnout	71·3%	74·6%
Lab	34,956 64·8%	71·8%
C	10,811 20·0%	28·2%
L	8,186 15·2%	—
Lab maj	24,145 44·7%	43·5%
Swing	+3·3%	+0·6%

Mr Roy Mason, Opposition spokesman on Trade and Civil Aviation since 1970, and chairman of the PLP miners' group. President of the Board of Trade from 1969-70. Minister of Power, 1968-69; Postmaster-General, April-June, 1968; Minister of Defence (Equipment), 1967-68; Minister of State, Board of Trade, 1964-67. Returned at a by-election in March, 1953. B April, 1924; ed at elementary schools and London School of Economics. Miner, 1938-53. Member, Yorkshire Miners' Council, 1949-53; branch official, NUM, 1947-53. *Appointed Secretary of State for Defence, March 1974.*

Mr George England, barrister, called to the Bar, 1972. B 1947; ed Barnsley Holgate Grammar School and Sheffield University. Secretary, Barnsley Conservative Association.

BARROW-IN-FURNESS   same

Electorate 54,246   1970: 54,126

*Booth, A. E. (Lab)	19,925
Bloomer, D. G. P. (C)	14,818
Benjamin, M. (L)	8,470
Lab majority	5,107

No change

	1970		1974	
Total Vote	39,936		43,213	
Turnout	73·8%		79·7%	
Lab	22,400	56·1%	46·1%	
C	17,536	43·9%	34·3%	
L	—	—	19·6%	
Lab maj	4,864	12·2%	11·8%	
Swing		+4·2%	+0·2%	

Mr Albert Booth, chairman of Select Committee on Statutory Instruments since 1970. An opposition spokesman on trade and industry since December, 1973. Elected 1966, contested Tynemouth in 1964. B May, 1928; ed St Thomas's, Winchester, South Shields Marine School, Rutherford College of Technology. Member, Tynemouth Borough Council, 1961-64; constituency party secretary, 1952-58; chairman, 1958-63. Sponsored by AUEW, technical and supervisory section. *Appointed Minister of State for Employment, March 1974.*

Mr David Bloomer, managing director of a scientific publishing company and barrister (Gray's Inn). B 1941; ed Marlborough College and Lincoln College, Oxford.

Mr Malvyn Benjamin, solicitor. B November, 1936; ed Dulwich College Preparatory School, St Paul's School and King's College, University of London. Contested Luton, 1963. Executive member, Jewish communal organizations.

BARRY   major

Electorate 69,358

*Gower, Sir R. (C)	25,326
Brooks, J. E. (Lab)	19,779
Lloyd, Dr Jennifer (L)	10,048
Wynne-Williams, Mrs V. (Pl Cymru)	1,924
C majority	5,547

	1974			974
Total Vote	57,077	L		17·6%
Turnout	82·3%	Pl Cymru		3·4%
C	44·4%	C maj		9·7%
Lab	34·6%			

Sir Raymond Gower was elected in 1951; contested Ogmore, 1950. Solicitor. Chairman, *Penrayy Press and Barry Herald* newspaper 1955-64; director, Nicholson Construction, 1957-66; Welsh Dragon Securities since 1961; Broughton and Company (Bristol) since 1961; Welsh Dragon Unit Trust (Management Co), 1962-67; Deane-Spence Ltd, Cranleigh and London SW1 (merchant bankers) since 1963: Association of Conservative Clubs, 1962-65. B August, 1916; ed Cardiff High School; University College, Cardiff.

Mr John Brooks, plasterer. B April, 1927; ed Harlech College, and University College, Cardiff. Leader, South Glamorgan County Council. TGWU.

Dr Jennifer Lloyd is an assistant psychiatrist in a centre for alcoholism and drug addiction. B April, 1937; ed Howell's School, Llandaff, Benenden School, Kent, and London University. Member, committee, Addiction Research Foundation of Wales; chairman, Cardiff and District Branch, Migraine Trust.

Mrs Valerie Wynne-Williams, television actress and company director. Ed Pontardawe Grammar School; studied physiotherapy King's College Hospital, London.

Former schoolgirl hurdles champion. Member, Equity.

BASILDON major

Electorate 90,412

Moonman, E. (Lab)	33,499
Denney, R. C. (C)	22,832
Fortune, E. (L)	17,794
Lab majority	10,667

	1974		1974
Total Vote	74,125	C	30·8%
Turnout	82·0%	L	24·0%
Lab	45·2%	Lab maj	14·4%

Mr Eric Moonman, industrial adviser, was MP for Billericay, 1966-70 and contested Chigwell, 1962. B April, 1929; ed elementary and secondary schools, and Liverpool and Manchester Universities. Vice-Chairman Labour Parliamentary Association since 1967. Former member, Select Committee on Science and Technology, founder and chairman of all-party Parliamentary mental health unit (1968-70). Leader, Stepney Council until reorganization of London boroughs in 1965; member, Tower Hamlets Council, 1964-68. Member NGA since 1944.

Mr Ronald Denney, lecturer, consultant chemist and author. B June, 1936; ed South East Essex Technical College and Sir John Cass College, London. Contested Poplar, 1970. Associate of the Royal Institute of Chemistry. Manager of three schools in Tower Hamlets.

Mr Edward Fortune, operational research analyst. B September, 1943; ed Yarm Grammar School, Yorkshire, and Imperial College, London University. Former councillor, Upton by Chester, 1967.

BASINGSTOKE major

Electorate 86,039

*Mitchell, D. B. (C)	30,886
Hunt, T. (Lab)	23,089
Whitbread, N. (L)	17,598
C majority	7,797

	1974		1974
Total Vote	71,573	Lab	32·2%
Turnout	83·2%	L	24·6%
C	43·1%	C maj	10·9%

Mr David Mitchell, Opposition Whip, 1965-67, was elected in 1964; contested St Pancras North in 1959. Wine shipper and director of firm of wine merchants. B June, 1928; ed Aldenham. Member, St Pancras Borough Council, 1956-59. Secretary, Conservative parliamentary labour committee, 1968-70.

Mr Terry Hunt, teacher. B June, 1942; ed Great Yarmouth Grammar School and Liverpool and Sheffield universities. Member, Basingstoke Borough Council, 1970-74.

Mr Neville Whitbread, chartered accountant. B June, 1938; ed Eton.

BASSETLAW same

Electorate 71,115   1970: 68,942

*Ashton, J. W. (Lab)	33,724
Heading, R. C. (C)	22,490
Lab majority	11,234

No change

	1970		1974
Total Vote	52,782		56,214
Turnout	76·5%		79·0%
Lab	28,959	54·9%	60·0%
C	20,698	39·2%	40·0%
L	3,125	5·9%	—
Lab maj	8,261	15·6%	20·0%
Swing		+3·7%	−2·1%

Mr Joseph Ashton, an estimating engineer, was returned at a by-election in October, 1968. B October, 1933; ed High Storrs Grammar School. Sheffield, and Rotherham Technical College. Member Sheffield City Council, 1962-69. Select Committee on Statutory Instruments, 1968-69. Vice-chairman, PLP public building and works group. Weekly political columnist with *Sheffield Star* since 1970 and other national and regional papers. Columnist in *Labour Weekly*. Sponsored by AUEW, technical and supervisory section. Member of its parliamentary panel.

Mr Roger Heading, farmer. B 1942; ed Repton, Clare College, Cambridge. Committee member, NFU; urban district councillor since 1967. Chairman, Isle of Ely Conservative Association.

BATH minor

Electorate 61,762 1970: 59,141

*Brown, Sir E. J. (C)	20,920
Downey, P. (L)	15,738
Bishop, M. L. (Lab)	14,296
de Laterriere, H. B. (Ind C)	204
Young, G. (Ind)	118
C majority	5,182

	1970		1974
Total Vote	45,634		51,276
Turnout	77·1%		83·0%
C	22,344	49·0%	40·8%
Lab	16,493	36·1%	27·9%
L	5,957	13·0%	30·7%
World Govt	840	1·8%	—
Ind C	—	—	0·4%
Ind	—	—	0·2%
C maj	5,851	12·8%	10·1%
Swing		+5·5%	+0·0%

Sir Edward Brown, elected in 1964, contested Stalybridge and Hyde, 1959. Company chairman and director. B April, 1913; ed elementary school, Camberwell, and Morley College, Lambeth. C h a i r m a n, National Union of Conservative and Unionist Associations, 1959-61. Member, Tottenham Borough Council, 1956-64. Joint secretary, Conservative Parliamentary committee on labour matters, 1965-68. Former member, ASSET and of London Trades Council.

Mr Peter Downey, company director. B July, 1942; ed Downside School; city and district councillor.

Mr Malcolm Bishop, barrister. B October, 1944; ed Grammar School and Oxford.

Mr Gilbert Young, retired insurance representative, stood for world government and the OAP movement.

BATLEY AND MORLEY same

Electorate 61,336 1970: 63,035

*Broughton, Sir A. D. D. (Lab)	21,495
Crone, N. (C)	14,404
Wrigley, P. (L)	11,470
Jarratt, G. (Ind Dem All)	828
Lab majority	7,091

No change

	1970		1974
Total Vote	45,670		48,197
Turnout	72·4%		78·6%
Lab	23,024	50·4%	44·6%
C	15,753	34·5%	29·9%
L	6,893	15·1%	23·8%
Ind Dem L	—	—	1·7%
Lab maj	7,271	15·9%	14·7%
Swing		+5·6%	+0·6%

Sir Alfred Broughton, member of Speaker's panel of chairmen since 1964, has represented the constituency since gaining it at a by-election in 1949. Physician. B October, 1902; ed Rossall School, Downing College, Cambridge, and the London Hospital. Member Batley Borough Council, 1946-49. Opposition whip, 1959-64. Deputy Lieutenant, West Riding of Yorkshire. Trustee, Leeds Trustee Savings Bank.

Mr Neil Crone, solicitor. B 1937; ed Scarborough College. Chairman, Batley and Morley Conservative Political Centre.

Mr Peter Wrigley, teacher. B September, 1937; ed Batley Grammar School, Borough Road College, and London and Bradford Universities. Contested Batley and Morley, 1970.

BEACONSFIELD major

Electorate 67,937

*Bell, R. M. (C)	26,040
Eastwell, W. H. (L)	14,792
Jones, P. M. (Lab)	11,691
C majority	11,248

	1974			1974
Total Vote	52,523		L	28·2%
Turnout	77·3%		Lab	22·2%
C	49·6%		C maj	21·4%

Mr Ronald Bell, QC, was MP for South B u c k i n g h a mshire, 1950-74. Contested Caerphilly by-election, 1939; won Newport by-election 1945, losing the seat two months later at the general election. Barrister (Gray's Inn, 1938); QC, 1966. B April, 1914; ed Cardiff High School and Magdalen College, Oxford. Member Select Committee on Education 1968-70; on Statutory Instruments, 1953-74.

Mr William Eastwell, teacher. B June, 1931; ed Slough Grammar School and Culham College. Member, Buckinghamshire County Council, since 1973. NUT.

Mr Peter Jones, lecturer in politics, Reading University. B January, 1945; ed Birkenhead School, University College, Swansea and London School of Economics. Member Reading Council since 1972 and Berkshire Council since 1973. ASTMS.

D

BEBINGTON AND ELLESMERE PORT   major

Electorate 86,091

Bates, A. (Lab)	31,850
*Cockeram, E. P. (C)	27,388
Handley, P. (L)	12,372
Lab majority	4,462

	1974		1974
Total Vote	71,610	C	38·2%
Turnout	83·2%	L	17·3%
Lab	44·5%	Lab maj	6·2%

Mr Alfred Bates, senior lecturer in mathematics. Contested Northwich, 1970. B June, 1944; ed Stretford Grammar School, Manchester and Cambridge Universities. Member, Stretford borough council since 1971.

Mr Eric Cockeram won Bebington for the Conservatives in 1970. Company director. B July, 1924; ed The Leys School, Cambridge. Member, Commons select committee on corporation tax, 1972. Chairman, Liverpool NHS executive, 1969-70. Governor, United Liverpool Hospitals. President, Menswear Association of Britain, 1964-65.

Mr Philip Handley is a lecturer. B September, 1937; ed Helsby Grammar School, University College, Bangor, and Leicester University. Member, ATTI.

BEDFORD   minor

Electorate 73,466   1970: 67,317

*Skeet, T. H. H. (C)	26,082
Colling, G. (Lab)	19,861
Griffiths, J. (L)	15,405
C majority	6,221

No change

	1970		1974
Total Vote	52,121		61,348
Turnout	77·3%		83·5%
C	26,330	50·5%	42·5%
Lab	21,051	40·4%	32·4%
L	4,740	9·1%	25·1%
C maj	5,279	10·1%	10·1%
Swing		+5·4%	+0·0%

Mr Trevor Skeet won the seat for the Conservatives in 1970. Conservative MP for Willesden, East, 1959-64. Contested Llanelli, 1955, and Stoke Newington and Hackney, North, 1951. Barrister (Inner Temple, 1947), industrial consultant and writer. B January, 1918; ed King's College, Auckland, and University of New Zealand. Chairman, Conservative trade and industry committee 1972-74; secretary of Commons all-party groups on minerals and airships. Chairman, Middle East sub-committee of Foreign and Commonwealth Affairs Committee.

Mr Gordon Colling, newspaper linotype operator and official of National Graphical Association. B March, 1933; ed Ruskin College, Oxford. Leader Labour group, Bedford District Council.

Mr John Griffiths, chairman, Squash Club development company and a public relations firm. B April, 1934; ed Uppingham, and Peterhouse, Cambridge. Contested Ludlow, 1964, and Wanstead and Woodford, 1966. Former chairman, National League of Young Liberals 1960-62.

BEDFORDSHIRE Mid   minor

Electorate 74,518   1970: 73,030

*Hastings, S. L. E. (C)	28,973
Harrowell, D. F. (Lab)	17,862
Meyer, P. W. (L)	17,151
C majority	11,111

No change

	1970		1974
Total Vote	56,504		63,986
Turnout	77·3%		85·9%
C	29,670	52·5%	45·3%
Lab	19,035	33·7%	27·9%
L	7,799	13·8%	26·8%
C maj	10,635	18·8%	17·4%
Swing		+6·4%	−0·7%

Mr Stephen Hastings was elected at a by-election in November, 1960. Director of three companies, chairman of one. B May, 1921; ed Eton and Sandhurst. Vice-chairman, horticulture sub-committee of Conservative agriculture committee since 1973, former secretary; member, executive, 1922 Committee. Regular Officer in the Scots Guards, 1939; aide-de-camp to the Minister of State in

the Middle East, 1943; served with Special Air Service Regiment in Africa, 1944-45, and then in the Special Forces. Assistant military attaché, Helsinki, 1950-53. Worked in Foreign Office 1953-55, and 1955-58 at the Embassy in Paris; with the political office, Middle East Forces Cyprus, 1958-60.

Mr David Harrowell, commercial sales manager. Contested the seat in 1970. B February, 1930; ed Luton Grammar School, King's College, London. Vice-chairman Bedfordshire county council and member Bedfordshire police authority. ASTMS.

Mr Percy Meyer, assistant sales office manager. B December, 1925; ed Hall School, Hampstead, Ardingly College, Sussex. Contested Hornsey, 1966, and Surrey East, 1970. Member, Finchley Borough Council, 1962-65.

BEDFORDSHIRE South   major

Electorate 63,701

*Madel, W. D. (C)	21,380
Penwarden D. (L)	16,622
Tinnion, P. F. (Lab)	15,847
C majority	4,758

No change

	1974			1974
Total Vote	53,849		L	30·9%
Turnout	84·5%		Lab	29·4%
C	39·7%		C maj	8·8%

Mr David Madel, publishing executive, won the seat for the Conservatives in 1970; contested Erith and Crayford, 1965 by-election and 1966. B August, 1938; ed Uppingham School, Keble College, Oxford. Member Bow Group Council, 1966-67; a member of the  group's standing committee on education. Secretary, Conservative parliamentary home affairs committee, 1972-73.

Mr David Penwarden. Contested West Ham, North, 1955, and Deptford by-election, 1963. Director of training, *Guardian* Newspaper Group business services. B September, 1932; ed Taunton School and Keble College, Oxford. Member West Ham Council, 1960-63, and Reading Council, 1965-66. Former member, NUT branch executive committee.

Mr Paul Tinnion, computer programmer. B November, 1946; ed Friends' School,

Saffron Walden and Bristol University. Member Saffron Walden Borough Council 1971-74.

BEDWELLTY   same

Electorate 49,747   1970: 49,096

*Kinnock, N. G. (Lab)	26,664
Yeo, T. S. K. (C)	5,027
Morgan, R. (L)	5,020
Moore, A. (Pl Cymru)	3,048
Lab majority	21,637

No change

	1970		1974
Total Vote	37,657		39,759
Turnout	76·7%		79·9%
Lab	28,078	74·6%	67·1%
C	5,799	15·4%	12·6%
Pl Cymru	3,780	10·0%	7·7%
L	—	—	12·6%
Lab maj	22,279	59·2%	54·4%
Swing		+6·6%	+2·3%

Mr Neil Kinnock, a trade union tutor with the Workers' Educational Association, was elected in 1970. B March, 1942; ed Lewis School, Pengam, Glamorgan, and University College, Cardiff. Member, Commons expenditure committee, 1971-73. Member, Tribune  group. National executive member, Anti-Apartheid Movement. President, University College, Cardiff, Socialist Society, 1962-65. Sponsored by TGWU.

Mr Timothy Yeo, chairman and investment manager of Securities Selection. B March 1945; ed Charterhouse and Emmanuel College, Cambridge.

Mr Rowland Morgan, chartered civil engineer and university teacher. B December, 1934; ed Tredegar Grammar School and Manchester University.

Mr Andrew Moore, research biochemist. B July 1947; ed Grammar School and Balliol College, Oxford.

BEESTON   major

Electorate 73,635

Lester, J. (C)	26,487
Gardner, A. J. (Lab & Co-op)	23,943
Reddish, S. (L)	12,091
C majority	2,544

	1974			1974
Total Vote	62,521		Lab & Co-op	38·3%
Turnout	84·9%		L	19·3%
C	42·4%		C maj	4·1%

Mr James Lester, director of footwear distributing company. B May, 1932; ed Nottingham High School. Contested Bassetlaw in the 1968 by-election and in 1970. Member, Nottinghamshire County Council since 1966; appointed chairman, Salary and Establishment Committee, 1967, and Finance and General Purposes Committee, 1969. Member, CCPRE management committee for Nottinghamshire international water sports centre, and management committee, Portland Training College for the Disabled. President, Wholesale Footwear Distributors' Association, Southern Branch.

Mr Antony Gardner, director of the Social Work Advisory Service. Former Co-operative official. Was Labour MP for Rushcliffe 1966-70; contested Wolverhampton, South-West, 1964. B December, 1927; ed Co-operative College and Southampton University (president of the union and of the university Labour Club, 1957-58).

Mr Stuart Reddish, Post Office administrator. B May, 1948; ed High Pavement Grammar School. Parish councillor, Holme Pierrepont since 1973. POEU Secretary, Nottingham East Liberal Association.

BELFAST East   **major**

Electorate 80,032

Craig, W. (Vanguard)	27,817
*McMaster, S. R. (UU Pro Assembly)	20,077
Bleakley, D. (NILP)	8,122
Gillespie, D. (SDLP)	1,502
Vanguard majority	7,740

	1974		1974
Total Vote	57,518	NILP	14·1%
Turnout	71·9%	SDLP	2·6%
Vanguard	48·4%	Vanguard maj	13·4%
UU Pro Assem	34·9%		

Mr William Craig, leader of the Vanguard Party, was elected to Stormont for Larne in 1960. A 49-year-old solicitor, he is an Assembly member for North Antrim. He was Minister of Home Affairs, Minister of Health, Minister of Local Government and Minister of Development in the Stormont Government.

Mr Stanley McMaster was elected at a by-election in March, 1959. Barrister, Lincoln's Inn, 1953. B September, 1926; ed at Campbell College, Belfast, and Trinity College, Dublin. Vice-Chairman, Ulster Unionist MPs 1972-74; vice-chairman, Shipping and Shipbuilding sub-committee of Conservative trade and industry committee. Former secretary, Conservative Aviation Committee.

Mr David Bleakley was Stormont MP for the Victoria division of Belfast, 1958-65. Aged 48. Appointed Minister of Community Relations by Mr Brian Faulkner in April, 1971, and served in that capacity for six months.

Mr Desmond Gillespie is an SDLP Assembly member for West Belfast. Aged 60, he is a member of the consultative committees of the Northern Ireland Assembly for health and social services and housing.

BELFAST North   **major**

Electorate 72,178

Carson, J. (UUUC)	21,531
Smyth, D. (UU Pro Assembly)	12,755
Donnelly, T. (SDLP)	12,003
Scott, S. (NILP)	2,917
UUUC majority	8,776

	1974		1974
Total Vote	49,206	SDLP	24·4%
Turnout	68·2%	NILP	5·9%
UUUC	43·7%	UUUC maj	17·8%
UU Pro Assem	25·9%		

Mr John Carson is a 40-year-old draper. Member, Belfast Corporation since 1971. Member, Orange Order.

Mr David Smyth, barrister, aged 25, was a research officer at Unionist headquarters in Belfast. Research officer, Conservative headquarters in London since 1973. Member, Unionist Party's standing committee and adviser to Mr Brian Faulkner's team at the Darlington conference.

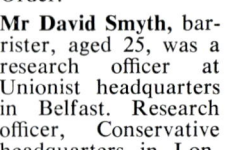

Mr Tom Donnelly is a member of the SDLP executive and of Belfast Corporation. Honorary treasurer, Belfast District Road Safety Committee and trustee, Ulster Transport and Folk Museum. Aged 34, he is employed as a development officer with ICI Fibres Ltd.

Mr Sandy Scott was awarded the MBE in 1970 for services in aid of community peace. He is a shop steward in the Belfast shipyards. Member, BBC Regional Advisory Council for Northern Ireland since 1971.

BELFAST South — major

Electorate 75,443

Bradford, Rev R. (UUUC)	22,083
*Pounder, R. (UU Pro Assembly)	18,085
Cooke, D. (Alliance)	5,118
Caraher, B. (SDLP)	4,149
Holmes, E. (NILP)	2,455
UUUC majority	3,998

	1974		1974
Total Vote	51,890	Alliance	9·9%
Turnout	68·8%	SDLP	8·0%
UUUC	42·5%	NILP	4·7%
UU Pro Assem	34·8%	UUUC maj	7·7%

The Rev Robert Bradford, a 33-year-old Methodist minister, has spent the past four years working in the Lenadoon area of Belfast. Unsuccessful Vanguard candidate in the Assembly elections. A soccer blue at Queen's University.

Mr Rafton Pounder was returned at a by-election in October, 1963. Chartered accountant. B May, 1933; ed Charterhouse and Christ's College, Cambridge. Member, European Parliament, 1973-74. Vice-chairman, Conservative Party Technology Committee, since 1970; secretary, Conservative Party Power Committee, 1969-70. Member, Select Committee on Public Accounts, 1970-72. Member, British delegation to Consultative Assembly of Council of Europe and WEU, 1965-68. Chairman, Cambridge University Conservative and Unionist Association, 1954. Secretary, Ulster Unionist Parliamentary Party, 1964-67.

Mr David Cooke, a founder member of the Alliance Party, is its Joint Honorary Treasurer. Elected to Belfast City Council, 1973. A solicitor, he runs an advice centre in South Belfast.

Mr Ben Caraher, Vice-chairman of the Social Democratic and Labour Party, was a member of the committee which organized the party in the Belfast area and drafted its constitution. He teaches economics and politics in a Belfast grammar school. Unsuccessful candidate for Belfast South in the Assembly elections.

Mr Erskine Holmes is the organizer for the Northern Ireland Labour Party and a former chairman. Unsuccessful contender in the Westminster elections in Belfast, South in 1966 and Armagh in 1970. Former teacher. B February, 1940; ed Annadale Grammar School, Belfast.

BELFAST West — major

Electorate 66,639

*Fitt, G. (SDLP)	19,554
McQuade, J. (UUUC)	17,374
Price, A. (Ind Repub)	5,662
Brady, J. (Repub Clubs)	3,088
Boyd, W. (NILP)	1,989
SDLP majority	2,180

	1974		1974
Total Vote	47,667	Ind	11·9%
Turnout	71·5%	Repub Clubs	6·5%
SDLP	41·0%	NILP	4·2%
UUUC	36·4%	SDLP maj	4·6%

Mr Gerard Fitt is leader of the Social Democratic and Labour Party in Northern Ireland and deputy chief of the Northern Ireland Executive. He won Belfast West from the Ulster Unionists in 1966. B April, 1926; ed Christian Brothers School, Belfast. MP for Dock constituency in Belfast until Stormont ceased to function. Served in Merchant Navy, 1941-53. Belfast City Councillor.

Mr John McQuade is an Assembly member for North Belfast. Elected to Stormont in 1966 and joined the Democratic Unionist party in 1971.

Mr Albert Price, 59, is the father of Dolores and Marion Price, who are at present serving sentences in England for their part in the London bomb incidents. Mr Price has the backing of the provisional IRA.

Mr Jack Brady joined the Republican movement in 1929 and was actively involved in the Republican congress in 1930. With Mr Gerard Fitt, he was a founder member of the All-Ireland Council of Labour. Shop steward with the Amalgamated Transport and General Workers' Union since 1959. He was interned from 1940 to 1945.

Mr William Boyd represented Woodvale at Stormont, 1958-65. He has been an alderman of Belfast Corporation. Lay preacher in the Methodist Church and a member of the Amalgamated Union of Engineering Workers.

BELPER — major

Electorate 70,677

MacFarquhar, R. L. (Lab)	30,611
*Stewart-Smith, D. G. (C)	28,577
Lab majority	2,034

	1974			1974
Total Vote	59,188	C		48·3%
Turnout	83·7%	Lab maj		3·4%
Lab	51·7%			

Mr Roderick Mac-Farquhar, research scholar and freelance journalist and broadcaster. B December, 1930; ed Fettes, Oxford and Harvard. Contested Ealing, South, 1966 and Meriden by-election 1968. NUJ.

Mr Geoffrey Stewart-Smith won the seat for the Conservatives in 1970. Publisher. B December, 1933; ed Winchester College and Sandhurst. Member, Select Committee on Nationalized Industries; member, backbench party committees on energy, defence, agriculture and aviation.

BERWICK & EAST LOTHIAN same

Electorate 56,949   1970: 55,252

Ancrum, Earl of (C)		21,234
*Mackintosh, J. P. (Lab)		20,694
Simpson, D. (Scot Nat)		6,956
C majority		540

C gain

	1970		1974
Total Vote	46,308		48,884
Turnout	83·8%		85·8%
Lab	21,107	45·6%	42·3%
C	20,466	44·2%	43·4%
Scot Nat	4,735	10·2%	14·2%
Lab maj	641	·4%	—
C maj	—		1·1%
Swing		+1·2%	+1·2%

The Earl of Ancrum (Mr Michael Ancrum), advocate. B 1945; ed Ampleforth, Oxford, and Edinburgh Universities. Contested West Lothian, 1970. First chairman, Thistle Group. Eldest son of Marquess of Lothian.

Mr John Mackintosh won the seat for Labour in 1966 after contesting it in 1964, and Edinburgh, Pentlands, in 1959. University professor. B August, 1929; ed Melville College, Edinburgh; Edinburgh University; Balliol College, Oxford, and Princeton University. Member, Select Committee on Procedure, 1966-70, Select Committee on Scottish Affairs, 1968-70 and Select Committee on Agriculture, 1967-69.

Mr David Simpson, reader in economics at Stirling University. B 1936; ed George Watson's College, Edinburgh, Gordonstoun, and Edinburgh University.

BERWICK UPON TWEED same

Electorate 41,553   1970: 41,669

*Beith, A. J. (L)	15,732
Hardie, D. (C)	15,289
Adam, G. J. (Lab)	4,326
L majority	443

No change

	1970		1974
Total Vote	30,712		35,347
Turnout	73·7%		85·1%
C	15,558	50·6%	43·2%
Lab & Co-op	8,413	27·4%	—
Lab	—		12·2%
L	6,741	21·9%	44·5%
C maj	7,145	23·3%	—
L maj	—		1·2%
Swing		+4·3%	+3·9%

1973 by-election: Total Vote 31,297 (75.0%)—L 12,489 (39·9%), C 12,432 (39·7%), Lab 6,178 (19·8%), New Ind 126 (0·4%), Eng Resurgence 72 (0·2%)—L maj 72 (0·2%).

Mr Alan Beith won the seat for the Liberals at the by-election in 1973; contested it in 1970. Liberal spokesman on home affairs. B April, 1943; ed King's School, Macclesfield, Balliol and Nuffield Colleges, Oxford. University lecturer. Member of general advisory council of BBC; Tynedale District Council, and Hexham Rural Council. Also from March 1974, Liberal spokesman on Northern Ireland.

Mr Donald Hardie contested the by-election in the constituency in 1973, when it was won by the Liberals. Contested Berwick and East Lothian in 1970 and Stirlingshire, West in 1966. Company director. B September, 1926; ed Beckenham Grammar School, Kent, and St Andrews and Indiana Universities. Member, Executive and Central Council, Conservative Party in Scotland; Scottish Conservative Trade Union Advisory Committee.

Mr Gordon Adam contested the seat in the 1973 by-election, and Tynemouth, 1966. Mining engineer. B March, 1934; ed Carlisle Grammar School and Leeds University. Member, Whitley Bay Borough Council, and chairman, North Tyneside Metropolitan District Council.

BEXLEY Bexleyheath major

Electorate 50,558

Townsend, C. D. (C)	18,541
Cartwright, J. C. (Lab & Co-op)	14,675
Pickard, W. (L)	9,575
C majority	3,866

	1974		1974
Total Vote	42,791	Lab & Co-op	34·3%
Turnout	84·6%	L	22·4%
C	43·3%	C maj	9·0%

Mr Cyril Townsend, employed in the Conservative research department. B December, 1937; ed Bradfield College, Berkshire, Royal Military Academy; captain in the Durham Light Infantry to 1968.

Mr John Cartwright, director, Royal Arsenal Co-operative Society Ltd. Contested Bexley in 1970. B November, 1933; ed Woking County Grammar School. Executive civil servant, 1952-55; Labour Party Organizer, 1955-67; Political secretary, 1967-72. Chairman, National Union of Labour Organizers, 1969-70. Leader of Greenwich Borough Council and Chief Whip, London Boroughs Association, both since 1971.

Mr Wilfrid Pickard, journalist and investment analyst. B April, 1934; ed Skipton Grammar School, Bootham School, Yorks, and London School of Economics. Contested Skipton, 1964 and 1966, and Harborough, 1970. Former Councillor, Barnoldswick Urban District Council, 1962-69.

BEXLEY Erith and Crayford minor

Electorate 60,041   1970: 57,696

*Wellbeloved, A. J. (Lab)	22,632
Raitt, R. I. (C)	15,551
Vince, S. (L)	10,951
Lab majority	7,081

No change

	1970		1974
Total Vote	41,170	71·3%	81·8%
Lab	23,012	55·9%	46·1%
C	18,158	44·1%	31·6%
L	—	—	22·3%
Lab maj	4,854	11·8%	14·4%
Swing		+4·6%	−1·3%

Mr James Wellbeloved was elected in the 1965 by-election. Commercial consultant. B July, 1926; ed elementary school and South East London Technical College. Member, Erith Borough Council, 1956-65. Former Leader of the Council of the London Borough of Bexley, 1972-73. Opposition whip, 1972-73.

Mr Ian Raitt is managing director of his own public relations firm. B June, 1933; ed Loretto School, Scotland, and St John's College, Cambridge.

Mr Stanley Vince, corporate communications consultant. B April, 1927; ed elementary school, South West Essex Technical College, and the Polytechnic, Regent Street. Contested Erith and Crayford, 1964; 1965 by-election, 1966.

BEXLEY Sidcup major

Electorate 49,095

*Heath, E. R. G. (C)	20.448
Hargrave, C. F. (Lab)	10,750
Moxon, O. (L)	9,847
Bennett, Air Vice-Marshal D. (Anti EEC)	613
C majority	9,698

	1974		1974
Total Vote	41,658	L	23·6%
Turn-out	84·8%	Anti-EEC	1·5%
C	49·1%	C maj	23·3%
Lab	25·8%		

Mr Edward Heath, Leader of the Opposition from March 1974, was Prime Minister from 1970. He became Leader of the Opposition and Leader of the Conservative Party on August 2, 1965, after securing an overall majority over his two rivals in the ballot of Conservative MPs, under the Parliamentary Party's new electoral process. Following the 1964 general election, he led for the Opposition on Treasury and economic affairs; was appointed chairman of the party's policy committee and research department. Secretary of State for Industry, Trade and Regional Development, and President of the Board of Trade, October 1963-64. Lord Privy Seal, 1960-63, and principal Foreign Office spokesman in the Commons, leading the British team in negotiations to join the Common Market,

Minister of Labour, October 1959-July 1960; Parliamentary Secretary to the Treasury, 1955-59; Deputy Chief Whip, 1952-55. Elected 1950. B July, 1916; ed Chatham House School, Ramsgate, and Balliol College, Oxford; president of the Union, 1939. Musician; chairman, trustee of London Symphony Orchestra, 1963-70; vice-president Bach Choir, since 1970. International yachtsman, won Sydney to Hobert race, 1969; captain Britain's Admiral's Cup team, 1971.

Mr Colin Hargrave is a schoolmaster and barrister (Lincoln's Inn, 1969). B October, 1943; ed Christ's College, Finchley, Mid-Essex Technical College and London School of Economics.

Mr Oliver Moxon contested Brighton, Kemptown 1970 and Hove 1966 and 1965 by-election. Author and company director. B June, 1922; ed Gresham's School.

BIRKENHEAD   major

Electorate 59,880

*Dell, E. (Lab)	20,696
Pyke, J. S. (C)	13,702
Lindsay, G. (L)	11,410
Lab majority	6,994

	1974		1974
Total Vote	45,808	C	29·9%
Turnout	76·5%	L	24·9%
Lab	45·2%	Lab maj	15·3%

Mr Edmund Dell, Chairman of the Public Accounts Committee since 1972, was formerly an Opposition spokesman on government relations with industry, monopolies and restrictive practices. Minister of State, Employment and Productivity, 1969-70;

Minister of State, Board of Trade, 1968-69; Under-Secretary, Department of Economic Affairs, 1967-68; Parliamentary Secretary, Ministry of Technology, 1966-67. Elected in 1964, contested Middleton and Prestwich, 1955. B August, 1921; ed Owen's School, London, and Queen's College, Oxford. Executive with ICI 1949-63, Member, Manchester City Council, 1953-60. President Manchester and Salford Trades Council, 1958-61. Sponsored by ASTMS. *Appointed Paymaster General, March 1974, attached to the Treasury.*

Mr John Pyke, jeweller and director of family jewellery firm. B February, 1940; ed Birkenhead School, Bromsgrove School and Trinity Hall, Cambridge. Member, Birkenhead CBC 1970-71 and 1972-74.

Mr Gordon Lindsay is a solicitor. B June, 1933; ed Loretto School, Scotland, and Liverpool University. Member, Birkenhead Borough Council, Merseyside County Council and Wirral Metropolitan District Council.

BIRMINGHAM   Edgbaston   major

Electorate 69,631

*Knight, Mrs. J. C. J. (C)	25,914
Hannah, J. G. (Lab)	19,994
Marshall, L. W. (Ind)	2,391
C majority	5,920

	1974		1974
Total Vote	48,299	Lab	41·4%
Turnout	69·4%	Ind	4·9%
C	53·6%	C maj	12·2%

Mrs Jill Knight, joint vice-chairman Conservative parliamentary health and social security committee since 1972, was elected in 1966; contested Northampton, 1959 and 1966. Housewife, lecturer and broadcaster. B July, 1927, ed Fairfield School, Bristol;

King Edward Grammar School, Birmingham. Member, Northampton Borough Council, 1955-66. Piloted Design Copyright Act 1968 through Parliament.

Mr John Hannah, Gas Board sales officer. B March, 1946; ed George Dixon Grammar School, Birmingham College of Commerce. Member, Birmingham City Council since 1969; West Midlands Metropolitan County Council since 1973. Member, NALGO.

BIRMINGHAM   Erdington   major

Electorate 65,231

*Silverman, J. (Lab)	22,978
Harvey, Miss C. F. (C)	16,050
Humphrey, P. T. (L)	6,991
Finnegan, T. M. (Nat Front)	1,145
Lab majority	6,928

	1974		1974
Total Vote	47,164	L	14·8%
Turnout	72·3%	Nat Front	2·4%
Lab	48·7%	Lab maj	14·7%
C	34·0%		

Mr Julius Silverman, a barrister (Gray's Inn, 1931), was elected in 1945 to the former Erdington seat abolished in 1955; then represented Aston 1955-74. Contested Moseley, 1935. B December, 1905, ed Leeds Central High School. First employed as a warehouseman, but later read for the Bar. Birmingham City Councillor, 1934-45.

Miss Caroline Harvey, political research officer at Conservative research department. B November, 1946; ed St Clare School, Penzance, and St Hugh's College, Oxford. Member, Oxford City Council.

Mr Patrick Humphrey, transport official. B August, 1926; ed Vaughan School, Kensington, and King's College, London. Contested Dagenham, 1964.

BIRMINGHAM Hall Green major

Electorate 66,524

*Eyre, R. E. (C)	27,280
Jamieson, D. C. (Lab)	21,036
C majority	6,244

	1974		1974
Total Vote	48,316	Lab	43·5%
Turnout	72·6%	C maj	12·9%
C	56·5%		

Mr Reginald Eyre, Under Secretary (Housing and Construction) for Environment 1972-74; Comptroller of HM Household 1970-72; Lord Commissioner of the Treasury, 1970. Was returned by a by-election in May, 1965; contested Birmingham, Northfield, 1959.

Solicitor. B May, 1924; ed King Edward's Camp Hill School, Birmingham, and Emmanuel College, Cambridge. National chairman, Conservative Political Centre, 1964-66. Opposition whip 1966-70.

Mr David Jamieson, teacher. B May, 1947; ed Tudor Grange Grammar School, Solihull, St Peter's College of Education, Saltley, Birmingham. Member, Solihull Council since 1970.

BIRMINGHAM Handsworth major

Electorate 45,399

Lee, J. M. H. (Lab)	14,290
*Chapman, S. B. (C)	12,667
Tilsley, P. (L)	5,566
Thompson, Miss S. (Marxist-Leninist)	334
Lab majority	1,623

	1974		1974
Total Vote	32,857	L	16·7%
Turnout	72·4%	Marx-Lenin	1·0%
Lab	43·5%	Lab maj	4·9%
C	38·5%		

Mr John Lee, barrister (Middle Temple, 1960), was MP for Reading, 1966-70 and contested that division in 1964. B August, 1927; ed Reading School, Christ's College, Cambridge, and School of Oriental and African Studies, London University. Administrative Officer, Colonial Service, Ghana 1951-58; on staff of BBC 1959-65. TGWU.

Mr Sydney Chapman, an architect and town planner, was elected in 1970. Member, Council of Royal Institute of British Architects, since 1972; secretary, Conservative Parliamentary Committee on local government and development. Instigator of National Tree Planting Year, 1973. Contested Stalybridge and Hyde, 1964. B October, 1935; ed Rugby School and Manchester University. Member, Executive Committee, National Union of Conservative and Unionist Associations, 1961-70; and vice-chairman, North-West area of Conservative and Unionist Associations 1966-70. National Chairman, Young Conservatives 1964-66. Associate partner in firm of architects and planning consultants; planning consultant, Home Builders' Federation.

Mr Paul Tilsley, sales representative. B March, 1945; ed Brandwood Secondary School and Lordswood Grammar-Technical School, Birmingham. Birmingham councillor since 1968; member, West Midlands Metropolitan County Council since 1973.

BIRMINGHAM Ladywood major

Electorate 40,155

*Walden, A. B. (Lab)	15,126
Lawn, R. (C)	6,164
Hardeman, K. G. (L)	3,753
Davis, J. A. A. (Nat Front)	751
Lab majority	8,962

	1974			1974
Total Vote	25,794	L		14·5%
Turnout	64·2%	Nat Front		2·9%
Lab	58·6%	Lab maj		34·7%
C	23·9%			

Mr Brian Walden, an Opposition spokesman on defence 1970-71 and on Treasury matters 1971-74, represented Birmingham All Saints 1964-74; fought Oswestry by-election, 1961. University tutor. B July, 1932; ed West Bromwich Grammar School, Queen's College and Nuffield College, Oxford (president of the Union, 1957).

Mr Richard Lawn, engineer and licensee. B June, 1921; ed Suffolk Street Technical College.

Mr Kenneth Hardeman, technical education adviser. B January, 1936; ed secondary modern school. Member, Birmingham City Council since 1966, alderman since 1971; Birmingham District Council since 1973.

Mr John Davis, plastics inspector. B January, 1942; ed at secondary modern school and Handsworth Technical School, Birmingham.

BIRMINGHAM Northfield major

Electorate 76,900

*Carter, R. J. (Lab)	31,704
Butcher, J. P. (C)	23,175
Newman, M. (Ind)	1,237
Robinson, D. W. (Comm)	368
Lab majority	8,529

	1974			1974
Total Vote	56,484	Ind		2·2%
Turnout	73·4%	Comm		0·6%
Lab	56·1%	Lab maj		15·1%
C	41·0%			

Mr Raymond Carter, electrical engineer, was elected in 1970. Contested Warwick 1968 by-election, and and Leamington, Wokingham, 1966. B September, 1935; ed Reading College of Technology and Stafford College of Technology. Member, Public Accounts Committee; Parliamentary and Scientific Com-

mittee, economic and finance group, trade and industry, power and steel and other groups. Chairman, Wokingham Labour Party, 1967-69. Member, Easthampstead Rural Council, 1963-68. TGWU.

Mr John Butcher, freelance sales consultant. B 1946; ed Huntingdon Grammar School; Birmingham University. Member, Birmingham City Council, since 1972.

Mr Derek Robinson, aged 46, is a toolmaker with BLMC. Contested the seat in 1966 and 1970. AEUW; shop steward since 1950; chairman, shop stewards' committee since 1957; deputy chairman, works committee; chairman, joint toolroom organization; and central services organization.

BIRMINGHAM Perry Barr major

Electorate 52,116

Rooker, J. W. (Lab)	17,960
*Kinsey, J. R. (C)	15,937
Hovers, K. J. (L)	6,044
Shorthouse, A. (Nat Front)	853
Lab majority	2,023

	1974			1974
Total Vote	40,794	L		14·8%
Turnout	78·3%	Nat Front		2·1%
Lab	44·0%	Lab maj		4·9%
C	39·1%			

Mr Jeffrey Rooker, chartered engineer and lecturer in industrial relations and organization of production at Lanchester Polytechnic. B June, 1941; ed Handsworth Technical College, College of Advanced Technology (now Aston University) and Warwick University. Co-opted member, Birmingham education committee 1972-74. ASTMS.

Mr Joseph Kinsey, retail florist, won the seat for the Conservatives in 1970; contested Birmingham, Aston, 1966. B August, 1921; ed at Church of England schools. Magistrate. Secretary, Perry Barr Conservative Association 1959-69. Alderman, Birmingham City Council, 1969.

Mr Kenneth Hovers, life assurance broker. B April, 1922; ed King Edward VI High School, Birmingham. Former Liberal Councillor on Birmingham City Council, 1956-61.

BIRMINGHAM Selly Oak   major

Electorate 62,357

*Gurden, H. E. (C)	19,705
Litterick, T. (Lab)	16,823
Grant, R. A. (L)	9,718
C majority	2,882

	1974		1974
Total Vote	46,246	Lab	36·4%
Turnout	74·2%	L	21·0%
C	42·6%	C maj	6·2%

Mr Harold Gurden, chairman, Commons Committee of Selection and member of Speaker's panel of chairmen, has held the seat since 1959. Company director in dairying and food industry. Vice-chairman, Conservative parliamentary education committee, 1965-66. B June, 1903; ed Lyttelton School, Birmingham, and Birmingham University. Former president of Birmingham Dairymen's Association and former chairman of the Society of Dairy Technology. Member, Birmingham City Council, 1946-56.

Mr Thomas Litterick is a lecturer in industrial relations. B May, 1929; ed Dundee School of Economics and St Andrews University. ASTMS.

Mr Roger Grant, education welfare officer. B October, 1946; ed King's Hill Secondary School, Lichfield and Walsall and Staffs College of Technology. Councillor for Aldridge-Brownhills UDC since 1970.

BIRMINGHAM Small Heath   major

Electorate 51,038

*Howell, D. H. (Lab)	19,319
Minnis, D. G. (L)	7,441
O'Connor, R. (C)	6,941
Lab majority	11,878

	1974		1974
Total Vote	33,701	L	22·1%
Turnout	66·0%	C	20·6%
Lab	57·3%	Lab maj	35·2%

Mr Denis Howell, Opposition spokesman on housing, local government and sport since 1970, was Minister of State for Housing and Local Government 1969-70. Under-Secretary for Education and Science, 1964-69. From 1964 he had special responsibility for sport; unofficially known as Minister for Sport. Returned at a by-election, March, 1961; represented the All Saints division, 1955-59, and contested former King's Norton division in 1951. B September, 1923; ed elementary school and Handsworth Grammar School, Birmingham. Member, Birmingham City Council, 1946-56, and the Albemarle Committee on the youth services. Football League referee. President, APEX. *Appointed Minister of State (Sport), Department of Environment, March 1974.*

Mr Dennis Minnis, travel executive. B September, 1938; ed Mary St Junior School and St Albans C of E School, Birmingham. Contested Birmingham, All Saints, 1970. Member, Birmingham City Council 1969-74, West Midlands Metropolitan Council, since 1973 and Birmingham District Council, since 1973 (Leader, Liberal group).

Mr Roman O'Connor is a company director. B June, 1947; ed grammar school and London and Birmingham Universities. Member, Birmingham City Council and chairman, Youth Employment Committee.

BIRMINGHAM Sparkbrook   major

Electorate 49,344

*Hattersley, R. S. G. (Lab)	19,939
Savage, D. J. (C)	12,534
Lab majority	7,405

	1974		1974
Total Vote	32,473	C	38·6%
Turnout	65·8%	Lab maj	22·8%
Lab	61·4%		

Mr Roy Hattersley, Opposition spokesman on education since 1972, was spokesman for foreign and Commonwealth affairs, 1970-72, and defence, 1972. Minister of Defence for Administration, 1969-70; Under Secretary, Department of Employment and Productivity, 1968-69; Parliamentary Secretary, Ministry of Labour, 1967-68. Elected in 1964; contested Sutton Coldfield, 1959. Health service executive. B December, 1932; ed Sheffield City Grammar School and Hull University. ASMTS. *Appointed Minister of State for Foreign and Commonwealth Affairs, March 1974.*

Mr David Savage, solicitor. B August, 1939; ed Hurstpierpoint College, College of Law. Member, Farnborough UDC, 1964-74 (vice-chairman 1971-72); Rusmoor Council since 1973. Chairman, Aldershot constituency association, 1969-73. Member, Swinton College Advisory Council since 1973; Commissioner of Income Tax since 1969.

BIRMINGHAM Stechford   major

Electorate 62,005

*Jenkins, R. H. (Lab)	23,704
Wedgwood, D. J. (C)	13,472
Gopsill, G. A. (L)	7,221
Bull, R. (WRP)	280
Lab majority	10,232

	1974		1974
Total Vote	44,677	L	16·2%
Turnout	72·0%	WRP	0·6%
Lab	53·0%	Lab maj	22·9%
C	30·1%		

Mr Roy Jenkins was re-elected to the Shadow Cabinet, 1973, having resigned as Deputy Leader of the Parliamentary Labour Party in April 1972 in disagreement with Labour policy towards the Common Market. Opposition spokesman on Home Office affairs since 1973. Chancellor of the Exchequer 1967-70; Home Secretary, 1965-67; Minister of Aviation, 1964-65. Economist, author, and journalist. Elected 1950. B November, 1920; ed Abersychan County School and Balliol College, Oxford; secretary and librarian, Oxford Union Society. Contested Solihull, 1945; represented Southwark, 1948-50. Chairman, Fabian Society, 1957-58. Member, Committee of Management, Society of Authors, 1956-60. Promoted Obscene Publications Act, 1959. Director of financial operations, John Lewis Partnership, 1962-64. Chairman, Labour European Committee; President, United Kingdom Council of European Movement. *Appointed Home Secretary, March 1974.*

Mr David Wedgwood is a consultant in public and industrial relations. B August, 1945; ed Bideford Grammar School, Crewkerne School, and Exeter College, Oxford. NUJ.

Mr Graham Gopsill, insurance agent. B December, 1938; ed Moseley School of Art, Birmingham. Member, Birmingham City Council since 1969; Birmingham District Council since 1973.

Mr Royston Bull, journalist. B 1935; ed grammar school and Leeds University. Chairman, Fleet Street Branch, NUJ, 1971-73.

BIRMINGHAM Yardley   major

Electorate 58,596

Tierney, S. (Lab)	20,580
*Coombs, D. M. (C)	18,633
Aldridge, J. (L)	6,912
Lab majority	1,947

	1974		1974
Total Vote	46,125	C	40·4%
Turnout	78·7%	L	15·0%
Lab	44·6%	Lab maj	4·2%

Mr Sydney Tierney, an officer and member of USDAW. Former milkman. Member, Co-operative Party. B September, 1923; ed Dearne Secondary Modern School and Plater College, Oxford.

Mr Derek Coombs won the seat for the Conservatives in 1970. Joint managing director of a family-controlled public company operating stores and mail order business. B August, 1931; ed Rydal School, Colwyn Bay, and Bromsgrove School.

Mr John Aldridge, insurance broker and consultant. B August, 1944; ed at Moseley Grammar School. Former Treasurer, Birmingham Regional Liberal Party.

BISHOP AUCKLAND   major

Electorate 72,924

*Boyden, H. J. (Lab)	27,101
Etheridge, D. W. (C)	19,226
Frise, Mrs. J. (L)	10,044
Lab majority	7,875

	1974		1974
Total Vote	56,371	C	34·1%
Turnout	77·3%	L	17·8%
Lab	48·1%	Lab maj	14·0%

Mr James Boyden was Under-Secretary for Defence (Army), 1967-69; Parliamentary Secretary, Public Building and Works, 1965-67; and Under Secretary, Education and Science, 1964-65. Returned in 1959. Director of extramural studies at Durham University. B October, 1910; ed Tiffin's School, Kingston upon Thames, and King's College, London, of which he is a Fellow. Called to the Bar (Lincoln's Inn), 1947. Member, Defence sub-committee of Public Expenditure Committee; Durham County Council, 1952-60; Newcastle RHB, 1958-64. Chairman of executive, National Institute for Adult Education, 1958-61. NUGMW.

Mr Donald Etheridge, management consultant. B August, 1936; ed Whitgift School. Member Godstone Council, 1970-72.

Mrs **Jill Frise**, teacher. B April, 1938; ed Bishop Auckland Grammar School and Bingley Training College. Member, Darlington and Croft Rural District and Chairman, Great Aycliffe Parish Council. Member, Rydale District Council since 1973.

	1970		1974
Total Vote	42,210		42,049
Turnout	75·6%		77·1%
Lab	22,473	53·2%	48·4%
C	19,737	46·7%	33·4%
L	—	—	14·0%
Nat Front	—	—	4·2%
Lab maj	2,736	6·5%	15·0%
Swing		+5·0%	−4·2%

BLABY   major

Electorate 64,534

*Lawson, N. (C)	26,892
Broad, G. (L)	14,594
Lack, D. E. (Lab)	13,749
C majority	12,298

	1974			1974
Total Vote	55,235	L		26·4%
Turnout	85·6%	Lab		24·9%
C	48·7%	C maj		22·3%

Mr **Nigel Lawson**, journalist, contested Eton and Slough, 1970. B March, 1932; ed Westminster School, Christ Church, Oxford. Editor of the *Spectator,* 1966-70. Was special assistant to Sir Alec Douglas-Home, then Prime Minister, in 1963-64; Editorial staff, *Financial Times,* 1956-60; City Editor, *The Sunday Telegraph,* 1961-63; Special Political Adviser, Conservative Party H.Q., 1973-74; Quondam Fellow of Nuffield College, Oxford.

Mr **Gordon Broad** is principal of Burleigh College, Loughborough. B June, 1914; ed Tonbridge School and King's College, London. Member, Leicestershire Education Committee.

Mr **David Lack**, teacher. B November, 1942; ed St Mary Cray secondary modern, Central School of Arts and Craft, City of Leicester College of Education. Member, Braunstone Parish Council. NUT.

Mrs **Barbara Castle**, chief Opposition spokesman on employment 1970-71 and security 1971-72, when she failed to be elected to Shadow Cabinet and returned to back benches. First Secretary and Secretary of State for Employment and Productivity, 1968-70; Minister of Transport, 1965-68; Minister of Overseas Development, 1964-65. Member, National Executive of Labour Party since 1950, chairman, 1958-59. One of two Blackburn MPs from 1945, elected for East Blackburn in 1950, and for the single member division in 1955. Journalist. B October, 1911; ed Bradford Girls' Grammar School and St Hugh's College, Oxford. *Appointed Secretary of State for Social Services, March 1974.*

Mr **Ian McGaw** is an insurance broker. Contested St Helens 1970. B August, 1940; ed Anfield Road Primary School and Collegiate School, Liverpool. Member, Young Conservatives National Advisory Committee, 1966-70.

Mr **Frank Beetham**, toolmaker. B March, 1932; ed St Albans Higher Grade Roman Catholic School and Blackburn Technical College. Contested Heywood and Royton, 1970. Councillor on Blackburn Borough Council since 1964 and Leader of the Liberal Group. Member, Blackburn District Council since 1973.

Mr **J. Kingsley Read**, textile manufacturers' agent, aged 37. Ed Christ Church infants' and primary schools, Blackburn Technical High School and Leeds University. Qualified AAA honorary coach and athletics judge.

BLACKBURN   same

Electorate 54,531   1970: 55,811

*Castle, Mrs B. A. (Lab)	20,340
McGaw, I. D. (C)	14,040
Beetham, F. (L)	5,891
Kingsley Read, J. (Nat Front)	1,778
Lab majority	6,300

No change

BLACKPOOL North   same

Electorate 59,290   1970: 58,865

*Miscampbell, N. A. (C)	23,942
Taylor, I. J. (Lab)	15,788
Nickson, P. B. (Ind L)	3,720
C majority	8,154

No change

	1970		1974
Total Vote	40,306		43,45 !
Turnout	68·5%		73·3%
C	22,298	55·3%	55·1%
Lab	13,062	32·4%	36·3%
L	4,946	12·3%	—
Ind L	—		8·6%
C maj	9,236	22·9	18·8%
Swing		+4·9%	−2·0%

Mr Norman Miscampbell, secretary Conservative parliamentary legal committee 1971-73, was returned at a by-election in March, 1962. Contested Newton in 1955 and 1959. Barrister (Inner Temple, 1952); B February, 1925; ed St Edward's School, Oxford, and Trinity College, Oxford. Member, Hoylake Urban District Council, 1955-61. PPS to Attorney-General 1973-74.

Mr Ivan Taylor, an engineer in the aircraft industry. Member, Blackpool District Council since 1973 and Blackpool Borough Council, 1966-73. B July, 1939. AUEW.

BLACKPOOL South   same

Electorate 57,576   1970: 58,937

*Blaker, P. A. R. (C)	20,107
Wynne, E. E. (L)	12,016
Atkins, M. (Lab)	11,739
Mills, E. (Nat Ind)	229
C majority	**8,091**

No change

	1970		1974
Total Vote	40,270		44,091
Turnout	68·3%		76·6%
C	21,273	52·8%	45·6%
Lab	13,267	32·9%	26·2%
L	5,730	14·2%	27·2%
Nat Ind	—		0·5%
C maj	8,006	19·9%	18·3%
Swing		+5·6%	−0·4%

Mr Peter Blaker, Under-Secretary for Foreign and Commonwealth Affairs, 1974, and Under-Secretary for Defence for the Army, 1972-74, was elected in 1964. B October, 1922; ed Shrewsbury School, Toronto University, and New College, Oxford, President of the Union and University Law Society. Barrister (Lincoln's Inn 1952); farmer; Foreign Service 1953-64. Assistant Opposition whip, 1966-67. On executive of 1922 Committee 1967-72. Joint secretary,

Conservative parliamentary trade committee, 1967-72.

Mr Edmund Wynne, a former Mayor of Blackpool, is a soft drinks manufacturer and sporting club proprietor. B February, 1917; ed Uddingstone Grammar School, Scotland. Member, Blackpool Borough Council (Mayor, 1972-73), Blackpool District Council and Lancashire County Council.

Mr Michael Atkins, civil engineer. B January, 1942; ed Earls Colne Grammar School, Wandsworth and Chelmsford Technical Colleges. Member, Preston Borough Council and Preston District Council. Member, Nalgo.

BLAYDON   same

Electorate 56,701   1970: 54,804

*Woof, R. E. (Lab)	27,279
Craig, A. A. (C)	15,705
Lab majority	**11,574**

No change

	1970		1974
Total Vote	39,650		42,984
Turnout	72·3%		75·8%
Lab	25,724	64·9%	63·5%
C	13,926	35·1%	36·5%
Lab maj	11,798	29·7%	26·9%
Swing		+4·3%	+1·4%

Mr Robert Woof, a miner and trade union official, was returned at a by-election in February, 1956. B October, 1911; ed Durham county school. Member, Durham County Council, 1947-56. Former official of National Union of Mineworkers, and sponsored by them.

Mr Alan Craig, executive, Slater Walker Securities. B 1945; ed Kingston Grammar School, Newcastle University, Manchester Business School. Political officer of the Bow Group.

BLYTH   minor

Electorate 73,984   1970: 67,911

*Milne, E. J. (Ind Lab)	22,918
*Richard, I. S. (Lab)	16,778
Shipley, J. (L)	10,214
Griffiths, B. (C)	8,888
Ind Lab majority	**6,140**

Ind Lab gain

	1970		1974
Total Vote	48,668		58,798
Turnout	71·7%		79·5%
Lab	36,118	74·2%	28·5%
C	12,550	25·8%	15·1%
Ind Lab	—	—	39·0%
L	—	—	17·4%
Lab maj	23,568	48·4%	—
Ind Lab maj	—	—	10·4%
Swing		+4·0%	

Mr Edward Milne, who was returned for Labour in the 1960 by-election, stood in 1974 as Independent when the constituency association decided to select a new candidate. C o n t e s t e d R u t h e r g l e n for Labour 1959. Trade union official. B October, 1915; ed Robert

Gordon's College, Aberdeen. Area organizer, Union of Shop, Distributive and Allied Workers, 1952-60. Vice-chairman, Parliamentary Labour Party, 1967-68; member of Speaker's panel of chairmen, 1965-66.

Mr Ivor Richard was MP for Barons Court 1964-74. An Opposition spokesman on Foreign and Commonwealth Affairs and formerly on posts and telecommunications. Under-Secretary of Defence for the Army, 1969-70. Contested Kensington, South, in 1959. Barrister (called by Inner Temple 1955). B May, 1932; ed St Michael's School, Llanelli, Cheltenham College, and Pembroke College, Oxford. *Appointed Permanent UK Representative at United Nations, March 1974.*

Mr John Shipley, administrator with the Open University. B July, 1946; ed Whitby Grammar School and University College, London. Member, Liberal Party's education panel. Former President of University College's student union. AUT. Northumberland FA referee; former secretary, Northern Liberal Party, 1973-74; agent, Mid Northumberland Liberal Association, 1970-73.

Mr Brian Griffiths, lecturer in politics at London School of Economics. Member, Bow Group.

BODMIN   major

Electorate 55,087

Tyler, P. (L)		20,283
*Hicks, R. (C)		20,274
Lonsdale, Mrs G. (Lab)		5,328
L majority		9

	1974		1974
Total Vote	45,885	C	44·2%
Turnout	83·3%	Lab	11·6%
L	44·2%	L maj	0·0%

Mr Paul Tyler, parliamentary adviser to Royal Institute of British Architects. B October, 1941; ed Mount House School, Tavistock, Sherborne School and Exeter College, Oxford. Contested Bodmin, 1970 and Totnes, 1966. Member, D e v o n County Council, 1964-

70; Devon and Cornwall Police Authority, 1966-70. Vice-chairman, Dartmoor National Park Committee, 1965-70. Appointed Liberal spokesman on housing and transport, March 1974.

Mr Robert Hicks, technical college lecturer, won the seat for the Conservatives in 1970. Assistant Government whip 1973-74. Contested Aberavon in 1966. B January, 1938; ed Queen Elizabeth Grammar School, Crediton, and University College, London. Joint vice-chairman, Conservative parliamentary agriculture, fisheries and food committee, 1972-73; joint secretary, West Country Conservative MPs, 1972-73. National vice-chairman of Young Conservatives, 1964-66; vice-chairman national advisory committee on education, 1965-67. Fellow of the Royal Geographical Society.

Mrs G. Lonsdale is a lecturer in social work at Plymouth Polytechnic; formerly a social worker with Cornwall County Council. Aged 38; ed state schools and London University.

BOLSOVER   same

Electorate 51,384   1970: 52,552

*Skinner, D. E. (Lab)	30,787
Dix, A. R. (C)	9,474
Lab majority	21,313

No change

	1970		1974
Total Vote	37,201		40,261
Turnout	70·8%		78·3%
Lab	28,830	77·5%	76·5%
C	8,371	22·5%	23·5%
Lab maj	20,459	55·0%	52·9%
Swing		+4·5%	+1·0%

Mr Dennis Skinner, former miner and president of Derbyshire National Union of Mineworkers since 1966, was elected in 1970. B February, 1932; ed Tupton Hall Grammar School and Ruskin C o l l e g e. Former member, Clay Cross Urban District Council and Derby-

shire County Council. Sponsored by NUM.

Mr **Alan Dix**, marketing director of a chemical company. B August 1947. Former officer of Greater London Young Conservatives; former divisional chairman, Cities of London and Westminster Young Conservatives and St Marylebone Young Conservatives.

BOLTON East   same

Electorate 59,723   1970: 61,243

Young, D. W. (Lab)	19,833
*Reed, L. D. (C)	18,220
Ackroyd, T. (L)	8,728
Booth, G. (Nat Front)	1,259
Lab majority	1,613

Labour gain

	1970		1974
Total Vote	45,067		48,040
Turnout	73.6%		80.4%
C	22,769	50.5%	37.9%
Lab	22,298	49.5%	41.3%
L	—	—	18.2%
Nat Front	—	—	2.6%
C maj	471	1.0%	
Lab maj	—	—	3.3%
Swing		+9.7%	−2.2%

Mr **David Young**, teacher, contested Bath, 1970, Banbury, 1966, and South Worcestershire, 1959. B October, 1930; ed Greenock Academy, Glasgow University and St Paul's College, Cheltenham. Alderman, Nuneaton Borough Council, and councillor, Nuneaton District Council. Chairman, Coventry East Labour Party 1964-68.

Mr **Laurance Reed** won the seat for the Conservatives in 1970. B December, 1937; ed Gresham's School and University College, Oxford. Worked in the Conservative Party public sector research unit, 1967-69. Member, Society for Underwater Technology; Select Committee on Science and Technology.

Mr **Tim Ackroyd**, barrister. B July, 1947; ed Kirtham Grammar School, Manchester University. Member, Guildford Borough Council, 1971-72.

Mr **Geoffrey Booth**, Journalist. B April 1932; ed Burnage High School Manchester, College of Commerce, Bristol. Member, NUJ; national executive member, 1963-64.

BOLTON West   same

Electorate 50,407   1970: 50,254

*Redmond, R. S. (C)	16,562
Taylor, Mrs. W. A. (Lab)	15,959
Linney, P. (L)	8,264
C majority	603

No change

	1970		1974
Total Vote	37,206		40,785
Turnout	74.0%		80.9%
C	19,225	51.7%	40.6%
Lab	17,981	48.3%	39.1%
L	—		20.3%
C maj	1,244	3.3%	1.5%
Swing		+8.1%	−0.9%

Mr **Robert Redmond**, management consultant, won the seat for the Conservatives in 1970. B September, 1919; ed Liverpool College. Vice-chairman, Conservative parliamentary employment committee since 1972. Member, Select Committee on nationalized industries. President, Alderley Edge branch, Royal British Legion.

Mr **Philip Linney**, chairman and managing director. B August, 1932; ed at Rivington and Blackrod Grammar School. Member, Turton Urban District Council since November 1963; chairman, 1969-70; member, Blackburn District Council since 1973.

BOOTLE   major

Electorate 63,463

*Mahon, S. (Lab)	27,301
Burrows, J. F. (C)	12,366
Fjortoft, Mrs H. (L)	6,258
Morris, R. (Comm)	586
Lab majority	14,935

	1974		1974
Total Vote	46,511	L	13.4%
Turnout	73.3%	Comm	1.2%
Lab	58.7%	Lab maj	32.1%
C	26.6%		

Mr **Simon Mahon** was elected in 1955. Opposition Whip, 1959-61. Ship repairer and contractor. An alderman of Bootle Borough Council; Mayor of Bootle, 1962-63. B April, 1914; ed St Joseph's Irish Christian Brothers School and St James' School, Bootle. Commissioned Royal Engineers, 1939-45. Trustee, Far Eastern Prisoners of War Fund. TGWU.

Mr **James Burrows**, company director. B 1924; ed elementary schools. Chairman, Bootle county borough education committee, 1968-71. Conservative chief whip, Bootle Council from 1970.

Mrs Helen Fjortoft, housewife. B May, 1925. Former hon. secretary, Merseyside Regional Liberal Party.

Mr Ronald Morris, aged 45, shop steward in the building industry. Secretary, All Bootle Rent Action Committee, 1972-73. Member, Merseyside area committee of the Communist Party; secretary of Bootle branch.

BOSWORTH   minor

Electorate 83,120   1970: 78,192

*Butler, A. (C)	28,151
Sloman, M. G. M. (Lab)	26,464
Galton, M. (L)	16,859
C majority	1,687

No change

	1970		1974
Total Vote	60,409		71,474
Turnout	77·1%		86·0%
C	30,732	50·9%	39·4%
Lab	29,677	49·1%	37·0%
L	—	—	23·6%
C maj	1,055	1·7%	2·4%
Swing		+8·0%	+0·3%

Mr Adam Butler, second son of Lord Butler, won the seat for the Conservatives in 1970. Assistant Government Whip, 1974. B October, 1931; ed Eton and Pembroke College, Cambridge. Was employed by Courtaulds Ltd 1955-73. Farmer. Member Commons Public Expenditure Centre, 1970-72.

Mr Martyn Sloman, National Coal Board economist. B July, 1946; ed Hywel DDA School, Cardiff, and University of Lancaster. Contested Leominster, 1970. Member, London Borough of Brent, 1971-74. APEX.

Mr Maurice Galton is a university lecturer. B May, 1937; ed Salesian College, Oxford, and Newcastle and Leeds Universities.

BOTHWELL   major

Electorate 58,697

*Hamilton, J. (Lab)	22,326
McAllister, D. (C)	12,725
Fisher, G. (Scot Nat)	6,710
Park, J. (L)	5,362
Bolton, D. (Comm)	562
Lab majority	9,601

	1974		1974
Total Vote	47,685	Scot Nat	14·1%
Turnout	81·2%	L	11·2%
Lab	46·8%	Comm	1·2%
C	26·7%	Lab maj	20·1%

Mr James Hamilton, chairman, trade union group Parliamentary Labour Party, 1969-70, assistant Government Whip 1969-70, and Opposition Whip, 1970, was elected in 1964. B March, 1918; ed senior secondary schools. Member, Lanarkshire County Council, 1955-65.

President, Constructional Engineering Union, 1968-70; member of its national executive, 1958-70. Chairman, Bothwell Trades Council, 1953-65. Sponsored by AUEW, construction section. *Appointed Lord Commissioner of the Treasury (Government Whip), March 1974.*

Mr David McAllister, marketing manager. B July, 1943; ed Bellshill and Uddingston Grammar School.

Mr Gerald Fisher, computer manager. Aged 44; ed Whitehill School and Glasgow University. Treasurer, British Computer Society, chairman of London branch; chairman, Holiday Fellowship Ltd.

Mr James Park, careers officer and ex-worker. B December 1948; ed Dalziel High School, Motherwell and Strathclude University.

Mr David Bolton, a miner for 35 years. Joined Communist Party 1951; elected vice-president of Scottish area NUM in 1969. B September, 1923; ed Holytown and Chapelhall High School.

BOURNEMOUTH East   major

Electorate 56,673

*Cordle, J. H. (C)	22,319
Musgrave, G. (L)	13,005
Lock, D. E. (Lab)	7,423
Hayes, M. (Nat Front)	875
Reynolds, A. (Anti-EEC)	834
C majority	9,314

	1974		1974
Total Vote	44,456	Lab	16·7%
Turnout	78·4%	Nat Front	2·0%
C	50·2%	Anti-EEC	1·9%
L	29·2%	C maj	20·9%

Mr John Cordle represented Bournemouth East and Christchurch 1959-74; contested the Wrekin division, 1951. Chairman, E. W. Cordle and Son Ltd, linen and cotton manufacturers, since 1968; chairman, Surgical Medical Laboratories Ltd; director of three

other companies. Member of Lloyd's. B October, 1912; ed at the City of London School. Member, Church Assembly, 1946-53.

Mr George Musgrave contested Bournemouth, East and Christchurch in 1970. Managing director of his own firm, Gemodels Ltd. B October, 1915; ed Hornsey County School and Nottingham University. Served with Commonwealth Missionary Society, British Guiana 1943-55.

Mr Desmond Lock, lecturer. B September, 1930; ed Henry Thornton Grammar School, Clapham, and London School of Economics. Local official, ATTI, since 1963.

Mr Michael Hayes, builder and decorator. B July, 1930; ed Bournemouth Grammar School.

BOURNEMOUTH West   major

Electorate 60,843

*Eden, Sir J. B. (C)	23,473
Richards, T. (L)	12,655
Bennett, L. F. (Lab)	10,062
C majority	10,818

	1974		1974
Total Vote	46,190	L	27·4%
Turnout	75·9%	Lab	21·8%
C	50·8%	C maj	23·4%

Sir John Eden, Minister of Posts and Telecommunications 1972 to 1974, was Minister for Industry 1970-72; and Minister of State for Technology June to October, 1970. Returned at a by-election in February, 1954; contested Paddington, North, December, 1953. Former company director. B September, 1925; ed Eton and in the United States. President, Independent Schools Association, 1969-71 and Vice-President, National Chamber of Trade, 1968-70.

Mr Terence Richards, manager of a company of paper merchants. B September, 1947; ed Oakmead School for Boys, Bournemouth, and Bournemouth College of Technology.

Mr Lionel Bennett, chartered engineer, contested the seat in 1970 and 1966. B July, 1929, Newport, Isle of Wight; ed County Grammar School, Southampton University and Bournemouth College of Technology. Member, Bournemouth Council, 1962-67 and since 1972; Bournemouth District Council since June, 1973, and leader of Labour group; Dorset County Council since April, 1973, and deputy leader of Labour group. ASTMS.

BRADFORD North   major

Electorate 64,524

*Ford, B. T. (Lab)	22,381
Thompson, H. P. (C)	15,764
Lishman, G. (L)	13,115
Marriott, A. (Ind)	386
Lab majority	6,617

	1974		1974
Total Vote	51,646	L	25·4%
Turnout	80·0%	Ind	0·7%
Lab	43·3%	Lab maj	12·8%
C	30·5%		

Mr Benjamin Ford was elected in 1964. Engineer. B April, 1925; ed Rowan Road Central School, Surrey. Alderman, Essex County Council, 1959-65. Member Clacton UDC, 1960-63. Vice-chairman, British-Latin American parliamentary group; chairman, Anglo-Portuguese, Anglo-Vietnam and Anglo-Malaysian groups. Vice-chairman, All-Party Wool Textile Group. AUEW sponsored. Member, executive, UK branch of Inter-Parliamentary Union, and of executive, trade union group, PLP.

Mr Patrick Thompson, teacher. B October, 1935; ed Felsted School, Essex, and Emmanuel College, Cambridge. Deputy chairman, North Norfolk Conservative Association; chairman, Eastern Area Committee of National Advisory Committee on Education.

Mr Gordon Lishman, charity organizer. B November, 1947; ed Colne Grammar School and Manchester University. Former vice-chairman National League of Young Liberals, 1969-73. Chairman, North-West Community Newspapers Ltd.

BRADFORD South   major

Electorate 71,507

*Torney, T. W. (Lab)	25,875
Dwyer, P. G. (C)	18,222
Holmstedt, Miss M. (L)	12,961
Pearson, R. (Ind Powellite)	749
Lab majority	7,653

	1974		1974
Total Vote	57,807	L	22·4%
Turnout	80·8%	Ind Powell	1·3%
Lab	44·8%	Lab maj	13·2%
C	31·5%		

Mr Thomas Torney,
elected in 1970, was
Derby and District
area organizer of the
Union of Shop, Dis-
tributive and Allied
Workers for over 20
years. B July, 1915.
Member, general
management commit-
tee, Derby Labour
Party; and Select
Committee on Race
Relations. Sponsored by USDAW.

Mr Paul Dwyer, public relations and marketing consultant. B May, 1940; ed St
Peter's Court, Broadstairs, St George's,
Cape Town, and Royal Agricultural College. Former councillor, London Borough
of Hammersmith.

Miss Margareta Holmstedt, part-time
university lecturer, translator and writer.
July 1941; ed Stockholm University.
Former Parliamentary Secretary, Swedish
Liberal Party in Parliament. Attache,
Swedish Embassy in London. World
President, World Federation of Liberal
and Radical Youth, 1968-70. Married to
Mr Michael Steed, Liberal candidate for
Manchester, Central.

BRADFORD West major

Electorate 61,282

*Lyons, E. (Lab)	20,787
*Wilkinson, J. A. D. (C)	18,568
Taylor, R. F. (L)	7,216
Merrick, J. (Anti-Immigration)	1,164
Herbert, R. O. (Ind Dem All)	200
Lab majority	2,219

	1974		1974
Total Vote	47,935	L	15·0%
Turnout	78·2%	Anti-Immig	2·4%
Lab	43·4%	Ind Dem All	0·4%
C	38·7%	Lab maj	4·6%

Mr Edward Lyons
represented Bradford,
East, 1966-74. Mem-
ber of the Select
Committee on Race
Relations and Immi-
gration 1968-70. Bar-
rister (Lincoln's Inn,
1952). Recorder since
1972. B May, 1926;
ed City of Leeds
School, Roundhay
High School and
Leeds University. Member, Society of
Labour Lawyers and Fabian Society.
Russian interpreter, 1946-48, attached to
Control Commission, Germany. Member,
PLP Home Affairs Group since 1966,
deputy chairman since 1970.

Mr John Wilkinson won Bradford, West,
for the Conservatives in 1970. Joint Secretary, Conservative parliamentary aviation
committee; secretary, defence committee
since 1972. B September, 1940; ed Eton,
RAF College, Cranwell, and Churchill
College, Cambridge. Member, Select Committees for Science and Technology and
for Race Relations and Immigration. Head
of Universities Department, Conservative
Central Office, 1967-68; aviation specialist,
Conservative Research Department, 1969.

Mr Roderick Taylor, handloom weaver.
B March, 1938; ed Bradford schools.

BRAINTREE major

Electorate 64,979

Newton, A. H. (C)	20,797
Kyle, J. K. (Lab)	18,796
Scott, D. (L)	15,204
C majority	2,001

	1974		1974
Total Vote	54,797	Lab	34·3%
Turnout	84·3%	L	27·7%
C	37·9%	C maj	3·6%

Mr Antony Newton
contested Sheffield,
Brightside in 1970.
Economist. Formerly
Assistant Director of
the Conservative Re-
search Department.
B August, 1937; ed
Friends' School, Saf-
fron Walden, and
Trinity College, Ox-
ford.

Mr Keith Kyle,
television journalist and member of the
staff of the Royal Institute of International
Affairs. B August, 1925; ed Chafyn Grove
School, Salisbury, Bromsgrove School and
Magdalen College, Oxford. Contested St
Albans, 1966. Former Washington correspondent and political and parliamentary
correspondent of *The Economist*. NUJ
and NUGMW.

Mr David Scott, newspaper sports editor.
B December, 1947; ed Ermysteds Skipton
Grammar School.

BRECON AND RADNOR same

Electorate 53,857   1970: 52,629

*Roderick, C. E. (Lab)	18,180
Davies, L. H. (C)	15,903
Thomas, N. (L)	8,741
Gittins, D. N. (Pl Cymru)	2,099
Lab majority	2,277

No change

	1970		1974
Total Vote	43,146		44,923
Turnout	82·0%		83·4%
Lab	18,736	43·4%	40·5%
C	13,892	32·3%	35·4%
L	8,169	18·9%	19·4%
Pl Cymru	2,349	5·4%	4·7%
Lab maj	4,844	11·2%	5·1%
Swing		+4·9%	+3·0%

Mr Caerwyn Roderick, elected in 1970, was a lecturer at Cardiff College of Education. B July, 1927; ed University College of North Wales. Was member, local executive NUT; national advisory committee for comprehensive schools and Welsh secondary committee of the NUT. Senior master, Hartridge High, Newport, 1960-69.

Mr Lloyd Havard Davies contest Carmarthen, 1970. Farmer, journalist and television commentator. B November, 1919; ed Llandovery Secondary School and Avoncroft Agricultural College, Worcestershire.

Mr Noel Thomas, lecturer. B December, 1929; ed Grove Park Grammar School, University of Wales in Bangor, University of Bristol, and University of Birmingham. Taught in Finland, Cyprus, Swaziland, South Africa.

Mr Dafydd Gittins, executive with Lufthansa airline trade union. B December, 1949; ed Brecon High School, Knightsbridge Computer College and Lufthansa training base, Hamburg.

BRENT East major

Electorate 62,811

*Freeson, R. (Lab)	21,063
Young, G. K. (C)	13,441
Perry, W. (L)	8,204
Lab majority	7,622

	1974		1974
Total Vote	42,708	C	31·5%
Turnout	68·0%	L	19·2%
Lab	49·3%	Lab maj	17·8%

Mr Reginald Freeson, Parliamentary Secretary, Ministry of Housing and Local Government, 1969-70; Parliamentary Secretary, Ministry of Power, 1967-69, was MP for Willesden, East, 1964-74. An Opposition spokesman on housing and construction, 1970 to 1974. B February, 1926; ed Jewish Orph-

anage, West Norwood, and Private study. Leader, Willesden Borough Council, 1958-65; chairman Brent Borough Council, 1964-65; alderman, Willesden and Brent, 1955-68. NUJ. *Appointed Minister for Housing and Construction, Department of Environment, March 1974.*

Mr George Young, merchant banker, served in Diplomatc and Civil Service, and resigned as Deputy Secretary in 1961. Former chairman, Monday Club economic policy group and Society for Individual Freedom. B April, 1911; ed Dumfries Academy, and St Andrew's, Dijon, Giessen, and Yale Universities.

Mr Woolf Perry, merchant banker. B October, 1919; ed Sir Walter and St John's School, London, and London University. Former vice-president, World Jewish Congress; member, Board of Deputies of British Jews; vice-chairman, Central Council for Jewish Education.

BRENT North major

Electorate 71,542

Boyson, R. (C)	25,700
Goudie, T. J. C. (Lab)	17,759
Harrison, F. (L)	12,537
Smith, A. (Nat Front)	1,570
C majority	7,941

	1974		1974
Total Vote	57,566	L	21·8%
Turnout	80·5%	Nat Fron:	2·7%
C	44·6%	C maj	13·8%
Lab	30·8%		

Mr Rhodes Boyson, headmaster Highbury Grove Comprehensive School, and publisher, fought Eccles, 1970. B May, 1925; ed Haslingden Grammar School, Cardiff, Manchester, London and Cambridge Universities. Chairman, National Council for Educational standards. Member, Waltham Forest Borough Council, since 1968.

Mr James Goudie, barrister, is Deputy Leader of Brent Council and chairman of its housing committee. Member since 1967. B June, 1942; ed Dean Close School, Cheltenham, and London School of Economics.

Mr Frederick Harrison, journalist. B March, 1944; ed University College, Oxford, Ruskin College, Oxford, and Birkbeck College, London.

Mr Alan Smith, marketing director. B July 1943; ed Southgate County Grammar School. Chairman, Kingsbury and Kenton branch, National Federation of Old Age Pensioners; member, National Trust.

BRENT South   major

Electorate 60,804

*Pavitt, L. A. (Lab & Co-op)	22,975
Holt, J. R. (C)	12,351
Waschauer, H. (L)	5,804
Harrison-Broadley, Sq Ldr J. (Nat Front)	1,852
Burt, L. (Comm)	380
Lab majority	10,624

	1974		1974
Total Vote	43,362	L	13·4%
Turnout	71·3%	Nat Front	4·3%
Lab & Co-op	53·0%	Comm	0·9%
C	28·5%	Lab & Co-op maj	24·5%

Mr Laurence Pavitt, MP, Willesden, West, 1959-74, was national organizer of the Medical Practitioners' Union, 1956-59. B February, 1914; ed elementary and central schools. Member, Medical Research Council, 1969-72; Hearing Aid Council; and Select Committee on Overseas Aid. Chairman, of PLP health group since 1964. Member, executive United Kingdom branches of Inter-Parliamentary Union and Commonwealth Parliamentary Association; Ilford Borough Council, 1949-52. NUPE. *Appointed Assistant Government Whip, March 1974.*

Mr James Holt is a personnel manager. B 1931; ed Wembley County Grammar School and Hendon and Harrow Technical Colleges. Member, Brent Borough Council since 1964.

Mr Harry Waschauer, a journalist. B November, 1924; ed grammar schools in Germany and Czechoslovakia. Member NUJ; ADM delegate.

Sq Ldr John Harrison-Broadley, car hire company executive. B October, 1920; ed Cheltenham College and HMS Conway. Contested Hove by-election, 1973; British bobsleigh champion, 1948.

Mr Les Burt, electrician and shop steward, working for London Transport. Borough secretary of the Communist Party and member of the district committee.

BRENTWOOD AND ONGAR   major

Electorate 56,949

*McCrindle, R. A. (C)	22,545
Wernick, L. (L)	13,452
Rosen, Dr M. H. (Lab)	12,398
C majority	9,093

	1974		1974
Total Vote	48,395	L	27·8%
Turnout	85·0%	Lab	25·6%
C	46·6%	C maj	18·8%

Mr Robert McCrindle, an insurance broker, was MP for Billericay, 1970-74. Contested Thurrock 1964 and Dundee, East, 1959. B September, 1929; ed Allan Glen's School, Glasgow. Associate of the Chartered Insurance Institute and Fellow of the Corporation of Insurance Brokers. Vice-chairman, Conservative parliamentary trade committee, 1972-73. Director, City and Western, merchant bankers; Cometco, commodity brokers; and life assurance and investment consultant companies. Vice-president, Corporation of Mortgage and Finance Brokers Ltd.

Mr Lionel Wernick, managing director. B November, 1928; ed at Wolverhampton Grammar School; King's College, London. Contested Billericay. 1966.

Dr Maurice Rosen, medical practitioner. B March, 1939; ed Hamorean Grammar School, Northern Polytechnic and St Mary's Hospital Medical School. MPU/ASTMS. Co-founder Junior Hospital Doctors' Action Group.

BRIDGWATER   same

Electorate 69,190   1970: 66.067

*King, T. J. (C)	24,830
Undy, R. (Lab)	16,786
Wyatt, J. (L)	15,269
C majority	8,044

No change

	1970		1974
Total Vote	50,975		56,885
Turnout	77·1%		82·2%
C	26,685	52·3%	43·6%
Lab	18,224	35·7%	29·5%
L	6,066	11·9%	26·8%
C maj	8,461	16·6%	14·1%
Swing		+5·1%	−1·2%

Mr Tom King won the by-election in March, 1970. Chairman, Sale, Tilney & Co Ltd; general manager E. S. and A. Robinson Ltd, Bristol, 1964-69. B June, 1933; ed Rugby and Emmanuel College, Cambridge. While at university he led an Oxford and Cambridge overland expedition to East Africa and when their vehicle burnt out in the Cameroons he and a companion hitch-hiked 2,000 miles to Kenya.

Mr Roger Undy is a research officer in industrial relations. Formerly a maintenance fitter. B November 1938; ed Huntingdon Street Secondary Modern School, Nottingham, and Ruskin College and Wadham College, Oxford. AUEW.

Mr John Wyatt, senior computer programmer. B May, 1950; ed Kingswood Grammar School. Member, Nalgo.

BRIDLINGTON minor

Electorate 65,453   1970: 61,716

*Wood, R. F. (C)		25,711
Cherry, J. M. (L)		14,715
Dix, A. A. W. (Lab)		9,780
C majority		10,996

No change

	1970		1974	
Total vote	43,096		50,206	
Turnou	69·7%		76·7%	
C	25,053	58·1%		51·2%
Lab	11,546	26·8%		19·5%
L	6,497	15·1%		29·3%
C maj	13,507	31·3%		21·9%
Swing		+3·2%		+0·2%

Mr Richard Wood was appointed Minister of Overseas Development, June, 1970, and in October of that year when the Ministry was merged with the Foreign and Commonwealth Office, he remained as Minister. B October, 1920, younger son of Earl of Halifax. Ed St Cyprians, Eastbourne, Eton and New College, Oxford. Formerly director of Hargreaves Ltd, F. J. C. Lilley Ltd, Yorkshire Conservative Newspapers Ltd and Hulton Press. Elected 1950, he was Minister of Pensions and National Insurance, 1963-64; Minister of Power, 1959-63; Parliamentary Secretary, Ministry of Pensions and National Insurance, 1955-58; Parliamentary Secretary, Ministry of Labour, 1958-59. Governor, Queen Elizabeth's Foundation for the Disabled.

Mr John Cherry, marketing director. B October, 1932. Member, East Riding County Council since 1970, and Beverley Borough Council since 1970. Member, Humberside County Council since 1973, and Beverley District Council since 1973.

Mr Anthony Dix, barrister. Member, Merton Borough Council since 1971. B

November, 1930; ed Tonbridge School. Member, Society of Labour Lawyers.

BRIGG AND SCUNTHORPE same

Electorate 89,473   1970: 87,058

Ellis, J. (Lab)		28,803
Riddell, J. P. S. (C)		25,729
Harris, J. (L)		15,484
Lab majority		3,074

No change

	1970		1974	
Total Vote	58,883		70,016	
Turnout	67·6%		78·2%	
Lab	31,434	53·4%		41·1%
C	27,449	46·6%		36·7%
L	—			22·1%
Lab maj	3,985	6·8%		4·4%
Swing		+6·7%		+1·2%

Mr John Ellis, MP for Bristol, North-West, 1966-70. Contested Wokingham, 1964. Member relations officer, Bristol and Bath Cooperative Retail Services. B October, 1934; ed Doncaster Grammar School, Rastrick Grammar School, Brighouse. Vice-chairman, staff side, Air Ministry, Whitley Council, 1961-63. TGWU. Member, Bristol City Council.

Mr Peter Riddell is an insurance broker. B March, 1936; ed Charterhouse and University of Western Ontario.

Mr John Harris, grocer and dairyman. B April, 1930; ed New Mills, Derbyshire, and Old Clee, Lincolnshire Grammar Schools.

BRIGHOUSE & SPENBOROUGH same

Electorate 62,403   1970: 61,560

Jackson, G. C. (Lab)		22,107
*Proudfoot, G. W. (C)		20,561
Robertshaw, P. G. (L)		11,029
Milner, Mrs S. (Ind Dem Alliance)		169
Lab majority		1,546

Labour gain

	1970		1974	
Total Vote	49,628		53,866	
Turnout	80·6%		86·3%	
C	22,953	46·2%		38·2%
Lab	22,894	46·1%		41·0%
L	3,781	7·6%		20·5%
Ind Dem All	—			0·3%
C maj	59	0·1%		
Lab maj	—			2·9%
Swing		+4·6%		−1·4%

Mr Colin Jackson represented the constituency 1964-70. Contested it, 1970 and 1960; King's Lynn 1959; and Newbury 1950 and 1951. Barrister, lecturer and writer. B December, 1921; ed Tewkesbury Grammar School and St John's College, Oxford. Joint-chairman, Council for Advancement of Arab British Understanding. NUJ.

Mr Wilfred Proudfoot won the seat for the Conservatives in 1970; MP for Cleveland, 1959-64; contested Cleveland, 1955, and Hemsworth, 1951. Supermarket operator; director, retailer-owned buying group. B December, 1921; ed Crook Council School and Scarborough College. Member, Scarborough Borough Council, 1952-58. Former managing director of commercial radio station.

Mr Patrick Robertshaw, barrister. B July, 1945; ed Hipperholme Grammar School and Southampton University.

BRIGHTON Kemptown same

Electorate 64,879 1970: 65,414

*Bowden, A. (C)	23,504
Hobden, D. (Lab)	19,484
Hall, D. (L)	7,954
Buckle, J. (Marx-Leninist)	170
C majority	4,020

No change

	1970		1974
Total Vote	49,146		51,112
Turnout	75·1%		78·8%
C	24,208	49·2%	46·0%
Lab	21,105	42·9%	38·1%
L	3,833	7·8%	15·6%
Marx-Lenin	—		0·3%
C maj	3,103	6·3%	7·9%
Swing		+3·9%	+0·8%

Mr Andrew Bowden, a personnel consultant, won the seat for the Conservatives in 1970; contested the seat in 1966, Kensington, North, 1964 and Hammersmith, North, 1955. Managing director of Personnel Assessment Ltd, 1969-71; and Haymarket Personnel Selections

Ltd, 1969-71. B April, 1930; ed Ardingly College, Sussex, National chairman, Young Conservatives, 1960-61. USDAW. Member, Wandsworth Borough Council, 1956-62. Member, Expenditure Committee

since 1973-74; joint chairman, All-party parliamentary Old Age Pensions Group, 1972-73.

Mr Dennis Hobden represented the constituency 1964-70, becoming Labour's first Sussex MP. He is a postal officer. B January, 1920; ed elementary. Member, Brighton Town Council since 1956 and East Sussex County Council since 1973 and leader of Labour group on each. Member, Union of Post Office Workers Parliamentary Panel.

Mr David Hall, information Officer. B November, 1947; ed Collyer's Grammar School, Horsham, Sussex, and Heriot-Watt University, Edinburgh; former President, University Students' Association, 1969-70.

BRIGHTON Pavilion same

Electorate 56,981 1970: 59,086

*Amery, H. J. (C)	21,910
Tonks, F. (Lab)	11,292
Hooper, K. (L)	9,764
Beaumont, R. (Ind)	428
C majority	10,618

No change

	1970		1974
Total Vote	39,341		43,394
Turnout	66·6%		76·1%
C	24,365	61·9%	50·5%
Lab	13,771	35·0%	26·0%
Ind	1,205	3·1%	1·0%
L	—		22·5%
C maj	10,594	26·9%	24·5%
Swing		+5·3%	−1·2%

Mr Julian Amery, Minister of State, Foreign and Commonwealth Office since 1972; Minister for Housing and Construction, Department of the Environment, 1970-72; Minister of Public Building and Works, June to October, 1970. Returned at by-election in

March, 1969, was Minister of Aviation, 1962-64; Secretary of State for Air from October, 1960; Under-Secretary, Colonial Office from 1958; and Under-Secretary, War Office, from 1957. Held Preston, North from 1950-66; contested the two-member Preston seat in 1945. B March, 1919; ed Eton and Balliol College, Oxford.

Mr Francis Tonks, lecturer. B September, 1926; ed St John's Leatherhead, Leeds University. Contested the seat 1970; former branch chairman ATTI.

Mr Keith Hooper, publisher and company director. B December, 1938; ed schools in USA, South Africa, University of South Africa, University of Stellenbosch, Kingston Technical College.

Mr Robert Beaumont, hotelier. Aged 45.

BRISTOL North-East major

Electorate 51,628

*Palmer, A. M. F. (Lab and Co-op)	18,625
Cox, R. (C)	12,538
Watts Miller, W. (L)	8,127
Lab and Co-op majority	6,087

	1974		1974
Total Vote	39,290	C	31·9%
Turnout	76·1%	L	20·7%
Lab & Co-op	47·4%	Lab & Co-op maj	15·5%

Mr Arthur Palmer was chairman, Select Committee on Science and Technology, 1966-70 and member since 1970, being chairman of one of its sub-committees. Repre-  sented Bristol, Central, 1964-74; Wimbledon, 1945-50; and Cleveland, 1952-59; contested Merton and Morden, 1950 and 1951. Chartered electrical engineer, national official of the Electrical Power Engineers' Association since 1945. B August, 1912; ed Ashford Grammar School and Brunel Technical College. Member, Select Committee on Nationalized Industries, 1964-66. Chairman, Parliamentary and Scientific Committee.

Mr Richard Cox, publisher and journalist. B March, 1931; ed Stowe School and St Catherine's College, Oxford. Member, Chelsea Borough Council, 1962-65.

Mr William Watts Miller, lecturer. B January, 1944; ed King's Park School and Edinburgh University. Bristol District councillor.

BRISTOL North-West minor

Electorate 65,697   1970: 65,003

*McLaren, M. (C)	21,569
Thomas, R. R. (Lab)	20,919
David, E. (L)	11,312
Wetherall, T. (Ind)	440
C majority	650

No change

	1970		1974
Total Vote	50,725		54,240
Turnout	78·1%		82·6%
C	24,124	47·5%	39·8%
Lab	23,075	45·5%	38·6%
L	3,299	6·5%	20·8%
Comm	227	0·4%	—
Ind.	—	—	0·8%
C maj	1,049	2·1%	1·2%
Swing		+1·7%	−0·4%

Mr Martin McLaren, a director of English China Clays Ltd regained the seat for the Conservatives in 1970. He won the seat from Labour in 1959 and represented it until 1966. A Lord Commissioner of the Treasury, 1963-64; Opposition whip, 1964-66. B January, 1914; ed Eton, New College, Oxford and Harvard University. Member, Commons committee on selection.

Mr Ronald Thomas, a university lecturer, is a member, Bristol City and Bristol District Councils. B March, 1929; ed Ruskin and Balliol Colleges, Oxford. Member, ASTMS.

Mr Edward David, university lecturer. B May, 1944; ed Dynevor Grammar School, Swansea; University College, Swansea and St John's College, Cambridge. Author, various articles on Liberal Party history. Member, Association of University Teachers.

BRISTOL South minor

Electorate 60,393   1970: 61,502

*Cocks, M. F. L. (Lab)	24,909
Kelleway, R. (C)	11,742
Stevens, J. (L)	7,499
Gannaway, P. (Nat Front)	1,006
Lab majority	13,167

No change

	1970		1974
Total Vote	39,936		45,156
Turnout	65·0%		74·8%
Lab	24,682	61·8%	55·2%
C	15,254	38·2%	26·0%
L	—		16·6%
Nat Front	—		2·2%
Lab maj	9,428	23·6%	29·1%
Swing		+5·3%	−2·8%

Mr Michael Cocks, elected in 1970, contested South Gloucestershire, 1964 and 1966 and Bristol, West, 1959. Lecturer. B August, 1929; ed Bristol University. President, Bristol Borough Labour Party, 1961-63. Sponsored by NUGMW. *Appointed Assistant Government Whip, March 1974.*

Mr Richard Kelleway general manager, freight company. B 1945; ed Presentation College, Reading, and Pembroke College, Cambridge. Bromley borough councillor since May, 1971.

Mr John Stevens, systems development manager, Unigate Ltd. B May, 1943; ed Trowbridge Boys' High School and Brunel College of Advanced Technology. Contested Bristol North West, 1970.

BRISTOL South-East major

Electorate 68,923

*Benn, A. N. W. (Lab)	26,540
Reece, N. G. (C)	18,628
Grayson, D. (L)	9,870
Bale, R. (Nat Front)	757
Robertson, J. (Social Dem)	668
Lab majority	7,912

	1974		1974
Total Vote	56,463	L	17·5%
Turnout	81·9%	Nat Front	1·3%
Lab	47·0%	Social Dem	1·2%
C	33·0%	Lab maj	14·0%

Mr Wedgwood Benn, chief Opposition spokesman on trade and industry 1970 to 1974, was Minister of Technology, 1966-70; Postmaster General, 1964-66. Elected in 1950. Debarred from the Commons on the death of his father, Viscount Stansgate, in November, 1960, he contested and won the by-election in May, 1961, but an Election Court declared his Conservative opponent elected. He renounced his title under the Peerage Act and was re-elected in August, 1963. Member of Labour Party executive, 1959-60 and since 1962; chairman, 1971-72. Elected to Shadow Cabinet, 1970; unsuccessfully contested deputy leadership of PLP in November, 1971. Journalist. B April, 1925; ed Westminster and New College, Oxford. NUJ. *Appointed Secretary of State for Industry, and Minister for Posts and Telecommunications, March 1974.*

Mr Norman Reece contested Swindon,

1966 and 1964. Company director. B June, 1913; ed St Peter's School, Wolverhampton, and Wolverhampton and Staffordshire Technical College. Chairman, Avon County Council Education Committee.

Mr David Grayson, managing director. B June, 1932; ed St George Grammar School, Bristol.

Mr Reginald Bale is a scaffolding contractor. B August, 1936; ed secondary modern school.

Mr James Robertson, aged 45, is honorary treasurer of the Campaign for Social Democracy and has been responsible for coordinating its policy studies. Has had no previous connexion with any political party.

BRISTOL West major

Electorate 60,133

*Cooke, R. G. (C)	21,140
Stacey, R. (L)	13,076
Malos, J. (Lab)	9,526
C majority	8,064

	1974		1974
Total Vote	43,742	L	29·9%
Turnout	72·7%	Lab	21·8%
C	48·3%	C maj	18·4%

Mr Robert Cooke was returned at a by-election in 1957; contested Bristol, South-East, 1955. Vice-chairman (1972) and former chairman, Conservative parliamentary broadcasting and communications committee; vice-chairman, arts and amenities group, 1964-72, chairman since 1972. Director of Westward Television; member, executive committee of Historic Houses Association. Landowner and horticulturist. B May, 1930; ed Downs School, Wraxhall; Harrow, and Christ Church College, Oxford.

Mr Robert Stacey contested the seat in 1966 and 1970. B August, 1926; ed Hornsey County School and Stationers' Company School, Hornsey. Port worker; member TGWU.

Mr John Malos is a reader in physics at the University of Bristol. B February, 1927; ed University of Queensland and Sydney. Member, AUT and ASTMS.

BROMLEY Beckenham major

Electorate 58,988

*Goodhart, P. C. (C)	22,976
Mitchell, G. (L)	12,821
Sharp, N. J. (Lab)	11,018
C majority	10,155

	1974			1974
Total Vote	46,815		L	27·4%
Turnout	79·3%		Lab	23·5%
C	49·1%		C maj	21·7%

Mr Philip Goodhart, a journalist, was re-turned for Becken-ham at a by-election in March, 1957; con-tested Consett, 1950. B November, 1925; ed Hotchkiss School, United States, and Trinity College, Cam-bridge. Joint hon. Secretary 1922 Com-mittee since 1960.

Chairman from 1972-74 of Conservative backbench committee on defence. Mem-ber, Select Committee on Overseas Aid 1969-74, Council of the Consumers' Association since 1959. Vice-chairman de-fence centre from March 1974.

Mr Graham Mitchell contested Finchley in 1970. Management services controlled. B April, 1938; ed St Andrew's College. Dublin, and Glasgow University.

Mr Nick Sharp, senior computer pro-grammer. B April, 1948; ed Beckenham and Penge Grammar School and Wadham College, Oxford. ASTMS.

BROMLEY Chislehurst   major

Electorate 53,169

Sims, R. E. (C)		20,595
MacDonald, A. H. (Lab)		15,102
Webster, R. (L)		9,127
C majority		5,493

	1974			1974
Total Vote	44,824		Lab	33·7%
Turnout	84·3%		L	20·4%
C	45·9%		C maj	12·2%

Mr Roger Sims is an export manager. Con-tested Shoreditch and Finsbury, 1966 and 1970. B January, 1930; ed City Boys' Grammar School, Leicester, and St Olave's Grammar School, London. Mem-ber, Chislehurst and Sidcup UDC 1956-62 Member, Royal Choral Society.

Mr Alistair Macdonald represented Chisle-hurst 1966-70. Contested Beckenham, 1964. Assistant company secretary. B May, 1925; ed Dulwich College, Enfield Tech-nical College and Corpus Christi, Cam-bridge. Member, Chislehurst UDC, 1958-62 and Bromley Borough Council, 1964-68 and since 1971. Member, National Union Bank Employees.

Mr Robert Webster, company director, contested Sevenoaks, 1970. B August, 1927; ed Bromley County School.

BROMLEY Orpington   minor

Electorate 65,006   1970: 65,112

*Stanbrook, I. R. (C)	26,435
Young, R. (L)	22,771
Grant, D. I. (Lab)	6,752
C majority	3,664

No change

	1970		1974
Total Vote	51,546		55,958
Turnout	79·1%		86·1%
C	24,385	47·3%	47·2%
L	23,063	44·7%	40·7%
Lab	4,098	7·9%	12·1%
C maj	1,322	2·6%	6·5%
Swing		+3·0%	−2·1%

Mr Ivor Stanbrook, a barrister, won Orp-ington for the Con-servatives in 1970; contested East Ham, South, 1966. B Janu-ary, 1924; ed Willes-den Central School, University College, London, and Pem-broke College, Ox-ford. Colonial district officer in Nigeria,

1950-60. Secretary Conservative parlia-mentary home affairs committee.

Mr Robin Young contested Rye in 1970. Journalist on staff of *The Times.* B December, 1939; ed Peter Symonds' School, Winchester, and Brasenose College, Oxford. Founder and unpaid administra-tor, De Beauvoir charitable housing asso-ciation, North London.

Mr David Grant contested Orpington in 1970. Teacher. B May, 1938; ed Trinity School, Croydon, Jesus College, Oxford, and London Institute of Education. NUT.

BROMLEY Ravensbourne   major

Electorate 48,110

*Hunt, J. L. (C)	20,420
Crowe, D. (L)	11,523
Hession, Dr H. A. (Lab)	6,943
Parker, G. (Nat Front)	786
C majority	8,897

	1974		1974
Total Vote	39,672	Lab	17·5%
Turnout	82·5%	Nat Front	2·0%
C	51·5%	C maj	22·4%
L	29·0%		

Mr John Hunt, MP for Bromley, 1964-74, contested Lewisham, South, in 1959. Director public relations firm. B October, 1929; ed Dulwich College. Mayor of Bromley, 1963 - 64; member, Bromley Borough Council 1953-65. Joint vice-chairman, Great-

er London Conservative MPs, since 1972. Chairman, British and Caribbean Association, from 1968; chairman, Indo-British Parliamentary group.

Mr David Crowe contested Bromley in 1970. Solicitor. B August, 1939; ed Cranleigh School, Surrey, and Christ Church, Oxford.

Dr Michael Hession, consultant child psychiatrist. B May, 1939; ed St Laurence's Hospital, Ramsgate, Christ's College, Cambridge, and St Bartholomew's and King's College Hospitals, London. MPU and ASTMS.

Mr Geoffrey Parker, insurance clerk. B December, 1928; ed Bromley County School.

BROMSGROVE AND REDDITCH
minor

Electorate 87,113	1970: 83,877
Miller, H. D. (C)	33,125
*Davis, T. A. G. (Lab)	29,536
Cartwright, G. E. (L)	10,726
C majority	3,589

C gain

	1970		1974
	64,214		73,378
Turnout	76·5%		84·2%
C	37,544	58·5%	45·1%
Lab	26,670	41·5%	40·2%
L	—		14·6%
C maj	10,874	16·9%	4·9%
Swing		+5·5%	−6·0%

1971 by-election: Total Vote 57,750 (66·3%)—Lab 29,809 (51·6%), C 27,941 (48·4%)—Lab maj 1,868 (3·2%).

Mr Hilary Miller contested the Bromsgrove by-election in 1971 and Barrow-in-Furness in 1970. Company director. B March, 1929; ed Eton, Merton College, Oxford, and London University. With the Colonial Service, 1955-68. Fellow of the Economic Devel-

lopment Institute of the World Bank.

Mr Terence Davis, former company executive, won Bromsgrove for Labour at the by-election in 1971; contested the seat in 1970. B January, 1938; ed King Edward VI Grammar School, Stourbridge; London University; and University of Michigan. Member, Yeovil RDC, 1967-68. ASTMS.

Mr Geoffrey Cartwright, swimming pool manufacturer. B July, 1930; ed Stourbridge Grammar School, Worksop College.

BUCKINGHAM
major

Electorate 78,466	
*Benyon, W. R. (C)	27,179
Maxwell, I. R. (Lab)	24,056
Crooks, S. (L)	15,519
C majority	3,123

	1974		1974
Total Vote	66,754	Lab	36·0%
Turnout	85·3%	L	23·2%
C	40·7%	C maj	4·7%

Mr William Benyon, a farmer, won the seat for the Conservatives in 1970. B January, 1930; ed Royal Naval College, Dartmouth. Member, Berkshire County Council, 1964-74; Bradfield Rural Council, 1960 - 62; Council of Reading University; Berkshire College of Agricul-

ture; Council of Bradfield College. Served in the Royal Navy for nine years.

Mr Robert Maxwell, publisher, contested the constituency in 1959, elected in 1964, returned in 1966 and defeated in 1970. B June, 1923; self educated. Chairman, Labour National Fund Raising Foundation, 1960-70; chairman, Labour working party on science, government and industry, 1963-64; member, Council of Europe United Kingdom delegation and vice-chairman of its committee on science and technology, 1968. Member, Estimates Committee, 1964-66, and chairman, Commons catering sub-committee. Elected Fellow, Harvard University at the Kennedy Institute of Politics School of Government, 1971; elected hon member, International Academy of Astronautics, 1973. Founder, Pergamon Press, 1949. ASTMS.

Mr Samuel Crooks, administrator with the Open University. B December, 1946; ed Campbell College, Belfast, Jesus College, Cambridge.

BURNLEY same

Electorate 52,483   1970: 56,036

*Jones, D. (Lab)	21,108
Pickup, A. (C)	11,268
Mews, S. (L)	9,471
Lab majority	9,840

No change

	1970		1974
Total Vote	42,492		41,847
Turnout	75·8%		79·7%
Lab	24,200	56·9%	50·4%
C	14,846	34·9%	26·9%
L	3,446	8·1%	22·6%
Lab maj	9,354	22·0%	23·5%
Swing		+5·3%	−0·7%

Mr Daniel Jones, engineer and AEF official for 20 years has represented the constituency since 1959; contested Barry, 1955. B September, 1908; ed Ynyshir (Rhondda) School and National Council of Labour Colleges, where he became a lecturer. Member, Select Committee for Parliamentary Commissioner. Sponsored by AUEW, engineering section.

Mr Albert Pickup is a trade representative. B May, 1916; ed Heasandford Junior School, Burnley. Member, Burnley Borough Council since 1955. Minister of the Church of Jesus Christ of Latter Day Saints.

Mr Stuart Mews, university lecturer. B May, 1944; ed Burnley Grammar School; Leeds University and Cambridge University.

BURTON same

Electorate 67,170   1970: 66,725

Lawrence, I. J. (C)	28,343
Hill, D. R. (Lab)	25,040
C majority	3,303

No change

	1970		1974
Total Vote	50,491		53,383
Turnout	75·7%		79·5%
C	27,428	54·3%	53·1%
Lab	23,063	45·7%	46·9%
C maj	4,365	8·6%	6·2%
Swing		+4·0%	−1·2%

Mr Ivan Lawrence, barrister. B December, 1936; ed Brighton, Hove and Sussex Grammar School, Christ Church, Oxford. Contested Peckham in 1966 and 1970.

Mr David Hill, political researcher. B February, 1948; ed King Edward School, Birmingham; and Brasenose College, Oxford. Former industrial relations officer with Unigate. ASTMS.

BURY AND RADCLIFFE same

Electorate 78,316   1970: 74,545

*Fidler, M. M. (C)	31,113
White, F. R. (Lab)	30,768
C majority	345

No change

	1970		1974
	56,388		61,881
Turnout	75·6%		79·0%
C	29,796	52·8%	50·3%
Lab	26,592	47·2%	49·7%
C maj	3,204	5·7%	0·5%
Swing		+7·0%	−2·5%

Mr Michael Fidler regained the seat for the Conservatives in 1970. B February, 1916; ed Salford Grammar School and Salford Royal Technical College. Prestwich councillor, 1951-63, alderman since 1963, mayor, 1957-58. Business interests in merchant banking. President, Board of Deputies of British Jews, 1967-73; vice-chairman, World Conference of Jewish Organizations, 1967-73.

Mr Frank White, industrial relations adviser. B November, 1939; ed Bolton Technical College. Member, Bolton County Council since 1963; elected, Greater Manchester County Council, 1973. NUGMW, and of Institute of Personnel Management.

BURY ST EDMUNDS same

Electorate 86,601   1970: 77,519

*Griffiths, E. W. (C)	33,424
Stephenson, J. K. (Lab)	20,171
Boulton, B. (L)	16,772
C majority	13,253

No change

	1970		1974	
Total Vote	59,974		70,367	
Turnout	77·4%		81·2%	
C	36,688	61·2%		47·5%
Lab	23,286	38·8%		28·7%
L	—			23·8%
C maj	13,402	22·3%		18·8%
Swing		+6·6%		−1·8%

Mr Eldon Griffiths, Under-Secretary for the Environment, with special responsibility for sport, 1970-74, and with responsibilities for planning applications, was returned at a by-election in May, 1964. Parliamentary Secretary, Ministry of Housing and Local Government, June to October, 1970. Journalist; Parliamentary adviser to the Police Federation of England and Wales, 1966-70. B May, 1925; ed Ashton Grammar School; Emmanuel College, Cambridge; and Yale University. Served in the Conservative research department. Chief European correspondent of *Washington Post*, 1961-63.

Mr John Stephenson is a lecturer. B May, 1939; ed Barrow-in-Furness Grammar School, London School of Economics and London Institute of Education. Member, AMA.

Mr Barry Boulton, sales engineer. B April, 1941; ed Leiston Grammar School and Borough Polytechnic. Former member, Malling Rural District Council, 1971-74.

CAERNARVON   same

Electorate 42,226   1970: 41,560

Wigley, D. (Pl Cymru)	14,103
*Roberts, G. O. (Lab)	12,375
Garel-Jones, T. W. A. (C)	5,803
David, G. H. (L)	2,506
Pl Cymru majority	1,728

Pl Cymru gain

	1970		1974
Total Vote	33,965		34,787
Turnout	81·7%		82·4%
Pl Cymru	11,331	33·4%	40·5%
Lab	13,627	40·1%	35·6%
C	6,812	20·0%	16·7%
L	2,195	6·5%	7·2%
Lab maj	2,296	6·7%	
Pl Cymru maj	—		5·0%
Swing		+6·9%	—

Mr Dafydd Wigley, aged 30, senior cost accountant and industrial economist with manufacturing firm in Merthyr. Ed Manchester University. Vice-chairman of Plaid Cymru, party spokesman on finance and taxation. Member, Merthyr Borough Council.

Mr Goronwy Roberts, an Opposition spokesman on Foreign and Commonwealth Affairs, 1970-74, was Minister of State, Board of Trade 1969-70; Minister of State, Foreign and Commonwealth Affairs, 1967-69; Minister of State, Education and Science, 1966-67; Minister of State, Welsh Office, 1964-66. Elected in 1945. University lecturer. B September, 1913; ed Ogwen Grammar School and universities of London and Wales. *Made life peer. Appointed Under Secretary of State for Foreign and Commonwealth Affairs March 1974.*

Mr Tristan Garel-Jones, school principal and company director. B 1941; ed Llangennech Primary School and King's School, Canterbury. Founded firm of language schools in Spain.

Mr Gerald David, managing director of a telecommunications consultancy. B August 1934; ed Newcastle Emlyn, Swansea Grammar School and Cardiff. Chairman, Little Kingshill Village Society.

CAERPHILLY   major

Electorate 55,995

*Evans, A. T. (Lab)	24,838
Williams, P. (Pl Cymru)	11,956
Everest, R. (C)	5,912
Bevan, D. H. (Ind)	711
Lab majority	12,882

	1974			1974
Total Vote	43,417	C		13·6%
Turnout	77·5%	Ind		1·6%
Lab	57·2%	Lab maj		29·7%
Pl Cymru	27·5%			

Mr Alfred Evans was returned at a by-election in July, 1968; contested Stroud, 1959, and Leominster, 1955. Former headmaster. B February, 1914; ed Bargoed Grammar School and University of Wales, Cardiff. Former member, Gelligaer Urban Council. Has served on Estimates Committee and backbench committees for disabled persons, social services and the Middle East.

Mr Phil Williams, 35, lecturer in electronics, University College, Aberystwyth. Ed Lewis School, Pengam, Clare College, Cambridge. Plaid Cymru spokesman on industrial development.

Mr Roger Everest, barrister. B 1939; ed Llandaff Cathedral School; Kingswood School, Bath; and University of Wales. Member, Bow Group.

CAITHNESS & SUTHERLAND same

Electorate 28,571   1970: 28,709

*MacLennan, R. A. R. (Lab)	8,574
Burnett, M. R. (L)	6,222
Bell, Mrs S. (C)	5,104
Sutherland, E. A. (Scot Nat)	3,814
Lab majority	2,352

No change

	1970		1974	
Total Vote	23,855		23,714	
Turnout	83·1%		83·0%	
Lab	8,768	36·7%		36·1%
L	6,063	25·4%		26·2%
C	5,334	22·4%		21·5%
Scot Nat	3,690	15·5%		16·1%
Lab maj	2,705	11·3%		9·9%
Swing		+1·4%		−0·1%

Mr Robert MacLennan, an Opposition spokesman on Scottish affairs, 1970-72, and defence 1972 to 1974, won the seat for Labour in March, 1966. Barrister (Gray's Inn, 1962). B June, 1936; ed Glasgow Academy, Balliol College, Oxford, Trinity College, Cambridge,

and Columbia University, New York. Member, Estimates Committee, 1967-69; Scottish Labour Committee for Europe; 1963 Club; Fabian Society. *Appointed Under Secretary for Prices and Consumer Protection, March 1974.*

Mr Michael Burnett is a farmer and Scottish Liberal Party spokesman on agriculture. B July, 1935; ed Morrison's Academy, Crieff, and Edinburgh University. Member of SLP's national executive since 1969; council member, NFU; member, Agricultural Wages Board, Agricultural Training Board and Sutherland County Council. Lay preacher in Church of Scotland.

Mrs Susan Bell contested Motherwell in 1970. Company secretary of Scottish Direct Limited, of which her husband, Mr Arthur Bell, Conservative candidate for Kirkcaldy, is managing director. B August, 1946; ed Wishaw High School and Glasgow College of Commerce and Distribution.

Mr Eric Sutherland, aged 52, solicitor.

CAMBRIDGE same

Electorate 76,200   1970: 65,500

*Lane, D. W. S. S. (C)	24,119
Curran, J. (Lab)	19,443
O'Loughlin, M. (L)	15,491
Inkster, Miss S. E. (Ind)	369
C majority	4,676

No change

	1970		1974	
Total Vote	47,443		59,422	
Turnout	72·4%		78·0%	
C	26,252	55·3%		40·6%
Lab	21,191	44·7%		32·7%
L	—			26·1%
Ind	—			0·6%
C maj	5,061	10·7%		7·9%
Swing		+6·3%		−1·3%

Mr David Lane. Under - Secretary, Home Office 1972 to 1974, regained the seat for the Conservatives at a by-election in 1967, after contesting it in 1966, and Vauxhall, 1964.

Barrister, called by Middle Temple, 1955. Formerly employed by British Iron and Steel Federation (1948-59, secretary from 1956) and by Shell International Petroleum Company (1959 to 1967). B September, 1922; ed Eton, Trinity College, Cambridge, and Yale University. Secretary Conservative parliamentary education committee, 1969-70. An Opposition spokesman on home affairs from March 1974.

Mr James Curran, Research Fellow of Open University. Former market research executive; contested Huntingdonshire in 1970. B March, 1945; ed Cambridge University. Chairman, Cambridge housing and rail action groups.

Mr Michael O'Loughlin, contested Huntingdonshire, 1970, and Cambridge, 1966 and 1964. Technical college lecturer. B January, 1923; ed Marlborough College and Christ's College, Cambridge. Founder member, British Epilepsy Association.

CAMBRIDGESHIRE minor

Electorate 84,756   1970: 78,271

*Pym, F. L. (C)	32,638
Jakobi, S. (L)	18,826
Farley, M. P. (Lab)	17,930
C majority	13,812

No change

	1970		1974	
Total Vote	59,118		69,394	
Turnout	75·5%		81·9%	
C	32,264	54·6%	47·0%	
Lab	19,993	33·8%	25·8%	
L	6,861	11·6%	27·1%	
C maj	12,271	20·7%	19·9%	
Swing		+5·6%	+0·2%	

Mr Francis Pym, Secretary of State for Northern Ireland since December, 1973, was returned in the 1961 by-election. Was Parliamentary Secretary to the Treasury and Government Chief Whip, 1970-73. Contested Rhondda West, 1959. Former company director and farmer. B February, 1922; ed Eton and Magdalene College, Cambridge. Assistant Government whip 1962-64; Opposition whip, 1964-67; Opposition deputy Chief Whip, 1967-70. Member, Herefordshire County Council, 1958-61. Appointed Opposition spokesman on Agriculture and Fisheries and on Northern Ireland, March 1974; in Shadow Cabinet.

Mr Stephen Jakobi, solicitor. B March, 1935; ed Malvern College, Clare College, Cambridge, and Swansea College of Technology. Contested Battersea North, 1964; Cities of London and Westminster, 1965 by-election, and Windsor, 1966. Member, Liberal Party's Panel on Immigration.

Mr Michael Farley contested Reigate in 1970. Lecturer. B July, 1942; ed King's Norton Grammar School, Birmingham, and Birmingham and Exeter Universities. Former chairman, Surrey Federation of Labour Parties.

CAMDEN Hampstead   minor

Electorate 63,865   1970: 71,918

*Finsberg, G. (C)	19,536
Clarke, A. J. (Lab)	17,279
Longland, R. A. (L)	8,323
C majority	2,257

No change

	1970		1974	
Total Vote	45,604		45,138	
Turnout	63·4%		70·7%	
C	21,264	46·6%	43·3%	
Lab	20,790	45·6%	38·3%	
L	3,550	7·8%	18·4%	
C maj	474	1·0%	5·0%	
Swing		+2·8%	+2·0%	

Mr Geoffrey Finsberg gained Hampstead for the Conservatives in 1970; contested Islington, East, 1955. B June, 1926; ed City of London School. Member, Hampstead Borough Council, 1949-65; and Camden Borough Council, 1964-74, leader 1968-70. Vice-chairman, Conservative parliamentary committee on trade, since 1972, and joint vice-chairman, Greater London committee of Conservative MPs. Industrial relations adviser. Member, executive, 1922 Committee, from March 1974.

Mr Anthony Clarke is a Post Office worker. B April, 1932; ed St Dominic's School, Southampton Road, NW5. Member, London Borough of Camden Council, Secretary, London District Council, Union of Post Office Workers.

Mr Ronald Longland contested Spelthorne in 1970. Engineer. B August, 1935; ed Mountjoy School, Dublin, and Twickenham College of Technology. Member, ASTMS.

CAMDEN Holborn and St Pancras South   minor

Electorate 38,964   1970: 41,741

*Jeger, Mrs L. M. (Lab)	12,414
Parsons, R. F. J. (C)	8,223
Hibbert, T. (L)	4,632
Lab majority	4,191

No change

	1970		1974	
Total Vote	22,573		25,269	
Turnout	54·0%		64·8%	
Lab	12,448	55·1%	49·1%	
C	10,125	44·8%	32·5%	
L	—	—	18·3%	
Lab maj	2,323	10·3%	16·6%	
Swing		+4·3%	−3·1%	

Mrs Lena Jeger, journalist, was returned in 1964. Elected for constituency, 1953, at a by-election caused by the death of her husband, but lost it in 1959. Member, Labour Party National Executive since 1968. B November, 1915; ed Southgate County School and London University. Speaks Russian and was assistant editor in Moscow of *British Ally.* Member, Speaker's panel of chairmen.

Chairman, working party on sewage disposal.

Mr Robert Parsons is a solicitor. B August, 1935; ed Kingswood School and Downing College, Cambridge. Member, Frimley and Camberley UDC since 1962 and Surrey County Council since 1970.

Mr Thomas Hibbert, principal, community centre. B March, 1925; ed Hawick High School, Cheshire Commercial College, Morley College, London, and Tavistock Institute of Human Relations. NUT.

CAMDEN St Pancras North   major

Electorate 41,427

*Stallard, A. W. (Lab)	14,761
Major, J. (C)	7,926
Medlicott, P. J. (L)	4,825
McLennan, G. (Comm)	466
Lab majority	6,835

	1974		1974
Total Vote	27,978	L	17·2%
Turnout	67·5%	Comm	1·7%
Lab	52·7%	Lab maj	24·4%
C	28·3%		

Mr Albert Stallard was elected in 1970; formerly a technical training officer. B November, 1921; ed Lowaters School and Hamilton Academy. Member, St. Pancras Borough Council, 1953-65, and Camden Council since that date. Member, AUEW. Chairman, Camden Town Disablement Committee and Mental Health Association. Sponsored by AUEW (engineering section).

Mr John Major is a banker. B March, 1943; ed Rutlish Grammar School. Member, London Borough of Lambeth Council, 1968-71.

Mr Paul Medlicott, journalist. B May, 1946; ed Westminster School and Trinity Hall, Cambridge. Former Editor, Liberal News. NUJ

Mr Gordon McLennan. Fought Glasgow, Govan, 1959, 1964, 1966; West Lothian by-election, 1963; St Pancras, North, 1970. Political organizer and trade union official. B May, 1924; ed Hamilton Crescent School, Glasgow and Glasgow Technical College. Trade union branch official, Trades Council delegate.

CANNOCK   major

Electorate 56,059

Roberts, G. E. (Lab)	23,869
King, R. D. (C)	12,805
Windridge, M. (L)	9,709
Lab majority	11,064

	1974		1974
Total Vote	46,383	C	27·6%
Turnout	82·7%	L	20·9%
Lab	51·5%	Lab maj	23·8%

Mr Gwilym Roberts was MP for Bedfordshire, South, 1966-70. Contested Conway, 1964, and Ormskirk, 1959. B August, 1928; ed Brynefail Grammar School and University of Wales. Principal lecturer Hendon College of Technology, 1957-66. Industrial consultant, market and operational research.

Mr Roger King, motor sales executive. B 1943; ed Solihull School; served engineering apprenticeship with the British Motor Corporation. Former youth club leader.

Mr Michael Windridge, executive of a publishing firm. B August, 1947; ed Repton.

CANTERBURY   same

Electorate 84,841   1970: 80,373

*Crouch, D. L. (C)	34,341
Goulden, Mrs S. (L)	17,300
Fuller, M. F. (Lab)	15,751
McKilliam, K. (Nat Front)	831
C majority	17,041

No change

	1970		1974
Total Vote	59,947		68,223
Turnout	74·6%		80·4%
C	33,222	55·4%	50·3%
Lab	15,172	25·3%	23·1%
L	11,553	19·3%	25·3%
Nat Front	—		1·2%
C maj	18,050	30·1%	25·0%
Swing		+4·2%	−1·4%

Mr David Crouch, a director of Pfizer Ltd, was elected in 1966; contested Leeds, West, 1959. B June, 1919; ed University College School, London. Member, Institute of Marketing. Former vice-president, West Leeds Conservative Association. Member, Select Committee on Nationalized Industries since 1970. Chair-

man, all-party parliamentary group for chemical industry. Vice-chairman Conservative Party industry committee since 1972.

Mrs Sarah Goulden, barrister. B January, 1934; ed Benenden School, and Law Society College of Law.

Mr Michael Fuller, university lecturer. B October, 1945; ed Lewes County Grammar School and St John's College, Cambridge. Member, Canterbury City Council, since 1970, and Canterbury District Council since 1973. Chairman, city council planning committee; Sheriff of Canterbury for 1973-74. AUT and NUPE.

Mr Keneth McKilliam, schoolmaster. B October, 1911; ed University College, London. Formerly in Overseas Civil Service.

CARDIFF North   major

Electorate 46,997

Grist, I. (C)	14,659
Collins, J. (Lab)	10,806
Thomas, T. A. D. (L)	7,139
Richards, P. (Pl Cymru)	1,586
C majority	3,853

	1974		1974
Total Vote	34,190	L	20·9%
Turnout	73·4%	Pl Cymru	4·6%
C	42·9%	C maj	11·3%
Lab	31·6%		

Mr Ian Grist, an information officer at the Welsh Conservative Party office, contested Aberavon in 1970. B December, 1938; ed Repton and Jesus College, Cambridge.

Mr John Collins, a teacher. B March, 1945; ed Preston Grammar School and University College, Cardiff. NUT.

Mr David Thomas, staff tutor, Open University. B May, 1931; ed Llandysul County Grammar School, St David's University College, Lampeter, St Catherine's College, Oxford, Serampore University, India. AUT.

Mr Philip Richards, barrister. B August, 1946; ed Cardiff High School and Bristol University. Member, Association of Law Teachers.

CARDIFF North-West   major

Electorate 41,511

*Roberts, M. H. A. (C)	16,654
Blewett, C. A. (Lab)	10,641
O'Brien, H. (L)	7,109
Palfrey, C. (Pl Cymru)	1,227
C majority	6,013

	1974		1974
Total Vote	35,631	L	19·9%
Turnout	87·1%	Pl Cymru	3·4%
C	46·7%	C maj	16·9%
Lab	29·9%		

Mr Michael Roberts was MP for Cardiff, North, which he won for the Conservatives, from 1970 to 1974. Contested Cardiff, South-East in 1959 and 1955, and Aberdare in the 1954 by-election. Former headmaster. B May, 1927; ed Neath Grammar School and University College, Cardiff. Chairman Conservative education committee; past president, Cardiff Association, National Union of Teachers. Joint-vice-chairman, Conservative education committee, from March 1974.

Mr Charles Blewett, secretary of Penallta Lodge, NUM. Pit-boy at 14, miner, colliery manager and mine under-manager. Aged 52; elementary education. Member, Institute of Mining and Chartered Engineers.

Mr Howard O'Brien, solicitor. B January, 1947; ed King's College, London. Contested Cardiff North, 1970.

Mr Colin Palfrey, adult education tutor. B July, 1939; ed Whitchurch Grammar School, Cardiff, University College, Cardiff, and King's College, London. Member, Caerphilly Urban Council. NAS.

CARDIFF South-East   major

Electorate 57,556

*Callaghan, L. J. (Lab)	20,641
Terlezki, S. (C)	13,495
Bailey, C. (Ind L)	3,800
Christon, B. (L)	2,978
Bush, K. (Pl Cymru)	1,254
Lab majority	7,146

	1974		1974
Total Vote	42,168	Ind L	9·0%
Turnout	73·3%	L	7·1%
Lab	48·9%	Pl Cymru	3·0%
C	32·0%	Lab maj	16·9%

Mr James Callaghan was chief Opposition spokesman on foreign and Commonwealth affairs 1972 - 74; employment 1971-72; Home Office matters, 1970-71. Home Secretary 1967-70, and Chancellor of the Exchequer 1964 - 67, Chairman of the Labour Party; member, national executive, 1957-67, and party treasurer since 1967, Parliamentary Secretary to the Admiralty, 1950-51, after three years as Parliamentary Secretary to the Ministry of Transport. Labour spokesman on Treasury affairs, 1961-64. Elected for South Cardiff, 1945, and for Cardiff, South-East, 1950. B March, 1912; ed at elementary and Portsmouth Northern Secondary Schools. *Appointed Secretary of State for Foreign and Commonwealth Affairs, March 1974.*

Mr Stefan Terlezki, hotelier. B October, 1927; ed High School and College of Food Technology and Commerce, Cardiff. Member, South Glamorgan and Cardiff District Council.

Mr Bernard Christon contested Blackpool, North, 1970. Pharmaceutical sales manager. B April, 1937; ed Selby and Bradford Technical Colleges.

Mr Keith Bush, civil engineer. B May, 1948; ed The County School, Tregaron, Cardiganshire, and Imperial College, London. AUEW, Technical and Supervisory Section.

CARDIFF West   major

Electorate 52,311

*Thomas, T. G. (Lab)	16,712
Neale, G. J. (C)	13,366
James, R. M. (L)	5,812
Hughes, D. (Pl Cymru)	2,093
Lab majority	3,346

	1974			1974
Total Vote	37,983		L	15·3%
Turnout	72·6%		Pl Cymru	5·5%
Lab	44·0%		Lab maj	8·8%
C	35·2%			

Mr George Thomas, Secretary of State for Wales, 1968-70, was Opposition chief spokesman for Wales 1970-74. Elected in 1945 for Cardiff, Central, and in 1950 for Cardiff, West. Minister of State, Commonwealth Office, 1967-68; Minister of State, Welsh Office, 1966-67; Under Secretary, Home Office,

1964-66. Teacher. B January, 1909; ed at Tonypandy Secondary School and University College, Southampton. Chairman, Welsh Parliamentary Party, 1958-59. Vice-President, Methodist Conference, 1960-61. Elected Fellow, University College of Cardiff, 1973. Sponsored by NUT. Appointed Chairman of Ways and Means and Deputy Speaker, March, 1974.

Mr Gareth Neale contested Brecon and Radnor in 1970 and the Rhondda, West by-election, 1967. Management services manager and industrial relations consultant. B April, 1935; ed Barry Grammar School and University of Wales, Aberystwyth. Chairman, Cardiff and District Business Enterprise Group; member, South Glamorgan County Council.

Mr Michael James, director of an estate agency and finance broking company. B March 8, 1934; ed elementary, Cardiff College of Technology and part time study at Cardiff University.

Dr Dafydd Hughes, 38, psychiatrist. Qualified at Welsh National School of Medicine. First Plaid Cymru member, Cardiff City Council.

CARDIGAN   same

Electorate 43,039   1970: 40,302

Howells, G. W. (L)	14,371
*Morgan, D. E. (Lab)	11,895
Llewellyn, T. W. (C)	4,758
Davies, C. (Pl Cymru)	4,754
L majority	2,476

L gain

	1970		1974
Total Vote	33,076		35,778
Turnout	82·1%		83·1%
Lab	11,063	33·4%	33·2%
L	9,800	29·6%	40·2%
Pl Cymru	6,498	19·6%	13·3%
C	5,715	17·3%	13·3%
Lab maj	1,263	3·8%	
L maj	—	—	6·9%
Swing		+0·8%	−1·9%

Mr Geraint Howells, chairman of the Welsh Liberal Party. Farmer. Contested Brecon and Radnor 1970. B April 1925; ed Ardwyn Grammar School. Member, Cardiganshire County Council since 1952. Served as Welsh Board member, British Wool Marketing Board, and Ponterwyd Eisteddfod secretary. Appointed Liberal spokesman on Wales, March 1974.

Mr Elystan Morgan was an Opposition spokesman on Wales, 1973-74 and on the Home Office, 1970-73. Under Secretary, Home Office, 1968-70. Won the seat for Labour in 1966. As a Pl Cymru candidate

contested Merioneth in 1964, and Wrexham, 1959, and the general election and by-election, 1955. Solicitor. B December, 1932; ed Ardwyn Grammar School, Aberystwyth, and University College of Wales, Aberystwyth.

Mr Trefor Llewellyn, chartered accountant. B July, 1947; ed University College, Cardiff.

Mr Clifford Davies contested Gower, 1970. Teacher. B December, 1939; ed Ystalyfera Grammar School and University College, Swansea.

CARLISLE   same

Electorate 51,842   1970: 52,294

*Lewis, R. H. (Lab)	23,119
White, E. M. (C)	18,139
Wild, J. (Ind Soc)	628
Lab majority	4,980

No change

	1970		1974	
Total Vote	41,107		41,886	
Turnout	78·6%		80·8%	
Lab	21,866	53·2%	23,119	55·2%
C	19,241	46·8%	18,139	43·3%
Ind Soc	—	—		1·5%
Lab maj	2,625	6·4%		11·9%
Swing		+2·9%		−2·7%

Mr Ronald Lewis, elected in 1964, contested West Derbyshire, 1951, South Northants, 1955, and Darlington, 1959. Worked in shops section of British Rail. B July, 1909; ed elementary schools and Cliff Methodist College. Member, Derbyshire County Council since 1949; Blackwell RDC since 1940, being chairman twice. Member, Select Committee on Expenditure. Sponsored by NUR.

Mr Earl White contested Wallsend in 1970. Company director and barrister (Lincoln's Inn). B April, 1932; ed Clifton College and New College, Oxford. Executive committee member, Northern Area Conservative Council.

CARLTON   major

Electorate 71,211

*Holland, P. W. (C)	27,305
Murray, J. (Lab)	20,147
Lange, D. (L)	11,282
Marriott, C. (Nat Front)	1,449
C majority	7,158

	1974			1974
Total Vote	60,183	L		18·7%
Turnout	84·5%	Nat Front		2·4%
C	45·4%	C maj		11·9%
Lab	33·5%			

Mr Philip Holland has represented the constituency since 1966; MP for Acton, 1959-64; contested Birmingham, Yardley, 1955. Industrial relations consultant. B March, 1917; ed Sir John Deane's Grammar School, Northwich. Joint secretary, Conservative parliamentary employment and productivity committee, 1967-70. Member, Public Accounts Committee. Served on Kensington Borough Council, 1955-59. President, Conservative trade union national advisory committee.

Mr James Murray, works convenor, Vickers Engineering, Newcastle. Contested Louth, 1970. B September, 1929. Member, Gateshead Borough Council, 1958-67. Sponsored by AEUW.

Mr Donald Lange, production engineer. B September, 1942.

Mr Cyril Marriott, engineering inspector. B September, 1923; ed Carlton Higher Standard School.

CARMARTHEN   same

Electorate 59,964   1970: 58,823

*Jones, G. G. (Lab)	17,165
Evans, G. R. (Pl Cymru)	17,162
Jones, D. O. (L)	9,698
Dunn, W. J. N. (C)	6,037
Lab majority	3

No change

	1970		1974	
Total Vote	49,213		50,062	
Turnout	83·7%		83·5%	
Lab	18,719	38·0%	17,165	34·3%
Pl Cymru	14,812	30·1%	17,162	34·3%
L	10,707	21·7%	9,698	19·4%
C	4,975	10·1%	6,037	12·0%
Lab maj	3,907	7·9%		0·0%
Swing		+3·3%		+2·8%

Mr Gwynoro Jones regained the seat for Labour, 1970. Former Labour Party research and public relations officer, Wales. B November, 1942; ed Gwendraeth Grammar School and Cardiff University. Member, Expenditure Committee. Member of Nalgo.

Mr **Gwynfor Evans,** president of Plaid Cymru since 1945, was MP for Carmarthen 1966-70; contested it in March, 1966 and 1964, Merioneth in 1945, 1950, 1955 and 1959 and the Aberdare by-election in 1954. B September, 1912; ed Barry County School; University College of Wales, Aberystwyth; and St John's College, Oxford. Farmer and market gardener.

Mr **David Owen-Jones,** barrister. B March, 1949; ed Llandovery College, Carmarthenshire, and University College, London.

Mr **William Newton Dunn,** shipping company executive. B October, 1941; ed Marlborough College, Gonville and Caius College, Cambridge, and business school, Fontainebleau.

CHEADLE   major

Electorate 64,942

*Normanton, T. (C)	27,556
Green, C. (L)	21,332
Castle, P. D. (Lab)	6,584
C majority	**6,224**

	1974		1974
Total Vote	55,472	L	38·4%
Turnout	85·4%	Lab	11·9%
C	49·7%	C maj	11·2%

Mr **Tom Normanton**
won the seat for the
Conservatives in
1970; contested Rochdale in 1964 and
1959. Industrialist and
company director. B
March, 1917; ed Manchester Grammar
School, Manchester
University and Manchester College of
Technology. Secre-

tary, Conservative Parliamentary committee on industry, 1972-74; member, European Parliament, since 1973. Appointed employer representative, National Board for Prices and Incomes, 1967-69. Immediate Past President, British Textile Employers' Association; Vice-President, International Textile Federation. Secretary, Conservative parliamentary energy committee since January 1974. Member Textile Industry Training Board, 1967-70, and, since 1968, of Central Training Council under Secretary of State for Employment.

Mr **Christopher Green** contested Surbiton, 1970. Journalist. B May, 1943; ed Wrekin College and King's College, London University.

Mr **Paul Castle,** writer on industrial and management affairs. B September, 1945; ed Leamington College for Boys and Pembroke College, Oxford. Councillor, Borough of Sale, 1971-74. NUJ.

CHELMSFORD   major

Electorate 79,297

*St John-Stevas, N. A. F. (C)	28,560
Mole, S. G. (L)	21,929
Morrell, Mrs F. (Lab)	16,063
C majority	**6,631**

	1974		1974
Total Vote	66,552	L	32·9%
Turnout	83·9%	Lab	24·1%
C	42·9%	C maj	10·0%

Mr **Norman St John-Stevas,** Minister of State for Education and Science with responsibility for the arts, 1973-74; Under Secretary for Education and Science, 1972-73. Elected in 1964; contested Dagenham in 1951. Barrister, author and journalist. B May,

1929; ed Ratcliffe College, Fitzwilliam College, Cambridge (president of the Union, 1950), Christ Church, Oxford, and Yale University. Called by Middle Temple, 1953. Member Select Committee on Race Relations and Immigration, 1968-69; executive, 1922 Committee, from March 1974.

Mr **Stuart Mole,** lecturer in government and politics. B January, 1949; ed St Paul's Cathedral Choir School, St John's School, Leatherhead, and Nottingham, Oxford and London Universities. Member, Chelmsford Borough Council since 1972 and of new district council. ATTI.

Mrs **Frances Morrell,** housewife and part-time press officer. B December, 1937; ed Queen Anne Grammar School, York, and Hull University. NUJ.

CHELTENHAM   same

Electorate 62,043   1970: 60,141

*Dodds-Parker, Sir A. D. (C)	21,723
Rodger, F. C. (L)	15,811
Gray, H. (Lab)	12,971
C majority	**5,912**

No change

	1970		1974
Total Vote	45,467		50,505
Turnout	75·6%		81·4%
C	22,823	50·2%	43·0%
Lab	14,213	31·3%	25·7%
L	8,431	18·5%	31·3%
C maj	8,610	18·9%	11·7%
Swing		+6·0%	−0·8%

Sir Douglas Dodds-Parker, elected for the seat in 1964, represented Banbury, 1949-59. Under-Secretary, Foreign Office, 1953-54 and 1955-57; Under - Secretary, Commonwealth Relations Office, 1954-55. Chairman (1972) and former vice-chairman, Conservative parliamentary foreign affairs committee. Member, European Parliament since 1973. Company director. B July, 1909; ed Winchester and Magdalen College, Oxford. Joined Sudan Political Service, 1930; assistant district commissioner; assistant private secretary to Governor General, Khartum, 1934-35; Public Security Department, Khartum, 1938-39.

Mr Frederick Rodger, ophthalmic surgeon, explorer, author and broadcaster. B June, 1916; ed Kelvinside and Glasgow University. Former professor of ophthalmology, Aligarh University, India; and director of Royal Commonwealth Society for the Blind; WHO consultant; member international committee for prevention of blindness.

Mr Hugh Gray was MP for Yarmouth, 1966-70; contested Aylesbury, 1959; Cheltenham, 1964. Lecturer at University of London. B April 19, 1916; ed Battersea Grammar School, London School of Economics and School of Oriental and African Studies.

CHERTSEY & WALTON major

Electorate 67,017

Pattie, G. E. (C)		26,603
Brady, N. J. (Lab)		14,640
Insoll, R. H. (L)		13,626
C majority		11,963

	1974		1974
Total Vote	54,869	Lab	26·7%
Turnout	81·9%	L	24·8%
C	48·5%	C maj	21·8%

Mr Geoffrey Pattie, company director. B January, 1936; ed Durham and St Catharine's College, Cambridge. Barrister-at-law (Gray's Inn). Contested Barking, 1970 and 1966. GLC member for Lambeth, 1967-70; chairman, Inner London Education Authority finance committee, 1968-70. Member, General Synod, Church of England, and

MCC. Director, leading British advertising agency.

Mr Nicholas Brady, economist. Member, Walton and Weybridge Urban District Council since 1971. Former shop assistant, laboratory assistant and electronics engineer. AScW and TGWU.

Mr Richard Insoll, contested Merton and Morden, 1970. Trade association director. B June, 1927; ed Beaumont College and London University.

CHESHAM & AMERSHAM major

Electorate 62,745

*Gilmour, I. H. J. L. (C)		27,035
Stoddart, D. (L)		16,619
Warshaw, B. M. (Lab)		9,700
C majority		10.416

	1974		1974
Total Vote	53,354	L	31·1%
Turnout	85·0%	Lab	18·2%
C	50·7%	C maj	19·5%

Mr Ian Gilmour, Secretary of State for Defence, 1974; Minister of State for Defence, 1972 - 74; Minister of State for Defence Procurement, 1971-72; Under-Secretary for Defence for the Army, 1970-71. MP for Norfolk, Central, 1962-74; contested Hounslow,

West by-election, 1962. Journalist and barrister. Editor, **Spectator,** 1954-59. B July, 1926; ed Eton and Balliol College, Oxford. Called to the Bar (Inner Temple), 1952. Appointed Opposition spokesman on defence, March 1974; in Shadow Cabinet.

Mr Douglas Stoddart, senior lecturer in management. B January, 1936; ed Sedburgh School, Magdalen College, Cambridge, PMD Harvard Business School, and Wadham College, Oxford.

Mr Brian Warshaw, sales manager. B May, 1939; ed Willesden Technical College. Councillor, London Borough of Harrow. NUGMW.

CHESTER, CITY OF minor

Electorate 68,963   1970: 68,069

Morrison, P. H. (C)		24,527
Crawford, J. (Lab)		17,759
Green, R. (L)		13,098
C majority		6,768

No change

	1970		974	
Total Vote	49,727		55,384	
Turnout	73·1%		80·3%	
C	25,877	52·0%	44·3%	
Lab	18,872	37·9%	32·1%	
L	4,978	10·0%	23·6%	
C maj	7,005	14·1%	12·2%	
Swing		+4·0%	−0·9%	

Mr Peter Morrison is an investment manager and company director. B 1944; ed Eton College and Keble College, Oxford. Personal assistant to Mr Peter Walker 1966-67; investment manager with Slater Walker Securities Ltd 1968-70. Partner in farming enterprise in Scotland. Member of organizations for the mentally handicapped. Younger brother of Mr Charles Morrison, Conservative MP for Devizes.

Mr John Crawford, local government officer. B April, 1915; ed local schools. Contested Chester, 1970 and 1966 and Northwich 1964 and 1959. Director, Birkenhead and District Cooperative Society; member and former branch secretary, NALGO.

Mr Ralph Green, lecturer at college of education. B February, 1932; ed Scarborough High School, Christ's Cellege, Cambridge. Member, ATCDE.

CHESTERFIELD   same

Electorate 70,659   1970: 71,051

*Varley, E. G. (Lab)	31,040
Taylor, J. D. (C)	15,644
Brown, M. (L)	9,937
Lab majority	15,396

No change

	1970		1974	
Total Vote	51,494		56,621	
Turnout	72·5%		80·1%	
Lab	30,386	59·0%	54·8%	
C	16,217	31·5%	27·6%	
L	4,891	9·5%	17·5%	
Lab maj	14,169	27·5%	27·2%	
Swing		+3·9%	+0·1%	

Mr Eric Varley, an Opposition spokesman on regional policy, 1970-72; chief spokesman on fuel and power, 1972-74; chairman, PLP trade union group, 1972-74. Minister of State, Technology and Power, 1969-70; assistant Government whip, 1967-69. Elected in

1964. Craftsman in mining industry. B August, 1932; ed secondary school, technical college, and Ruskin College, Oxford. Member, Derbyshire area executive of National Union of Mineworkers, 1955-64. Sponsored by NUM. *Appointed Secretary of State for Energy, March 1974.*

Mr John Taylor, wholesale bulb merchant and director of family agricultural and horticultural business. B November, 1943; ed Bedford School. President and former chairman, East Midlands Young Conservatives.

Mr Maurice Brown, medical representative. B July, 1934; ed Bemrose Grammar School, Derby, and Liverpool Medical School. Member, Derbyshire Council.

CHESTER-LE-STREET   minor

Electorate 68,109   1970: 63,829

*Radice, G. H. (Lab)	33,534
Herd, D. J. (L)	14,808
Balfour, N. (C)	8,291
Lab maj	18,726

No change

	1970		1974	
Total Vote	47,057		56,633	
Turnout	73·7%		83·1%	
Lab	33,694	71·6%	59·2%	
C	13,363	28·4%	14·6%	
L	—	—	26·1%	
Lab maj	20,331	43·2%	33·1%	
Swing		+5·4%	−0·7%	

1973 by-election: Total Vote 48,774 (71·4%)—Lab 25,874 (53·0%), L 18,808 (38·6%), C 4,092 (8·4%)—Lab maj 7,066 (14·4%).

Mr Giles Radice was returned at the 1973 by-election. Fought Chippenham, 1964 and 1966. Head of research department, NUGMW, 1966-73. Member, Labour economic and finance committee and of trade union group. B October, 1936; ed Magdalen College, Oxford.

Mr David Herd, lecturer. B October, 1940; ed Kirkcaldy High School, University of Aberdeen. Member of national executive committee, ATCDE, 1971-73.

Mr Neil Balfour, barrister and merchant banker, contested the seat in the by-election in 1973. B August, 1944; ed Ampleforth College, Yorks; and University College, Oxford. Council member, New Horizon Youth Centre.

CHICHESTER   major

Electorate 69,242

*Chataway, C. J. (C)	29,127
Jeffs, G. (L)	17,714
Smith, N. J. M. (Lab)	7,854
C majority	11,413

	1974		1974
Total Vote	54,695	L	32·4%
Turnout	79·0%	Lab	14·3%
C	53·2%	C maj	20·9%

Mr Christopher Chataway, Minister for Industrial Development, 1972-74; Minister of Posts and Telecommunications, 1970-72. Elected in 1969 by-election; MP for Lewisham, West 1959-66. Became Under Secretary for Education and Science in 1964 reorganization of department; formerly Parliamentary Secretary for Education. Broadcaster, journalist. B January, 1931; ed Sherborne and Magdalen College, Oxford. Alderman and leader, Inner London Education Authority, 1967-69; member, LCC, 1958-61. Held world record for 5,000 metres, 1954; represented Britain in Olympic Games, 1952 and 1956. Former Director, Haymarket Press Ltd and of National Advertising Corporation. An Opposition spokesman on industry from March 1974.

Mr Graham Jeffs, chartered accountant. B December, 1946; ed Godalming Grammar School, articled in London. Member, Surrey County Council since 1973.

Mr Nigel Smith, Oxford post-graduate student. B October, 1948; ed Manchester Polytechnic and Kent State University, Ohio. Former branch secretary, USDAW; member, NUT.

CHIPPENHAM   minor

Electorate 67,282   1970: 63,055

*Awdry, D. E. (C)	24,645
Banks, R. E. J. (L)	21,553
Whiles, J. (Lab)	9,395
C majority	3,092

No change

	1970		1974
Total Vote	49,011		55,593
Turnout	77·4%		82·6%
C	24,371	49·7%	44·3%
L	13,833	28·2%	38·8%
Lab	10,807	22·0%	16·9%
C maj	10,538	21·5%	5·6%
Swing		+5·1%	−0·1%

Mr Daniel Awdry was returned at 1962 by-election. Solicitor. B September, 1924; ed Winchester College and Sandhurst College. Member Chippenham Council, 1950-63, mayor 1956-57. President, Southern Boroughs Association, 1957-58. Vice-chairman Conservative Parliamentary transport committee, 1967-73. PPS Minister of State, Trade, 1963-64; Solicitor General, 1973-74.

Mr Ronald Banks, contested Croydon, North-West 1964, 1966 and 1970. Finance consultant and lecturer in economics. B April, 1933; ed John Ruskin Grammar School, Croydon, and RAF College, Cranwell.

Mr John Whiles is a railway staff administrator. B May, 1927; ed Collegiate School, Bridgwater. Mayor of Calne, Wiltshire, 1966-67 and 1967-68. TSSA.

CHORLEY   same

Electorate 74,349   1970: 71,220

Rodgers, G. (Lab)	25,440
*Monks, Mrs C. M. (C)	25,035
Orrell, Mrs N. (L)	12,652
Lab majority	405

Labour gain

	1970		1974
Total Vote	56,239		63,127
Turnout	79·0%		84·9%
C	26,577	47·2%	39·6%
Lab	24,900	44·3%	40·3%
L	,428	7·9%	20·0%
Ind	334	0·6%	—
C maj	1,677	3·0%	—
Lab maj	—		0·6%
Swing		+6·2%	−1·8%

Mr George Rodgers is a welder. B November, 1925. Member, Huyton with Roby UDC. AUEW.

Mrs Constance Monks won the seat for the Conservatives in 1970; contested it in 1966. A former teacher, is partner with her husband in a newspaper business. B May, 1911; ed Chorley Grammar School and City of Leeds Training College. Chorley borough councillor, 1947-67; alderman since 1967, mayor 1959-60. Member, Conservative backbench committees on education, arts and amenities, and health and social services.

Mrs Neva Orrell, deputy head teacher, primary school. B July, 1915; ed High School for Girls, Wigan, and Brighton Municipal Training College. Former member, Leyland UDC. Member, Lancashire County Council and South Ribble District Council. NUT.

CHRISTCHURCH & LYMINGTON
major

Electorate 54,823

*Adley, R. J. (C)	25,908
Kyrle, M. (L)	11,274
Reed, B. S. (Lab)	7,471
C majority	14,634

	1974		1974
Total Vote	44,653	L	25·2%
Turnout	76·4%	Lab	16·7%
C	58·0%	C maj	32·8%

Mr Robert Adley, marketing director of international hotel group, was MP for Bristol, North-East, 1970-74; contested Birkenhead in 1966. B March, 1935; ed Uppingham School. Member, Slough Borough Council, 1965 - 68. Former chairman, Sunningdale Conservative Association. Member Bow Group. Vice-chairman, West Country Conservative MPs 1972. Secretary, all-party tourism committee; First chairman and founder member, Brunel Society. Member, steering committee, SS Great Britain project. Treasurer, Anglo-Chinese parliamentary group.

Mr Martin Kyrle, teacher. B March, 1933; ed Southampton and Sussex Universities. Chairman, Hampshire Area Liberal Group; president, Eastleigh and District Branch NAS; executive committee member, Eastleigh Trades Council.

Mr Bruce Reed, freelance journalist and lecturer. B April, 1945; ed Rutherford Grammar School, Newcastle upon Tyne, and Southampton University. Consultant to Open University. Southampton city and district councillor since 1972; NUGMW and NUJ.

CIRENCESTER & TEWKESBURY
minor

Electorate 79,804   1970: 72,980

*Ridley, N. (C)	31,163
Otter, R. G. (L)	20,962
Fox, R. G. (Lab)	13,775
C majority	10,201

No change

	1970		1974
Total Vote	53,941		65,900
Turnout	73·0%		82·6%
C	30,217	56·0%	47·3%
Lab	16,131	29·9%	20·9%
L	7,593	14·1%	31·8%
C maj	14,086	26·1%	15·5%
Swing		+4·8%	+0·1%

Mr Nicholas Ridley was Under Secretary for Trade and Industry, 1970-72; Parliamentary Secretary, Ministry of Technology, June to October, 1970. Chairman, Conservative parliamentary finance committee 1972-73. An Opposition spokesman on technology and trade, 1969-70 and on defence 1955-66. Elected 1959. Contested Blyth, 1955. Civil engineer and company director. B February, 1929; ed Eton and Balliol College, Oxford.

Mr Robin Otter contested Worcestershire, South, 1966, and Westbury, 1970. Solicitor. B February 25, 1926; ed Marlborough and University College, Oxford. Retired district commissioner, Kenya.

Mr Roger Fox is a senior economics lecturer. B February, 1939; ed Ruskin College, Oxford and Warwick University. Formerly economics and industrial relations adviser, Office of Manpower and Economics; industrial relations assistant, National Board for Prices and Incomes. Member, Kensington and Chelsea Borough Council since 1971. TGWU.

CITIES OF LONDON AND WESTMINSTER, City of London and Westminster South
minor

Electorate 51,943   1970: 58,798

*Tugendhat, C. S. (C)	16,945
Turner, P. J. (Lab)	8,698
Underwood, T. (L)	6,015
Wertheim, C. D. (Ind C)	134
Eckley, R. E. (Dem Cap)	44
Boaks, Lt Cdr W. G. (Ind)	35
C majority	8,427

No change

	1970		1974
Total Vote	32,171		31,871
Turnout	54·5%		61·3%
C	19,102	59·4%	53·2%
Lab	10,062	31·3%	27·3%
L	2,708	8·4%	18·9%
Anti-Lab	157	0·5%	—
Young Ideas	142	0·4%	—
Ind C	—	—	0·4%
Dem Capital	—	—	0·1%
Ind	—	—	0·1%
C maj	9,040	28·1%	25·9%
Swing		+4·2%	−1·1%

Mr **Christopher Tu-gendhat** represented Cities of London and Westminster, 1970-74. Member, Select Committee on Science and Technology. Director, Sunningdale Oils Ltd; Phillips Petroleum International (UK) Ltd. Author and Journalist. B February, 1937; ed Ampleforth College, Gonville and Caius College, Cambridge. President, Cambridge Union, 1960. Member of NUJ.

Mr Philip Turner is Head of Manpower Planning, National Coal Board. B June, 1939; ed Beckenham and Penge Grammar School for Boys and University College, London. Member, Camden Borough Council, since 1971. ASTMS.

Mr Trevor Underwood, economic consultant. B July, 1943; ed Clacton-on-Sea County High School, Clare College, Cambridge, London School of Economics, University of Rochester, New York, Harvard University, Massachusetts.

Mr Christopher Wertheim, aged 35, managing director of a Sauna and an authority on massage.

Lieut-Commander William Boaks contested Clapham, 1970, and Walthamstow, East, 1951. B May, 1904; ed elementary school and Royal Naval College, Greenwich. Also contested, in 1974, Lambeth, Streatham and Merton, Wimbledon.

CITIES OF LONDON AND WEST-MINSTER, City of Westminster, Paddington   major

Electorate 58,253

*Latham, A. C. (Lab)		17,293
*Scott, N. P. (C)		16,421
Lewis, N. (L)		6,441
Lab majority		**872**

	1974		1974
Total Vote	40,155	C	40·9%
Turnout	69·0%	L	16·0%
Lab	43·0%	Lab maj	2·1%

Mr Arthur Latham was MP for Paddington, North, 1969-74. Contested Rushcliffe, 1964, and Woodford, 1959. Lecturer in further education. B August, 1930; ed Romford Royal Liberty School, Garnett College of Education. Member, Havering Council (formerly Romford Borough Council) since 1952 and alderman since 1962; former leader,

Labour group. Member, CAWU, TGWU, ATTI.

Mr Nicholas Scott, Under-Secretary for Employment, 1974. Represented Paddington, South, 1966-74; contested Islington, South-West, 1964 and 1959. Former managing director of a printing company. B August, 1933; ed Clapham College. Vice-chairman, Conservative backbench committee on employment until 1972 and former chairman of Westminster Community Relations Council. National chairman, Young Conservatives, 1963 and president, Greater London Young Conservatives. Member, Holborn Borough Council, 1956-59 and 1962-65.

Mr Neville Lewis, barrister. B March, 1945; ed Radley College and Pembroke College, Oxford.

CITIES OF LONDON AND WEST-MINSTER, City of Westminster, St Marylebone   same

Electorate 43,472   1970: 47,640

*Baker, K. W. (C)		15,683
Merriton, Mrs J. (Lab)		6,966
Silver, B. (L)		5,599
Davies, Dr W. (Ind Powell)		470
C majority		**8,717**

No change

	1970		1974	
Total Vote	28,407		28,718	
Turnout	59·6%		66·1%	
C	17,639	62·1%		54·6%
Lab	8,325	29·3%		24·2%
L	2,443	8·6%		19·5%
Ind Powell	—	—		1·6%
C maj	9,314	32·8%		30·3%
Swing		+3·3%		−1·2%

1970 by-election: Total Vote 16,828 (35·3%)—C 10,684 (63·5%), Lab 4,542 (27·0%, L 1,038 (6·2%), Nat Front 401 (2·4%), Fourth World Group 163 (1·0%)— C maj 6,142 (36·5%).

Mr Kenneth Baker, Parliamentary Secretary, Civil Service Department, 1972-74. Elected, 1970 by-election. MP for Acton, 1968-70 and contested the seat in 1966; fought Poplar 1964. Industrial consultant. B Nov, 1934; ed St. Paul's School and Magdalen College,

Oxford. Member, Twickenham Borough Council, 1960-62; Public Accounts Committee, 1969-70.

Mrs Jean Merriton, administrative worker. B September, 1927; ed Sherwood School, Epsom, London School of Economics. Member, Westminster City Council and GLC; ASTMS.

Mr Bernard Silver, managing director,

Silver Advertising Ltd. B October, 1937; ed Kilburn Grammar School and College for Distributive Trades.

CLEVELAND & WHITBY   major

Electorate 60,408

Brittan, L. (C)	21,090
Hewitson, Miss J. B. (Lab)	17,448
Watson, G. (L)	11,030
C majority	3,642

	1974		1974
Total Vote	49,568	Lab	35·2%
Turnout	82·0%	L	22·2%
C	42·5%	C maj	7·3%

Mr Leon Brittan, barrister (called to the Bar, 1962). B September, 1939; ed Haberdashers' Aske's School, Trinity College, Cambridge (president of Union) and Yale University. Contested Kensington, North, 1970 and 1966. Vice-chairman, National Association of School Governors and Managers; member, advisory committee on housing of Community Relations Commissions. Chairman Bow Group 1964 and 1965. Editor of *Crossbow* 1966-68. Member political Committee, Carlton Club.

Miss Jean Hewitson, contested Scarborough and Whitby, 1970. Social worker. B 1944; ed Leeds University. Quaker; has done social work among Puerto Rican immigrants in New York.

Mr Geoffrey Watson, curator; chairman and honorary director, Yorkshire Field Studies Centre; broadcaster, natural history, archaeology and the countryside.

CLITHEROE   same

Electorate 51,592   1970: 49,753

*Walder, A. D. (C)	20,613
Walsh, M. (Lab)	12,085
Roberts, C. W. (L)	10,438
C majority	8,528

No change

	1970		1974
Total Vote	39,553		43,136
Turnout	79·5%		83·6%
C	20,430	51·6%	47·8%
Lab	14,158	35·8%	28·0%
L	4,965	12·5%	24·2%
C maj	6,272	15·8%	19·8%
Swing		+4·9%	+2·0%

Mr David Walder, assistant Government whip, 1973-74. Returned in 1970; represented High Peak, 1961-66; contested Leicester, South-West, 1959. Barrister, author and publisher. B November, 1928; ed Latymer School and Christ Church, Oxford. Chairman, Wembley South Conservative Association, 1958-59. Vice-chairman, Parliamentary home affairs committee. Former member, publishing and economic directorate of CBI. Joint secretary, Conservative defence committee from March 1974.

Mr Michael Walsh is a systems analyst. B July, 1944; ed St Joseph's College, Blackpool and University College, London. ASTMS.

Mr Bill Roberts, personnel manager. B July, 1943; ed Royal Masonic School, Bushey, Herts and St David's University, Lampeter, Cards. Member, Barrowford Urban District Council since 1969. (Leader of the Liberal-controlled council.) Member, Pendle District Council since 1973.

COATBRIDGE & AIRDRIE   major

Electorate 59,246

*Dempsey, J. (Lab)	24,945
Anderson, Mrs. C. M. (C)	13,162
Hill, R. (Scot Nat)	7,961
Lab majority	11,783

	1974		1974
Total Vote	46,068	C	28·6%
Turnout	77·7%	Scot Nat	17·3%
Lab	54·1%	Lab maj	25·6%

Mr James Dempsey, elected in 1959, was a clerk with a haulage firm, later a lecturer on political economy and a writer on local government. B February, 1917; ed Holy Family School, Mossend, Cooperative College, Loughborough, and National Council of Labour Colleges. Member, Lanarkshire County Council since 1945.

Mrs Christine Anderson, housewife and investment consultant. B June, 1943; ed Ilkley Grammar School and Keighley Technical College and School of Art.

Mr Russell Hill, industrial therapy manager. B 1932. Member, Stirling County Council since 1967; former vice-convenor of the roads committee.

COLCHESTER same

Electorate 82,784   1970: 74,991

*Buck, A. (C)	29,072
Whytock, D. (Lab)	22,210
Thomas, D. W. (L)	15,737
C majority	6,862

No change

	1970	1974
Total Vote	58,135	67,019
Turnout	77·5%	80·9%
C	30,562	52·6% 43·4%
Lab	20,325	35·0% 33·1%
L	7,248	12·5% 23·5%
C maj	10,237	17·6% 10·2%
Swing		+7·8% −3·6%

Mr Antony Buck, Under Secretary for Defence for the Royal Navy, 1972-74, was returned at a by-election in 1961. Barrister (Inner Temple, 1954) and former director of family agricultural merchants business. B December, 1928; ed King's School, Ely, and Trinity Hall, Cambridge. Legal adviser, National Association of Parish Councils, 1957-59. Committee member of the Bow Group for four years and secretary for two. Secretary, Conservative Home Affairs Committee, 1964-70; Member, Select Committee on Parliamentary Commission for Administration, 1970-72.

Mr David Whytock, university lecturer. B May, 1940; ed Lawside School, Dundee, and St Andrew's University. Member, Colchester Borough Council since 1971.

Mr David Wynford Thomas, lecturer in law. B March 10, 1948; ed Gowerton Grammar School, Swansea, and University College of Wales, Aberystwyth. Executive member Welsh Liberal Party; member, Liberal Party Council; secretary, Association of Liberal lawyers.

COLNE VALLEY same

Electorate 60,276   1970: 58,604

Wainwright, R. S. (L)	20.984
*Clark, D. G. (Lab)	20,265
Davy, K. E. (C)	10,864
L majority	719

L gain

	1970	1974
Total Vote	47,353	52,113
Turnout	80·8%	86·4%
Lab	18,896	39·9% 38·9%
L	18,040	38·1% 40·3%
C	10,417	22·0% 20·8%
Lab maj	856	1·8% —
L maj	—	— 1·4%
Swing		+8·4% −0·1%

Mr Richard Wainwright won the seat for the Liberals in 1966, after contesting it in 1964, at the 1963 by-election and in 1959. He lost it to Labour in 1970. Chief Liberal parliamentary spokesman on economic and industrial affairs, 1966-70. Chartered accountant (President, Leeds, Bradford and District Chartered Accountants, 1965-66). B April, 1918; ed Shrewsbury School and Clare College, Cambridge. Appointed Liberal spokesman on trade and industry. March 1974.

Mr David Clark, an Opposition spokesman on agriculture and food, won the seat for Labour in 1970. University lecturer, contested Manchester, Withington, 1966. B October, 1939; ed Windermere Grammar School and Manchester University, chairman of university Labour Club and president of the Union, 1963-64. Vice-chairman of PLP environment group, secretary of all-party wool textile group. NUPE.

Mr Kenneth Davy contested the seat in 1970. Financial consultant. B 1941; ed Filey. Huddersfield councillor.

CONSETT same

Electorate 58,616   1970: 58,246

*Watkins, D. J. (Lab)	27,401
Wilkinson, T. (C)	9,058
McClure, R. (L)	8,384
Lab majority	18,343

No change

	1970	1974
Total Vote	40,899	44,843
Turnout	70·2%	76·5%
Lab	28,985	70·9% 61·1%
C	11,914	29·1% 20·2%
L	—	— 18·7%
Lab maj	17,071	41·7% 40·9%
Swing		+2·4% +0·4%

Mr David Watkins was elected in 1966. Contested Bristol, North-West, 1964. Engineer. B August, 1925; ed secondary school and Bristol College of Technology. Member, Bristol City Council, 1954-57, and Bristol Education Committee, 1958-66. Member, Select Com-

mittee on Nationalized Industries, 1967-69. Vice-chairman PLP power and steel group. Sponsored by AUEW, and secretary of union's parliamentary group.

Mr Trevor Wilkinson, insurance executive, is chairman of North-East branch of Bow Group. Member, Newcastle City Council.

Mr Ray McClure, office manager. B September, 1931; ed Southern College of Art and Queen Elizabeth College, Leatherhead. Contested Morpeth, 1970. Member, Blyth Borough Council since 1969.

CONWAY same

Electorate 51,361   1970: 48,662

*Roberts, T. W. P. (C)	16,763
Rees, The Rev. D. B. (Lab)	12,214
Jones, Dr D. T. (L)	8,546
Farmer, M. (Pl Cymru)	4,203
C majority	4,549

No change

	1970		1974
Total Vote	39,888		41,726
Turnout	82.0%		81.2%
C	16,927	42.4%	40.2%
Lab	16,024	40.2%	29.3%
Pl Cymru	4,311	10.8%	10.1%
L	2,626	6.6%	20.5%
C maj	903	2.3%	10.9%
Swing		+1.8%	+4.3%

Mr Wyn Roberts, television executive and journalist, won the seat for the Conservatives in 1970. B July, 1930; ed Beaumaris County School, Harrow and University College, Oxford. Formerly Welsh Controller, TWW Ltd, and a former executive of Harlech Television.

The Rev David Rees. B August, 1937; ed Llanddewi Beefi CP School, Tregaron Grammar School, University College of Wales, Aberystwyth, and United Theological College. Minister of Religion, writer and lecturer.

Dr David Jones, medical administrator. B June, 1931; ed Llanrwst Grammar School and Leeds University.

Mr Michael Farmer, barrister. B May, 1944; ed King's College, London.

CORNWALL North major

Electorate 51,376

*Pardoe, J. W. (L)	25,667
Gardner, Mrs R. T. (C)	16,938
Benjamin, J. B. (Lab)	1,726
L majority	8,729

No change

	1974		1974
Total Vote	44,331	C	38.2%
Turnout	86.3%	Lab	3.9%
L	57.9%	L maj	19.7%

Mr John Pardoe, Liberal spokesman on economic affairs and deputy Liberal Whip until 1974, won seat from Conservatives in 1966; contested Finchley, 1964. Treasurer, Liberal Party, 1968-69. B July, 1934; ed Sherborne School and Corpus Christi College, Cambridge. Former consultant to National Association of Schoolmasters. Member, Independent Broadcasting Authority's general advisory council, since 1973. Director, International Metal Co. Appointed Liberal spokesman on Treasury matters, March 1974.

Mrs Trixie Gardner, dental surgeon. B July, 1927; ed University of Sydney. Contested Blackburn, 1970. Member, Westminster City Council since 1968; GLC, 1970-73, Cordon Bleu.

Mr John Benjamin, accountant. B November, 1944; ed Chipping Sodbury Grammar School and London Polytechnic. ASTMS.

COVENTRY North-East major

Electorate 62,869

Park, G. M. (Lab)	30,496
Forman, N. F. (C)	15,069
Pickard, A. (People)	1,332
Hosey, J. (Comm)	838
Lab majority	15,427

	1974		1974
Total Vote	47,735	People	2.8%
Turnout	75.9%	Comm	1.7%
Lab	63.9%	Lab maj	32.3%
C	31.6%		

Mr George Park, an engineer, is leader of Coventry Borough Council and Coventry District Council. Member, West Midlands Metropolitan County Council. B September, 1914; ed Onslow Drive Secondary School, Glasgow, Whitehill Grammar School, Glasgow and

Coventry Technical College. Former convener of shop stewards, Chrysler UK Ltd. Member and former branch president, AUEW.

Mr Nigel Forman, member of Conservative research department. B March, 1943; ed Shrewsbury School, New College, Oxford, College of Europe, Harvard, and Sussex University.

Mr Alan Pickard, a computer technician at Warwick University. Aged 23. Coventry area organizer of People.

Mr John Hosey, convenor at Standard Triumph Works, Coventry, for automotive group, TGWU. Contested Coventry, East, 1970. B. 1919. Member, national committee, Anti-Apartheid Movement.

Mrs Lesley Whittaker, solicitor. B 1944. National Secretary, People.

COVENTRY North-West   major

Electorate 48,896

*Edelman, M. (Lab)	22,089
Wade, C. L. (C)	15,431
Whittaker, Mrs. L. (People)	1,542
Lab majority	6,658

	1974		1974
Total Vote	39,062	C	39·5%
Turnout	79·9%	People	3·9%
Lab	56·5%	Lab maj	17·0%

Mr Maurice Edelman has held the seat since 1950. Represented Coventry, West, 1945-50. Journalist and author. B March, 1911; ed Cardiff High School and Trinity College, Cambridge. Vice-chairman of the British Council, 1951-67. Vice-president, Franco-British Parliamentary Committee; Member, European Consultative Assembly 1949-51 and 1965-70. Chairman, Socialist Group, Western European Union, 1965-70.

Mr Charles Wade, company director. B July, 1937; ed Harrow. Contested Birmingham, Ladywood, 1970. Member, Warwick council, 1967-71.

Mrs Lesley Whittaker, solicitor. B 1944. National Secretary, People.

COVENTRY South-East   major

Electorate 50,525

*Wilson, W. (Lab)	22,217
Taylor, I. C. (C)	11,466
Prem, Dr D. (L)	4,472
Lab majority	10,751

	1974		1974
Total Vote	38,155	C	30·0%
Turnout	75·5%	L	11·7%
Lab	58·2%	Lab maj	28·2%

Mr William Wilson was elected in 1964. Contested Warwick and Leamington in 1951, 1955, 1957 (by-election), and 1959. B June, 1913; ed elementary school, Coventry Technical College, and Birmingham University. Solicitor. Member, Warwickshire County Council,

1958-70 and since 1972. Member, Joint Consolidation Committee 1964-67 and Race Relations and Immigration 1970-74.

Mr Ian Taylor is manager of European department in firm of stockbrokers. B April 1945; ed Whitley Abbey School, Coventry, Keele University and LSE. Vice-chairman, Greater London CPC, 1970-71. Member, Conservative Overseas Bureau since 1972.

Dr Dhani Prem, medical practitioner. B September 1904 in India; ed National University, Banares, India; the College of Physicians, Bombay and King's College Hospital Medical School and the School of Tropical Medicine. Treasurer, Liberal Candidates' Association. Member, Birmingham City Council, 1945-52.

COVENTRY South-West   major

Electorate 67,396

Wise, Mrs A. (Lab)	22,985
Jeffrey, J. R. (C)	22,472
Chapple, N. B. (L)	11,348
Lab majority	513

	1974		1974
Total Vote	56,805	C	39·5%
Turnout	84·3%	L	20·0%
Lab	40·5%	Lab maj	0·9%

Mrs Audrey Wise, lecturer on political matters. B 1935; ed Rutherford High School. Member of a borough council at age of 21. Member, Institute for Workers' Control.

Mr John Jeffrey, civil airline pilot and company director. B December, 1922; ed Johnstone High School, Renfrewshire. Chairman, BALPA, 1962-66.

Mr Brian Chapple, senior lecturer. B May 1926; ed Stationers' Company's School and

Merton College, Oxford. Former member, Bushey UDC, 1962-64; member, Solihull County Borough County since 1972; member, West Midlands Metropolitan County Council for Solihull since 1973. Member, West Midlands Passenger Transport Advisory Committee. AMA.

CREWE   minor

Electorate 58,788   1970: 57,515

Dunwoody, Mrs G. P. (Lab)	21,259
Park, J. G. (C)	16,136
Hulland, D. J. (L)	8,313
Lab majority	5,123

No change

	1970		1974
Total Vote	40,838		45,708
Turnout	71·0%		77·7%
Lab	22,160	54·3%	46·5%
C	18,678	45·7%	35·3%
L	—		18·2%
Lab maj	3,482	8·5%	11·2%
Swing		+6·7%	−1·3%

Mrs Gwyneth Dunwoody, Parliamentary Secretary, Board of Trade, 1967-70, sat for Exeter, 1966-70, after contesting it in 1964. B December, 1930; ed Fulham County Secondary School and the Convent of Notre Dame. Director, Film Producers' Association of Great Britain since 1970.

Mr Graham Park is a solicitor and director of a retail meat business. B April, 1941; ed Wadham House School, Malvern College, and Manchester University.

Mr Derek Hulland, leather merchant. B October 1941. Member, Executive Committee, Crewe Chamber of Trade.

CROSBY   major

Electorate 78,328

*Page, R. G. (C)	32,519
Hughes, S. F. (Lab)	16,949
Woodcock, G. (L)	12,842
C majority	15,570

	1974		1974
Total Vote	62,310	Lab	27·2%
Turnout	79·5%	L	20·6%
C	52·2%	C maj	25·0%

Mr Graham Page, Minister for Local Government and Development within the Department of the Environment, 1970-74; Minister of State for Housing and Local Government, June to October, 1970. Opposition spokesman on land and housing, 1964-70. Returned at by-election in 1953; contested Islington, North, 1950 and 1951. B June, 1911; ed Magdalen College School, Oxford, and London University. Solicitor. Chairman of Select Committee on Statutory Instruments, 1964-70.

Mr Sean Hughes, teacher. B May, 1946; ed St Aloysius' Primary School, West Park Grammar School, St John's College, Southsea, and Liverpool University. Member, Huyton Urban Council and Merseyside Metropolitan County Council. NAS.

Mr Geoffrey Woodcock, university lecturer. B April, 1936; ed Liverpool College and Liverpool University.

CROYDON Central   major

Electorate 66,120

Moore, J. E. M. (C)	21,353
Rosser, R. A. (Lab)	20,039
Maxwell, I. H. (L)	11,346
C majority	1,314

	1974		1974
Total Vote	52,738	Lab	38·0%
Turnout	79·8%	L	21·5%
C	40·5%	C maj	2·5%

Mr John Moore, investment banker and stockbroker. B November, 1937; ed Licensed Victuallers' School, Slough, London School of Economics (President of the union, 1959-60). Member, London borough council of Merton, 1971-74.

Mr Richard Rosser, trade union research officer. B October, 1944; ed St Nicholas Grammar School, Northwood, Middlesex, and Commerce Degree Bureau, Senate House, London, Councillor, London Borough of Hillingdon, since 1971; member, Fabian Society; TSSA and APEX research officer, TSSA since 1968.

Mr **Ian Maxwell**, barrister. B April 1938; ed University College School, Hampstead, and University College, University of London.

CROYDON North-East   major

Electorate 57,951

*Weatherill, B. B. (C)		19,395
Coyne, C. R. (Lab)		15,575
Streeter, P. (L)		10,659
C majority		3,820

	1974		1974
Total Vote	45,629	Lab	34·1%
Turnout	78·7%	L	23·4%
C	42·5%	C maj	8·4%

Mr **Bernard Weatherill**, Government Deputy Chief Whip, 1973-74; Comptroller of the Household (whip), 1972-73 and Lord Commissioner of the Treasury (whip), 1970-72. Opposition whip, 1967-70. Elected in 1964. A master tailor and former vice-chairman, Bernard Weatherill Ltd. Freeman of the City of London. B November, 1920; ed Malvern College. Member, National Union of Conservative Party 1963-64; chairman, Guildford Conservative Association, 1959-63; vice-chairman, South-Eastern Area Council, 1962-64.

Mr **Charles Coyne**, management consultant and economist, contested Central Norfolk, 1970. B January, 1933; ed Riley High School, Hull, Hull Municipal Technical College and London University. Member GMWU.

Mr **Patrick Streeter**, chartered accountant and bank executive. B August, 1946; ed Harrow School.

CROYDON North-West   major

Electorate 54,759

*Taylor, R. G. (C)		17,887
Boden, S. J. (Lab)		14,816
Pitt, W. H. (L)		9,707
C majority		3,071

No change

	1974		1974
Total vote	42,410	Lab	34·9%
Turnout	77·4%	L	22·9%
C	42·2%	C maj	7·2%

Mr **Robert Taylor** was elected in 1970. An architectural ironmonger. Contested Battersea North, 1964 and 1959. B December, 1932; ed Cranleigh School. Director of G. and S. Allgood Ltd. and associated companies; chairman of G. and S. Allgood (Pty) Ltd. Former Sussex county rugby player. Member, Committee of Building Materials Export Group. TA parachutist.

Mr **Stan Boden**, teacher, fought the seat, 1970. B September, 1935; ed London and Birmingham Universities. Member, Croydon Borough Council since 1971.

Mr **William Pitt**, lighting engineer. B July, 1937; ed Heath Clark School, Croydon, and London Nautical School. Secretary, local Liberal Association.

CROYDON South   major

Electorate 59,450

*Clark, W. G. (C)		28,915
Coleman, Mrs J. P. (L)		13,048
Hodge, H. E. (Lab)		6,965
C majority		15,867

	1974		1974
Total Vote	48,928	L	26·7%
Turnout	82·3%	Lab	14·2%
C	59·1%	C maj	32·4%

Mr **William Clark** was MP for Surrey, East, from 1970 to 1974. Contested Northampton in 1955 and was MP for Nottingham, South, 1959-66. B October, 1917; ed London secondary school. Member, Wandsworth Borough Council, 1949-53. Accountant and financial director of sugar producing companies.

Mrs **Jean Coleman**, solicitor. B August, 1924; ed St Anne's College, Sanderstead, and Law Society School of Law.

Mr **Henry Hodge**, aged 30, is a solicitor

for the Child Poverty Action Group and vice-chairman of the National Council for Civil Liberties.

DARLINGTON   minor

Electorate 62,414   1970: 62,580

*Fletcher, E. J. (Lab)	20,546
Hord, B. H. (C)	18,477
Freitag, P. (L)	11,398
Lab majority	2,069

No change

	1970		1974
Total Vote	47,877		50,421
Turnout	76·4%		80·8%
Lab	23,208	48·5%	40·7%
C	19,447	40·6%	36·6%
L	5,222	10·9%	22·6%
Lab maj	3,761	7·8%	4·1%
Swing		+0·6%	+1·9%

Mr Edward Fletcher, elected in 1964, contested Middlesbrough, West in 1959. Trade union official. B February, 1911; ed elementary school and Fircroft College, Birmingham. Member of Newcastle City Council since 1960. Member, estimates committee, 1964-66, Expenditure Committee, 1964-70, and 1969-70 area secretary, CAWU.

Mr Brian Hord, chartered surveyor. B June, 1934; ed Purley County Grammar School and Regent Street Polytechnic, London.

Mr Peter Freitag, financial planning consultant. B April 23, 1929; ed Haberdasher's Aske's School. County councillor. Chairman, Association of Liberal Clubs.

DARTFORD   major

Electorate 56,527

Irving, S. (Lab & Co-op)	19,803
*Trew, P. J. E. (C)	16,149
Josephs, I. R. (L)	10,273
Aldous, R. (Nat Front)	945
Lab & Co-op majority	3,654

	1974			1974
Total Vote	47,170	L		21·8%
Turnout	83·4%	Nat Front		2·0%
Lab & Co-op	42·0%	Lab & Co-op		
C	34·2%	maj		7·7%

Mr Sydney Irving held the seat from 1955 to 1970. Deputy Speaker and Chairman of Ways and Means, 1968-70; Deputy Chairman of Committee of Ways and Means, 1966-68; Treasurer of the Household and Deputy Chief Whip, 1964-66. Teacher and lecturer. B July, 1918; ed Pendower School, Newcastle upon Tyne, and London School of Economics. Deputy Pro Chancellor, University of Kent, 1968-70; Alderman, Dartford Borough Council, 1952-70. Chairman, Dartford District Council since 1973.

Mr Peter Trew won the seat for the Conservatives in 1970; contested it in 1966. Civil engineer and director of companies in the Rush and Tompkins construction and property development group. B April, 1932; ed Diocesan College, Rondebosch, Cape Province and Royal Naval College, Dartmouth. Joint secretary, Conservative parliamentary finance committee, 1972-74.

Mr Ian Josephs, hotelier and proprietor of a language school. B January 1932; ed Charterhouse and Oxford University. Contested Isle of Thanet, 1970 as an independent. Member, Kent County Council, 1961-66.

Mr Roy Aldous, builder. B February, 1937; ed local schools.

DARWEN   same

Electorate 70,004   1970: 66,494

*Fletcher-Cooke, C. (C)	25,495
Campbell-Saviours, D. N. (Lab)	16,185
Cooper, A. (L)	15,060
C majority	9,310

No change

	1970		1974
Total Vote	51,025		56,740
Turnout	76·7%		81·0%
C	26,728	52·4%	44·9%
Lab	17,634	34·5%	28·5%
L	6,663	13·0%	26·5%
C maj	9,094	17·8%	16·4%
Swing		+7·2%	−0·7%

Mr Charles Fletcher-Cooke, QC was elected in 1951. Under Secretary, Home Office, 1961-63. Contested East Dorset as Labour candidate, 1945. B May, 1914; ed Malvern College and Peterhouse, Cambridge; president of the union, 1936. Barrister (Lincoln's Inn, 1938), QC 1958. Legal adviser to the Government at the Danube Conference in 1948. Vice-chairman, Conservative Trade and Industry Committee since 1966; member, Select Committee on Parliamentary Commissioner since 1967. Director, Hulton Publications Ltd.

Mr Campbell-Saviours is a company secretary. B August, 1943; ed Keswick School and the Sorbonne. Member, Ramsbottom UDC, since 1972. TGWU.

Mr Alan Cooper, headmaster. B 1927; ed St Andrews School, Eccles, Didsbury Training College, Manchester and Liverpool University. Contested Rossendale, 1959, Bolton East, 1964, Altrincham and Sale, 1966 and Darwen, 1970. Member, Eccles Borough Council since 1958.

DAVENTRY   major

Electorate 82,535

*Jones, A. (C)	31,273
Jones, P. (Lab)	21,524
Smout, P. (L)	16,802
C majority	9,749

	1974			1974
Total Vote	69,599	Lab		30·9%
Turnout	84·3%	L		24·1%
C	44·9%	C maj		14·0%

Mr Arthur Jones represented Northamptonshire South, 1962-74; contested Wellingborough, 1955. Estate agent with an interest in a number of private companies. B October, 1915; ed Bedford Modern School. Member Bedford Borough Council since 1949, former Mayor; Bedfordshire County Council 1956-67. Member, Select Committee on Race Relations and Immigration, and Expenditure Committee. Chairman, Conservative Party backbench committee on local government and development; chairman, Conservative Party local government

National Advisory Committee, 1963-73. Member, executive committee, Town and Country Planning Association.

Mr Peter Jones, personnel manager. B November, 1943; ed Pontardane Grammar School, Swansea University and London School of Economics. Contested Worcester, 1970. NUGMW.

Mr Peter Smout contested Northants, South, 1970. Deputy headmaster. B November 14, 1929; ed Leys School, Cambridge; Clare College, Cambridge, and Birmingham University.

DEARNE VALLEY   same

Electorate 62,698   1970: 62,935

*Wainwright, E. (Lab)	34,727
Hargreaves, P. (L)	7,873
Lord Irwin (C)	6,950
Wilson, A. E. (Ind)	906
Lab majority	26,854

No change

	1970		1974
Total Vote	45,240		50,456
Turnout	71·9%		80·5%
Lab	33,966	75·1%	68·8%
C	6,848	15·1%	13·8%
L	4,426	9·8%	15·6%
Ind	—	—	1·8%
Lab maj	27,118	59·9%	53·2%
Swing		+4·0%	+2·5%

Mr Edwin Wainwright, secretary of the PLP trade union group since 1966. Elected in 1959. B August, 1908; ed Darfield Council School and Wombwell and Barnsley Technical College. Miner and branch official of the National Union of Mineworkers for 26 years. Member, National Executive Committee, NUM 1952-59 and sponsored by NUM. Secretary, Yorkshire group of Parliamentary Labour Party since 1966.

Mr Peter Hargreaves, company director. B December 1935; ed Secondary Modern School. Contested Dearne Valley, 1966 as an Independent, and in 1970 as a Liberal. Former member, Wombwell UDC 1965-69; Member, Wombwell UDC since 1970 and District Council, since 1973.

Lord Irwin, bank executive. B 1944; ed Eton and Christchurch, Oxford. Member, General Council, National Society for Cancer Relief; chairman, Greater London Committee for Cancer Relief since 1970; trustee, Magdalen Hospital Trust.

DENBIGH same

Electorate 63,025   1970: 60,732

*Morgan, W. G. O. (C)	21,258
Williams, Dr D. L. (L)	15,243
Sherrington, E. J. (Lab)	10,141
Matthews, G. (Pl Cymru)	4,103
C majority	6,015

No change

	1970		1974
Total Vote	47,673		50,745
Turnout	78·5%		80·5%
C	21,246	44·6%	41·9%
Lab	12,537	26·3%	20·0%
L	8,636	18·1%	30·0%
Pl Cymru	5,254	11·0%	8·1%
C maj	8,709	18·3%	11·8%
Swing		−2·2%	+1·8%

Mr Geraint Morgan, QC, was elected in 1959, contested Merioneth in 1951 and Huyton, 1955. A barrister (Gray's Inn, 1947), QC 1971. B November, 1920; ed University College of Wales, Aberystwyth, and Trinity Hall, Cambridge, Vice-chairman of Welsh Conservative MPs since 1972.

Dr David Williams, general practitioner. B December, 1926; ed Birkenhead School and Liverpool University. Member, Flintshire County Council; member General Medical Services Committee, BMA.

Mr Emlyn Sherrington, lecturer. B December, 1938; ed Llanberis Council School, Brynrefail School, University College of Wales, Aberystwyth. County councillor. ASTMS.

Mr Gwyn Matthews contested the seat in 1970. Teacher. B October, 1943; ed Denbigh Grammar School and University College, Bangor. President of the Union, 1967-68.

DERBY North major

Electorate 82,088

*Whitehead, P. (Lab)	26,029
Penfold, D. J. (C)	24,736
Peel, M. (L)	13,995
Lab majority	1,293

	1974			1974
Total Votes	64,760		C	38·2%
Turnout	78·9%		L	21·6%
Lab	40·2%		Lab maj	2·0%

Mr Phillip Whitehead, television producer and writer. Elected 1970; contested West Derbyshire in 1966. B May, 1937; ed Lady Manners Grammar School, Bakewell, and Exeter College, Oxford. Member, Fabian Society executive committee, and NUJ.

Mr David Penfold, sales development manager. B April, 1935; ed Burton Grammar School, Highgate School and in France. Contested Nottingham, West, 1966. Member, Burton-on-Trent Borough Council, 1964-71; former leader, Conservative majority; chairman, finance committee.

Mr Malcolm Peel, training manager. B February, 1931; ed Sheffield University and Magdalene College, Cambridge. Member of Derby District Council.

DERBY South major

Electorate 73,864

*Johnson, W. H. (Lab)	26,613
Clements, R. S. W. (C)	19,470
Mills, Mrs J. (L)	10,121
Lab majority	7,143

	1974			1974
Total Vote	56,204		C	34·6%
Turnout	76·1%		L	18·0%
Lab	47·3%		Lab maj	12·7%

Mr Walter Johnson, staff training executive with London Transport, was elected in 1970; contested Acton in the 1968 by-election, South Bedfordshire, 1959, and Bristol West, 1955. B November, 1917; ed Devon House School, Margate. Brentford and Chiswick councillor for six years. Sponsored by, and member of, TSSA. Treasurer, National Federation of Professional Workers since 1965.

Mr Ronald Clements, company director. B October, 1935; ed Greenhill Preparatory School and Wyggeston School. Member, Leicester City Council, 1964-71.

Mrs Julia Mills, part-time teacher. B August, 1915; ed King Edward VI School, Camp hill, Birmingham, and Victoria (London) College of Music, County Councillor since 1964, and Mayoress of Sutton Coldfield.

DERBYSHIRE North-East — major

Electorate 66,297

*Swain, T. (Lab)		29,602
Ramsden, J. C. (C)		22,320
Lab majority		7,282

	1974		1974
Total Vote	51,922	C	43·0%
Turnout	78·3%	Lab maj	14·0%
Lab	57·0%		

Mr Thomas Swain, was elected in 1959. B October, 1911; ed at Broadway School, Burton - on - Trent. Miner; held various offices in National Union of Mine-workers, including vice-presidency of the Derbyshire area executive; sponsored by NUM. Served on Staveley Urban Council and Derbyshire County Council.

Mr John Ramsden, incorporated insurance broker and company director. B September, 1927; ed Dronfield Grammar School. Contested Chesterfield, 1970. Alderman, Derbyshire County Council, 1970-74.

DERBYSHIRE South-East — major

Electorate 53,350

*Rost, P. L. (C)		20,016
Wardle, J. W. (Lab)		16,981
Fry, F. (L)		8,378
C majority		3,035

	1974		1974
Total Vote	45,375	Lab	37·4%
Turnout	85·0%	L	18·5%
C	44·1%	C maj	6·7%

Mr Peter Rost, stockbroker, won the seat for the Conservatives in 1970; contested Sunderland, North, in 1966. B September, 1930; ed Aylesbury Grammar School and Birmingham University. Former teacher and financial journalist. Joint secretary, Conservative parliamentary committee on trade since 1972.

Mr John Wardle, assistant railway station manager. B February 1922; ed Wolverley Sebrigt Endowed School and trade union scholarships. Contested Kidderminster, 1966, and Hereford, 1959. Member, Joint Steering Group for Railways, 1966-67, Kidderminster RDC since 1949, Hereford and Worcester County Council since 1973. South Midlands District Secretary, ASLEF, for 11 years.

Mr Frederick Fry, cost and works accountant. B April 1936.

DERBYSHIRE West — same

Electorate 48,763   1970: 47,811

*Scott-Hopkins, J. S. R. (C)		19,941
Worboys, P. (L)		11,481
Inglis, F. C. (Lab)		9,529
C majority		8,460

No change

	1970		1974
Total Vote	36,668		40,951
Turnout	76·7%		84·0%
C	22,692	61·9%	48·7%
Lab	13,976	38·1%	23·3%
L	—	—	28·0%
C maj	8,716	23·8%	20·6%
Swing		+5·7%	+0·8%

Mr James Scott-Hopkins was elected at a by-election in 1967; MP for North Cornwall, 1959-66; contested Bedwellty in 1955. Parliamentary Secretary, Ministry of Agriculture, Fisheries and Food 1962-64. A marketing consultant. B November, 1921; ed Eton and New College, Oxford, and Emmanuel College, Cambridge. Farmer. Member of European Parliament since 1973.

Mr Peter Worboys, solicitor. B March, 1947; ed Perse School, Cambridge, Selwyn College, Cambridge.

Mr Frederick Inglis, university lecturer, contested the seat in 1970. B May, 1937; ed Oundle and Caius College, Cambridge. NUT.

DEVIZES — minor

Electorate 77,033   1970: 72,116

*Morrison, C. A. (C)		27,878
Faulkner, R. O. (Lab)		17,980
Crawford, J. (L)		16,753
C majority		9,898

No change

	1970		1974	
Total Vote	55,127		62,611	
Turnout	76·4%		81·3%	
C	28,475	51·6%		44·5%
Lab	20,442	37·1%		28·7%
L	6,210	11·3%		26·7%
C maj	8,033	14·6%		15·8%
Swing		+4·5%		+0·6%

Mr Charles Morrison, a farmer, has represented the constituency since a by-election in 1964. B June, 1932; ed Eton and Royal Agricultural College, Cirencester. Member, South West Regional Sports Council, 1966-68. Secretary, Conservative Committee for Education and Science, 1965-66. Chairman, Conservative parliamentary agriculture, fisheries and food committee 1972-74. Chairman, trustees of Young Volunteer Force Foundation. Elder brother of Mr Peter Morrison, Conservative MP for City of Chester. Joint vice-chairman agriculture committee, and vice-chairman, 1922 Committee, from March 1974.

Mr Richard Faulkner, director of public affairs consultancy. B March, 1946; ed Merchant Taylors' School and Worcester College, Oxford. Contested seat in 1970. Councillor, London Borough of Merton, since 1971. TGWU and NUJ.

Mr John Crawford, teacher. B December, 1932; ed Holyhead Grammar School, Bangor Normal College, and Furzedown College, London. Contested Howden, 1964. Former member, Whitby UDC 1961-64. Associate, College of Preceptors.

DEVON North   major

Electorate 73,037

*Thorpe, J. J. (L)	34,052
Keigwin, T. (C)	22,980
Marston, T. K. (Lab)	6,140
L majority	11,072

	1974		1974
Total Vote	63,172	C	36·4%
Turnout	86·5%	Lab	9·7%
L	53·9%	L maj	17·5%

Mr Jeremy Thorpe was elected Leader of the Liberal Party in 1967 following the resignation of Mr Jo Grimond. Hon treasurer of the Liberal Party, 1965-67. Won the seat from the Conservatives in 1959; contested it in 1955. B April, 1929; ed in United States, Eton

and Trinity College, Oxford (President of the Union, 1951). Barrister (Inner Temple, 1954), Member, Committee of Privileges. Resigned directorships of London and County Securities, Capital Securities and other companies in December, 1973. Father and grandfather were MPs.

Mr Timothy Keigwin, farmer and broadcaster, contested the seat in 1966 and 1970. B October, 1921; ed Harrow and Corpus Christi College, Cambridge. Vice-chairman, North Devon Conservative Association. Member, NFU; Country Landowners' Association.

Mr Terence Marston, metallurgist. Contested Torrington, 1970. B March, 1937; ed Bradford Institute of Technology. EPEA. Associate member, Institute of Metallurgists.

DEVON West   major

Electorate 56,976

*Mills, P. M. (C)	23,524
Pinney, A. (L)	18,256
Duffin, J. B. H. (Lab)	5,089
C majority	5,268

	1974		1974
Total Vote	46,869	L	38·9%
Turnout	82·3%	Lab	10·8%
C	50·2%	C maj	11·2%

Mr Peter Mills, Under Secretary, Northern Ireland Office, 1972-74; Parliamentary Secretary, Agriculture Fisheries and Food, April to November, 1972. Represented Torrington, 1964-74. B September, 1921; ed Epsom College and Wye College. Farmer and formerly a farm company director. Former member, Church Assembly and House of Laity, Exeter Diocese and former vice-president, Parish Councils Association and Rural District Councils Associations. Member, Select Committee on Agriculture, 1967-69. Joint vice-chairman, Conservative agriculture committee, from March 1974.

Mr Aza Pinney, property consultant. B July 1936; ed at Eton, Christ Church, Oxford, and Dorset Farm Institute. Contested West Dorset, 1964, 1966, West Derbyshire, 1967; founder member, Dorset Grassland Society. Official speaker, European Movement.

DEWSBURY same

Electorate 60,991   1970: 60,544

*Ginsburg, D. (Lab)	21,186
Humphrey, I. J. (C)	15,774
Allsop, A. (L)	12,899
Lab majority	5,412

No change

	1970		1974
Total Vote	45,171		49,859
Turnout	74·6%		81·7%
Lab	22,015	48·7%	42·5%
C	17,468	38·7%	31·6%
L	5,688	12·6%	25·9%
Lab maj	4,547	10·1%	10·8%
Swing		+7·4%	−0·4%

Mr David Ginsburg, elected in 1959. Market research consultant. Previously secretary, Labour Party research department, and of home policy sub-committee of National Executive. Deputy chairman, Parliamentary and Scientific Committee; member, Select Committee on Science and Technology. B March, 1921; ed University College School, Hampstead; Balliol, Oxford. Member, Institute Professional Civil Servants, 1946-52. T & GWU since 1952. Labour Party representative on Economics Committee of TUC, 1952-59.

Mr Ivor Humphrey, company representative. B January, 1927; ed Creswell Secondary School. Contested Bolsover, 1970. Member, National Executive, USTRA.

Mr Alan Allsop, purchasing manager. B August 1929; ed Batley Technical College. Contested Dewsbury, 1964, 1966 and 1970. Member, Dewsbury Borough Council since 1965. President, Dewsbury Divisional Liberal Party.

DONCASTER same

Electorate 58,919   1970: 59,755

*Walker, H. (Lab)	23,041
Tunnicliffe, K. I. (C)	17,565
Davison, W. (L)	7,490
Lab majority	5,476

No change

	1970		1974
Total Vote	44,737		48,096
Turnout	74·9%		81·6%
Lab	22,658	50·6%	47·9%
C	19,431	43·4%	36·5%
L	2,648	5·9%	15·6%
Lab maj	3,227	7·2%	11·4%
Swing		+3·1%	−2·1%

Mr Harold Walker, an Opposition spokesman on employment since 1970, was Under Secretary, Department of Employment and Productivity, April, 1968-70; Assistant Government whip, 1967-68. Elected in 1964. Engineer. B July, 1927; ed at council school and Manchester College of Technology. *Appointed Under Secretary for Employment, March 1974.*

Mr Ian Tunnicliffe contested Morpeth in 1970. Schoolmaster. B June 1943; ed Wyggeston School, Leicester, and Bede College, Durham. Member, Sunderland Borough Council, 1967-70.

Mr Wilfrid Davison, lecturer in business studies. B June, 1938; ed St Mary's College, Great Crosby, Liverpool and Liverpool University. ATTI.

DON VALLEY same

Electorate 87,856   1970: 83,618

*Kelley, R. (Lab)	48,737
Le Bosquet, P. J. (C)	20,792
Lab majority	27,945

No change

	1970		1974
Total Vote	61,169		69,529
Turnout	73·1%		79·1%
Lab	42,496	69·5%	70·1%
C	18,673	30·5%	29·9%
Lab maj	23,823	38·9%	40·2%
Swing		+5·0%	−0·6%

Mr Richard Kelley, a miners' union secretary for 10 years, was returned in 1959. B July, 1904; ed elementary school. Served on the West Riding County Council 1949-59. Member Select Committee on Nationalized Industries. Sponsored by NUM.

Mr Peter Le Bosquet, director and chief executive. B December, 1947; ed High Pavement Grammar School and Clarendon College, Nottingham. Chairman, Nottingham Young Conservatives; executive member, West Nottingham Conservative Association; vice-chairman, Nottingham Conservative Federation.

DORKING same

Electorate 58,402   1970: 58,889

*Sinclair, Sir G. E. (C)	24,803
Andrews, S. (L)	14,490
Spiers, J. R. (Lab)	8,961
C majority	10,313

No change

	1970		1974
Total Vote	43,019		48,254
Turnout	73·0%		82·6%
C	25,393	59·0%	51·4%
Lab	10,523	24·5%	18·6%
L	7,103	16·5%	30·0%
C maj	14,870	34·6%	21·4%
Swing		+4·5%	−0·8%

Sir George Sinclair, elected in 1964, was a colonial administrator from 1936-61. Deputy-Governor, Cyprus, 1955-60. B November, 1912; ed Abingdon School and Pembroke College, Oxford. Member, Select Committees on Race Relations and Immigration Overseas Aid and Procedure. Member Commonwealth Affairs Committee (joint sec, 1966-68), and the national executive committee of the United Nations Association. Served on Wimbledon Borough Council, 1962-65; overseas political consultant, 1961-63. Joint secretary, Conservative education committee, March 1974.

Mr Stuart Andrews, lecturer in politics and economics. B May 19, 1944; ed Haileybury and Imperial Service College, Hertford; Exeter University. Trustee, Cambridge Tutors' Educational Trust, Croydon.

Mr John Spiers, publisher. B September, 1941; ed Redhill School, East Sutton, Catford College of Commerce and University of Sussex. ACSS.

DORSET North same

Electorate 70,738   1970: 62,614

*James, D. P. (C)	30,288
Watkins, P. G. (L)	23,405
Smith, T. G. (Lab)	6,032
C majority	6,883

No change

	1970		1974
Total Vote	49,192		59,725
Turnout	78·5%		84·4%
C	28,471	57·9%	50·7%
L	12,095	24·6%	39·2%
Lab	8,626	17·5%	10·1%
C maj	16,376	33·3%	11·5%
Swing		+4·4%	+0·1%

Mr David James was elected in 1970. He represented Brighton, Kemptown, for the Conservatives from 1959 to 1964 when he was defeated by seven votes. Sec, Northern Ireland Committee, Shipping and Shipbuilding Committee. B December, 1919; ed Eton and Balliol College, Oxford. An author. Underwriting member of Lloyd's. Member, 1945-46, Antarctic expedition; polar adviser for film, Scott of the Antarctic. Council member, Outward Bound Trust 1948-73; trustee, National Maritime Museum 1953-65.

Mr Philip Watkins, chartered accountant. Hon treasurer, Liberal Party. B November 1930; ed Bristol Grammar School and Brasenose College, Oxford. Fought Bridgwater, 1959, 1964, 1966; North Dorset, 1970.

Mr Trevor Smith, hospital social worker. B December, 1949; ed Holy Trinity and Priory Schols, Taunton, and Taunton Technical College. Member, Somerset County Council since 1973. Nalgo and COHSE; member Christian Socialist Movement and Fabian Society.

DORSET South same

Electorate 68,923   1970: 66,953

*King, E. M. (C)	26,933
Chedzoy, A. (Lab)	18,318
Broomfield, D. T. (L)	12,140
C majority	8,615

No change

	1970		1974
Total Vote	52,976		57,391
Turnout	79·1%		82·2%
C	27,580	52·1%	46·9%
Lab	20,716	39·1%	31·9%
L	4,680	8·8%	21·1%
C maj	6,864	12·9%	15·0%
Swing		+4·6%	+1·0%

Mr Evelyn King was elected in 1964, having joined the Conservative Party in 1951 and contested Southampton, Itchen, in 1959. Labour MP for Penryn and Falmouth, 1945-50, and Parliamentary Secretary, Ministry of Town and Country Planning, 1947-50. A former headmaster, he now farms and

manages Embley Estates. B May, 1907; ed Cheltenham College and King's College, Cambridge. Served on Select Committee on Overseas Aid. Member, Conservative Foreign and Commonwealth Affairs Committee and Agriculture Committee.

Mr Alan Chedzoy, college lecturer. B March, 1935; ed Beckenham Grammar School, Bognor Regis Training College, and Reading University. Member, Weymouth and Portland District Council. NUT.

Mr David Broomfield, postman. B March 1930; ed elementary schools. Member, Ringwood RDC since 1966; chairman, Ringwood Parish Council. Member, UPOW.

DORSET West   minor

Electorate 53,116   1970: 50,651

Spicer, J. W. (C)	21,634
Angus, R. (L)	14,183
Cross, M. F. (Lab)	8,333
C majority	7,451

No change

	1970		1974
Total Vote	38,921		44,150
Turnout	76·0%		83·1%
C	21,081	54·2%	49·0%
Lab	10,526	27·0%	18·9%
L	7,314	18·8%	32·1%
C maj	10,555	27·1%	16·9%
Swing		+5·5%	+1·4%

Mr James Spicer, company director and farmer. B 1925; ed Latymer. Contested the Southampton, Itchen by-election in 1971. Director, Conservative Group for Europe; member of National Executive since 1966; vice-chairman, Wessex Area CPC Committee;  chairman, National CPC Advisory Committee, 1969-72. Member, Institute of Strategic Studies and British Atlantic Committee. President, Beaminster British Legion.

Mr Roger Angus, lecturer. B April 1943; ed Winchester College and New College, Oxford.

Mr Martin Cross, senior lecturer. B December, 1945; ed Downside School and Worcester College, Oxford. Branch Secretary, ATTI, 1970-73. Lewes Borough Councillor since 1971, and member Lewes DC since 1973.

DOVER AND DEAL   same

Electorate 76,552   1970: 72,580

*Rees, P. W. I. (C)	27,033
Bishop, L. J. A. (Lab)	22,183
Young, R. S. (L)	12,832
Stone W. (Ind Soc Dem)	661
C majority	4,850

No change

Dover & Deal

	1970		1974
Total Vote	58,557		62,709
Turnout	80·7%		81·9%
C	30,103	51·4%	43·1%
Lab	28,454	48·6%	35·4%
L	—	—	20·5%
Ind Soc Dem	—	—	1·0%
C maj	1,649	2·8%	7·7%
Swing		+4·3%	+2·4%

Mr Peter Rees, QC, won the seat in 1970; he contested Liverpool, West Derby, in 1966, and Abertillery in 1965 by-election, and in 1964. Barrister (Inner Temple, 1953). B December, 1926; ed Stowe School and Christ Church,  Oxford. Member, Select Committee on Company Taxation; officer of Conservative Finance and Legal Committees. Member, Institute of Taxation and Inns of Court Conservative and Unionist Society. Joint secretary, Conservative finance committee, March 1974.

Mr Leonard Bishop contested Isle of Thanet 1970 and 1966. Chartered accountant. B November, 1937; ed St Marylebone Grammar School. Leader of Labour groups on Ramsgate Borough Council and Thanet District Council.

Mr Scot Young, businessmann and farmer. B May, 1935; self-educated. Chairman and president of companies in Britain and Canada.

DOWN North   major

Electorate 94,069

*Kilfedder, J. A. (UUUC)	38,169
Bradford, R. H. (UU Pro Assembly)	21,943
Curran, D. (SDLP)	2,376
UUUC majority	16,226

	1974		1974
Total Vote	62,488	Pro Assem	35·1%
Turnout	66·4%	SDLP	3·8%
C	61·1%	C maj	26·0%

Mr James Kilfedder,
was returned as
Ulster Unionist in
1970; represented Bel-
fast, West, 1964-66. B
July 1928; ed Portora
Royal School, Ennis-
killen, and Dublin
University. Barrister
(King's Inn, Dublin,
1952, and Gray's Inn,
1958). Joint Secretary,
Conservative Parlia-
mentary Committee on Northern Ireland
since 1972; secretary, Ulster Unionist MPs,
1972. Member of Northern Ireland Assembly.

Mr Roy Bradford is Minister of Environment in the Northern Ireland Executive.
Elected Unionist MP for Victoria at Stormont in 1962. Former Minister of Development and Minister of Commerce. Aged
43, he is a writer and broadcaster.

Mr Dermott Curran is an SDLP councillor in Ardglass, co Down. Aged 34.

DOWN South   same

Electorate 91,792   1970: 87,079

*Orr, Capt L. P. S. (UUUC)	31,088
Holywood, S. (SDLP)	25,486
Golding, H. (Repub Clubs)	3,046
UUUC majority	5,602

UUUC Gain

	1970		1974
Total Vote	64,317		59,620
Turnout	73·9%		64·9%
UUUC	—		52·1%
UU	34,894	54·2%	—
Nat Unity	21,676	33·7%	—
L	7,747	12·0%	—
SDLP	—		42·7%
Repub Clubs	—		5·1%
UU maj	13,218	20·5%	—
UUUC maj	—		9·4%

Capt. Lawrence Orr,
chairman of the Ul-
ster Unionist MPs,
1964-74. Elected in
1950. B September,
1918; ed Campbell
College, Belfast, and
Trinity College, Dub-
lin, Past Imperial
Grand Master of
Orange Order. Direc-
tor, Associated Lei-
sure Ltd. Vice-chair-
man, Conservative Northern Ireland Committee.

Mr Sean Holywood, became a Newry
councillor in May, 1973. Prominent in the
civil rights movement, he was responsible
for the organization of protest marches
in Newry following the "bloody Sunday"
incident in Londonderry. Aged 29. Graduate of Queen's University and has taught
at St Colman's College, Newry since 1967.

Mr Hugh Golding contested the constituency as a National Unity candidate in
1970. Printer; aged 54. Was a member of
Newry Council until it was dissolved and
also of Down Rural District Council and
Down County Council. Former member,
executive, Northern Ireland Labour
Party.

DUDLEY East   major

Electorate 59,827

*Gilbert, J. W. (Lab)	27,417
Taylor, J. M. (C)	15,795
Lab majority	11,622

	1974		1974
Total Vote	43,212	C	36·5%
Turnout	72·2%	Lab maj	26·9%
Lab	63·4%		

Mr John Gilbert was
MP for Dudley 1970-
74; contested the
1968 by-election, and
Ludlow, 1966. An
Opposition spokesman
on Treasury matters
1972 to 1974. B
April, 1927; ed Mer-
chant Taylors' School,
Northwood, St John's
College, Oxford, and
New York Univer-
sity. NUGMW. *Appointed Financial
Secretary to the Treasury, March 1974*

Mr John Taylor, solicitor. B August, 1941;
ed Bromsgrove School, College of Law.
Member, Solihull County Borough Council, 1971-74, and West Midlands Metropolitan County Council since 1973. Secretary, Birmingham Law Students Society,
1964-65. Director, several private companies, particularly travel and fuel.

DUDLEY West   major

Electorate 74,212

Phipps, C. B. (Lab)	29,143
*Montgomery, F. (C)	24,474
Thirlby, M. (Ind L)	5,971
Lab majority	4,669

	1974		1974
Total Vote	59,588	C	41·1%
Turnout	80·3%	Ind L	10·0%
Lab	48·9%	Lab maj	7·8%

Mr Colin Phipps contested the Walthamstow, East by-election in 1969. Petroleum geologist and chairman of Dr Colin Phipps and Partners Ltd and Phipps Oil Ltd. B July, 1934; ed Acton County School, Bishop Gore School, Swansea, and London and Birmingham Universities. NUGMW.

Mr Fergus Montgomery was MP for Brierley Hill from the by-election in 1967 until 1974; represented Newcastle, East, 1959-64 contested Consett, 1955. Teacher. B November, 1927; ed Hebburn Methodist elementary school, Jarrow Grammar School, and Bede College, Durham. Member, Hebburn UDC, 1950-58; chairman, Young Conservatives, 1957-58.

DUMFRIES same

Electorate 61,304   1970: 60,939

*Monro, H. S. P. (C)	21,707
Wheatley, J. F. (Lab)	12,739
Whitley, L. (Scot Nat)	9,186
Reive, D. H. (L)	5,642
C majority	8,968

No change

	1970		1974
Total Vote	46,427		49,274
Turnout	76·2%		80·3%
C	24,661	53·1%	44·0%
Lab	15,555	33·5%	25·8%
Scot Nat	6,211	13·4%	18·6%
L	—		11·4%
C maj	9,106	19·6%	18·2%
Swing		+4·9%	−0·7%

Mr Hector Monro, Under Secretary for Health and Education, Scottish Office, 1971-74; Lord Commissioner of the Treasury (whip), 1970-71. Opposition whip, 1967-70. Elected in 1964. B October, 1922; ed Canford School and King's College, Cambridge.

Member, Dumfries County Council, 1952-67. Former member of party committees on Scotland, agriculture, and aviation. Former chairman, Century Aluminium. Manager, Scottish rugby XV during tour of Australia. An Opposition spokesman on Scotland from March 1974.

Mr John Wheatley, advocate. B May 1941; ed Holy Cross Academy, Mount St Mary's College, Edinburgh University.

Mr Laurence Whitley, prospective minister of religion. B September, 1949; ed Edinburgh Academy and Edinburgh and St Andrews Universities.

Mr Duncan Reive, Director of Child Guidance and education officer. B 1919; ed Cumnock Academy, Edinburgh University, and Glasgow University. Elder, Maxweltown West Church, Dumfries.

DUNBARTONSHIRE Central major

Electorate 48,998

*McCartney, H. (Lab)	16,439
Hirst, M. (C)	9,775
Reid, J. (Comm)	5,928
Welsh, A. (Scot Nat)	5,906
Harvey, C. (L)	2,583
Hammond, S. (WRP)	52
Lab majority	6,664

	1974		1974
Total Vote	40,683	Scot Nat	14·5%
Turnout	83·0%	L	6·3%
Lab	40·4%	WRP	0·1%
C	24·0%	Lab maj	16·4%
Comm	14·6%		

Mr Hugh McCartney, sales representative, was MP for Dunbartonshire, East, 1970-74. B January, 1920; ed secondary school and Royal Technical College, Glasgow. Member, Dunbarton County Council; burgh councillor since 1955. Member, TGWU.

Mr Michael Hirst, chartered accountant. B January 1946; ed Glasgow Academy; Glasgow University; University of Iceland, Reykjavik. National vice-chairman, Scottish Young Conservatives, 1972-73. President, Glasgow University Conservative Club.

Mr James Reid, engineer at Marathon shipyard, Clydebank. B 1933. Contested Dunbartonshire East, 1970. Spokesman for the Upper Clyde Shipyard workers during the "work-in" to prevent the closing of Clyde shipyards. Clydebank councillor. Rector of Glasgow University. Former shop stewards' convenor at Polar Engine Works.

Mr Andrew Welsh, teacher. B 1944; ed Govan High School, Glasgow, and Glasgow University. Chairman, Stirling branch SNP.

Mr Colin Harvey, teacher, social worker and author. B July 1931; ed Edinburgh University, Oxford University, London School of Economics and Glasgow University.

Mr **Stephen Hammond** is news editor of the WRP's daily newspaper *Workers' Press*. Aged 28; ed Bristol University.

DUNBARTONSHIRE East   major

Electorate 61,266

Henderson, J. S. B. (C)	19,092
McGarry, E. F. (Lab)	15,416
Bain, Mrs M. (Scot Nat)	11,635
Cameron, J. (L)	5,936
C majority	3,676

	1974		1974
Total Vote	52,079	Scot Nat	22·3%
Turnout	85·0%	L	11·4%
C	36·6%	C maj	7·0%
Lab	29·6%		

Mr **Barry Henderson**, marketing executive for international computer manufacturer. B April, 1936; ed Lathallan School, Fife and Stowe. Contested East Dunbartonshire, 1970; Edinburgh, East, 1966.

Mr **Edward McGarry** is a gear cutter. Contested Burton-on-Trent, 1959. Ed St Bridget's RC School and Motherwell High School. Member of Coventry City Council, 1951-54; member, TGWU.

Mrs **Margaret Bain**, remedial teacher. B September, 1945; ed Biggar High School, Glasgow and Strathclyde universities, and Jordanhill College of Education. Stirling and district regional officer, SWTA. Former secretary, Cumbernauld, North, branch, SNP.

Mr **Jim Cameron**, training adviser. B November, 1944; ed St Mungo Academy.

DUNBARTONSHIRE West   major

Electorate 51,565

*Campbell, I. (Lab)	16,247
Carse, Miss M. (C)	13,638
Murray, A. (Scot Nat)	11,144
Lab majority	2,609

	1974		1974
Total Vote	41,029	C	33·2%
Turnout	79·6%	Scot Nat	27·2%
Lab	39·6%	Lab maj	6·3%

Mr **Ian Campbell**, electrical power engineer with South of Scotland Electricity Board, 1953-70, was elected in 1970. B April, 1926; ed Dunbarton Academy, Royal Technical College (now Strathclyde University). Member, all - party whisky group; Dunbarton Council, 1958-70; provost of Dunbarton, 1962-70; EPEA and NUGMW.

Miss **Moira Carse**, teacher. B August, 1939; ed Glasgow University (Queen Margaret President). ALCM. Was chairman, Shawlands Young Conservatives.

Mr **Alexander Murray**, sheep farmer. B December, 1930; ed Beauly, Inverness. Joined SNP, 1962; chairman, West Dunbartonshire Constituency Association, 1967. County Councillor, 1967-72. NFU.

DUNDEE East   same

Electorate 62,597   1970: 61,533

Wilson, G. (Scot Nat)	20,066
*Machin, G. (Lab)	17,100
Clyde, J. J. (C)	13,371
Gourlay, J. (Ind)	220
Scot Nat majority	2,966

Scot Nat gain

	1970		1974
Total Vote	46,819		50,757
Turnout	76·1%		81·1%
Lab	22,630	48·3%	33·7%
C	19,832	42·3%	26·3%
Scot Nat	4,181	8·9%	39·5%
Anti-War	176	0·4%	
Ind	—		0·4%
Lab maj	2,798	6·0%	
Scot Nat maj	—		5·8%
Swing	—	+3·3%	−0·7%

1973 by-election: Total Vote 44,014 (70·6%)—Lab 14,411 (32·7%), Scot Nat 13,270 (30·2%), C 11,089 (25·2%) L 3,653 (8·3%), Lab Pty of Scotland 1,409 (3·2%), Ind 182 (0·4%)—Lab maj 1,141 (2·5%).

Mr **Gordon Wilson** contested the seat in the March, 1973, by-election. Partner in a law practice. B April, 1938; ed Douglas High School and Edinburgh University. Senior vice-chairman, SNP; director, party's oil campaign. Appointed Deputy Leader, SNP Parliamentary Party

and spokesman on energy and oil, March 1974.

Mr George Machin, a former Sheffield engineering inspector, shop steward and city councillor, retained the seat for Labour at the March, 1973 by-election. B December, 1932; ed Marlcliffe School.

Mr James Clyde, QC (1971). Advocate. B January, 1932; ed Edinburgh Academy, Corpus Christi, Oxford, and Edinburgh University. Called to Bar, 1959. Advocate Depute, 1973.

Mr Harry McLevy. Contested Dundee, West, 1970. Fitter. B August, 1936; ed Logie Junior Secondary School, Dundee.

DUNFERMLINE   major

Electorate 60,219

*Hunter, A. (Lab)	19,201
Fraser, J. M. (C)	14,791
Patrick, R. R. (Scot Nat)	8,695
Valentine, M. (L)	6,153
Lab majority	4,410

	1974		1974
Total Vote	48,840	Scot Nat	17·8%
Turnout	81·1%	L	12·6%
Lab	39·3%	Lab maj	9·0%
C	30·3%		

Mr Adam Hunter was elected in 1964. A miner and executive member of the National Union of Mineworkers, Scottish area. B November, 1908; ed at elementary school. Member of Fife County Council, 1961-64; Secretary of Fife Cooperative Association for 17 years. Tutor, National Council of Labour Colleges. Sponsored by NUM.

Mr James Fraser, building contractor and chartered surveyor. B January, 1920; ed Dunfermline High School and Heriot-Watt College, Edinburgh. Past president, Scottish National Federation of Building Trades Employers; immediate past president, Dundee Chamber of Commerce.

Mr Robert Patrick, teacher. B 1927; ed Beath High School and Edinburgh University.

Mr Malcolm Valentine, director of marketing and export company. B February 1938; ed Clifton Hall, near Edinburgh.

DUNDEE West   minor

Electorate 63,464   1970: 66,767

*Doig, P. M. (Lab)	22,193
Tomison, Miss M. (C)	15,745
Fairlie, J. (Scot Nat)	12,959
McLevy, H. (Comm)	673
Lab majority	6,448

No change

	1970		1974
Total Vote	50,970		51,570
Turnout	76·3%		81·2%
Lab	26,271	51·5%	43·0%
C	19,449	38·1%	30·5%
Scot Nat	4,441	8·7%	25·1%
Comm	809	1·6%	1·3%
Lab maj	6,822	13·4%	12·5%
Swing		+1·7%	+0·4%

Mr Peter Doig was returned at a by-election in November, 1963. Contested Aberdeen, South, in 1959. Sales supervisor. B September, 1911; ed Blackness School, Dundee. A member of Dundee Town Council for 10 years, and hon. city treasurer, 1959-63. Member Transport and General Workers Union since 1936. Former member, Scottish Select Committee and Estimates Committee.

Miss Maureen Tomison, political consultant for Granada TV, journalist and author. B May, 1941; ed George Watson's, Edinburgh, Linlithgow Academy, St Andrew's University. Former lobby correspondent, *Bristol Evening Post;* political and diplomatic correspondent *The Sun* and then for the *Daily Sketch.*

Mr James Fairlie, student teacher. B May, 1940; ed Dundee University. Vice-chairman, Perth and East Perthshire SNP constituency association.

DURHAM   major

Electorate 75,045

*Hughes, W. M. (Lab)	31,405
Kirkhope, T. J. R. (C)	16,202
Heesom, A. (L)	12,235
Lab majority	15,203

	1974		1974
Total Vote	59,842	C	27·1%
Turnout	79·7%	L	20·4%
Lab	52·5%	Lab maj	25·4%

Mr Mark Hughes, elected in 1970, was lecturer in economic history at Durham University, 1964-70. B December, 1932; ed Stowcliffe School, Durham School, and Balliol College, Oxford. Served on Durham Rural Council. Member, Select Committee on Parliamentary Commissioner for Administration, and Public Expenditure Committee.

Mr Timothy Kirkhope, solicitor. B April, 1945; ed Royal Grammar School, Newcastle upon Tyne, College of Law, Guildford. Chairman, Tyneside hospital broadcasting service.

Mr Alan Heesom, university lecturer. B May, 1941; ed Oundle School and Corpus Christi College, Cambridge.

DURHAM North-West   major

Electorate 60,686

*Armstrong, E. (Lab)	28,326
Riddell, Sir J. (C)	10,865
Forster, J. K. (L)	8,809
Lab majority	17,461

	1974		1974
Total Vote	48,000	C	22·6%
Turnout	79·1%	L	18·3%
Lab	59·0%	Lab maj	36·4%

Mr Ernest Armstrong, an Opposition spokesman on education and science 1973-74; was an Opposition whip 1970-73. Lord Commissioner of the Treasury, 1969-70; Assistant Government whip, 1967-69. Elected in 1964; contested Sunderland, South, in 1955 and 1959. Head-

master. B January, 1915; ed Wolsingham Grammar School and City of Leeds Teacher Training College. Member, Public Accounts Committee, 1964-66. Chairman, Labour Education Committee 1965-70. Member, Sunderland Town Council 1956-65, NUGMW and NUT. A Methodist preacher. *Appointed Under Secretary, Education and Science, March 1974.*

Sir John Riddell, international banker. B January, 1934; ed Eton; Christ Church, Oxford. Member, Fulham Housing Improvement Association.

Mr James Forster, chief technical officer. B December, 1926; ed Blaydon Grammar School, County Durham, and Emmanuel College, Cambridge.

EALING Acton   major

Electorate 56,366

Young, Sir G. (C)	18,492
*Spearing, N. J. (Lab)	17,041
Uziell-Hamilton, M. R. (L)	7,160
C majority	1,451

	1974		1974
Total Vote	42,693	Lab	39·9%
Turnout	75·7%	L	16·8%
C	43·3%	C maj	3·4%

Sir George Young, economist. B July, 1941; ed Eton and Christ Church, Oxford. Member, Greater London Council, 1970-73; Lambeth Borough Council, 1968-71. Economic adviser, Post Office Corporation, since 1969.

Mr Nigel Spearing, teacher. B October, 1930; ed Latymer Upper School, Hammersmith, and St Catherine's College, Cambridge University. Regained the seat for Labour in 1970; contested Warwick and Leamington, 1964. Was member, Select Centre on Overseas Development; secretary, PLP education group and all-party waterways group. Co-opted member, GLC committees 1966-73. NUT.

Mr Mario Uziell-Hamilton, solicitor and company director. B May, 1922; ed Brentwood School, Sorbonne, St Catherine's College, Cambridge. Contested Wandsworth, Central, 1966 and Paddington, North, 1970.

EALING North   major

Electorate 73,327

*Molloy, W. J. (Lab)	25,387
Patterson, Dr M. J. L. (C)	22,939
Phillips, C. (L)	10,922
Smith, P. (Royal Repub)	93
Lab majority	2,448

	1974		1974
Total Vote	59,341	L	18·4%
Turnout	80·9%	Royal Repub	0·1%
Lab	42·8%	Lab maj	4·1%
C	38·6%		

Mr William Molloy was elected in 1964. B October, 1918; ed elementary school in Swansea and University of Wales. Industrial secretary. Member, Estimates Committee, 1967-70; member, Select Committee on Housing. Leader of Fulham Borough Council, 1956-64. Member, Hammersmith Council, 1964-67.

Member Assemblies, Council of Europe and WEU, 1969-73. Former staff-side chairman, Foreign Office Departmental Whitley Council. Fellow, Royal Geographical Society. Member of the court, Reading University.

Dr Mark Patterson, consultant pathologist. B March, 1934; ed St. Bartholomew's Hospital. Member, GLC, 1970-73.

Mr Clive Philips, furnisher, decorator and interior designer. B May, 1932; ed Brighton Grammar School.

EALING Southall   major

Electorate 70,328

*Bidwell, S. J. (Lab)	25,726
Gilbey, W. A. (C)	16,914
Arnold, I. (L)	8,640
Chahal, B. S. (Anti-Helmet)	310
Lab majority	8,812

	1974		1974
Total Vote	51,590	L	16·7%
Turnout	73·3%	Anti-Helmet	0·6%
Lab	49·9%	Lab maj	17·1%
C	32·8%		

Mr Sydney Bidwell was elected in 1966. B January, 1917; ed elementary school and evening classes. Contested Hertfordshire, South-West, 1964; Hertfordshire, East, 1959. Member, Select Committee on Race Relations and Immigration. Former tutor and organizer for the  National Council of Labour Colleges, previously railway worker. Former NUR, and now TGWU.

Mr Walter Gilbey, wine and spirit merchant. B February, 1935; ed Heatherdown, Ascot; Eton. Member, Berkshire County Council, chairman of finance committee.

Mr Ian Arnold, dairy farmer, was in the Indian Civil Service from 1939 to 1947. B November, 1916; ed Portsmouth Grammar School; Royal Masonic Senior School, Bushey; Gonville and Caius College, Cambridge. With Shaw Wallace group in India from 1947-68 when he retired as joint managing director of parent company.

Mr Baldev Singh Chahal, GPO telephonist, aged 37. Convenor, Turban Action Committee, UK.

EASINGTON   major

Electorate 63,211

*Dormand, J. D. (Lab)	33,637
Smailes, J. S. (C)	13,107
Lab majority	20,530

	1974		1974
Total Vote	46,744	C	28·0%
Turnout	73·9%	Lab maj	43·9%
Lab	72·0%		

Mr John Dormand was elected in 1970. B August, 1919; ed Wellfield Grammar School, Bede College, Durham, Loughborough College, Oxford University, Harvard University. Member, Easington RDC, 1949-52; education officer for Easington RDC, 1963-70. Member, Se-  lect Committee on Nationalized Industries. Former president, Horden and District NUT. *Appointed Assistant Government Whip, March, 1974.*

Mr Stephen Smailes, maintenance engineer. B May, 1940; ed Newham Grange schools, Stockton and Billingham College. Member, Teesside Council since 1967. AUEW.

EASTBOURNE   major

Electorate 74,260

Gow, I. R. E. (C)	31,462
Terrell, S. (L)	23,987
Dawson, D. S. (Lab)	5,874
C majority	7,475

	1974		1974
Total Vote	61,323	L	39·1%
Turnout	82·6%	Lab	9·6%
C	51·3%	C maj	12·2%

Mr Ian Gow is a solicitor. Contested Coventry, East, 1964 and Clapham, 1966. B February, 1937; ed Winchester. Has served as member of Bow Group, Conservative Commonwealth Council and South-wark Diocesan Conference. Special interests: pensions and welfare.

Mr Stephen Terrell, QC, fought the seat in 1964, 1966 and 1970. B June, 1916; ed Trinity College, Glenalmond and University College, London. President of the Liberal Party 1971-72. Made Deputy-Lieutenant of Middlesex in 1961 and now of Greater London.

Mr David Dawson, personnel development and recruitment manager. B April, 1944; ed Peter Symonds' School, Winchester, Southampton University and London School of Economics. ASTMS.

EAST GRINSTEAD   major

Electorate 55,063

*Johnson Smith, G. (C)	23,928
Billenness, P. (L)	15,351
Short, W. J. (Lab)	5,629
C majority	8,577

	1974		1974
Total Vote	44,908	L	34·2%
Turnout	81·5%	Lab	12·5%
C	53·3%	C maj	19·1%

Mr Geoffrey Johnson Smith, Parliamentary Secretary, Civil Service Department, November, 1972-74; Under Secretary of Defence for the Army, 1971-72. Elected at a by-election in 1965; represented Holborn and St Pancras, South, 1959-64, Vice-chairman, Conservative Party organization with special responsibility for Young Conservatives, 1965-71. Opposition Whip, 1965-66. Freelance writer and broadcaster. B April, 1924; ed Charterhouse and Lincoln College, Oxford. Information officer, British Consulate in San Francisco, 1950-52.

Mr Peter Billenness, economics graduate and marketing consultant. Former Vice-chairman and treasurer, National League of Young Liberals. B May, 1927; ed Roborough School, Eastbourne, Eastbourne Grammar School, Eastbourne College, Cheltenham Technical College, University College, London. Contested Hendon South in 1959 and 1964; Bromley, 1966; Epsom, 1970. Member, Market Research Society.

Mr William Short, head of social studies faculty in London comprehensive school. B July, 1942; ed Ilford and Westcliff High Schools, Dudley College of Education, and Woolwich Polytechnic. Secretary, Labour Political Studies Centre. NUT.

EAST KILBRIDE   major

Electorate 66,092

*Miller, Dr M. (Lab)	23,424
Parvin, G. W. (C)	15,456
MacQuarie, D. P. (Scot Nat)	13,819
McDowell, D. (Comm)	693
Lab majority	7,968

	1974		1974
Total Vote	53,392	Scot Nat	25·9%
Turnout	80·8%	Comm	1·3%
Lab	43·9%	Lab maj	14·9%
C	28·9%		

Dr Maurice Miller, was MP for Glasgow, Kelvingrove, 1964-74, and an assistant Government whip, 1968-69. Medical practitioner. B August, 1920; ed Shawlands Academy, Glasgow, and Glasgow University. Member, Glasgow Corporation, 1950-64. Bailie, 1954-57. Chairman, Glasgow and West of Scotland Socialist Medical Association.

Mr Gilmour Parvin, Investment analyst. B September, 1949; ed Queen's Park Secondary School, Glasgow, and Glasgow University. Vice-chairman, Cathcart Conservatives and Chairman, Scottish Young Conservatives, 1971-73.

Mr Don MacQuarie, freelance journalist, aged 31. Ed Coatbridge Secondary School and Hamilton Academy. Joined SNP, 1962; director, SNP's Scottish anthem campaign.

Mr David McDowell, lecturer. Aged 51. Miner for 11 years and then full-time Communist Party member. Graduated from Glasgow University at 41.

EASTLEIGH   major

Electorate 75,469

*Price, D. E. C. (C)	28,512
Presman, E. (Lab)	18,402
Johnson, D. (L)	17,178
C majority	10,110

	1974		1974
Total Vote	64,092	Lab	28·7%
Turnout	84·9%	L	26·8%
C	44·5%	C maj	15·8%

Mr David Price was Under Secretary for Aerospace, Department of Trade and Industry, 1971-72; Parliamentary Secretary, Ministry of Aviation Supply, 1970-71; Parliamentary Secretary, Ministry of Technology, June to October, 1970. Opposition spokesman on  technology and science 1964-70, Parliamentary Secretary, Board of Trade, 1962-64. Elected 1955. B November, 1924; ed Eton, Trinity College, Cambridge, and Yale University (Research Fellow), president, Cambridge Union, 1948. Economist and industrial executive. General consultant, Institution of Works Managers. Member, Select Committee on Science and Technology. Chairman, Parliamentary Scientific Committee.

Mr Elkan Presman is a publicity consultant. B November, 1937; ed City of London School and Oxford University. Former head of Oxfam's National Publicity and Appeals Department. Member, ASTMS.

Mr David Johnson, headmaster. B July, 1937; ed Shaftesbury Grammar School, Dorset, and King Alfred's College, Winchester. Member, Romsey Borough Council, since 1967. Elected, Test Valley District Council, 1973.

Mr Michael Foot was elected to the Shadow Cabinet in 1970 and became Opposition spokesman on the power and steel industries until 1971; shadow Leader of the House principally concerned with Common Market legislation 1971-72; from  1972-4 concerned with EEC only. Unsuccessfully contested Deputy Leadership of PLP in July 1970 and November, 1971. Was returned for Ebbw Vale at a by-election in November, 1960. MP for Plymouth, Devonport, 1945-55, he contested the seat in 1959, and Monmouth, 1935. Journalist, managing director of Tribune. B July, 1913; ed Forres School, Swanage, Leighton Park School, Reading and Wadham College, Oxford; president of Union, 1933. Member, Labour Party National executive, 1947-50 and since 1972. *Appointed Secretary of State for Employment, March 1974.*

Mr Angus Donaldson, hotelier. B 1928; ed Bassaleg Grammar School. Contested Ebbw Vale, 1970, and Merthyr Tydfil 1972 by-election. Member, Tredegar Urban District Council since 1966; member, Monmouthshire County Council since 1967.

Mr Jonathan Evans, lawyer. B June 1950; ed Howardian High School, Cardiff; Law Society College of Law. Member Cardiff Civic Society.

Mr John Rogers, teacher. B February, 1943; ed Glyndwr Secondary Modern, Rhyl, Rhyl Grammar, St Mary's College, Crosby and Leeds University.

EBBW VALE   same

Electorate 37,386. 1970: 38,461

*Foot, M. M. (Lab)	20,660
Donaldson, A. (L)	4,996
Evans, J. P. (C)	2,303
Rogers, J. D. (Pl Cymru)	1,767
Lab majority	15,664

No change

	1970		1974
Total Vote	30,139		29,726
Turnout	78·4%		79·5%
Lab	21,817	72·4%	69·5%
L	4,371	14·5%	16·8%
C	2,146	7·1%	7·7%
Pl Cymru	1,805	6·0%	5·9%
Lab maj	17,446	57·9%	52·7%
Swing		+2·4%	+1·7%

ECCLES   same

Electorate 57,552. 1970: 59,135

*Carter-Jones, L. (Lab)	22,538
Dunn, R. (C)	14,752
Collier, Mrs A. M. (L)	7,966
Keenan, T. (Comm)	404
Lab majority	7,786

No change

	1970		1974
Total Vote	43,014		45,660
Turnout	72·7%		79·3%
Lab	23,913	55·6%	49·4%
C	18,458	42·9%	32·3%
Comm	643	1·5%	0·9%
L	—		17·4%
Lab maj	5,455	12·7%	17·0%
Swing		+4·6%	−2·2%

Mr Lewis Carter-Jones, elected in 1964, contested the City of Chester in the 1956 by-election and in 1959. Teacher, lecturer and industrial training adviser. B November, 1920; ed Bridgend Grammar School and University College of Wales, Aberystwyth.  Member of Estimates Committee since 1965. Secretary, Indo-British and Anglo-Colombian parliamentary groups; vice-chairman, all-party Disabled Drivers' Group, and member, all-party Disablement Group. Member, committee for research into aids for disabled run by National Fund for Crippling Diseases, and management committee, Royal Orthopaedic Hospitals; chairman, Possum Research Foundation. Sponsored by TGWU.

Mr Terry Keenan, teacher. Contested the seat in 1970. B August 16, 1942; ed Barrow-in-Furness Grammar School and Manchester College of Education.

Mrs Maureen Collier, teacher. B August, 1935; ed Adelphi House Grammar School, Salford, Sedgley Park teacher training college, Prestwich.

Mr Robert J. Dunn, management trainee. B July, 1946; ed Manchester Polytechnic and Salford University.

EDINBURGH Central   major

Electorate 40,780

Cook, R. F. (Lab)	11,354
Jones, P. (C)	10,393
Scott, C. (L)	4,180
Rae, S. (Scot Nat)	4,074
Lab majority	961

	1974		1974
Total Vote	30,001	L	13·9%
Turnout	73·6%	Scot Nat	13·6%
Lab	37·8%	Lab maj	3·2%
C	34·6%		

Mr Robin Cook, a tutor and organizer in adult education, contested Edinburgh, North, in 1970. B February, 1946; ed Aberdeen Grammar School, Royal High School, Edinburgh and Edinburgh University. Councillor, Holyrood ward since  1971; chairman housing committee since 1973. Member, TGWU; delegate Edinburgh and district trades council.

Mr Peter Jones, investment research manager. B May, 1945; ed St Mary's College, Middlesbrough, and Strathclyde University, Glasgow (President, Students' Association). Manager, Wood Mackenzie & Co (Stockbrokers), Edinburgh and London.

Mr Christopher Scott, farmer and writer. Contested Galloway, 1970 and South Angus 1964. B October, 1924; ed Eton and King's College, Cambridge. Lloyds underwriter.

Mr Alexander Rae contested Midlothian, 1966 and Edinburgh Pentlands, 1970. Solicitor. B June, 1941; ed George Watson's College, Edinburgh, Dundee High School, and Edinburgh University. Voluntary Service Overseas in Ghana 1967-68; member, Edinburgh executive of United Nations Association and Edinburgh Community Relations Council. Member, Nalgo.

EDINBURGH East   minor

Electorate 56,953. 1970: 57,350

*Strang, G. S. (Lab)	20,163
May, D. J. (C)	14,614
MacDougall, G. (Scot Nat)	7,128
Melling, J. (L)	3,998
Swan, Mrs I. (Comm)	274
Lab majority	5,549

No change

	1970		1974	
Total Vote	42,743		46,177	
Turnout	74·4%		81·1%	
Lab	22,171	51·9%		43·7%
C	16,657	39·0%		31·6%
Scot Nat	3,502	8·2%		15·4%
Comm	413	0·9%		0·6%
L	—			8·6%
Lab maj	5,514	12·9%		12·0%
Swing		+4·0%		+0·4%

Mr Gavin Strang, elected in 1970. Member, Select Committee on Science and Technology from 1970 to 1974. An Opposition spokesman on trade and industry from 1973 to  1974. Agricultural scientist. B July, 1943; ed Morrison's Academy, Edinburgh University and Churchill College, Cambridge. Member, ASTMS, Fabian Society and Cooperative Party; and of Tayside Economic Planning Consultative Group. 1966-68. *Appointed Under Secretary for Oil, Department of Energy, March 1974.*

Mr Douglas May, advocate. B May, 1946; ed George Heriots School and Edinburgh University. Former president, Edinburgh University Conservative Club, and vice-chairman, Federation of Conservative Students. Former vice-chairman, Scottish Young Conservatives.

Mr George MacDougall, journalist. Chairman, Broughton-Calton SNP. B March, 1928; ed Edinburgh Corporation Primary and secondary schools. Vice-chairman, Edinburgh Branch NUJ; Father of NUJ Chapel, *The Scotsman.*

Mr John Melling, nurse administrator. B April, 1934; ed Bootham School, York. Contested Hertford, 1970. Former chairman, Scottish Liberal Party's transport policy committee.

Mrs Irene Swann, health visitor with Edinburgh Corporation. Contested Edinburgh East, 1970, and West Lothian, 1964 and 1966. Chairman, Communist Party national executive committee. B April, 1932; ed Northumberland County Modern School. NUPE.

EDINBURGH Leith   major

Electorate 39,157

*Murray, R. K. (Lab)		12,604
Percy, W. R. V. (C)		11,883
Miller, H. (Scot Nat)		6,569
Lab majority		721

	1974			1974
Total Vote	31,056	C		38·3%
Turnout	79·3%	Scot Nat		21·1%
Lab	40·6%	Lab maj		2·3%

Mr Ronald King Murray, QC, elected in 1970, was Opposition spokesman on Scottish legal matters 1970-74. He was a lecturer in law who contested Roxburgh, Selkirk and Peebles in 1965 by-election and 1964 general election; Edinburgh North, in 1960 by-election, and Caithness and Sutherland, 1959. B June, 1922; ed George Watson's College, Edinburgh, and Edinburgh University. Called to Scottish bar, 1953. Chairman, Edinburgh City Labour Party since 1968-71. *Appointed Lord Advocate, March 1974.*

Mr William Percy, business consultant. B May, 1945; ed Melville College, Edinburgh, and Edinburgh University. Territorial Army officer. Employed by Industrial Development Council in Scotland. Member, Edinburgh City Council.

Mr Hugh Miller, construction machine engineer. B October, 1928; ed Blairgowrie

High School. Secretary, West Leith branch SNP. ASTMS.

EDINBURGH North   major

Electorate 46,936

*Fletcher, A. (C)		16,417
Cairns, R. (Lab)		9,404
Guild, R. H. (L)		5,487
Lynch, J. (Scot Nat)		4,550
C majority		7,013

	1974			1974
Total Vote	35,858	L		15·3%
Turnout	76·4%	Scot Nat		12·7%
C	45·8%	C maj		19·5%
Lab	26·2%			

Mr Alex Fletcher, chartered accountant and company director, won the by-election in 1973. B August 1929; ed Greenock High School and Institute of Chartered Accountants. Contested West Renfrewshire, 1970. Member, East Kilbride Development Corporation, 1971-73. Church of Scotland elder. Business consultant, former IBM executive.

Mr Robert Cairns fought Edinburgh, North by-election 1973. Assistant editor, Scottish National Dictionary. B July, 1947; ed Morgan Academy, Dundee, Edinburgh University. Member, ASTMS and Edinburgh and District Trades Council.

Mr Ronald Guild, schoolteacher. B June, 1921; ed Trinity College, Glenalmond, Trinity College, Oxford, Edinburgh University. Contested Edinburgh South in 1964, 1970 and by-election, 1973. Member, Edinburgh Liberal Party executive.

Mr James Lynch, management accountant. B October, 1934; ed Lawside Academy, Dundee.

EDINBURGH Pentlands   major

Electorate 54,504

Rifkind, M. (C)		18,162
McWilliam, J. D. (Lab)		13,560
Ross Smith, S. (L)		6,870
Forest, T. (Scot Nat)		4,951
C majority		4,602

	1974			1974
Total Vote	43,543	L		15·8%
Turnout	79·9%	Scot Nat		11·4%
C	41·7%	C maj		10·6%
Lab	31·1%			

H

Mr Malcolm Rifkind, advocate. B June 1946; ed George Watson's College, Edinburgh and Edinburgh University. Contested, Edinburgh Central in 1970. Member, Edinburgh Council since 1970. Chairman, Thistle Group, 1969-70. Lecturer in politics, University College of Rhodesia, 1967-69. Returned to Scotland and was called to the Bar.

Mr John McWilliam, Post Office engineer. Member Edinburgh Corporation since 1970. B May, 1941; ed Leith Academy, Herriot Watt College of Science and Technology, Napier College of Science and Technology. POEU.

Mr Stanley Ross-Smith, architect. B June, 1919; ed Edinburgh Academy and Edinburgh College of Art. Member, Scottish Inland Waterways Association.

Mr Thomas Forest, accountant. B October, 1947; ed Lindsay High School, Bathgate Technical College and Edinburgh College of Commerce. Chairman, Bathgate branch SNP; general secretary, ASNTU.

Government, 1949-54. National president, Scottish Young Unionists, 1960-62, and vice-chairman, Scottish Unionist members' parliamentary committee, 1965-66, 1968-69 and chairman 1970-71. Company director. Member, Select Committee on Scottish Affairs.

Mr Trevor Davies, University administrator. B January, 1944; ed University of Leicester. Edinburgh councillor since 1971. Member, APEX.

Mr Nat Gordon, contested Dundee East in 1973. Personnel manager. B July, 1944; ed James Gillespie's School, George Heriot's School, University of Strathclyde. Former chairman, Scottish Young Liberals; former member, Scottish Liberal Party Executive Committee; member, Edinburgh Council since 1973.

Mr Robert Shirley, senior research Fellow in finance, Heriot Watt University. B March, 1928; ed Beardsden Academy and Glasgow University.

EDINBURGH West   major

Electorate 52,044

*Stodart, J. A. (C)	18,908
Taylor, W. J. (Lab)	10,431
Gorrie, D. C. E. (L)	9,189
Moore, Mrs R. (Scot Nat)	4,241
C majority	8,477

	1974		1974
Total Vote	42,769	L	21·5%
Turnout	82·2%	Scot Nat	9·9%
C	44·2%	C maj	19·8%
Lab	24·4%		

Mr Anthony Stodart, Minister of State for Agriculture, Fisheries and Food, 1972-74; Parliamentary Secretary, Ministry of Agriculture, Fisheries and Food, 1970-72; Under Secretary, Scottish Office, 1963-64. Elected in 1959; contested Berwick and East Lothian as a Liberal in 1950, and Midlothian and Peebles, 1951, and Midlothian, 1955, as a Conservative. Farmer. B June, 1916; ed Wellington College. Writer, lecturer and broadcaster on farming. An Opposition spokesman on agriculture from March 1974.

Mr Bill Taylor, a barrister, is an Edinburgh town councillor. B September, 1944; ed Robert Gordon's College, Aberdeen and Aberdeen University. TGWU.

Mr Donald Gorrie. Contested seat 1970. Administrative director, Scottish Liberal Party and former teacher. B April, 1933; ed Oundle and Corpus Christi College,

EDINBURGH South   same

Electorate 55,708. 1970: 55,675

*Hutchison, A. M. C. (C)	18,784
Davies, T. J. (Lab)	12,403
Gordon, N. (L)	8,073
Shirley, R. (Scot Nat)	5,770
C majority	6,381

No change

	1970		1974
Total Vote	41,252		45,030
Turnout	74·1%		80·8%
C	19,851	48·1%	41·7%
Lab	15,071	36·5%	27·5%
L	3,469	8·4%	17·9%
Scot Nat	2,861	6·9%	12·8%
C maj	4,780	11·6%	14·2%
Swing		−1·0%	+1·3%

Mr Michael Clark Hutchison was returned at a by-election in May, 1957. He contested Motherwell in 1955. B February, 1914; ed Eton and Trinity College, Cambridge. Barrister (Gray's Inn, 1937). Colonial Service, Palestine, 1946-48; Political officer in the Aden

Oxford. Member, Edinburgh Town Council since 1971.

Mrs Catherina Moore, maths teacher, contested Edinburgh Central, 1970. B 1937; ed Holy Cross Academy and Edinburgh University. Member, education policy committee of SNP.

ENFIELD Edmonton   minor

Electorate 61,018. 1970: 63,203

Graham, T. E. (Lab and Co-op)	20,837
Gordon, J. (C)	15,114
Greenwood, Miss P. (L)	8,186
Bruce, D. J. (Nat Front)	1,765
Pittard, L. R. (Ind)	98
Lab majority	5,723

No change

	1970		1974
Total Vote	42,244		46,000
Turnout	66·8%		75·4%
Lab	20,626	48·8%	
Lab & Co-op	—		45·3%
C	18,481	43·7%	32·8%
L	3,137	7·4%	17·8%
Nat Front	—	—	3·8%
Ind	—	—	0·2%
Lab maj	2,145	5·1%	—
Lab & Co-op maj	—		12·4%
Swing		+6·0%	−3·7%

Mr Edward Graham, National Secretary of the Cooperative Party, contested Enfield West in 1966; former Labour Group Leader on Enfield Council and chairman, Housing and Redevelopment Committee, 1961-68. B March 1925; ed elementary schools, Cooperative College, WEA and Open University. Member, National Association of Cooperative Officials.

Mr Jeffrey Gordon, solicitor. Contested Southwark, 1970 and 1972 by-election. Chairman, British Legal Association since 1973; general secretary, 1972-73. B January, 1934; ed elementary schools in Chingford and High Wycombe; Sir George Monoux Grammar School, Walthamstow; King's College, London. Member, Chingford Council 1961-65.

Mrs Patricia Greenwood, interior designer. B December, 1938; ed Royal Adacemy of Music, London University; Colorado College, USA; Cheshunt College, Cambridge.

Mr David Bruce, salesman. B January, 1940; ed Northampton Secondary School,

London. Member, United Road Transport Union.

ENFIELD North   major

Electorate 67,327

Davies, B. (Lab)	20,690
Parkinson, C. de H. (C)	17,274
Curtis, Mrs S. (L)	13,682
Robinson, K. T. (Nat Front)	1,372
Lab majority	3,416

	1974			1974
Total Vote	53,018		L	25·8%
Turnout	78·7%		Nat Front	2·6%
Lab	39·0%		Lab maj	6·4%
C	32·6%			

Mr Bryan Davies, contested Norfolk Central 1966. Lecturer. B November, 1939; ed Redditch High School, University College, London, Institute of Education, London, and London School of Economics. Member, ATTI.

Mr Christopher Parkinson is a marketing executive with a national civil engineering and building contractor. B May, 1938; ed in Bermuda and the Cathedral School, Truro. Member, Lambeth Borough Council, 1964-68; member, Hertfordshire County Council, 1969-74.

Mrs Sarah Curtis, journalist. B May, 1936; ed Roedean School and St Hugh's College, Oxford. Member, UK executive, UNICEF.

Mr Kenneth Robinson, experimental chemist. B January 31, 1943; ed Edmonton County Grammar School; South Bank Polytechnic.

ENFIELD Southgate   major

Electorate 70,404

*Berry, A. G. (C)	28,260
Bridge, G. (L)	13,806
Sealey, F. (Lab)	10,945
Pell, B. W. (Nat Front)	1,192
C majority	14,454

	1974			1974
Total Vote	54,203		Lab	20·2%
Turnout	77·0%		Nat Front	2·2%
C	52·1%		C maj	26·7%
L	25·5%			

Mr Anthony Berry, merchant banker, was elected in 1964. Deputy Chairman, Leopold Joseph and Sons Ltd; director, Thanet and Anglo Welsh Investment Trusts. Formerly assistant editor of The Sunday Times and director of Kemsley Newspapers Ltd, 1954-59. B February 1925; ed Eton and Christ Church, Oxford. PPS to Mr Peter Walker, 1970-74, as Secretary of State for Environment and then for Trade and Industry. Secretary and later vice-chairman, Conservative Transport Committee 1967-70; joint secretary, Conservative London members' Committee, 1966-70. Member, Anglo Israel Council.

Mr George Bridge, produce merchant. B April, 1917; ed St Ignatius School and Trinity College of Music, London University. Contested the seat in 1955, 1959, 1964, 1966 and 1970.

Mr Francis Sealey, BBC producer and former teacher. B January, 1944; ed Dr Morgan's Grammar School, Bridgwater, Woolwich Polytechnic and McMaster University, Ontario. ABS.

Mr Bruce Pell, building industry employee, 24.

EPPING FOREST major

Electorate 62,470

*Biggs-Davison, J. A. (C)	24,290
Sheaff, W. J. (Lab)	16,123
Wood, D. F. (L)	11,478
C majority	8,167

	1974		1974
Total Vote	51,891	Lab	31·1%
Turnout	83·1%	L	22·1%
C	46·8%	C maj	15·7%

Mr John Biggs-Davison was MP for Chigwell, South in 1951. Author, journalist and broadcaster. B June, 1918; ed Clifton College and Magdalen College, Oxford. Assistant Commissioner and magistrate in the Punjab, 1954, he was political officer, deputy commissioner, and commandant, border military police, Baluchistan frontier. Joint vice-chairman (1972) and former secretary, Conservative Foreign and Commonwealth affairs committee; vice-chairman, Northern Ireland

Committee; vice-president, Pan-European Union; and chairman, British Commonwealth Union. Fellow of the Royal Geographical Society. Co-founder of Pakistan Society, 1951. Governor, Clifton College, 1972.

Mr William Sheaff contested Chigwell, 1970. Teacher. B October, 1922; ed St Austell Grammar School and St Luke's College, Exeter. Served three years on Stevenage UDC; Methodist lay preacher.

Mr Derek Wood, contested Ealing, North, 1964. Senior partner, Euroculture International Cultural Services. B April, 1937; ed Preston Manor County Grammar School and London University. Member, London Tourist Board and Institute of Race Relations.

EPSOM AND EWELL same

Electorate 78,742. 1970: 79,874

*Rawlinson, Sir P. A. G. (C)	35,823
Griffiths, D. (L)	18,899
Kearney, N. J. (Lab)	10,787
C majority	16,924

No change

	1970		1974
Total Vote	57,871		65,509
Turnout	72·4%		83·2%
C	35,541	61·4%	54·7%
Lab	12,767	22·1%	16·5%
L	9,563	16·5%	28·8%
C maj	22,774	39·3%	25·8%
Swing		+4·3%	−0·5%

Sir Peter Rawlinson, QC, Attorney General 1970-74. Opposition chief spokesman on law, 1967-70; spokesman on broadcasting, 1965-66. Solicitor General, 1962-64. Elected in 1955; contested Hackney, 1951. B June, 1919; ed Downside and Christ's College, Cambridge. Barrister (Inner Temple 1946), QC 1959; Bencher, 1962, member Bar Council 1965-67, senate Inns of Court, 1967-69.

Mr David Griffiths is secretary, British group of the Liberal international. Fought Portsmouth, Langstone, 1966. Public relations consultant. B July, 1936; ed Purbrook Park County Grammar School and Portsmouth College of Technology. Member, Liberal Party foreign affairs panel.

Mr Neil Kearney, trade union administrative officer. Former branch secretary, and currently staff representative, APEX.

ESHER major

Electorate 47,131

*Mather, D. C. M. (C)	21,775		
Byers, C. (L)	11,060		
Barnham, G. A. (Lab)	5,970		

C majority	10,715

	1974		1974
Total Vote	38,805	L	28·5%
Turnout	82·3%	Lab	15·4%
C	56·1%	C maj	27·6%

Mr Carol Mather was elected in 1970. Member, Conservative Research Department, 1962-70. Contested Leicester, North-West, in 1966; B January, 1919; ed Harrow and Trinity College, Cambridge. Member of Lloyd's. Served in Welsh Guards, 1940-62, and was liaison officer to General Montgomery in the Western Desert campaign, the Normandy landings, and the advance into Europe. Member Eton RDC, 1966. Joint Secretary, Conservative Parliamentary Foreign and Commonwealth affairs committee since 1972 and of Northern Ireland committee, since 1972.

Mr Charles Byers, barrister. B March, 1949; ed Westminster School and Christ Church, Oxford.

Mr Glen Barnham, trade union official, NATTKE. B April, 1945. Member, Ealing Council since 1971. Chairman, social committee, 1973-74; vice chairman, nursery school committee; governor, three comprehensive schools.

ESSEX, SOUTH-EAST major

Electorate 75,421

*Braine, Sir B. R. (C)	28,644		
Jones, D. B. (Lab)	19,379		
Alexander, Mrs F. (L)	13,891		

C majority	9,265

	1974		1974
Total Vote	61,914	Lab	31·3%
Turnout	82·1%	L	22·4%
C	46·3%	C maj	15·0%

Sir Bernard Braine, chairman of the Select Committee on Overseas Development, is a former Conservative spokesman on foreign and Commonwealth affairs and overseas development; Parliamentary Secretary, Ministry of Health, 1962-64; Under-Secretary, Commonwealth Relations Office, 1961-62, and Parliamentary Secretary, Ministry of Pensions and National Insurance, October, 1960. Elected for the seat in 1955; represented Billericay from 1950; contested Leyton East, 1945. Management consultant. B June, 1914; ed Hendon County School. Chairman, British Commonwealth Producers' Organisation, 1958-60. Treasurer, UK branch of Commonwealth Parliamentary Association, 1965-68; deputy chairman, 1964-65; deputy chairman of CPA since 1970. Chairman, Anglo-Ethiopian Society, and of National Council on Alcoholism. Member, executive, 1922 Committee.

Mr Bryn Jones is an industrial correspondent. Aged 34; ed London and Indiana Universities. Member, NUJ executive representing Fleet Street journalists.

Mrs Frances Alexander, teacher of nursing studies. B November, 1935; ed Brentwood County High School, London Hospital, Weymouth Training College. Member, national private nurses committee, Royal College of Nursing.

ETON AND SLOUGH same

Electorate 63,153. 1970: 62,875

*Lestor, Miss J. (Lab)	22,919		
Dolland, S. (C)	16,028		
Goldenberg, P. (L)	10,051		
Coniam, A. (Nat Front)	1,541		
Crevald, S. H. (Ind C)	344		

Lab majority	6,891

No change

	1970		1974
Total Vote	48,946		50,883
Turnout	77·8%		80·6%
Lab	24,103	49·2%	45·0%
C	21,436	43·8%	31·5%
L	3,407	7·0%	19·7%
Nat Front	—	—	3·0%
Ind C	—	—	0·7%
Lab maj	2,667	5·4%	13·5%
Swing		+2·1%	−4·0%

Miss Joan Lestor, an Opposition spokesman on education 1970-74, was Under Secretary, Department of Education and Science, 1969-70. Won the seat for Labour in 1966; contested Lewisham, West, 1964. Teacher. B November, 1931; ed Blaenavon Secondary School, Monmouth, William Morris High School, Walthamstow and London University. Member national executive of the Labour Party since 1967; Wandsworth Borough Council, 1958-66, and London County Council, 1962-64. *Appointed Under Secretary for Foreign and Commonwealth Affairs, March 1974.*

Mr Steven Dolland, industrial consultant. B November, 1943; ed Quintin School, London, Lincoln College, Oxford, and Harvard Business School. Barrister (Middle Temple, 1973).

Mr Philip Goldenberg, solicitor. B April, 1946; ed St Paul's School, London, and Pembroke College, Oxford.

Mr Andrew Coniam, schoolteacher. B September, 1946; ed Royal Grammar School, High Wycombe, and Milton Keynes College of Education.

EXETER   major

Electorate 66,583

*Hannam, J. G. (C)	22,762
Powell, G. (Lab)	17,686
Morrish, D. (L)	16,322
C majority	**5,076**

	1974		1974
Total Vote	56,770	Lab	31·1%
Turnout	85·3%	L	28·7%
C	40·1%	C maj	8·9%

Mr John Hannam won the seat for the Conservatives in 1970. B August, 1929; ed Yeovil Grammar School. Member Somerset County Council, 1967-69. Chairman, British Motels Federation, 1967-72; member, council of British Travel Association, 1968-69. Sec-

retary, Conservative Parliamentary Trade Committee, 1971-72. Formed his own company to develop motels and restaurants. Member Somerset County Council, 1967-69.

Mr Graham Powell, railway guard. B July, 1925; ed elementary and grammar

schools. Member, Devon County Council since 1963. Branch secretary, NUR.

Mr David Morrish contested the seat in 1970. College lecturer. B May, 1931; ed Sutton High School, Plymouth, and Exeter and Wisconsin universities. Member, Exeter City Council since 1961, and member, Devon County Council.

EYE   same

Electorate 65,227. 1970: 63,623

*Harrison, Sir H. (C)	23,486
Robinson, D. (L)	15,811
Manley, R. E. (Lab)	13,937
Goldsmith, E. (People)	395
Kingham, A. A. (Ind Dem All)	220
C majority	**7,675**

No change

	1970		1974
Total Vote	49,796		53,849
Turnout	78·3%		82·5%
C	26,099	52·4%	43·6%
Lab	17,735	35·6%	25·9%
L	5,962	12·0%	29·4%
People	—	—	0·7%
Ind Dem All	—	—	0·4%
C maj	8,364	16·8%	14·2%
Swing		+4·6%	+0·4%

Sir Harwood Harrison was Comptroller of the Household, 1959-61, after being a Lord Commissioner of the Treasury from 1956. Won the seat in 1951 after contesting it in 1950. Company director. B June, 1907; ed Northampton Grammar School and Trinity College, Oxford, PPS to Mr Harold Macmillan, 1953. Assistant Government Whip 1954. Former vice-chairman, Conservative trade and industry committee. Member, Defence and External Affairs sub-committee, Public Expenditure Committee, since 1971. Chairman, Inter-Parliamentary Union, British Branch.

Mr Denys Robinson, senior English master, New College School, Oxford; contested Cirencester and Tewkesbury, 1970. B July, 1943; ed William Hulme's Grammar School, Manchester, and Brasenose College, Oxford.

Mr Roy Manley, social administrator. Contested the seat in 1970 and Lewes in 1966. B February, 1930; ed Merchant Taylors School, Crosby, and Reading University. NUGMW.

Mr Edward Goldsmith, author and journalist. Aged 45. Founder and editor, "Ecologist" magazine.

FALMOUTH & CAMBORNE   same

Electorate 66,418.   1970: 62,001

*Mudd, W. D. (C)	22,500
Dalling, M. G. (Lab)	18,236
Davey, A. G. S. T. (L)	13,000
C majority	4,264

No change

	1970		1974
Total Vote	48,234		53,736
Turnout	77·8%		80·9%
C	21,477	44·5%	41·9%
Lab	19,954	41·4%	33·9%
L	5,843	12·1%	24·2%
Mebyon Kernow	960	2·0%	
C maj	1,523	3·1%	7·9%
Swing		+5·1%	+2·4%

Mr David Mudd, journalist and broadcaster, won the seat for the Conservatives in 1970. B June, 1933; ed Truro Cathedral School. Member, Tavistock Urban Council, 1963-65. Secretary, Westcountry group of MPs. Member NUJ 1952-54, 1959-70; Father of Westward Television Chapel, 1968-70.

Mr Michael Dalling contested Gloucestershire, South, in 1970 and Cirencester and Tewkesbury, 1966. Solicitor. B June, 1935; ed St Boniface College, Plymouth. Member, Gloucester City Council since 1966. NUGMW.

Mr Alfred Davey, teacher and lecturer. Contested the seat in 1970. B May, 1914; ed Redruth Grammar School and Exeter University. Member, Cambourne-Redruth UDC (chairman, 1964-65); Kerrier District Council since 1973.

FAREHAM   major

Electorate 56,859

*Bennett, Dr R. F. B. (C)	22,303
Smith, P. (L)	14,426
Horne, Miss J. (Lab)	8,237
Boulden, W. P. (Ind C)	1,879
C majority	7,877

	1974			1974
Total Vote	46,845	Lab		17·6%
Turnout	82·4%	Ind C		4·0%
C	47·6%	C maj		16·8%
L	30·8%			

Dr Reginald Bennett represented Gosport and Fareham 1950-74; contested East Woolwich, 1945. Psychiatrist and businessman; international yachtsman. B. July, 1911; ed Winchester and New College, Oxford, St George's Hospital and Maudsley Hospital. Chairman, catering sub-committee of Commons services committee since 1970. Chairman, Anglo-Italian Parliamentary Group, and Vice-President, Franco-British Parliamentary Relations Committee.

Mr Peter Smith, personal finance adviser. B June, 1938; ed Strodes Grammar School, Egham. Contested Gosport and Fareham, 1970.

Miss Jennie Horne, freelance broadcaster. B February 1949; ed London School of Economics; training as a barrister. Member, Camden Council since 1971. TGWU.

FARNHAM   same

Electorate 62,136.   1970: 60,120

*Macmillan, M. (C)	25,686
Davies, F. (L)	19,224
Hodge, Miss H. C. (Lab)	6,347
Dane, Maj N. (Ind.)	251
C majority	6,462

No change

	1970		1974
Total Vote	44,108		51,508
Turnout	73·4%		82·9%
C	25,113	56·9%	49·9%
L	10,178	23·1%	37·3%
Lab	8,817	20·0%	12·3%
Ind	—	—	0·5%
C maj	14,935	33·9%	12·5%
Swing		+5·6%	+0·3%

Mr Maurice Macmillan was Paymaster General, attached to the Treasury, from 1973-74; Secretary of State for Employment 1972-73; Chief Secretary to the Treasury 1970-72. Elected in 1966, after being MP for Halifax 1955-64. Contested Seaham, 1945, Lincoln, 1951, and Wakefield (by-election), 1957. Economic Secretary to the Treasury 1963-64. B January, 1921; ed Eton and Balliol College, Oxford. Chairman, Macmillan and Company Ltd, 1966-70. Son of Mr Harold Macmillan. President, United Kingdom Council of the European Move-

FAR

ment, 1961-63. Former chairman, Wider
Share Ownership Council and later, chairman, executive committee of WSOC.
Appointed to Shadow Cabinet and a
spokesman on Treasury and economic
affairs, March 1974.

Mr Philip Davies, director of printing and
publishing company. B September, 1945;
ed Woking County Grammar School.
Member, Farnham UDC, 1970-74; Surrey
County Council and Waverley District
Council, since 1973.

Miss Hilary Hodge, dental surgeon. B
November, 1945. European lawn tennis
tournaments winner and Berkshire Ladies
county player. NUPE.

FARNWORTH same

Electorate 70,350.   1970: 69,494

*Roper, J. F. H. (Lab and Co-op)	28,068
Royse, A. S. (C)	15,431
Rothwell, Mrs M. P. (L)	12,918
Lab majority	12,637

No change

	1970		1974
Total Vote	50,259		56,417
Turnout	72·3%		80·2%
Lab & Co-op	29,392	58·5%	49·7%
C	20,867	41·5%	27·3%
L	—		22·9%
Lab & Co-op maj	8,525	17·0%	22·4%
Swing		+7·7%	−2·7%

Mr John Roper was
elected in 1970; con-
tested High Peak in
1964. Economist. B
September, 1935; ed
William Hulme's
Grammar School,
Manchester; Reading
School, Magdalen Col-
lege, Oxford, and
University of Chicago.
Member, Commons
Select Committee on
Expenditure, 1970; Select Committee on
Corporation Tax, 1972; Secretary, North
West group of Labour MPs. Director, Co-
operative Wholesale Society Ltd and Co-
operative Insurance Society Ltd. Member,
Association of University Teachers. Chair-
man, General Council of the United Na-
tions Association since 1973.

Mr Albert Royse contested the seat, 1964
and 1959 and Burnley, 1966. Accountant.
B April, 1917; ed Bolton County Grammar School. Member, Farnworth Borough
Council since 1950; mayor, 1960.

Mrs Margaret Rothwell, teacher. B June,
1931; ed Farnworth Grammar School and
Manchester College of Housecraft. Member, Kearsley Urban Council since 1971
(Chairman, 1971-72).

120

FAVERSHAM same

Electorate 75,529.   1970: 71,677

*Moate, R. D. (C)	26,316
Freedman, M. (Lab)	20,909
Morgan, P. (L)	14,927
Dignan, E. (Community)	151
C majority	5,407

No change

	1970		1974
Total Vote	56,017		62,303
Turnout	78·1%		82·5%
C	29,914	53·4%	42·2%
Lab	26,103	46·6%	33·6%
L	—		23·9%
Community	—		0·2%
C maj	3,811	6·8%	8·7%
Swing		+5·9%	+0·9%

Mr Roger Moate won
the seat for the Con-
servatives in 1970; an
insurance broker, con-
tested the seat in
1966. B May, 1938;
ed Latymer Upper
School, Hammer-
smith. Vice-chairman,
Greater London area
Young Conservatives,
1964-66. Director,
Alexander Howden
and Swann Limited (Insurance).

Mr Michael Freedman, personnel manager. B October, 1942; ed Kingsbury
County Grammar, University College,
London, St Edmund Hall, Oxford, University of Saskatchewan, Canada. ASTMS.

Mr Peter Morgan, teacher. B May, 1926;
ed Monmouth School, Lewis School, Pen-
gam, St Paul's teacher training college,
Cheltenham. Member, Swale District
Council; president of local branch of
NUT, 1963-72.

FERMANAGH & SOUTH TYRONE same

Electorate 69,775.   1970: 70,381

West, H. (UUUC)	26,858
*McManus, F. (Unity)	16,229
Haughey, D. (SDLP)	15,410
Brown, H. (UU Pro Assembly)	3,157
UUUC majority	10,629

	1970		1974
Total Vote	64,203		61,654
Turnout	91·2%		88·4%
Unity	32,813	51·1%	26·3%
UU	31,390	48·9%	—
UUUC	—		43·6%
SDLP	—		25·0%
Pro Assem	—		5·1%
Unity maj	1,423	2·2%	—
UUUC maj	—		17·2%

Mr Harry West, chairman of the United Ulster Union-ist Parliamentary Coa-lition from March 1974, is leader of the Unionist party in the Northern Ireland Assembly. Member, Orange Order. Repre-sented Enniskillen at Stormont and was Minister of Agricul-ture under three successive Prime Ministers.

Mr Frank McManus won the seat in 1970. Contesting his first parliamentary seat, he defeated Mr Austin Currie, Nationalist member for East Tyrone at Stormont. Teacher. B August, 1942; ed St Michael's, Enniskillen, and Queen's University, Bel-fast. Chairman, Fermanagh civil rights movement.

Mr Denis Haughey is chairman of the SDLP. Graduate of Queen's University. Aged 29.

Mr Hubert Brown, aged 64, is a former chief welfare officer of Co Fermanagh.

FIFE Central   major

Electorate 57,903

*Hamilton, W. W. (Lab)	24,418
Livingstone, D. (Scot Nat)	10,324
Eyres, S. R. (C)	9,098
Maxwell, A. (Comm)	2,019
Lab majority	14,094

	1974		1974
	1970		1970
Total Vote	45,859	C	19.8%
Turnout	79.2%	Comm	4.4%
Lab	53.2%	Lab ma	30.7%
Scot Nat	22.5%		

Mr William Hamil-ton was MP for West Fife, 1950-74, and contested that seat in 1945. Member, Es-timates Committee, 1953-70, chairman, 1964-70. Teacher. B June, 1917; ed Wash-ington Grammar School, co. Dur-ham, and Sheffield University. Member,

Public Expendtiure Committee. Vice-chair-man, Parliamentary Labour Party, 1964-70. Member, NUT. Sponsored by Confe-deration of Health Service Employees.

Mr David Livingstone, planning engineer. Aged 48; ed Kirkcaldy High School. Chairman, Lothian Regional Council, SNP, and West Lothian constituency.

Mr Stephen Eyres, tutor, Swinton Conser-vative College. B December, 1948; ed St Andrews University. Deputy chairman, Selsdon Group. Editor, *Swinton Journal.*

Mr Alex Maxwell is a workshops superin-tendent. Member, Cowdenbeath town council since 1965. B November, 1931; ed Airdrie Academy and Coatbridge Tech-nical College.

FIFE East   minor

Electorate 56,050.   1970: 53,155

*Gilmour, Sir J. E. (C)	21,172
Braid, J. (Scot Nat)	8,593
Pickard, W. (L)	7,766
Maan, B. A. (Lab)	6,634
C majority	12,579

No change

	1970		1974
Total Vote	39,618		44,165
Turnout	74.4%		78.9%
C	21,619	54.6%	47.9%
Lab	9,756	24.6%	15.0%
Scot Nat	4,666	11.8%	19.4%
L	3,577	9.0%	17.6%
C maj	11,863	29.9%	28.5%
Swing		+1.5%	+1.4%

Sir John Gilmour was elected at a by-elec-tion in 1961; con-tested East Stirling-shire and Clackman-nan, 1945. Market gardener. B October, 1912; ed Eton and Trinity Hall, Cam-bridge, and Dundee School of Economics. Chairman, Scottish Unionist Party, 1965-

67; Fife County Council, 1955-61. Mem-ber, Select Committee on Scottish Affairs; Member, Royal Company of Archers. Vice-chairman, Conservative Parliamen-tary agricultural committee, 1963-64 and 1969-70, Scottish Conservative MPs since March 1974.

Mr James Braid, sales supervisor. B April, 1912; ed Waid Academy. Member, SNP National Executive and National Assem-bly. Provost for St Monans; Fife county councillor.

Mr Willis Pickard, journalist, contested East Fife, 1970. B May, 1941; ed Daniel Stewarts College, Edinburgh, St Andrews University. Features editor, *The Scots-man.* NUJ.

Mr Bashir Maan, company director. First coloured Labour candidate chosen by a Scottish constituency. B October, 1926; ed Panjab University, Pakistan. Came to Britain 1953. Member, Glasgow City Council since 1970. Magistrate of the City of Glasgow, and sub-convener of Police Committee since 1971. TGWU.

FLINT East
same

Electorate 68,691. 1970: 64,793

*Jones, S. B. (Lab & Co-op)	27,663
Penston, M. J. A. (C)	18,811
Carlile, A. (L)	10,653
Taylor, N. (Pl Cymru)	1,135
Lab majority	8,852

No change

	1970		1974
Total Vote	52,592		58,262
Turnout	81·2%		84·8%
Lab & Co-op	24,227	46·1%	47·5%
C	20,145	38·3%	32·3%
L	5,888	11·2%	18·3%
Pl Cymru	2,332	4·4%	1·9%
Lab & Co-op maj	4,082	7·8%	15·2%
Swing		+5·0%	−3·7%

Mr Barry Jones was elected in 1970. Teacher. B June, 1938; ed Hawarden Grammar School and Bangor College of Education. Contested Northwich, 1966. UK delegate to Council of Europe and WEU. Member, Hawarden Rural District Council. Regional organizer, NUT. *Appointed Under Secretary, Welsh Office, March 1974.*

Mr Michael Penston, solicitor. B 1938; ed Holyhead Grammar School and Law Society School of Law.

Mr Alexander Carlile, barrister. B February, 1948; ed Epsom College and King's College, London University.

Mr Neil Taylor, lawyer. Aged 32; ed John Bright Grammar School, Llandudno. Member, Denbigh Borough Council. Member, Plaid Cymru Steel Action Group. Founder and chairman of the first club dedicated to promoting Welsh language and culture.

FLINT West
same

Electorate 63,900. 1970: 58,115

*Meyer, Sir A. J. C. (C)	22,039
Harries, N. B. (Lab)	14,897
Brighton, P. (L)	12,831
Hughes, G. (Pl Cymru)	2,296
C majority	7,142

No change

	1970		1974
Total Vote	45,199		52,063
Turnout	77·8%		81·5%
C	20,999	46·4%	42·3%
Lab	13,655	30·2%	28·6%
L	7,437	16·4%	24·6%
Pl Cymru	3,108	6·9%	4·4%
C maj	7,344	16·2%	13·7%
Swing		+4·5%	−1·2%

Sir Anthony Meyer, former diplomat, was elected in 1970; represented Eton and Slough, 1964-66. B October, 1920; ed Eton and New College, Oxford. Trustee of the National Theatre; founder and director, political journal, Solon. Joint Secretary, British Council of European Movement. Member, Foreign Service, 1946-62. Conservative Research centre, 1968. Joint Secretary, backbench housing committee 1964-66.

Mr Norman Harries, lecturer. Ed Caerphilly Grammar School, Cardiff Technical College.

Mr Paul Brighton, teacher. B July, 1942; ed University of Exeter and University of Sussex. School convenor, Nat Assoc. of Schoolmasters.

Mr Gwilym Hughes, teacher, contested Conway 1964 and West Flint 1966 and 1970. B March, 1934; ed Gyfun School, Amlwch, Anglesey, and Normal College, Bangor; Member, Rhuddlan Council since 1968.

FOLKESTONE & HYTHE
same

Electorate 64,285. 1970: 61,067

*Costain, A. P. (C)	23,400
Budd, B. (L)	14,890
Butler, M. J. S. (Lab)	11,412
C majority	8,510

No change

	1970		1974
Total Vote	42,022		49,702
Turnout	68·8%		77·3%
C	27,031	64·3%	47·1%
Lab	13,772	32·8%	23·0%
Ind	1,219	2·9%	
L			29·9%
C maj	13,259	31·6%	17·1%
Swing		+6·1%	−3·7%

Mr Albert Costain was elected in 1959. Chairman of Richard Costain Ltd, 1966-69. B July, 1910; ed King James' Grammar School, Knaresborough, and the College of Estate Management, Fellow of the Institute of Builders; Vice-President, International Prestressed  Concrete Development Group, 1952. London treasurer, National Children's Home, 1950-60. Former chairman, Conservative arts and amenities committee. Member, Estimates Committee, 1965-70.

Mr Bernard Budd, QC, contested Dover in 1966 and 1964. Barrister (Gray's Inn, 1952). B December, 1912; ed Cardiff High School, West Leeds High School, and Pembroke College, Cambridge.

Mr John Butler, university lecturer. B March, 1943; ed Bec School, Wolverhampton College of Technology, City of London College, University of Kent, Canterbury. Member, Canterbury City Council; chairman, Marlow Theatre Trust; Canterbury District Council since 1973. AUT and NUPE.

GAINSBOROUGH minor

Electorate 61,672. 1970: 59,099

*Kimball, M. (C)		22,177
Blackmore, R. (L)		15,967
Lansbury, T. J. (Lab)		12,011
C majority		6,210

No change

	1970		1974	
Total Vote	44,160		50,155	
Turnout	74·6%		81·3%	
C	22,163	50·2%		44·2%
Lab	14,454	32·7%		23·9%
L	7,543	17·1%		31·8%
C maj	7,709	17·4%		12·4%
Swing		+3·9%		+1·4%

Mr Marcus Kimball, land-owner, farmer and Lloyd's underwriter, was returned at a by-election in 1956; contested Derby, South, 1955. B October, 1928; ed Eton and Trinity College, Cambridge. Member, Rutland County Council, 1955-62. Chairman, East Midland Area Young Conservatives, 1954-58. Chairman, British Field Sports Society since 1964. Joint master and huntsman.

Cottesmore Hounds, 1953-58, and Fitzwilliam, 1951-52. Member, Nature Conservancy Wild Fowl Conservation Committee. Privy Council representative on Royal College of Veterinary Surgeons, 1969-70.

Mr Roger Blackmore, lecturer in government, contested Gainsborough 1970. B December, 1941; ed Shebbear College, North Devon, and Leicester University. Branch officer, ATTI.

Mr Terry Lansbury, farmer. B June, 1926; ed London University and Magdalene College, Cambridge. NUAAW.

GALLOWAY same

Electorate 39,082. 1970: 38,669

*Brewis, H. J. (C)		13,316
Thompson, G. H. (Scot Nat)		9,308
Hannay, Dr D. R. (L)		4,643
Chalmers, Mrs H. (Lab)		3,091
C majority		4,008

No change

	1970		1974	
Total Vote	27,852		30,358	
Turnout	72·0%		77·8%	
C	14,003	50·3%		43·9%
Scot Nat	5,723	20·5%		30·7%
Lab	5,665	20·3%		10·2%
L	2,461	8·8%		15·3%
C maj	8,280	29·7%		13·2%
Swing		+3·0%		+1·8%

Mr John Brewis, vice-chairman, Scottish Conservative MPs 1972-74; member, European Parliament, 1972-74; member, to Council of Europe, 1965-68. Elected at a by-election in April, 1959. Barrister (Middle Temple, 1964), farmer and company director, Deputy-  lieutenant for Wigtownshire. B April, 1920; ed Eton and New College, Oxford. Member, Wigtown County Council, 1955-59. Member of Commons Chairmen's panel since 1965.

Mr George Thompson, a former SNP assistant national secretary, teaches modern languages at Kirkcudbright High School. B 1928; ed Dalry School, Kirkcudbright Academy and Edinburgh University.

Dr David Hannay, doctor of medicine and lecturer. B January, 1939; ed Winchester College, Trinity College, Cambridge, St George's Hospital, London. Runs a hill farm in Galloway. Vice-chairman Galloway Liberal Association 1969-70; member, executive committee of Scottish Liberal Party since 1972.

Mrs Helen Chalmers, medical secretary and receptionist. B January, 1927; ed Strathairn Academy. Member, Lanark County Council, 1970-73. TGWU.

GATESHEAD East   same

Electorate 62,881.   1970: 62,011

*Conlan, B. (Lab)	27,269
Ryder, R. A. (C)	11,970
Buckingham, K. A. (L)	10,196
Lab majority	15,299

No change

	1970		1974
Total Vote	44,013		49,435
Turnout	71·0%		78·6%
Lab	28,524	64·8%	55·2%
C	15,489	35·2%	24·2%
L	—		20·6%
Lab maj	13,035	29·6%	30·9%
Swing		+4·8%	−0·7%

Mr Bernard Conlan was elected in 1964; contested High Peak, 1959. Engineer. B October, 1923; ed Manchester primary and secondary schools. Member, Manchester City Council 1954-66; officer of Amalgamated Engineering Union 1944-66. Sponsored by AUEW engineering section. Member, Defence and External Affairs sub-committee, Public Expenditure Committee.

Mr Richard Ryder, senior partner in a firm dealing in pharmaceuticals, property and publicity. B 1949; ed Radley College, Oxford, Magdalene College, Cambridge. Former chairman, Cambridge University Conservative Association; personal assistant to Mr Francis Pym at 1970 general election.

Mr Kenneth Buckingham, master baker. B March, 1921; ed Jarrow Central School. Member, Felling Urban District Council since 1967; member, Durham County Council since 1970; member, Tyne-Wear Metropolitan District Council since 1973.

GATESHEAD West   same

Electorate 30,572.   1970: 34,398

*Horam, J. R. (Lab)	13,839
Heddle, B. J. (C)	5,372
Bennison, J. (L)	3,474
Lab majority	8,467

No change

	1970		1974
Total Vote	22,950		22,685
Turnout	66·7%		74·2%
Lab	15,622	68·1%	61·0%
C	7,328	31·9%	23·7%
L	—		15·3%
Lab maj	8,294	36·1%	37·3%
Swing		+6·7%	−0·5%

Mr John Horam, economic consultant, was elected in 1970; contested Folkestone and Hythe in 1966. B March, 1939; ed Silcoates School, Wakefield, and St Catharine's College, Cambridge. Founder-director Commodities Research Unit Ltd. Chairman, Circle Thirty-Three Housing Trust Ltd. Sponsored by TGWU. Feature and leader writer, *Financial Times,* 1962-65, *The Economist,* 1965-68, and contributor to *Tribune,* 1966-68.

Mr John Heddle, surveyor, company director and underwriting member of Lloyds. B September 1941; ed Bishops Stortford College and the College of Estate Management (London University). Member Kent County Council, Council and Fellow of Incorporated Society of Valuers & Auctioneers, Rating and Valuation Association, and Institute of Directors. Chairman,Burlington Housing Society Ltd. Vice-president, Gateshead Conservative Association.

Mr Joseph Bennison, company director. B September, 1922; ed Technical College. Member, Gateshead Borough Council since 1970.

GILLINGHAM   same

Electorate 61,717.   1970: 59,742

*Burden, F. F. A. (C)	20,934
Sayer, R. (L)	15,052
Clother, H. G. N. (Lab)	14,850
C majority	5,882

No change

	1970		1974
Total Vote	43,870		50,836
Turnout	73·4%		82·4%
C	25,813	58·8%	41·2%
Lab	18,057	41·2%	29·2%
L	—		29·6%
C maj	7,756	17·7%	11·6%
Swing		+4·9%	−2·8%

Mr Frederick Burden was elected in 1950; contested South Shields 1935, Finsbury 1945, and Rotherhithe, in 1947 by-election. Chairman, Parliamentary animal welfare group and vice-chairman, RSPCA. Company director. B December, 1905; ed Sloane

Grammar School, Chelsea.

Mr Robert Sayer, manager. B August, 1939. Member, Kent County Council since 1973; member, Gillingham District Council since 1973; leader, Liberal Group.

Mr Henry Clother, Head of Publicity and Public Relations Department, NUT, contested Woking, 1964 and Canterbury, 1970. B January, 1931; ed Gillingham Grammar School and Jesus College, Cambridge. NUJ member since 1959.

GLASGOW Cathcart   major

Electorate 49,346

*Taylor, E. M. (C)	18,247
McCann, P. T. (Lab)	16,152
Ewing, A. (Scot Nat)	5,410
C majority	2,095

	1974		1974
Total Vote	39,809	Lab	40·6%
Turnout	80·7%	Scot Nat	13·6%
C	45·8%	C maj	5·3%

Mr Edward Taylor, Under-Secretary (Development) Scottish Office, 1974; Under-Secretary, Scottish Office, 1970-71, when he resigned in disagreement with Government's policy on the EEC. Elected in 1964; contested Glasgow, Springburn, 1959. Industrial relations officer and journalist. B April, 1937; ed Glasgow High School and Glasgow University. Member, Glasgow City Council, 1959-64. Chairman, Conservative parliamentary consumer protection committee, 1972; former joint-secretary, Conservative parliamentary shipbuilding committee, former vice-chairman, transport committee. An Opposition spokesman on Scotland from March 1974.

Mr Peter McCann, solicitor. B August, 1924; ed St Mungo's Academy, Glasgow University. Member, Glasgow Corporation since 1961. TGWU.

Mr Alex Ewing, publicity and promotions assistant. B February, 1942; ed Holyrood School and Glasgow School of Art. Joined SNP, 1963; former secretary, Cathcart branch, and chairman, Gorbals constituency. SLADE.

GLASGOW Central   major

Electorate 25,426

*McMillan, T. M. (Lab)	9,400
Gourlay, M. (C)	3,435
Ewing, S. (Scot Nat)	2,211
Brodie, A. (L)	982
Lab majority	5,965

	1974		1974
Total vote	16,028	Scot Nat	13·8%
Turnout	63·0%	L	6·1%
Lab	58·6%	Lab maj	37·2%
C	21·4%		

Mr Thomas McMillan, formerly a wood machinist at Cowlairs railway workshops, was elected in 1966. B February, 1919; ed secondary education. Member, Glasgow City Council since 1962. Magistrate and Bailie of Burgh, 1964. Secretary, Glasgow Central CLP. Sponsored by NUR.

Mr Len Gourlay, store supervisor. B October, 1920; ed Whitehall Senior Secondary School, Glasgow. Served for 10 years in the Royal Navy.

Mr Stewart Ewing, chartered accountant and senior lecturer, Strathclyde University. Aged 48; ed Glasgow University. Married to Mrs Winifred Ewing, SN candidate for Moray and Nairn and MP for Hamilton, 1967-70.

Mr Alexander Brodie, accounts clerk. B September, 1916; ed Dunbarton Academy. Former secretary and chairman, West Dunbarton Liberal Association, 1951-58. Past president, Bathgate toastmasters' club. Acting chairman, West Lothian Liberal Association. ACTS.

GLASGOW Craigton   major

Electorate 43,949

*Millan, B. (Lab)	18,055
Scouller, A. M. (C)	10,817
Hooston, G. (Scot Nat)	6,303
Lab majority	7,238

	1974		1974
Total Vote	35,175	C	30·7%
Turnout	80·0%	Scot Nat	17·9%
Lab	51·3%	Lab maj	20·6%

Mr Bruce Millan, an opposition spokesman on Scottish affairs, 1973-74 and on industry, 1970-73, was Under-Secretary of State for Scotland, 1966-70; Under-Secretary of Defence for the Royal Air Force, 1964-66. Elected in 1959; contested the seat 1955 and West Renfrewshire, 1951. Chartered accountant. B October, 1927; ed Harris Academy, Dundee. Sponsored by APEX. *Appointed Minister of State for Scotland, March 1974.*

Mr Alastair Scouller, freelance writer and interpreter. B May, 1950; ed Jordanhill College School, Glasgow, University of Glasgow, University of Besancon, France, University of Zurich, Switzerland. Active in Young Conservatives since 1965. President, Glasgow University Conservative Club, 1971-72.

Mr Robert Hooston, shippinng agent, aged 25. Member, Vice-chairman, Craigton Constituency Association, SNP.

GLASGOW Garscadden major

Electorate 54,267

*Small, W. W. (Lab)		21,035
Rae, J. G. (C)		9,771
McRury, M. (Scot Nat)		8,789
Barr, S. (Comm)		635
Lab majority		11,264

	1974		1974
Total Vote	40,230	Scot Nat	21·8%
Turnout	74·1%	Comm	1·6%
Lab	52·3%	Lab maj	28·0%
C	24·3%		

Mr William Small re-presented Glasgow, Scotstoun, 1959-74. Engineer. B October, 1909; elementary education at Motherwell. Member, Ayr County Council, 1945-52, and of national committee, Amalgamated Engineering Union, 1955-57; past president, West Ayrshire district
AEU. Sponsored by AUEW engineering section.

Mr Grant Rae, training officer in an engineering firm. B November, 1944; ed Rutherglen Academy and Stow College of Engineering. Vice-chairman, Scottish Conservative Trade Union Advisory Committee. ASTMS.

Mr Malcolm McRury, electronics engineer. B April, 1936; ed Daliburgh secondary school and James Watt Memorial College, Greenock. Stow College, Glasgow. Merchant seaman for 10 years.

Mr Samuel Barr, welder, aged 42. Shop stewards' convenor at Govan Shipbuilders' Scotstoun division. Secretary, Clyde district committee, Amalgamated Society of Boilermakers. Member, Glasgow Trades Council.

GLASGOW Govan major

Electorate 31,928

Selby, H. (Lab)		10,326
*Macdonald, Mrs M. (Scot Nat)		9,783
Mair, J. (C)		3,049
McMillan, P. (L)		763
Lab majority		543

	1974		1974
Total Vote	23,921	C	12·7%
Turnout	74·9%	L	3·2%
Lab	43·2%	Lab maj	2·3%
Scot Nat	40·9%		

Mr Harry Selby, aged 60, contested Govan by-election, 1973. Glasgow councillor since 1972; Chairman, Govan constituency Labour Party for 11 years.

Mrs Margo Macdonald, teacher, won the seat from Labour in the November, 1973 by-election. Contested Paisley, 1970. B April, 1944; ed Hamilton Academy and Dunfermline College. Joined SNP in 1966; vice-chairman, policy.

Mr John Mair, lawyer. B May, 1929; ed Oxford and Glasgow universities. Hember, Glasgow City Council since 1970. Founder member of ratepayers' and residents' associations.

Mr Peter McMillan, club manager. Born 1929. Chairman, Kilmarnock Liberal Association. Member, Scottish Liberal Party since 1960. Contested the seat in the 1973 by-election. Member, Kilmarnock, Town Council.

GLASGOW Hillhead major

Electorate 41,553

*Galbraith, T. G. D. (C)		14,378
Welsh, D. (Lab)		7,997
Steedman, Mrs L. (L)		6,644
Bovey, K. S. (Scot Nat)		3,702
C majority		6,381

	1974		1974
Total Vote	32,721	L	20·3%
Turnout	78·7%	Scot Nat	11·3%
C	43·9%	C maj	19·5%
Lab	24·4%		

Mr Thomas Galbraith
was Parliamentary Secretary, Ministry of Transport, 1963-64; Under-Secretary, Scottish Office from 1959, resigned in November, 1962. Civil Lord of the Admiralty from 1957; Treasurer of the Household, 1955; Comptroller of the Household, 1954. Re-
turned at a by-election in 1948; contested Paisley, 1945, and East Edinburgh by-election in the same year. An Opposition spokesman on transport, 1964-65; vice-chairman, Conservative parliamentary transport committee, 1966-68, Chairman of Scottish Conservative MPs' committee, 1971-72. B March, 1917; son and heir of Lord Strathclyde; educated Aytoun House, Glasgow; Wellington College; Christ Church, Oxford; and Glasgow University.

Mr David Welsh, teacher. B April, 1939; ed Hillhead High School and Glasgow University. Member, Educational Institute of Scotland.

Mrs Louise Steedman, housewife. B May, 1923; ed York and studied singing in York, London, Glasgow and Rome. Chairman, Glasgow Committee British Sailors' Society; vice-chairman, Glasgow West Conservative Society.

Mr Keith Bovey, solicitor. B July, 1927; ed Paisley Grammar School, School of Oriental and African Studies, London University, and Glasgow University.

GLASGOW Kelvingrove major

Electorate 42,505

*Carmichael, N. G. (Lab)		13,115
Kenyon, Dr A. R. T. (C)		10,717
MacKellar, C. M. (Scot Nat)		5,666
Lab majority		2,398

	1974		1974
Total Vote	29,498	C	36·3%
Turnout	69·4%	Scot Nat	19·2%
Lab	44·5%	Lab maj	8·1%

Mr Neil Carmichael,
an Opposition spokesman on Scottish affairs 1970-74, was Parliamentary Secretary, Ministry of Technology, 1969-70; and to Ministry of Transport, 1967-69. MP for Glasgow, Woodside, 1962-74. Engineer. B October, 1921; ed Estbank Aca-

demy and Royal College of Science and Technology, Glasgow. Formerly employed by Gas Board in planning department. Member Glasgow City Council, 1962-63. Member Select Committee on Nationalised Industries. NUGMW. *Appointed Under Secretary, Department of Environment, March 1974.*

Dr Tom Kenyon, is a general practitioner. B June, 1937; ed Medical College of St Bartholomew's. As an RAMC officer he served with the Argylls in Aden, and then trained Australians and Vietnamese at jungle warfare school. Served with the Special Air Service as a parachutist. Served in Ulster.

Mr Colin Mackellar, engineering inspector. Born 1936. Chairman, Partick East branch, SNP.

GLASGOW Maryhill major

Electorate 51,236

Craigen, J. M. (Lab & Co-op)		20,303
MacIntosh, A. (Scot Nat)		8,920
Taylor, S. (C)		6,625
Lab majority		11,383

	1974		1974
Total Vote	35,848	C	18·5%
Turnout	70·0%	Lab & Co-op	
Lab & Co-op	56·6%	maj	31·7%
Scot Nat	24·9%		

Mr James Craigen,
industrial liaison officer, contested Ayr, 1970. B August, 1938; ed Shawlands Academy, Glasgow, and University of Strathclyde. Member, Glasgow Corporation, 1965-68; Bailie, 1966-68; convenor, Printing Committee 1967-68. Head of Organization
and Social Services at the Scottish Trades Union Congress, 1964-68; Member, Glasgow City Labour Party Executive, 1963-68; Race Relations Board, Scottish Committee, 1967-70; Scottish Ambulance Service Board, 1966-71; and of Scottish Police Advisory Board, and governor of the Scottish Police College since 1970.

Mr Angus MacIntosh, joiner. B 1927. Chairman, Glasgow Maryhill Constituency Association, SNP; SNP councillor for Glasgow Cowcaddens, 1968-71.

Mr Stewart Taylor, teacher. B 1941; ed Glasgow University and Jordanhill College. Member of special constabulary.

GLASGOW Pollock   same

Electorate 59,019.   1970: 57,501

*White, J. (Lab)	21,090
Lang I. B. (C)	17,684
D'Arcy Conyers, M. (Scot Nat)	6,584
Bigam, T. (Comm)	377
Lab majority	3,406

No change

	1970		1974
Total Vote	41,752		45,735
Turnout	72·6%		77·5%
Lab	19,311	46·2%	46·1%
C	18,708	44·8%	38·7%
Scot Nat	3,733	8·9%	14·4%
Comm	—	—	0·8%
Lab maj	603	1·4%	7·4%
Swing		+1·7%	−3·0%

Mr James White won the seat for Labour in 1970. B April, 1922; ed Knightswood Senior Secondary School. Managing director, Glasgow Car Collection Ltd.

Mr Ian Lang, insurance broker, contested Central Ayrshire in 1970. B June, 1940; ed Rugby and Sidney Sussex College, Cambridge. A trustee of the Savings Bank of Glasgow.

Mr Matthew D'Arcy Conyers, teacher. B 1928; ed Glasgow university and Jordanhill College of Education. Chairman, Pollok North branch, SNP.

Mr Thomas Biggam, shop steward at Prestcold factory in Hillington. Contested Glasgow, Govan, 1970. B 1932. Member, Scottish committee, Communist Party. President, AUEW branch.

GLASGOW Provan   major

Electorate 54,454

*Brown, H. D. (Lab)	23,154
Edwards, R. (Scot Nat)	7,367
Malone, G. (C)	6,324
Jackson, J. (Comm)	749
Lab majority	15,787

	1974		1974
Total Vote	37,594	C	16·8%
Turnout	69·0%	Comm	2·0%
Lab	61·6%	Lab maj	42·0%
Scot Nat	19·6%		

Mr Hugh Brown was elected in 1964. Former civil servant, Ministry of Pensions and National Insured Allan Glen's ance. B May, 1919; School and Whitehill Secondary School, Glasgow. Member, Glasgow Corporation, 1954-64; Secretary, indoor postal section, Glasgow branch. Union of Post Office Workers. 1946-47. Chairman, Social Services Group. PLP, 1966-68, and of Scottish Labour group since 1973.

Mr Ronald Edwards, teacher. Aged 43; ed Strathclyde University. Former treasurer of Cumbernauld Burgh Council. Contested Glasgow, Craigton, 1970.

Mr Gerald Malone, lawyer. B July, 1950; ed Glasgow University; former office bearer of the Federation of Conservative Students.

Mr John Jackson, paperworker. Contested general elections in 1966, 1970. B September, 1924; ed Kent Road School, Glasgow, and Finnieston Street School, Glasgow. Member, Glasgow Trades Council committee.

GLASGOW Queen's Park   major

Electorate 38,556

*McElhone, F. (Lab)	15,883
Shearer, W. (C)	7,517
MacKellar, D. G. (Scot Nat)	4,394
Kay, J. (Comm)	372
Purdie, R. (Int Marxist)	90
Lab majority	8,366

	1974		1974
Total Vote	28,256	Scot Nat	15·5%
Turnout	73·3%	Comm	1·3%
Lab	56·2%	Int Marx	0·3%
C	26·6%	Lab maj	29·6%

Mr Frank McElhone was MP for Glasgow, Gorbals, 1969-74. Member, Glasgow City Council since 1963. Glasgow magistrate, 1966-68, senior magistrate, 1968-69. B April, 1929; ed St Bonaventure's Secondary School. USDAW.

Mr William Shearer contested Glasgow,

Gorbals in a 1969 by-election and in 1970. B June, 1910. Member, Glasgow Corporation, 1967-70 and since 1972. Glasgow magistrate. Master slater. Ed Glasgow Govan High School.

Mr David Mackellar, company director. B 1937. Spent six years as training officer with an East African newspaper. Vice-chairman, West Renfrewshire Constituency Association, SNP.

Mr John Kay, draughtsman and now full-time Glasgow secretary of Communist Party. Contested Glasgow, Gorbals, 1970 and 1969 by-election. B June, 1926. Former Scottish secretary, Association of Scientific Workers. ASTMS and DATA.

GLASGOW Shettleston major

Electorate 38,176

*Galpern, Sir M. (Lab)	14,208
Turpie, L. (C)	6,472
Lindsay, W. (Scot Nat)	5,834
Lab majority	**7,736**

	1974			1974
Total Vote	26,514	C		24·4%
Turnout	69·4%	Scot Nat		22·0%
Lab	53·6%	Lab maj		29·2%

Sir Myer Galpern has represented the constituency since 1959. Member, Glasgow Corporation, 1932-60; Lord Provost, and Lord Lieutenant for the County of the City of Glasgow, 1958-1959. House furnisher. B 1903; ed elementary school and Glasgow University. Member, Court of Glasgow University; Advisory Committee on Education in Scotland; and National Committee for Training of Teachers. Member, Speaker's Panel of Chairmen.

Mr Leonard Turpie, solicitor. B April, 1934; ed Glasgow High School and Glasgow University. Contested Greenock as a Unionist in 1959. Glasgow councillor since 1958; Leader, Glasgow Tory group; former convenor of planning of Glasgow Corporation.

Mr William Lindsay, sales manager, contested Shettleston, 1970 and 1966. B 1936; ed Woodside Secondary School, Glasgow. Shettleston councillor, 1968-71.

GLASGOW Springburn major

Electorate 47,790

*Buchanan, R. (Lab)	18,067
Morton, W. (Scot Nat)	7,672
McCune, N. (C)	7,452
McLellan, N. (Comm)	478
Lab majority	**10,395**

	1974			1974
Total Vote	33,669	C		22·1%
Turnout	70·4%	Comm		1·4%
Lab	53·7	Lab maj		30·9%
Scot Nat	22·8			

Mr Richard Buchanan was elected in 1964. Engineer. B May, 1912; ed St Mungo's Academy and the Royal College of Science and Technology (now Strathclyde University). Member, Glasgow Corporation, 1949-64. Chairman, Scottish Central Library. Former secretary, Glasgow City Labour Party. Director, Glasgow Citizens' Theatre. Sponsored by NUR. President, Scottish Library Association.

Mr William Morton, maintenance engineer. Aged 41; ed Allan Glen's School, Glasgow. Former Glasgow councillor.

Mr Norman McCune, managing director of road haulage company. B August, 1942.

Mr Neil McLellan, shop steward in railway workshop, contested the seat in 1970. B 1922. Chairman of NUR branch and delegate to Glasgow Trades Council. Member, Glasgow committee, Communist Party.

GLOUCESTER major

Electorate 62,060

*Oppenheim, Mrs S. (C)	23,052
Pegler, A. E. (Lab)	18,215
Halford, D. (L)	10,155
Gordon-Storkey, B. (C Powell)	366
C majority	**4,837**

	1974			1974
Total Vote	51,788	L		19·6%
Turnout	83·4%	C-Powell		0·7%
C	44·5%	C maj		9·3%
Lab	35·2%			

I

Mrs Sally Oppenheim won the seat for the Conservatives in 1970. B July, 1928; ed Sheffield High School, Lowther College, North Wales, and the Royal Academy of Dramatic Art. Member, BBC Advisory Council since 1971; chairman, Conservative Parliamentary Consumer Protection Committee since 1972. National Vice-President, Royal Society for Prevention of Accidents, the Association of Townswomen's Guilds and the National Mobile Homes Residents Association. Member, executive committee of National Council for the Single Woman and Her Dependants. Member, Select Committee on Anti-Discrimination.

Mr Alf Pegler, engineering components inspector, contested Horsham in 1959 and 1964. B January, 1924; ed elementary school, Cork Street, and Oliver Goldsmith. Member, Crawley UDC since 1956. AUEW.

Mr David Halford, nylon process operator. B May, 1944; ed Crypt Grammar School, Gloucester, Gloucester Technical College, TGWU.

Mr Bryan Gordon-Storkey, driving school proprietor, aged 36.

GLOUCESTERSHIRE South major

Electorate 79,795

Cope, J. (C)	27,602
McDonald, Miss O. A. (Lab)	21,143
Short, D. (L)	17,276
C majority	6,459

	1974			1974
Total Vote	66,021	Lab		32·0%
Turnout	82·7%	L		26·2%
C	41·8%	C maj		9·8%

Mr John Cope, a chartered accountant, contested Woolwich, East, in 1970. B May, 1937; ed Oakham School, Rutland. Conservative research department, 1965-67. Personal assistant to Mr Barber, 1967-70, and special assistant to Mr Peter Walker, 1972-74.

Miss Oonagh McDonald is a lecturer in Moral Philosophy at Bristol University. Secretary, index for community action, an index of voluntary organizations in Bristol.

Mr David Short, insurance consultant. B March, 1943; ed Gravesend Grammar School for Boys and Kingsway Day Continuation College. Free Church lay preacher; member, Hereford City Council, Hereford County Council, and Hereford and Worcester County Council. ASTMS.

GLOUCESTERSHIRE West minor

Electorate 66,770. 1970: 63,599

*Loughlin, C. W. (Lab)	22,765
Marland, P. (C)	21,141
MacGregor, A. I. (L)	11,856
Hart, Dr S. S. (Ind)	171
Lab majority	1,624

No change

	1970		1974	
Total Vote	49,099		55,933	
Turnout	77·0%		83·8%	
Lab	22,637	46·1%	40·7%	
C	21,530	43·8%	37·8%	
L	4,932	10·0%	21·2%	
Ind	—	—	0·3%	
Lab maj	1,107	2·2%	2·9%	
Swing		+7·4%	−0·3%	

Mr Charles Loughlin, Parliamentary Secretary, Ministry of Public Building and Works, 1968-70; Parliamentary Secretary, Ministry of Social Security, 1967-68; Parliamentary Secretary, Ministry of Health, 1965-67. Elected in 1959. B February, 1914; ed St Mary's

School, Grimsby, and National Council of Labour Colleges. Area organizer, Union of Shop Distributive and Allied Workers, 1946-59. Sponsored by USDAW.

Mr Paul Marland contested Bedwellty in 1970. Farmer. B March, 1940; ed Gordonstoun and Trinity College, Dublin. Member, North Cotswold RDC. Member, Monday Club

Mr Alasdair MacGregor, agricultural journalist and farmer. B June, 1930; ed Stowe School; Lycee Jaccard, Lausanne; Trinity College, Cambridge and Uppsala University, Sweden. NFU.

GOOLE   same

Electorate 64,825.   1970: 63,111

*Marshall, E. I. (Lab)	30,245
Kemp, N. P. (C)	17,020
Clarkson, J. T. (Ind)	2,150
Lab majority	13,225

No change

	1970		1974
Total Vote	43,881		49,415
Turnout	69·5%		76·2%
Lab	26,424	60·2%	61·2%
C	17,457	39·8%	34·4%
Ind	—		4·3%
Lab maj	8,967	20·4%	26·8%
Swing		+4·6%	−3·2%

1971 by-election: Total Vote 35,313 (55·6%)—Lab 24,323 (68·9%), C 10,990 (31·1%)—Lab maj 13,333 (37·8%).

Mr Edmund Marshall,
a mathematician, was elected in May, 1971. Contested Louth as a Liberal in 1964 and 1966; joined Labour Party 1967. B May, 1940; ed Humberstone Foundation School, Clee; Magdalen College, Oxford; Liverpool University. Member, Expenditure Committee; Methodist local preacher; member, British Council of Churches; treasurer Christian Socialist Movement.

Mr Noel Picarda Kemp, broadcaster, former city editor of *The Spectator,* and restaurateur. B December, 1937; ed Westminster School and Christ Church, Oxford.

GOSPORT   major

Electorate 48,614

Viggers, P. J. (C)	19,563
Hewitt, G. J. (Lab)	12,335
Rix, J. G. (L)	7,485
C majority	7,228

	1974		1974
Total Vote	39,383	Lab	31·3%
Turnout	81·0%	L	19·0%
C	49·7%	C maj	18·3%

Mr Peter Viggers,
merchant banker. B March, 1938 ed Alverstoke Primary School, Gosport; Portsmouth Grammar School, Trinity Hall, Cambridge. Director of Edward Bates and Sons Ltd and of other companies including Richardson Smith Ltd (chairman) and Pre-

mier Consolidated Oilfields Ltd; an underwriting member of Lloyd's. Solicitor.

Mr. Graham Hewitt, company manager. B February, 1939; ed Gosport Grammar School. Joined Labour Party in 1954; British national delegate to the International Union of Socialist Youth, 1960-64; member Gosport Borough Council since 1963, Labour leader since 1968 and chairman; Mayor Elect of Gosport to take office April, 1974; member Western Authorities Orchestral Society.

Mr John Rix, investment analyst. Former, Chartered Accountant, 1956-73. B March, 1934; ed Sherborne School, Dorset.

GOWER   same

Electorate 56,481.   1970: 54,246

*Davies, I. (Lab)	23,856
George, D. F. R. (C)	8,780
Thomas, R. C. C. (L)	8,737
Harris, J. N. (Pl Cymru)	3,741
Lab majority	15,076

No change

	1970		1974
Total Vote	41,789		45,114
Turnout	77·0%		79·9%
Lab	26,485	63·4%	52·9%
C	9,435	22·6%	19·5%
Pl Cymru	5,869	14·0%	8·3%
L	—		19·4%
Lab maj	17,050	40·8%	33·4%
Swing		+6·8%	+3·7%

Mr Ifor Davies was Under Secretary, Welsh Office, 1966-69; Lord Commissioner of the Treasury, 1964-66. Elected in 1959. Industrial personnel officer. B June, 1910; ed Gowerton School, Swansea Technical College, and Ruskin College, Oxford. Member, Speaker's Panel of Chairmen. Member,

Glamorgan County Council, 1958-61. Chairman, Welsh Grand Committee; Council of Swansea University College. Member, Court of University of Wales, Board of Civic Trust for Wales. APEX.

Mr David George, who fought Cardiganshire in 1970, is a farmer. Chairman, livestock marketing company; seed growers' association; management committee of Welsh Growers Federation; and CPC for Wales. B May, 1937; ed Mill Hill School and Reading University.

Mr Clement Thomas, managing director of meat company. B January, 1929; ed Blundell's School and St. John's College, Cambridge. Former captain, Welsh Rugby Football Team; member, Welsh Council for the Disabled; committee member,

Welsh Sports Association for the Disabled; Rugby football correspondent of *The Observer* and Welsh Rugby correspondent of *The Guardian*.

Mr John Harris, lecturer in metallurgy. B June, 1924; ed University of Wales, Swansea. Director of two private companies.

GRANTHAM   minor

Electorate 77,747. 1970: 73,626

*Godber, J. B. (C)	31,910
Smedley, Mrs. S. M. (Lab)	20,567
Bailey, W. T. (Ind L)	10,781
C majority	11,343

No change

	1970		1974
Total Vote	56,366		63,258
Turnout	76·4%		81·4%
C	33,070	58·7%	50·4%
Lab	23,296	41·3%	32·5%
Ind L	—	—	17·0%
C maj	9,774	17·4%	17·9%
Swing		+6·6%	+0·2%

Mr Joseph Godber, Minister of Agriculture, Fisheries and Food 1972-74; Minister of State, Foreign and Commonwealth Office, 1970-72. Was Opposition chief spokesman on agriculture, 1965-70; previously spokesman on labour affairs. Minister of Labour, 1963-64; Secretary of State for War, June-October, 1963; Minister of State, Foreign Office, 1961-63 and joint Under-Secretary, 1960-61; joint Parliamentary Secretary, Ministry of Agriculture, Fisheries and Food, 1957-60; assistant whip, 1955-57. Elected in 1951. Farmer. B March, 1914; ed Bedford School. Member, Bedfordshire County Council, 1946-52.

Mrs Stella Smedley, housewife. B 1943; ed Queen Elizabeth's Girls Grammnar School, Mansfield; member of Newark District Council.

GRAVESEND   minor

Electorate 86,496. 1970: 84,046

Ovenden, J. F. (Lab)	29,571
*White, R. L. (C)	27,989
Mumford, D. C. (L)	13,136
Turner, J. D. (Nat Front)	1,726
Lab majority	1,582

Labour gain

	1970		1974
Total Vote	63,869		72,422
Turnout	75·9%		83·7%
C	29,924	46·8%	38·6%
Lab	28,711	44·9%	40·8%
L	5,234	8·2%	18·1%
Nat Front	—		2·4%
C maj	1,213	1·9%	—
Lab maj	—		2·2%
Swing		+4·9%	−2·0%

Mr John Ovenden, telecommunications engineer. B August, 1942; ed Chatham House Grammar School, Rasmgate. Gillingham councillor; former secretary, Kent Federation of Labour Party.

Mr Roger White won the seat for the Conservatives in 1970; contested it in 1966, and Stoke Newington and Hackney, North, 1959 and 1964. Company director. B June, 1928; ed St Joseph's College, Croydon. National vice-chairman, Young Conservatives, 1958-59; member, Council of London Borough of Bromley, 1964-68; Vice-chairman Conservative Parliamentary transport industries committee. Member, British Board of Boxing Control. Deputy chairman of Prison Board.

Mr David Mumford, field officer, Cyrenians (working with single homeless persons). B January, 1947; ed Kingswood School, Bath, and Merton College, Oxford.

Mr James Turner, chemical analyst, aged 29. Kent organizer, National Front.

GREENOCK & PORT GLASGOW
major

Electorate 63,594

*Mabon, Dr J. D. (Lab & Co-op)	20,565
Campbell, W. M. (L)	8,789
Scott Younger, F. (C)	7,892
Wright, K. (Scot Nat)	4,881
Murray, A. (Comm)	483
Lab majority	11,776

	1974			1974
Total Vote	42,610		Scot Nat	11·4%
Turnout	67·0%		Comm	1·1%
Lab & Co-op	48·3%		Lab & Co-op	
L	20·6%		maj	27·6%
C	18·5%			

Dr Dickson Mabon  was an Opposition spokesman on Scottish affairs, 1970-72; Minister of State, Scottish Office, 1967-70, and Under Secretary, Scottish Office, 1964-67. Returned at a by-election in December, 1955; contested West Renfrewshire, 1955 and Bute and North Ayrshire, 1951. Physician. B November, 1925; ed North Kelvinside School, Glasgow and Glasgow University. President, Scottish Union of Students, 1954-55. Secretary all party shipbuilding committee; vice-chairman, all party Scotch Whisky committee; vice-chairman, Labour backbench cane sugar refining committee. Director, Radio Clyde Ltd and advisor on Parliamentary and EEC legislation to several companies, Freeman, Worshipful Society of Apothecaries of City of London, 1972. Member, MPU, BMA and NUGMW.

Mr Menzies Campbell, advocate. B 1940; ed Hillhead High School, Glasgow and Glasgow University; past president, Glasgow University Liberal Association; former captain, British Olympic team; member, Clayson Committee, Royal Commission on Licensing Laws.

Mr F. Scott Younger, civil engineer. B December, 1940; ed Kelvinside Academy, Glasgow University and University of California; lecturer in civil engineering, Strathclyde University, 1965-72; director, Pre-construction Services Ltd; secretary, Institution of Civil Engineers, Glasgow, and West of Scotland Association.

Mr John Wright, chartered engineer. Aged 28; ed Greenock High School and Glasgow University. Member, Institute of Civil Engineers.

Mr Alex Murray, full-time Communist Party worker and former Rolls-Royce factory worker, contested the seat in 1970. B 1923. Former shop stewards' convenor.

GREENWICH Greenwich major

Electorate 52,390

*Barnett, N. G. (Lab)	20,164
Harold, Mrs S. M. S. (C)	11,294
Wilson, A. J. D. (L)	7,855
Lab majority	8,870

	1974		1974
Total Vote	39,313	C	28·7%
Turnout	75·0%	L	20·0%
Lab	51·3%	Lab maj	22·6%

Mr Guy Barnett re-  tained the seat for Labour in the by-election of July, 1971. MP for Dorset, South, 1962-64, contested Scarborough and Whitby, 1959. Schoolmaster. Former chief education officer of Commonwealth Institute. B August, 1928; ed Highgate School and St Edmund Hall, Oxford. Chairman, Oxford University Labour Party Group, 1951; Secretary, Oxford Union, 1953. Parliamentary consultant to Society to Civil Servants.

Mrs Suzette Harold, computer software executive. B April, 1940; ed Walthamstow Hall School for Daughters of Missionaries, and Lady Margaret Hall, Oxford; member, Oxford City Council 1965-71.

Mr Alastair Wilson, barrister. B May, 1946; ed Wellington College and Cambridge University.

GREENWICH Woolwich East major

Electorate 50,520

*Mayhew, C. P. (Lab)	20,967
Watson, B. H. (C)	8,990
Woodhead, D. J. (L)	6,390
Hanman, P. S. (Nat Front)	1,066
Murphy, J. R. (Exports)	191
Lab majority	11,977

	1974		1974
Total Vote	37,604	L	17·0%
Turnout	74·4%	Nat Front	2·8%
Lab	55·7%	Exports	0·5%
C	23·9%	Lab maj	31·8%

Mr Christopher May-  **hew,** Minister of Defence for the Royal Navy from 1964 until he resigned in 1966, was a party spokesman on foreign affairs from December, 1961 to 1964, and previously on War Office matters. Represented South Norfolk, 1945-50, returned for East Woolwich at a by-election, 1951. Under-Secretary for Foreign Affairs, 1946-50. B June, 1915; ed Haileybury and Christ Church, Oxford; President of the Union, 1937. Television broadcaster and writer. Chairman, Middle East International (Publishers) Ltd; and of National Association for Mental Health.

Mr Barry Watson, publicity manager of international engineering company. B June, 1935; ed Manchester Grammar School, Allan Glen's School, Glasgow, and Royal College of Science and Technology, Glasgow. Member of City of Westminster Council since 1968.

Mr David Woodhead, lecturer in politics. B March, 1944; ed Huddersfield New College; Manchester University and Durham University. ATTI.

Mr Philip Hanman, interviewer for computer consultancy. B January, 1952; ed St. Joseph's Academy, Blackheath, University of Lille. Former member of USDAW.

GREENWICH Woolwich West   major

Electorate 55,767

*Hamling, W. (Lab)	20,126
Bottomley, P. J. (C)	17,690
Johnson, J. P. (L)	7,833
Lab majority	2,436

	1974		1974
Total Vote	45,649	C	38·7%
Turnout	81·8%	L	17·1%
Lab	44·1%	Lab maj	5·3%

Mr William Hamling, was an Opposition spokesman on defence and Opposition whip 1970-73; assistant Government Whip, 1969-70. Elected in 1964. Contested Woolwich, West, 1955 and 1959, Torquay, 1956 by-election, Wavertree 1950, 1951 and Southport, 1945. Lecturer. B August, 1912; ed elementary school, Liverpool Institute and University of Liverpool. Member, Fabian Society, and Estimates Committee, 1965-66. Trustee, National Maritime Museum since 1967. Member, NUT and ATTI. PPS to Mr Harold Wilson, Prime Minister, 1974.

Mr Peter Bottomley, 29, employed by a London lighting and displays firm. Ed Westminster mixed comprehensive and Trinity College, Cambridge. TGWU.

Mr Paul Johnson contested Dartford, 1970. Insurance executive, Lloyds' syndicate. B March, 1942; ed Erith Technical School.

GRIMSBY   minor

Electorate 66,836.   1970: 65,581

*Crosland, C. A. R. (Lab)	21,585
Brown, K. (C)	15,914
Rigby, D. (L)	12,084
Kale, P. H. (C-Powell)	816
Lab majority	5,671

No change

	1970		1974
Total Vote	44,881		50,399
Turnout	68·4%		75·4%
Lab	23,571	52·5%	42·8%
C	17,460	38·9%	31·6%
L	3,850	8·6%	24·0%
C-Powell	—		1·6%
Lab maj	6,111	13·6%	11·2%
Swing		+2·1%	+1·2%

Mr Anthony Crosland, chief Opposition spokesman on the environment 1970-74; was elected to Shadow Cabinet in 1970; Secretary of State for Local Government and Regional Planning 1969-70 with Cabinet responsibilities for Ministry of Housing and Local

Government, Ministry of Transport, and for environment and pollution matters; President of the Board of Trade, 1967-69; Secretary of State for Education and Science, 1965-67; Economic Secretary to the Treasury, 1964-65. Elected in 1959; represented South Gloucestershire, 1950-55; contested Southampton, Test, 1955. Economist, university lecturer and writer. B August, 1918; ed Highgate School and Trinity College, Oxford (President of the Union, 1946). Chairman, Fabian Society, 1961-62. *Appointed Secretary of State for the Environment, March 1974.*

Mr Keith Brown, investment analyst and member of the Stock Exchange. B January, 1943; ed Forest School, Snaresbrook; member Havering Council; personal assistant to Lord Hailsham at 1970 general election. Former national vice-chairman Young Conservatives.

Mr Derek Rigby contested Isle of Ely, 1966. Process development manager, frozen foods. B May, 1934; ed Deytheur Grammar School, Montgomeryshire, and Wigan Technical College. Former member NUM and NACODS.

GUILDFORD   same

Electorate 71,678   1970: 68,154

*Howell, D. A. R. (C)	28,152
Fox, C. (L)	18,261
Crow, Mrs J. E. (Lab)	11,175
C majority	9,891

No change

	1970		1974
Total Vote	49,133		57,588
Turnout	72·1%		80·3%
C	27,203	55·4%	48·9%
Lab	13,108	26·7%	19·4%
L	8,822	17·9%	31·7%
C maj	14,095	28·7%	17·2%
Swing		+5·6%	+0·4%

Mr David Howell, Minister of State for Energy, 1974; Minister of State for Northern Ireland, November, 1972-74; Under Secretary for Northern Ireland, 1972; Lord Commissioner of the Treasury, 1970-71; Parliamentary Secretary, Civil Service Department, 1970-72 and Under Secretary for Employment, 1971-72. Elected in 1966; contested Dudley, 1964. Director of the Conservative Political Centre, 1964-66. B January, 1936; ed Eton and King's College, Cambridge. Editor of Crossbow, 1962-64; chairman, Bow Group, 1961. Served in the economic section of the Treasury, 1959-60; leader writer and special correspondent with *The Daily Telegraph,* 1960-64. An Opposition spokesman on energy from March 1974.

Mr Christopher Fox, chartered accountant. B June 1945; ed Peter Symond's School, Winchester and London School of Economics.

Mrs Jean Crow is a scientific officer with the UK Atomic Energy Authority. B December, 1943; ed RAF schools and St Joseph's Convent, Reading. IPCS.

HACKNEY Central   major

Electorate 48,288

	1974
*Davis, S. C. (Lab)	18,705
Lightwood, K. S. (C)	6,302
Snow, Mrs M. (L)	5,256
Lab majority	12,403

	1974		1974
Total Vote	30,263	C	20·8%
Turnout	62·7%	L	17·4%
Lab	61·8%	Lab maj	41·0%

Mr Clinton Davis, elected in 1970, contested Yarmouth in 1964 and 1959, and Portsmouth, Langstone, in 1955. Solicitor. B December, 1928; ed Mercer's School and King's College, London University (Chairman, Labour Society). Mayor, London borough of Hackney, 1968-69; Secretary, all-party solicitors group. *Appointed Under Secretary for Trade, March 1974.*

Mr Kenneth Lightwood contested the seat, 1970. Office manager. B May, 1940; ed Owen's School, Islington. Borough of Hackney alderman and deputy leader of opposition.

Mrs Margaret Snow, housewife and former teacher. B July 1933; ed at Buchan School, Isle of Man, The Mount School, Mill Hill, and Hendon Technical College, Kilburn. Organiser, Misery Campaign on the Northern Underground Line, 1970.

HACKNEY North & Stoke Newington   major

Electorate 52,564

*Weitzman, D. (Lab)	17,160
Wylson, A. J. (C)	7,826
Lyons, S. J. (L)	5,932
Lord, H. (Nat Front)	1,226
Goldman, M. (Comm)	532
Lab majority	9,334

	1974		1974
Total Vote	32,676	L	18·1%
Turnout	62·2%	Nat Front	3·7%
Lab	52·5%	Comm	1·6%
C	23·9%	Lab maj	28·6%

Mr David Weitzman, QC, was member for Stoke Newington, 1945-50, and elected for Stoke Newington and Hackney, North, in 1950; contested Stoke Newington, 1935. B June, 1898; ed Hutchesons' Grammar School, Glasgow, and Manchester University. Barrister (Gray's Inn, 1922), QC 1951.

Mr Anthony Wylson, architect. B July, 1932; ed King's School, Canterbury; School of Architecture, Bedford Square, London; British School at Rome. Member, Kent County Council, 1967-74.

Mr Simon Lyons, retailer. B April, 1911; ed Freeland School, Stoke Newington, and Cowper Street Secondary Modern School, City of London.

Mr Henry Lord, civil servant. B August, 1915; ed Barnsbury Central School.

Mr Monty Goldman, accountant, contested Stoke Newington and Hackney, North, in 1970 and 1966. B October, 1931; ed Parmiter's Grammar School. Secretary, Hackney branch, Communist Party.

HACKNEY South & Shoreditch major

Electorate 49,247

*Brown, R. W. (Lab)	18,580
Proctor, K. H. (C)	6,562
Bone, C. (L)	6,053
Lab majority	12,018

HAL

	1974			1974
Total Vote	31,195	C		21·0%
Turnout	63·3%	L		19·4%
Lab	59·6%	Lab maj		38·5%

Mr Ronald Brown, MP for Shoreditch and Finsbury, 1964-74, was an assistant Government whip, 1966-67. Senior lec-turer in electrical en-gineering, principal of Industrial Training School. Parliamentary adviser to Furniture, Timber and Allied Trade Union. B Sep-tember, 1921; ed elementary school, South London, and Borough polytechnic. Brother of Lord George-Brown. Alderman and leader, London borough of Southwark since 1964. Leader, Camberwell Borough Council, 1956-64.

Mr K. Harvey Proctor is executive director of Parliamentary Digest Ltd. B January, 1947; ed High School for Boys, Scar-borough and University of York.

Mr Clive Bone, chartered engineer. B May 1943; ed Weston Road Secondary School, Wimbledon Technical College, Kingston and Middlesex Polytechnics.

HALESOWEN & STOURBRIDGE
major

Electorate 81,620

*Stokes, J. H. R. (C)	26,514
Turner, D. (Lab)	22,465
Eden, L. (L)	17,471
C majority	4,049

	1974			1974
Total Vote	66,450	Lab		33·8%
Turnout	81·4%	L		26·3%
C	39·9%	C maj		6·1%

Mr John Stokes, management consul-tant, represented Old-bury and Halesowen, 1970-74. Fought Glou-cester, 1964, and Hit-chin, 1966. B July, 1917; ed Haileybury and Queen's College, Oxford (treasurer, Conservative Associa-tion). Member, Con-servative Parliamen-tary Defence Committee. Chairman, General Purposes Committee, Primrose League.

Mr Denis Turner, transport controller. B August, 1942; ed Bilston Stonefield Secon-dary School and Bilston College of Further Education. Member, West Midands County Council, Wolverhampton Borough and District Councils. Member, ISTC.

Mr Leonard Eden, district airline sales manager. B November, 1941; ed St Hubert's, Warley, and The Oratory, Bir-mingham. Member of Liberal Party trans-port advisory panel.

HALIFAX
same

Electorate 63,196   1970: 66,222

*Summerskill, Dr Shirley C. W. (Lab)	20,970
Lyons, S. R. (C)	17,967
Clegg, A. (L)	12,300
Lab majority	3,003

No change

	1974		1974
Total Vote	48,701		51,237
Turnout	73·5%		81·1%
Lab	24,026	49·3%	40·9%
C	23,828	48·9%	35·1%
L	—		24·0%
ILP	847	1·7%	—
Lab maj	198	0·4%	5·9%
Swing		+5·8%	−2·7%

Dr Shirley Summers-kill, an Opposition spokesman on health 1970-74, was elec-ted in 1964; contested Blackpool, North, in 1962 by-election. Me-dical practitioner. B September, 1931; ed St Paul's School; Somerville College, Oxford; and St Thomas' Hospital.

Vice-president, Socialist Medical Associa-tion; chairman, PLP health group, 1969-70, previously vice-chairman, 1964-69. United Kingdom delegate to the UN Status of Women Commission, 1968 and 1969. Daughter of Lady Summerskill. MPU. *Appointed Under Secretary, Home office, March, 1974.*

Mr Stuart Lyons, managing director of John Collier Tailoring Ltd, has been a Leeds city councillor since 1970 and mem-ber, Yorkshire and Humberside Economic planning council since 1971. B October, 1943; ed Rugby and King's College, Cam-bridge.

Mr Allen Clegg, textile physicist, contested Bradford, South, 1964. B May, 1938; ed Heath Grammar School, Halifax, and Durham, Bradford and Salford uni-versities. Member Halifax County Borough Council 1963-74, Calderdale District Council since 1973. APEX.

136

HALTEMPRICE   minor

Electorate 76,268   1970: 74,813

*Wall, P. H. B. (C)	31,720
Walker, R. (L)	19,896
Cross, L. (Lab)	11,031
C majority	11,824

No change

	1970		1974
Total Vote	56,033		62,647
Turnout	74·8%		82·1%
C	30,042	53·6%	50·6%
Lab	15,862	28·3%	17·6%
L	10,129	18·1%	31·7%
C maj	14,180	25·3%	18·9%
Swing		−0·7%	+3·8%

Mr Patrick Wall was returned at a by-election in February, 1954; contested Cleveland, 1951 and 1952 by-election. B October, 1916; ed Downside. Vice-chairman of Conservative parliamentary committee on defence, 1965-70 and 1972, and for many years vice-chairman of the party's Commonwealth committee and overseas bureau. Executive member, United Kingdom branch of the Inter-Parliamentary Union. Chairman of the Conservative sub-committee on fisheries since 1972 and Southern Africa sub-committee. Member Westminster City Council, 1953-63. Member of defence committee of WEU, Military Committee of NAA and of Council of Europe. Served with Royal Marines, 1935-50. Joint vice-chairman, Conservative defence committe, from March 1974.

Mr Robert Walker was in the diplomatic service for 25 years and in 1972 became Deputy Registrar of Hull University. B May, 1924; ed Sowerby Bridge Grammar School and Peterhouse College, Cambridge.

Mr Laurie Cross, economics lecturer. B July, 1940; ed Willerby County Secondary School, Hull University and Hull College of Education. ATCDE.

HAMILTON   major

*Wilson, A. (Lab)	19,070
MacDonald, I. (Scot Nat)	12,692
Douglas-Hamilton, Lord James (C)	7,977
Lab majority	6,378

	1974		1974
Total Vote	39,739	Scot Nat	31·9%
Turnout	79·7%	C	20·1%
Lab	48·0%	Lab maj	16·0%

Mr Alexander Wilson, a miner, regained the seat for Labour in 1970, contested the 1967 by-election. B June, 1917; ed Forth Grammar School. Member third district council Lanarkshire for 11 years. Sponsored by NUM.

Mr Ian MacDonald contested Glasgow, Bridgeton, 1961 by-election, and Stirlingshire, East and Clackmannan, 1970. Dry cleaner. B November, 1934; ed Glasgow Academy and Glasgow University. National organizer, Scottish National Party, 1962-69.

Lord James Douglas-Hamilton, brother of the Duke of Hamilton, is an advocate. B July, 1942; ed Strathavon and Balliol College, Oxford. Boxing blue and former president of the Oxford Union.

HAMMERSMITH Fulham   major

Electorate 57,981

*Stewart, M. (Lab)	20,995
Stevens, M. (C)	17,446
Dowden, G. (L)	6,105
Smithies, H. (Nat Front)	966
Lab majority	3,549

	1974		1974
Total Vote	45,512	L	13·4%
Turnout	78·5%	Nat Front	2·1%
Lab	46·1%	Lab maj	7·8%
C	38·3%		

Mr Michael Stewart, Chairman, Select Committee on Parliamentary Commission for Administration, since 1970, was Secretary of State for Foreign and Commonwealth Affairs 1968-70; Secretary of State for Foreign Affairs, March to October, 1968; First Secretary of State, 1967-68; Secretary of State for Economic Affairs, 1966-67; Secretary of State for Foreign Affairs, 1965-66; Secretary of State for Education and Science, 1964. Labour spokesman on housing and local government, 1959-64 and previously on education. Elected Fulham, 1950; contested West Lewisham in 1931 and 1935; represented Fulham East, 1945-50. Vice-Chamberlain of the Household, 1946-47; Comptroller, 1946-47; Under Secretary for War, 1947-51; Parliamentary Secretary, Ministry of Supply, May to

October, 1951. B November, 1906; ed Christ's Hospital and St John's College, Oxford; president of the Union, 1929. Former teacher at the Merchant Taylors' and the Coopers' Company Schools.

Mr Martin Stevens, European chief executive of international marketing consultants, contested Dulwich, 1966, 1964. B July, 1929; ed Bradfield and Trinity College, Oxford. Former London county councillor.

Mr Gerald Dowden, landscape gardener, contested Lewes in 1966 and 1964. B October, 1926; ed Lord Weymouth Grammar School, Warminster.

Mr Arnold Smithies, French-speaking telephonist, GPO International Exchange, aged 52.

HAMMERSMITH North major

Electorate 52,063

*Tomney, F. (Lab)	18,970
Beckett, R. G. (C)	11,929
Knott, S. (L)	7,460
Lab majority	7,041

	1974		1974
Total Vote	38,359	C	31·1%
Turnout	73·7%	L	19·4%
Lab	49·4%	Lab maj	18·3%

Mr Frank Tomney has represented this constituency since 1950. Industrial consultant. B May, 1908; ed at primary and technical school. Former member, Watford Borough Council and Hertfordshire County Council. NUGMW Member, European Movement; delegate, Western European Union, 1960-64 and 1973-74.

Mr Richard Beckett, barrister. Has special interests in children, crime and environment. B March, 1944; ed Eton and Oxford.

Mr Simon Knott, member of the Stock Exchange and director of several public companies. B June 1931; ed Malvern College, Trinity College, Cambridge, and the Middle Temple. Contested Barons Court, 1959, 1964, 1966 and 1970. Hammersmith Borough councillor, 1967-68; first Liberal councillor in inner London. Committee member, Association of Liberal Councillors.

HARBOROUGH major

Electorate 65,223

*Farr, J. A. (C)	27,974
Reynolds, N. (L)	15,501
Robinson, J. W. (Lab)	11,579
C majority	12,473

	1974		1974
Total Vote	55,054	L	28·1%
Turnout	84·4%	Lab	21·0%
C	50·8%	C maj	22·6%

Mr John Farr was elected in 1959; contested Ilkeston, 1955. B September, 1922; ed Harrow. Member of Lloyd's, landowner and farmer. Secretary, Conservative agricultural, fisheries and food committee; all-party conservation committee; and Anglo-Irish Parliamentary group. Former member, East Midlands Land Tribunal.

Mr Norman Reynolds, plant manager. B June, 1922; ed Leicester University College and London University. Member, Wigston Urban Council, 1963-74 (chairman, 1968-69), elected Oadby and Wigston District Council, 1973.

Mr John Robinson, sheet metal worker. B September, 1941; ed Westfield Secondary Modern School, Wellingborough and Leicester Technical Colleges, and the Open University. County councillor. SMWU.

HARINGEY Hornsey same

Electorate 58,070   1970: 64,683

*Rossi, H. A. L. (C)	18,792
Kuczynski, I. (Lab)	16,584
O'Brien, P. (L)	8,676
C majority	2,208

No change

	1970	1974
Total Vote	43,614	44,052
Turnout	67·4%	75·9%
C	21,434 49·1%	42·6%
Lab	17,645 40·4%	37·6%
L	3,755 8·6%	19·7%
Comm	624 1·4%	—
SPGB	156 0·4%	—
C maj	3,789 8·7%	5·0%
Swing	+3·7%	−1·8%

Mr Hugh Rossi, Under Secretary for the Environment 1974; Lord Commissioner of the Treasury, 1972-74; Assistant Govt. Whip, 1970-72. Elected in 1966. Solicitor. B June 1927; ed Finchley Catholic Grammar School and King's College, London University. Member,

Haringey Borough Council, 1964-68; Hornsey Borough Council, 1956-65 (deputy mayor, 1964-65). Middlesex County Council, 1961-65. Joint secretary, Conservative Parliamentary housing, land and local government group, 1968-70. Former member, executive committee, Society of Conservative lawyers. Government whip for Europe, 1971-72. Deputy leader, delegation to Council of Europe and WEU, 1972. An Opposition spokesman on the environment from March 1974.

Mr Irving Kuczynski, economics lecturer at South Bank Polytechnic. B February, 1947; ed state schools and Manchester University. Member of Camden Borough Council since 1971; Inner London Education Authority. ASTMS.

Mr Patrick O'Brien, barrister. B June, 1945; ed St Joseph's Academy, Blackheath, and Queen's College, Cambridge.

Mr Norman Atkinson, elected in 1964, contested Wythenshawe in 1955; Altrincham and Sale, 1959. Design engineer at Manchester University. B March, 1923; ed elementary and technical schools. Member, Manchester City Council, 1945-49.

Sponsored by AUEW, engineering section. Member, Tribune Group.

Mr John Croft, electrical engineer and auctioneer. B 1933; ed West Sussex County Jubilee School. Former Haringey councillor.

Miss Katherine Papatheodotou, part-time clerical officer studying law at London University. B December, 1940, in Cyprus. Former teacher. Chairman of an Anglo-Greek society.

Mr Roy Painter, managing director, Industrial Contract Cleaning Company. B May, 1933; ed secondary modern school; council member, Contract Cleaning and Maintenance Association.

Mr John Martin, managing director of a business research company. Contested Worcester for Labour, 1964. B. April, 1936; ed grammar school and London School of Economics. Former finance committee chairman, Haringey Borough Council, and former secretary, Consumer Council.

HARINGEY Tottenham same

Electorate 47,327   1970: 51,258

*Atkinson, N. (Lab)	16,999
Croft, J. A. (C)	7,873
Miss K. Papatheodotou (L)	2,478
M. P. Coney (Nat Ind Anti-Com Mkt)	1,373
Painter, R. (Nat Front)	1,270
Martin, J. (Soc Dem)	763
Squire, K. (Ind C)	274
Lab majority	9,126

No change

	1970		1974
Total Vote	28,342		31,030
Turnout	55·3%		65·6%
Lab	17,367	61·3%	54·8%
C	10,975	38·7%	25·4%
L	—	—	8·0%
Nat Ind	—	—	4·4%
Nat Front	—	—	4·1%
Social Dem	—	—	2·4%
Ind C	—	—	0·9%
Lab maj	6,392	22·5%	29·4%
Swing		+4·0%	−3·4%

HARINGEY Wood Green same

Electorate 51,734   1970: 53,653

*Butler, Mrs J. S. (Lab and Co-op)	18,594
Malynn, P. (C)	10,950
Walton, M. (L)	7,194
Lab majority	7,644

No change

	1970		1974
Total Vote	32,688		36,738
Turnout	60·9%		71·0%
Lab & Co-op	18,666	57·1%	50·6%
C	14,022	42·9%	29·8%
L	—	—	19·6%
Lab & Co-op maj	4,644	14·2%	20·8%
Swing		+3·7%	−3·3%

Mrs Joyce Butler has represented the seat since 1955. House-wife. B December, 1910; ed King Edward's High School, Birmingham, and Woodbrooke College. Member, Wood Green Borough Council, 1947-64. Alderman and first chairman of London Borough of Haringey; Mayoress, 1965-66. A vice-chairman of the Parliamentary Labour Party, 1965-70. Member, Speaker's panel of chairmen. Chairman, Cooperative group of MPs. President, Spurs ladies' football team; London Passenger Action Conference. Joint Chairman, Parliamentary committee on pollution.

Mr Peter Malynn, managing director of his family company, Parfums Le Galion Ltd. B December, 1929; ed Queen Elizabeth's Grammar School, Wimborne, The Blue School, Wells, Sydney University. Member, Watford RDC 1955-58; GLC, 1967-73. Member, executive, London Council of Social Service.

Mr Michael Walton contested Guildford, 1970. Teacher. B August, 1938; ed Harrow County Grammar School and Oxford and Birmingham Universities. Member, Windsor Borough Council, 1962-65 and 1966-69. NUT.

HARLOW   major

Electorate 61,027

Newens, A. S. (Lab and Co-op)	25,814
Goldstone, B. (L)	13,280
Smith, J. (C)	13,016
Lab majority	12,534

	1974		1974
Total Vote	52,110	L	25·5%
Turnout	85·4%	C	25·0%
Lab & Co-op	49·5%	Lab & Co-op maj	24·0%

Mr Stanley Newens, a teacher, was MP for Epping, 1964-70. B February, 1930; ed Buckhurst High School, University College, London, and Westminster Teacher Training College. Director of LCS (London Co-operative Society). Member NUM 1952-56 and NUT since 1956.

Mr Basil Goldstone contested Norfolk, South in 1970, Peterborough, 1966, Basingstoke, 1964, Dover, 1950, Petersfield, 1945, and Hendon, 1935. Hospital officer. B October, 1909; ed Dover College. Member, King's Lynn Borough Council since 1971.

Mr James Smith, European director of a company servicing the turbo-machinery industry. Chairman of Mitcham and Morden Conservative Association. B 1937; ed King Edward VI School, Lichfield, and Imperial College, London.

HARROGATE   same

Electorate 64,174   1970: 62,570

Banks, R. G. (C)	27,517
Bayley, I. de C. (L)	15,728
Wheaton, M. A. (Lab)	6,084
Brons, A. H. (Nat Front)	1,186
Stringfellow, J. E. (Dem Christian)	875
C majority	11,789

No change

	1970		1974
Total Vote	43,789		51,390
Turnout	70·0%		80·1%
C	26,167	59·7%	53·5%
L	8,825	20·1%	30·6%
Lab	8,797	20·1%	11·8%
Nat Front	—		2·3%
Dem Christian	—	—	1·7%
C maj	17,342	39·6%	22·9%
Swing		+3·4%	+1·0%

Mr Robert Banks, a horticultural nursery man and farmer, was a Paddington councillor, 1959-65. B 1937; ed Haileybury. Naval reserve officer; former executive in publishing, now partner in an investment company.

Mr Ian Bayley, businessman with interests in insurance and road haulage. B October, 1938; ed Cranleigh School and Trinity College, Dublin. Member, Harrogate District Council.

Mr Michael Wheaton, University lecturer in politics. Chairman of Humberside County Council social services committee. B September, 1944; ed Cathays High School for Boys, Cardiff, and University College of Swansea.

Mr Andrew Brons, college lecturer. B June, 1947; ed Harrogate Grammar School and York University. Member, ATTI.

HARROW Central — minor

Electorate 44,913   1970: 45,863

*Grant, J. A. (C)	15,320
Offenbach, D. M. (Lab)	12,403
Montgomerie, R. S. (L)	7,635
Donin, J. (Nat Front)	823
C majority	2,917

No change

	1970		1974
Total Vote	32,893		36,181
Turnout	71·6%		80·5%
C	16,525	50·2%	42·3%
Lab	12,561	38·2%	34·3%
L	3,449	10·5%	21·1%
Ind	358	1·1%	
Nat Front	—		2·3%
C maj	3,964	12·0%	8·1%
Swing		+3·7%	−2·0%

Mr Anthony Grant, Under-Secretary for Trade and Industry 1970-74; Parliamentary Secretary, Board of Trade, June to October, 1970. Elected in 1964; contested Hayes and Harlington in 1959. Solicitor. B May, 1925; ed St Paul's School and Brasenose College, Oxford. Liveryman of the Worshipful Company of City Solicitors. Freeman, City of London; member, Court of Guild of Freemen. Joint honorary secretary, Conservative Parliamentary Legal Committee, 1965-66. Opposition whip, 1966-70.

Mr David Offenbach contested New Forest, 1970. B August, 1943; ed St Marylebone Grammar School and London University. Solicitor. Member, Camden Borough Council since 1968. ASTMS.

Mr Ronald Montgomerie, solicitor. B May, 1929; ed Rutherglen Academy, Glasgow, John Lyon School, Harrow, and University College, London. Chairman, group of housing societies, and Harrow Central Liberal Association.

Mr Jeffrey Donin is an auditor. B February, 1946; ed Brookside House Secondary Grammar School.

HARROW East — minor

Electorate 48,878   1970: 50,363

*Dykes, H. J. M. (C)	17,978
Childerhouse, K. W. (Lab)	13,485
McDonnell, J. (L)	8,805
C majority	4,493

No change

	1970		1974
Total Vote	38,270		40,268
Turnout	75·9%		82·4%
C	19,517	51·0%	44·6%
Lab	15,496	40·5%	33·5%
L	3,185	8·3%	21·9%
Ind	72	0·2%	
C maj	4,021	10·5%	11·1%
Swing		+5·7%	+0·3%

Mr Hugh Dykes, stockbroker, won the seat for the Conservatives in 1970; contested Tottenham, 1966. B May, 1939; ed Weston - super - Mare Grammar School, and Pembroke College, Cambridge, where he was chairman of University Conservative Association 1962. Research secretary. Bow Group, 1965-66. Secretary Conservative Finance Committee, 1970.

Mr Kenneth Childerhouse, lecturer, contested Wembley, North, 1970 and 1966, Harrow, West, 1964. B February, 1939; ed Boys' County School, Harrow, London School of Economics, and University of London Institute of Education. Harrow councillor 1964-68. Chairman, Chiswick Polytechnic branch, ATTI.

Mr Joseph McDonnell, departmental secretary, National Coal Board; B June, 1919; councillor in Northumberland for eight years; member, British Association of Colliery Management.

HARROW West — same

Electorate 56,122   1970: 57,374

*Page, J. A. (C)	23,950
Bell, R. E. (L)	12,081
Wagner, L. (Lab)	10,430
C majority	11,869

No change

	1970		1974
Total Vote	41,769		46,461
Turnout	72·8%		82·8%
C	24,867	59·5%	51·5%
Lab	11,462	27·4%	22·4%
L	5,440	13·0%	26·0%
C maj	13,405	32·1%	25·5%
Swing		+3·9%	−1·5%

Mr John Page was returned in a by-election in March, 1960; contested Eton and Slough, 1959. Chairman (former secretary) of Conservative parliamentary employment committee 1972. Company director. B September, 1919; ed Harrow and Magdalene College, Cambridge. President, Greater London area Conservative trade unionists; vice-chairman, Conservative home affairs committee. Chairman, Council of Europe budget committee.

Mr Robert Bell, university lecturer; B February, 1930; ed Carlisle Grammar School, Pembroke College, Cambridge, Trinity College, Dublin, Edinburgh University; contested Clackmannan and East Stirlingshire, 1970.

Mr Leslie Wagner, university lecturer. Chairman of Harrow education committee since 1971. B February, 1943; ed Salford Grammar School and Manchester University. AUT.

HARTLEPOOL   minor

Electorate 64,619   1970: 64,403

*Leadbitter, E. L. (Lab)	26,988
Freeman, N. (C)	22,700
Lab majority	4,288

No change

	1970		1974
Total Vote	47,892		49,688
Turnout	74%		76·9%
Lab	27,704	57·8%	54·3%
C	20,185	42·2%	45·7%
Lab maj	7,516	15·6%	8·6%
Swing		+1·7%	+3·5%

Mr Edward Leadbitter was elected in 1964. Member, Select Committee on Science and Technology. President Hartlepool Constituency Labour Party. Teacher. B June, 1919; ed state schools and Cheltenham Teacher Training College. Member, West Hartlepool Borough Council 1954-67. Sponsored by NUPE.

Mr Nicholas Freeman, barrister. B 1939; ed Stoneygate School, Leicester; Kings School, Canterbury. Member, Kensington and Chelsea Borough Council since 1968; Society of Conservative Lawyers.

HARWICH   same

Electorate 89,007   1970: 82,117

*Ridsdale, J. E. (C)	32,452
Cadman, D. (L)	19,989
Fryer, J. B. (Lab)	18,697
C majority	12,463

No change

	1970		1974
Total Vote	61,196		71,138
Turnout	74·5%		79·9%
C	32,754	53·5%	45·6%
Lab	19,923	32·5%	26·3%
L	8,518	13·9%	28·1%
C maj	12,831	21·0%	17·5%
Swing		+4·2%	−0·8%

Mr Julian Ridsdale was returned at a by-election in February, 1954. Company director. Under-Secretary for Defence for the Royal Air Force after the 1964 reorganization; Under-Secretary, Air Ministry, in July, 1962. Contested Paddington, North, 1951. B June, 1915; ed Tonbridge, the Royal Military College, Sandhurst, and the London University School of Oriental Languages. Chairman of the British Japanese Parliamentary group. Member Select Committee of Public Accounts, 1970-71.

Mr David Cadman, chartered surveyor and managing director. B December, 1941; ed Friends' School, Saffron Walden, Essex, and London University (College of Estate Management). Member, Liberal Party housing panel.

Mr John Fryer, journalist. B February, 1945; ed Chigwell School. Branch secretary, NUJ.

HASTINGS   same

Electorate 56,696   1970: 55,213

*Warren, K. R. (C)	20,075
Foster, M. J. (Lab)	12,992
Cass, M. G. (L)	11,690
C majority	7,083

No change

	1970		1974
Total Vote	40,237		44,757
Turnout	72·9%		79·0%
C	20,364	50·6%	44·8%
Lab	13,549	33·7%	29·0%
L	6,324	15·7%	26·1%
C maj	6,815	16·9%	15·8%
Swing		+5·3%	−0·5%

Mr Kenneth Warren was elected in 1970. Contested St Pancras, North in 1964. Aeronautical engineer. Member Select Committee on Science and Technology and chairman sub-committee on Sea-Bed Technology. Vice-chairman Conservative Parliamentary aviation com-

mittee; chairman, United States section of Conservative Foreign Affairs Committee. Member, NUGMW, 1954-57; member of union side on joint negotiating panel, BOAC, 1955-57. B August, 1926; ed Midsomer Norton Grammar School, Aldenham School, De Havilland Aeronautical Technical School, King's College, London, and London School of Economics.

Mr Michael Foster is chairman of the constituency Labour Party.

Mr Gerald Cass contested Hendon, North in 1970, 1966. Former chairman of the London Liberal Party. B August, 1929; ed secondary school. Company director; associate member, Chartered Institute of Secretaries.

HAVANT & WATERLOO   major

Electorate 75,804

*Lloyd, I. S. (C)	27,397
Brewin, S. (L)	18,209
Acklaw, J. T. (Lab)	13,367
Wakeford, R. E. (Ind)	675
C majority	9,188

	1974		1974
Total Vote	59,648	Lab	22·4%
Turnout	78·7%	Ind	1·1%
C	45·9%	C maj	15·4%
L	30·5%		

Mr Ian Lloyd represented Portsmouth, Langstone, 1964-74. Economist and chairman of International Shipping Information Services. B May, 1921; ed Michaelhouse, Natal, Witwatersrand University, King's College, Cambridge, and Administrative Staff College, Henley. Fellow of the Royal Statistical Society. Economic adviser to Central Mining and Investment Corporation, 1949-53; member, South African Board of Trade and Industries, 1953-56, and director, Acton Society Trust, 1956. Former president, Cambridge Union.

Mr Sydney Brewin, chartered accountant. B April, 1931; ed Burton-on-Trent Grammar School. East Sussex county councillor 1961-64. East Grinstead district councillor 1960-64.

Mr John Acklaw, educational psychologist, member, Havant District Council. B November, 1940; ed Kilburn Grammar School, Manchester University and University College, Swansea. Member, executive of Association of Educational Psychologists.

HAVERING Hornchurch   major

Electorate 60,052

*Williams, A. L. (Lab)	21,763
Jackson, J. (C)	15,567
McCarthy, B. (L)	10,391
Percy-Davis, B. (People)	619
Lab majority	6,196

	1974		1974
Total Vote	48,340	L	21·5%
Turnout	80·5%	People	1·3%
Lab	45·0%	Lab maj	12·8%
C	32·2%		

Mr Alan Lee Williams, a lecturer, was MP for Hornchurch, 1966-70; contested Epsom, 1964. Director British Atlantic Committee. B November 1930; ed Roan School, Greenwich, and Ruskin College, Oxford. Member PLP Defence Group, 1966-70. Vice-chairman, Labour Party Foreign Affairs Group, 1968-70. Secretary, all party River Thames Group. Joint chairman, Railways Reform Society. Head of United Nations Association, Youth Department, 1962-66; member, Greenwich Borough Council, 1951-53; national youth officer, Labour Party, 1955-62. Freeman, City of London, 1969; Company of Watermen and Lightermen, 1945-51.

Mr John Jackson, journalist on the London *Evening News,* contested Erith and Crayford in 1970. B September, 1937; ed Hackney Downs Grammar School. Member, London Borough Council of Redbridge since 1968.

Mr Brian McCarthy, computer specialist. B June, 1939; ed Whitechapel Grammar School and West Ham College of Technology. Contested West Ham, North, 1970. Former Newham borough councillor.

Mr Ben Percy-Davis, retired farmer; national council member, The Conservation Society; founder and chairman, Essex Conservation Society; former county councillor.

HAVERING Romford   major

Electorate 54,660

Neubert, M. J. (C)	17,134
O'Flynn, D. R. (Lab)	14,061
Hurlstone, T. (L)	12,190
Bates, E. (Ind)	374
C majority	3,073

	1974			1974
Total Vote	43,759	L		27·8 %
Turnout	80·0%	Ind		0·8%
C	39·1%	C maj		7·0%
Lab	32·1%			

Mr Michael Neubert contested Romford 1970, Hammersmith, North, 1966. B September 1933; ed Queen Elizabeth's School, Barnet, Bromley Grammar School and Downing College, Cambridge. Member of Bromley Council since 1960 (Leader, 1967-70, Mayor 1972-73).  Organizer of holiday air tours all over the world.

Mr Denis O'Flynn, a machine moulder in the car industry, is a member of AUEW (Foundry Section). B 1934; ed St Patrick's School, Cork.

Mr Terry Hurlstone, educationist. B September, 1939; ed Hendon Grammar School, Brentwood College of Education. NAS.

HAVERING Upminster   major

Electorate 63,716

*Loveridge, J. W. (C)		21,003
Whysall, J. E. D. (Lab)		19,995
Merton, A. (L)		11,596
C majority		**1,008**

	1974		1974
Total Vote	52,594	Lab	38·0%
Turnout	82·5%	L	22·0%
C	39·9%	C maj	1·9%

Mr John Loveridge, a college principal and farmer, was MP for Hornchurch, 1970-74; fought Aberavon in 1951. B September, 1925; ed privately and St John's College, Cambridge. Member, Hampstead Borough Council, 1953-59. Secretary, Conservative Smaller Businesses  Committee; member, Select Committees on Expenditure and Procedure.

Mr John Whysall is a teacher and former lecturer in communications. Member, Havering Borough Council since 1971. B April, 1943; ed Trinity College, Dublin. Member ATTI and Fabian Society.

Mr Andrew Merton, schoolmaster. B June, 1946; ed Thurrock Technical College, Barking teacher training college. NAS.

HAZEL GROVE   major

Electorate 67,962

Winstanley, Dr M. P. (L)	26,966
Arnold, T. R. (C)	24,968
Roberts, A. (Lab)	6,315
L majority	**1,998**

	1974		1974
Total Vote	58,249	C	42·9%
Turnout	85·7%	Lab	10·8%
L	46·3%	L maj	3·4%

Dr Michael Winstanley, medical practitioner, television and radio broadcaster, journalist. Contested Stretford, 1964, MP for Cheadle, 1966-70. B August, 1918; ed Manchester Grammar School, Manchester University (president of the union). Former member, Commons  select committee for the Parliamentary Commissioner for Administration. NUJ. Appointed Liberal spokesman on Social Services and Deputy Whip, March, 1974.

Mr Tom Arnold, impressario, contested Manchester, Cheetham, in June, 1970. B January, 1947; ed Bedales, Le Rosey (Switzerland), and Pembroke College, Oxford. Member, Society of West End Theatre Managers and Association of Touring and Producing Managers.

Mr Allan Roberts, senior social worker. B October, 1943; ed Droysden Secondary Modern School, Didsbury College of Education, Manchester University. Member, Manchester City and Metropolitan District Councils, chairman of housing committee.

HEMEL HEMPSTEAD   major

Electorate 83,000

*Allason, J. H. (C)	27,572
Corbett, R. (Lab)	27,385
Baron, Miss C (L)	15,682
C majority	**187**

	1974		1974
Total Vote	70,639	Lab	38·8%
Turnout	85·1%	L	22·2%
C	39·0%	C maj	0·3%

Mr James Allason was elected in 1959; contested Hackney, Central, 1955. Chairman, Conservative parliamentary housing and construction committee since 1972. Chairman, Environment and Home Office Sub-Committee, Commons expenditure committee since 1972.

Insurance broker. B September, 1912; ed Haileybury and the Royal Military Academy, Woolwich. Member, Kensington Borough Council, 1956-65. Regular Army officer for 22 years. Chairman, Allason Investments, Ltd.

Mr Robin Corbett, publishing executive. B December, 1933; ed Holly Lodge Grammar School, Smethwick. Contested the seat in 1966 and West Derbyshire by-election in 1967; member, national executive council of NUJ, 1965-69.

Miss Christina Baron, research student and part-time university tutor. B October, 1950; ed St Leonards School, St Andrews; The City University, London.

HEMSWORTH same

Electorate 68,961   1970: 69,059

Woodall, A. (Lab)	44,093
Kerr, R. F. (C)	9,152
Lab majority	34,941

No change

	1970		1974
Total Vote	49,547		53,245
Turnout	71·7%		77·2%
Lab	40,013	80·7%	82·8%
C	9,534	19·2%	17·2%
Lab maj	30,479	61·5%	65·6%
Swing		+4·6%	−2·0%

Mr Alec Woodall, colliery surface foreman. B September, 1918; ed Southmoor Road County School, Hemsworth. Member, Hemsworth Urban District Council since 1966. Life member NUM.

Mr Richard Kerr, tutor at Swinton Conservative College since 1972. Has studied economic development in poor countries. B 1949 ed Boston and Bourne Grammar schools, Grantham College of Further Education, and Bradford University.

HENLEY major

Electorate 61,605

*Heseltine, M. R. D. (C)	24,367
Evans, S. C. (L)	15,467
Alexander, A. (Lab)	10,500
C majority	8,900

	1974			1974
Total Vote	50,334		L	30·7%
Turnout	81·7%		Lab	20·9%
C	48·4%		C maj	17·7%

Mr Michael Heseltine, Minister for Aerospace and Shipping 1972-74; Under Secretary for the Environment, 1970-72; Parliamentary Secretary, Ministry of Transport, June to October 1970. Represented Tavistock, 1966-74; contested Coventry, North, 1964, and

Gower, 1959. B March, 1933; ed Shrewsbury and Pembroke College, Oxford. President, Oxford Union, 1954. Publisher; former chairman of Haymarket publishing group. President, Federation of Devon Young Conservatives, 1966. Director, Bow Publications, 1961-65. An Opposition spokesman on Trade from March 1974.

Mr Simon Evans, financial adviser. B August, 1923; ed Aberdare Grammar School, Saltley College, Birmingham, and St. Luke's College, Birmingham. Contested Abingdon, 1970.

Mr Alan Alexander, lecturer in politics, University of Reading. B December, 1943; ed Glasgow secondary schools and Glasgow University. Member, Reading Borough Council (chairman, housing committee since 1972); and of New Berkshire County Council since 1973.

HEREFORD minor

Electorate 57,389   1970: 56,363

*Gibson-Watt, D. (C)	18,676
Tannant Nash, C. B. (L)	15,238
Geffen, I. E. (Lab)	11,299
C majority	3,438

No change

	1970		1974
Total Vote	41,374		45,213
Turnout	73·4%		78·8%
C	22,011	53·2%	41·3%
Lab	14,410	34·8%	25·0%
L	4,953	12·0%	33·7%
C maj	7,601	18·4%	7·6%
Swing		+5·7%	−1·0%

Mr David Gibson-Watt, Minister of State, Welsh Office 1970 - 74. Party spokesman on Wales, 1964-70. Returned at a by-election in 1956; contested Brecon and Radnor, 1950 and 1951; assistant Government whip, 1957-59; a Lord Commissioner of the Treasury, 1959-61. Farmer and forester. B September, 1918; ed Eton and Trinity College, Cambridge. Former member, Radnor County Council; Deputy Lieutenant for Radnorshire. Had responsibility for British Agricultural Exhibition, Moscow, 1964. Member, Council of Fellows of Royal Agricultural Societies.

Mr Brian Tannant Nash, chairman and managing director. B February, 1937. Fellow, British Computer Society.

Mr Ivan Geffen, solicitor, fought Newcastle upon Tyne, North, 1951, Thirsk and Malton, 1950. Former member, editorial board, *Peace News.* B March, 1920; ed Westminster School and University of London.

from 1970. General Secretary, Fabian Society, 1960-64. Chairman, Labour Committee for Europe, 1965; member, Estimates Committee, 1956-66. CAWU. *Appointed Secretary of State for Prices and Consumer Protection, March 1974.*

Mr Vivian Bendall, surveyor and valuer. B December, 1938; grammar school, Croydon. Member, GLC, 1970-73; and of London Borough of Croydon, 1964-74. Chairman, Greater London Area Young Conservatives, 1967-68; member, executive committee of the national union representing Greater London area, 1970-72. Executive committee member, Greater London Conference for the Care of the Elderly; committee member, Southern Regional Association for the Blind; member, Central Council for the Care of the Disabled.

Mr Tom Willis, lecturer. B 1944; ed Caterham School, Surrey, University of Sussex, and London University. Contested Hitchin, 1970. A.T.T.I.

HERTFORD & STEVENAGE major

Electorate 79,516

*Williams, Mrs. S. V. T. B. (Lab)	30,343
Bendall, V. (C)	22,167
Willis, T. N. (L)	15,444
Lab majority	8,176

	1974		1974
Total Vote	67,954	C	32·6%
Turnout	85·4%	L	22·7%
Lab	44·6%	Lab maj	12·0%

Mrs Shirley Williams was MP for Hitchin, 1964-74. Chief Opposition spokesman for the social services, 1970-71, when she was elected to the Shadow Cabinet; spokesman on Home Affairs, 1971-73 and on prices 1973-74; Minister of State, Home Office, 1969-70;

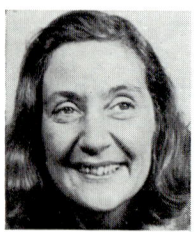

Minister of State, Education and Science, 1967-69; Parliamentary Secretary, Ministry of Labour, 1966-67. Contested Harwich in 1954 by-election and 1955, and Southampton, Test, 1959. Economist. B July, 1930; ed Summit School, Minnesota, St Paul's School, Hammersmith, Somerville College, Oxford (first woman chairman, University Labour Club), and Columbia University, New York. Member, Labour Party NEC

HERTFORDSHIRE East   major

Electorate 88,035

*Walker-Smith, Sir D. (C)	32,032
Keir, M. M. (Lab)	20,674
Clark, P. (L)	18,546
C majority	11,358

	1974		1974
Total Vote	71,252	Lab	29·0%
Turnout	80·9%	L	26·0%
C	44·9%	C maj	15·9%

Sir Derek Walker-Smith, QC, was Minister of Health, 1957-59; Parliamentary Secretary, Board of Trade, 1955-56; Economic Secretary to the Treasury, 1956-57; and Minister of State, Board of Trade, 1957. Represented Hertford 1945-55 and East Hertfordshire since

1955. Called by Middle Temple, 1934; QC, 1955. B April, 1910; ed Rosall and Christ Church, Oxford. Member Committee of Privileges. Chairman of the 1922 Committee, 1951-55 and vice-chairman Conservative Parliamentary arts and amenities committee since 1972. Member European Parliament since 1973. Chairman of Society of Conservative Lawyers; Associate of Royal Institution of Chartered Surveyors. Honorary vice-president National House Builders' Registration Council. Former chairman, National Advisory Committee on Local Government.

Mr Malcolm Keir, lecturer; contested Harrow elections, 1964. B November, 1937; ed Harrow Weald Grammar School and Keele and Essex universities.

Mr Peter Clark, bank clerk. B November, 1947; ed Friends' School, Saffron Walden. Member, Stansted Parish Council, 1970-73; chairman, Quendon and Rickling Parish Council, and member, Uttlesford District Council since 1973. Member of NUBE.

HERTFORDSHIRE South major

Electorate 63,877

*Parkinson, C. (C)	21,190
Dubs, A. (Lab)	18,104
Henchley, J. (L)	13,356
C majority	3,086

	1974		1974
Total Vote	52,650	Lab	34·4%
Turnout	82·4%	L	25·4%
C	40·2%	C maj	5·9%

Mr Cecil Parkinson was MP for Enfield, West from 1970-74; contested Northampton, 1970. Chartered accountant. Founder and chairman Parkinson Hart Securities Ltd. B September, 1931; ed Royal Grammar School, Lancaster and Emmanual College, Cambridge. Secretary, Parliamentary Conservative Finance Committee. Assistant Government whip, 1974.

Mr Alfred Dubs, industrial market researcher. B December, 1932; ed Cheadle Hulme School and London School of Economics. Member, Westminster City Council since 1971; chairman, Westminster Community Relations Council. Contested Cities of London and Westminster in 1970.

Mr John Henchley, sales manager. Contested Barnet for the Liberals, in 1970, and Croydon, North-East, 1966. B December, 1934; ed Clifton College. Rugby Union referee.

HERTFORDSHIRE South-West major

Electorate 75,201

Dodsworth, G. H. (C)	26,563
Mitchell, J. E. (Lab)	18,465
Jarrett, J. E. S. (L)	17,987
C majority	8,098

Total Vote	63,015	Lab 29·3%
Turnout	83·8%	L 28·5%
C	42·1%	C maj 12·8%

Mr Geoffrey Dodsworth, merchant banker, director of W. Brandt's Sons & Co Ltd. contested Hartlepools in 1964 and Don Valley, 1959. B 1928; ed St. Peter's School, York. Member, executive committee, National Union of Conservative and Unionist Associations; Primrose League, Bow Group, and York City Council, 1959-65.

Mr Jim Mitchell, lecturer in history at Dacorum College of Further Education, Hemel Hempstead. Contested Aylesbury, 1970. B March, 1927; ed Sir Walter St John's School, London, and University College, Exeter. Hemel Hempstead borough councillor since 1967 (Labour group leader, 1970-72).

Mr John Jarrett, deputy director of the British Epilepsy Association; contested the seat in 1970. B September, 1924; ed Westminster City School and Pembroke College, Cambridge.

HEXHAM same

Electorate 65,432 1970: 62,564

*Rippon, A. G. F. (C)	24,059
Wade, E. (Lab)	16,129
Cairncross, R. L.	12,730
C majority	7,930

No change

	1970		1974
Total Vote	47,182		52,918
Turnout	75·4%		80·9%
C	24,516	52·0%	45·5%
Lab	16,645	35·3%	30·5%
L	6,021	12·8%	24·0%
C maj	7,871	16·7%	15·0%
Swing		+2·8%	-0·8%

Mr Geoffrey Rippon, QC, Secretary of State for the Environment 1972-74; Chancellor of Duchy of Lancaster with responsibility for Common Market negotiations, 1970-72; Minister of Technology, June-July, 1970. Opposition spokesman on defence, 1968-70. Elected in 1966; represented Norwich, South, 1955-64; contested Shoreditch and Finsbury, 1950 and 1951. Minister of Public Build-

ing and Works, 1962-64, joining Cabinet in 1963; Parliamentary Secretary, Ministry of Housing and Local Government, 1961-62, and to Ministry of Aviation, 1959-61; Opposition spokesman on housing and local government, 1966-68. Called by Middle Temple, 1948, QC 1964. B May, 1924; ed King's College, Taunton, and Brasenose College, Oxford. Mayor of Surbiton, 1951-52; leader, Conservative Party on LCC 1957-59. President, Conservative Party National Advisory Committee on Local Govt; member, Court of London University. Appointed to Shadow Cabinet and a spokesman on Foreign and Commonwealth Affairs and Europe, March 1974.

Mr Eric Wade, Open University staff tutor in social science. Northumberland county councillor since 1972; Newcastle metropolitan district councillor from May, 1973. B June, 1939; ed Dukes Grammar School, Alnwick, County Technical College, Ashington, King's College University of Durham, and University of Newcastle upon Tyne. Coal miner for three years.

Mr Roy Cairncross contested Tynemouth in 1955. Public relations officer. B May, 1924. Member of Whitley Bay Council 1963-66 and of North Tyneside Metropolitan District Council since 1973.

HEYWOOD & ROYTON   same

Electorate 73,798   1970: 72,048

*Barnett, J. (Lab)	28,216
MacGregor, I. (C)	21,054
Bingham, V. (L)	14,392
Lab majority	7,162

No change

	1970		1974
Total Vote	54,879		63,662
Turnout	76·2%		86·3%
Lab	25,081	45·7%	44·3%
C	24,178	44·0%	33·1%
L	5,620	10·2%	22·6%
Lab maj	903	1·6%	11·2%
Swing		+4·7%	−4·7%

Mr Joel Barnett, returned in 1964, contested Runcorn in 1959. An Opposition spokesman on the Treasury since 1970. Member, Public Expenditure Committee, 1971-74; Select committees on the Civil List and Tax Credits. Accountant. B October, 1923; ed Jewish School, Derby Street, Manchester, and Manchester Central High School. TGWU. Served on Prestwich Borough Council, 1956-59. Chairman (1967-70) and vice-chairman (1966-67) **PLP** economic and finance group. Member, Public Accounts Committee 1965-71. *Appointed Chief Secretary to the Treasury, March 1974.*

Mr Ian MacGregor contested the constituency in 1970. Personal assistant to textile company director. B July, 1930; ed Queen Elizabeth's Grammar School, Blackburn.

Mr Vivian Bingham is a personnal director. B April, 1932; ed King Edward's School, Birmingham, and New College, Oxford.

HIGH PEAK   same

Electorate 56,665   1970: 55,308

*Le Marchant, S. (C)	19,231
Jackson, P. M. (Lab)	16,956
Scott, Mrs. N. (L)	12,117
C majority	2,275

No change

	1970		1974
Total Vote	44,731		48,304
Turnout	80·9%		85·2%
C	19,558	43·7%	39·8%
Lab	18,054	40·4%	35·1%
L	7,119	15·9%	25·1%
C maj	1,504	3·4%	4·7%
Swing		+2·6%	+0·7%

Mr Spencer Le Marchant, member of the Stock Exchange, elected to the seat, 1970. B 1931; ed Eton. Governor, United Westminster Schools; former member, Westminster City Council. Joint secretary of Conservative energy committee from March 1974.

Mr Peter Jackson won High Peak for Labour in 1966; defeated in 1970. University lecturer. B October, 1928; ed Durham, Leicester and Hull Universities. Former vice-chairman **PLP** Communications group; former member, Select Committee on Agriculture. Member, Derbyshire County Council, and executive, National Trust. TGWU.

Mrs Nora Scott, vicar's wife. B March, 1920; ed Morpeth High School for Girls, Newcastle upon Tyne Conservatoire of Music, and Royal Academy of Music. Rural district councillor. Musicians' Union.

HILLINGDON Hayes & Harlington   major

Electorate 55,547

*Sandelson, N. D. (Lab)	24,682
Watherston, P. D. (C)	14,634
Fairhurst, J. S. (Nat Front)	2,721
Lab majority	10,048

	1974			1974
Total Vote	42,037	C		34·8%
Turnout	75·7%	Nat Front		6·5%
Lab	58·7%	Lab maj		23·9%

Mr Neville Sandelson retained the seat for Labour in the 1971 by-election. Barrister. B November, 1923; ed Westminster and Trinity College, Cambridge. Contested Chichester, 1970. Leicester, South-West by-election, 1967, Heston and Isleworth, 1966, Rushcliffe, 1959, Beckenham by-election, 1957, and Ashford, 1950, 1951 and 1955. Member, LCC, 1952-58; Society of Labour Lawyers. Fabian Society. NUGMW.

Mr Peter Watherston, merchant banker. B May, 1942; ed Winchester and London School of Economics.

Mr John Fairhurst, aged 41. Organizer, Hayes branch, National Front.

HILLINGDON Ruislip-Northwood
minor

Electorate 53,855   1970: 54,702

*Crowder, F. P. (C)	21,995
Race, D. A. G. (Lab)	10,574
Arram, Miss J. (L)	10,311
Hobday, Mrs. P. (Ind C)	1,439
C majority	11,421

No change

	1970		1974	
Total Vote	39,976		44,319	
Turnout	73·0%		82·3%	
C	24,247	60·6%	49·6%	
Lab	11,541	28·9%	23·8%	
L	4,188	10·5%	23·3%	
Ind C	—		3·2%	
C maj	12,706	31·8%	25·8%	
Swing		+6·8%	−2·9%	

Mr Petre Crowder, QC, won the seat in 1950; contested North Tottenham by-election, 1945. Barrister (Inner Temple, 1948); QC, 1964. B July, 1919; ed Eton and Christ College, Oxford. Deputy chairman, Hertfordshire Quarter Sessions, 1959-63; appointed chairman, 1963. Former recorder of Gravesend, 1960; Recorder of Colchester since 1967.

Mr Reginald Race, research officer, National Union of Public Employees. B June, 1947; ed Sale Grammar School, University of Kent, and University of Essex. Former secretary, Kent Committee for the Defence of Trade Unions; former director, Canterbury Social Rights Campaign, and former chairman, University Labour Club, Kent. APEX.

Miss Joyce Arram, legal executive, contested the seat in 1970, and South-East Essex, 1966. B March, 1935; ed Camden High School for Girls, North Western Polytechnic, Holborn College of Law.

HILLINGDON Uxbridge
major

Electorate 59,510

*Shersby, J. M. (C)	20,542
Sykes, Miss A. M. P. H. (Lab)	18,127
Pincham, J. S. (L)	10,150
C majority	2,415

	1974			1974
Total Vote	48,819	Lab		37·1%
Turnout	82·4%	L		20·8%
C	42·1%	C maj		4·9%

Mr Michael Shersby held the seat for the Conservatives in the 1972 by-election. Director, British Sugar Bureau. B February, 1933; ed John Lyon School, Harrow-on-the-Hill. Joint Secretary, Conservative Party Industry Committee since 1972. Member, Paddington Borough Council, 1959-64 and Westminster City Council, 1964-71. (Deputy Lord Mayor, 1967-68.)

Miss Manuela Sykes contested the seat for Labour at the by-election in 1972, and for the Liberals Falmouth and Camborne, 1966, Ipswich, 1964, 1959 and the 1957 by-election, and Finchley, 1955. Lecturer, writer and public relations adviser. B January, 1925; ed Richmond County School for Girls and University College, London.

Mr John Pincham, insurance broker. B May, 1932; ed Wimbledon Park Primary School, Kingston Grammar School. Fellow, Chartered Insurance Institute. Principle shareholder, JS Pincham & Co. Ltd., international insurance/re-insurance brokers.

HITCHIN major

Electorate 72,144

Stewart, I. (C)	27,222
Mallalieu, Miss A. (Lab)	23,204
Beavan, D. (L)	10,824
Bianchi, P. (Ind)	467
C majority	4,018

	1974		1974
Total Vote	61,717	L	17·5%
Turnout	85·5%	Ind	0·7%
C	44·1%	C maj	6·5%
Lab	37·6%		

Mr Ian Stewart, banker, director of Brown Shipley & Co Ltd. Fought Hammersmith, North, 1970. B January, 1935; ed Haileybury and Jesus College, Cambridge. Director, British Numismatic Society since 1965. Treasurer, Westminster Committee for Protection of Children since 1961.

Miss Ann Mallalieu, barrister. B November, 1945; ed Holton Park Girls' Grammar School, Wheatley, Oxon, Newnham College, Cambridge; first woman President of the Union. Daughter of Mr J. P. W. Mallalieu, MP for Huddersfield, East, since 1945. TGWU.

Mr David Beavan, journalist. B August, 1951; ed Stowe School and Essex University. NUJ.

HOLLAND WITH BOSTON minor

Electorate 79,774   1970: 77,184

*Body, R. (C)	30,561
Cornish, M. (Lab)	18,180
Stephenson, G. R. (L)	15,466
C majority	12,381

No change

	1970		1974
Total Vote	57,821		64,207
Turnout	74·8%		80·5%
C	33,580	58·1%	47·6%
Lab	24,241	41·9%	28·3%
L	—	—	24·1%
C maj	9,339	16·1%	19·3%
Swing		+7·8%	+1·5%

Mr Richard Body, elected in 1966, represented Billericay from 1955-59. Contested Leek in 1951, Rotherham, 1950, and Abertillery by-election, 1950. Barrister (Middle Temple, 1949) and farmer. B May, 1927; ed Reading School. Former officer of Conservative backbench sub-committee on horticulture; chairman, Open Seas Forum since 1970.

Mr Michael Cornish contested Lowestoft in 1966, Saffron Walden in 1964 and the by-election in 1965. Editor of an industrial magazine. B June, 1937; ed grammar school, King's College, Cambridge, and University College of Wales. Member, West Suffolk County Council since 1964 and leader of Labour group; elected, 1973, to new county council, deputy leader of Labour group. Deputy general secretary, Fabian Society 1968-73.

Mr Ray Stephenson, solicitor. B January, 1925; ed Horncastle Grammar School and London University. Member, GLC since 1973. Former branch secretary of NALGO.

HONITON major

Electorate 72,606

*Emery, P. F. H. (C)	32,429
Howell, V. (L)	18,306
Newitt, M. D. D. (Lab)	8,791
C majority	14,123

	1974		1974
Total Vote	59,526	L	30·7%
Turnout	82·0%	Lab	14·8%
C	54·5%	C maj	23·7%

Mr Peter Emery, Under-Secretary for Energy 1974; Under-Secretary for Trade and Industry, 1972-74, with responsibility for industry. Returned at by-election in 1967. An Opposition spokesman on Treasury, economic affairs and trade, 1964-65. Elected for Reading in 1959; defeated in 1966; contested Poplar, 1951, and Lincoln, 1955. Joint founder and first secretary of Bow Group. Manufacturer. B February, 1926; ed Scotch Plains, New Jersey, and Oriel College, Oxford. Served on Hornsey Borough Council for eight years (deputy mayor, 1957-58). Director of Institute of Purchasing and Supply, 1961-72, and Phillips Petroleum Companies in United Kingdom,

1964-72; Secretary-General, European Federation of Purchasing, 1962-72. Chairman, Consultative Council of Professional Management Organizations, 1967-72.

Mr Victor Howell, director/partner in family building firm. Teacher. B August, 1945; ed Kelly College, Tavistock, Whitelands Teacher Training College, Putney and Exeter Technical College. Member, Exeter City Council since 1970 and Exeter District Council since June 1973.

Mr Malyn Newitt, university lecturer, contested the seat in 1970. B January, 1940; ed Winchester College and Balliol College, Oxford.

HORNCASTLE same

Electorate 49,528.   1970: 46,959

*Tapsell, P. H. B. (C)	19,344
Miller, R. (L)	12,555
Berry, A. J. R. (Lab)	6,791
Iszatt, E. P. (Ind Dem All)	367
C majority	6,789

No change

	1970		1974
Total Vote	34,866		39,057
Turnout	74·2%		78·8%
C	19,299	55·3%	49·5%
Lab	8,860	25·4%	17·4%
L	6,707	19·2%	32·1%
Ind Dem All	—	—	0·9%
C maj	10,439	29·9%	17·4%
Swing		+6·6%	+1·1%

Mr Peter Tapsell was elected in 1966. MP for Nottingham, West, 1959-64; contested Wednesbury, 1957 by-election. Partner in a firm of stockbrokers. B February, 1930; ed Tonbridge School and Merton College, Oxford. Former member, Advisory Council of the Midland Region of the BBC, and council of the Tennyson Society. Personal assistant to the then Prime Minister, Sir Anthony Eden, during 1955 election campaign.

Mr Roger Miller, industrial relations executive, tobacco and joint proprietor of a pipe company. B February, 1938; ed Harrow School and Trinity College, Oxford. Contested Horncastle, 1970. Citizen of London and Liveryman of the Carpenters Company.

Mr Tony Berry, lecturer at Northampton College of Technology and a counsellor with the Open University. B May, 1942; ed Wandsworth Comprehensive School, Southampton and Cambridge universities. Northampton district councillor and chairman, Finance Committee, 1973.

HORSHAM & CRAWLEY major

Electorate 89,910

*Hordern, P. M. (C)	31,802
Leighton, R. (Lab)	25,028
Gill, A. (L)	18,167
C majority	6,774

	1974			1974
Total Vote	74,997		Lab	33·4%
Turnout	83·4%		L	24·2%
C	42·4%		C maj	9·0%

Mr Peter Hordern, MP for Horsham 1964-74, was elected in 1964. Chairman Conservative parliamentary committee on finance 1970-72. Member Public Accounts Committee, 1969. Member of London Stock Exchange and company director. B April, 1929; ed Geelong Grammar School, Australia, and Christ Church, Oxford. Joint vice-chairman, Conservative finance committee, from March 1974. Member, executive, 1922 Committee.

Mr Ronald Leighton, a printer, born January, 1930, ed elementary and Ruskin College. Contested Middleton and Prestwich, 1964.

Mr Tony Gill, export consultant, contested Horsham, 1970. B May, 1936; ed St Helen's College, Thames Ditton.

HOUGHTON-LE-SPRING major

Electorate 59,315

*Urwin, T. W. (Lab)	34,263
Ritchie, R. C. (C)	10,300
Lab majority	23,963

	1974			1974
Total Vote	44,563		C	23·1%
Turnout	75·1%		Lab maj	53·8%
Lab	76·9%			

Mr Thomas Urwin, Minister of State, Local Government and Regional Planning, 1969-70; Minister of State, Department of Economic Affairs, 1968-69. Elected in 1964. B June, 1912; elementary education. Houghton-le-Spring Urban Council, 1949-65, chairman, 1954-55. Formerly full-time organizer, Amalgamated Union of Building Trade Workers, 1954-64; branch officer, 1933-54. Sponsored by AUBTW.

Mr Richard Ritchie. B September, 1949; ed Harrow School and Ealing School of Business and Social Studies. Engaged in marketing department of oil company; Spelthorne district councillor.

HOUNSLOW Brentford & Isleworth
major

Electorate 71,451

*Hayhoe, B. J. (C)	22,690
*Barnes, M. C. J. (Lab)	21,964
Blackburn, D. C. (L)	9,502
Benford, T. (Nat Front)	1,741
C majority	726

	1974			1974
Total Vote	55,897	L		17·0%
Turnout	78·2%	Nat Front		3·1%
C	40·6%	C maj		1·3%
Lab	39·3%			

Mr Barney Hayhoe was MP for Heston and Isleworth from 1970-74; contested Lewisham, South, 1964. Mechanical engineer. B August, 1925; ed elementary school and Stanley Technical School, South Norwood. Vice-chairman, Conservative Group for

Europe, and member, executive committee and general purposes committee, European Movement. Secretary, Conservative employment committee, 1970-71, and member, Select Committee on Race Relations and Immigration, 1971-73. Vice-chairman, Young Conservatives, 1951-53; area chairman, Conservative Political Centre, 1962-64; vice-chairman, Conservative Party International Office, since 1973.

Mr Michael Barnes, MP for Brentford and Chiswick, 1966-74. Contested Wycombe, 1964. Marketing consultant. B September, 1932; ed Malvern College and Corpus Christi College, Oxford, Chairman, PLP social security group, 1969-70; member, Public Accounts Committee since 1967; Chairman, ASTMS Parliamentary Committee, 1970-71.

Mr David Blackburn, merchant and investment banker and company director.

Mr Thomas Benford, local government officer. B July 1936; ed Plaistow Grammar School.

HOUNSLOW Feltham & Heston
major

Electorate 79,364

*Kerr, R. W. (Lab)	27,519
Ground, R. P. (C)	19,464
Quinn, J. A. (L)	10,952
Reid, Mrs J. (Nat Front)	2,653
Lab majority	8,055

	1974			1974
Total Vote	60,588	L		18·1%
Turnout	76·3%	Nat Front		4·4%
Lab	45·4%	Lab maj		13·3%
C	32·1%			

Mr Russell Kerr, an air charter executive, was MP for Feltham, 1966-74. Contested Horsham, 1951, Merton and Morden, 1959, and Preston, North, 1964. B February, 1921; ed Shore School, Sydney, and Sydney University. Former chairman of the Tribune group of

Labour backbenchers; director Tribune Publications Ltd. National executive member, ASTMS, 1964-73. Member, Select Committee on Nationalized Industries since 1967; vice-chairman since 1970. Member, PLP Northern Ireland and aviation groups. War-time member of RAF pathfinder force.

Mr Patrick Ground is a barrister. Member, Hammersmith Council, chairman, health and social services committees, 1968-71. B August, 1932; ed Beckenham and Penge County Grammar School, Selwyn College, Cambridge, and Magdalen College, Oxford (former president, Oxford University Conservative Association).

Mr John Quinn, industrial security officer. B September, 1932; ed Beckett Grammar School, Nottingham. Member, Hounslow Education Advisory Committee; member, Mayor's Charity Committee.

Mrs Josephine Reid, housewife. B October, 1915; ed Lomond Grove School, Camberwell. Contested GLC elections in 1973.

HOVE
same

Electorate 73,423.   1970: 74,789

*Sainsbury, T. (C)	30,451
Wilson, D. (L)	18,942
Wallis, R. A. (Lab)	6,374
Budden, E. (Nat Front)	442
C majority	11,509

No change

	1970		1974
Total Vote	49,926		56,209
Turnout	66·7%		76·5%
C	34,287	68·7%	54·2%
Lab	15,639	31·3%	11·3%
L	—	—	33·7%
Nat Front	—	—	0·8%
C maj	18,648	37·3%	20·5%
Swing		+2·9%	+2·7%

1973 by election: Total vote 46,166 (62·3%)—C 22,070 (47·8%), L 17,224 (37·3%), Lab 5,335 (11·6%), Nat Front 1,409 (3·0%), Comm 128 (0·3%)—C maj 4,846 (10·5%)

Mr Timothy Sains-bury, director of J. Sainsbury, Ltd, was elected at the 1973 by-election. B June, 1932; ed Eton and Worcester College, Oxford. Member, Public Expenditure Committee.

Mr Des Wilson, jour-nalist, director of Shelter, 1967-71. Con-tested Hove, 1973 by-election. B March, 1941 in New Zealand.

Mr Ronald Wallis contested the seat in the 1973 by-election. Member, Eastbourne Borough Council since 1972 and Brighton District Council and East Sussex County Council since 1973. B November, 1947; ed Brighton Secondary Modern School. Post Office clerical assistant. APEX and CPSA.

Mr Edward Budden, engineering worker, aged 47. Brighton area organizer, Na-tional Front.

HOWDEN   minor

Electorate 56,672.   1970: 54,592

*Bryan, Sir P. E. O. (C)	21,892
Haywood, S. (L)	15,681
Kirkwood, J. (Lab)	7,259
C majority	6,211

No change

	1970		1974
Total Vote	38,774		44,832
Turnout	70·8%		79·1%
C	22,102	57·0%	48·8%
Lab	9,567	24·7%	16·2%
L	6,951	17·9%	35·0%
Ind	154	0·3%	—
C maj	12,535	32·3%	13·8%
Swing		+4·3%	+0·1%

Sir Paul Bryan, Min-ister of State for Em-ployment 1970-72, has been chairman of the Conservatives' back-bench employment committee since 1973. Elected in 1955. B August, 1913; ed St

John's School, Lea-therhead, and Gon-ville and Caius Col-lege, Cambridge. As-sistant whip, 1956; a Lord Commissioner of the Treasury, 1958-61. Contested Sow-erby 1951, 1950 and 1949 (by election). Director, Granada Television and Greater Manchester Independent Radio Limited. Vice-chairman of the Conservative Party Organization, 1961-65. Member, Sowerby Bridge UDC, 1947-50.

Mr Stuart Haywood, university lecturer, contested the seat in 1970. B September, 1936; ed Queen Elizabeth's Grammar School, Mansfield, and Hull University. Leader of Liberals on Beverley District Council.

Mr James Kirkwood, secretary, Driffield Trades Council; member, Driffield Urban Council and AUEW.

HUDDERSFIELD East   same

Electorate 53,163.   1970: 54,496

*Mallalieu, J. P. W. (Lab)	20,224
Taylor, C. J. H. (C)	12,920
Lee, M. (L)	8,530
Mear, N. (Nat Front)	796
Drake, A. (Comm)	246
Lab majority	7,304

No change

	1970		1974
Total Vote	41,138		42,716
Turnout	75·5%		80·3%
Lab	20,629	50·1%	47·3%
C	15,632	38·0%	30·2%
L	4,569	11·1%	20·0%
Comm	308	0·8%	0·6%
Nat Front	—	—	1·9%
Lab maj	4,997	12·1%	17·1%
Swing		+7·7%	−2·5%

Mr J. P. W. Malla-lieu, Minister of State, Ministry of Technology 1968-69; Minister of State, Board of Trade, 1967-68; Minister of Defence for the Royal Navy, 1966-67, and Under-Secretary, 1964-66. Elected for Huddersfield in 1945 and returned for East

division in 1950. Journalist and author.

B June, 1908; ed Cheltenham College, Trinity College, Oxford, and University of Chicago; President of Oxford Union in 1930 and a rugby blue. NUJ.

Mr Cyril Taylor, founder president, American Institute for Foreign Study, responsible for its activities outside USA. B May, 1935; ed St Marylebone Grammar School, London, Trinity Hall, Cambridge, and Harvard Business School. Deputy chairman, Kensington Conservative Association.

Mr Malcolm Lee, co-ordinator of post-graduate studies in education. B 1933; ed Kirkburton Secondary Modern School, Millhouse Secondary Modern School, Huddersfield College of Technology and Westminster College, London. Contested Huddersfield, 1966 and 1970. National Vice-chairman, Teachers in Colleges and Departments of Education.

Mr Norman Mear, chartered engineer, aged 59.

Mr Tony Drake, teacher of economics at comprehensive school in Huddersfield. Aged 24; ed Wadham College, Oxford. Chairman and education organizer, Huddersfield branch, Communist Party. NUT.

HUDDERSFIELD West same

Electorate 53,176. 1970: 53,107

*Lomas, K. (Lab)	17,434
Stansfield, J. M. (C)	16,804
Hasler, Mrs K (L)	9,790
Lab majority	630

No change

	1970		1974
Total Vote	41,094		44,028
Turnout	77·4%		82·8%
Lab	16,866	41·0%	39·6%
C	16,673	40·6%	38·2%
L	6,128	14·9%	22·2%
Nat Front	1,427	3·5%	—
Lab maj	193	0·5%	1·4%
Swing		+5·2%	−0·5%

Mr Kenneth Lomas, elected in 1964, contested Macclesfield in 1955 and Blackpool, South, in 1951. Former assistant regional Transfusion Service, 1955-64. B November, 1922; ed Ashton-under-Lyne council and modern schools. Former member Select Committee on Race Relations and Immigration, Speaker's Conference and Select Committee on Parliamentary Commissions.

Mr John Stansfield, schoolmaster, head of the careers department at Wheelwright Grammar School, Dewsbury. Contested Dewsbury in 1970. B February, 1938; ed Batley Grammar School and Birmingham University. Leader, Ossett Council Conservative group for four years.

Mrs Kathleen Hasler, supervisor pre-school playgroups. B March, 1939; ed Exeter University. Married to Methodist minister.

HUNTINGDONSHIRE minor

Electorate 80,124. 1970: 66,505

*Renton, Sir D. L. M. (C)	29,042
Rowe, D. (L)	19,040
Ormerod, P. A. (Lab)	17,066
C majority	10,002

No change

	1970		1974
Total Vote	50,068		65,148
Turnout	75·2%		81·3%
C	27,398	54·7%	44·6%
Lab	17,588	35·1%	26·2%
L	5,082	10·1%	29·2%
C maj	9,810	19·6%	15·3%
Swing		+3·6%	−0·6%

Sir David Renton, QC, a member of the Royal Commission on the Constitution, was Minister of State, Home Office, 1961-62; Under-Secretary, Home Office, 1958-61; and Parliamentary Secretary, Ministry of Power, 1955-58. Elected in 1945. Called to the Bar (Lincoln's Inn), 1933; QC, 1954; elected Bencher in November, 1962. B August, 1908; ed Oundle School and University College, Oxford.

Major Dennis Rowe, retired Army officer and schoolmaster. Ed Drayton Manor Grammar School, Hanwell; Larkfield teachers' training college, Dunmurry, Northern Ireland.

Mr Paul Ormerod, economist. B March, 1950; ed Manchester Grammar School, Christ's College, Cambridge, and St Catherine's College, Oxford. Member, ASTMS.

HUYTON major

Electorate 71,302

*Wilson, J. H. (Lab)	31,767
Benyon, T. (C)	16,462
Snowden, N. (L)	7,584
Smith, H. (Ind)	234
Lab majority	15,305

	1974			1974
Total Vote	56,047	L		13·5%
Turnout	78·6%	Ind		0·4%
Lab	56·7%	Lab maj		27·3%
C	29·4%			

Mr Harold Wilson, became Prime Minister again on March 4, 1974, having been Leader of the Opposition, 1970-74. Prime Minister and First Lord of the Treasury, 1964-70. Elected Leader of the Labour Party in February, 1963, after the death of Mr Hugh Gaitskell.

Unsuccessfully contested the leadership in 1960. Was principal Opposition spokesman on foreign affairs from November, 1961, and previously on Treasury subjects. Elected to the national executive of the party in 1952; chairman, 1961-62. From 1945 to 1950 represented Ormskirk; elected for Huyton in 1950. B March, 1916; ed Milnsbridge Council School, Royds Hall School, Huddersfield, Wirral Grammar School, and Jesus College, Oxford. Economic assistant to the War Cabinet Secretariat, 1940-41; director of economics and statistics, Ministry of Fuel and Power, 1943-44. Parliamentary Secretary, Ministry of Works, 1945; Secretary for Overseas Trade, March, 1946; President of the Board of Trade, September, 1947; resigned in 1951 over Labour's budgetary policy. Chairman, Public Accounts Committee, 1959-63. Chancellor, Bradford University, 1966.

Mr Thomas Benyon, banker. B 1941; ed Wellington College. Member, Bow Group.

Mr Neil Snowden, general management trainee. B June, 1949. Member, Liverpool District Council since 1973; chairman, Land Management Committee; member, Policy and Finance and Personnel Committees.

ILKESTON   same

Electorate 74,364.   1970: 74,080

*Fletcher, L. R. (Lab)		31,500
Morrell, P. R. (C)		17,320
Pool, G. (L)		11,734
Lab majority		14,180

No change

	1970		1974
Total Vote	54,988		60,554
Turnout	74·2%		81·4%
Lab	32,961	59·9%	52·0%
C	15,870	28·9%	28·6%
L	6,157	11·2%	19·4%
Lab maj	17,091	31·1%	23·4%
Swing		+4·6%	+3·8%

Mr Raymond Fletcher was elected in 1964; contested Wycombe, 1955. Journalist and author. B December, 1921; secondary education and university extra-mural classes. Sponsored by the T & GWU since 1964, member since 1954. Columnist on the *Guardian*. Chairman,

parliamentary airships group, and parliamentary branch, Labour Friends of Israel.

Mr Peter Morrell, solicitor and company director. Born May, 1944; ed Westminster School and University College, Oxford.

Mr Geoffrey Pool, lecturer. B October, 1940; ed Nottingham High School, Sheffield Teacher Training College and Leicester University.

INCE   minor

Electorate 76,630.   1970: 66,723

*McGuire, M. T. (Lab)		39,822
Dyson, J. (C)		17,063
Lab majority		22,759

No change

	1970		1974
Total Vote	47,172		56,885
Turnout	70·7%		74·2%
Lab	32,295	68·5%	70·0%
C	14,877	31·5%	30·0%
Lab maj	17,418	36·9%	40·0%
Swing		+5·1%	−1·5%

Mr Michael McGuire, elected in 1964, was wholetime NUM branch secretary (Sutton Manor Colliery, St Helens, Lancashire), 1957-64. B May, 1926; elementary education. Executive member, St Helens Trades and Labour Council, 1957-

64. Sponsored by NUM. Served on Select Committee on Nationalized Industries 1967-70 and executive, PLP trade union group.

Mr John Dyson, chartered accountant and lecturer in accountancy. B 1939; ed Arnold School, Blackpool and Liverpool University. Chairman, North West area Bow Group; member, Warrington branch of United Nations Association and Housing Centre Trust.

INVERNESS same

Electorate 57,368. 1970: 54,258

*Johnston, D. R. (L)	16,903
Henderson, R. E. (C)	11,680
Cameron, D. J. (Lab)	7,816
Gibson, R. M. (Scot Nat)	7,258
L majority	5,223

No change

	1970		1974
Total Vote	39,249		43,657
Turnout	72·3%		76·1%
L	15,052	38·3%	38·7%
C	12,378	31·5%	26·7%
Lab	9,038	23·0%	17·9%
Scot Nat	2,781	7·1%	16·6%
L maj	2,674	6·8%	12·0%
Swing			

Mr Russell Johnston, elected in 1964, was the first United Kingdom Liberal MP in the European Parliament delegation; is Liberal spokesman on foreign affairs and defence. B July, 1932; ed Portree High School, Isle of Skye, and Edinburgh University. Former teacher and research assistant with the Scottish Liberal Party. Chairman, Scottish Liberal Party since 1970; vice-president, European Liberal group, group spokesman on regional aid. Parliamentary adviser to Scottish Police Federation; member, Royal Commission on Local Government in Scotland.

Mr Robert Henderson, an advocate; has taught law at Glasgow and Edinburgh universities. B March, 1937; ed Larchfield School, Helensburgh, Morrison's Academy, Grieff, and Glasgow University. An honorary Sheriff Substitute; Standing Junior Counsel in Scotland to the Department of Trade and Industry.

Mr David Cameron, economics lecturer. B January, 1947; ed Inverness Royal Academy and Strathclyde and Manchester universities. Member ATTI.

Mr Robert Gibson is a teacher. B October, 1945; ed The High School of Glasgow; Dundee University; Dundee College of Education. Member of the party's land policy and education committees.

IPSWICH same

Electorate 86,928. 1970: 86,404

*Money, E. D. (C)	29,893
Weetch, K. T. (Lab)	29,634
Knott, Mrs J. (L)	11,857
Brown, Dr D. (Nat Dem)	1,161
C majority	259

No change

	1970		1974
Total Vote	62,864		72,545
Turnout	72·7%		83·4%
C	27,704	44·1%	41·2%
Lab	27,691	44·0%	40·8%
L	5,147	8·2%	16·3%
Nat Dem	2,322	3·7%	1·6%
C maj	13	0·0%	0·3%
Swing		+5·7%	+0·1%

Mr Ernle Money, barrister, won the seat for the Conservatives in 1970. B February, 1931; ed Marlborough College and Oriel College, Oxford. Member, general council of the Bar, 1962-66. Secretary, Conservative Parliamentary Arts and Amenities Committee, 1972-74; member, Advisory Committee on Theatres, 1974; Secretary, Committee for Association Football.

Mr Kenneth Weetch, college lecturer, contested Saffron Walden, 1970. B September, 1933; ed Newbridge Grammar School and London School of Economics. Former national executive member, National Association of Schoolmasters; member, Association of Teachers in Colleges and Departments of Education.

Mrs Joan Knott, housewife. B May, 1921; ed Glendale Grammar School, London. Contested Great Yarmouth, 1970. Member, National Executive Committee of the Liberal Party.

ISLE OF ELY major

Electorate 68,794

*Freud, C. R. (L)	27,647
Stevens, J. (C)	19,300
Ferris, M. (Lab)	9,478
L majority	8,347

	1974		1974
Total Vote	56,425	C	34·2%
Turnout	82·0%	Lab	16·8%
L	49·0%	L maj	14·8%

Mr Clement Freud won the seat for the Liberals at the 1973 by-election. Writer and Broadcaster. Consultant and director to hotel and restaurant companies. B April, 1924; ed Dartington Hall and St Paul's School. Liberal spokesman on education since 1973.

Mr John Stevens, a stockbroker, contested the Isle of Ely by-election, July,

1973, and Birmingham, Stechford, 1970. B March, 1938; ed University College School, Hampstead, and Bristol University. Senior vice-chairman, Federation of University Conservative and Unionist Associations, 1963-64. Personal assistant to Mr Edward Heath, 1966-68.

Mr Michael Ferris, agricultural engineer. B January, 1938; ed grammar school and technical college. Member, Norwich City Council. ASTMS.

ISLE OF WIGHT   same

Electorate 85,211. 1970: 80,537

Ross, S. (L)	34,808
*Woodnutt, H. F. M. (C)	27,042
Bisson, T. C. (Lab)	7,495
L majority	7,766

Liberal gain

	1970		1974
Total Vote	58,038		69,345
Turnout	72·0%		81·4%
C	30,437	52·4%	39·0%
Lab	13,111	22·6%	10·8%
L	12,883	22·2%	50·2%
Vectis Nat	1,607	2·8%	—
C maj	17,326	29·8%	—
L maj	—		11·2%
Swing		+5·1%	−0·8%

Mr Stephen Ross, chartered surveyor and farmer; contested the seat, 1970, and 1966. B July, 1926; ed Bedford School. Isle of Wight county councillor and chairman policy and resources committee. Appointed Liberal spokesman on local government and planning, March 1974.

Mr Mark Woodnutt was elected in 1959. Chartered secretary and company director. B November, 1918; ed Isleworth Grammar School. Member, Isle of Wight County Council, since 1952; county alderman, 1957. Member, all-party Anglo-Czechoslovakia group; all-party tourists and resorts group. Vice-chairman all-party hover group.

Mr Tony Bisson, contested Bournemouth, East and Christchurch, 1970. Teacher. B December, 1935; ed Newport (I.o.W.) Secondary Grammar School, Borough Road College of Education, Isleworth, and Open University. President, Eastleigh branch NUT, 1969.

ISLINGTON Central   major

Electorate 45,094

*Grant, J. D. (Lab)	15,687
Devonald-Lewis, R. (C)	6,996
Stuart, I. (L)	6,447
Lab majority	8,691

	1974			1974
Total Vote	29,130	C		24·0%
Turnout	64·6%	L		22·1%
Lab	53·8%	Lab maj		29·8%

Mr John Grant, MP for Islington East, 1970-74, was an Opposition spokesman on broadcasting and other media. Contested Beckenham in 1966. Former journalist. B October, 1932; ed grammar school and Stationers' Company's School, Hornsey. Member, Select Committee on Expenditure; member PLP Committees on employment, posts and telecommunications, environment, economics and finance; Parliamentary consultant to Civil and Public Services Association, NUJ and TGWU. *Appointed Parliamentary Secretary, Civil Service Department, March 1974.*

Mr Richard Devonald-Lewis, mortgage broker; contested Islington, East, 1970. B January, 1940; ed Bryanston School and Royal Marines Officers' Training School. Islington borough councillor, 1968-71.

Mr Ian Stuart, cargo-handler. Chairman, Joint Shop Stewards Liaison Committee. B March, 1926; ed Lewes Grammar School. Contested Uxbridge, 1972 by-election. Former member, Liberal Party Finance and Administration Board, 1971-73. Former chairman, Association of Liberal Trade Unionists, 1971-73.

ISLINGTON North   major

Electorate 41,202

*O'Halloran, M. J. (Lab)	13,332
Wolfson, G. M. (C)	6,704
Davenport, M. (L)	4,503
Score, J. (Nat Front)	871
Fallon, D. (Lab and Dem)	570
Lab majority	6,628

	1974			1974
Total Vote	25,980	L		17·3%
Turnout	63·0%	Nat Front		3·3%
Lab	51·3%	Lab & Dem		2·2%
C	25·8%	Lab maj		25·5%

Mr Michael O'Hallo-
ran was returned at
the by-election in Oc-
tober, 1969. Building
worker. B August,
1928; ed elemen-
tary school. Former
member, Islington
Borough Council.
TGWU.

Mr Geoffrey Wolfson,
head of personnel,
Hambros Bank. B
1934; ed King's School, Bruton, Eton
and Pembroke College, Cambridge. Lieutenant commander in Royal Navy reserve
special branch; head of youth services,
Industrial Society, 1966-69.

Mr Michael Davenport, division head,
European Economic Commission. B
August, 1940; ed Abbey School, Fort
Augustus, University of Edinburgh, Uni-
versity of Pennsylvania.

Mr John Score, hairdresser. B July, 1941;
ed Sir Phillip Magnus Technical College.

ISLINGTON South and Finsbury
major

Electorate 41,869

*Cunningham, G. (Lab)	15,064
Szemerey, J. (C)	6,473
Adams, R. (L)	5,415
Betteridge, Mrs M. (Comm)	492
Lomas, A. (Ind)	293
Lab majority	8,591

	1974			1974
Total Vote	27,737	L		19·5%
Turnout	66·2%	Comm		1·8%
Lab	54·3%	Ind L		1·0%
C	23·3%	Lab maj		31·0%

Mr George Cunning-
ham was MP for Is-
lington South-West
from 1970-74; con-
tested Henley, 1966.
B June, 1931; ed
Dunfermline High
School, Blackpool
Grammar School and
Manchester Univer-
sity. Commonwealth
officer for Labour
Party. Member, Se-

lect Committee on Overseas Development,
1973-74; and Expenditure Committee,
1971-74. TGWU.

Mr John Szemerey, journalist and senior
executive with European Commission,
Brussels. Contested Islington, South-West,
1970. Former Islington Borough councillor. B August, 1940; ed Uppingham,
Hotchkiss School Conn, USA, and London University.

Mr Robin Adams, director of research,
commodity research unit. B September,
1946; ed Falcon College, Essexvale, Rhodesia, Magdalen College, Oxford.

Mrs Marie Betteridge contested Islington, South-West in 1970. Executive member, Islington Committee for Community
Relations. APEX.

JARROW
minor

Electorate 54,265   1970: 54,652

*Fernyhough, E. (Lab)	27,740
Bolam, Mrs. B. (C)	13,848
Lab majority	13,892

No change

	1970		1974	
Total Vote	40,708		41,588	
Turnout	74·4%		76·6%	
Lab	25,861	63·5%	66·7%	
C	14,847	36·5%	33·3%	
Lab maj	11,014	27·0%	33·4%	
Swing		+4·1%	−3·2%	

Mr Ernest Ferny-
hough was Parliamen-
tary Secretary, Minis-
try of Labour, 1967-
68, and Under-Secre-
tary, Department of
Employment and Pro-
ductivity, 1968-69. Re-
turned at a by-elec-
tion, 1947. Former
miner. Full-time offi-
cial, National Union
of Distributive and
Allied Workers, 1935-47. B December,
1908; elementary education.

Mrs Beatrice Bolam, teacher. B 1919;
ed Jarrow Grammar School, Newcastle
College of Education. Jarrow borough
councillor for 28 years; contested the seat
1950, 1951.

KEIGHLEY
same

Electorate 51,284. 1970: 51,140

Cryer, G. R. (Lab)	18,595
*Hall, Miss J. V. (C)	17,717
Whittaker, W. K. (L)	7,820
Binns, J. (Soc Dem)	348
Lab majority	878

Labour gain

	1970		1974	
Total Vote	41,298		44,480	
Turn-out	86·7%		86·7%	
C	20,957	50·7%	39·8%	
Lab	20,341	49·2%	41·8%	
L	—		17·6%	
Social Dem	—		0·8%	
C maj	616	1·5%		
Lab maj	—		2·0%	
Swing		+5·7%	−1·7%	

Mr Robert Cryer is a technical college teacher. Member, Keighley Borough Council since 1971. B December, 1934; ed Salt High School, Shipley and Hull University. Member TGWU and ATTI.

Miss Joan Hall, a secretary, won the seat for the Conservatives in 1970; contested Barnsley in 1966 and 1964. B August, 1935; ed Queen Margaret's School, Escrick Park, York, and Ashridge House of Citizenship, Berkhampstead. Vice-chairman, Greater London Young Conservatives, 1963. Won 1959 London Ideal Secretary competition.

Mr Wilfred Whittaker, lecturer. B January, 1946; ed Victoria County Secondary School, Morley Grammar School, Hull University, St John's College, York.

Mr John Binns, former Labour MP, represented Keighley, 1964-70. Engineer. B June, 1914; ed Holycroft Secondary School, Keighley.

KENSINGTON & CHELSEA Chelsea
major

Electorate 64,357

*Worsley, Sir M. (C)	23,320
Clarke, N. (L)	8,012
Ward, Mrs S. (Lab)	6,839
Barclay, J. (Ind C)	416
C majority	15,308

	1974		1974
Total Vote	38,587	Lab	17·7%
Turnout	59·9%	Ind C	1·1%
C	60·4%	C maj	39·7%
L	20·8%		

Sir Marcus Worsley was elected for Chelsea in 1966. MP for Keighley, 1959-64; contested Keighley, 1955. Farmer, landowner, director of an investment trust. B April, 1925; ed Eton and New College, Oxford. Programme assistant BBC European Service, 1950-53. Chairman, Conservative Health and Social Security Committee since 1972; chairman, Greater London committee of Conservative MPs since 1972. Second Church Estates Commissioner since 1970. Member, Select Committee on Tax Credit Scheme; executive, 1922 Committee.

Mr Nicholas Clarke, restaurateur. B March, 1933; ed Eton.

Mrs Susan Ward, a community worker and former conciliation officer with Race Relations Board. B September, 1949; ed St James' School, West Malvern; Oxford University. Member, Wandsworth Borough Council since 1972. ACTSS.

KENSINGTON & CHELSEA
Kensington   major

Electorate 60,856

*Rhys Williams, Sir B. M. (C)	18,425
Tilley, J. V. (Lab)	13,293
Lefever, Dr R. (L)	8,270
C majority	5,132

No change

	1974		1974
Total Vote	39,988	Lab	33·2%
Turnout	65·7%	L	20·7%
C	46·1%	C maj	12·8%

Sir Brandon Rhys Williams, an industrial consultant, represented Kensington, South, 1968-74. Member, European Parliament, since 1973. Contested Pontypridd, 1959 and Ebbw Vale, 1960 by-election and 1964. B November, 1927; ed Eton. Chairman of the National Birthday Trust. Assistant director (appeals) Spastics Society, 1962-63. Formerly with ICI Ltd. Former vice-chairman, parliamentary health and social security committee; former secretary, parliamentary finance committee. Rapporteur for economic and monetary union in European Parliament.

Mr John Tilley, journalist. B June, 1941. Member, Wandsworth Borough Council since 1971. NUJ.

Dr Robert Lefever, medical practitioner. B March, 1937; ed Mill Hill School, Corpus Christi College, Cambridge, Middlesex Hospital, Royal College of Music. Member, British Medical Association and of Equity.

KETTERING
major

Electorate 84,981

*de Freitas, Sir G. (Lab)	31,659
Reed, G. D. (C)	21,872
Haigh, A. J. W. (L)	15,393
Lab majority	9,787

	1974			1974
Total Vote	68,924	C		31·7%
Turnout	81·1%	L		22·3%
Lab	45·9%	Lab maj		14·2%

Sir Geoffrey de Freitas, elected in 1964, was High Commissioner in Kenya until September, 1964, when he resigned to re-enter politics. MP for Nottingham, Central, 1945-50 and Lincoln until 1961. High

Commissioner in Ghana, 1961; appointed High Commissioner to proposed East African Federation, 1963. Under-Secretary for Air, 1946-50, and Under-Secretary, Home Office, 1950-51. B April, 1913; ed Haileybury and Clare College, Cambridge (president of Union, athletic blue), and Yale University, Barrister (Cholmeley Scholar) 1937. President, Assembly of Council of Europe, 1966-69. President of Gauche Européenne. Former chairman, Labour Group for Europe.

Mr George Reed, solicitor; member Berkshire County Council, 1970-73. B December, 1935; ed Canford School and St John's College, Cambridge. Former vice-chairman Windsor and Maidenhead Conservative Association. Member, Berkshire County Council 1970-73.

Mr James Haigh contested the seat in 1970, Bromley as nuclear disarmament candidate in 1964, and Birmingham, Ladywood, as Fellowship Party candidate, 1969 by-election. Schoolteacher. B December, 1937; ed Marlborough, and Leeds and Oxford universities.

KIDDERMINSTER minor

Electorate 78,398. 1970: 72,360

Bulmer, J. E. (C)	27,065
Jones, R. H. (Lab)	18,380
Batchelor, A. J. (L)	18,230
C majority	8,685

No change

	1970		1974
Total Vote	53,466		63,675
Turnout	73·8%		81·2%
C	27,667	51·7%	42·5%
Lab	18,297	34·2%	28·9%
L	7,502	14·0%	28·6%
C maj	9,370	17·5%	13·6%
Swing		+5·4%	−1·9%

Mr Esmond Bulmer, director of H. P. Bulmer Ltd, cider makers. B May, 1935; ed Rugby and Kings College, Cambridge. Member, National Farmers Union.

Mr Reginald Jones, solicitor. Aged 43; ed grammar school. Member, Kidderminster Borough Council, 1971-73.

Mr Anthony Batchelor, a senior lecturer; leader of Liberals on Kidderminster Borough Council and Wyre Forest District Council. Contested Worcestershire, South, 1964. B April, 1941; ed King Charles I School, Kidderminster, Birmingham Polytechnic University College, London and Keele University.

KILMARNOCK major

Electorate 59,898

*Ross, W. (Lab)	23,544
Ross, K. A. (C)	13,817
MacInnes, A. (Scot Nat)	7,644
Wight, A. J. (L)	4,878
Lab majority	9,727

	1974			1974
Total Vote	49,883	Scot Nat		15·3%
Turnout	83·3%	L		9·8%
Lab	47·2%	Lab maj		19·5%
C	27·7%			

Mr William Ross, chief Opposition spokesman for Scotland 1970 to 1974; was Secretary of State for Scotland, 1964-70. Won the seat at a by-election in 1946; contested Ayr Burghs in 1945. Schoolmaster. B April, 1911; ed Ayr Academy and Glasgow University. Chairman Regional Economic Advisory Council for Scotland 1965-70. Hon Fellow EIS. *Appointed Secretary of State for Scotland, March 1974.*

Mr Kenneth Ross, solicitor. B April, 1949; ed Hutcheson's Boys Grammar School and Edinburgh University. President, Edinburgh University Union, 1970-71.

Mr Alastair MacInnes, an engineering surveyor, contested Kilmarnock, 1970. B July, 1927; ed Glenwood High School, Durban, and in Aberdeen. Member, Kilmarnock Town Council 1966-69.

Mr Archibald Wight, garage and motor agent, fought the seat in 1970. B December, 1931; ed Biggar High School, Lanarkshire. Member, executive, Scottish Liberal Party; former member, Darvel Burgh Council, 1965-70.

KINGSTON UPON HULL Central
major

Electorate 64,167

*McNamara, J. K. (Lab)	26,855
Carver, P. W. J. (C)	19,236
Lab majority	7,619

	1974			1974
Total Vote	46,091		C	41·7%
Turn-out	71·8%		Lab maj	16·5%
Lab	58·3%			

Mr Kevin McNamara was MP for Kingston upon Hull, North, 1966-74; contested Bridlington, 1964. Vice-chairman, Parliamentary Labour Party committee on Northern Ireland. Lecturer in law. B September, 1934; ed St Mary's College, Crosby, and Hull University. Former member, Public Accounts Committee, Statutory Instruments Committee. Secretary, National Association of Labour Student Organizations, 1956-57. Sponsored by TGWU.

Mr Peter Carver, a farmer. B June, 1938; ed Uppingham School. Member, East Riding County Council since 1971; former member, North Cave Parish Council. Deputy chairman, Howden Conservative Association, 1972-73.

KINGSTON UPON HULL East
major

Electorate 83,006

*Prescott, J. L. (Lab)	41,300
Tod, Dr E. D. M. (C)	17,707
Lab majority	23,593

	1974			1974
Total Vote	59,007		C	30·0%
Turnout	71·1%		Lab maj	40·0%
Lab	70·0%			

Mr John Prescott was an official of the National Union of Seamen. Elected in 1970; contested Southport in 1966. Agent at Chester in 1964. B May, 1938; ed Grange Secondary Modern School, Ellesmere Port, Ruskin College, Oxford, and University of Hull. Sponsored by NUS. Member Select Committee on Nationalized Industries.

Dr David Tod, medical practitioner; former Wandsworth councillor. B March, 1930; ed Hymers College and Edinburgh University.

KINGSTON UPON HULL West
minor

Electorate 58,946. 1970: 59,511

*Johnson, J. (Lab)	20,719
Taylor, C. M. K. (C)	12,788
Silverwood, I. (L)	8,497
Lab majority	7,931

No change

	1970		1974
Total Vote	38,587		42,004
Turnout	64·8%		71·2%
Lab	24,050	62·3%	49·3%
C	14,537	37·7%	30·4%
L	—		20·2%
Lab maj	9,513	24·6%	18·9%
Swing		+2·5%	+2·8%

Mr James Johnson was returned in 1964; represented Rugby, 1950-59. Teacher and lecturer. B September, 1908; ed Duke's School, Alnwick, and Leeds and London Universities. Chairman, PLP Commonwealth committee since 1968; and of the fisheries committee since 1965. Member of the executive, Commonwealth Parliamentary Association. Has served on Coventry City Council and Fabian Society executive. Was overseas officer for NUGMW, organizing African trade unions of local government workers and civil servants in Kenya. Sponsored by NUGMW.

Mr Maxwell Taylor, a chartered accountant; computer manager, salary administrator and Common Market coordinator for Unigate Ltd. Fought Chester-le-Street, 1966. B April, 1937; ed Eton and Trinity College, Cambridge. Member, Westminster City Council.

Mr Trevor Silverwood, inshore fisherman. B December, 1929; ed Barnsley Holgate Grammar School. Contested Bridlington, 1966 and 1970. Member, Bridlington Borough Council since 1966, North Wolds District Council since 1973.

KINGSTON UPON THAMES
Kingston upon Thames   same

Electorate 58,951.   1970: 59,737

*Lamont, N. H. S. (C)	23,006
Wells, S. (L)	12,699
Mullin, C. J. (Lab)	11.369
Christie, M. J. (Anti EEC)	288
C majority	10,307

No change

	1970		1974
Total Vote	41,338		47,362
Turnout	69·2%		80·3%
C	23,426	56·7%	48·6%
Lab	13,090	31·7%	24·0%
L	4,822	11·7%	26·8%
Anti-EEC	—	—	0·6%
C maj	10,336	25·0%	21·8%
Swing		+3·6%	-0·2%

1972 by-election: Total vote 31,877—C 16,679 (52·3%), Lab 9,892 (31·0%), L 3,601 (11·3%), Ind C 1,705 (5·4%) —C maj 6,787 (21·3%).

Mr Norman Lamont, a merchant banker, was returned at a by-election in May, 1972; contested East Hull in 1970. Secretary, Conservative Parliamentary Health and Social Security Committee, 1972-74. B May, 1942; ed Loretto School and Fitzwilliam College, Cambridge. President, Cambridge Union, 1964. Chairman, Bow Group, 1971-72. Joint secretary, Conservative finance committee, from March 1974.

Mr Stephen Wells contested the seat in 1970 and in by-election, 1972. Managing director, market research company. B September, 1946; ed Worcester Royal Grammar School and Chelsea College, London University.

Mr Chris Mullin, freelance journalist, contested North Devon, 1970. B December, 1947; ed Hull University. Member, Society for Anglo-Chinese Understanding. NUT and ASTMS.

KINGSTON UPON THAMES
Surbiton   same

Electorate 45,828.   1970: 47,661

*Fisher, Sir N. T. L. (C)	17,176
Brooke, D. (L)	10,676
Mackinlay, A. S. (Lab)	9,813
C majority	6,500

No change

	1970		1974
Total Vote	33,561		37,665
Turnout	70·4%		82·2%
C	17,359	51·7%	45·6%
Lab	10,469	31·2%	26·0%
L	4,027	12·0%	28·3%
Ind	1,706	5·1%	—
C maj	6,890	20·5%	17·2%
Swing		+2·3%	-0·4%

Sir Nigel Fisher, a company director, is chairman of All-Party East Africa Group of Commonwealth Parliamentary Association, and member of the Executive Committee of CPA. Spokesman on Commonwealth Affairs, 1964-66, and Under Secretary, Commonwealth Relations and Colonies, 1963-64; Under Secretary for the Colonies, 1962-63. Elected for Surbiton, 1955; represented Hitchin, 1950-55; contested Chislehurst 1945. Member, executive 1922 Committee and former member of Conservative Party national executive committee. B July, 1913; ed Eton and Trinity College, Cambridge.

Mr David Brooke, managing director of a retail house furnishing group. Leader, opposition group, borough of West Ham since 1965. B October, 1920; ed Chalkwell Hall School and Southend Municipal College.

Mr Andrew Mackinlay, local government officer. B April, 1949; ed Tolworth Catholic Primary School, Surbiton, and Salesian College, Chertsey. Member, Kingston-upon-Thames Borough Council since 1971.

KINGSWOOD   major

Electorate 55,488

Walker, T. W. (Lab)	18,616
Irving, C. G. (C)	16,975
Aspinwall, J. H. (L)	12,471
Lab majority	1,641

	1974			1974
Total Vote	48,062		C	35·3%
Turnout	86·6%		L	25·9%
Lab	38·7%		Lab maj	3·4%

Mr Terence Walker, an accountant. B October, 1935; ed Clarks Grammar School, Bristol. Member TGWU.

Mr Charles Irving, company director and director of public relations for Dowty group of companies, contested Bilston 1970. Former hotel kitchen boy. Member of Cheltenham Borough Council and Gloucestershire County Council since 1948. Mayor, Cheltenham 1958-60, 1971-72. B May, 1926; ed Lucton School and Cheltenham Grammar School. Chairman of regional council for South Wales and Severnside. Member, National Council for the Care and Resettlement of Offenders. Founder and chairman, National Victims Association.

Mr Jack Aspinwall, company director. B February, 1933; ed Prescot Grammar School, Lancashire, Marconi College, Chelmsford. Elected Avon County Council, April, 1973.

KINROSS & WEST PERTHSHIRE
minor

Electorate 35,020. 1970: 33,944

*Douglas-Home, Sir A. (C)	14,356
Murray, D. C. (Scot Nat)	6,274
Barrie, D. (L)	3,807
Skene, D. G. (Lab)	2,694
C majority	8,082

No change

	1970		1974	
Total Vote	25,159		27,131	
Turnout	74·0%		77·5%	
C	14,434	57·4%	52·9%	
Scot Nat	4,670	18·6%	23·1%	
Lab	3,827	15·2%	9·9%	
L	2,228	8·8%	14·0%	
C maj	9,764	38·8%	29·8%	
Swing		+0·0%	+0·4%	

Sir Alec Douglas-Home, Secretary of State for Foreign and Commonwealth Affairs 1970-74, was Prime Minister from October 19, 1963, until the general election in October, 1964. Resigned as Leader of the Conservative Party on July 22, 1965, and became chief spokesman on external affairs. The last party leader chosen by "the customary process of consultation" which he replaced with an election procedure. When he became Prime Minister he was the fourteenth Earl of Home. On October 23, 1963, he disclaimed all his titles under the Peerage Act, 1963, and the new session was postponed from October 29 to November 12 to enable him to contest the by-election at Kinross on November 6. As Lord Home he had been Secretary of State for Foreign Affairs from July, 1960; Lord President of the Council and Leader of the House of Lords from 1957; Secretary of State for Commonwealth Relations, 1955-60. B July, 1903; ed Eton and Christ Church, Oxford. As Lord Dunglass was MP for South Lanark, 1931-45, when

he succeeded to the Earldom. Parliamentary Private Secretary to Mr Neville Chamberlain, 1935-40. Under Secretary, Foreign Office in the 1945 caretaker Government; Minister of State, Scottish Office, 1951-55. Appointed to Shadow Cabinet as Chief Opposition spokesman on Foreign and Commonwealth affairs and Europe, March 1974.

Mr Duncan Murray, hill farmer. B 1916; ed Hymers College, Hull, and Oriel College, Oxford. County councillor and chairman of Badenoch District Council. Former Indian civil servant; served and travelled in Tibet, Kashmir and North-West Frontier before returning to Strathspey in 1950.

Mr David Barrie, a teacher; treasurer and secretary, Glasgow University Liberal Club. Chairman, North Glasgow Young Liberals. B 1947; ed Coatbridge High School and Glasgow University (President of Union, 1970). ETS.

Mr Danus Skene, hotelier. B April, 1944; ed Sussex University and Chicago University. ASTMS.

KIRKCALDY
major

Electorate 60,251

*Gourlay, H. P. H. (Lab)	22,469
Bell, A. (C)	13,087
Knox, R. (Scot Nat)	12,311
Lab majority	9,382

	1974			1974
Total Vote	47,867	C		27·3%
Turnout	79·4%	Scot Nat		25·7%
Lab	46·9%	Lab maj		19·6%

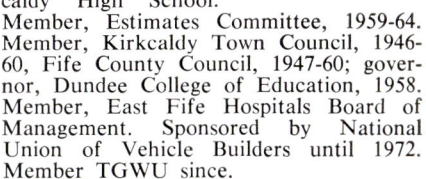

Mr Harry Gourlay, elected 1959, contested South Angus, 1955. Deputy Chairman of Ways and Means, 1968-70; a Lord Commissioner of the Treasury, 1966-68; assistant Government whip, 1964-66. Vehicle examiner. B July, 1916; ed Kirkcaldy High School. Member, Estimates Committee, 1959-64. Member, Kirkcaldy Town Council, 1946-60, Fife County Council, 1947-60; governor, Dundee College of Education, 1958. Member, East Fife Hospitals Board of Management. Sponsored by National Union of Vehicle Builders until 1972. Member TGWU since.

Mr Arthur Bell, managing director of company promoting crafts by mail order. B October, 1946; ed Brechin High School, The Royal High School, Edinburgh, and Edinburgh University. Former vice-chairman, Scottish Young Conservatives. Joint author of three books including a guide to Edinburgh pubs.

Mr Roger Knox, lecturer in computer education, Moray House College of Education, Edinburgh. Aged 31; ed St Andrew's University.

KNUTSFORD major

Electorate 54,724

*Davies, J. E. H. (C)	23,632
Lomax, B. (L)	12,542
McColgan, B. W. (Lab)	8,840
C majority	11,090

	1974		1974
Total Vote	45,014	L	27·9%
Turnout	82·2%	Lab	19·6%
C	52·5%	C maj	24·6%

Mr John Davies was Chancellor of the Duchy of Lancaster 1972-74, with special responsibility for European affairs, being Britain's continuing representative on the Council of Ministers. Secretary of State for Trade and Industry, 1970-72. Elected in 1970. Former banker and former Director General of the Confederation of British Industry. Former vice-chairman and managing director, Shell-Mex and BP; director, Hill, Samuel group. B January, 1916; ed Windlesham House School, Sussex, and St Edward's School, Oxford. Member, NEDC, 1964-69; National Joint Advisory Council, Ministry of Labour, 1964-69; British Productivity Council, 1964-69; British National Export Council, 1964-69 and Public Schools Commission, 1966-68. Member, Council of Industrial Design, 1966-70.

Mr Brian Lomax, probation officer (involved in research on the problem of battered babies). B March, 1948; ed De La Salle College, Salford, and Pembroke College, Cambridge. Contested Oldham West, 1970. Past president, Cambridge University Liberal Club.

Mr Barry McColgan, chartered accountant. Aged 27; ed secondary modern school and Hull University.

LAMBETH Central major

Electorate 48,571

*Lipton, M. (Lab)	15,954
Patten, C. F. (C)	8,585
Thwaites, E. (L)	5,226
Smart, S. (WRP)	337
Brome, E. (Marxist-Leninist)	107
Lab majority	7,369

	1974		1974
Total Vote	30,209	L	17·3%
Turnout	62·2%	WRP	1·1%
Lab	52·8%	Marx-Lenin	0·3%
C	28·4%	Lab maj	24·4%

Mr Marcus Lipton, MP for Brixton 1945-74, contested Brixton 1935. Barrister (Gray's Inn, 1926). B October, 1900; ed Bede Grammar School, Sunderland, and Merton College, Oxford. Member, House of Commons Committee on Petitions, since 1966, and of PLP committees on defence, finance, housing and local government since 1945. Alderman, Lambeth Borough Council, 1937-56; member, Stepney Borough Council, 1934-37. Chairman, Anglo-Nepalese and Anglo-Bulgarian Parliamentary groups.

Mr Christopher Patten, personal assistant to Lord Carrington. B May 1944; ed St Benedict's, Ealing, and Balliol College, Oxford. Conservative Research Department, 1966-70; Cabinet Office, 1970-72.

Mr Eric Thwaites, civil engineer, contested Islington, North in 1964, 1966 and the 1969 by-election, and Clapham, 1970. B July, 1909; ed Merchant Taylors' School.

Mr Sylvester Smart, instrument mechanic. B 1952; ed Balham County Secondary School. AUEW.

LAMBETH Norwood minor

Electorate 52,676. 1970: 53,412

*Fraser, J. D. (Lab)	17,320
Hancock, Miss B. (C)	13,298
Drake, M. (L)	6,885
Lab majority	4,022

No change

	1970		1974
Total Vote	35,073		37,503
Turnout	64·4%		71·2%
Lab	16,634	47·4%	46·2%
C	16,003	45·6%	35·4%
L	2,436	6·9%	18·3%
Lab maj	631	1·8%	10·7%
Swing		+2·0%	−4·5%

Mr John Fraser, an Opposition spokesman on the Home Office 1971-74, won the seat in 1966 and contested it in 1964. Solicitor. B June, 1934; ed Sloane Grammar School and Law Society College. NUGMW, Chairman, PLP. Greek Democratic Committee, Member, Select Committee on Education and Science, Broadacsting Proceedings of House of Commons. Vice-chairman, PLP Environment Group. Member, Lambeth Borough Council, 1962-66 and Council of London Borough of Lambeth until 1968. Founder member, Co-ownership Development Society. *Appointed Under Secretary for Employment, March 1974.*

Miss Brenda Hancock, employed by the Conservative research department, specializing in housing. B 1932, Tsingtao, China; ed St Felix School, Southwold, Bedford College, University of London. Former headmistress.

Mr Michael Drake, company director. B January, 1935. Contested GLC and borough elections. Member of ASTMS.

LAMBETH Streatham   major

Electorate 56,320

*Shelton, W. J. M. (C)	18,457
Gaffin, Mrs J. (Lab)	13,982
Silver, R. (L)	7,456
Lamb, T. (Nat Front)	937
Boaks, Lt Cdr W. G. (Ind)	45
C majority	4,475

	1974		1974
Total Vote	40,877	L	18·2%
Turnout	72·6%	Nat Front	2·3%
C	45·1%	Ind	0·1%
Lab	34·2%	C maj	10·9%

Mr William Shelton was MP for Clapham 1970-74. Chairman of an advertising agency. B October, 1929; ed Radley College, Worcester College, Oxford, and Texas University, USA. Member GLC, 1967-70; chief whip, ILEA, 1968. Joint secretary, Greater London Conservative MPs since 1972. Governor, Henry Thornton School, Clapham.

Mrs Jean Gaffin, teacher. B August, 1936; ed Stratford Grammar School, secretarial college, and London School of Economics. ATTI.

Mr Robert Silver, publisher's representative. B April, 1949; ed Wheatley Hills High School and Technical College, Doncaster.

Mr Thomas Lamb. Contested Battersea, South, 1970. Electrician. B March, 1917; ed Benfieldside Board School, Consett. Member EETPU.

LAMBETH Vauxhall   major

Electorate 46,314

*Strauss, G. R. (Lab)	16,135
Marshall, Miss M. (C)	7,494
Cousins, E. (L)	5,139
Lab majority	8,641

	1974		1974
Total Vote	28,768	C	26·0%
Turnout	62·1%	L	17·9%
Lab	56·1%	Lab maj	30·0%

Mr George Strauss, the Father of the House of Commons, was first elected for North Lambeth in 1929 (he was beaten by 29 votes in 1924). He was defeated in 1931, reelected 1934, and returned for Vauxhall after the 1950 redistribution. Parliamentary Secretary, Ministry of Transport, 1945-47, and Minister of Supply, 1947-51. Chairman, Select Committee on Members' Interests (Declaration) 1969 and member, Committee of Privileges. Chairman, PLP arts, cultural activities, leisure and sport committee. Member LCC, 1925-45. B July, 1901; ed Rugby. Retired businessman.

Miss Margaret Marshall, chartered secretary. B February, 1934; ed Laurel Bank School, Glasgow, and St Andrews University. Member, ASTMS.

Mr Edward Cousins, barrister. B October, 1943; ed Wimbledon College, Lycee Francais de Londres, Council of Legal Education, Liverpool University.

LANARK   major

Electorate 48,059

*Hart, Mrs J. C. M. (Lab)	16,823
MacDougall, A. C. S. (C)	14,723
McAlpine, T. (Scot Nat)	8,803
Lab majority	2,100

	1974		1974
Total Vote	40,349	C	36·5%
Turnout	83·9%	Scot Nat	21·8%
Lab	41·7%	Lab maj	5·2%

Mrs Judith Hart, Opposition spokesman on overseas development 1970-74; Minister of Overseas Development, 1969-70; Paymaster General, 1968-69, with seat in Cabinet; Minister of Social Security, 1967-68; Minister of State, Commonwealth Office, 1966-67; Under Secretary, Scottish Office, 1964-66. Won seat for Labour, 1959; contested Bournemouth, West, 1951; Aberdeen, South, 1955. B September, 1924; ed Royal Grammar School, Clitheroe; London School of Economics, and London University. Member, Labour Party National Executive since 1969. *Appointed Minister of Overseas Development, March 1974.*

Mr Alan MacDougall contested constituency in 1970. Insurance and mortgage broker. B August, 1934; ed Kilmarnock Academy and George Watson's College, Edinburgh. Former provost and senior magistrate.

Mr Thomas McAlpine contested Bothwell, 1970. Managing director of engineering company. B September, 1929; ed Dalziel High School, Motherwell, and Glasgow University. Member, Hamilton Council, 1960-63. Vice-chairman, Scottish National Party.

LANARKSHIRE North   major

Electorate 53,541

*Smith, J. (Lab)	21,448
Pickering, A. M. S. (C)	14,664
Watt, Mrs P. (Scot Nat)	8,187
Lab majority	6,784

	1974		1974
Total Vote	44,299	C	33·1%
Turnout	82·7%	Scot Nat	18·5%
Lab	48·4%	Lab maj	15·3%

Mr John Smith, elected in 1970, is an advocate. B September, 1938; ed Dunoon Grammar School and Glasgow University. Chairman, university Labour Club 1959-60. Contested East Fife in by-election 1961 and in 1964. Member, executive, Scottish Labour Group; Select Committee on Scottish Affairs, 1971-72. NUGMW.

Mr Alan Pickering, chairman of a new Scottish industrial group; Helensburgh councillor. B October, 1939; ed grammar school, Oxford and Cambridge Universities.

Mrs Phyllis Watt, aged 42, practising midwife.

LANCASTER   same

Electorate 49,288.   1970: 47,576

*Kellett-Bowman, Mrs M. E. (C)	17,666
Owen, D. (Lab)	15,197
Drury, A. (L)	6,898
Wallace, P. E. (Ind L)	631
Darnton, G. (Ind)	245
C majority	2,469

No change

	1970		1974
Total Vote	37,863		40,637
Turnout	79·6%		82·4%
C	18,584	49·1%	43·5%
Lab	16,843	44·5%	37·4%
L	2,436	6·4%	17·0%
Ind L	—		1·5%
Ind	—		0·6%
C maj	1,741	4·6%	6·1%
Swing		+4·9%	+0·7%

Mrs Elaine Kellett-Bowman won the seat in 1970. Barrister and farmer. Contested Buckingham, 1966 and 1964, South West Norfolk, 1959, and the 1959 by-election, and Nelson and Colne, 1955. B July, 1924; ed Queen Mary's School, Lytham; The Mount, York; and St Anne's College, Oxford. Called to Middle Temple, 1964. Alderman of Borough of Camden since 1968. Member of Press Council, 1964-68.

Mr David Owen, legal assistant, contested South Fylde, 1966. B March, 1941; ed Baines Grammar School, Poulton-le-Fylde and Manchester University. TGWU sponsored; chairman, Preston clerical branch.

Mr Anthony Drury, 47, former freelance photographer, now studying photography at Blackpool Technical College.

LEEDS East   major

Electorate 67,091

*Healey, D. W. (Lab)	25,550
Nelson, R. A. (C)	15,036
Marsh, S. (L)	9,906
Lab majority	10,514

	1974		1974
Total Vote	50,492	C	29·8%
Turnout	75·2%	L	19·6%
Lab	50·6%	Lab maj	20·8%

Mr Denis Healey, chief Opposition spokesman on Treasury matters 1972-74; chief Opposition spokesman on foreign and Commonwealth affairs, 1970-72; Secretary of State for Defence, 1964-70. Elected for Leeds, South-East, at a by-election in 1952, and
for Leeds, East, in 1955; contested Pudsey and Otley, 1945. B August, 1917; ed Bradford Grammar School and Balliol College, Oxford. Member, Labour Party national executive committee since 1970. Secretary of the Labour Party international department, 1946-52; councillor, Royal Institute of International Affairs, 1948-60; councillor, Institute of Strategic Studies, 1958-61; member of the executive of the Fabian Society, 1954-61. *Appointed Chancellor of the Exchequer, March 1974.*

Mr Anthony Nelson, a merchant banker; vice-chairman St Marylebone Conservative Association. Member, Bow Group Council. B June, 1948; ed Harrow, Christ's College, Cambridge.

Mr Sydney Marsh, group building supervisor. B March, 1941; ed at secondary school.

LEEDS North-East   major

Electorate 58,499

*Joseph, Sir K. (C)		20,822
Gunnell, J. (Lab)		13,562
Greenfield, C. (L)		8,839
Lord, C. (People)		300
C majority		7,260

	1974		1974
Total Vote	43,523	L	20·3%
Turnout	74·4%	People	0·7%
C	47·8%	C maj	16·7%
Lab	31·2%		

Sir Keith Joseph, Secretary of State for Social Services 1970-74; Minister of Housing and Local Government and Minister for Welsh Affairs, 1962-64; Parliamentary Secretary, Ministry of Housing and Local Government, 1959-61, and Minister of State,
Board of Trade, 1961-62. Former deputy chairman, Bovis Holdings Ltd. Returned at a by-election in February, 1956; contested Barons Court, 1955. B January, 1918; ed Harrow and Magdalen College,

Oxford. Called to the Bar (Middle Temple) 1946; Fellow of All Souls, 1946-60; Common Councilman and Alderman of City of London, 1946-49; founder and first chairman, Mulberry Housing Trust; a founder and first chairman, Foundation for management Education. Appointed to Shadow Cabinet, March 1974.

Mr John Gunnell, lecturer, Leeds University. B October, 1933; ed King Edward's School, Birmingham and Leeds University.

Mr Christopher Greenfield, research officer. B December 1948; ed Kingswood Grammar School, University of Leeds. Member, Leeds Metropolitan District Council since 1973.

Mr Clive Lord, probation and after-care officer in Morley, Yorkshire. Aged 39. Founder, Yorkshire area group of People.

LEEDS North-West   major

Electorate 64,511

*Kaberry, Sir D. (C)		21,995
Fenwick, L. C. K. (Lab)		15,324
Waldenberg, S. (L)		11,853
C majority		6,671

	1974		1974
Total Vote	49,172	Lab	31·2%
Turnout	76·2%	L	24·1%
C	44·7%	C maj	13·6%

Sir Donald Kaberry was elected in 1950. Member Speaker's Conference on Electoral Reform; Chairman of the Association of Conservative Clubs. Vice-chairman Conservative Party Organization, 1955-61;
chairman, Association of Conservative Clubs since 1961. Solicitor and company director. B August, 1907; ed Leeds Grammar School. Parliamentary Secretary, Board of Trade, April-October, 1955; assistant Government whip, 1952-55. Member, Leeds City Council, 1930-39 and 1946-51. Chairman, Yorkshire Conservative MPs, since 1972. Member, Select Committee on Nationalized Industries.

Mr Keith Fenwick, university lecturer in education. B May, 1941; ed Derby School, London and Manchester universities. Formerly British Council officer. AUT.

Mr Stephen Waldenberg, company accountant. B September, 1945; ed Roundhay School, Leeds and Leeds College of Commerce.

LEEDS South   major

Electorate 52,307

*Rees, M. (Lab)	21,365
Pedder, D. (L)	9,505
Harmer, P. D. (C)	7,810
Lab majority	11,860

	1974		1974
Total Vote	38,680	L	24·6%
Turnout	73·9%	C	20·2%
Lab	55·2%	Lab maj	30·7%

Mr Merlyn Rees was chief Opposition spokesman on Northern Ireland 1972-74; an Opposition spokesman on the Home Office, 1970-72. Elected to Shadow Cabinet, 1972. Under Secretary, Home Office, 1968-70; Under Secretary for Defence for the RAF, 1966-68;

Under Secretary for Defence for the Army, 1965-66. Returned at a by-election in June, 1963. Contested Harrow, East, 1955 and 1959. Economics lecturer. B December, 1920; ed Harrow Weald Grammar School, Goldsmith's College, and London School of Economics, NUT and GMWU. *Appointed Secretary of State for Northern Ireland, March 1974.*

Mr Denis Pedder, consultant microbiologist. B October, 1927; ed Church of England School for Boys, Lancaster; Municipal College, Burnley; University of Leeds. Contested Leeds, West, 1964, and 1966. Member Leeds City Council since 1969, West Yorkshire Metropolitan District Council since 1973 and Leeds District Council since 1973.

Mr David Harmer, marketing representative. B 1940; ed University College School and Leeds University. Member, Bedfordshire County Council since 1970; former member, Leighton-Linslade UDC. Former member, Young Conservative National Advisory Committee.

LEEDS South-East   major

Electorate 49,501

*Cohen, S. (Lab)	17,827
Sexton, Mrs M. (C)	8,373
Clay, Miss M. (L)	6,981
Innes, W. (Comm)	405
Lab majority	9,454

	1974		1974
Total Vote	33,586	L	20·8%
Turnout	67·8%	Comm	1·2%
Lab	53·1%	Lab maj	28·1%
C	24·9%		

Mr Stanley Cohen, British Railways clerical officer, was elected in 1970; contested Barkston Ash, 1966. B July, 1927; ed St Patrick and St Charles Roman Catholic Schools, Leeds. Alderman, Leeds City Council and member for 18 years. Sponsored by TSSA.

Mrs May Sexton contested the seat in 1970. Engaged in family bakery business. B 1924; ed Belle Vue School. Member, Leeds City Council, 1960-63 and 1965-71. Former chairman, South East Leeds Women's Advisory Committee. Member, YMCA management committee. Family Service Unit, and Council of Social Service.

Miss Margaret Clay, careers officer. B April, 1947; ed Lewes County Grammar School; universities of Sheffield and Leeds.

Mr William Innes, maintenance fitter. B July, 1946; ed Whitehill Secondary School, Glasgow. Shop steward and member district committee, AUEW.

LEEDS West   minor

Electorate 59,893. 1970: 63,442

Dean, J. (Lab)	19,436
Meadowcroft, M. (L)	15,451
Hall, Dr D. (C)	11,246
Lab majority	3,985

No change

	1970		1974
Total Vote	41,708		46,133
Turnout	65·7%		77·0%
Lab	21,618	51·8%	42·1%
C	14,749	35·4%	24·4%
L	5,341	12·8%	33·5%
Lab maj	6,869	16·5%	8·6%
Swing		+3·9%	−0·6%

Mr Joseph Dean, engineer. Aged 51. Leader of Manchester City Council; leader of Leeds District Council. Shop steward, AUEW.

Mr Michael Meadowcroft, assistance secretary, Joseph Rowntree Social Service Trust. B March, 1942; ed King George V School, Southport. Member, Leeds City Council, 1968-74, and Leeds Metropolitan

District Council and West Yorkshire Metropolitan County Council.

Dr David Hall, general practitioner, has been a Leeds City councillor since 1967. Member, Leeds metropolitan district council. Fought Colne Valley, 1966. B October, 1934; ed Shrewsbury School and Leeds University.

LEEK   major

Electorate 83,237

*Knox, D. L. (C)	31,526
Roebuck, R. D. (Lab)	25,794
Burman, R. M. (L)	11,860
C majority	5,732

	1974			1974
Total Vote	69,180		Lab	37·3%
Turnout	83·1%		L	17·1%
C	45·6%		C maj	8·3%

Mr David Knox, economist and management consultant, won the seat for the Conservatives in 1970. B 1933; ed Lockerbie and Dumfries Academies and London University. Editor, Young Conservative report on Law, Liberty and Licence. Contested Stechford, 1964

and 1966; Nuneaton by-election, 1967; Jnt Secretary, Conservative Finance Committee, 1972-73.

Mr Roy Roebuck, journalist, MP for Harrow, East, 1966-70. Contested Altrincham and Sale, 1964, and by-election, 1965. B September, 1929. Member, Select Committee on Estimates, Select Committee on Parliamentary Commissioner. NUJ and GMWU. Ed State Schools and Manchester College of Commerce.

Mr Richard Burman, a management services manager, contested the seat 1970. Leader, Liberal group, Stoke-on-Trent District Council. B August, 1930; ed Oundle, Leeds College of Technology and Regent Street Polytechnic.

LEICESTER East   major

Electorate 63,175

*Bradley, T. G. (Lab)	23,474
Reeves, K. G. (C)	22,061
Sanders, K. (Nat Front)	3,662
Lab majority	1,413

	1974			1974
Total Vote	49,197		C	44·8%
Turnout	77·9%		Nat Front	7·4%
Lab	47·7%		Lab maj	2·9%

Mr Tom Bradley was an Opposition spokesman on transport 1970-74. He was elected at a by-election in July, 1962; contested Rutland and Stamford in 1950, 1951 and 1955 and Preston, South, in 1959. Railway clerk. B April, 1926; ed Kettering Central

School. President, Transport Salaried Staffs Association since 1964; treasurer 1961-64. Member, Labour Party national executive since 1966. Sponsored by TSSA.

Mr Ken Reeves, a headmaster, fought Stoke, Central, 1966 and Southall, 1970. B June, 1932; ed Drayton Manor Grammar School, King's College, and University of London Institute of Education. Member, London Head Teachers' Association.

LEICESTER South   major

Electorate 71,939

*Boardman, T. G. (C)	22,943
Marshall, J. (Lab)	21,177
Willey, G. (L)	9,148
Kynaston, J. (Nat Front)	1,639
C majority	1,766

	1974			1974
Total Vote	54,907		L	16·7%
Turnout	76·3%		Nat Front	3·0%
C	41·8%		C maj	3·2%
Lab	38·6%			

Mr Tom Boardman, Chief Secretary to the Treasury 1974. Minister for Industry, 1972-74. Won Leicester, South-West in a by-election in November, 1967; contested the constituency in 1966 and 1964. B January, 1919; ed Bromsgrove School. Solicitor, formerly finance director,

Allied Breweries, and chairman, Chamberlain-Phipp. Ex-chairman of Parliamentary Panel of the Institute of Directors. Member, executive, 1922 committee, from March 1974.

Mr James Marshall, lecturer, contested Harborough, 1970. B March, 1941; ed Sheffield City Grammar School and Leeds University. NUAWW, ATTI and Co-operative Party.

Mr Gordon Willey, economist. B March, 1948; ed Rutherford Grammar School and Leicester University. Member, NALGO district council.

LEICESTER West   major

Electorate 64,050

*Janner, G. E. (Lab)	27,195
Simpson, A. (C)	18,543
Newcombe, W. (Nat Front)	2,579
Lab majority	8,652

	1974		1974
Total Vote	48,317	C	38·4%
Turnout	75·4%	Nat Front	5·3%
Lab	56·3%	Lab maj	17·9%

Mr Greville Janner, QC, was elected in 1970. Contested Wimbledon, 1955. B 1928; ed Bishop's College School, Quebec; St Paul's School, London; Trinity Hall, Cambridge, and Harvard Law School. President of the Cambridge Union and Chairman of the University Labour Club. Hon. Sec, Jewish Ex-Servicemen's Association. Member, Public Accounts Committee, 1970-74; Hendon, South Labour Party, and NUJ. Founder and Chairman, Committee for Homeless and Rootless People.

Mr Anthony Simpson is a barrister. B October, 1935; ed Rugby School and Magdalene College, Cambridge. Member, Oadby UDC, 1968-71.

Mr William Newcombe, butcher. B September, 1938; ed Humberstone primary school and Moat Road Secondary Grammar School.

LEIGH   same

Electorate 64,552.   1970: 64,149

*Boardman, H. (Lab)	26,310
Lewisham, Lord (C)	12,663
Pemberton, R. (L)	12,594
Lab majority	13,647

No change

	1970		1974
Total Vote	45,715		51,567
Turnout	71·3%		79·9%
Lab	26,625	58·2%	51·0%
C	15,314	33·5%	24·5%
Ratepayers	3,776	8·2%	—
L	—		24·4%
Lab maj	11,311	24·7%	26·5%
Swing		+6·3%	−0·9%

Mr Harold Boardman has represented the seat since 1945. Official of the Union of Shop, Distributive and Allied Workers. B 1907; elementary education. Member, Derby Town Council. Former chairman, Derby Labour College. Sponsored by USDAW.

Viscount Lewisham, accountant. B 1949; ed Eton and Christ Church, Oxford. President of debating and political societies at Eton; former president of the Oxford Union and Edmund Burke Society. Member, Bow Group arts and communications standing committee.

Mr Roy Pemberton, dyehouse manager. B November, 1946; ed Keighley Boys Grammar School, Beath Senior High School; Scottish College of Textiles.

LEOMINSTER   minor

Electorate 43,742.   1970: 41,719

Temple-Morris, P. (C)	16,221
Pincham, R. (L)	14,602
Lindley, C. D. (Lab)	4,172
C majority	1,619

No change

	1970		1974
Total Vote	30,413		34,995
Turnout	72·8%		80·0%
C	17,630	58·0%	46·3%
L	6,462	21·2%	41·7%
Lab	6,321	20·8%	11·9%
C maj	11,168	36·8%	4·6%
Swing		+4·0%	−1·4%

Mr Peter Temple-Morris, barrister. B February, 1938; ed Malvern and St Catharine's College, Cambridge. Contested Norwood, Lambeth, 1970, and Newport, 1964 and 1966. Member, Iran Society Council. Former chairman, Cambridge University Conservative Association. Member, Afro-Asian Expedition, 1961.

Mr Roger Pincham, stockbroker. B October, 1935; ed Kingston Grammar School. Contested Leominster, 1970. Partner, Phillips and Drew, stockbrokers.

Mr Clive Lindley, managing director of his own multiple catering firm. Aged 39; ed Lancaster University.

LEWES major

Electorate 71,631

Rathbone, J. R. (C)		30,423
Holt, M. (L)		16,166
Little, J. F. (Lab & Co-op)		10,875
C majority		14,257

	1974		1974
Total Vote	57,464	L	28·1%
Turnout	80·2%	Lab & Co-op	18·9%
C	52·9%	C maj	24·8%

Mr John Rathbone is an advertising executive. B March, 1933; ed Eton, Christ Church, Oxford, and Harvard Business School. Deputy-Chairman, Charles Barker Advertising. Director, Charles Barker and Sons Ltd. Chief Publicity and Public Relations Officer, Conservative Central Office, 1966-68.

Mr Malcolm Holt, company director. B May, 1944; ed Douai School, Woolhampton. Contested Lewes, 1970.

Mr James Little, market researcher with British Rail. B October, 1927; ed St Mary's Secondary School, Belfast. Served on five different local authorities. TSSA.

LEWISHAM Deptford major

Electorate 60,673

*Silkin, J. E. (Lab)		22,699
Cross, C. H. (C)		11,070
Steele, M. (L)		8,181
Lab majority		11,629

	1974		1974
Total Vote	41,950	C	26·4%
Turnout	69·1%	L	19·5%
Lab	54·1%	Lab maj	27·7%

Mr John Silkin, Opposition spokesman on health and social security from 1972-74 and on local government and development, 1970-72, was returned at a by-election in 1963. Solicitor. B March, 1923; ed Dulwich College, University of Wales, and Trinity Hall, Cambridge. Minister of Public Building and Works, 1969-70; Parliamentary Secretary to the Treasury, in which post he became Deputy Leader of the House, a new appointment, and Government Chief

Whip, 1966-69; Treasurer of the Household and Government deputy Chief Whip, April-July, 1966; Lord Commissioner of the Treasury, 1966; Government Whip, 1964-66. Contested St Marylebone, 1950; Woolwich, West, 1951; and Nottingham, South, in 1959. Sponsored by TGWU. *Appointed Minister for Planning and Local Government, Department of Environment, March 1974.*

Mr Cecil Cross, actor and script writer. B 1925; ed Abbey and Stanhope School and Royal Academy of Dramatic Art.

Mr Michael Steele, lobby correspondent. B October, 1936; ed Guildford Grammar School, Perth, Australia, and University College of North Staffordshire, Keele. Liberal Party chief press officer, 1966-72. NUJ.

LEWISHAM East major

Electorate 68,861

*Moyle, R. D. (Lab)		24,339
Marshall, J. L. (C)		18,033
Minter, M. (L)		10,543
Carey, C. (Ind)		269
Hansford-Miller, F. (Freedom Pty)		203
Lab majority		6,306

	1974		1974
Total Vote	53,387	L	19·7%
Turnout	77·5%	Ind	0·5%
Lab	45·6%	Freedom Pty	0·4%
C	33·8%	Lab maj	11·8%

Mr Roland Moyle represented Lewisham, North, 1966-74. Opposition spokesman on higher education, 1971-74. Lawyer and industrial relations executive. B March, 1928; ed elementary school, Bexleyheath; county school Llanidloes, Montgomeryshire; University College of Wales, Aberystwyth, Trinity Hall, Cambridge, Grays Inn. Chairman, Cambridge University Labour Club, 1953. Member, Greenwich Borough Council, 1964-66. Member, Select Committee on Race Relations and Immigration, 1968-72. Vice-chairman Parliamentary Labour Party Defence Committee, 1968-72. Sponsored by National Union of Public Employees. *Appointed Parliamentary Secretary, Ministry of Agriculture, Fisheries and Food, March 1974.*

Mr John Marshall contested Dundee, East, 1966 and 1964. Investment analyst. B 1940; ed Harris Academy, Dundee, Glasgow Academy and St. Andrew's University (President, Conservative Society). Member, Aberdeen council, 1968-70, Ealing council since 1971.

Mr Michael Minter contested Clapham, Wandsworth, 1966. Chartered accountant. Chairman of society for protection of unborn children. B June, 1937; ed Ipswich School.

Mr Charles Carey, barrister (Inner Temple, 1959). B 1937; ed St Edmund's College, Old Hall, Hertfordshire, and Trinity College, Cambridge. Free from party ties.

Mr Frank Hansford-Miller, head of Department of Mathematics, Statistics and Computer Science, Haverstock Comprehensive School, Chalk Farm, NW3. B November 1916; ed elementary school, Colfe's Grammar School, Lewisham, and London University. Member, London Borough of Lewisham Council, 1959-68. Founded John Hampden New Freedom Party in 1966.

LEWISHAM West   major

Electorate 61,870

Price, C. (Lab)	21,118
*Gummer, J. S. (C)	18,716
Eagle, J. D. (L)	7,974
Williams, P. (Nat Front)	1,000
Lab majority	2,402

	1974		1974
Total Vote	48,808	L	16·3%
Turnout	78·9%	Nat Front	2·0%
Lab	43·3%	Lab maj	4·9%
C	38·3%		

Mr Christopher Price, freelance journalist and broadcaster, represented Birmingham, Perry Barr for Labour, 1966-70. Contested Shipley, 1964. Member, Education and Science Select Committee, 1967-70. B January, 1932; ed Leeds Grammar School and Queen's College, Oxford (secretary, Labour Club, 1953). Member, Sheffield City Council, 1962-66. Editor, *New Education,* 1967-68; education correspondent, *New Statesman,* since 1968. Member, NUJ.

Mr Selwyn Gummer, a vice-chairman of the Conservative Party, won the seat for the Conservatives in 1970; contested Greenwich, 1966 and 1964. Publisher and journalist. B November, 1939; ed King's School, Rochester, and Selwyn College, Cambridge (president of the Union, 1962). Co-opted member, Inner London Education Authority, 1967-70.

Mr James Eagle, postal officer. B February, 1937; ed Leo County Secondary School. UPOW.

Mr Peter Williams, medical administrator, aged 53. Member, National Front Directorate; area organizer, S.E. London.

LICHFIELD & TAMWORTH   major

Electorate 89,000

*d'Avigdor-Goldsmid, Maj-Gen J. A. (C)	30,659
Grocott, B. J. (Lab)	28,852
Elliott, Mrs D. (L)	14,151
C majority	1,807

	1974		1974
Total Vote	73,662	Lab	39·2%
Turnout	82·8%	L	19·2%
C	41·6%	C maj	2·4%

Major General James (Jack) d'Avigdor-Goldsmid, regular Army officer for 35 years, won the seat for the Conservatives in 1970. B December, 1912; ed Harrow and Sandhurst. Member, defence sub-committee of Expenditure Committee and Speaker's Conference on Electoral Law. Vice-chairman, Conservative parliamentary defence committee, since 1972. Colonel of his former regiment, 4th/7th Royal Dragoon Guards, since 1963. Member, Jockey Club, and steward at various race meetings.

Mr Bruce Grocott contested South-West Hertfordshire, 1970. Polytechnic lecturer. B November, 1940; ed Hemel Hempstead Grammar School and Leicester and Manchester Universities. Former London County Council organization and methods officer. Member, ASTMS.

Mrs Doreen Elliott, county organizer for national charity. B October, 1932; ed Ashington Secondary Girls' School.

LINCOLN   minor

Electorate 52,897. 1970: 52,827

*Taverne, D. (Soc Dem)	14,780
Jackson, Miss M. M. (Lab)	13,487
Moran, P. M. (C)	13,299
Dem Lab majority	1,293

No change

	1970		1974
Total Vote	39,367		41,566
Turnout	74·4%		78·6%
Lab	20,090	51·0%	32·4%
C	15,340	39·0%	32·0%
Ind	3,937	10·0%	—
Social Dem	—		35·5%
Lab maj	4,750	12·1%	—
Social Dem maj	—		3·1%
Swing	—	+2·3%	

1973 by-election: Total vote 37,738 (72·5%)—Dem Lab 21,967 (58·2%), Lab 8,776 (23·3%), C 6,616 (17·5%), Dem C Against Common Mkt 198 (0·5%), Maj Rule 100 (0·3%), Ind for Hanratty Inquiry 81 (0·2%)—Dem Lab maj 13,191 (34·9%).

Mr Dick Taverne, QC, was re-elected as a Democratic MP at a by-election in 1973 after resigning from the Labour Party over policy towards the EEC. He was Financial Secretary to the Treasury, 1969-70; Minister of State, Treasury, 1968-69; Under - Secretary, Home Office, 1966-68. Returned for Lincoln in a March, 1962 by-election. Contested Putney, 1959. Barrister, called by Middle Temple, 1954. B October, 1928; ed Charterhouse; Balliol College, Oxford. Chairman, University Labour Club, 1949. WEA lecturer in international affairs, 1955-58. NUGMW. Chairman of the General Sub-Commitee of the Public Expenditure Committee, 1971-72. Member, European Parliament, since 1973.

Miss Margaret Jackson is a Labour Party research assistant. B January, 1943; ed Notre Dame High School, Norwich, and Manchester College of Science and Technology. Former experimental officer, department of metallurgy, Manchester University. TGWU.

Mr Peter Moran, solicitor. B August, 1936; ed St Edward's College, Liverpool, and Liverpool University. Clerk to Horncastle magistrates, 1967-72; president, Lincolnshire branch, Justices' Clerks' Society, 1970-72. Assistant adviser for magistrates' training courses.

LIVERPOOL Edge Hill — major

Electorate 40,706

*Irvine, Sir A. J. (Lab)	12,979
Alton, D. (L)	7,229
Perry, S. (C)	6,871
Lab majority	5,750

	1974		1974
Total Vote	27,079	L	26·7%
Turnout	66·5%	C	25·4%
Lab	47·9%	Lab maj	21·2%

Sir Arthur Irvine, QC, Solicitor General, 1967-70. Won seat in 1947 by-election; contested Kincardine and West Aberdeenshire, 1935 and 1939 as a Liberal, and Twickenham, 1945 and South Aberdeen, 1946 as Labour candidate. B July, 1909; ed Edinburgh Academy, Edinburgh University, and Oriel College, Ox-

ford; president of the union, 1932. Secretary to Lord Chief Justice, 1935-40. Called by Middle Temple, 1935; QC, 1958. Member of the Inner Temple. Recorder of Colchester, 1965-67. Chairman, Select Committee on Procedure, 1964-65.

Mr David Alton, teacher. B March, 1951; ed Edmund Campion Grammar School, Hornchurch and Christ College of Education, Liverpool. Member, Liverpool City Council since 1972; Merseyside Metropolitan District Council since 1973 and Liverpool District Council since 1973. Chairman, North West Young Liberal Federation, 1971. NUT.

Mr Stephen Perry, accountant. B 1944; ed Ellesmere College, Shropshire. Chairman, Cheshire Young Conservatives.

LIVERPOOL Garston — same

Electorate 80,103. 1970: 75,674

Loyden, E. (Lab)	25,332
Laville, N. (C)	24,651
Black, G. (L)	9,834
Lab majority	681

Labour gain

	1970		1974
Total Vote	49,837		59,817
Turnout	65·8%		74·7%
C	28,381	56·9%	41·2%
Lab	21,456	43·0%	42·3%
L	—	—	16·4%
C maj	6,925	13·9%	—
Lab maj	—	—	1·1%
Swing	—	+2·5%	-7·5%

Mr Edward Loyden, President of Liverpool Trades Council since 1966, is a port authority motor launch driver. B May 1923; elementary education. Member, Liverpool City Council since 1960; present District and Metropolitan councillor. Member of dis-

trict and national committees of the Docks/Waterways section, TGWU; branch chairman of union. Member social security appeals tribunal and mental health review tribunal.

Mr Nigel Laville is a computer consultant. Manager of Management Information and Computer Services. B 1934; ed Britannia Royal Naval College, Dartmouth. Served in Royal Navy, 1948-67.

Mr Geoffrey Black, chartered accountant. B December, 1948; ed Quarry Bank School, Liverpool.

LIVERPOOL Kirkdale major

Electorate 44,973

*Dunn, J. A. (Lab)	16,443
Gillin, J. (C)	9,918
Mahon, P. (L)	4,866
Lab majority	6,525

	1974			1974
Total Vote	31,227	C		31·8%
Turnout	69·4%	L		15·6%
Lab	52·6%	Lab maj		20·9%

Mr James Dunn, an Opposition whip, was elected in 1964. Engineer. B January, 1926; ed St Teresa's School, Liverpool, and the London School of Economics. Member, Liverpool City Council, 1958-65. Estimates Committee, 1964-70; Select Committee on Procedure, 1964-67; Episcopal Commission for International Justice and Peace, 1967-70. Secretary, Anglo-Spanish Parliamentary Group. Member of North Atlantic Assembly since 1968. President Merseyside Association for Brain Damaged Children. Member, Catholic Education Council. Sponsored by TGWU. *Appointed Lord Commissioner of the Treasury (Government Whip), March 1974.*

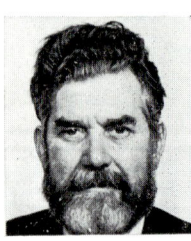

Mr James Gillin, confectioner and tobacconist. B 1921; ed Walton Lane County School, Liverpool. Member, Liverpool City Council.

Mr Paul Mahon, partner in family business (newsagents and tobacconists). B May, 1950; ed St Mary's College, Crosby, and Silesian College, Oxford. Member, Merseyside Metropolitan County Council since 1973 and Liverpool District Council since 1973.

LIVERPOOL Scotland Exchange
major

Electorate 34,823

*Parry, R. (Lab)	15,295
Charles, R. S. (C)	2,963
Mahon, D. (L)	1,596
O'Hara, R. (Comm)	505
Lab majority	12,332

	1974			1974
Total Vote	20,359	L		7·8%
Turnout	58·5%	Comm		2·5%
Lab	75·1%	Lab maj		60·6%
C	14·5%			

Mr Robert Parry, building trade worker. B January, 1933; ed Bishop Goss Roman Catholic School, Liverpool. Member of Liverpool City Council since 1963 and former full-time organizer for NUPE. Member of Co-operative Party and TGWU. Represented Liverpool Exchange, 1970-74.

Mr Ralph Charles, director of a multiple retail company of fish merchants. B 1940; ed Liverpool College. Chairman, Liverpool and District Fish Merchants Association. Member, Liverpool City Council, 1969-72. Member, South West Lancashire Valuation Panel.

Mr David Mahon, north-west organizer for Shelter. B June, 1939; ed St Mary's College, Crosby and St Joseph's College, Durham. Contested Fylde South for Labour in 1970.

Mr Roger O'Hara, engineer; contested the seat in 1970. B December, 1932; ed St Vincents De Paul and St Teresa's secondary modern school. AUEW shop steward and convenor.

LIVERPOOL Toxteth major

Electorate 45,603

*Crawshaw, R. (Lab)	14,354
Malins, H. J. (C)	8,797
Jones, T. (L)	6,678
Hunter, W. (WRP)	263
Lab majority	5,557

	1974			1974
Total Vote	30,092	L		22·2%
Turnout	66·0%	WRP		0·9%
Lab	47·7%	Lab maj		18·5%
C	29·2%			

Mr Richard Crawshaw was elected in 1964. Barrister (Inner Temple, 1948). B September, 1917; ed Pendleton Grammar School, Tatterford School, Pembroke College, Cambridge and London University. Member, Liverpool City Council, 1956-65. Member, Speaker's panel of chairmen.

Mr Humphrey Malins, solicitor. B. 1945; ed St. John's School, Leatherhead, and Brasenose College, Oxford. Chairman, Running Into Europe 1973 committee which organized a charity run from the South East to Brussels.

Mr **Trevor Jones,** President of the Liberal Party, 1972-73, is a ship's chandler. Elected to Liverpool City Council in 1968, and to the Liverpool District Council in 1973. Deputy Leader of the Liverpool Liberal Group. Member, Merseyside Metropolitan Council and leader of that Liberal Group.

Mr **William Hunter,** factory worker. Aged 53. Former member of the Revolutionary Communist Party and of the Labour Party, from which he was expelled in 1954 when a member of Islington Borough Council. AUEW.

Mr **John Watton,** accountant. B May, 1952; ed City of London School, Jesus College, Cambridge. Elected to Merseyside Metropolitan County Council and Liverpool district council in 1973.

Mr **Colin Gibbon,** garage proprietor. B May, 1936; ed Pontypridd Grammar School.

LIVERPOOL Walton   same

Electorate 51,470.   1970: 53,824

*Heffer, E. S. (Lab)	20,057
Rollins, R. W. (C)	11,841
Watton, J. (L)	4,842
Gibbon, C. (Nat Front)	647
Lab majority	8,216

No change

	1970		1974
Total Vote	36,654		37,387
Turnout	68·1%		72·6%
Lab	20,530	56·0%	53·6%
C	16,124	44·0%	31·7%
L	—	—	12·9%
Nat Front	—	—	1·7%
Lab maj	4,406	12·0%	22·0%
Swing		+1·3%	−4·9%

Mr **Eric Heffer** joined the Opposition Front Bench team on the Industrial Relations Bill, 1970-71. An Opposition spokesman on employment, 1971-73. Member, Shadow Cabinet, 1972. Elected for Walton in 1964. Carpenter and joiner. B January 1922; elementary education.

Past chairman, Huyton branch, Amalgamated Society of Woodworkers; past president, Liverpool Trades Council and Labour Party; member, Liverpool City Council, 1960-66. Member, Select Committee on Race Relations and Immigration; Select Committee on Procedure, 1965-66. Sponsored by ASW. *Appointed Minister of State for Industry, March 1974.*

Mr **Richard Rollins** contested Barrow in Furness, 1966. Property supervisor for an oil company. B March, 1938; ed Morecambe Grammar School and Liverpool University. Member, Liverpool City Council, 1960-63, and of Morecambe Borough Council since 1964. Chairman, North West Area Conservative Political Committee.

LIVERPOOL Wavertree   same

Electorate 59,186.   1970: 59,131

Steen, A. D. (C)	19,027
Levin, I. I. (Lab)	13,752
Carr, C. (L)	11,450
C majority	5,275

No change

	1970		1974
Total Vote	41,030		44,229
Turnout	69·4%		74·7%
C	19,127	46·6%	43·0%
L	11,650	28·4%	25·9%
Lab	10,253	25·0%	31·1%
C maj	7,477	18·2%	11·9%
Swing		+3·6%	−4·8%

Mr **Anthony Steen,** Lloyds Underwriter and barrister. Former lecturer in law, Council of Legal Education and Ghana High Commission. Defence counsel for Ministry of Defence, British forces. Founder of Task Force and Young Volunteer Force Foundation.

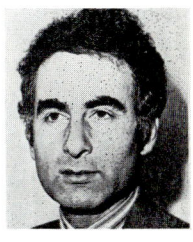

Consultant on employment and youth problems to Canadian federal and provincial governments. B 1939; ed Westminster School and University College, London. Member, Kensington Conservative Association.

Mr **Ian Levin,** solicitor. B August, 1914; ed Liverpool Collegiate School and Liverpool University. Member, Liverpool City Council, since 1946; Lord Mayor, 1970-71; alderman; chairman, Health Committee; member, Social Services, Housing and other committees. ASTMS.

Mr **Cyril Carr,** immediate past chairman of the Liberal Party, contested the seat in 1970, 1966 and 1964. Solicitor. B July, 1926; ed Liverpool College, Ridley College, Canada, and Liverpool University. Member, Liverpool City Council, since 1962; chairman and leader, Liverpool Metropolitan District Council, since 1973, Member, Merseyside Metropolitan County Council. Immediate past chairman, Association of Liberal Councillors.

LIVERPOOL West Derby same

Electorate 58,140. 1970: 60,484

*Ogden, E. (Lab)	22,689
Last, J. (C)	12,716
Gilchrist, P. (L)	5,701
Pascoe, D. (People)	388
Lab majority	9,973

No change

	1970		1974	
Total Vote	38,943		41,494	
Turnout	64·4%		71·4%	
Lab	22,324	57·3%	54·7%	
C	16.619	42·7%	30·6%	
L	—		13·7%	
People	—		0·9%	
Lab maj	5,705	14·6%	24·0%	
Swing		−0·8%	−4·7%	

Mr Eric Ogden, a former miner, was elected in 1964. B August, 1923; ed Queen Elizabeth's Grammar School, Middleton, Leigh Technical College and Wigan and District Mining and Technical College. First candidacy sponsored by Lancashire miners outside mining areas. Member, Middleton Borough Council, 1958-64. Parliamentary adviser to Council of the Pharmaceutical Society of Great Britain. Hon secretary, all-party Channel Tunnel group.

Mr John Last, food buyer for a stores chain. B 1940; ed Sutton Grammar School and Trinity College, Oxford. Member, Hoylake Urban District Council and Merseyside County Council.

Mr Phillip Gilchrist, trainee teacher. B November, 1951; ed King's School, Chester, University of York.

Mr David Pascoe, deputy head teacher. Aged 28; ed Edge Hill College. Member of Friends of the Earth.

LLANELLI same

Electorate 64,011. 1970: 64,616

*Davies, D. J. D. (Lab)	28,941
Richards, G. (C)	7,496
Evans, E. J. (L)	7,140
Williams, R. (Pl Cymru)	6,020
Hitchon, R. (Comm)	507
Lab majority	21,445

No change

	1970		1974	
Total Vote	49,999		50,104	
Turnout	77·4%		78·3%	
Lab	31,398	62·8%	57·8%	
Pl Cymru	8,387	16·8%	12·0%	
C	5,777	11·5%	15·0%	
L	3,834	7·7%	14·2%	
Comm	603	1·2%	1·0%	
Lab maj	23,011	46·0%	42·8%	
Swing		+2·5%	+4·2%	

Mr Denzil Davies, barrister, was elected in 1970. B October 1938; ed Carmarthen Grammar School and Pembroke College, Oxford University. Member Select Committees on Corporation Tax and Joint Select Committees on Delegated Legislation. Lectured at Chicago and Leeds Universities. Practises in North Wales and Chester circuits.

Mr Gywlym Richards, solicitor. B 1930; ed Llendywsul Grammar School and St Catherine's College, Oxford. Chairman, Carmarthen Conservative Association.

Mr John Evans, carpet retailer. B June, 1951; ed Pontardawe Grammar School.

Mr Raymond Williams, teacher. Ed Llanelli Boys' Grammar School, University of Wales. Former Welsh Independent Church minister and extra-mural university teacher.

Mr Robert Hitchon contested seat in 1970, 1966 and 1964. Engineering worker. B July, 1938; ed Llanelly Grammar School and Llanelli Technical College. Shop steward in local BMC factory.

LONDONDERRY same

Electorate 93,680. 1970: 90,302

Ross, W. (UUUC)	33,060
Logue, H. (SDLP)	23,670
Montgomery, M. (Repub Clubs)	4,889
Foster, R. (Lab and Trade Union)	1,162
UUUC majority	9,390

UUUC gain

	1970		1974
Total Vote	73,712		62,781
Turnout	81·6%		67·0%
UU	39,141	53·1%	—
Nat Unity	27,006	36·6%	—
Derry Lab	7,565	10·3%	—
UUUC	—		52·6%
SDLP	—		37·7%
Repub Clubs	—		7·8%
Lab & TU	—		1·8%
UU maj	12,135	16·5%	
UUUC maj	—		14·9%

Mr **William Ross** has been secretary of the Mid - Londonderry Unionist Association for the past four years. Farmer, in mid-forties. Member of Orange Order.

Mr **Hugh Logue** is an SDLP member of the N. Ireland Assembly. Aged 26, he taught for three years in St Patrick's and St Brigid's School, Londonderry, before election to the Assembly.

Mr **Michael Montgomery** is a local councillor. Aged 38. He was interned for a year from August, 1971.

Mr **Richard Foster** is a shop-owner in Londonderry. Aged 47.

LOUGHBOROUGH minor

Electorate 69,629.   1970: 63,564

*Cronin, J. D. (Lab)	22,643
Yorke, R. M. (C)	21,946
Bennett, M. (L)	14,096
Lab majority	697

No change

	1970		1974
Total Vote	50,263		58,685
Turnout	78·9%		84·3%
Lab	22,806	45·4%	38·6%
C	22,272	44·3%	37·4%
L	5,185	10·3%	24·0%
Lab maj	534	1·1%	1·2%
Swing		+6·0%	+0·0%

Mr **John Cronin** was elected in 1955. Consultant surgeon and company director. B March, 1916; ed London University. Employed by Malta Government in 1957 to report on the island's medical services, make recommendations for national health service.

Former surgeon, Royal Free and Prince of Wales Hospitals. Member, London County Council, 1950-53. Opposition whip, 1959-62. Front bench spokesman for air, 1961-62; spokesman on aviation, 1962-64. Secretary, Anglo-French Parliamentary Relations Committee, 1964-70.

Mr **Richard Yorke**, QC, contested Durham in 1966. He is a Recorder of the Crown Court and President of the Civil Aviation Review Board. B 1930; ed Solihull School, Balliol College, Oxford and Grays Inn. Called to the Bar, 1956. Member, Bar of New South Wales and High Court of Australia.

Mr **Maurice Bennett**, owner of small printing firm. B August, 1935; ed Liverpool Collegiate Grammar School. Member, Loughborough borough council and Charnwood District Council. Chairman, Loughborough and District Consumer Group.

LOUTH minor

Electorate 71,013.   1970: 67,443

*Archer, J. H. (C)	25,158
Sellick, J. (L)	15,440
Dowson, A. G. (Lab)	15,148
C majority	9,718

No change

	1970		1974
Total Vote	48,341		55,746
Turnout	71·6%		78·5%
C	25,659	53·1%	45·1%
Lab	16,403	33·9%	27·2%
L	6,279	13·0%	27·7%
C maj	9,256	19·1%	17·4%
Swing		+4·8%	−0·6%

Mr **Jeffrey Archer**, elected at by-election in 1969, is a freelance journalist. B April, 1940; ed Wellington and Oxford. Defeated Sir William (now Lord) Fiske to become youngest-ever member of Greater London Council, 1966. Chairman, Arrow Enterprises, a public relations company.

Mr **John Sellick**, company director with farming interests. B October, 1943; ed Knossington Grange, and Oakham School, Rutland.

Mr **Alan Dowson**, lecturer in liberal studies. B May, 1938; ed Boundary Road Secondary School and Constantine Technical College, Middlesbrough, Nottingham Technical College and Bath University. Member, Peterborough City Council since 1971 and Peterborough District Council since 1973. ATTI.

LOWESTOFT same

Electorate 76,396.   1970: 72,458

*Prior, J. M. L. (C)	26,157
Baker, D. A. (Lab)	22,553
Hancock, P. (L)	15,261
C majority	3,604

No change

	1970	1974
Total Vote	56,898	63,971
Turnout	78·5%	83·7%
C	28,842 50·7%	40·9%
Lab	23,319 41·0%	35·2%
L	4,737 8·3%	23·8%
C maj	5,523 9·7%	5·6%
Swing	+4·5%	−2·0%

Mr James Prior, Lord President of the Council and Leader of the House of Commons 1972-74; Minister of Agriculture, Fisheries and Food, 1970-72. Deputy Chairman, Conservative Party organization 1972-74. He was elected in 1959, and was Vice-Chairman of the Conservative Party, April to August, 1965, when he resigned to become PPS to Mr Edward Heath. Farmer and land agent. B October, 1927; ed Charterhouse and Pembroke College, Cambridge. Director, F. Lambert and Son, Ltd, 1958-70, and IDC Group 1968-70. Appointed to Shadow Cabinet as Opposition spokesman on home affairs, March 1974.

Mr Douglas Baker contested the seat, 1970. University lecturer. B June, 1931; ed Braintree County High School and London University. Member AUT and Fabian Society.

Mr Peter Hancock, deputy headmaster and counsellor, Open University. B October, 1929; ed Moseley Grammar School, Birmingham University. Suffolk County councillor.

LUDLOW   major

Electorate 48,268

*More, J. E. (C)		18,674
Robinson, E. (L)		10,687
Martin, T. G. (Lab)		9,035
C majority		7,987

	1974		1974
Total Vote	38,396	L	27·8%
Turnout	79·5%	Lab	23·5%
C	48·6%	C maj	20·8%

Mr Jasper More was Vice-Chamberlain of the Household, 1970-71, when he resigned in disagreement with government policy on EEC. Opposition whip 1964-70. Elected at a by-election in November, 1960. B July, 1907; ed Eton and King's College, Cambridge. Barrister (Lincoln's Inn and Middle Temple, 1930), landowner, farmer and forester. Intro-

duced Deer Act, 1963, to protect deer not kept in enclosed parks. Member Shropshire County Council, 1958 and since 1973; chairman, county branch, County Landowners' Association, 1955-60, and member of the headquarters executive committee.

Mr Eric Robinson, lecturer, contested Wolverhampton, South-West, 1970. B July, 1930; ed Hanley Grammar School, Stoke on Trent, Edinburgh University. Member, Shropshire County Council.

Mr Thomas Martin, businessman. B July, 1940; ed elementary school, Newry Grammar School, Queen's University, Belfast. Member, General Advisory Council of BBC. NUGMW.

LUTON East   major

Electorate 52,980

Clemitson, I. M. (Lab)		17,137
*Simeons, C. F. C. (C)		15,712
Fisher, J. (L)		9,680
Bard, J. M. (Ind)		155
Lab majority		1,425

	1974		1974
Total Vote	42,684	L	22·7%
Turnout	80·6%	Ind	0·4%
Lab	40·1%	Lab maj	3·3%
C	36·8%		

Mr Ivor Clemitson, research officer for the National Graphical Association. Aged 42; ed Old Luton Grammar School and London University. Served for three years in Sheffield as Church of England priest, and afterwards as industrial chaplain in Luton. Has taught from time to time in Luton schools and College of Technology.

Mr Charles Simeons won Luton in 1970; contested it in 1966 and 1964. Pollution control consultant. B September, 1921; ed Oundle and Queens' College, Cambridge. President, Luton, Dunstable and District Chamber of Commerce, 1967-68. Chairman, Ampthill Cheshire Home, British Empire Cancer Campaign for Research and Action for Crippled Child. Governor, Luton Industrial College. Governor, Rotary International, 1967-68.

Mr James Fisher, systems analyst with BAC. B January, 1936; ed Headlands Grammar School, Swindon and Nottingham University. Liberal group leader, Luton District Council. Liberal group chairman, Bedfordshire County Council.

Mr Jules Bard campaigned on behalf of the Committee for Prevention of Police State.

LUTON West major

Electorate 57,698

	1974			1974
Sedgemore, B. C. J. (Lab)	20,083			
Atkins, R. (C)	15,041			
Dolling, M. (L)	12,669			
Lab majority	5,042			

	1974			1974
Total Vote	47,793	C		31·5%
Turnout	82·8%	L		26·5%
Lab	42·0%	Lab maj		10·5%

Mr Brian Sedgemore, barrister. Wandsworth councillor since 1971. B March 1937; ed Hewton Primary School, Heles School, Exeter, Oxford University. Former private secretary to Mr Robert Mellish. Member, Society of Labour Lawyers, Fabian Society, National Council for Civil Liberties and Child Poverty Action Group. Chairman, Wandsworth Council for Community Relations.

Mr Robert Atkins, computer systems salesman. B February, 1946; ed Highgate School. Member Haringey Council since 1968; member, Young Conservatives National Advisory Committee and Management Committee; vice-chairman, Greater London Young Conservatives; chairman, Association of Young Conservative Councillors; member, National Union executive committee, General Purposes Committee; Haringey Community Relations Advisory Committee, Conservative group for Europe, London Europe Society and United Europe Association.

Mr Michael Dolling, taxi proprietor. B July, 1938; ed secondary school and motor engineer apprenticeship. Chairman, Luton Taxi Owners Association; member, executive committee, National Federation of Taxicab Associations.

MACCLESFIELD major

Electorate 79,487

*Winterton, N. R. (C)	32,638		
Silverman, B. H. (Lab)	18,352		
Berry, A. J. (L)	15,926		
C majority	14,286		

	1974		1974
Total Vote	66,916	Lab	27·4%
Turnout	84·2%	L	23·8%
C	48·8%	C maj	21·3%

Mr Nicholas Winterton, elected in 1971 by-election. Sales and general manager of a plant hire firm from 1960-71. Contested Newcastle - under - Lyme in October, 1969, and 1970. B March, 1938; ed Bilton Grange School and Rugby School. Member, Warwickshire County Council, 1967-72. Vice-chairman Conservative education committee; secretary, Anglo-Danish Parliamentary Group.

Mr Barry Silverman contested Ruislip-Northwood in 1970. Marketing manager. B October, 1931; ed Pinner County Grammar School. Former borough councillor. Former secretary and branch chairman, executive staffs branch, ASTMS.

Mr Anthony Berry, lecturer at Manchester University. B August, 1939; ed St Brendan's College, Bristol, and Bath, London, Seattle and Manchester Universities. Member, Disley RDC.

MAIDSTONE same

Electorate 88,871 1970: 84,440

*Wells, J. J. (C)	31,334	
Harrison, E. (L)	23,678	
Arndell, R. (Lab)	16,006	
C majority	7,656	

No change

	1970		1974
Total Vote	60,956		71,018
Turnout	72·2%		79·9%
C	31,316	51·4%	44·1%
Lab	18,473	30·3%	22·5%
L	11,167	18·3%	33·3%
C maj	12,843	21·1%	10·8%
Swing		+5·8%	+0·2%

Mr John Wells was elected in 1959; contested Smethwick, 1955. Joint vice-chairman of the Conservative backbench agricultural committee from 1970, and chairman of the party's horticultural committee 1964-67. Marine engineer, director, and owner of a horticultural business. B March, 1925; ed Heath Mount School, Hertford, Eton and Corpus Christi College, Oxford.

Mr **Edward Harrison,** journalist and broadcaster, contested Bexley, 1970. B April, 1948; ed Grenville College, Bideford, and University of Kent. NUJ.

Mr **Richard Arndell,** barrister (Middle Temple, 1968). B February, 1944; ed Trinity College, Cambridge.

MALDON   major

Electorate 61,267

Wakeham, J. (C)	22,088
Beale, R. (L)	14,866
Morris, Miss V. (Lab)	13,368
C majority	7,222

	1974		1974
Total Vote	50,322	L	29·5%
Turnout	82·1%	Lab	26·6%
C	43·9%	C maj	14·3%

Mr **John Wakeham,** a chartered accountant, contested Putney, Wandsworth 1970 and Coventry, East 1966. Director of public and private companies. B June 1932; ed Charterhouse. Member, Young Europeans Association and English Speaking Union.

Mr **Roderic Beale,** lecturer. Contested the division in 1970 and Cambridgeshire, 1966. B October, 1932; ed Culford School, Bury St Edmunds; Leighton Park School, Reading, and London School of Economics. ATTI.

Miss **Vera Morris,** economist and lecturer in economics. B June, 1936; ed grammar school and university. ASTMS.

MANCHESTER Ardwick   major

Electorate 47,544

*Kaufman, G. B. (Lab)	16,110
Hargreaves, R. H. (C)	11,215
Maffia, A. (L)	4,590
Lab majority	4,895

	1974		1974
Total Vote	31.915	C	35·1%
Turnout	67·1%	L	14·4%
Lab	50·5%	Lab maj	15·3%

Mr **Gerald Kaufman,** elected in 1970, was Parliamentary press liaison officer to the Labour Party until that year. Contested Bromley in 1955, and Gillingham, 1959. B June, 1930; ed Leeds Grammar School and Queen's College, Oxford. Assistant secretary, Fabian Society, 1954-55; former political correspondent, *New Statesman. Appointed Under Secretary, Department of Environment, March 1974.*

Mr **Ruslyn Hargreaves,** solicitor. Contested Huddersfield, West, 1966; Manchester, Moss Side 1964, 1961; Howden, 1959. B August, 1923; ed William Hulme's Grammar School and Manchester University. Secretary, Manchester Liberal Federation, 1963-66.

Mr **Anthony Maffia,** company chairman. B May, 1942; ed Our Lady of Grace Roman Catholic School and Heys Boys' Secondary Modern School.

MANCHESTER Blackley   minor

Electorate 53,644   1970: 57,917

*Rose, P. B. (Lab)	19,369
Samuel, H. (C)	13,863
Roche, H. (L)	8,155
Lab majority	5,506

No change

	1970		1974
Total Vote	40,275		41,387
Turn·ut	69·5%		77·1%
Lab	21,437	53·2%	46·8%
C	18,838	46·8%	33·5%
L	—		19·7%
Lab maj	2,599	6·4%	13·3%
Swing		+4·4%	−3·4%

Mr **Paul Rose** was elected in 1964. Former chairman, Labour Party home affairs group. Former Opposition spokesman on aviation supply and employment, including Industrial Relations Bill. B December, 1935; ed Bury Grammar School and Manchester University. Barrister (Gray's Inn 1950). Member, British delegation to Council of Europe and Western European Union, 1968-69. Former chairman, North West Sports Council.

Mr **Hugh Samuel,** solicitor, contested Lewisham, North, in 1970. B May, 1933; ed Westminster School and St John's College, Cambridge. Member, London Borough of Merton Council, 1964-69, and Wimbledon Borough Council, 1958-62.

Mr **Harry Roche,** production control manager. B April, 1921; ed St Anne's Grammar School, Liverpool. Vice-president, Licensed Victuallers' Association. JP.

MANCHESTER Central   major

Electorate 39,495

*Lever, N. H. (Lab)	15,075
Horne, C. (C)	5,071
Steed, M. (L)	4,281
Lab majority	10,004

	1974		1974
Total Vote	24,427	C	20·7%
Turnout	61·8%	L	17·5%
Lab	61·7%	Lab maj	40·9%

Mr **Harold Lever,** Opposition spokesman on European affairs, 1970-72; chairman, Public Accounts Committee, 1970-74. Elected to Shadow Cabinet 1970 and resigned in April 1972 in protest at Party's EEC policy; reelected to Shadow Cabinet in December, 1972, and

until 1974 had responsibility for company law, mergers and competition, civil aviation and shipping. Paymaster General, 1969-70, with a seat in Cabinet, serving in the Ministry of Technology with special responsibility for power matters; Financial Secretary to the Treasury, 1967-69; Under-Secretary, Department of Economic Affairs, January-August, 1967. Member, Speaker's panel of chairmen, 1964-66. B January, 1914; ed Manchester Grammar School and Manchester University. *Appointed Chancellor of the Duchy of Lancaster, March 1947.*

Mr **Christopher Horne,** chartered accountant and magazine publisher. B 1947; ed Watford Boys' Grammar School and Eton. Member, Hammersmith Borough Council, 1968-71, and chairman of the Highway Planning Committee.

Mr **Michael Steed,** university lecturer, contested the Manchester, Exchange, by-election in 1973, Truro in 1970 and the Brierley Hill 1967 by-election. B January, 1940; ed Corpus Christi College, Cambridge, and Nuffield College, Oxford. AUT.

MANCHESTER Gorton   minor

Electorate 55,450   1970: 61,563

*Marks, K. (Lab)	22,276
Waley-Cohen, S. (C)	13,300
Brooks, R. (L)	7,906
Lab majority	8,976

No change

	1970		1974	
Total Vote	44,286		43,482	
Turnout	71·9%		78·4%	
Lab	23,679	53·5%		51·2%
C	17,594	39·7%		30·6%
L	3,013	6·8%		18·2%
Lab maj	6,085	13·7%		20·6%
Swing		+3·2%		−3·4%

Mr **Kenneth Marks,** returned at a by-election in November, 1967; contested Moss Side, 1955. Headmaster. B June, 1920; ed Central High School, Manchester, Didsbury College of Education, Manchester. Vice-chairman,

Parliamentary Labour Party education group and former chairman, social security group. Opposition Whip, 1970-71. Member, Select Committee on Education and Science, 1968-70; Denton (Lancs) UDC, 1957-66 (chairman, 1962-63). NUT, member of its advisory committee for secondary schools.

Mr **Stephen Waley-Cohen** is a director of a financial publishing company and former financial journalist. B 1946; ed Wellesley House, Broadstairs; Eton College and Magdalene College, Cambridge.

Mr **Robert Brooks,** chairman and organiser of community association. B August, 1938; ed Yew Tree Secondary School, Wythenshawe. Macclesfield district councillor.

MANCHESTER Moss Side   major

Electorate 50,967

*Hatton, F. (Lab)	14,715
*Taylor, F. H. (C)	12,323
Wallace, W. (L)	7,979
Pushkin, Miss R. (Marx-Leninist)	206
Lab majority	2,392

	1974		1974
Total Vote	35,223	L	22·6%
Turnout	69·1%	Marx-Lenin	0·6%
Lab	41·8%	Lab maj	6·8%
C	35·0%		

Mr Frank Hatton, personnel officer, was elected for Manchester, Exchange, at the June, 1973, by-election; contested Manchester, Moss Side 1970. Ed Manchester Central High School. Member, Manchester City Council. Former secretary, Manchester, Exchange Labour Party. TGWU. B September 1921. Director, Manchester Ship Canal Company.

Mr Frank Taylor was returned at a by-election in 1961; contested Newcastle-under-Lyme, 1955, and Chorley, 1959. B October, 1907; ed at Rutlish School, Merton. Principal of two firms of chartered accountants. Member, Worshipful Company of Bakers, and Guild of Air Pilots, Governor of Rutlish School. Financial director, Ministry of Food, 1942-45.

Mr William Wallace, university teacher. B March, 1941; ed St Edward's School, Oxford; Kings College, Cambridge, Cornell University, US, and Nuffield College Oxford. Contested Huddersfield, West in 1970.

MANCHESTER Openshaw   minor

Electorate 42,223   1970: 50,401

*Morris, C. R. (Lab)	16,478
Rosen, A. (C)	9,021
Wood, A. (L)	4,467
Hulse, J. (Nat Front)	541
Widdall, P. (Comm)	312
Lab majority	7,457

No change

	1970		1974
Total Vote	32,245		30,819
Turnout	64·0%		73·0%
Lab	19,397	60·1%	53·5%
C	12,296	38·1%	29·3%
Comm	552	1·7%	1·0%
L	—		14·5%
Nat Front	—		1·7%
Lab maj	7,101	22·0%	24·2%
Swing		+6·1%	−1·1%

Mr Charles Morris, Parliamentary Private Secretary to Mr Harold Wilson since 1970. Treasurer of the Household (deputy Chief Government Whip), 1969-70; Whip, 1966-69. Elected in 1962, by-election; contested Cheadle, 1959. Formerly a postal and telegraph officer and member of the executive council of the Union of Post Office Workers, 1959-63. B

December, 1926; ed Brookdale Park School, Manchester. *Appointed Minister of State for Urban Affairs, Department of the Environment, March 1974.*

Mr Aubrey Rosen, lecturer on British Constitution at Metropolitan Police Cadet College, Hendon. B 1937; ed Queen's University, Belfast and London School of Economics.

Mr Arthur Wood, architectural assistant and designer/photographer. B June, 1940; ed Winnington Park School, Northwich, Manchester College of Science and Technology.

Mr John Hulse, shopkeeper. Aged 48. Secretary, Manchester branch Regimental Association; former service secretary, Beswick and Bradford British Legion.

MANCHESTER Withington   major

Electorate 57,750

Silvester, F. (C)	17,997
Moxley, S. N. M. (Lab)	13,584
McWilliam-Fowler, I. (L)	10,877
C majority	4,413

	1974		1974
Total Vote	42,458	Lab	32·0%
Turnout	73·5%	L	25·6%
C	42·4%	C maj	10·4%

Mr Frederick Silvester held Walthamstow, West for the Conservatives, 1967-70, contesting the seat 1966. Advertising executive and barrister (Grays Inn, 1957). B September, 1933; ed Sir George Monoux Grammar School, Walthamstow and Sidney Sussex College, Cambridge. Member Walthamstow Borough Counncil, 1961-65. CPC political education officer, 1957-60.

Mr Sholto Moxley, teacher. B September 1928; ed Bournemouth Grammar School and New College, Oxford. Member, Fabian Society and Co-operative Party; executive member, Socialist Educational Association.

Mr Ian McWilliam-Fowler, journalist. B June, 1939; ed Merchant Taylors School, Crosby.

MANCHESTER Wythenshawe   major

Electorate 55,306

*Morris, A. (Lab & Co-op)	26,900
Hill, Mrs J. (C)	14,462
Blond, A. (L)	6,905
Lab majority	12,438

	1974			1974
Total Vote	48,267	C		30·0%
Turnout	73·9%	L		14·3%
Lab & Co-op	55·7%	Lab & Co-op maj	25·8%

Mr Alfred Morris was elected in 1964; contested seat in 1959 and Liverpool, Garston, in 1951. Parliamentary adviser to the Police Federation. Promoted Chronically Sick and Disabled Persons Act, 1970. Received the first Lord Harding award for services to the disabled. B March, 1928; ed Manchester elementary schools, Ruskin College and St Catherine's College, Oxford and post graduate studies at University of Manchester. Chairman of the Food and Agriculture group of the Parliamentary Labour Party and Labour MPs' disablement group, both 1970-74. *Appointed Under Secretary for Disabled, Department of Health and Social Secretary, March 1974.*

Mrs Joyce Hill, member of Manchester City Council since 1968; elected to Metropolitan District Council for Manchester, 1973. Ed Loreto Convent High School, India, and St Hilary's, Wimbledon. Member, executive council, Radio Manchester.

Mr Anthony Blond, publisher. B March, 1928; ed Eton College and New College, Oxford. Contested City of Chester in 1964 for Labour Party. Company director and director of Greater Manchester Independent Radio.

MANSFIELD   same

Electorate 68,890   1970: 67,233

*Concannon, J. D. (Lab)	34,378
Thompson, H. J. (C)	18,236
Westacott, F. (Comm)	675
Lab majority	16,142

No change

	1970		1974	
Total Vote	46,209		53,289	
Turnout	68·7%		77·3%	
Lab	30,554	66·1%		64·5%
C	15,027	32·5%		34·2%
Comm	628	1·3%		1·3%
Lab maj	15,527	33·6%		30·3%
Swing		+4·2%		+1·6%

Mr Dennis Concannon, Opposition whip, 1970-74; assistant Government whip, 1968-70. Returned in 1966. Miner and official of the NUM, 1953-66. B May 1930; ed Rossington Secondary School, Doncaster Technical School, WEA, Nottingham University. Member,

Mansfield council, 1962-68. Member, Labour Party parliamentary committees on power and steel, defence, and social services. *Appointed Vice-Chamberlain of the Household, 1974.*

Mr John Thompson, state registered chiropodist. B August, 1927; ed Alfred Sutton School and Reading Technical College. Member, Luton Borough Council for four years. Chairman of governors of group of high schools.

Mr Frederick Westacott contested Mansfield 1970, 1966 and Leicester, 1950. East Midlands District Secretary, Communist Party. B September, 1917; ed Nantybwch Primary School.

MELTON   major

Electorate 81,357

Latham, M. (C)	32,239
Pick, J. (L)	19,490
Mayhew, R. W. S. (Lab)	16,228
C majority	12,749

	1974			1974
Total Vote	67,957	L		28·7%
Turnout	83·5%	Lab		23·9%
C	47·4%	C maj		18·8%

Mr Michael Latham, freelance consultant. Contested Liverpool, West Derby, 1970. B November, 1942; ed Marlborough College, King's College, Cambridge. Director and chief executive of the House Builders Federation, 1971-73 and Parliamentary Liaison Officer, National Federation of Building Trades Employees, 1967-73. Conservative Research Department, 1965-67. Member, Westminster City Council, 1968-71.

Mr John Pick, author and company director. B December, 1921; ed Sidcot School, Somerset and Emmanuel College, Cambridge. Contested the seat, 1970.

Mr Royston Mayhew, a former shoe worker. B March, 1943; ed secondary school, Ruskin College, Oxford and Sussex University.

MERIDEN   major

Electorate 96,380

Tomlinson, J. E. (Lab)	40,541
*Speed, H. K. (C)	36,056
Lab majority	4,485

	1974			1974
Total Vote	76,597		C	47·1%
Turnout	79·5%		Lab maj	5·8%
Lab	52·9%			

Mr John Tomlinson, lecturer in industrial relations, contested Walthamstow, East, 1970, and Bridlington, 1966. B August, 1939; ed Westminster City School and Co-operative College. Formerly political organizer and head of research department, AUEW. Member, Sheffield City Council, 1964-67, and Dartford Borough Council since 1970. TGWU and ATTI.

Mr Keith Speed, Under Secretary for the Environment 1972-74; assistant Government whip, 1970-72. Won seat for the Conservatives in 1968 by-election. Regular naval officer, 1947-56; sales and marketing manager and management training adviser. B March, 1934; ed Greenhill School, Evesham. Bedford Modern School, and Royal Naval Colleges, Dartmouth and Greenwich. Joined Conservative research department in 1965 with special responsibility to Mr Heath and Mr Barber on parliamentary affairs. National vice-chairman, Young Conservatives, 1963-65.

MERIONETH   same

Electorate 26,566   1970: 26,434

Thomas, D. E. (Pl Cymru)	7,823
*Edwards, W. H. (Lab)	7,235
Jones, I. A. E. (L)	4,153
Owen, R. R. (C)	3,392
Pl Cymru majority	588

Pl Cymru Gain

	1970		1974
Total Vote	22,285		22,603
Turnout	84·3%		85·1%
Lab	8,861	39·8%	32·0%
Pl Cymru	5,425	24·3%	34·6%
L	5,034	22·6%	18·4%
C	2,965	13·3%	15·0%
Lab maj	3,436	15·4%	
Pl Cymru maj	—		2·6%
Swing		+4·4%	+4·7%

Mr Dafydd Thomas, university lecturer, contested Conway, 1970. B October 1946; ed University College of North Wales. Plaid Cymru spokesman on rural development and agriculture. Member, TGWU.

Mr William Edwards, Opposition spokesman on Welsh Affairs,

1970-74. Elected in 1966; contested Flint, West in 1964. Solicitor. B January, 1938; ed Amlwch Grammar School. Sir Thomas Jones Comprehensive School, Liverpool University and the London College of Law. Visiting lecturer at Liverpool College of Commerce. Member, Historic Building Council of Wales.

Mr Iolo Jones is an audio visual aid officer for Merioneth education authority. B January 1937; ed Middle Rhymney Council School, Dolgellau Primary School and Dolgellau Grammar School.

Mr Roy Owen, administration services manager for Quinton Hazell Ltd. B November, 1941; ed John Bright School, Llandudno and Open University.

MERTHYR TYDFIL   same

Electorate 39,462   1970: 41,291

*Rowlands, E. (Lab)	20,486
Roberts, E. (Pl Cymru)	7,336
Knowles, M. (C)	2,622
Bettell-Higgins, D. (L)	1,002
Jones, A. (Comm)	369
Battersby, R. (WRP)	160
Lab majority	13,150

No change

	1970		1974
Total Vote	32,18?		31,975
Turnout	77·9%		81·0%
Ind Lab	16,701	51·9%	—
Lab	9,234	28·7%	64·1%
C	3,169	9·8%	8·2%
Pl Cymru	3,076	9·5%	22·9%
Ind Lab maj	7,467	23·2%	
L	—	—	3·1%
Comm	—	—	1·1%
WRP	—	—	0·5%
Lab maj	—	—	41·1%
Swing		+20·8%	−18·5%

1973 By-election: Total vote 32,064—Lab 15,562 (48·5%) Pl Cymru 11,852 (37·0%), C 2,366 (7·4%), Comm 1,519 (4·7%), L 765 (2·4%)—Lab maj 3,710 (11·5%).

Mr Edward Rowlands won the seat in the 1972 by-election. MP for Cardiff, North, 1966-70; Under-Secretary, Welsh Office, 1969-70. Former lecturer, Welsh College of Advanced Technology. B January, 1940; ed Rhondda Grammar School, Wirral Grammar School, King's College, London. Former member, Estimates Committee. *Appointed Under Secretary, Welsh office, March 1974.*

Mr Emrys Roberts, public relations consultant, contested the seat in 1972 by-election. Ed University College, Cardiff (President of Students' Union 1954-55).

Editor of group of South Wales local newspapers.

Mr Michael Knowles, export executive. B May, 1942; ed Clapham College. Member, Kingston-upon-Thames council; vice-chairman, housing, policy and resources committee.

Mr David Bettell-Higgins, director of a do-it-yourself business. B July 1944; ed Blackwood Secondary Modern School, Pontypool Technical College and Crosskeys Technical College.

Mr Arthur Jones contested the constituency in the 1972 by-election, and Rhondda, 1970. Toolmaker. B July, 1916; ed technical college. Former member, Merthyr Borough Council. Branch secretary, AUEW.

Mr Roy Battersby, television and film director. Aged 37; ed grammar school, University College, London and London School of Economics. Member, Central Committee of the WRP; ACTT.

MERTON Mitcham & Morden   major

Electorate 64,894

*Douglas-Mann, B. L. H. (Lab)	21,771
Harris, D. A. (C)	18,546
Spratling, P. C. (L)	10,462
French, S. E. (Comm)	507
Lab majority	3,225

	1974		1974
Total Vote	51,286	L	20·4%
Turnout	79·0%	Comm	1·0%
Lab	42·4%	Lab maj	6·3%
C	36·2%		

Mr Bruce Douglas-Mann was MP for Kensington, North, 1970-74; contested Maldon in 1966 and St Albans in 1964. Solicitor. B June, 1927; ed in Canada and Jesus College, Oxford. Vice-chairman PLP Environment Group since 1972. Member, Kensington Borough Council, 1962-65; Kensington and Chelsea Council, 1966-68.

Mr David Harris, a political correspondent of *The Daily Telegraph.* B November, 1937; ed Mount Radford School, Exeter. Member, GLC (Bromley, Ravensbourne) since 1968; chairman, GLC Thamesmead committee, 1971-73. NUJ (former chairman and secretary Parliamentary branch).

Mr Peter Spratling, commercial engineer. B October, 1936; ed Surbiton County Scondary School and Wimbledon Technical College.

Mr Sidney French, Surrey Communist Party secretary. B 1921. NUGMW.

MERTON Wimbledon   major

Electorate 70,235

*Havers, Sir R. M. O. (C)	26,542
Bill, K. (Lab)	14,329
Searby, K. (L)	13,478
Boaks, Lt-Cdr W. G. (Ind)	240
C majority	12,213

	1974		1974
Total Vote	54,589	L	24·7%
Turnout	77·7%	Ind	0·4%
C	48·6%	C maj	22·4%
Lab	26·2%		

Sir Michael Havers, QC, Solicitor-General 1972-74. Elected in 1970. B March, 1923; ed Westminster School and Corpus Christi College, Cambridge. Called to the Bar (Inner Temple), 1948. Recorder of Dover, 1962-68; Recorder of Norwich in 1968. Appointed Shadow Law Officer, March 1974.

Mr Keith Bill, journalist and author. B November, 1939; ed Woodhouse Grammar School, Finchley. Trustee of drug abuse centre.

Mr Keith Searby, contested Dorset, South, 1970. Public relations consultant. B April, 1947; ed Henbury Comprehensive School, Bristol, and Trowbridge Boys' High School. Former national vice-chairman, Young Liberals.

MIDDLETON & PRESTWICH   same

Electorate 75,968   1970: 76,750

Callaghan, J. (Lab)	24,357
*Haselhurst, A. G. B. (C)	23,840
Harrison, J. P. (L)	12,946
Lab majority	517

Labour gain

	1970		1974
Total Vote	57,193		61,143
Turnout	74·5%		80·5%
C	25,030	43·8%	39·0%
Lab	23,988	41·9%	39·8%
L	8,175	14·3%	21·2%
C maj	1,042	1·8%	—
Lab maj	—		0·8%
Swing		+4·5%	−1·3%

Mr James Callaghan is an art lecturer at a college in Manchester. Aged 47; ed secondary. Member, Middleton borough council.

Mr Alan Haselhurst won the seat for the Conservatives in 1970. An industrial executive. Chairman, Young Conservative National Advisory Committee 1966-68. B June, 1937; ed King Edward VI School, Birmingham, Cheltenham College, and Oriel College, Oxford. President, University Conservative Association.

Mr J. Philip Harrison, company director in marketing, textile and paper industries. B September 1943. Ed Moseley Hall Grammar School and Didsbury College, Manchester.

MIDLOTHIAN   minor

Electorate 88,409   1970: 76,931

*Eadie, A. (Lab)	32,220
Mowat, Dr D. (C)	20,478
McKinlay, J. G. (Scot Nat)	19,450
Lab majority	11,742

No change

	1970		1974
Total Vote	58,177		72,148
Turnout	75·4%		81·6%
Lab	30,802	52·9%	44·6%
C	18,328	31·5%	28·4%
Scot Nat	9,047	15·5%	26·9%
Lab maj	12,474	21·4%	16·3%
Swing		+4·2%	+2·6%

Mr Alexander Eadie, an Opposition spokesman on energy, is a former chairman, PLP miners' group, and of the Parliamentary power and steel group. Elected in 1966. Contested Ayr in 1964 and 1959. Former miners' agent and for 20 years in Fife local govern-

ment. B June, 1920; ed Buckhaven Senior Secondary School, Fife, and Technical College. Member, Scottish executive committee, Labour Party and joint vice-chairman of the Parliamentary Labour Party trade union group. Member, NUM. *Appointed Under Secretary for Coal, Department of Energy, March 1974.*

Dr David Mowat, physician. B November, 1948; ed Paisley and Colchester and Edinburgh University (secretary of the union).

Mr John McKinlay, contested Aberdeenshire, West, in 1970. Hospitals group domestic manager. B May, 1921; ed Exeter School and Skerry's Commercial College, Glasgow.

MONMOUTH   minor

Electorate 75,188   1970: 75,546

*Stradling Thomas, J. (C)	27,269
Thompson, F. R. (Lab)	22,707
Hando, D. (L)	11,506
Spanswick, E. H. (Pl Cymru)	930
C majority	4,562

No change

	1970		1974
Total Vote	60,831		62,412
Turnout	80·5%		84·2%
C	28,312	46·5%	43·7%
Lab	26,957	44·3%	36·4%
L	4,061	6·7%	18·4%
Pl Cymru	1,501	2·5%	1·5%
C maj	1,355	2·2%	7·3%
Swing		+3·8%	+2·5%

Mr John Stradling Thomas won the seat for the Conservatives in 1970. Assistant Government whip, 1971-73; Lord Commissioner of the Treasury (whip) **1973-74.** Contested Cardiganshire in 1966; Aberavon in 1964. Farmer. B June, 1925; ed Rugby and London

University. Member, Bow Group; Carmarthen Borough Council 1961-64. NFU council 1963-70; Select Committee on Civil List.

Mr Frank Thompson, contested Wells, 1970, and Norfolk, South, 1964. Lecturer at East Monmouthshire College of Further Education. B January, 1938; ed Magnus Grammar School, Newark and Hull University. NUT, Fabian Society and Co-operative Party.

Mr David Hando, deputy headmaster. B 1938; ed St Julian's High School; London School of Economics and the University of Wales. Contested Monmouth, 1970.

Mr Edward Spanswick, engineer. Has been a shop steward in the electricity generating industry. Convener of Plaid Cymru's Gwent Regional Council.

MONTGOMERYSHIRE same

Electorate 33,415   1970: 32,304

*Hooson, H. E. (L)	12,495
Williams-Wynne, W. R. C. (C)	7,844
Harries, P. W. (Lab)	4,888
Jones, A. (Pl Cymru)	2,274
L majority	4,651

No change

	1970		1974
Total Vote	26,573		27,501
Turnout	82·2%		82·3%
L	10,202	38·4%	45·4%
C	7,891	29·7%	28·5%
Lab	5,335	20·1%	17·8%
Ply Cymru	3,145	11·8%	8·3%
L maj	2,311	8·7%	16·9%
Swing		+3·5%	+0·5%

Mr Emlyn Hooson, QC, Leader of the Welsh Liberal Party, was elected at a by-election in April, 1962. Member Liberal Party Executive since 1964. Party spokes-man on Wales, law, and agriculture. Con-tested Conway, 1950 and 1951. Barrister (Gray's Inn, 1949),  QC 1960. Hill farmer in Montgomeryshire. B March, 1925; ed Denbigh Grammar School and University College of Wales. Chairman of former Merioneth Quarter Sessions and former member, Bar Council. Appointed Liberal spokesman on agricul-ture and prices, March 1974.

Mr William Williams-Wynne, farmer, chartered surveyor, auctioneer. B Feb-ruary, 1947; ed Abermad, Aberystwyth, and Eton.

Mr Peter Harries, lecturer. B October, 1940; ed Ebbw Vale Grammar School, University College, Cardiff, and Manage-ment Centre, Bradford University. Chair-man, Montgomeryshire ATTI and Powys liaison committee, ATTI.

Mr Arwel Jones, a teacher. Aged 38; ed Barmouth Grammar School and University College, Bangor. Member, Llandiloes Borough Council.

MORAY & NAIRN same

Electorate 41,380   1970: 39,242

Ewing, Mrs. W. M. (Scot Nat)	16,046
*Campbell, G. T. C. (C)	14,229
Smith, E. G. (Lab)	2,299
Scot Nat majority	1,817

Scot Nat gain

	1970		1974
Total Vote	28,331		32,574
Turnout	72·2%		79·8%
C	13,994	49·4%	43·7%
Scot Nat	7,885	27·8%	49·3%
Lab	6,452	22·8%	7·0%
C maj	6,109	21·6%	—
Scot Nat maj	—		5·6%
Swing		+6·3%	—

Mrs Winifred Ewing, vice-president of the SNP, won Hamilton from Labour at the by-election in Novem-ber, 1967; defeated in 1970. B July, 1929;  ed Queen's Park Senior Secondary School, Glasgow and Glasgow University. Solicitor. Lecturer in law, Scottish College of Commerce, 1954-56; secretary, Glasgow Bar Association, 1961-67. Wife of Mr Stewart Ewing, SNP candidate for Glasgow Central. Appointed SNP spokesman on EEC and home affairs, March 1974.

Mr Gordon Campbell, Secretary of State for Scotland 1970-74. Under-Secretary, Scottish Office, 1963-64; Lord Commis-sioner of the Treasury, 1962-63. Elected in 1959. B June, 1921; ed Wellington. Joined Foreign Service, 1946 and served until 1957. Seconded to Cabinet Office, 1954-56. Member of permanent delegation to United Nations, 1949-52.

Mr Edward Smith, teacher. B November, 1939; ed Elgin Academy, Aberdeen and Glasgow Universities.

MORECAME & LONSDALE same

Electorate 68,014   1970: 66,305

*Hall-Davis, A. G. F. (C)	27,704
Wates, B. N. (L)	12,948
Carron, T. (Lab)	12,782
C majority	14,756

No change

	1970		1974
Total Vote	48,150		53,434
Turnout	72·6%		78·6%
C	27,442	57·0%	51·8%
Lab	13,916	28·9%	23·9%
L	6,792	14·1%	24·2%
C maj	13,526	28·1%	27·6%
Swing		+3·0%	−0·1%

Mr Alfred Hall-Davis, assistant Government whip 1973-74. Elec-ted in 1964; contested Chorley in 1955 and 1951 and St Helen's, 1950. Former chair-man and managing director of a brewery company. B June, 1924; ed Terra Nova School, Birkdale, and Clifton College, Bris-tol.

Mr **Bernard Wates,** deputy director of education, Westmorland. B October, 1920; ed Mill Hill School; Trinity Hall, Cambridge, Department of Education, Oxford.

Mr **Terence Carron,** lecturer in further education. B March, 1937; ed St Mary's College, Crosby; Hull, London and Liverpool universities. Member, Seaforth council, Liverpool. ATTI.

MORPETH   same

Electorate 48,043   1970: 47,556

*Grant, G. (Lab)	22,026
Currey, D. (C)	8,992
Devereux, H. (L)	8,035
Lab majority	13,034

No change

	1970		1974	
Total Vote	36,166		39,053	
Turnout	76·0%		81·3%	
Lab	21,826	60·3%		56·4%
C	9,515	26·3%		23·0%
L	4,825	13·3%		20·6%
Lab maj	12,311	34·0%		33·4%
Swing		+7·4%		+0·3%

Mr **George Grant,** elected in 1970, was a miner and for eight years a conciliation officer in the NUM northern area. B October, 1924; ed elementary school, WEA and evening classes. Chairman, Bedlingtonshire Urban Council, member since 1959; Chairman and Compensation secretary, Ashington branch, NUM; chairman, Ashington Miners' Federation.

Mr **David Curry,** journalist. B June, 1944; ed Ripon Grammar School, Corpus Christi College, Oxford, Kennedy School of Government, Harvard.

Mr **Humphrey Devereux,** electricity board purchasing officer. B May, 1930; ed Marlborough College and Exeter College, Oxford. Local councillor. Member NALGO.

MOTHERWELL & WISHAW   major

Electorate 52,401

*Lawson, G. M. (Lab)	18,310
Caldwell, J. W. (C)	11,997
Nicholson, G. (Scot Nat)	7,852
Sneddon, J. (Comm)	1,066
Lab majority	6,313

	1974			1974
Total Vote	39,225	Scot Nat		20·0%
Turnout	77·1%	Comm		2·7%
Lab	46·7%	Lab maj		16·1%
C	30·6%			

Mr **George Lawson** was MP for Motherwell, 1954-74. Treasurer of the Household (Deputy Government Chief Whip), 1966-67; Lord Commissioner of the Treasury, whip, 1959-64. B July, 1906; ed St Bernard's and North Merchiston elementary schools.

Member, joint committee on delegated scottish legislation. Staff tutor with the National Council of Labour Colleges, 1937-40, and West of Scotland organizer, 1940-50. Secretary, Edinburgh Trades Council, 1950-54.

Mr **James Caldwell,** solicitor. B January, 1923; ed Glasgow University.

Mr **George Nicholson,** science teacher, contested Ross and Cromarty, 1970. Aged 42; ed Edinburgh and Aberdeen universities.

Mr **James Sneddon** contested the seat in 1970, 1966 and 1964. Stel works maintenance engineer. B Sptember, 1918; ed Calder Primary School and Dalziel High School. AUEW convenor. President, Dalziel Cooperative Society.

NANTWICH   minor

Electorate 60,676   1970: 56,880

Cockcroft, J. H. (C)	21,474
Bailey, A. E. (Lab)	16,306
Glidewell, Mrs H. (L)	11,668
C majority	5,168

No change

	1970		1974	
Total Vote	44,116		49,448	
Turnout	77·5%		81·5%	
C	20,397	46·2%		43·4%
Lab	15,124	34·3%		33·0%
L	8,595	19·5%		23·6%
C maj	5,273	11·9%		10·4%
Swing		+3·0%		−0·7%

Mr **John Cockcroft,** a leader writer for the *Daily Telegraph.* Member, Conservative Bureau Foreign Affairs Forum; Conservative Commonwealth and Overseas Council; National Association of Youth Clubs. B July 1934; ed Oundle and St John's College, Cambridge.

Mr **Adrian Bailey** contested Worcester-shire, South in 1970. Librarian. B December, 1945; ed Cheltenham Grammar School, Exeter University, and Loughborough College of Librarianship. Member, NALGO.

Mrs **Hilary Glidewell**, housewife. B November, 1923; ed St George's School, Clarens, Switzerland, and Finch College, New York. Member, Knutsford Urban Council. Former member, NUJ.

NEATH   same

Electorate 51,919   1970: 52,667

*Coleman, D. R. (Lab)	25,351
Evans, H. G. (Pl Cymru)	8,758
Walters, L. J. (C)	6,616
Lab majority	16,593

No change

	1970		1974
Total Vote	39,734		40,725
Turnout	75·4%		78·4%
Lab	28,378	71·4%	62·2%
C	6,765	17·0%	16·2%
Pl Cymru	4,012	10·1%	21·5%
Comm	579	1·4%	—
Lab maj	21,613	54·4%	40·7%
Swing		+4·6%	+4·2%

Mr **Donald Coleman**, elected in 1964, was an Opposition whip 1970-74. Member, Select Committee on Overseas Aid since 1969 and delegate Council of Europe and Western European Union since 1968. Metallurgist; sponsored by British Iron, Steel and Kin-

dred Trades Association. B September, 1925; ed Cadoxton School, Barry, and Cardiff Technical College. Tenor soloist and former member, Welsh National Opera Company. *Appointed Lord Commissioner of the Treasury (Government Whip), March 1974.*

Mr **Huw Evans**, 30, public health inspector, Neath Borough Council. Member, West Glamorgan County Council.

Mr **Leslie Walters**, analytical chemist. B 1937; ed Cowbridge Grammar School, Bridgend and Morgan Technical College. Member, Penybont RDC; Ogwr district council; chairman, Penybont, South, Conservative branch.

NELSON & COLNE   same

Electorate 47,941   1970: 49,501

*Waddington, D. C. (C)	15,692
Hoyle, E. D. H. (Lab)	15,515
Greaves, A. (L)	9,166
C majority	177

No change

	1970		1974
Total Vote	38,352		40,373
Turnout	78·2%		84·2%
C	19,881	51·8%	38·9%
Lab	18,471	48·2%	38·4%
L	—	—	22·7%
C maj	1,410	3·7%	0·4%
Swing		+7·9%	−1·5%

Mr **David Waddington, QC,** won the seat for the Conservatives at 1968 by-election; contested Heywood and Royton, 1966, Nelson and Colne, 1964, and Farnworth, 1955. Barrister (Gray's Inn, 1951), QC, 1971.

B August, 1929; ed Sedbergh School and Hertford College, Oxford. President, University Conservative Association, 1950; vice-chairman, north-west area, Young Conservatives, 1956-57. Member, Public Accounts Committee; secretary, Conservative Parliamentary legal and transport committees. Textile company director.

Mr **Eric Hoyle**, sales engineer, contested Clitheroe 1964 and Nelson and Colne 1970. B February 1929; ed Adlington School, Horwich Technical College and Bolton Technical College. Joined Labour Party, 1945. Member, national executive, ASTMS since 1968, member, since 1958.

Mr **Anthony Greaves**, teacher. B July 1942; ed Wakefield Grammar School, Hertford College, Oxford and Manchester University. Elected, Colne Borough Council, May, 1972; Lancashire County Council, April, 1973; Pendle District Council, June, 1973.

NEWARK   same

Electorate 70,734   1970: 67,947

*Bishop, E. S. (Lab)	31,586
Cargill, D. H. (C)	27,089
Lab majority	4,497

No change

	1970		1974
Total Vote	51,690		58,675
Turnout	76·1%		82·9%
Lab	26,455	51·2%	53·8%
C	25,235	48·8%	46·2%
Lab maj	1,2 :0	2·4%	7·7%
Swing		+5·4%	−2·6%

Mr Edward Bishop, an Opposition spokesman on trade, industry and aerospace, was elected in 1964. Contested Gloucestershire, South, 1955, Exeter, 1951, and Bristol, West, 1950. Assistant Government whip 1966-67. Aeronautical design draughtsman. B October, 1920; ed South Bristol Central School, Merchant Venturers' Technical College, and Bristol University. Chairman of the all-party Parliamentary Equal Rights Group. Member of Bristol City Council for 17 years.

Mr David Cargill, art gallery director and famer, contested Normanton in 1970. B April, 1936; ed Gresham's School, Holt, Norfolk.

NEWBURY major

Electorate 71,899

*McNair-Wilson, M. (C)	24,620
Clouston, D. (L)	23,419
Fletcher, Mrs C. A. (Lab)	10,035
C majority	**1,201**

	1974		1974
Total Vote	58,074	L	40·3%
Turnout	80·8%	Lab	17·3%
C	42·4%	C maj	2·1%

Mr Michael McNair-Wilson won Walthamstow, East for the Conservatives in 1969 by-election. Contested Lincoln in 1964. Chairman, Conservative parliamentary aviation committee from 1972, and joint secretary, 1969-72. B October, 1930; ed Eton. Director of firm of public relations consultants; former provincial newspaper reporter and aircraft company press officer. Brother of MP for New Forest.

Mr Dane Clouston contested the seat in 1970. Mature student, New College, Oxford. Former banker. B September, 1938; ed Marlborough College and Royal Naval College, Dartmouth.

Mrs Celia Fletcher, assistant secretary of the GLCSA. Member, Merton Borough Council since 1971. B February 1943; ed Stoke Park Grammar School, Coventry and St Mary's Teachers' Training College, Cheltenham. ASTMS.

NEWCASTLE-UNDER-LYME minor

Electorate 71,177 1970: 69,811

*Golding, J. (Lab)	28,603
Bonsor, N. (C)	22,955
Fyson, R. (L)	8,861
Rowe, S. (United Kingdom)	228
Lab majority	**5,648**

No change

	1970		1974
Total Vote	45,700		60,647
Turnout	65·5%		85·2%
Lab	22,329	48·8%	47·2%
C	20,223	44·2%	37·8%
L	1,954	4·3%	14·6%
S Dem	1,194	2·6%	
Utd Kingdom	—	—	0·4%
Lab maj	2,106	4·6%	9·3%
Swing		+9·5%	−2·4%

Mr John Golding, an Opposition whip 1970-74, was elected at the 1969 by-election. Member, Select Committee on Nationalized Industries. B March, 1931; ed City Grammar School, Chester, University College of North Staffordshire, and London School of Economics. Assistant secretary, Post Office Engineering Union. Member Select Committee on Statutory Instruments, 1969-70. *Appointed Lord Commissioner of the Treasury (Government Whip), March 1974.*

Mr Nicholas Bonsor, barrister and farmer. B December, 1942; ed Eton and Keble College, Oxford. Boxing Blue.

Mr Robert Fyson, lecturer in liberal studies and history. B March, 1940; ed Christ's Hospital and Hertford College, Oxford. Member, Newcastle-under-Lyme Borough Council since 1970; Newcastle-under-Lyme District Council, since 1973; ATTI.

NEWCASTLE UPON TYNE Central same

Electorate 25,023 1970: 31,494

*Short, E. W. (Lab)	12,182
Jack, M. (C)	4,180
Lab majority	**8,002**

No change

	1970		1974
Total Vote	19'360		16,362
Turnout	61·5%		65·4%
Lab	13,671	70·6%	74·4%
C	4,256	22·0%	25·5%
L	1,433	7·4%	—
Lab maj	9,415	48·6%	48·9%
Swing		+3·1%	−0·1%

Mr Edward Short, Deputy Leader of the Opposition, April, 1972-74, succeeding Mr Roy Jenkins. November, 1972-74 "sha-dow" leader of the House. Secretary of State for Education and Science, 1968-70, Postmaster General, 1966-68; Parliamentary Secretary to the Treasury and Government chief whip 1964-66. Elected in 1951. Former head-master of a secondary school. B December, 1912; ed Bede College, Durham. Leader of the Labour group, Newcastle City Council, 1950. Sponsored by NUT. *Appointed Lord President of the Council and Leader of the House of Commons, March 1974.*

Mr Michael Jack, export shipper with detergent manufacturing firm. Aged 27. Ed Leicester University. Chairman, Northern Area Young Conservatives; has twice contested local government elections in the area.

NEWCASTLE UPON TYNE East
same

Electorate 45,292   1970: 47,090

*Rhodes, G. W. (Lab & Co-op)	20,439
Hill, M. (C)	14,347
Lab & Co-op majority	6,092

No change

	1970		1974
Total Vote	35,444		34,786
Turnout	75·3%		76·8%
Lab & Co-op	20,612	58·1%	58·7%
C	14,832	41·8%	412%
Lab & Co-op maj	5,7 0	16·3%	17·5%
Swing		+1·6%	−0·6%

Mr Geoffrey Rhodes won the seat in 1964; contested Barkston Ash, 1955 and Battersea, South, 1959. Member of the Council of Europe 1967-70 and chairman, Labour Party national working group on higher education, 1968-72. B November, 1928 ed Cockburn High School, Leeds and Leeds University (presi-

dent of the Union, 1954). Member of Leeds City Council, 1953-58; former head of department of business studies at a technical college; broadcaster and jour-nalist, lecturer in political science.

Mr Martyn Hill, marketing executive for Procter and Gamble Ltd. B May, 1944; ed Walford Grammar School, Queen's Col-lege, St Andrew's University.

NEWCASTLE UPON TYNE North
same

Electorate 40,063   1970: 42,053

*Elliott, R. W. (C)	12,793
Eccles, R. G. (Lab)	9,813
Wood, C. (L)	6,772
C majority	2,980

No change

	1970		1974
Total Vote	28,496		29,378
Turnout	67·8%		71·9%
C	15,978	56·1%	43·5%
Lab	12,518	43·9%	33·4%
L	—	—	23·0%
C maj	3,460	12·1%	10·1%
Swing		+1·7%	−1·0%

Mr R. W. Elliott, vice-chairman of the Conservative Party Organization from 1971, was Comptroller of the Household (whip) since 1970; an Opposition whip, 1964-70. Elected at 1957 by-election; con-tested Morpeth 1955 and 1954 by-election. Farmer. B December, 1920; ed King Edward VI Grammar School, Morpeth. President of the Nor-thern area Young Conservative Council, 1953.

Mr Robert Eccles, permanent way design assistant with British Rail. B February, 1928; ed Nunthorpe Grammar School and York Technical College. Contested New-castle upon Tyne, North, 1970. Member, Rydale District Council since 1973, Flaxton RDC since 1964. Chairman, Council TSSA since 1966; chairman, management-staff joint council for British Rail (Eastern Region) since 1972.

Mr Christopher Wood, civil engineer. B December, 1940. Ed Bury Grammar School, Lancs, Durham University. Mem-ber, Bishop Auckland UDC, 1967-74. Elected, Wear Valley District Council, 1973, Durham County Council, 1973.

NEWCASTLE UPON TYNE West
same

Electorate 76,271   1970: 74,154

*Brown, R. C. (Lab)	33,829
Stewart, R. M. (C)	22,433
Lab majority	11,396

No change

	1970	1974
Total Vote	52,449	56,262
Turnout	70·7%	73·8%
Lab	30,805	58·7% 60·1%
C	21,644	41·3% 39·9%
Lab maj	9,161	17·5% 20·2%
Swing		+4·0% −1·4%

Mr Robert Brown, Opposition front bench spokesman on environment until 1974. Former vice-chairman, Parliamentary Labour Party trade union group. Parliamentary Secretary, Ministry of Transport, 1968-70. Elected in 1966. B May, 1921; ed elementary and secondary technical schools. Secretary of constituency Labour Party and election agent, 1950-66. Councillor and alderman, Newcastle City Council for 10 years. NUGMW official parliamentary panel. *Appointed Under Secretary for Social Security, Department of Health and Social Security, March 1974*

Mr Robin Stewart, barrister. B August, 1938; ed Winchester and New College, Oxford. Member, Hexham UDC, 1972-74; Tyndedale Council since 1973. Experience of international business and managerial consultancy.

NEW FOREST
major

Electorate 77,761

*McNair-Wilson, P. M. E. D. (C)	30,567
Hayes, A. (L)	19,185
Bailey, M. V. C. (Lab)	12,737
C majority	11,382

	1974		1974
Total Vote	62,489	L	30·7%
Turnout	80·4%	Lab	20·4%
C	48·9%	C maj	18·2%

Mr Patrick McNair-Wilson was vice-chairman of the Conservative fuel and power committee. Elected at 1968 by-election; represented Lewisham, West, 1964-66. Director of the London Municipal Society 1960-63. Company director. B May 1929 ed Eton. Member, Select Committee on Science and Technology, 1968-70. Brother of MP for Newbury.

Mr Andrew Hayes, health service administrator. B June, 1943 ed Merchant Taylors School, Queen's University, Belfast, and London School of Economics. Hampshire county councillor since 1973. NALGO.

Mr Malcolm Bailey, former merchant seaman, is an official and member, NUS. Member, New Forest Rural District Council for nine years. B April 1925; ed Royal Air Force School, Egypt.

NEWHAM North-East
major

Electorate 65,522

*Prentice, R. E. (Lab)	24,200
Stroud, T. J. (C)	10,869
Cohen, L. H. (L)	8,486
Redgrave, Miss V. (WRP)	760
Ross, J. M. (Int Marxist)	202
Lab majority	13,331

	1974		1974
Total Vote	44,517	L	19·1%
Turnout	67·9%	WRP	1·7%
Lab	54·4%	Int Marx	0·4%
C	24·4%	Lab maj	29·9%

Mr Reginald Prentice, Chief Opposition spokesman on employment 1971-74. Represented East Ham, North, 1957-74; contested Streatham, 1955, Croydon, North, in 1950 and 1951. In October, 1969, he resigned after four days in office as Minister of State, Technology and Power; Minister of Overseas Development, 1967-69; Minister of Public Building and Works, 1966-67; Minister of State for Education and Science, 1964-66. B July, 1923; ed Whitgift School, and London School of Economics. Scientific instrument maker, and former adviser to Transport and General Workers' Union. Sponsored by TGWU. *Appointed Secretary of State for Education and Science, March 1974.*

Mr Tim Stroud, company director. B February, 1945; ed Clifton College School, King's College, London, Inns of Court Law School. Called to Bar (Lincoln's Inn), 1971. Contested same constituency for GLC, 1973.

Mr Lionel Cohen, research student and part-time university tutor. B November, 1932; ed Hendon County Grammar School; Lancaster and Sheffield Universities.

Miss **Vanessa Redgrave,** the actress, left the Labour Party in 1965 and joined the Workers Revolutionary Party in 1973. B 1937.

NEWHAM North-West major

Electorate 53,202

*Lewis, A. W. J. (Lab)	18,898
Bigg, D. C. (L)	6,350
Atkinson, D. A. (C)	6,301
Lab majority	12,548

	1974		1974
Total Vote	31,549	L	20·1%
Turnout	59·3%	C	20·0%
Lab	59·9%	Lab maj	39·8%

Mr Arthur Lewis, elected for Upton in 1945, and represented West Ham, North, from 1950 to 1974. Director of family business. Former trade union official (NUG MW) and chairman of the Eastern Regional group of Labour MPs. B February, 1917; ed elementary school and Borough Polytechnic, National Council of Labour Colleges and WEA. Former member of the London Labour Party executive committee. Member, Estimates Committee. Member NUGMW, APEX, ASTMS.

Mr David Bigg, company secretary. B January 1947 ed Exhall Grange School, Coventry. Member, Association of Certified Accountants, Institute of Book-keepers.

Mr David Atkinson, company director. B March, 1940; ed Southend College of Technology. Member, Essex County Council since 1973.

NEWHAM South major

Electorate 57,354

*Jones, Sir F. E. (Lab)	23,952
Shipley, I. W. I. (L)	5,369
Fox, F. (C)	4,422
Lobb, M. (Nat Front)	2,511
Lab majority	18,583

	1974		1974
Total Vote	36,254	C	12·2%
Turnout	63·2%	Nat Front	6·9%
Lab	66·1%	Lab maj	51·2%
L	14·8%		

Sir Elwyn Jones, QC, Opposition spokesman on legal matters 1970-74, was Attorney General, 1964-70. Elected for Plaistow in 1945 and represented West Ham, South, from 1950 to 1970. B October, 1909; ed Llanelli Grammar School, University College of Wales and Gonville and Caius College, Cambridge. Called to the Bar (Gray's Inn), 1935; QC 1953. Former member, British War Crimes Executive, and General Council of the Bar; former treasurer of Justice and trustee of Amnesty. *Appointed Lord Chancellor, March 1974. Made life peer.*

Mr Ivor Shipley, pharmacy proprietor. B January, 1923. Ed Eggar's Grammar School, Alton, Chelsea College of Science and Technology; Open University. Contested Bromley, 1964, Bromley councillor, 1963-64; member, NPU; founder and chairman, Open University Society for Medical Sciences.

Mr Frank Fox, accountant. B June, 1944; ed St Bonaventure's Grammar School, London. Vice-chairman, South-Eastern Area, Young Conservatives, 1971-72. Member, Margate council, 1968-74 and of Kent County Council since 1973.

NEWPORT minor

Electorate 74,551   1970: 71,520

*Hughes, R. J. (Lab)	29,384
Price, G. (C)	18,002
Morgan, J. H. (L)	11,868
Cox, Mrs P. (Pl Cymru)	936
Lab majority	11,382

No change

	1970		1974	
Total Vote	54,134		60,190	
Turnout	75·5%		80·7%	
Lab	30,132	55·7%	48·8%	
C	22,005	40·6%	29·9%	
Pl Cymru	1,997	3·7%	1·5%	
L	—		19·7%	
Lab maj	8,127	15·0%	18·9%	
Swing		+2·2%	−1·9%	

Mr Roy Hughes was elected in 1966. Former administrative officer in a Coventry car firm, and officer in Transport and General Workers' Union, 1959-66. B June, 1925; ed at Pontllanfraith County Grammar School, and Ruskin College, Oxford. Member, Cov-

entry City Council and secretary, Coventry Labour Party, 1962-66.

Mr Gerald Price, barrister. Aged 24; ed Hailebury and Middle Temple. Chairman, Barry Young Conservatives; committee member, Welsh Conservative Political Centre.

Mr John Morgan, director and chartered engineer. B February 1929; ed Tredegar Gammar and Pembroke College, Cambridge.

Mrs Phyllis Cox, assistant cashier. B July, 1935; ed Open University. Former shop steward.

NEWTON — minor

Electorate 94,360   1970: 89,413

Evans, J. (Lab)	38,369
Porter, H. (C)	23,599
Leather, W. N. (L)	15,939
Lab majority	14,770

No change

	1970		1974
Total Vote	66,414		77,907
Turnout	74·1%		82·6%
Lab	34,873	52·5%	49·2%
C	25,863	38·9%	30·3%
L	5,678	8·5%	20·4%
Lab maj	9,010	13·6%	18·9%
Swing		+6·0%	−2·6%

Mr John Evans is a fitter. B October, 1930; ed Jarrow Central School. Member, Hebburn Urban District Council for 12 years, and of South Tyneside Metropolitan District Council since 1973. AUEW.

Mr Barry Porter contested the Liverpool, Scotland by-election in 1971. Solicitor. B 1939; ed Birkenhead School and University College, Oxford. Member, Birkenhead Borough Council, 1967-72.

Mr William Leather, lecturer in government and social science. B February, 1940; ed Wade Deacon Grammar School, Widnes, Liverpool Polytechnic.

NORFOLK North — major

Electorate 89,725

*Howell, R. F. (C)	35,684
Mason, Rev D. M. (Lab)	21,394
Moore, R. G. (L)	17,853
C majority	14,290

	1974			1974
Total Vote	74,931		Lab	28·5%
Turnout	83·5%		L	23·8%
C	47·6%		C maj	19·1%

Mr Ralph Howell, joint vice-chairman Conservative back-bench committee on agriculture and on employment. Won the seat for the Conservatives in 1970; contested it in 1966. Farmer. B May, 1923; ed Diss Grammar School. Former local NFU chairman; specialized knowledge of agriculture and local government; member of Nutford and Launditch Rural Council since 1961.

The Rev David Mason, Methodist minister and community worker. B May, 1926; ed Mercers' School, London University and Boston University (Fulbright Scholar). Member, Kensington and Chelsea Borough Council and GLC. Member, NCHSE and TGWU.

Mr Richard Moore, political secretary to Mr Jeremy Thorpe. B February, 1931. Ed Highfield School, Liphook, Radley and Trinity College, Cambridge. Contested Tavistock, 1955, 1959; Cambridgeshire, 1961 by-election and 1964; North Antrim, 1966, 1970. Former clerk to NUJ chapel on *News Chronicle*.

NORFOLK North-West — major

Electorate 79,156

*Brocklebank-Fowler, C. (C)	27,823
Page, J. D. (Lab)	27,020
Walker, R. A. (L)	10,852
C majority	803

	1974			1976
Total Vote	65,695		Lab	41·1%
Turnout	83·0%		L	16·5%
C	42·3%		C maj	1·2%

Mr Christopher Brocklebank - Fowler, MP for King's Lynn 1970-74, marketing and advertising consultant. B 1935; ed Perse School, Cambridge. Former chairman and secretary of Bow Group. Member, Junior Carlton Club; joint secretary, United Nations parliamentary group, since 1971; chairman, Conservative Horticulture Committee. Contested West Ham, North, 1963. Member, Select Committee on Overseas Aid since 1973.

Mr Derek Page was MP for King's Lynn 1964-70; contested Isle of Ely 1959 and Northwich, 1955. Export agent and consultant. B August, 1927; ed St Bede's College, Manchester, and London University. Member, Select Committee on Agriculture, 1968-69. Member, Lymm Urban Council, 1954-57.

Mr Reginald Walker contested Ruislip-Northwood in 1966, 1964 and 1959. Company director. B June, 1917; ed Waterloo Grammar School, Liverpool, and Cambridge University. Member, Liberal Party Council, 1960-63.

NORFOLK South   major

Electorate 90,043

MacGregor, J. R. R. (C)	33,059
Truman, R. J. (Lab)	22,040
Scott, M. (L)	19,115
Fairhead, C. C. (Ind Progressive)	337
C majority	11,019

	1974		1974
Total Vote	74,551	L	25·6%
Turnout	82·8%	Ind Progress	0·4%
C	44·3%	C maj	14·8%
Lab	29·6%		

Mr John MacGregor is a merchant banker. Was chairman of the Federation of Conservative and Unionist Associations. Bow Group, and Conservative and Christian Democratic Youth Community. B 1933; ed Merchiston Castle School, Edinburgh, St Andrews University,

and King's College, London. Served in Conservative Research Department; special assistant to Sir Alec Douglas-Home when Prime Minister, and head of Mr Heath's private office, 1965-68.

Mr Ron Truman, insurance official, fought Burton, 1970, Wallasey 1966 and North Fylde 1964. B May, 1923; ed Bishophalt Grammar School, Hillingdon, and King's School, Peterborough. Member TGWU. Member of board, Leicester Co-operative Society Ltd.

Mr Malcolm Scott, clothing and textile retailer. B November, 1946; ed St Joseph's College, Birkfield, Norwich City College.

NORFOLK South-West   same

Electorate 53,351   1970: 48,145

*Hawkins, P. L. (C)	20,430
Toch, H. (Lab)	14,387
Nash, K. W. (L)	8,986
McNee, Mrs M. M. (Ind Powellite)	380
C majority	6,043

No change

	1970		1974
Total Vote	38,792		44,183
Turnout	80·6%		82·8%
C	22,220	57·3%	46·2%
Lab	16,572	42·7%	32·6%
L	—		20·3%
Ind Powell	—		0·9%
C maj	5,648	14·5%	13·7%
Swing		+6·2%	−0·5%

Mr Paul Hawkins was appointed Vice-Chamberlain of the Household (whip) in December, 1973; Lord Commissioner of the Treasury (whip), 1972-73; assistant Government whip, 1970-72. Elected 1964. Auctioneer and chartered surveyor. B August, 1912; ed

Cheltenham College. Member, Norfolk County Council for 21 years. Member, Select Committee on Agriculture, 1968-69, and Conservative Party agriculture and broadcasting committees.

Mr Henry Toch contested Rutland and Stamford in 1970 and Poole in 1964. Lecturer and tax consultant. B August, 1923; ed elementary and grammar schools and London School of Economics.

Mr Keith Nash, chartered patent agent. B December 1942; ed Judd School, Tonbridge and University of St Andrew's.

NORMANTON   same

Electorate 58,459   1970: 58,047

*Roberts, A. (Lab)	29,621
Marlow, A. R. (C)	14,447
Lab majority	15,174

No change

	1970		1974
Total Vote	41,553		44,068
Turnout	71·6%		75·4%
Lab	28,421	68·4%	67·2%
C	13,132	31·6%	32·8%
Lab maj	15,289	36·8%	34·4%
Swing		+8·0%	+1·2%

Mr Albert Roberts
was elected in 1951.
Mining engineer;
NUM branch secretary, 1935-41; mines
inspector, 1941-51. B
May, 1908; ed Woodlesford County School
and Whitwood Technical College. Rothwell Urban Council
1937-51, chairman
1948-49. Chairman,
International Parliamentary Union (British
branch). Deputy Lieutenant, West Riding,
1967.

Mr Antony Marlow. B June, 1940; ed
Wellington, RMA Sandhurst, St Catharine's College, Cambridge. Retired Army
officer, planning and development manager
for grain distribution and agriculture.

NORTHAMPTON North major

Electorate 48,603

Colquhoun, Mrs M. M. (Lab)	16,321
Jackson, C. M. (C)	15,288
Baker, R. B. (L)	8,475
Lab majority	1,033

	1974		1974
Total Vote	40,084	C	38·1%
Turnout	82·5%	L	21·1%
Lab	40·7%	Lab maj	2·6%

Mrs Maureen Colquhoun, literary research assistant, contested Tonbridge in
1970. B August, 1928;
ed convent, Eastbourne, commercial
college, Brighton, and
London School of
Economics. Member,
Shoreham council
since 1965. Member,
NUGMW.

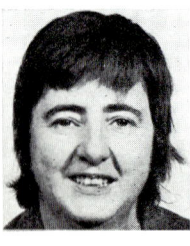

Mr Christopher Jackson, paint group
senior executive, fought East Ham South,
1970. B May 1935; ed Rye Grammar
School, Kingswood School, Bath, Magdalen College, Oxford, Frankfurt University and London School of Economics.
Former voluntary welfare officer, St. Martin-in-the-Fields social service unit.

Mr Robert Baker, teacher. B August,
1917; ed Northampton Grammar School
and Faltley Church of England Training
College.

NORTHAMPTON South major

Electorate 44,003

Morris, M. W. L. (C)	14,321
Dilks, J. (Lab)	14,142
Miller, R. F. (L)	7,099
C majority	179

	1974		1974
Total Vote	35 562	Lab	39·8%
Turnout	80·8%	L	20·0%
C	40·3%	C maj	0·5%

Mr Michael Morris,
director of advertising
agency. B November,
1936; ed Bedford
School and St Catharine's College, Cambridge. Contested
Islington, North, 1966.
Alderman, London
Borough of Islington;
member, Islington
Council since 1968
(leader, 1969-71).

Member, Lord Chancellor's Advisory
Committee on Courts Act (Greater London) and of fund-raising advisory committee of National Council of Social
Services.

Mr John Dilks contested the Lincoln by-election in March, 1973, and West Derbyshire in 1964, and the by-election in 1962.
Member relations and education officer,
Derby and Burton Co-operative Society.
B June, 1933; ed secondary school, and
Derby Junior College of Technology.
Leader, Derby County Borough Council
since 1972. Member, national executive,
USDAW, 1967-73.

Mr Rhett Miller, former local goverment officer, is studying at London School
of Economics. B June 1945; ed secondary
modern school, Northampton, and Birmingham University.

NORTH FYLDE same

Electorate 71,713   1970: 71,558

*Clegg, W. (C)	36,577
Sparks, D. H. (Lab)	16,919
C majority	19,658

	1970		1974
Total Vote	48,902		53,496
Turnout	68·3%		74·6%
C	33,667	68·8%	68·4%
Lab	15,235	31·1%	31·6%
C maj	18,432	37·7%	36·7%
Swing		+7·5%	−0·4%

Mr Walter Clegg,
Lord Commissioner
of the Treasury
(whip), 1970-72; Vice-Chamberlain of the
Household (whip),
1972-73; Comptroller
of the Household
(whip), 1973-74. Elected in 1966; contested
Ince, 1959. Solicitor.
B April, 1920; ed
Bury Grammar

School, Arnold School, and Manchester University Law School. Joint secretary, Conservative parliamentary housing and local government committee, 1967-69. Member, Lancashire County Council, 1955-61.

Mr David Sparks, trainee careers advisor. B November 1948; ed Fisher More Secondary School, Widnes, Wade Deacon Grammar School, and Lancaster University. Member, Warrington Trades and Labour Council. NUGMW and NALGO.

NORTHWICH   minor

Electorate 52,118   1970: 50,608

Goodlad, A. (C)	19,778
Benyon, S. G. (Lab & Co-op)	13,485
Reaper, R. (L)	10,344
C majority	6,293

No change

	1970		1974
Total Vote	39,716		43,607
Turnout	66·6%		83·7%
C	20,366	51·3%	45·3%
Lab	15,746	39·6%	—
Lab & Co-op	—		30·9%
L	3,604	9·1%	23·7%
C maj	4,620	11·6%	14·4%
Swing		+4·8%	+1·3%

Mr Alistair Goodlad contested Crewe in 1970. B 1943; ed St Faith's School, Cambridge, Marlborough College, and King's College, Cambridge. Was personal assistant to Mr Peter Walker when Opposition spokesman on transport.

Mr Stanley Benyon, training officer with the Co-operative Society. B February, 1933; ed Aberdare Grammar School and the Co-operative College. Member, Pontypridd Parish Council. Secretary, Trades and Labour Council, Aberdare. USDAW.

Mr David Reaper is a teacher. B April, 1947; ed Robert Richardson Grammar School and Sunderland College of Education. Member, Vale Royal District Council since 1973.

NORWICH North   minor

Electorate 44,723   1970: 43,562

Ennals, D. H. (Lab)	17,111
Doe, T. P. (C)	9,817
Wheeler, M. (L)	7,773
Goold, Mrs G. (Nat Front)	544
Lab majority	7,294

No change

	1970		1974
Total Vote	31,090		35,245
Turnout	71·3%		78·8%
Lab	18,564	59·7%	48·5%
C	11,868	38·2%	27·8%
Ind Prog	658	2·1%	—
L	—	—	22·0%
Nat Front	—	—	1·5%
Lab maj	6,696	21·5%	20·7%
Swing		+4·8%	+0·4%

Mr David Ennals, represented Dover, 1964-70. Minister of State for Health and Social Security, 1968-70, was Under - Secretary, Home Office, 1967-68, and Under-Secretary of State for Defence (Army), 1966-67. Contested Richmond as a Liberal in 1950 and 1951. B August, 1922;

ed Queen Mary's Grammar School, Walsall, and at Windsor, Connecticut. Campaign director, National Association for Mental Health until 1974. Secretary, United Nations Association, 1952-57. Overseas Secretary, Labour Party, 1958-64. *Appointed Minister of State for Foreign and Commonwealth Affairs, March 1974.*

Mr Timothy Doe, schoolmaster. B 1943; ed Wymondham College, RAF College, Cranwell, London University and Keswick College of Education. Chairman, Norfolk Conservative Educational Advisory Committee. Member, Norfolk County Council.

Mr Michael Wheeler, educational consultant and publisher. B March, 1929; ed Tollington School, London; London, Graz and Madrid Universities. Contested St Marylebone 1959, 1963 by-election; Sudbury and Woodbridge, 1964, 1966, 1970.

Mrs Gillian Goold, housewife. B January, 1945; ed Roxeth Manor Secondary School and Kilburn Polytechnic Commercial College.

NORWICH South   major

Electorate 44,467   1970: 46,402

Garrett, J. L. (Lab)	15,393
*Stuttaford, Dr I. T. (C)	14,741
Parker, Mrs. L. (L)	7,183
Lab majority	652

	1974		1974
Total Vote	37,317	L	19·2%
Turnout	83·9%	Lab maj	1·7%
Lab	41·2%	Swing	−2·0%
C	39·5%		

Mr John Garrett, management consultant: B September 1931; ed Sir George Monoux Grammar School, Walthamstow, University College, Oxford and University of California. Member, Greenwich Council. TGWU.

Dr Thomas Stuttaford, general practitioner, won the seat for the Conservatives in 1970. Member of the Select Committee on Science and Technology since 1970; former secretary, Conservative parliamentary committee for health and social services. B May, 1931; ed Greshams School, Brasenose College, Oxford and West London Hospital. Member, Norwich City Council; Blofield and Flegg RDC. Member, MPU.

Mrs Lesley Parker, housewife, fought the seat in 1970. B May, 1921; ed Wychwood School, Oxford, and Somerville College, Oxford.

NOTTINGHAM East major

Electorate 53,551

*Dunnett, J. J. (Lab)	17,324
Shepherd, R. C. S. (C)	13,346
Rowan, T. (L)	6,294
Lab majority	3,978

	1974		1974
Total Vote	36,964	C	36·1%
Turnout	69·0%	L	17·0%
Lab	46·9%	Lab maj	10·8%

Mr Jack Dunnett represented Nottingham, Central, 1964-74. Solicitor. B June, 1922; ed Whitgift Middle School, Croydon; Downing College, Cambridge. Member, Middlesex County Council, 1958-61, Enfield Borough Council, 1958-63, Greater London Council, 1964-67.

Member, NUGMW from 1961. Chairman, Notts County Football Club.

Mr Richard Shepherd, director of food companies, is a member of the South-East Economic Planning Council. B December, 1942; ed Woolverstone Hall, London School of Economics, The Johns Hopkins University.

Mr Edward Rowan, nurse. B May, 1939; ed secondary school in Ireland. Member, NUPE and ALTU.

NOTTINGHAM North major

Electorate 75,990

*Whitlock, W. C. (Lab)	25,435
Spungin, M. F. (C)	20,990
Edwards, Mrs P. (L)	9,623
Peck, J. (Comm)	754
Lab majority	4,445

	1974		1974
Total Vote	56,802	L	16·9%
Turnout	74·7%	Comm	1·3%
Lab	44·8%	Lab maj	7·8%
C	36·9%		

Mr William Whitlock was Under Secretary for Foreign and Commonwealth Affairs, 1967-69; Deputy Chief Whip and Lord Commissioner of the Treasury, March-July, 1967; Comptroller of the Household, 1966-67; Lord Commissioner of the Treasury March-July, 1966;

Vice-Chamberlain of the Household, 1964-66. Elected in 1959. Opposition whip, 1962-64. Former area organizer of the Union of Shop, Distributive and Allied Workers. B June, 1918; ed Itchen Grammar School, Southampton, and Southampton University. President, Leicester Labour Party, 1956-57; president, East Midlands regional council, 1962-63.

Mr Michael Spungin, solicitor and company director, fought Grimsby, 1970; Derbyshire, North-East, 1966 and 1964. B. September, 1936; ed Mundella Grammar School, Nottingham, and Wadham College, Oxford. Member, Nottingham City Council, since 1967, Nottinghamshire County Council from 1973.

Mrs Peggy Edwards, housewife, contested the seat in 1970, Ilkeston, 1964, and West Derbyshire, 1966. B June, 1921; ed private. Member, West Derbyshire District and Matlock UDC.

Mr John Peck contested constituency in 1970, 1966, 1964, 1959 and 1955. Nottingham Cooperative Society employee. B August, 1922; ed Scunthorpe Grammar School. USDAW.

NOTTINGHAM West major

Electorate 77,051

*English, M. (Lab)	27,592
Lloyd, P. R. C. (C)	21,795
Johnson, A. (L)	11,260
Lab majority	5,797

	1974			1974
Total Vote	60,647	C		35·9%
Turnout	78·7%	L		18·6%
Lab	45·5%	Lab maj		9·5%

Mr Michael English won the seat for Labour, 1964; contested Shipley, 1959. B December, 1930; ed King George V Grammar School, Southport and Liverpool University. Member, Rochdale Borough Council, 1953-65. Member, official parliamentary panel, NUGMW.

Member expenditure committee since 1970; chairman, Parliamentary Affairs Group of the Parliamentary Labour Party since 1970.

Mr Peter Lloyd, a marketing manager. B November, 1937; ed Tonbridge School and Pembroke College, Cambridge. Chairman, Bow Group, 1972-73; former chairman, Cambridge University Conservative Association.

Mr Andrew Johnson, geologist. B January, 1939; ed St Albans School, Luton College of Technology.

NUNEATON

minor

Electorate 77,082   1970: 75,048

*Huckfield, L. J. (Lab)	34,258
Samuel, D. (C)	16,765
Inman, D. (L)	12,591
Lab majority	17,493

No change

	1970		1974
Total Vote	57,246		63,614
Turnout	76·2%		82·5%
Lab	32,877	57·4%	53·8%
C	18,767	32·8%	26·3%
L	5,602	9·8%	19·8%
Lab maj	14,110	24·6%	27·5%
Swing		−1·1%	−1·4%

Mr Leslie Huckfield was elected at the 1967 by-election; contested Warwick and Leamington, 1966. B April, 1942; ed Prince Henry's Grammar School, Evesham, Keble College, Oxford and Birmingham University. Lecturer in economics, Birmingham College of Commerce, 1963-67. Parliamentary adviser,

British Safety Council since 1970. Member, Association of Teachers in Technical Institutions and T&GWU. Member, Estimates Committee.

Mr David Samuel, property consultant. B 1939; ed Randwick High School, Sydney. Member, Kensington and Chelsea Borough Council, since 1968; and of Housing Committee, Association of Municipal Corporations.

Mr David Inman, solicitor. B May, 1936; ed King Edward's School Birmingham, and University College, London University. Member, Hinckley and Bosworth District Council, Leicestershire County Council and Hinckley UDC. Deacon of a Baptist Church.

OGMORE

minor

Electorate 67,354   1970: 65,666

*Padley, W. E. (Lab)	28,372
Gibbs, Mrs J. (L)	10,819
Jones, R. K. (C)	9,416
Merriman, E. J. (Pl Cymru)	5,139
Lab majority	17,553

No change

	1970		1974
Total Vote	49,679		53,746
Turnout	75·6%		79·8%
Lab	33,436	67·3%	52·8%
C	10,415	21·0%	17·5%
Pl Cymru	5,828	11·7%	9·6%
L	—	—	20·1%
Lab maj	23,021	46·3%	32·6%
Swing		+5·2%	+5·5%

Mr Walter Padley, elected in 1950, was Minister of State, Foreign Office, 1964-67. Chairman, Labour Party 1965-66; member, national executive since 1956 and chairman of overseas committee 1963-71. Contested Acton by-election 1943 as an ILP candidate. B July, 1916; ed Chipping Norton Grammar

School and Ruskin College, Oxford. President, Union of Shop, Distributive and Allied Workers, 1948-64. Represents Labour Party on Bureau of Socialist International.

Mrs Jennie Gibbs, company representative, hygiene consultant and former teacher, fought the seat in 1966. B October, 1920; ed Maesteg Grammar School, University College of Wales, Aberystwyth. Partner in serigraphics. Maestag. Member, Ogwr District Council and Mid-Glamorgan County Council, since 1973; Maestag UDC since 1963 and Glamorgan CC since 1967.

Mr Roger Jones, solicitor. B September, 1945; ed Bridgend Grammar Technical School, Glamorgan, and Wadham College, Oxford. Secretary, Cardiff Law Society.

Mr Edward Merriman, clerk with National Coal Board; former miner. Member, Mid-Glamorgan County Council and Ogmore District Council.

OLDHAM East   same

Electorate 50,462   1970: 51,012

*Lamond, J. A. (Lab)	18,548
McGrandle, L. (C)	12,246
Hilyer, C. (L)	7,667
Lab majority	6,302

No change

	1970		1974
Total Vote	33,280		38,461
Turnout	65·2%		76·2%
Lab	17,020	51·1%	48·2%
C	16,260	48·8%	31·8%
L	—	—	19·9%
Lab maj	760	2·3%	16·4%
Swing		+6·5%	−7·0%

Mr James Lamond, design draughtsman, was elected in 1970. B November, 1928; ed Burrelton School, Coupar Angus junior secondary school. Member, Aberdeen town council since 1959-70; leader of the Labour group 1967-70; Lord Provost 1970-71; Lord Lieutenant of Aberdeen 1970-71. Sponsored by AUEW Technical and Supervisory Section. Member, Public Accounts Committee.

Mr Leith McGrandle, journalist. B April, 1943; ed Glasgow High School and Glasgow University. Deputy city editor of *The Sunday Telegraph.* Member of Bow Group since 1965 and Editor of *Crossbow* since 1972.

Mr Christopher Hilyer, architect. B March, 1940; ed Prescot Grammar School, Manchester School of Architecture.

OLDHAM West   same

Electorate 47,793   1970: 49,823

*Meacher, M. H. (Lab)	17,933
Trippier, D. (C)	11,628
Limont, A. (L)	7,505
Lab majority	6,305

No change

	1970		1974
Total Vote	33,393		37,066
Turnout	67·0%		77·5%
Lab	16,062	48·1%	48·4%
C	14,387	43·1%	31·4%
L	2,944	8·8%	20·2%
Lab maj	1,675	5·0%	17·0%
Swing		+8·7%	−6·0%

Mr Michael Meacher regained the seat for Labour in 1970; contested Colchester, 1966. B November, 1939; ed Berkhampstead School, New College, Oxford, and London School of Economics. Lecturer in social administration York University, 1966-69 and London School of Economics, 1970. Member, Fabian Society; chairman Hull branch ASTMS. *Appointed Under Secretary for Industry, March 1974.*

Mr David Trippier, stockbroker and lecturer in stock exchange economics, contested Rochdale by-election in 1972. B 1946; ed Bury Grammar School.

Mr Anthony Limont, barrister. B February, 1942; ed Fettes College and Liverpool University. Member, Liverpool City Council, Merseyside Metropolitan Council, Liverpool District Council.

ORKNEY & SHETLAND   same

Electorate 26,087   1970: 24,707

*Grimond, J. (L)	11,491
Firth, J. (C)	4,186
Wills, W. J. G. (Lab)	2,865
L majority	7,305

No change

	1970		1974
Total Vote	16,812		18,542
Turnout	68·0%		71·0%
L	7,896	47·0%	62·0%
C	5,364	31·9%	22·6%
Lab	3,552	21·1%	15·4%
L maj	2,532	15·1%	39·4%
Swing		+3·5%	—

Mr Jo Grimond, who was Leader of the Liberal Party from 1956 to 1967, won the seat in 1950; contested it in 1945, Liberal spokesman on Scottish Affairs, energy and the arts. Barrister (Middle Temple, 1937); director, The Manchester Guardian and Evening News Ltd from 1967. B July, 1913; ed Eton and Balliol College, Oxford. Secretary, Scottish National Trust, 1947-49; Rector, Edinburgh University, 1960-63; Chancellor, University of Kent since 1970. President, Scottish Liberal Party, 1970. Appointed Liberal spokesman on energy and Scotland, March 1974.

Mr John Firth, lecturer in neuro-surgery at National Hospital for Nervous Diseases, London. Contested the seat in 1970, 1966 and 1964. B May, 1936; ed Harrow, Hertford College, Oxford, and St Thomas's Hospital, London.

Mr Jonathan Wills is a writer, artist and crofter. B June, 1947; ed Warwick School, Anderson Institute, Lerwick and Edinburgh University (Rector, 1971-72). TGWU.

ORMSKIRK   major

Electorate 95,688

Kilroy-Silk, R. (Lab)	34,807
*Soref, H. B. (C)	27,004
Parry, D. (L)	11,949
Lab majority	7,803

	1974		1974
Total Vote	73,760	C	36·6%
Turnout	77·1%	L	16·2%
Lab	47·2%	Lab maj	10·6%

Mr Robert Kilroy-Silk, university lecturer, contested the seat in 1970. B May, 1942; ed Saltley Grammar School, Birmingham, London School of Economics, and London University.

Mr Harold Soref, managing director of an export shipping company, was elected

in 1970; contested Rugby in 1955 and Dudley, 1951. B December, 1916; ed St Paul's School, Queen's College, Oxford. Founder member, Conservative Commonwealth Council. Member, executive council, Monday Club and chairman of its Africa Group. Member, council, Anglo-Jewish Association.

Mr David Parry, architect. B November, 1937; ed Bluecoat School, Liverpool, Sheffield University.

OSWESTRY   major

Electorate 55,901

*Biffen, W. J. (C)	20,438
Evans, D. (L)	13,428
Bishton, J. (Lab)	9,685
C majority	7,010

No change

	1974		1974
Total Vote	43,551	L	30·8%
Turnout	77·9%	Lab	22·2%
C	46·9%	C maj	16·1%

Mr John Biffen was returned at a by-election in 1961; contested Coventry, East, 1959. Economist. B November, 1930; ed Dr Morgan's Grammar School, Bridgwater, Jesus College, Cambridge. Member of executive 1922 Committee. Chairman, Conservative industry committee. Librarian, Bow Group, 1961-62. Member, Public Accounts Committee, 1964-67. An economic adviser and a director of firm of management consultants. Treasurer, Anglo-Italian party group.

Mr David Evans, college lecturer, contested Wallasey, 1970. B February, 1947; ed Teignmouth Grammar School and Liverpool University.

Mr John Bishton, social worker. B 1946; ed Wolverhampton Municipal Grammar School, University College, Swansea, London School of Economics, Birmingham University. NALGO.

OXFORD   same

Electorate 77,591   1970: 70,986

*Woodhouse, C. M. (C)	23,967
Luard, D. E. T. (Lab)	23,146
Butler, Mrs M. (L)	13,094
C majority	821

No change

	1970		1974
Total Vote	52,965		60,207
Turnout	74·6%		77·6%
C	24,873	47·0%	39·8%
Lab	22,989	43·4%	38·4%
L	5,103	9·6%	21·7%
C maj	1,884	3·5%	1·4%
Swing		+4·1%	−1·1%

Mr Christopher Woodhouse, who regained the seat for the Conservatives in 1970, was MP for the constituency, 1959-66. Under Secretary, Home Office, 1962-64, and Parliamentary Secretary, Ministry of Aviation, 1961-62. Member, Speaker's panel of chairmen since 1971. B May, 1917; ed Winchester and New College, Oxford. Director, IDC Group Ltd and writer. President, Classical

Association, 1968-69. Director-general, Royal Institute of International Affairs, 1955-59. Foreign Service, 1950-55. Member, Expenditure Committee, 1970-72.

Mr Evan Luard was MP for the constituency, 1966-70, contested it, 1964. Under-Secretary for Foreign and Commonwealth Affairs, 1969-70. B October, 1926; ed Felsted and King's College, Cambridge. Fellow, St Anthony's College, Oxford. Member, Oxford City Council, 1958-61.

Mrs Margaret Butler, housewife. B February, 1926; ed Oxford Central Girls' School. County and district councillor.

OXON, MID   major

Electorate 58,464

Hurd, D. R. (C)	22,148
Parsloe, E. (Lab)	14,175
Sparrow, R. (L)	12,160
Myhill, J. (Ind C)	488
C majority	7,973

	1974		1974
Total Vote	48,971	L	24·8%
Turnout	83·8%	Ind C	1·0%
C	45·2%	C maj	16·3%
Lab	28·9%		

Mr Douglas Hurd, head of Mr Edward Heath's political office since 1968. B March, 1930; ed Eton and Cambridge University. Worked in the foreign service in China, the United States and Europe, reaching the position of first secretary. Author of four successful political thrillers.

Mr Eric Parsloe is Deputy Secretary-General, International Voluntary Service. B 1938; ed grammar schools and Oxford University. Former member, Andover Borough Council, AUEW.

Mr Robert Sparrow, solicitor. B August, 1941; ed Denstone College and the College of Law, London. Employed by Royal Bank of Scotland. Member, Association of Liberal Lawyers research group, Law Society, British Legal Association, NUBE.

PAISLEY   minor

Electorate 68,881   1970: 65,740

*Robertson, J. (Lab)	23,820
Workman, J. (C)	14,923
Rollo, D. (Scot Nat)	10,455
Lab majority	8,897

No change

	1970		1974
Total Vote	47,011		49,198
Turnout	71·5%		71·4%
Lab	25,429	54·1%	48·4%
C	15,232	32·4%	30·3%
Scot Nat	3,432	7·3%	21·2%
L	2,918	6·2%	
Lab maj	10,197	21·7%	18·1%
Swing		+7·5%	+1·8%

Mr John Robertson was returned at a by-election in 1961; contested Glasgow Scotstoun, 1951. Toolmaker. B February, 1913; ed Motherwell Central School. Assistant divisional organizer, AUEW. West Scotland, 1954-61. Former member, Speaker's panel of chairmen. Lanarkshire County Council, Motherwell and Wishaw Town Council, 1946-52. Sponsored by AUEW, engineering section.

Mr John Workman, company secretary, contested the seat in 1970. B May, 1944; ed Abercorn School and Paisley Grammar School. Member, Paisley Council, 1969-72.

Mr David Rollo, chartered electrical engineer. Contested Hamilton, 1959; Glasgow, Woodside, 1970. B 1919; ed Lenzie Academy and Glasgow University.

PEMBROKE   same

Electorate 71,476   1970: 70,649

*Edwards, R. N. (C)	22,268
Parry, G. S. D. (Lab)	20,789
Jones, P. E. C. (L)	12,340
Davies, R. V. (Pl Cymru)	2,820
C majority	1,479

No change

	1970		1974
Total Vote	55,055		58,217
Turnout	77·9%		81·4%
C	19,120	34·7%	38·2%
Lab	17,889	32·5%	35·7%
Dem	11,824	21·5%	—
Pl Cymru	3,681	6·7%	4·8%
L	2,541	4·6%	21·2%
C maj	1,231	2·2%	2·5%
Swing		+7·0%	+0·1%

Mr Nicholas Edwards won the seat for the Conservatives in 1970. Insurance broker. B February, 1934; ed Westminster School and Trinity College, Cambridge. Secretary, Welsh group of Conservative MPs since 1972. Chairman, William Brandt's (Insurance Holdings) Ltd

and subsidiary companies; director, William Brandt's Sons and Co Ltd, merchant bankers. Member of Lloyd's and of Commons Public Expenditure Committee.

Mr Gordon Parry, contested Monmouth, 1959, and Pembroke, 1970. Warden, Pembrokeshire Teachers' Centre. B November, 1925; ed Pembroke Dock intermediate school, Trinity College, Carmarthen, Liverpool University.

Mr Patrick Jones, chief medical laboratory technologist. B June, 1939; ed Narberth Grammar School; University College of Wales, Aberystwyth. Member, Pembrokeshire County Council. ASTMS.

Mr Richard Davies, university lecturer, contested Cardiff South-East in 1970. B September, 1946; ed Milford Haven Grammar School and Sidney Sussex College, Cambridge.

PENISTONE   major

Electorate 66,286

*Mendelson, J. J. (Lab)	27,797
Wilkinson, A. D. (C)	14,084
Chadwick, D. (L)	13,140
Eaden, M. (Soc Dem)	867
Lab majority	13,713

	1974		1974
Total Vote	55,888	L	23·5%
Turnout	84·3%	Social Dem	1·5%
Lab	49·7%	Lab maj	24·5%
C	25·2%		

Mr John Mendelson, elected at by-election, 1959. University lecturer in political science. B July, 1917; ed London University and abroad. Former vice-president, Sheffield Trades and Labour Council; former chairman Sheffield Hallam, Labour Party. Member, Public Accounts Committee, 1964-66, and Speaker's conference on electoral law.

Mr Andrew Wilkinson, assistant bank inspector. B May, 1946; ed Roundhay Grammar School, Leeds and Leeds College of Commerce. Chairman, Yorkshire Young Conservatives.

Mr David Chadwick contested Blackpool, South, 1970, and Nelson and Colne by-election, 1968. Lecturer. B September, 1939; ed Blackpool College of Technology, Art and Design, Bolton College of Education. Member, Blackpool council, 1968-73. ATTI.

Mr Martin Eaden, social worker. B 1949; ed Lancaster University; expelled from Labour Party, 1973, for acting as agent for his father, who stood as an independent

steelworker in the district and metropolitan county elections against the official Labour candidate and was elected.

PENRITH & THE BORDER   same

Electorate 54,428   1970: 54,251

*Whitelaw, W. S. I. (C)	26,433
Weedall, J. N. D. (Lab)	9,095
Alexander, P. (L)	8,202
Hesmondhalgh, W. (Ind)	235
C majority	17,338

No change

	1970		1974	
Total Vote	40,372		43,965	
Turnout	74·4%		80·8%	
C	23,800	58·9%		60·1%
Lab	10,256	25·4%		20·7%
L	6,316	15·6%		18·6%
Ind	—			0·5%
C maj	13,544	33·5%		39·4%
Swing		+5·5%		+2·9%

Mr William Whitelaw was Secretary of State for Employment, 1973-74; Secretary of State for Northern Ireland, 1972-73, and Lord President of the Council and Leader of the House of Commons, 1970-72. President, National Union of Conservative and Unionist Associations, 1971. Opposition Chief Whip, 1964-70; Parliamentary Secretary, Ministry of Labour, 1962-64. Elected 1955; contested East Dunbartonshire, 1950 and 1951. B June, 1918; ed Winchester and Trinity College, Cambridge. Appointed to Shadow Cabinet as Opposition spokesman on employment, March 1974.

Mr Joseph Weedall, schoolmaster. B January, 1935; ed Ellesmere College, Shropshire. Member, Border RDC since 1967, Cumberland County Council since 1970 and Carlisle District Council since 1973. NUT.

Mr Peter Alexander, writer. B January, 1929; ed Eton and Oxford.

PERTH & EAST PERTHSHIRE
minor

Electorate 57,206   1970: 56,984

*MacArthur, I. (C)	21,167
Crawford, G. D. (Scot Nat)	12,192
Friel, Miss V. A. (Lab)	6,784
Smith, Mrs K (L)	4,644
C majority	8,975

No change

	1970		1974
Total Vote	41,955		44,787
Turnout	73·5%		78·3%
C	21,860	52·1%	47·3%
Lab	9,972	23·8%	15·1%
Scot Nat	7,112	16·9%	27·2%
L	3,011	7·2%	10·4%
C maj	11,888	28·3%	20·0%
Swing		−0·1%	+1·9%

Mr Ian MacArthur, Chairman, Scottish Conservative MPs, 1972-73; member Speaker's Conference on electoral law since 1973; and Opposition spokesman on Scottish affairs, 1965-70, and Opposition Scottish whip, 1964-65; a Lord Commissioner of the Treasury (whip), 1963-64, and an assistant Government whip, 1962-63. Elected, 1959; contested Greenock in 1955 and the December by-election of that year. Associate director, J. Walter Thompson Co Ltd. B May, 1925; ed Cheltenham College and Queen's College, Oxford. Vice-chairman, Scottish Conservative Party since 1972; chairman, all-party whisky industry committee; member, Select Committee on Scottish Affairs, 1970-72. Secretary, Scottish Conservative MPs, from March 1974.

Mr Douglas Crawford, joint managing director of a group of economic and development consultants with branches in Edinburgh, London and Cardiff. B 1941; ed Glasgow Academy and Cambridge University.

Miss Valerie Friel, lecturer. B December, 1937; ed St Ninian's High School, Kirkinilloch, and Glasgow University. Contested the seat in 1970; former executive member, West Stirlingshire constituency Labour Party.

Mrs Kathleen Smith, housewife, was formerly a journalist. B May, 1922; ed Dundee School of Economics. Chairman, Tayside Regional Council, and member, SLP executive. Secretary, Dundee branch, Disablement Income Group (Scotland).

PETERBOROUGH   major

Electorate 62,641

*Nicholls, Sir H. (C)	20,353
Ward, M. J. (Lab)	20,331
Boizot, P. (L)	10,772
C majority	22

	1974		1974
Total Vote	51,456	Lab	39·5%
Turnout	82·1%	L	20·9%
C	39·5%	C maj	0·0%

Sir Harmar Nicholls, elected in 1950, was Parliamentary Secretary, Ministry of Agriculture, Fisheries and Food, 1955-58, and Ministry of Works, 1958-61. Member, executive, 1922 Committee since 1970. Contested Nelson and Colne, 1945, and Preston, South, 1946.

Chairman and a director of Malvern Festival Theatre Trust Ltd, and a director of International Life Assurance Co (UK) Ltd, J. and H. Nicholls (Paints) Ltd, Midland and East Anglia Trust Ltd, Nicholls and Hennessy (Hotels) Ltd, Radio Luxembourg (London) Ltd, and Winkfields Estates Ltd, Lloyds underwriter. B November, 1912; ed Queen Mary's School, Walsall.

Mr Michael Ward contested the seat 1966 and 1970. Local government press officer and former local government officer, Labour Party. B April, 1931; ed Royal Liberty Grammar School, Romford, and Manchester University. Member, Romford Borough Council since 1958 and London Borough of Havering since 1964. Member, GMWU, and Fabian Society.

Mr Peter Boizot, company director. B November, 1929; ed King's School, Peterborough and St Catherine's College, Cambridge. Vice-chairman, Save Piccadilly Campaign; leader, Soho Society Traders Section. Managing director, Pizza Express Ltd.

PETERSFIELD   minor

Electorate 73,716   1970: 69,608

*Quennell, Miss J. M. (C)	30,732
Slack, T. W. (L)	21,152
Whiteley, P. F. (Lab)	7,703
Bishop, P. H. H. (Tech Consultant)	101
C majority	9,580

No change

	1970		1974
Total Vote	50,270		59,688
Turnout	72·1%		81·0%
C	30,414	60·5%	51·5%
Lab	10,307	20·5%	12·9%
L	7,783	15·5%	35·4%
Ind	1,766	3·5%	—
Tech Consult	—		0·2%
C maj	20,107	40·0%	16·0%
Swing		+5·7%	−0·7%

Miss Joan Quennell was returned at by-election, November, 1960. B December, 1923; ed Bedales School, Petersfield. Member, Public Accounts Committee, select committee on EEC secondary legislation and Speaker's Panel of Chairmen. Member, West Sussex County Council, 1951-61. Past governor, Area Technical College, Crawley and Teachers' Training College, Bognor Regis. Company director.

Mr Timothy Slack, teacher, held several posts in schools abroad and has been headmaster of Bedales School, Petersfield, since 1962. B April, 1928; ed Winchester College and New College, Oxford. Member, Headmasters' Association and other professional bodies; board of visitors, Foston Detention Centre, 1956-59; council of Britain-Burma Association, since 1962.

Mr Paul Whiteley, polytechnic lecturer. B. February, 1946; ed Sheffield and Essex Universities and Garnett College of Education. ATTI.

PLYMOUTH Devonport major

Electorate 49,802

*Owen, Dr D. A. L. (Lab)		15,819
*Vickers, Dame J. H. (C)		15,382
Banks, M. (L)		6,298
Lab majority		437

	1974			1974
Total Vote	37,499		C	41·0%
Turnout	75·3%		L	16·8%
Lab	42·2%		Lab maj	1·2%

Dr David Owen represented Plymouth, Sutton, 1966-74. He was an Opposition spokesman on defence, 1970-72, when resigned over disagreement on EEC policy. Under-Secretary of Defence for the Royal Navy, 1968-70. Contested Torrington 1964. B July, 1938; ed Bradfield College, Berkshire, Sidney Sussex College, Cambridge, and St Thomas's Hospital. Governor, Charing Cross Hospital, 1966-68. Patron, Disablement Income Group. Member, ASTMS (MPU section).

Member, defence and external affairs sub-committee, Public Expenditure Committee. *Appointed Under Secretary for Health, Department of Health and Social Security, March 1974.*

Dame Joan Vickers was elected in 1955; contested South Poplar, 1945. Lecturer. B 1907; ed St Monica's College, Burgh Heath, Surrey and in Paris. Served with British Red Cross in South East Asia, area welfare officer, Social Welfare Department in Malaya. Member of London County Council, 1937-45; United Kingdom delegate to Status of Women Commission at United Nations, 1962-63. Member, United Kingdom delegation to Council of Europe and Western European Union since 1967. Netherlands Red Cross Medal.

Mr Michael Banks, explorer, mountaineer and author. B December, 1922; ed Chippenham Grammar School. Contested Tavistock, 1970. Member, Dartmoor Rescue Group.

PLYMOUTH Drake major

Electorate 55,109

*Fookes, Miss J. (C)		18,417
Taylor, F. K. (Lab)		15,806
Castle, Miss M. (L)		8,784
C majority		2,611

	1974			1974
Total Vote	43,007		Lab	36·7%
Turnout	78·0%		L	20·4%
C	42·8%		C maj	6·1%

Miss Janet Fookes represented Merton and Morden 1970-74. Teacher. Former member of Hastings Borough Council. B February, 1936; ed Hastings and St Leonards Ladies' College, Hastings High School and Royal Holloway College, University of London. Member, expenditure committee, public petitions committee; secretary, Conservative Parliamentary Education Committee and of all-party deserted families group.

Mr Keith Taylor contested Plymouth, Devonport, in 1970, and Tiverton in 1966. Teacher, previously a civil servant. B September, 1941; ed St Luke's College, Exeter. Member, Exeter City Council, 1966-72. NUPE and NUT.

Miss Maureen Castle, Home Office Criminologist (barrister and psychologist). B January, 1937; educated at Exeter and London universities. Contested St Ives, 1970 for Labour Party.

PLYMOUTH Sutton major

Electorate 61,230

Clark, A. K. M. (C)	21,649
Fletcher, B. W. (Lab)	13,545
Banks, S. (L)	12,683
C majority	8,104

	1974		1974
Total Vote	47,877	Lab	28·3%
Turnout	78·2%	L	26·5%
C	45·2%	C maj	16·9%

Mr Alan Clark, military historian, son of Lord Clark. B April, 1928; ed Eton and Christ Church, Oxford. Barrister, Inner Temple, 1955. Member, Institute for Strategic Studies. Governor, St Thomas's Hospital.

Mr Brian Fletcher, a teacher. Director, Nuffield Education Project in South-West. Member, NAS. B March, 1942; ed King Edward VI Grammar School, Birmingham, Birmingham University and King's College, London.

Mr Simon Banks, teacher. B November, 1946; ed Grammar School, Welwyn Garden City; King's College, Cambridge; Bristol University. Committee member, Plymouth and E. Cornwall Group, Conservation Society; Plymouth Housing Action Group; NUT.

PONTEFRACT & CASTLEFORD
same

Electorate 59,809   1970: 60,146

*Harper, J. (Lab)	34,409
Needham, R. F. (C)	10,605
Lavery, B. (WRP)	991
Lab majority	23,804

No change

	1970		1974
Total Vote	42,461		46,005
Turnout	70·6%		76·9%
Lab	31,774	74·8%	74·8%
C	10,687	25·2%	23·0%
WRP	—		2·1%
Lab maj	21,087	49·7%	51·7%
Swing		+3·6%	−1·1%

Mr Joseph Harper, an Opposition whip, 1970-74, was a Lord Commissioner of the Treasury (whip) 1966-70, and an assistant Government whip, 1964-66. Elected in a by-election in 1962. Miner. B March, 1914; elementary education and WEA. Member, Featherstone Urban Council for 14 years, chairman, 1955-56 and 1961-62. Member, Yorkshire area NUM executive committee, 1947-48 and 1950-52; Pontefract and Castleford Hospital Management Centre. *Appointed Comptroller of the Household, March 1974.*

Mr Richard Needham, co-founder Monday Club, and first chairman, Home Affairs Group. Left Monday Club in 1964 after break-up of Rhodesia Federation and joined PEST. Company chairman. B 1942; ed Lincoln's Inn and Harvard Business School.

Mr Brian Lavery, aged 44, underground mechanic at Wheldale Colliery, Yorkshire.

PONTYPOOL same

Electorate 54,727   1970: 53,821

*Abse, L. (Lab)	25,133
Mathias, E. A. R. (L)	7,668
Wallace, T. (C)	7,497
Tanner, R. (Pl Cymru)	1,308
Williams, G. (Comm)	498
Lab majority	17,465

No change

	1970		1974
Total Vote	38,759		42,104
Turnout	72·0%		76·9%
Lab	27,402	70·7%	59·7%
C	8,869	22·9%	17·8%
Pl Cymru	2,053	5·3%	3·1%
Comm	435	1·1%	1·2%
L	—		18·2%
Lab maj	18,533	47·8%	41·5%
Swing		+4·3%	+2·9%

Mr Leopold Abse was returned at a by-election in November, 1958; contested Cardiff, North, 1955. Solicitor. B April, 1917; ed Howard Gardens High School, Cardiff, and London School of Economics. Chairman, Cardiff Labour Party 1951-53; member, Cardiff City Council 1953-58. Member, Home Office Advisory Council for Penal Reform; Council of Institute for Study and Treatment of Delinquency; National Council for the Unmarried Mother and her Child, departmental committee on adoption. Sponsor or co-sponsor of private members' Acts on divorce, homosexuality, family planning, legitimacy, and widows' damages.

Mr Robert Mathias contested Pontypool, 1950. Chartered civil engineer. B April, 1916; ed Abersycham Grammar School and Imperial College, London. NALGO.

Mr Theo Wallace, barrister. B April, 1938; ed Charterhouse and Christ Church, Oxford. Called to the Bar 1963. Deputy chairman, South Battersea Conservatives.

Mr Roger Tanner, planning officer. B October, 1949; ed Cardiff High School, University of Southampton and University of Wales, Bangor. NALGO.

Mr Graham Williams, convener of craftsmen's committee at Panteg Steel Works. B 1934. Former chairman, Pontypool Trades Council. AUEW.

PONTYPRIDD same

Electorate 69,685 1970: 65,191

*John, B. T. (Lab)		28,028
Jones, I. A. (C)		11,406
Murphy, Mrs M. G. (L)		9,889
Kemp, R. A. (Pl Cymru)		4,612
Lab majority		16,622

No change

	1970		1974
Total Vote	48,549		53,935
Turnout	74·5%		77·4%
Lab	28,414	58·5%	52·0%
C	8,205	16·9%	21·1%
L	6,871	14·1%	18·3%
Pl Cymru	5,059	10·4%	8·5%
Lab maj	20,209	41·6%	30·8%
Swing		+4·1%	+5·3%

Mr Brynmor John was elected in 1970. Solicitor. B April, 1934; ed Pontypridd Grammar School and University College, London. Specializes in industrial accident law. Governor of Pontypridd secondary schools. Former member, local trades council.

Mr Alun Jones, solicitor. B December, 1937; ed Gowerton School, and University College of Wales, Aberystwyth.

Mrs Mary Murphy, teacher. Ed Pontypridd Grammar School, Bangor Training College. Contested Pontypridd, 1970. Former secretary, Welsh Liberal Party. Member, Pontypridd UDC since 1963; elected to new council, 1973.

Mr Richard Kemp, mathematics lecturer. Ed Aberdare Grammar School and University College, Aberystwyth. Council member, Glamorgan Naturalists.

POOLE same

Electorate 83,781 1970: 77,927

*Murton, H. O. (C)		31,156
Goode, G. M. (L)		21,088
Hobbs, G. W. (Lab)		15,434
C majority		10,068

No change

	1970		1974
Total Vote	58,556		67,678
Turnout	75·1%		80·8%
C	31,100	53·1%	46·0%
Lab	17,610	30·1%	22·8%
L	9,846	16·8%	31·1%
C maj	13,490	23·0%	14·9%
Swing		+6·0%	+0·1%

Mr Oscar Murton was appointed Deputy Speaker and Second Deputy Chairman of Ways and Means in 1973 after serving as a Government whip. Member of Speaker's panel of chairmen, 1970-71. Elected in 1964. B May, 1914; ed Uppingham School. Member, Poole Borough Council, 1961-64. Formerly managing director of departmental stores in Newcastle and Sunderland. Former member, executive committee, Inter-Parliamentary Union (British Group). Appointed Deputy Chairman of Ways and Means and Deputy Speaker, March 1974.

Mr Maxwell Goode, farmer. B September, 1927; ed Kettering Grammar School, University College of Wales, Aberystwyth. Contested South Dorset, 1955; Central Norfolk, 1959, 1962 by-election and 1964; South Dorset, 1966; Poole, 1970.

Mr Garfield Hobbs, teacher. B December, 1945; ed Plymouth College, Exeter University. NUT, Cooperative Party and Fabian Society. Methodist local preacher.

PORTSMOUTH North major

Electorate 68,353

*Judd, F. A. (Lab)		23,847
Griffiths, P. H. S. (C)		23,527
Peaston, A. J. (L)		7,304
Lab majority		320

POR

	1974			1974
Total Vote	54,678	C		43·0%
Turnout	78·8%	L		13·3%
Lab	43·6%	Lab maj		0·6%

Mr Frank Judd repre-
sented Portsmouth,
West, 1966-74. An
Opposition defence
spokesman. Social ad-
ministrator. B March,
1935; ed City of Lon-
don School and Lon-
don School of Econo-
mics. Parliamentary
Private Secretary to
Mr Harold Wilson
1970-72. Member of
British delegation to Council of Europe
1970-73. Member, executive, Commonwealth Parliamentary Association. Chairman, Fabian International and Commonwealth Bureau. *Appointed Under Secretary of Defence for the Royal Navy,
March 1974.*

Mr Peter Griffiths was Conservative MP
for Smethwick, 1964-66. B May, 1928; ed
West Bromwich Grammar School, City of
Leeds Training College, and London and
Birmingham Universities. Senior Economic
lecturer, Portsmouth Polytechnic.

Mr Anthony Peaston, telecommunications
post and reprographic coordinator, IBM
(UK) Ltd. B July, 1944; ed St George's
School, Maida Vale.

PORTSMOUTH South   major

Electorate 71,345

*Pink, R. B. (C)	26,824
Lloyd, S. (Lab)	15,842
Williams, J. (L)	10,307
Rifkin, A. D. (Marx-Leninist)	394
C majority	10,982

	1974			1974
Total Vote	53,367	L		19·3%
Turnout	75·2%	Marx-Lenin		0·7%
C	50·3%	C maj		20·6%
Lab	29·7%			

Mr Bonner Pink, a
company director, was
elected in 1966. B
September, 1912; ed
Oundle. Member,
Estimates Committee,
1967-70; Public Ex-
penditure Committee
since 1971. Member
of Portsmouth City
Council from 1948
(Alderman, 1961);
Lord Mayor of Ports-

mouth, 1961-62. Chairman and other office

208

holder, constituency Conservative Association 1946-65; member, Conservative
Party Local Government Advisory Committee 1947-64. Vice-chairman, Wessex
Area Conservatives 1957-60, chairman
1960-63.

Mr Sydney Lloyd, polytechnic lecturer. B
January, 1931; ed Barnsley College of
Technology, Durham University and
Brighton Polytechnic. Member, Cuckfield
Urban District Council since 1971. ATTI.

Mr John Williams, retail executive. B
March, 1947; ed Mile End House School,
Portsmouth.

PRESTON North   same

Electorate 50,912   1970: 51,746

Atkins, R. H. (Lab)	16,797
*Holt, Miss M. (C)	16,542
Payne, G. (L)	7,099
Lab majority	255

Labour gain

	1970		1974
Total Vote	39,700		40,438
Turnout	76·7%		79·4%
C	20,102	50·6%	40·9%
Lab	17,140	43·2%	41·5%
L	2,458	6·2%	17·5%
C maj	2,962	7·5%	
Lab maj	—		0·6%
Swing		+6·7%	−4·0%

Mr Ronald Atkins
represented the con-
stituency 1966-70.
Contested Lowestoft,
1964. B June, 1916;
ed Barry County
School and London
University. Lecturer
in further education
college. Member,
NUT. Member Brain-
tree Rural District
Council 1952-61. For-

mer Executive member, National Council
on Inland Transport.

Miss Mary Holt won the seat for the Con-
servatives in 1970. Barrister. B 1924; ed
Park School, Preston, Girton College,
Cambridge. Former vice-chairman, Preston
North Conservative Association; member,
National Executive Council and of
Women's National Advisory Committee,
1969-70; North-West representative, Cen-
tral Council.

Mr Gordon Payne contested Chorley,
1970. Chartered secretary. B August, 1933;
ed Preston Grammar School. Leader,
Liberal group, Lancashire CC.

PRESTON South   same

Electorate 51,159   1970: 52,181

Thorne, S. G. (Lab)	17,354
*Green, A. (C)	15,467
Marshall, R. P. (L)	7,974
Lab majority	1,887

Labour gain

	1970		1974
Total Vote	39,629		40,795
Turnout	75·9%		79·7%
C	20,480	51·7%	37·9%
Lab	19,149	48·3%	42·5%
L	—		19·5%
C maj	1,331	3·3%	—
Lab maj	—		4·6%
Swing		+5·3%	−4·0%

Mr **Stanley Thorne**, lecturer in industrial sociology, contested Liverpool, Wavertree, 1964. B July, 1918; ed Ruskin College, Oxford, and Liverpool University. Deputy chairman, Liverpool education committee. Vice-president, Liverpool Labour Party. Governor, Liverpool Polytechnic. Member, ASTMS.

Mr **Alan Green**, company director, who regained the seat for the Conservatives in 1970, was MP for the constituency, 1955-64. Contested it in 1966, and Nelson and Colne, 1950 and 1951. Financial Secretary to the Treasury, 1963-64; Minister of State, Board of Trade, 1962-63, and Parliamentary Secretary, Ministry of Labour, 1961-62. B September, 1911; ed Brighton College and London University. Director, Martin's Bank, and other companies. President, North-West area Young Conservatives, since 1964. Member Select Committee on Nationalized Industries and chairman, North-West Committee of Conservative MPs.

Mr **Ronald Marshall**, lecturer in social studies and adult education. B March, 1927; ed Woodhouse Grove School, Apperley Bridge, Yorks, Handsworth College, Birmingham, and Manchester University. ATTI.

PUDSEY   same

Electorate 65,780   1970: 62,335

Shaw, J. G. D. (C)	21,750
Cooksey, S. J. (L)	18,011
Targett, K. (Lab)	15,267
C majority	3,739

No change

	1970		1974
Total Vote	49,375		55,028
Turnout	79·2%		83·6%
C	24,308	49·2%	39·5%
Lab	18,313	37·1%	27·7%
L	6,754	13·7%	32·7%
C maj	5,995	12·1%	6·8%
Swing		+3·5%	−0·1%

Mr **Giles Shaw**, who contested Kingston upon Hull West in 1966, is a marketing director, confectionery division, Rowntree Mackintosh Ltd. B November 1931; ed Sedbergh School and St John's College, Cambridge. (President of the Union, 1954.) Served on Flaxton Rural District Council for seven years. Joint secretary, Yorkshire Conservative MPs, from March 1974.

Mr **Stephen Cooksey**, university administrator, contested Leeds, South, 1970. B January 1944; ed Middlesbrough High School and University of Leeds. Secretary and later chairman, Leeds University Liberal Association. Elected Horsforth UDC, 1971, West Yorkshire County Council, 1973. Member, national executive and Council of Liberal Party.

Mr **Kenneth Targett**, poultry farmer and shopkeeper, contested Skipton, 1970. B January, 1928; ed elementary and secondary schools, Brasted Place Theological College and Queen's College, Birmingham. Ordained, 1957; former vicar of Bierley, Bradford. Member, Skipton RDC. NUAAW.

READING North   major

Electorate 64,021

Durant, R. A. B. (C)	19,984
Denby, Miss M. J. (Lab)	17,615
Burnett, J. (L)	13,137
C majority	2,369

	1974		1974
Total Vote	50,736	Lab	34·7%
Turnout	79·2%	L	25·9%
C	39·4%	C maj	4·7%

Mr **Anthony Durant** is general manager and company secretary of an audio visual aids firm. Contested Rother Valley, 1970. B January 1928; ed Dane Court Preparatory School and Bryanston School, Dorset. Member Woking Urban Council, 1968-74. Chairman, Woking education committee; member, Surrey education committee. Former director of film trade association.

Miss Maeve Denby, university graduate in psychology and sociology, lecturer. B February, 1945; ed Geneva, Cheltenham Ladies' College, University of Hull, and St Hugh's College, Oxford. Oxford city councillor; development officer for a national charity concerned with educationally sub-normal children. Contested Henley, 1970.

Mr Julian Burnett is general manager of a firm of scientific publishers. B August, 1925; ed Sevenoaks School and New College, Oxford. Contested Enfield East 1964 and 1966, Enfield West 1970.

READING South   major

Electorate 68,544

*Vaughan, Dr G. F. (C)	23,735
Bural, P. (L)	18.376
Kaufman, G. (Lab)	13,358
C majority	5,359

	1974		1974
Total Vote	55,469	L	33·1%
Turnout	80·9%	Lab	24·1%
C	42·8%	C maj	9·7%

Dr Gerald Vaughan, who won Reading for the Conservatives in 1970, is a specialist at Guy's Hospital and has acted as adviser to voluntary organizations, including the National Society for Autistic Children and the National Institute for the Deaf. Contested Poplar, 1955. B  June, 1923; ed privately in East Africa, London University and Guy's Hospital. Alderman, GLC, 1967-72, and LCC, 1955-64. Member, South-East Economic Planning Council, 1968-71. Joint Secretary, Conservative Parliamentary Health and Social Security Committee. An Opposition Whip from March 1974.

Mr Paul Bural is a publications manager. B February, 1940; ed Leys School, Cambridge, and London College of Printing. Member, Berkshire County Council since 1973. Member and group negotiator, ASTMS.

Mr Gerd Kaufmann, architect. B June, 1933; ed St Lawrence College, Ramsgate, and Architectural Association School of Architecture, London. Member, Elstree council, 1968-71, Hertfordshire council, 1968-74.

REDBRIDGE Ilford North   major

Electorate 64,651

*Iremonger, T. L. (C)	19,843
Miller, Mrs. M. (Lab)	19,558
Wilson, Gareth (L)	12,063
C majority	285

	1974		1974
Total Vote	51,464	Lab	38·0%
Turnout	79·6%	L	23·4%
C	38·5%	C maj	0·5%

Mr Thomas Iremonger was returned at a by-election in February, 1954. Contested Birmingham, Northfield, 1950. Editor and journalist. B March, 1916; ed Oriel College, Oxford. Served as district officer in Colonial Service in Western Pacific. Author of  books on penology and economics. Underwriting member of Lloyd's. Member of Royal Commission on the Penal System, 1963-66; of Home Secretary's Advisory Council on the Employment of Prisoners; and of General Council, Institute for the Study and treatment of Delinquency. Member, Chelsea Borough Council, 1952-55.

Mrs Millie Miller, social worker. B April, 1923; ed Dame Alice Owen's Girls' School. Mayor of Stoke Newington, 1957-58; Camden 1967-68 and leader of Camden council 1971-73. GMWU.

Mr Gareth Wilson, chartered accountant. B May, 1943; ed Ilford County High School. Contested Ilford, North, 1970.

REDBRIDGE Ilford South   same

Electorate 55,807   1970: 58,243

Shaw, A. J. (Lab)	17,201
*Cooper, A. E. (C)	16,058
Wilson, Gerald (L)	9,666
Lab majority	1,143

Labour gain

	1970		1974
Total Vote	39,714		42,925
Turnout	68·2%		76·9%
C	18,369	46·2%	37·4%
Lab	17,087	43·0%	40·1%
L	3,341	8·4%	22·5%
Nat Front	727	1·8%	—
Ind	190	0·5%	—
C maj	1,282	3·2%	
Lab maj	—		2·7%
Swing		+4·5%	−2·9%

Mr Arnold Shaw was MP for Ilford South 1966-70. Contested that division 1964, 1970. Teacher. B July, 1909; ed Cooper's Company School; Southampton and London universities. Member, Redbridge council since 1971 and from 1965-68; Ilford council, 1952-65 and Stepney, 1934-48. NUT.

Mr Albert Cooper, regained the seat for the Conservatives in 1970; MP for the constituency, 1950-66. Contested Dagenham, 1945. B September, 1910; ed London College of Choristers and in Australia and New Zealand. Member, Ilford Council, 1935-51; alderman from 1947. Managing director, Dispersions Ltd; director Ault & Wiborg (International) Ltd, McIntyre & Sons Ltd and S. Collier & Co Ltd.

Mr Gerald Wilson, director of London photographic organization. B June, 1913; ed King Henry VIII School, Coventry. Contested Ilford, South, 1970.

REDBRIDGE Wanstead & Woodford major

Electorate 57,927

*Jenkin, C. P. F. (C)	23,056
Gilby, D. (L)	11,155
Darlington, R. (Lab)	10,365
C majority	11,901

	1974		1974
Total Vote	44,576	L	25·0%
Turnout	76·9%	Lab	23·2%
C	51·7%	C maj	26·7%

Mr Patrick Jenkin was Minister for Energy 1974; Chief Secretary, Treasury, 1972-74; Financial Secretary to the Treasury, 1970-72. Elected in 1964. Barrister and former industrial adviser. Was an Opposition spokesman on finance, economic and trade affairs, 1965-70. B September, 1926; ed Clifton College and Jesus College, Cambridge. Member, Hornsey Borough Council, 1960-63. Appointed to Shadow Cabinet as Opposition spokesman on energy, March 1974.

Mr David Gilby, research engineer. B May, 1948; ed St Aloysius College, Highgate, and King's College, London University.

Mr Roger Darlington is personal assistant to Mr Merlyn Rees, MP. B June, 1948; ed Xaverian College, Manchester and Manchester University Institute of Science and Technology.

REIGATE & BANSTEAD major

Electorate 72,260

Gardiner, G. A. (C)	30,131
Bryan, A. C. (L)	16,071
Ormerod, M. G. (Lab)	13,547
Taggart, M. (Ind Dem)	254
C majority	14,060

	1974		1974
Total Vote	60,003	Lab	22·6%
Turnout	83·0%	Ind Dem	0·4%
C	50·2%	C maj	23·4%
L	26·8%		

Mr George Gardiner, journalist. Contested Coventry, South, 1970. B March, 1935; ed Harvey Grammar School, Folkestone, and Balliol College, Oxford. Senior political correspondent for Thomson Newspapers and broadcaster.

Mr Cyril Bryan, marketing manager. B February, 1938; ed Reigate Grammar School.

Mr Michael Ormerod is a research scientist. B September, 1938; ed Bradfield College, ASTMS.

Mr Mervyn Taggart, maker of films on democracy and peace. B March, 1918; ed Sedbergh School, Ottershaw College, and London University.

RENFREWSHIRE East major

Electorate 62,973

*Anderson, Miss M. B. H. (C)	25,713
Stewart, R. S. (Lab)	10,227
Craig, W. (L)	9,588
Watterson, Mrs S. (Scot Nat)	5,268
C majority	15,486

	1974		1974
Total Vote	50,796	L	18·9%
Turnout	80·7%	Scot Nat	10·4%
C	50·6%	C maj	30·5%
Lab	20·1%		

Miss Harvie Anderson served as Deputy Speaker and Deputy Chairman of Ways and Means, 1970-73, and was the first woman to sit in the Speaker's Chair. Member of Speaker's panel of Chairmen, 1966-70. Elected in 1959; contested West Stirlingshire in 1950 and 1951 and Sowerby, 1955. B 1915; ed St Leonard's School, St Andrews, Secretary, Conservative parliamentary arts, public building and works committee, 1965-66. Member, executive, 1922 Committee, 1962-70; Historic Buildings Council for Scotland, 1966; Royal Commission on Local Government in Scotland, 1966, Stirling County Council, 1945-59. RSNI Hospital Board, 1952-59, and Scottish Advisory Council on Education, 1955-59. President, Scottish Young Unionists, 1955-58. Member, executive, 1922 Committee, from March 1974.

Mr Robin Stewart, teacher. B February, 1949; ed Rutherglen Academy, Glasgow University, and Jordanhill College of Education. EIS.

Mr William Craig, export manager. Ed High School of Glasgow and Glasgow University. President, Glasgow University Liberal Club, 1949-50. Former member, Scottish Covenant Association.

Mrs Sheila Watterson, telephone receptionist. Secretary to the party on Glasgow District Council.

RENFREWSHIRE West   major

Electorate 69,114

*Buchan, N. F. (Lab)	22,178
Ross-Harper, J. (C)	19,510
Cameron, C. (Scot Nat)	8,394
Young, D. (L)	5,022
Lab majority	2,668

	1974		1974
Total Vote	55,104	Scot Nat	15·2%
Turnout	79·7%	L	9·1%
Lab	40·2%	Lab maj	4·8%
C	35·4%		

Mr Norman Buchan, an Opposition spokesman on agriculture, 1973-74 and Scottish Affairs, 1970-73, was Under Secretary, Scottish Office, 1967-70. Elected in 1964. Teacher. B October, 1922; ed Kirkwall Grammar School and Glasgow University. President of Ruther-

glen district, Educational Institute of Scotland. Lecturer in adult education; edited a collection of Scottish folk songs. *Appointed Minister of State for Agriculture, Fisheries and Food, March 1974.*

Mr Ross Harper, solicitor. B March, 1935; ed Hutcheson Boys' Grammar School and Glasgow University. Contested Hamilton, 1970.

Mr Charles Cameron, business controls analyst. B August, 1942; ed Hutchesons Boys' Grammar School. Member, Largs Town Council; works council chairman, IBM, Greenock. Former SNP organizer, Coatbridge, Largs and Coatbridge/Airdrie branches.

Mr David Young, schoolmaster. B November, 1937; ed Aberdeen University, Inverurie Academy, Aberdeenshire, Kilmarnock Academy.

RHONDDA   major

Electorate 65,352

*Jones, T. A. (Lab)	36,880
James, G. P. (Pl Cymru)	6,739
Leyshon, P. (C)	4,111
Austin, D. J. (L)	3,056
True, A. (Comm)	1,374
Lab majority	30,141

	1974		1974
Total Vote	52,160	C	7·9%
Turnout	79·8%	L	5·8%
Lab	70·7%	Comm	2·6%
Pl Cymru	12·9%	Lab maj	57·8%

Mr Alec Jones represented Rhondda West in 1967-74. Secretary, Welsh Labour Group; secretary, Welsh Parliamentary Party. Schoolteacher. B August, 1924; ed Rhondda Grammar School and Bangor Training College. Chairman, Parliamentary Labour Party

education group, 1969-70; former Wood Green borough councillor. NUT.

Mr Glyn James contested the former Rhondda East seat on three occasions. Mechanical engineer with the National Coal Board. Member, mid-Glamorgan County Council and Rhondda District Council.

Mr Peter Leyshon, art teacher. B 1933; ed Tonypandy Grammar School and Cardiff College of Art. Chairman, Rhondda Conservative Association; member, South Wales Mountain Rescue Association; former member, Sports Council for Wales.

Mr Dennis Austin, hotelier. B December, 1937; ed grammar school. Reached rank of Petty Officer in Royal Navy.

Mr **Arthur Trew**, electrician. B December 1920; ed elementary schools and Treherbert Boys' School. Contested two general elections and a by-election at Rhondda West. Member, borough and county councils; area committee member, ETU.

RICHMOND UPON THAMES
Richmond   same

Electorate 53,441   1970: 57,301

*Royle, A. (C)	19,534
Rundle, T. S. (L)	15,707
Palmer, A. R. (Lab)	8,322
Russell, E. (Nat Front)	570
C majority	3,827

No change

	1970		1974
Total Vote	40,894		44,133
Turnout	71·7%		82·6%
C	20,979	51·3%	44·3%
Lab	12,981	31·7%	18·8%
L	6,934	16·9%	35·6%
Nat Front	—		1·3%
C maj	7,998	19·5%	8·7%
Swing		+2·7%	+2·9%

Mr **Anthony Royle**, served as Under-Secretary of State for Foreign and Commonwealth Affairs, 1970-74. Elected in 1959; contested St Pancras, North, 1955, and Torrington by-election, 1958. Vice-chairman, Conservative committee on foreign affairs, 1965-67. Opposition whip 1967-70; B March, 1927; ed Harrow and Sandhurst.

Mr **Stanley Rundle**, consultant chemist and technical translator. B September, 1913. Ed Northampton School, Northampton College of Technology, universities of Milan and London. Member, Richmond upon Thames council since 1966; GLC since April, 1973. Contested Kingston upon Thames, 1964, Ipswich, 1966, and Richmond, 1970.

Mr **Tony Palmer** contested the seat in 1970. Personnel officer with NCB. B July, 1943; ed Brighton, Hove and Sussex Grammar School and Bristol University. Member, Richmond Borough Council since 1971. ASTMS.

Mr **Eric Russell**, Post Office overseas telegraph operator. B February, 1945; ed St Mary's secondary school. UPW.

RICHMOND UPON THAMES
Twickenham   minor

Electorate 71,683   1970: 73,974

*Jessel, T. (C)	27,595
Kramer, S. (L)	16.092
Taylor, R. M. (Lab)	15,909
C majority	11,503

No change

	1970		1974
Total Vote	52,499		59,596
Turnout	71·0%		83·1%
C	28,571	54·4%	46·3%
Lab	16,950	32·3%	26·7%
L	6,516	12·4%	27·0%
Ind	462	0·8%	—
C maj	11,621	22·1%	19·3%
Swing		+4·2%	−1·2%

Mr **Toby Jessel** was elected in 1970; contested Kingston-upon-Hull, North, at the by-election in 1966 and at the general election two months later. Fought Peckham in 1964. B July, 1934; ed Royal Naval College, Dartmouth, and Balliol College, Oxford. A member

of GLC for Richmond on Thames, 1967-73, and of Southwark Borough Council, 1964-66, Joint Secretary, Greater London group of Conservative MPs. Director of Jessel Securities, Secretary, Conservative Candidates' Association, 1961-66.

Mr **Stephen Kramer**, barrister. B September, 1947; ed Hampton Grammar School, Keble College, Oxford and University of Nancy, France.

Mr **Ronald Taylor**, political organizer, contested Woking, 1970. B April, 1938; ed Roundhay Grammar School, Leeds; Ruskin College, Oxford; former full-time official GMWU.

RICHMOND (YORKS)   major

Electorate 62,069   1970: 70,908

*Kitson, T. P. G. (C)	26,994
Graham, Miss B. (L)	11,727
Pearce, E. R. (Lab)	7,659
C majority	15,267

	1974			1974
Total Vote	46,380		L	25·3%
Turnout	74·4%		Lab	16·5%
C	58·2%		C maj	32·9%

Mr Timothy Kitson has been Parliamentary Private Secretary to Mr Heath, the Prime Minister, 1970-74. Opposition Whip, 1967-70. Elected in 1959. Farmer. B January, 1931; ed Charterhouse and the Royal Agricultural College, Cirencester.

Estimates Committee, 1964-66; North Riding County Council, 1955-60.

Miss Beth Graham contested Faversham in 1950. Senior lecturer in management, Huddersfield Polytechnic. B October, 1926; ed Settle and Skipton High Schools and Management Centre at University of Bradford. Press officer, Yorkshire division, ATTI; former treasurer. Member North Yorkshire County Council; Practitioner Committee for North Yorkshire area health authority.

Mr Edward Pearce contested Blackpool, South, in 1966. Technical college lecturer; former research assistant, International Department of the Labour Party. B March, 1939; ed Darlington Grammar School, St Peter's College, Oxford, and Stockholm University. NUGMW.

RIPON same

Electorate 49,579   1970: 47,395

Hampson, K. (C)		21,080
*Austick, D. (L)		16,745
English, D. M. (Lab)		4,643
C majority		4,335

C gain

	1970		1974	
Total Vote	34,941		42,468	
Turnout	73·7%		85·6%	
C	21,211	60·7%	49·6%	
Lab	9,147	26·2%	10·9%	
L	4,583	13·1%	3·4%	
C maj	12,064	34·5%	10·2%	
Swing		+4·1%	+2·1%	

1973 by-election: Total Vote 31,983 (64·3%)—L 13,902 (43·5%), C 12,596 (40·5%), Lab 4,435 (13·8%), Dem C Against EEC 690 (2·2%)—L maj 946 (3·0%).

Mr Keith Hampson, university lecturer, was personal assistant to Mr Heath in the 1966 General Election and also assisted him in the Bexley contest in 1970. B August, 1943; ed King James I Grammar School, Bishop Auckland, and at Bristol and Harvard Universities. After

serving in Mr Heath's private office at the Commons, in 1968, he was secretary to Sir Alec Douglas-Home's Scottish constitutional committee from 1968 to 1970. A former Young Conservative, he became chairman of Bristol University Conservative Association. Contested the seat at the by-election in July, 1973.

Mr David Austick gained the seat for the Liberals in the by-election in July, 1973. Party spokesman on health and social security and Northern Ireland. Deputy Leader, Liberal Group, West Yorkshire County Council; member, Leeds City Council and Leeds Metropolitan District Council. B May, 1920; ed City of Leeds School. Partner, Austicks Bookshops, Leeds; chairman, education board, Booksellers Association, 1960-65.

Mr David English, journalist, contested the seat in the by-election in July, 1973. B February, 1950; ed Ripon Grammar School and Pembroke College, Oxford. NUJ.

ROCHDALE same

Electorate 65,592   1970: 63,629

*Smith, C. (L)		25,266
Cunliffe, L. F. (Lab)		16,367
Green, Miss L (C)		7,933
Sellors, M. (Nat Front)		1,885
L majority		8,899

No change

	1970		1974	
Total Vote	46,301		51,451	
Turnout	72·8%		78·4%	
Lab	19,247	41·6%	31·8%	
L	14,076	30·4%	49·1%	
C	12,978	28·0%	15·4%	
Nat Front	—		3·7%	
Lab maj	5,171	11·2%	—	
L maj	—		17·3%	
Swing	—	+5·2%		

1972 by-election: Total Vote 45,633 (69·0%)—L 19,296 (42·3%), Lab 14,203 (31·1%), C 8,060 (17·7%), Ind 4,074 (8·9%)—L maj 5,093 (11·2%).

Mr Cyril Smith gained the seat for the Liberals in the by-election in October, 1972. Fought the seat in 1970. Party spokesman on employment. B June, 1928; ed Rochdale Grammar School. Managing director, Smith Springs (Rochdale) Ltd; director, G.A.

Electric Ltd, Rochdale. Mayor of Rochdale 1966-67; member of borough council since 1952. On parliamentary panel, TGWU, 1955-58.

Mr **Lawrence Cunliffe** contested the seat at the October, 1972 by-election.

Miss Lilian Green is director of a firm of wholesale fruit merchants. B 1933; ed Spring Bank Secondary Modern School, Rochdale. Member, United Europe Association.

Mr Michael Sellors, chartered accountant. B January, 1943; ed Burnage Grammar School.

ROCHESTER & CHATHAM same

Electorate 79,107   1970: 77,190

*Fenner, Mrs P. E. (C)	24,326
Kenward, R. R. (Lab & Co-op)	23,483
Fellowes, C. (L)	14,945
C majority	843

No change

	1970		1974	
Total Vote	55,185		62,754	
Turnout	71·5%		79·3%	
C	30,263	54·8%		38·8%
Lab	24,922	45·2%		
Lab & Co-op	—			37·4%
L	—			23·8%
C maj	5,341	9·7%		1·3%
Swing		+6·9%		−4·1%

Mrs Peggy Fenner, Parliamentary Secretary to the Ministry of Agriculture, Fisheries and Food, 1972-74. Won the seat for the Conservatives in 1970. Contested Newcastle-under-Lyme in 1966. B November, 1922; ed LCC elementary school, Brockley and Ide Hill School, Kent. Housewife. Chairman, Sevenoaks Council, 1962-63. Member, executive of Kent Borough and Urban District Councils' Association, 1967-71. Member, West Kent Divisional Executive Education Committee, 1963-72.

Mr Roger Kenward, teacher, contested Arundel and Shoreham in 1966 and at the 1970 by-election, and fought Portsmouth, Langstone, in 1970. Ed Shoreham Secondary School and Brighton Teachers' Training College. Member, Southwick UDC, 1963-1974.

Mr Colin Fellowes, manufacturer of electronic components. B October, 1938; ed Acton Central School and Brunel College of Technology.

ROSS & CROMARTY same

Electorate 29,134   1970: 26,947

*Gray, J. H. N. (C)	7,908
McRae, W. (Scot Nat)	5,037
Robertson, J. C. (L)	4,621
MacLean, R. D. (Lab)	4,336
C majority	2,871

No change

	1970		1974	
Total Vote	19,326		21,902	
Turnout	71·7%		75·2%	
C	6,418	33·2%		36·1%
L	5,617	29·1%		21·1%
Lab	5,023	26·0%		19·8%
Scot Nat	2,268	11·7%		23·0%
C maj	801	4·1%		13·1%
Swing		+5·0%		+4·5%

Mr Hamish Gray, who won the seat for the Conservatives in 1970, was a Lord Commissioner of the Treasury 1973-74 after serving two years as an assistant whip. Former director of a roofing and contracting firm. B June, 1927; ed Inverness Royal Academy. Member, Inverness Council 1965-70. Former member, council, Highland Chamber of Commerce and of Highlands and Islands Youth Employment Committee.

Mr William McRae, solicitor. B May, 1923; ed Falkirk High School and Glasgow University. Former Secretary and chairman, Falkirk Arts and Civic Council.

Mr John Robertson, farmer. B April, 1932; ed Merchiston Castle School and Cambridge University. Member, Ross and Cromarty CC; chairman, Liberal Highland Regional Council.

Mr Ronald MacLean contested the seat in 1970. Further education college teacher. B May, 1942; ed primary school, Inverness Royal Academy, Aberdeen University, and Jordanhill College of Education.

ROSSENDALE same

Electorate 50,055   1970: 49,900

*Bray, R. W. T. (C)	16,040
Noble, M. A. (Lab)	15,243
Hamilton, J. A. (L)	10,478
C majority	797

No change

	1970		1974	
Total Vote	39,016		41,761	
Turnout	78·2%		83·4%	
C	20,448	52·4%		38·4%
Lab	18,568	47·6%		36·5%
L	—			25·1%
C maj	1,880	4·8%		1·9%
Swing		+7·8%		−1·4%

Mr **Ronald Bray** won the seat for the Conservatives in 1970. Engineer, farmer, and Lloyd's underwriter. B January, 1922; ed Latymer Upper School, London. Contested Stockton-on-Tees in 1964. Former member of Woking Urban Council. Secretary, Conservative Parliamentary Employment Committee and of North-West Group of Conservative MPs since 1972.

Mr **Michael Noble,** contested Manchester, Withington, 1970. B March, 1935; ed Hull Grammar School, Sheffield and Hull universities. Tutor in industrial studies, WEA. Member, TGWU.

Mr **John Hamilton,** insurance broker. B 1931. Contested South Belfast, 1963 by-election and Mid Armagh, 1965 Stormont elections.

ROTHERHAM   minor

Electorate 60,774   1970: 60,460

*O'Malley, B. K. (Lab)	27,088
Lewis, D. (C)	10,354
Hughes, J. (L)	7,726
Lab majority	16,734

No change

	1970		1974
Total Vote	38,016		45,168
Turnout	62·9%		74·3%
Lab	25,246	66·4%	60·0%
C	12,770	33·6%	22·9%
L	—		17·1%
Lab maj	12,476	32·8%	37·0%
Swing		+3·3%	−2·1%

Mr **Brian O'Malley,** an Opposition spokesman on pensions and social security, 1970-74, was Under-Secretary, Health and Social Security, 1969-70. A Lord Commissioner of the Treasury, April 1967-69; became deputy Government Chief Whip in July, 1967; assistant Government whip, 1964-66. Represented the constituency since the by-election in March, 1963. Teacher and lecturer. B January, 1930; ed Mexborough Grammar School and Manchester University. Sponsored by Musicians' Union, of which he was a branch secretary. *Appointed Minister of State for Health and Social Security, March 1974.*

Mr **David Lewis,** chairman of a property development company, formerly a public relations officer. B 1936; ed Ampleforth College. Former chairman, North-West Leicester Young Conservatives and Leicester Conservative Trade Unionist Committee.

Mr **John Hughes,** managing director of a carpet company. B September, 1948; ed Abbeydale Grammar School, Sheffield.

ROTHER VALLEY   minor

Electorate 91,076   1970: 87,331

*Hardy, P. (Lab)	52,532
Waller, G. (C)	19,058
Lab majority	33,474

No change

	1970		1974
Total Vote	61,740		71,590
Turnout	70·6%		78·6%
Lab	44,322	71·8%	73·4%
C	17,418	28·2%	26·6%
Lab maj	26,904	43·6%	46·7%
Swing		+5·0%	−1·6%

Mr **Peter Hardy,** elected in 1970, was a teacher. B July, 1931; ed Wath upon Dearne Grammar School; Westminster College, London; Sheffield University. Contested Scarborough and Whitby, 1964, Sheffield, Hallam, 1966. Member, PLP agriculture, environment, power and education group; Wath upon Dearne Urban Council, 1960-70 (chairman, 1968-69); National Union of Public Employees, Past President, Don and Dearne Schoolmasters Association.

Mr **Gary Waller,** public relations consultant, was formerly personal assistant to Sir Keith Joseph. B 1945. GLC candidate for Leyton, 1973.

ROXBURGH, SELKIRK & PEEBLES
same

Electorate 57,478   1970: 57,180

*Steel, D. M. S. (L)	25,707
Thom, J. S. (C)	16,690
Purves, D. (Scot Nat)	3,953
Graham, D. A. (Lab)	3,089
L majority	9,017

No change

	1970		1974
Total Vote	46,202		49,439
Turnout	80·8%		86·3%
L	19,524	42·2%	52·0%
C	18,974	41·1%	33·7%
Lab	4,454	9·6%	6·2%
Scot Nat	3,147	6·8%	8·0%
Ind	103	0·3%	—
L maj	550	1·2%	18·2%

Mr David Steel, the Liberal Whip, won the seat from the Conservatives at the 1965 by-election; contested the seat in 1964. Sponsored the Abortion Act, 1967. Party spokesman on Commonwealth and Overseas Development, President of the Anti-Apartheid Movement in Great Britain, 1966-69. Director of advertising company. B. March, 1938; ed Prince of Wales School, Nairobi; George Watson's College, Edinburgh and Edinburgh University. Member of the British Council of Churches. President, National League of Young Liberals.

Mr Stuart Thom, contested Greenwich, 1970, and at the 1971 by-election. Business executive. B July, 1942; ed Dumfries Academy, George Watson's College, Edinburgh, Edinburgh University, and Manchester Business School. Member, Young European Management Association, Bow Group, and Royal Commonwealth Society.

Mr David Purves, agricultural chemist. B April 1924; ed Galashiels Academy and Edinburgh University.

Mr David Graham, teacher and part-time WEA tutor. B April, 1951; ed Royal Belfast Academical Institution and University of Edinburgh. President, University Labour Club, 1969-71; vice-chairman, national organization of Labour students, 1971; chairman, Edinburgh, South, constituency Labour Party. EIS.

ROYAL TUNBRIDGE WELLS major

Electorate 68,618

Mayhew, P. (C)	27,212
Owens, D. (L)	16,184
Short, M. F. (Lab)	11,734
C majority	11,028

	1974		1974
Total Vote	55,130	L	29·3%
Turnout	80·3%	Lab	21·3%
C	49·3%	C maj	20·0%

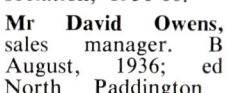

Mr Patrick Mayhew, a barrister, fought Dulwich, Camberwell in 1970. B September, 1929; ed Tonbridge School and Balliol College, Oxford. Vice-chairman, Sevenoaks Conservative Association, 1956-60.

Mr David Owens, sales manager. B August, 1936; ed North Paddington secondary central school.

Mr Michael Short, teacher. B May, 1946; ed East Grinstead County Grammar School, North-Western Polytechnic, London. NUT, Fabian Society, Public Enterprise Group.

RUGBY minor

Electorate 59,031 1970: 57,813

*Price, W. G. (Lab)	25,176
Boswell, M. T. E. (C)	19,022
Campbell, J. (L)	6,560
Frost, A. E. (Soc Credit)	106
Lab majority	6,154

No change

	1970		1974
Total Vote	47,381		50,864
Turnout	81·8%		86·2%
Lab	25,041	52·8%	49·5%
C	22,086	46·6%	37·4%
Social Credit	254	0·5%	0·2%
L	—		12·9%
Lab maj	2,955	6·2%	12·1%
Swing		−2·6%	−2·9%

Mr William Price won the seat for Labour in 1966. Journalist. Parliamentary Private Secretary to the Deputy Leader of the Opposition since 1972. B June, 1934; ed Forest of Dean Technical School and Gloucester Technical College. Former central Midlands secretary of the National Union of Journalists. *Appointed Parliamentary Secretary, Overseas Development, March 1974.*

Mr Timothy Boswell, farmer and economist. B December, 1942; ed Marlborough College and New College, Oxford; worked at Conservative research department 1966-73, head of economic section 1970-73.

Mr John Campbell contested Nuneaton 1959, 1964, and 1965 by-election. Iron moulder. B March, 1922; ed at elementary school. Former shop steward for Amalgamated Union of Foundry Workers.

RUNCORN same

Electorate 69,319   1970: 61,331

*Carlisle, M. (C)	26,374
Taylor, M. J. E. (Lab)	19,106
Brenton, P. M. (L)	12,020
C majority	7,268

No change

	1970	1974
Total Vote	47,217	57,500
Turnout	77·0%	82·9%
C	25,272	53·5%	45·9%
Lab	16,204	34·3%	33·2%
L	5,741	12·1%	20·9%
C maj	9,068	19·2%	12·6%
Swing		+3·7%	−3·2%

Mr Mark Carlisle, Minister of State, Home Office, 1972-74, was previously Under-Secretary, Home Office 1970-72. Elected in 1964. Contested St Helens in the 1958 by-election and in 1959. B July, 1929; ed Radley College and Manchester University. Barrister (Gray's Inn, 1954). Former chairman, Federation of University Conservative and Unionist Associations. Former member, Home Office Advisory Council on the Penal System.

Mr Michael Taylor, personnel manager, contested the seat in 1966 and 1970. B September 1937; ed Harrow and Emmanuel College, Cambridge.

Mr Michael Brenton, airline chief steward. B. September, 1941; ed St Bedes School and Vindicatrix training college. Member, Cookery and Food Association.

RUSHCLIFFE major

Electorate 63,366

*Clarke, K. H. (C)	29,828
Gallagher, M. (Lab)	12,119
Hamilton, J. (L)	11,719
C majority	17,709

	1974		1974
Total Vote	53,666	Lab	22·6%
Turnout	84·7%	L	21·8%
C	55·6%	C maj	33·0%

Mr Kenneth Clarke won the seat for the Conservatives in 1970. Lord Commissioner of the Treasury (Government whip), 1974; assistant whip, 1972-74. Contested Mansfield in 1964 and 1966. Barrister. B July, 1940; ed Nottingham High School and Gonville and Caius College, Cambridge. Called to the Bar by Gray's Inn, 1963. Research secretary, Birmingham Bow Group, 1966-67. President, Cambridge Union, 1963. Joint secretary, Conservative health and social security committee, from March 1974.

Mr Michael Gallagher, mature student. Mansfield Councillor. B July, 1934; ed St Mary Magdalene Junior School, Seaham; St Joseph's Seaham Secondary Modern School, WEA section, Nottingham University, Coleg Harlech, North Wales. Former miner.

Mr Julian Hamilton, chartered accountant. B August, 1939; ed Nottingham High School, Rugby School, and Cranfield Business School.

RUTHERGLEN major

Electorate 48,452

*Mackenzie, J. G. (Lab)	19,005
Thomson, J. (C)	14,852
Leslie, Mrs. L. (Scot Nat)	6,089
Lab majority	4,153

	1974		1974
Total Vote	39,946	C	37·2%
Turnout	82·4%	Scot Nat	15·2%
Lab	47·6%	Lab maj	10·4%

Mr Gregor Mackenzie, Opposition spokesman on Posts and Telecommunications, won the seat for Labour in the May, 1964, by-election; contested Kinross and West Perth, 1959, and East Aberdeenshire, 1950. Sales manager. B November, 1927; ed Queens Park School and School of Social Studies, Glasgow University. Glasgow Corporation, 1952-55 and 1956-64. Member, Fabian Society; Estimates Committee, 1964-66. *Appointed Under Secretary for Industry, March 1974.*

Mr John Thomson, headmaster. B December, 1934. Fellow in education of Winston Churchill Management Trust, 1970; first Conservative councillor in Motherwell; leader, Conservative group, Motherwell and Wishaw Town Council

Conservative group; member of national executive of Technical Teachers' Association.

Mrs Louisa Leslie, radiographer. B June, 1937; ed Shawlands School. Has fought Glasgow municipal elections for the party. Secretary, Pollokshaws North Branch, SNP.

RUTLAND & STAMFORD   minor

Electorate 54,204   1970: 50,287

*Lewis, K. (C)	21,088
Byrne, A. J. (Lab)	12,203
Howie, D. (L)	11,336
C majority	8,885

No change

	1970		1974
Total Vote	37,939		44,627
Turnout	75·4%		82·3%
C	22,803	60·1%	47·2%
Lab	15,136	39·9%	27·3%
L	—		25·4%
C maj	7,667	20·2%	19·9%
Swing		+6·7%	−0·1%

Mr Kenneth Lewis was elected in 1959; contested Ashton-under-Lyne, 1951, and Newton, 1945 and 1950. Member, Estimates Committee, 1966-68, and Committee of Selection, 1964-70. B July, 1916; ed Jarrow Central School and Edinburgh University. Chairman

of a shipping and travel organization. Treasurer, Commonwealth and Continental Church Society. Member, Middlesex County Council 1947-50.

Mr Anthony Byrne, administrative assistant, Central Lancashire New Town. B August, 1947; ed Caltham School, Rutland, and Lancaster, Colorado and Cambridge Universities. NUAAW.

Mr David Howie, contested Grantham, 1966. B June, 1941; ed Fettes, and Corpus Christie College, Cambridge.

RYE   same

Electorate 71,791   1970: 68,013

*Irvine, B. G. (C)	33,591
Moore, D. R. S. (L)	17,456
Harris, R. W. (Lab)	6,967
C majority	16,135

No change

	1970		1974
Total Vote	50,278		58,014
Turnout	73·9%		80·8%
C	32,300	64·2%	57·9%
Lab	9,031	18·0%	12·0%
L	8,947	17·8%	30·1%
C maj	23,269	46·3%	27·8%
Swing		+3·7%	−0·1%

Mr Godman Irvine was elected in 1955; contested Wood Green, 1951. Member, Speaker's panel of chairmen since 1966; Select Committee on Agriculture, 1966-69. Barrister (Inner Temple, 1932), farmer, and Companion, Institution of Civil Engineers. B in

Canada, July, 1909; ed St Paul's School, London, and Magdalen College, Oxford. Vice-chairman, Conservative Parliamentary Agriculture Committee,1964-70. Member, Executive, 1922 Committee, 1965-68, and vice-chairman Conservative Parliamentary Foreign and Commonwealth Affairs Committee; a United Kingdom representative on General Council, Commonwealth Parliamentary Association, 1969-70 and Treasurer of the Association since. President, Association of British Resorts since 1964. Hon Treasurer, 1922 Committee, from March 1974.

Mr Douglas Moore, management accountant. B September, 1925; ed County Technical College, Dartford, Kent. Member, Bognor Regis UDC.

Mr Robert Harris, teacher. B March, 1945; ed primary and grammar schools, Grey College, Durham University. NUT.

SAFFRON WALDEN   major

Electorate 61,926

*Kirk, P. M. (C)	23,013
Moore, F. P. D. (L)	15,468
Dowsett, J. (Lab)	13,138
C majority	7,545

	1974			1974
Total Vote	51,619		L	30·0%
Turnout	83·3%		Lab	25·4%
C	44·6%		C maj	14·6%

Mr Peter Kirk, chairman of the joint British and Danish Conservative group at the European Parliament since 1973, was also leader of the first Conservative delegation to the European Parliament. Under Secretary for Defence for the Royal Navy, 1970-72. He was re-

turned at a by-election in March, 1965; represented Gravesend, 1955-64; Under-Secretary for War, 1963-April, 1964, and Under-Secretary of Defence for the Army until October, 1964. Journalist and former director of Inter-Communication (P.R.) Ltd, Howard Rayner Holdings Ltd, and Slip Products Co Ltd. B May, 1928; ed Marlborough College and Trinity College, Oxford (President of the Union, 1949) and Zurich University. United Kingdom delegate to the Council of Europe and Western European Union, 1956-63, and since 1966-70.

Mr Francis Moore contested the constituency in 1970, 1966 and 1964. Agricultural engineer. B February, 1924; ed Wellington College. Parish councillor.

Mr John Dowsett, electronics engineer, contested Sutton and Cheam, 1970. B July, 1930; ed Mid-Essex Technical College. Member, Sutton Borough Council, 1964-68, Saffron Walden Borough Council, since 1971. ASTMS.

ST ALBANS   major

Electorate 67,489

*Goodhew, V. H. (C)	26,345
Shaw, A. C. (L)	17,924
Berstein, D. L. (Lab)	14,077
C majority	8,421

	1974		1974
Total Vote	58,346	L	30·7%
Turnout	86·4%	Lab	24·1%
C	45·1%	C maj	14·4%

Mr Victor Goodhew, Lord Commissioner of the Treasury (whip), 1970-73 and Assistant Government Whip, June to October, 1970, was elected in 1959. Vice-chairman of the Conservative committee on defence, 1964-70. He contested Paddington, North, in 1955. B November, 1919; ed King's College School. Member of Westminster City Council, 1953-59, and of LCC, 1958-61. Vice-chairman of Anglo-German Parliamentary Group and of Conservative Parliamentary Defence Committee.

Mr Charles Shaw contested the constituency in 1970. Commercial manager, chemical industry. B March, 1938; ed Sedbergh School, Yorkshire, Christ's College, Cambridge. Member of the Liberal Party's economic affairs panel.

Mr Daniel Bernstein, chartered accountant. B July, 1942; ed Carmel College, Wallingford, Berks. Councillor, London Borough of Enfield. ASTMS.

ST HELENS   same

Electorate 75,479   1970: 74,448

*Spriggs, L. (Lab)	32,621
Lycett, A. E. (L)	10,905
Bridgeman, K. J. (C)	10,752
Pike, Mrs M. (ILP)	991
Lab majority	21,716

No change

	1970		1974
Total Vote	48,096		55,269
Turnout	64·6%		73·2%
Lab	31,587	65·7%	59·0%
C	16,509	34·3%	19·4%
L	—	—	19·7%
ILP	—	—	1·8%
Lab maj	15,078	31·3%	39·3%
Swing		+5·0%	−4·1%

Mr Leslie Spriggs was returned at a by-election in 1958; contested North Fylde, 1955. Railwayman. B April, 1910; ed council school and through National Council of Labour Colleges. President, political section, north-west England district council of the NUR, 1954. Member of nine PLP groups and Cheshire region of Labour Party; lecturer at National Council of Labour Colleges.

Mr Alan Lycett, solicitor. B December, 1920; ed St Helens Secondary School and Liverpool University. Member, St Helens Borough Council 1958-74 (leader, Liberal group). Mayor of St Helens, 1972–73.

Mr Keith Bridgeman, insurance broker. B December, 1941: ed Dulwich College. Vice-chairman, Crawley UDC, 1970-71.

ST IVES   same

Electorate 51,092   1970: 48,567

*Nott, J. W. F. (C)	18,290
Tonkin, G. E. T. (L)	12,865
Tidy, B. M. (Lab)	9,231
Taylor, G. T. (Ind C)	177
C majority	5,425

No change

	1970		1974
Total Vote	36,475		40,563
Turnout	75·1%		79·4%
C	18,581	50·9%	45·1%
Lab	9,913	27·2%	22·7%
L	7,981	21·9%	31·7%
Ind	—	—	0·4%
C maj	8,668	23·8%	13·4%
Swing		+6·6%	−0·6%

Mr John Nott, Minister of State, Treasury 1972-74, was elected in 1966. B February, 1932—ed Bradfield College and Trinity College, Cambridge (President of the Union, 1959). Barrister (Inner Temple, 1960). Business consultant, general manager, S. G. Warburg

and Co Ltd, 1962-65, and director S. G. Warburg Finance and Developments, 1965-67 and former director of other companies.

Mr Terence Tonkin, schoolteacher. B January, 1936; ed Humphry Davy Grammar School, Penzance, and Loughborough College, Leicestershire. Member, St Ives Borough Council since 1969, and Penwith District Council since 1973.

Mr Bruce Malcolm Tidy, journalist, aged 26. Ed Exeter University.

SALFORD East   same

Electorate 39,851   1970: 45,701

*Allaun, F. (Lab)	14,426
Knightly, Mrs. B. (C)	7,495
Watkin, H. (L)	4,536
Lab majority	6,931

No change

	1970		1974
Total Vote	28,436		26,457
Turnout	62·2%		66·4%
Lab	15,853	55·7%	54·5%
C	9,583	33·7%	28·3%
L	3,000	10·5%	17·1%
Lab maj	6,270	22·0%	26·2%
Swing		+6·2%	−2·1%

Mr Frank Allaun was elected in 1955; contested Manchester, Moss Side, 1951. Deputy chairman, foreign affairs group of the Parliamentary Labour Party. B February, 1913; ed Manchester Grammar School. Has been engineer, shop assistant, foreign tours leader,

WEA lecturer, chartered accountant, journalist. Elected National Executive, Labour Party, 1967; chairman, Labour Peace Fellowship.

Mrs Betty Knightly, barrister (Gray's Inn 1951). B June, 1919; ed Perse School, Cambridge; Godolphin School, Salisbury. Vice-president, Married Women's Association; member, Holborn Borough Council, 1956-59.

Mr Howard Watkin, bank employee. B September, 1949; ed Hull Grammar School, Manchester University.

SALFORD West   same

Electorate 46,469   1970: 47,733

*Orme, S. (Lab)	16,808
Tillett, J. N. L. (C)	10,346
Arstall, A. E. (L)	5,591
Lab majority	6,462

No change

	1970		1974
Total Vote	31,296		32,745
Turnout	65·6%		70·5%
Lab	16,986	54·3%	51·3%
C	14,310	45·7%	31·6%
L	—	—	17·1%
Lab maj	2,676	8·5%	19·7%
Swing		+4·9%	−5·5%

Mr Stanley Orme, elected in 1964, was an Opposition spokesman on Northern Ireland, 1972-74. He contested Stockport, South, 1959. Engineer. B April, 1923; ed elementary and technical schools, National Council of Labour

Colleges and Workers' Educational Association classes. Member, Sale Borough Council 1958-64. Sponsored by AUEW, engineering section; shop steward, branch president for 21 years. Chairman of AUEW's parliamentary group of 22 MPs, and of Northern Ireland PLP group. *Appointed Minister of State for Northern Ireland, March 1974.*

Mr Jeffery Tillett, a teacher. Contested Ilkeston, 1964, and Nottingham, North, 1966. B December, 1927; ed Derby School, Nottingham University, Sheffield University, and Sheffield Polytechnic. Member, Derby Borough Council, 1957-74; alderman, 1968-74. NUT.

Mr Eddie Arstall is a curriculum development officer and a qualified pharmacist. B September, 1921; ed Urmston Grammar School, Salford Technical College, Manchester University and Alsager Training College. NUT.

SALISBURY   same

Electorate 62,223   1970: 61,104

*Hamilton, M. A. (C)	22,753
Lakeman, J. (L)	16,536
Connor, C. J. (Lab)	10,455
C majority	6,217

No change

	1970		1974
Total Vote	44,042		49,744
Turnout	72·1%		79·9%
C	26,549	60·3%	45·7%
Lab	17,493	39·7%	21·0%
L	—		33·2%
C maj	9,056	20·6%	12·5%
Swing		+5·3%	+2·0%

Mr Michael Hamilton was returned at a by-election in February, 1965. Represented Wellingborough, 1959-64. Lord Commissioner of the Treasury (whip), 1962-64; assistant whip, 1961-62. B July, 1918—ed Radley and University College, Oxford. Vice-chairman, Army and Navy Stores Ltd; member, Hops Marketing Board.

Mr John Lakeman, sociology teacher. B December, 1947; ed Bishop Wordsworth's School, Salisbury, and Exeter University. NAS.

Mr Christopher Connor, marketing engineer. Aged 34. Member, Basingstoke Borough Council.

SCARBOROUGH major

Electorate 58,750

*Shaw, M. N. (C)	21,858
Pitts, M. F. (L)	16,751
Taylor-Gooby, D. (Lab)	7,034
Ellis, Mrs M. J. (Ind)	114
Stoker, B. M. (Ind C)	102
C majority	5,107

	1974		1974
Total Vote	45,859	Lab	15·3%
Turnout	78·0%	Ind	0·2%
C	47·7%	Ind C	0·2%
L	36·5%	C maj	11·1%

Mr Michael Shaw was elected for Scarborough and Whitby in 1966. He represented Brighouse and Spenborough, 1960-64: contested that division in 1959 and Dewsbury, 1955. Chartered accountant. B October, 1920; ed Sedbergh. Chairman, Yorkshire Area Conservatives, 1965-66. Vice-chairman, Conservative Trade and Industry Committee, from 1967. Vice-chairman, Yorkshire Conservative MPs since 1972.

Mr Michael Pitts, teacher. B March, 1936; ed High School, Scarborough and Pembroke College, Oxford. Contested Warrington 1964; Cleveland 1966 and Scarborough 1970. Member Scarborough RDC since 1968; Scarborough District Council since 1973 (Leader of the Liberal group). National chairman of the Liberal Candidates' Association 1970-73 (now Vice-president).

Mr David Taylor-Gooby, teacher. Aged 28; ed Cambridge University. Director, Young Volunteers' Service in Newcastle, 1970-72. NUT.

SEVENOAKS major

Electorate 74,217

*Rodgers, Sir J. C. (C)	29,936
Bradley, I. (L)	16,223
Scanlan, J. (Lab)	14,987
Woolard, D. J. (Ind)	754
C majority	13,713

	1974		1974
Total Vote	61,900	Lab	24·2%
Turnout	83·4%	Ind	1·2%
C	48·4%	C maj	22·1%
L	26·2%		

Sir John Rodgers was elected in 1950. Member, Public Accounts Committee since 1970. Parliamentary Secretary, Board of Trade, 1958-60. Marketing consultant, company director and author. Consultant and former deputy chairman, J. Walter Thompson Co Ltd; director, History Today Ltd, Cocoa Merchants Ltd. B October, 1906; ed St Peter's, York, in France, Keble College, Oxford. Founder governor, Administrative Staff College. Member, Council Foundation for Management Education; past president, Institute of Practitioners in Advertising; founder and vice-president, Institute of Statisticians. Fellow, Royal Society of Arts.

Mr Ian Bradley, Research Fellow, New College, Oxford. B May 28, 1950; ed Tonbridge School and New College, Oxford. Member, Liberal Party Education Panel.

Mr James Scanlan, wine merchant. B May, 1940; ed Eareley Road Primary School, Hillbrook School for Boys, Brixton School of Building. Member, Dartford RDC since 1971; South Eastern England Development Board and Thameside Joint Local Authority Committee on Employment and Industry.

Mr Duncan Woolard, company vice-president. Aged 38; ed Sevenoaks School.

SHEFFIELD, ATTERCLIFFE   major

Electorate 63,419

*Duffy, A. E. P. (Lab)	34,120
Santhouse, Miss P. (C)	12,944
Tariq Ali (Int Marxist)	424
Lab majority	21,176

	1974		1974
Total Vote	47,488	C	27·2%
Turnout	74·9%	Int Marx	0·9%
Lab	71·8%	Lab maj	44·6%

Mr Patrick Duffy, was returned in 1970; MP for Colne Valley, 1963-66; contested Tiverton, 1955, 1951, and 1950. Economist and consultant. B June, 1920; ed London and Columbia Universities. NUGMU Chairman PLP economic affairs and finance group, 1965-66. Member, Select Committee on Public Expenditure, since 1970.

Miss Patricia Santhouse, medical secretary, contested the seat in 1970. B March, 1939; ed High Storrs Grammar School, Sheffield. Former vice-chairman of Yorkshire Young Conservatives. Member, Sheffield City Council, and chief whip of Conservative group.

SHEFFIELD Brightside   major

Electorate 56,251

*Griffiths, E. (Lab)	27,363
Smith, J. P. P. (C)	6,796
Blades, W. T. (L)	5,347
Gill, Miss V. A. (Comm)	513
Lab majority	20,567

	1974		1974
Total Vote	40,019	L	13·4%
Turnout	71·1%	Comm	1·3%
Lab	68·4%	Lab maj	51·4%
C	17·0%		

Mr Edward Griffiths, a director of the British Steel Corporation, was returned at a by-election in June, 1968; contested Denbigh, 1966. B March, 1929; ed University College of North Wales, Bangor. Industrial chemist. Member, House of Commons Services Committee. Member, Flintshire County Council, 1964.

Mr John Smith, Secretary to the Inland Waterways Amenity Advisory Council. B December 1943; ed at York and London universities. Member, Brighton County Borough Council and Brighton District Council. Group Convenor in ASTMS.

Mr Thomas Blades, clerical officer, British Rail. B 1924. Contested Doncaster, 1970. Chairman, Doncaster residents' association.

Miss Violet Gill, engineering worker and AUEW shop steward. B September, 1936; ed Sheffield, Woodside Council School and Burngreave Secondary Modern. Member, Executive Committee, Communist Party.

SHEFFIELD Hallam   major

Electorate 76,877

*Osborn, J. H. (C)	29,062
Blunkett, D. (Lab)	16,149
Johnson, M. A. K. (L)	14,160
C majority	12,913

	1974		1974
Total Vote	59,371	Lab	27·2%
Turnout	77·2%	L	23·8%
C	48·9%	C maj	21·7%

Mr John Osborn was elected in 1959. Joint secretary, 1922 Committee since 1968; chairman, Conservative parliamentary transport industries committee since 1972 and Anglo-Soviet Parliamentary Group; joint chairman All-Party Roads Study Group. Member, executive of the Inter-Parliamentary Union and Select Committee on Science and Technology 1970-72. Director, Samuel Osborn and Co Ltd, steel and engineering company, and subsidiary companies. B December, 1922; ed Rugby and Trinity Hall, Cambridge. A searcher of the Cutler's Company. Delegate to Council of Europe and Western European Union.

Mr David Blunkett, post-graduate student and formerly a clerk/typist. B June, 1947; ed Sheffield School for the Blind; Royal Normal College for the Blind, Shrewsbury; Shrewsbury Technical College; Richmond College, Sheffield; Sheffield University, Huddersfield College of Education. ATTI.

Mr Malcolm Johnson, rolling mill manager. B January, 1928; ed Aireborough Grammar School; Leeds College of Technology. Member, Aireborough UDC. 1961-64, Sheffield District Council since 1973.

SHEFFIELD Heeley   major

Electorate 64,790

Hooley, F. O. (Lab)	25,317
Ingle, R. J. (C)	18,732
Singleton, A. J. (L)	9,061
Lab majority	**6,585**

	1974		1974
Total Vote	53,110	C	35·3%
Turnout	82·0%	L	17·1%
Lab	47·7%	Lab maj	12·4%

Mr Frank Hooley was MP for the constituency from 1966-70. Contested it in 1964 and Skipton, 1959. Former member, Public Accounts Committee and Select Committee on Science and Technology. B November, 1923; ed King Edward's School, Birmingham and Birmingham University. Assistant registrar, Sheffield University, 1952-65, and senior assistant registrar, 1965-66.

Mr Robert Ingle, teacher. B April, 1931; ed Deacons School, Peterborough, City of Sheffield College of Education, and St Paul's College, Cheltenham. Member, Huddersfield County Borough Council, 1968-74.

Mr Anthony Singleton, National Coal Board official. B November, 1945; ed Kennington Boys' School, London. Contested the seat 1970. Member, British Association of Colliery Management.

SHEFFIELD Hillsborough   major

Electorate 51,687

Flannery, M. H. (Lab)	22,065
Williamson, B. (C)	10,785
Osner, R. C. (L)	6,863
Lab majority	**11,280**

	1974		1974
Total Vote	39,713	C	27·1%
Turnout	76·8%	L	17·3%
Lab	55·6%	Lab maj	28·4%

Mr Martin Flannery, headmaster. B March, 1918; ed elementary, grammar and Sheffield College of Education. Member, national executive committee, NUT.

Mr Brian Williamson, economist. B February 1945; ed Trinity College, Dublin. Political assistant to Mr Maurice Macmillan MP.

Mr Robin Osner, lecturer. B May, 1942; ed Stowe School, Buckingham; London University, Polytechnic of the South Bank. Secretary, technical advisory committee, Institute of Food, Science and Technology.

SHEFFIELD Park   major

Electorate 66,974

*Mulley, F. W. (Lab)	31,273
Butler, F. R. (L)	8,596
Crewe, T. E. (C)	7,731
Morton, C. (Comm)	521
Lab majority	**22,677**

	1974		1974
Total Vote	48,121	C	16·1%
Turnout	71·8%	Comm	1·1%
Lab	65·0%	Lab maj	47·1%
L	17·9%		

Mr Frederick Mulley, Opposition spokesman on transport 1970-74, Minister of Transport 1969-70; Minister of State, Foreign Office, 1967-69; Minister of Aviation, 1965-67; Deputy Secretary of State for Defence and Minister of Defence for the Army, 1964-65. Won the division in 1950; contested Sutton Coldfield in 1945. Member, Labour Party National Executive, 1957-58 and 1960-64 and since 1965. Vice-chairman of Labour Party 1973-74. Sponsored by APEX. Barrister (Inner Temple, 1954) and economist. B July, 1918; ed Warwick School, Christ Church, Oxford, and Fellow of St Catharine's College, Cambridge 1948-50. *Appointed Minister for Transport, Department of the Environment, March 1974.*

Mr Francis Butler, mature student. B May, 1941; ed Owler Lane, Sheffield, and Sheffield College of Art. Member, Sheffield City Council, Sheffield District Council, and South Yorkshire Metropolitan Council.

Mr Eric Crewe, assistant transport manager. B 1928; ed at grammar school. Sheffield city councillor.

Mr Cyril Morton is a convener of shop stewards at Ambrose Shardlows. B 1933. Former member, Communist Party NEC. AUEW.

SHIPLEY same

Electorate 51,538. 1970: 50,385

*Fox, J. M. (C)	19,439
Wedgeworth, Rev. M. J. (Lab)	15,284
Roberts, G. G. (L)	10,158
Campion, C. G. (Ind Dem All)	192
C majority	4,155

No change

	1970		1974
Total Vote	41,567		45,073
Turnout	82·5%		87·4%
C	20,938	50·4%	43·1%
Lab	16,161	38·9%	33·9%
L	4,468	10·7%	22·5%
Ind Dem All	—	—	0·4%
C maj	4,777	11·5%	9·2%
Swing		+3·8%	−1·1%

Mr Marcus Fox was elected in 1970; contested Dewsbury, 1959 and Huddersfield, West, 1966. Assistant whip, 1972-73; Lord Commissioner of the Treasury (whip), 1973-74. Member, Select Committee on Race Relations and Immigration, 1970; Secretary, party transport industries committee, 1970. Former company director and owner of textile finishing firm. B June, 1927; ed Wheelwright Grammar School, Dewsbury. Member, Dewsbury Borough Council, 1957-65.

The Rev Michael Wedgeworth, Methodist minister and teacher. B January, 1940; ed Bradford Grammar School and Nottingham and Cambridge universities. Member, Norwich City Council, 1971-72.

Mr Glyn Roberts, lecturer. B May, 1925; ed Monmouth School and London School of Economics. Member, ATTI.

SHOREHAM major

Electorate 67,178

*Luce, R. N. (C)	28,200
Bartram, P. F. (L)	18,442
Barry, Q. (Lab)	8,360
C majority	9,758

	1974			1974
Total Vote	55,002		L	33·5%
Turnout	80·7%		Lab	15·2%
C	51·3%		C maj	17·7%

Mr Richard Luce, MP for Arundel and Shoreham, 1971-74; contested Hitchin 1970; B Oct 14, 1936; ed Wellington College, Christ's College, Cambridge and Wadham College, Oxford. Overseas civil servant (Kenya) 1960-62. Branch manager Gallaher Ltd, 1963-65; marketing manager Spirella, 1965-68. Chairman, IFA Consultants Ltd, since 1972. Secretary Conservative Party Consumer Protection Committee and Latin American group. An Opposition Whip from March 1974.

Mr Peter Bartram, editor and journalist. B May, 1947; ed Steyning Grammar School and London School of Economics. West Sussex country councillor, Adur district councillor. Fought Arundel and Shoreham, 1970, 1971 (by-election).

Mr Quintin Barry, a solicitor, fought Lewes in 1970. B March, 1936; ed Tyttenhanger Lodge Preparatory School and Eastbourne College.

SHREWSBURY major

Electorate 59,614

*Langford-Holt, Sir J. (C)	21,095
Marsh, W. (L)	14,914
Woodvine, D. W. (Lab)	11,536
C majority	6,181

	1974			1974
Total Vote	47,545		L	31·4%
Turnout	79·7%		Lab	24·3%
C	44·4%		C maj	13·0%

Sir John Langford-Holt was returned in 1945. Secretary of the Conservative Parliamentary labour committee for five years. Member Public Accounts Committee and several Conservative backbench committees. B June, 1916; ed Shrewsbury School. Director, Siebe Gorman Holdings Ltd.

Mr William Marsh contested the constituency in 1966. Administrative assistant with the West Midlands Gas Board. B November, 1914; ed Smethwick Municipal College and Wolsey Hall. Member, Shrewsbury Borough Council since 1962, and Shrewsbury District Council and Salop County Council.

Mr Derek Woodvine, engineering turner. B 1932; ed St Mary's Secondary, Tunstall. Member, Shrewsbury Borough Council, since 1964, and Shropshire County Council, since 1972. AUEW.

SKIPTON   same

Electorate 52,837.   1970: 51,555

*Drayson, G. B. (C)	19,301
Brooks, Mrs K. C. (L)	17,185
Wheeler, T. V. (Lab)	8,079
C majority	2,116

No change

	1970		1974
Total Vote	40,561		44,565
Turnout	78·7%		84·3%
C	20,817	51·3%	43·3%
Lab	12,011	29·6%	18·1%
L	7,733	19·1%	38·6%
C maj	8,806	21·7%	4·7%
Swing		+5·3%	+1·7%

Mr Burnaby Drayson was elected in 1945. Company director. B March, 1913; ed Borlase School, Buckinghamshire. Member, Stock Exchange, 1935-54. Chairman, all party East-West Trade Committee. Member, Royal Agriculture Society. Member, Expenditure Committee since 1970.

Mrs Claire Brooks, solicitor, contested the seat in 1959. B June, 1931; ed Settle C of E School, Settle Girls' High School, Skipton Girls' High School, University College, London.

Mr Terence Wheeler is a training manager. B May, 1945; ed Leyton County High School for Boys, Leicester University and Queens University, Belfast. ASTMS.

SOLIHULL   major

Electorate 79,227

*Grieve, W. P. (C)	35,049
Windmill, J. A. (L)	17,686
Norman, D. A. (Lab)	11,608
C majority	17,363

	1974			1974
Total Vote	64,343		L	27·5%
Turnout	81·2%		Lab	18·0%
C	54·5%		C maj	27·0%

Mr Percy Grieve, QC, was elected in 1964; contested Lincoln by-election, March, 1962. B March, 1915; ed privately and at Trinity Hall, Cambridge. Barrister (Middle Temple, 1938), QC 1962. Recorder of Northampton since 1965; Assistant Recorder of Leicester, 1956-65, and deputy chairman, Lincoln (Holland) Quarter Sessions from 1962. Member, Select Committee on Race Relations and Immigration, 1968-70. Chairman, Anglo-French Parliamentary group; treasurer Anglo-Benelux Committee; delegate Council of Europe and Western European Union since 1969.

Mr John Windmill, solicitor. B July, 1938; ed Fairfield Preparatory School, Moseley Grammar School, Birmingham University and Guildford School of Law. Member, Solihull Borough Council, 1962-64; Solihull County Borough Council, 1964-65, 1966-69, 1970-74; Solihull Metropolitan District Council since 1973.

Mr David Norman, research officer. B September, 1943; ed Westcliff High School for Boys, London School of Economics, Oxford University. TGWU.

SOMERSET North   minor

Electorate 88,249.   1970: 84,808

*Dean, A. P. (C)	34,576
White, H. R. (Lab)	22,421
Bourne, Mrs J. (L)	18,023
C majority	12,155

No change

	1970		1974
Total Vote	67,096		75,020
Turnout	79·1%		85·0%
C	38,975	58·1%	46·1%
Lab	28,121	41·9%	29·9%
L	—		24·0%
C maj	10,854	16·2%	16·2%
Swing		+6·2%	0·0%

Mr Paul Dean, Under Secretary, Health and Social Security 1970-74, was elected in 1964. Contested Pontefract by-election, March, 1962. Farmer until 1956; resident tutor, Swinton College, 1956-57; joined Conservative research department, 1958; assistant director, 1962. B September, 1924; ed Ellesmere

College, Shropshire and Exeter College, Oxford. Former company executive and former member of the governing body of the Church of Wales.

Mr Haydn White, deputy headmaster at Blandford, fought Dorset, North, in 1970. Chairman, Dorset, North, Labour Party. B June, 1940; ed Maes-y-Dderwen Comprehensive School, Ystrad Gynlais, and University College of Wales, Aberystwyth.

Mrs Judith Bourne, housewife and State Registered nurse. B January, 1937; ed Dr Challoner's Grammar School, Amersham, and Middlesex Hospital.

SOUTHAMPTON Itchen   same

Electorate 81,208. 1970: 80,737

*Mitchell, R. C. (Lab)	27,557
James, P. T. (C)	21,967
Cherryson, J. (L)	13,173
Lab majority	5,590

No change

	1970		1974
Total Vote	43,792		62,697
Turnout	54·2%		77·2%
Speaker	29,417	67·2%	—
Nat Dem	9,581	21·9%	—
Ind	4,794	10·9%	—
Lab	—	—	43·9%
C	—	—	35·0%
L	—	—	21·0%
Maj	19,836	45·3%	
Lab maj	—	—	8·9%

1971 by-election: Total Vote 40,779 (49·6%)—Lab 22,575 (55·4%), C 12,900 (31·6%), Nat Dem 3,090 (7·6%), L 2,214 (5·4%)—Lab maj 9,675 (23·8%).

Mr Richard Mitchell, who won the 1971 by-election, was MP for Southampton, Test 1966-70, having unsuccessfully contested the seat in 1964. Contested New Forest 1959. Member, Labour backbench groups on education, environment, ports, shipping and shipbuilding. Member, Select committee on Education and Science, 1968-70, and chairman, education group, Parliamentary Labour Party, 1967-69. Deputy headmaster. B August, 1927; ed Godalming Grammar School and Southampton University. Member Southampton Council, 1955-67. NUT and NUGMW.

Mr Peter James, solicitor and company director. B April, 1941; ed St John's Preparatory School, Chepstow, and Hereford Cathedral School. Contested Pontypool, 1966.

Mr Joseph Cherryson, teacher, contested the seat, 1964 and 1971 by-election. B March, 1931; ed North Copernicus School, and University College, Dublin.

SOUTHAMPTON Test   minor

Electorate 73,455. 1970: 70,614

*Hill, S. J. A. (C)	23,742
Gould, B. C. (Lab)	22,339
Wallis, J. R. (L)	12,000
C majority	1,403

No change

	1970		1974
Total Vote	51,867		58,081
Turnout	73·3%		79·1%
C	24,660	47·5%	40·9%
Lab	22,858	44·1%	38·5%
L	4,349	8·4%	20·7%
C maj	1,802	3·5%	2·4%
Swing		+4·1%	−0·5%

Mr James Hill, company director. Won seat for Conservatives 1970. B December 1924; ed Regents Park School, Southampton, naval training college, North Wales and Southampton University. Member, Select Committee on Expenditure 1972-73; secretary, Conservative back-bench committee on housing and construction, 1971-73; delegate to European Parliament since 1973; member of committee on transport at European Parliament and chairman of committee for regional policy and transport since March, 1973; member of honorary committee for Europe Day of Council of Europe. Served with BOAC, 1947-58. Member, Southampton City Council, 1966-70; committee, South Hampshire Plan; committee, Southampton Conservative and Ratepayers Federation.

Mr Bryan Gould, fellow and tutor in law, Worcester College, Oxford. B February, 1939; ed Dannevirke High School, Auckland University, New Zealand and Oxford. Previously, British diplomatic service. AUT and Society of Labour Lawyers.

Mr Jack Wallis, insurance broker. B February, 1923; ed Wilson's Grammar School, Goldsmiths Teacher Training College, London, and Sidney Sussex College, Cambridge. Contested the seat in 1970 and Buckingham, 1964. Member, Harpenden Urban District Council, 1962-65.

SOUTHEND East same

Electorate 56,827. 1970: 57,663

*McAdden, Sir S. J. (C)	19,600
Burstin, M. (Lab)	14,648
Curry, J. W. J. (L)	9,979
C majority	4,952

No change

	1970		1974
Total Vote	41,090		44,227
Turnout	71·2%		77·8%
C	24,025	58·5%	44·3%
Lab	17,065	41·5%	33·1%
L	—		22·6%
C maj	6,960	16·9%	11·2%
Swing		+7·9%	−2·9%

Sir Stephen McAdden was elected in 1950. Export sales manager. B November, 1907; ed LCC schools and the Salesian School, Battersea. Member, Hackney Borough Council, 1935-45; Wanstead and Woodford Borough Council, 1945-48; and Essex County Council, 1947-48. Chairman, Anglo-Israel group and Anglo-Austrian group. ASSET. Business interests in pharmaceuticals and public relations.

Mr Motel Burstin contested Southend, West, in 1970 and 1966. B January, 1920; ed Warsaw and Municipal College, Southend. Director of organization providing specialized accommodation for the elderly. Leader, Labour group, Southend Borough Council.

Mr Michael Curry, travel agent. B September, 1923; ed Bankcrofts College.

SOUTHEND West same

Electorate 66,900. 1970: 68,940

*Channon, H. P. G. (C)	25,040
Greaves, W. (L)	19,885
Wright, A. N. (Lab)	8,720
C majority	5,155

No change

	1970		1974
Total Vote	48,800		53,645
Turnout	70·8%		80·2%
C	29,304	60·0%	46·7%
Lab	12,419	25·4%	16·2%
L	7,077	14·5%	37·1%
C maj	16,885	34·6%	9·6%
Swing		+5·5%	−2·0%

Mr Paul Channon was Minister for Housing and Construction 1972-74; Minister of State for Northern Ireland, March-November 1972; Under Secretary for the Environment 1970-72; Parliamentary Secretary, Ministry of Housing and Local Government, June to October, 1970. Elected at by-election in January, 1959, succeeding his father. Former director of Guinness brewery, and other companies. B October, 1935; ed Lockers Park, Hemel Hempstead, Eton and Christ Church, Oxford. Member of executive, 1922 Committee, 1965-66. An Opposition spokesman on consumer affairs from March 1974.

Mr Walter Greaves, manager, contested Harrogate in 1966 and 1970. B August, 1940; ed Harrogate Grammar School and University College, London.

Mr Anthony Wright, medical representative. B 1939; ed Christchurch Boys' Secondary Modern, Southport and Bromley Technical College. Member, Benfleet UDC since 1971. ACTSS.

SOUTH FYLDE same

Electorate 90,064. 1970: 85,186

*Gardner, E. L. (C)	41,028
Lawson, A. (L)	15,649
Knight, Miss K. E. (Lab)	13,474
C majority	25,379

No change

	1970		1974
Total Vote	62,027		70,151
Turnout	72·8%		77·9%
C	39,459	63·6%	58·5%
Lab	13,354	21·5%	19·2%
L	9,214	14·8%	22·3%
C maj	26,105	42·1%	36·2%
Swing		+6·1%	−1·4%

Mr Edward Gardner, QC, elected in 1970, was MP for Billericay from 1959 to 1966; contested Erith and Crayford in 1955. Called to the Bar (Gray's Inn) in 1947, admitted to the Nigerian and British Guianan Bars, 1962, and became a Master of the Bench of Gray's Inn in 1968. B May, 1912; ed Hutton Grammar School, Chairman of "Justice" working party on bail and remands in custody, 1967, and a member of the executive committee, 1968. Chairman,

Conservative Parliamentary Home Affairs Committee, since 1973. Chairman, Bar Council committee on Parliamentary Privilege, 1967. Governor, Thomas Coram Foundation for Children since 1962.

Mr Alan Lawson, director of St Albans teachers' centre. B May, 1930; ed Ormskirk Grammar School; King Alfred's College, Winchester; Liverpool University. Member, Rainford UDC, 1968-71; Tewin Parish Council.

Miss Kathleen Knight, lecturer. B July, 1948; ed Park School, Preston and University of Lancaster. Member, Preston District Council. Member, ATTI.

SOUTHPORT   same

Electorate 65,580. 1970: 64,772

*Percival, W. I. (C)	23,975
Fearn, R. (L)	20,093
Ward, P. R. (Lab)	6,690
C majority	3,882

No change

	1970		1974
Total Vote	45,717		50,758
Turnout	70·6%		77·4%
C	22,958	50·2%	47·2%
L	13,809	30·2%	39·6%
Lab	8,950	19·6%	13·2%
C maj	9,149	20·0%	7·6%
Swing		+4·4%	+1·7%

Mr Ian Percival, QC, was elected in 1959; contested Battersea, North, 1951 and 1955. Barrister (Inner Temple, 1948); QC, 1963. B May, 1921; ed Latymer School and St Catharine's College, Cambridge. Chairman, Conservative parliamentary legal committee since 1972; former vice-chairman, Fellow of Institute of Taxation. Member, Kensington Borough Council, 1952-59. Director of Research, Inns of Court Conservative and Unionist Society, 1963-65.

Mr Ronald Fearn, an assistant bank manager, fought the seat in 1970. Member, Southport Town Council, Sefton Metropolitan District Council, and Merseyside Metropolitan District Council. B February, 1931; ed Southport, Norwood Road County School and King George V Grammar School. NUBE.

Mr Peter Ward, an estimating engineer. Member, Preston Rural District Council since 1971. B April, 1934; ed Wigan College of Further Education. DATA.

SOUTH SHIELDS   same

Electorate 71,895. 1970: 75,032

*Blenkinsop, A. (Lab)	30,740
Smith, S. (C)	18,754
Owen, W. (Nat Front)	1,958
Lab majority	11,986

No change

	1970		1974
Total Vote	50,151		51,452
Turnout	66·8%		71·6%
Lab	30,191	60·2%	59·7%
C	19,960	39·8%	36·4%
Nat Front	—		3·8%
Lab maj	10,231	20·4%	23·3%
Swing		+4·5%	−1·4%

Mr Arthur Blenkinsop was elected in 1964; represented Newcastle-upon-Tyne, East, 1945-59. Parliamentary Secretary, Ministry of Health, 1949-51, and Ministry of Pensions, 1946-49. B June, 1911; ed Royal Grammar School, Newcastle, and College of Commerce, Newcastle. Chartered secretary. Former vice-chairman, Parliamentary Labour Party. Member, Advisory Committee on Misuse of Drugs; member of executive committee and former chairman, Fabian Society; Chairman, Labour parliamentary environment group; executive member, National Trust; chairman of Council of Town and Country Planning Association; vice-chairman, all party conservation group; secretary, Anglo-Polish parliamentary group.

Mr Stanley Smith, deputy regional organizer, blood transfusion service. Aged 45. Member, South Shield Town Council since 1959.

Mr William Owen, shopkeeper. Alderman, South Shields Council since 1970.

SOUTHWARK Bermondsey   major

Electorate 54,930

*Mellish, R. J. (Lab)	24,847
Flight, H. (C)	6,126
Hewittson, C. (L)	3,751
Davey, G. (Nat Front)	1,485
Lab majority	18,721

	1974			1974
Total Vote	36,209	L		10·3%
Turnout	65·9%	Nat Front		4·1%
Lab	68·6%	Lab maj		51·7%
C	16·9%			

Mr Robert Mellish, Opposition Chief Whip, 1970-74, became Minister of Housing and Local Government three weeks before the 1970 election. Parliamentary Secretary to the Treasury and Government Chief Whip, 1969-70; Minister of Public Building and  and Works, 1967-69; Parliamentary Secretary, Ministry of Housing and Local Government, 1964-67, with special responsibility for London housing. Elected for Rotherhithe in 1946; returned for Bermondsey in 1950. B March, 1913; elementary school education. Sponsored by Transport and General Workers' Union of which he was an official. Knighted by Pope John (Knight Commander of St Gregory) for services to Roman Catholic Church, 1959. Chairman, London Labour Party since 1961. *Appointed Parliamentary Secretary, Treasury, and Government Chief Whip, March 1974.*

Mr Howard Flight, company director and former investment adviser. B 1948; ed Brentwood School, Magdalene College, Cambridge, and Michigan University. Past chairman, Cambridge University Conservative Association.

Mr Chris Hewittson, bank official. B 1950; ed Uppington School, University of London. Arrested in Rhodesia in December, 1972; April, 1973, sentenced to five years' imprisonment in Rhodesia for attempting to overthrow the Smith regime; released January, 1974, and returned to Britain.

Mr Godfrey Davey is manager of an industrial catering company. B June, 1945; ed St Joseph's College, Croydon.

SOUTHWARK Dulwich   minor

Electorate 67,083.   1970: 66,265

*Silkin, S. C. (Lab)		22,530
Raffan, K. W. T. (C)		17,189
Pearson, W. H. (L)		9,851
Lab majority		5,341

No change

	1970		1974
Total Vote	42,696		49,570
Turnout	64·4%		73·9%
Lab	20,145	47·2%	45·4%
C	19,250	45·1%	34·7%
L	3,301	7·7%	19·9%
Lab maj	895	2·1%	10·8%
Swing		+5·6%	−4·3%

Mr Samuel Silkin, QC an Opposition spokesman on legal matters 1970-74 was elected in 1964. B March, 1918; ed Dulwich College and Trinity Hall, Cambridge. Barrister (Middle Temple, 1941). Chairman,  Select Committee on Parliamentary privilege, 1966-67. Vice-chairman PLP Legal and Judicial Group since 1970. President, Alcohol Education Centre; Governor, Maudsley Hospital. Member of the Royal Commission on the Penal System for England and Wales, 1965-66. *Appointed Attorney General, March 1974.*

Mr Keith Raffan, national chairman of PEST. B June, 1949; ed Robert Gordon's College, Aberdeen; Trinity College, Glenalmond, Perth, and Corpus Christi College, Cambridge.

Mr William Pearson, managing director of advertising agency. B May, 1927; ed Wellington College and Worcester College, Oxford. Chairman, West Horsley Parish Council.

SOUTHWARK Peckham   major

Electorate 62,897

*Lamborn, H. G. (Lab)		26,116
Baker, N. B. (C)		8,045
Saltmarsh, S. (L)		6,446
Lab majority		18,071

	1974			1974
Total Vote	40,607		C	19·8%
Turnout	64·6%		L	15·9%
Lab	64·3%		Lab maj	44·5%

Mr Harry Lamborn was elected for Southwark in May, 1972. B May, 1915; ed LCC secondary school. Member, Camberwell Borough Council, 1953-65, mayor, 1963-64; LCC, 1958-65; GLC since 1964; USDAW since 1933. Director, Royal Arsenal Co-operative  Society, 1965-72. Governor, King's College Hospital since 1965.

Mr Nicholas Baker, solicitor. B November, 1938; ed Clifton and Exeter College, Oxford.

Mr Sidney Saltmarsh, journalist. B April, 1915; ed grammar school in Bournemouth. NUJ.

SOWERBY   same

Electorate 48,246.   1970: 50,037

Madden, M. F. (Lab)	14,492
Thompson, D. (C)	14,377
Shutt, D. (L)	11,254
Labour majority	115

No change

	1970		1974
Total Vote	37,834		40,123
Turnout	75·6%		83·2%
Lab	16,583	43·8%	36·1%
C	16,114	42·6%	35·8%
L	5,137	13·6%	28·0%
Lab maj	469	1·2%	0·3%
Swing		+6·3%	+0·4%

Mr Max Madden, press and information officer for the British Gas Corporation. Contested Sudbury and Woodbridge, 1966. B October, 1941; ed Lascelles Secondary Modern School South Harrow; Pinner Grammar School and North-East Essex Technical College. Member, London Borough of Wandsworth Council. TGWU.

Mr Donald Thompson, butcher, contested Batley and Morley, 1970. B November, 1931; ed Hipperholme Grammar School. Member, West Riding County Council, since 1967. Director, local farmers' co-operative.

Mr David Shutt contested the constituency in 1970. Chartered accountant. B March, 1942; ed Pudsey Grammar School. Member, Caldergate Metropolitan District Council.

SPELTHORNE   same

Electorate 68,837.   1970: 68,579

*Atkins, H. E. (C)	24,772
Grant, J. (Lab)	16,713
Winner, P. (L)	13,632
Butterfield, E. (Nat Front)	1,339
C majority	8,059

No change

	1970		1974
Total Vote	50,297		56,456
Turnout	73·3%		82·0%
C	27,266	54·2%	43·9%
Lab	18,239	36·3%	29·6%
L	4,792	9·5%	24·1%
Nat Front	—	—	2·4%
C maj	9,027	17·9%	14·3%
Swing		+6·4%	−1·8%

Mr Humphrey Atkins, Treasurer of the Household, 1970-73, was Parliamentary Secretary to the Treasury and Government chief whip 1973-74. Opposition whip 1967-70. Represented Merton and Morden from 1955 to 1970; contested West Lothian, 1951. Former director of financial advertising agency. B August, 1922; ed Wellington College. Vice-chairman, management committee of Outward Bound Trust, 1966-70. Secretary, Conservative parliamentary defence committee, 1965-67. Appointed Treasurer of the Household, June, 1970. Opposition Chief Whip from March 1974.

Mr John Grant, wine shipper, contested Twickenham, 1970. B November, 1925; ed Stowe School, Buckingham. Member, Richmond-upon-Thames Borough Council.

Mr Paul Winner, chairman and managing director of a marketing and public relations consultancy. B July, 1934; ed St Lawrence College, Ramsgate; Westminster City Schools, La Sorbonne, Paris; St John's College, Oxford, and the LSE Department of Business Administration.

Mr Eric Butterfield, heavy goods driver and shop steward in the TGWU. B June, 1926; ed elementary and Army schools. Former regular soldier.

STAFFORD & STONE   minor

Electorate 78,110.   1970: 74,639

*Fraser, H. C. P. J. (C)	30,056
Cowlishaw, T. E. (Lab)	21,073
Martin, H. S. (L)	13,132
C majority	8,983

No change

	1970		1974
Total Vote	54,806		64,261
Turnout	73·4%		82·3%
C	30,056	54·8%	46·8%
Lab	20,380	37·2%	32·8%
L	4,370	8·0%	20·4%
C maj	9,676	17·6%	14·0%
Swing		+3·9%	−1·8%

Mr Hugh Fraser, a director of various companies, was appointed Secretary of State for Air in July, 1962, became Minister of Defence for the Royal Air Force in the 1964 re-organization. Under-Secretary, Colonial Office, 1960-62, War Office, 1958-60. Member for Stone from 1945 to 1950, when he was returned for Stafford and Stone. B January, 1918; ed Ampleforth, Balliol College, Oxford (president of the Union), and the Sorbonne.

Mr Terence Cowlishaw, former coal-miner. B June, 1930; ed Rugeley Grammar School and Wolverhampton College of Technology. Member, Staffordshire County Council since 1958 and Rugeley Urban District Council since 1952. Part-time lecturer, WEA, NUM and NUAAW.

Mr Harold Martin, executive sales manager. B February, 1944; ed Grove Park School, Wrexham. Member, Liberal Industrial Relations Association, West Midlands Liberal Executive Committee.

STAFFORDSHIRE South-West **major**

Electorate 60,587

*Cormack, P. T. (C)	23,878
Wymer, I. K. (Lab)	14,120
Freeman, E. (L)	10,408
Maxwell, D. (Eng Nat)	482

C majority	9,758

	1974		1974
Total Vote	48,888	L	21·3%
Turnout	80·7%	Eng Nat	1·0%
C	48·8%	C maj	19·9%
Lab	28·9%		

Mr Patrick Cormack, teacher, represented Cannock for the Conservatives from 1970-74. Contested Grimsby, 1966; Bolsover, 1964. B May, 1939; ed St James Choir and Havelock Schools, Grimsby; Hull University. Chairman, all-party parliamentary committee for Soviet

Jews. Member, Select Committee on Anti-Discrimination. Former Vice-chairman, East Midlands Area Young Conservatives, former member Council of Historical Association. Member, Select Committee on Anti-Discrimination.

Mr Ivor Wymer, head of Department of Social Studies, Art and General Education, Bilston College of Further Education. B 1938; ed Paston School, North Walsham; Leeds University. NAS.

Mr Eric Freeman, a sales manager. B June, 1937; ed Port Glasgow High School, Stockport Technical College.

STALYBRIDGE & HYDE **same**

Electorate 64,526. 1970: 63,823

*Pendry, T. (Lab)	24,922
Swerling, S. M. (C)	16,854
White, H. (Ind L)	10,850

Lab majority	8,068

No change

	1970		1974
Total Vote	46,906		52,626
Turnout	73·5%		81·5%
Lab	22,226	47·4%	47·3%
C	19,377	41·3%	32·0%
L	5,303	11·3%	
Ind L	—	—	20·7%
Lab maj	2,849	6·1%	15·3%
Swing		+3·8%	−4·6%

Mr Tom Pendry, an Opposition whip 1971-74, was a full-time official of the National Union of Public Employees 1960-70. He was elected in 1970. B June, 1934; ed St Augustine's School, Ramsgate, and Plater Hall, Oxford. Member, Paddington Borough Council, 1962-65.

Delegate Council of Europe, 1973; WEU 1973. *Appointed a Lord Commissioner of the Treasury (Government Whip), March 1974.*

Mr Sam Swerling, solicitor. B October, 1939; ed Repton and Trinity College, Dublin. Member, Society of Conservative Lawyers.

STIRLING, FALKIRK & GRANGEMOUTH **minor**

Electorate 64,046. 1970: 61,953

*Ewing, H. (Lab)	21,685
McIntyre, Dr R. D. (Scot Nat)	17,836
Campbell, G. (C)	12,228

Lab majority	3,849

No change

	1970		1974
Total Vote	45,309		51,749
Turnout	73·0%		81·2%
Lab	22,984	50·7%	41·9%
C	15,754	34·8%	23·6%
Scot Nat	6,571	14·5%	34·5%
Lab maj	7,230	15·9%	7·4%
Swing		+2·8%	−1·2%

1971 by-election: Total Vote 37,833 (60·0%)—Lab 17,536 (46·5%), Scot Nat 13,048 (34·6%), C 7,149 (18·9%)—Lab maj 4,488 (11·9%).

Mr Harry Ewing, MP for Stirling and Falkirk, 1971-74. Post office worker. B January 20, 1931; ed Beath High School, Cowdenbeath. Fought Fife, East, 1970. Member, Amalgamated Union of Foundryworkers, 1956-62. Various appointments in Union of Post Office Workers 1962-71, and Co-operative movement.

Dr Robert McIntyre, President of the Scottish National Party and Provost of Stirling since 1967, is a consultant chest physician. B December 1913; ed Hamilton Academy, Daniel Stewart's College, Edinburgh and Glasgow Universities. Member, Stirling Town Council, since 1956. Contested Motherwell, 1945 (twice) and 1950; Perth and East Perthshire, 1951, 1955, 1959 and 1964; West Stirlingshire, 1966 and 1970; Stirling and Falkirk, 1971.

Mr Geoffrey Campbell, chartered mechanical engineer. B September, 1926; ed Coupar Anglis, Perthshire, and Dundee Technical College. Member, Midlothian County Council; bailie, Penicuik Town Council; chairman, Conservative Trade Union Advisory Committee for Scotland; member, Scottish Conservative Group for Europe.

STIRLINGSHIRE East & Clackmannan   minor

Electorate 62,222.   1970: 61,811

Reid, G. N. (Scot Nat)	22,289
*Douglas, R. G. (Lab & Co-op)	18,679
Lester, A. H. (C)	9,994
Bolton, G. (Comm)	322
Scot Nat majority	3,610

Scot Nat gain

	1970		1974
Total Vote	46,790		51,284
Turnout	75·6%		82·6%
Lab & Co-op	23,729	50·7%	36·4%
C	13,178	28·2%	19·5%
Scot Nat	7,243	15·5%	43·5%
L	2,640	5·6%	—
Comm	—	—	0·6%
Lab & Co-op maj	10,551	22·5%	—
Scot Nat maj	—	—	7·0%
Swing		+4·1%	—

Mr George Reid, freelance journalist and broadcaster. Aged 34; ed Tullibody School and Dollar Academy, and St Andrew's University. Formerly head of features and documentaries, Scottish Television. SNP spokesman on housing, health and social services from March 1974.

Mr Dick Douglas, a lecturer, was elected in 1970. He contested Glasgow, Pollok in the 1967 by-election; Edinburgh, West, in 1966; South Angus in 1964. B January, 1932; ed senior secondary school, Co-operative College, Standford Hall, Loughborough, and University of Strathclyde. Member, AUEW.

Mr Anthony Lester, insurance inspector. B January, 1928; ed Morgan Academy, Dundee, and Royal Navy. Member, Edinburgh Council.

Mr Gordon Bolton, coal miner. Former secretary, Scottish Miners' Youth Committee. NUM.

STIRLINGSHIRE West   minor

Electorate 53,256.   1970: 48,885

*Baxter, W. (Lab)	17,730
Jones, Mrs J. (Scot Nat)	12,886
Price, T. (C)	12,789
Lab majority	4,844

No change

	1970		1974
Total Vote	38,628		43,405
Turnout	78·9%		82·8%
Lab	18,884	48·9%	40·8%
C	11,465	29·7%	29·5%
Scot Nat	8,279	21·4%	29·7%
Lab maj	7,419	19·2%	11·2%
Swing		+2·0%	+3·9%

Mr William Baxter was elected in 1959. Building contractor and farmer. B December, 1911; ed Banton public school. County councillor. Stirlingshire, 1932; Stirling representative on County Councils Association. Founder member, Western Region Hospital Board.

Mrs Janette Jones, housewife. B August, 1931. Chairman, West Stirlingshire SNP; vice-chairman, Kilsyth Branch. Kilsyth Burgh councillor since 1968.

Mr Timothy Price, industrial investment banker. B September, 1945; ed Ampleforth College and Magdalene College, Cambridge. Former assistant to Mr Peter Walker, MP.

STOCKPORT North   minor

Electorate 52,311.   1970: 52,647

Bennett, A. F. (Lab)	16,948
*Owen, I. W. (C)	16,745
Arnold, P. (L)	9,283
Lab majority	203

Lab gain from C

	1970		1974	
Total Vote	39,415		42,976	
Turnout	74·9%		82·1%	
C	18,132	46·0%	39·0%	
Lab	17,261	43·8%	39·4%	
L	4,022	10·2%	21·6%	
C maj	871	2·2%		
Lab maj	—		0·5%	
Swing		+5·3%	−1·3%	

Mr Andrew Bennett, teacher, contested Knutsford, 1970; member, Oldham Borough Council since 1964. B March, 1939; ed Birmingham University, NUT.

Mr Idris Owen won the seat for the Conservatives in 1970; contested it in 1966; Stalybridge and Hyde, 1955, and Manchester, Exchange, 1951. Company director in the construction industry. B 1912; ed Stockport School and College of Technology and Manchester School of Commerce. Fellow, Institute of Builders. Vice-president, National Federation of Building Trades Employers, 1965. Member, Stockport Borough Council since 1946; Mayor, 1962-63; vice-chairman, Conservative parliamentary housing and construction committee since 1972.

Mr Peter Arnold, teacher. B August, 1944; ed Carlisle grammar school, Didsbury College of Education and London University. Former member NUT; member Professional Association of Teachers.

STOCKPORT South   minor

Electorate 47,335. 1970: 49,142

*Orbach, M. (Lab)	15,722
Edwards, D. E. H. (C)	12,624
Carter, C. J. (L)	9,182
Lab majority	3,098

No change

	1970		1974	
Total Vote	36,039		37,528	
Turnout	73·3%		79·3%	
Lab	16,747	46·5%	41·9%	
C	14,679	40·7%	33·6%	
L	4,613	12·8%	24·5%	
Lab maj	2,068	5·7%	8·2%	
Swing		+2·9%	−1·2%	

Mr Maurice Orbach, elected for the constituency in 1964. Represented Willesden East, from 1945-59; contested that seat in 1935 and a 1938 by-election. Engineer-administrator. B July, 1902; ed high school in Cardiff and New York University. Member, Standing

Orders Committee; backbench groups on industry and health. Chairman, Atlantic and Pacific Mfg Co Ltd. Member, ASTMS; USDAW. Director-General, Trades Advisory Council; member, World Executive, World Jewish Congress.

Mr Elgan Edwards, barrister, contested Merioneth, 1970. B December, 1943; ed Rhyl Grammar School, University College of Wales, Aberystwyth, and Grays Inn. Member, Chester City Council and Chester District Council. President, Students Union, Aberystwyth, 1966-67.

Mr Christopher Carter, management accountant. B November, 1945; ed Queen Elizabeth's Grammar School, Bromyard, and University of Warwick. Member, Stockport Metropolitan District Council.

STOKE-ON-TRENT Central   minor

Electorate 60,701. 1970: 59,818

*Cant, R. B. (Lab)	27,171
Ashley, Mrs E. (C)	15,423
Lab majority	11,748

No change

	1970		1974	
Total Vote	29,985		42,594	
Turnout	50·0%		70·2%	
Lab	18,758	62·5%	63·8%	
C	11,227	37·4%	36·2%	
Lab maj	7,531	25·1%	27·6%	
Swing		+5·5%	−1·2%	

Mr Robert Cant was elected in 1966; contested Shrewsbury, 1950 and 1951. Lecturer. B July, 1915; ed Middlesbrough High School and London School of Economics. Member, Stoke City Council since 1953, new Staffordshire County Council since 1973, and PLP economic and financial affairs group.

Mrs Elsie Ashley, director of a firm of timber merchants, contested the seat in 1970. Born 1919; ed Newcastle-under-Lyme secondary modern schools and privately. Newcastle-under-Lyme borough councillor; Staffordshire County Council representative on the executive committee, West Midlands Sports Council; founder president, Newcastle Youth Athletic Association. North Staffordshire president, Spastics Society of Great Britain.

STOKE-ON-TRENT North   minor

Electorate 59,386. 1970: 58,780

*Forrester, J. S. (Lab)	28,177
Davies, J. (C)	15,718
Lab majority	12,459

No change

	1970		1974	
Total Vote	31,184		43,895	
Turnout	52·9%		73·9%	
Lab	20,642	66·2%		64·2%
C	10,542	33·8%		35·8%
Lab maj	10,100	32·4%		28·4%
Swing		+5·3%		+2·0%

Mr John Forrester was elected in 1966. Teacher. B June, 1924; ed Eastwood Council School, City School of Commerce, Stoke-on-Trent, and Alsager Teacher Training College. Member, NUT; executive committee member, Stoke-on-Trent and District Association; member Stoke-on-Trent city and district councils.

Mr John Davies. B November, 1927; ed St Chad's, Wolverhampton. Chairman of the Conservative group, Stoke City Council, 1969-70 and member 1960-63 and 1968-70. Member, Institute of Motor Industries.

STOKE-ON-TRENT South   minor

Electorate 72,010. 1970: 67,953

*Ashley, J. (Lab)	31,650
Newall, S. (C)	15,981
Smith, M. (L)	7,578
Lomas, S. (Comm)	481
Lab majority	15,669

	1970		1974	
Total Vote	34,475		55,690	
Turnout	50·5%		77·3%	
Lab	20,770	60·2%		56·8%
C	13,341	38·7%		28·7%
Comm	364	1·0%		0·9%
L	—	—		13·6%
Lab maj	7,429	21·5%		28·1%
Swing		+3·4%		−3·3%

Mr Jack Ashley, chairman of all-party Lords and Commons group on disablement, was elected in 1966. He contested Finchley, 1951. Sponsored by General and Municipal Workers' Union, former shop steward and member of national executive of Chemical Workers'

Union 1946-47. Borough councillor, Widnes, 1946-47. B December, 1922; ed elementary school, Ruskin College, Oxford and Gonville and Caius College, Cambridge (President of the Union). Chairman, all-party widows and single parents group.

Mr Simon Newall, dental surgeon. B 1945; ed Leek High School, Sheffield University. Member, Leek UDC since 1970, Bow Group, Conservative group for Europe Graduates Association.

Mr Martyn Smith, computer systems engineer. B February, 1946; ed Wiggeston Boys' School, Leicester; Jesus College, Cambridge. Member, Newcastle Borough Council, 1972-74. ASTMS, branch secretary. International Computers (Midlands) Branch.

Mr Sam Lomas contested constituency in 1970 and 1966. Building worker. B February, 1930; ed elementary school. Clerk of works for county. Local representative, NALGO.

STRATFORD-ON-AVON   major

Electorate 71,271

*Maude, A. E. U. (C)	30,106
Wright, M. (L)	16,885
Burton, M. (Lab)	11,165
C majority	13,221

	1974			1974
Total Vote	58,156	L		29·0%
Turnout	81·6%	Lab		19·2%
C	51·8%	C maj		22·7%

Mr Angus Maude was elected at a by-election in 1963. Conservative spokesman on aviation, 1964-65, and on colonies, 1965-66. Represented Ealing, South, 1950-58, when he resigned; contested South Dorset by-election in November, 1962. Author and journalist. B September, 1912; ed Rugby and Oriel College, Oxford. Director, Conservative Political Centre, 1951-55; editor, Sydney Morning Herald, 1958-61. Member, Select Committees on Procedure and European secondary legislation. Former chairman, Conservative parliamentary education committee. Member, executive, 1922 Committee, from March 1974.

Mr Michael Wright, lecturer. B April, 1926; ed St Albans School and Manchester and Birmingham universities. Member, Warwickshire County Council.

Mr Michael Burton, barrister and lecturer in law. B November, 1946; ed Eton and Oxford University.

STRETFORD same

Electorate 68,091. 1970: 71,006

*Churchill, W. S. (C)	23,630
Anthony, K. (Lab)	19,641
Wrigley, D. I. (L)	12,558
C majority	3,989

No change

	1970		1974
Total Vote	53,243		55,829
Turnout	75·0%		82·0%
C	28,629	53·8%	42·3%
Lab	24,614	46·2%	35·2%
L	—	—	22·5%
C maj	4,015	7·5%	7·1%
Swing		+7·0%	−0·2%

Mr Winston Churchill, journalist and author, won the seat for the Conservatives in 1970. He contested Manchester, Gorton, in by-election, November, 1967. B October, 1940; ed Eton and Christ Church College, Oxford. Member, Select Committee on Statutory Instruments; trustee, National Benevolent Fund for the Aged; PPS, Minister of Housing, 1970-72; PPS, Minister of State, Foreign Affairs, 1972-73; Joint Secy, Conservative Foreign Affairs committee.

Mr Kenneth Anthony, former trade union official. B January, 1943; ed Cooperative College, Loughborough, and Manchester University.

Mr Dennis Wrigley contested High Peak in 1970, 1966, 1964 and 1961 (by-election) and Oldham, East, 1959. Company market development director. B January, 1930; ed Manchester Grammar School and Manchester Regional School of Architecture. Former chairman, Liberal Transport Committee.

STROUD minor

Electorate 68,851. 1970: 66,072

*Kershaw, J. A. (C)	25,619
Maddocks, W. H. (Lab and Co-op)	17,148
Ritchie, Mrs S. A. (L)	15,521
Churchill, J. (Powell C)	470
C majority	8,471

No change

	1970		1974
Total Vote	53,046		58,758
Turnout	80·3%		85·3%
C	27,089	51·1%	43·6%
Lab	19,158	36·1%	—
L	6,799	12·8%	26·4%
Lab & Co-op	—	—	29·2%
C-Powell	—	—	0·8%
C maj	7,931	14·9%	14·4%
Swing		+5·9%	−0·3%

Mr Anthony Kershaw was Under Secretary, Defence (RAF) 1973-74; Under Secretary, Foreign and Commonwealth Office 1970-73; Parliamentary Secretary, Ministry of Public Building and Works, June-October 1970. He was elected in 1955; contested Gloucester, 1950 and 1951. Barrister (Inner Temple, 1939). B December, 1915; ed Eton and Balliol College, Oxford. Joint secretary, Conservative defence committee, 1964-67; member, executive committee, 1922 Committee, 1964-66. PPS to Mr Heath until 1970.

Mr William Maddocks, trade union official for the textile workers. B February, 1921. Director, Gloucester and Severnside Cooperative Society.

Mrs Anne Ritchie, housewife. B March, 1925; ed Hitchin Girls' Grammar School, Hatfield.

SUDBURY & WOODBRIDGE same

Electorate 83,792. 1970: 78,109

*Stainton, K. M. (C)	31,987
Lewis, N. (L)	18,286
Orriss, B. (Lab)	18,228
C majority	13,701

No change

	1970		1974
Total Vote	59,358		68,501
Turnout	76·0%		81·7%
C	32,393	54·6%	46·7%
Lab	19,829	33·4%	26·6%
L	7,136	12·0%	26·7%
C maj	12,564	21·2%	20·0%
Swing		+4·0%	−0·5%

Mr Keith Stainton, company director, was returned at by-election December, 1963. B November, 1921; ed Kendal Grammar School and Manchester University. Member, Estimates Committee. Select Committee on Science and Technology, since 1970. Promoted

Housebuilding (Protection of Purchasers) Bill, 1964 which led to strengthening of National Housebuilders Registration Council, *Financial Times* leader writer, 1949-53. Founder member, Bow Group.

Mr Neville Lewis contested Ipswich in 1970. Chartered surveyor. B October, 1935; ed Badingham College and London University. Member, Cosford RDC, 1970-74; chairman, Semer Parish Council. NALGO.

Mr Brian Orriss contested the seat in 1970. Personal secretary. B September, 1933; ed North-East Essex Technical College. Member, West Suffolk County Council, 1964-67.

SUNDERLAND North   major

Electorate 75,623

*Willey, F. T. (Lab)		28,933
Brown, D. J. S. (C)		17,533
Lennox, J. (L)		9,015
Lab majority		**11,400**

	1974		1974
Total Vote	55,481	C	31·6%
Turnout	73·4%	L	16·2%
Lab	52·1%	Lab maj	20·5%

Mr Frederick Willey, Minister of State, Ministry of Housing and Local Government, 1967; Minister of Land and Natural Resources, 1964-67. Barrister (Middle Temple, 1936). B November, 1910; ed Johnston School and St John's College, Cambridge (football

blue). Elected as Sunderland MP in 1945 and returned for North Division in 1950 after redistribution. Former chairman, Select Committee on Education and Science.

Mr John (Tim) Brown, solicitor. B January, 1941; ed Argyle House School, Sunderland, St Bees School, Cumberland, and Bristol University. Member, Sunderland County Borough Council since 1967; chairman, General Purposes Committee, 1971-72; deputy Conservative leader, Sunderland District Council.

Mr John Lennox, teacher. B June, 1947; ed grammar school, Sheffield University; De La Salle College of Education, Manchester, Durham University.

SUNDERLAND South   major

Electorate 76,547

*Bagier, G. A. T. (Lab)		28,296
Wright, M. (C)		19,700
Nicholson, J. (L)		9,098
Lab majority		**8,596**

	1974		1974
Total Vote	57,094	C	34·5%
Turn-out	74·6%	L	15·9%
Lab	49·6%	Lab maj	15·0%

Mr Gordon Bagier, who won the seat in 1964, was a signals inspector in British Railways. B July, 1924; ed Pendower Secondary Technical School, Newcastle-upon-Tyne. President, Yorkshire District Council, NUR, 1962-64. Member, Keighley Borough Council,

1956-60, and Sowerby Bridge Urban Council, 1962-65. Member, Estimates Committee, 1964-66.

Mr Mark Wright, economist, is manager of Barclays Bank group economic intelligence unit. B August, 1940; ed Durham School, Hatfield College, Durham University, and Oxford University. Church of England lay reader.

Mr John Nicholson, export sales administrator. B April, 1916; ed at Royal Grammar School, Newcastle upon Tyne. Elected to Northumberland County Council, April, 1973; Blyth Valley District Council, June, 1973.

SURREY East   major

Electorate 55,110

*Howe, Sir R. E. G. (C)		23,563
Vaus, K. S. (L)		15,544
Allonby, D. L. (Lab)		6,946
C majority		**8,019**

	1974		1974
Total Vote	46,053	L	33·7%
Turnout	83·6%	Lab	15·1%
C	51·2%	C maj	17·4%

Sir Geoffrey Howe, QC, Minister for Trade and Consumer Affairs with the Department for Trade and Industry, 1973-74; Solicitor General, 1970-73. Represented Reigate, 1970-74 and Bebington, 1964-66, contesting Aberavon, 1955 and 1959. Barrister, called by Middle

Temple, 1952. B December, 1926; ed Winchester and Trinity Hall, Cambridge. Former deputy chairman, Glamorgan Quarter Sessions; member, General Council of Bar, 1957-61; elected Bencher of Middle Temple, 1969. Founder, National Association of School Governors and Managers. Appointed to Shadow Cabinet as Opposition spokesman on Social Services, March 1974.

Mr Kenneth Vaus, dental surgeon, national chairman of the Liberal Party, contested East Surrey, 1959, Hereford, 1964 and 1966, Reigate, 1970. B September, 1928; ed Haberdashers' Aske's School and Sheffield University. Member, Liberal National executive, and finance and administration board.

Mr David Allonby, BBC broadcasting engineer. B February, 1933; ed Lancaster Royal Grammar School. Member, Association of Broadcasting Staffs, Fabian Society, and Co-operative Party.

SURREY North-West   major

Electorate 68,414

*Grylls, W. M. J. (C)		28,841
Sims, L. E. (L)		13,892
Clifton, A. A. (Lab)		11,608
Foster, D. B. (Nat Coalition)		463
C majority		14,949

	1974		1974
Total Vote	54,804	Lab	21·2%
Turnout	80·1%	Nat Coalition	0·8%
C	52·6%	C maj	27·3%
L	25·3%		

Mr Michael Grylls, MP for Chertsey, 1970-74, contested Fulham in 1964 and 1966. Chairman, H. & J. Wine Agencies Ltd. B February, 1934; ed Royal Naval College, Dartmouth, and universities in Paris and Madrid. Member, Expenditure Committee; Select Committee on Overseas Development. Member, GLC (Cities of London and Westminster), 1967-70; chief whip, ILEA, 1967-68; chairman, further and higher education sub-committee, 1968. Member, Conservative Political Centre and Conservative Commonwealth Council. Fellow, Royal Institute of International Affairs. Secretary, Conservative industry committee, from March 1974.

Mr Leslie Sims, heating engineer. B July, 1931; ed S.E. Essex Technical College. Association member, Institute Domestic Heating Engineers.

Mr Antony Clifton, baker and confectioner. B November, 1946; ed Fordingbridge Secondary Modern School, Salisbury and South Wiltshire College of Technology. Member, Bakers' Union.

SUSSEX Mid   major

Electorate 60,412

Renton, R. T. (C)		27,317
Symes-Schutzmann, R. (L)		15,162
Fraser, Miss M. R. (Lab)		7,993
C majority		12,155

	1974		1974
Total Vote	50,472	L	30·0%
Turnout	83·5%	Lab	15·8%
C	54·1%	C maj	24·1%

Mr Timothy Renton, merchant banker, contested Sheffield, Park, 1970. B May, 1932 ed Eton and Magdalen College, Oxford. Director of banking and mining companies; representative subscriber to the London Metal Exchange.

Mr Robert Symes-Schutzmann, writer, broadcaster and television producer. B May, 1924; ed Volksschule, Realgymnasium, Switzerland and Regent Street Polytechnic.

Miss Margaret Fraser, lecturer in public administration. B April, 1948; ed Nottingham High School for Girls, universities of Reading and Birmingham. NUGMW.

SUTTON Sutton & Cheam   minor

Electorate 60,012. 1970: 60,991

Macfarlane, N. (C)		22,555
*Tope, G. N. (L)		20,836
Rhodes, J. K. (Lab)		6,270
C majority		1,719

Conservative gain from L

	1970		1974
Total Vote	41,241		49,661
Turnout	67·5%		82·7%
C	23,957	58·1%	45·4%
Lab	11,261	27·3%	12·6%
L	6,023	14·6%	41·9%
C maj	12,696	30·8%	3·5%
Swing		+5·0%	+1·0%

1972 by-election: Total Votes 34,204 (56·2%)—L 18,328 (53·5%), C 10,911 (31·8%), Lab 2,973 (8·6%), Ind Anti-EEC 1,332 (3·8%), Nat Ind 660 (1·9%) L maj 7,417 (21·7%).

Mr Neil Macfarlane, oil company executive, contested East Ham, North, 1970, Sutton and Cheam by-election, 1972. B May, 1936; ed St Arbyns, Woodford Green, and Bancrofts School, Woodford Wells. Company director of private schools.

Mr Graham Tope, an insurance officer, won the by-election in December, 1972. Liberal spokesman on the environment. B November, 1943; ed Whitgift School, Croydon. Fought GLC elections in Sutton, 1970. Chairman, South East England Young Liberals, 1971-73. Vice-chairman, National League of Young Liberals, 1971-73.

Mr Jim Rhodes, personnel manager. B May, 1925; ed Caterham Valley Central School and Oxted Grammar School. Former member, Caterham and Warlingham UDC, 1952-55; member, Sutton Council since 1971; former soccer referee, 1948-68. ASTMS.

SUTTON Carshalton   major

Electorate 66,219

*Carr, L. R. (C)		24,440
Walker, P. J. (Lab)		18,750
Smallbone, Mrs H. (L)		11,695
C majority		5,690

	1974		1974
Total Vote	54,885	Lab	34·2%
Turnout	82·9%	L	21·3%
C	44·5%	C maj	10·4%

Mr Robert Carr, was Home Secretary, following the resignation of Mr Maudling, from 1972-74. Lord President of the Council, April-November, 1972 and Secretary of State for Employment, 1970-72. He was chief Opposition spokesman on employment and productivity and labour matters, 1967-70. Secretary for Technical Co-operation, 1963-64; Parliamentary Secretary, Ministry of Labour, December, 1955-April, 1958. PPS to Sir Anthony Eden, 1951-55. Represented Mitcham, 1950-74. B November, 1916; ed Westminster School and Gonville and Caius College, Cambridge. Metallurgist and industrialist, and former company director; Governor, St Mary's Hospital, Paddington, 1958-63; Imperial College of Science and Technology, 1959-63; St Mary's Medical School Council, 1958-63. Fellow of Institute of Metallurgists, 1957.

Appointed to Shadow Cabinet as Opposition spokesman on Treasury and economic affairs, March 1974.

Mr Peter Walker, political assistant to leader of GLC. B August, 1945; ed primary, secondary modern schools and London university (external degree). Member, London borough of Croydon Council, since 1971. TGWU.

Mrs Hester Smallbone contested Battersea, North in 1970. Housewife. B May, 1924; ed Ecclesfield Grammar School, Sheffield, and Somerville College, Oxford. Former member, Richmond Council, 1961-65.

SUTTON COLDFIELD   major

Electorate 59,918

*Fowler, P. N. (C)		28,355
Watson, Sir A. (L)		14,929
Little, R. A. (Lab)		6,028
C majority		13,426

	1974		1974
Total Vote	49,312	L	30·3%
Turnout	82·3%	Lab	12·2%
C	57·5%	C maj	27·2%

Mr Norman Fowler was MP for Nottingham, South, 1970-74; Home Affairs correspondent of *The Times* 1966-70. B 1938; ed King Edward VI School, Chelmsford and Trinity Hall, Cambridge. Member, Select Committee on Race Relations and Immigration since 1970; NUJ. Chairman, University Conservative Association, Former member, Bow Group Council; served on editorial board of Crossbow for eight years.

Sir Andrew Watson is a barrister (Inner Temple). B December, 1937; ed Eton.

Mr Raymond Little, production estimator with Hawker Siddeley Aviation. B January, 1949; ed secondary school and college of further education. Member, Hatfield Rural District Council since 1970. AUEW.

SWANSEA East   same

Electorate 59,019. 1970: 58,603

*McBride, N. (Lab)		28,537
Mercer, D. J. (C)		8,850
Ball, J. G. (Pl Cymru)		5,135
Jones, W. R. (Comm)		507
Lab majority		19,687

No change

	1970		1974	
Total Vote	41,125		43,029	
Turnout	70·2%		72·9%	
Lab	28,183	68·5%		66·3%
C	8,191	19·9%		20·6%
Pl Cymru	4,188	10·2%		11·9%
Comm	563	1·4%		1·2%
Lab maj	19,992	48·6%		45·7%
Swing		+5·6%		+1·4%

Mr Neil McBride was a Lord Commissioner of the Treasury, 1969-70; assistant Government whip, 1966-69. Elected at a by-election in March, 1963; contested High Peak, 1955, and Perth and East Perthshire, 1951. Brass finisher. B April, 1910; ed Paisley Grammar School and through National Council of Labour Colleges. Twice chairman of Paisley Labour Party, sponsored by AUEW, engineering section.

Mr David Mercer, solicitor. B 1950; ed Nottingham University. Member, Society of Conservative Lawyers; Lawn Tennis Umpires' Association.

Mr John Ball is a production supervisor. B December, 1947; ed Cwmbwrla elementary school and Dynevor Grammar. ASTMS.

Mr William Jones contested seat in 1970 and 1966. Insurance agent. B November, 1918; ed elementary school. Chairman, Swansea tenants' and residents' organization. USDAW.

Mr Alan Williams was an Opposition spokesman on education and science, 1970-73; consumer affairs, 1973-74. Chairman, all-party committee on minerals since 1972. Parliamentary Secretary, Ministry of Technology and Power 1969-70; Under Secretary, Department for Economic Affairs, 1967-69. Member, Public Accounts Committee, 1966-67. Won seat in 1964; contested Poole, 1959. B October, 1930; ed Cardiff High School, Cardiff College of Technology, and University College, Oxford. Radio and television broadcaster and freelance journalist. Member, Fabian Society and ATTI. Chairman, Welsh Labour Group, 1965-66. *Appointed Minister of State for Prices and Consumer Protection, March 1974.*

Mr David Lewis contested Gower in 1966. Assistant to works manager, structural engineering firm. B February, 1940; ed Mill Hill School and Swansea Technical College. Member, National Committee, Young Conservatives, 1964-66.

Mr Brian Keal, Chemical engineer. B May, 1939; ed Barnstaple Grammar School; University College, Swansea. Member, Glamorgan County Council and West Glamorgan County Council.

Mr Derrick Hearne, computer consultant in service of United Nations. B June, 1932; ed Ystalyfera Grammar School, Swansea and King's College, London.

SWANSEA West   same

Electorate 64,465. 1970: 64,686

*Williams, A. J. (Lab)	22,124
Lewis, D. R. O. (C)	18,786
Keal, B. E. (L)	8,248
Hearne, D. K. (Pl Cymru)	1,859
Lab majority	3,338

No change

	1970		1974	
Total Vote	49,039		51,017	
Turnout	75·8%		77·9%	
Lab	24,622	50·2%		43·4%
C	21,384	43·6%		36·8%
Pl Cymru	3,033	6·2%		3·6%
L	—			16·2%
Lab maj	3,238	6·6%		6·5%
Swing		+3·1%		+0·0%

SWINDON   minor

Electorate 62,170. 1970: 61,305

*Stoddart, D. L. (Lab)	24,093
Young, G. C. M. (C)	15,384
Hubbard, R. (L)	10,564
Blakeney, Mrs K. (WRP)	240
Lab majority	8,709

No change

	1970		1974	
Total Vote	46,342		50,281	
Turnout	75·6%		80·9%	
Lab	25,731	55·5%		47·9%
C	20,155	43·5%		30·6%
Comm	456	1·0%		—
L	—	—		21·0%
WRP	—	—		0·5%
Lab maj	5,576	12·0%		17·3%
Swing		+6·3%		−2·6%

Mr David Stoddart
won the seat for
Labour in 1970 after
contesting it unsuc-
cessfully at the 1969
by-election. Contested
Newbury, 1964 and
1959. Power station
administrative assis-
tant. B May, 1926; ed
St Clement Dane's
and Henley Grammar
Schools; Bromley

Technical College. Member, Select Committee on Nationalised Industries since
1970; Electrical, Electronic, Telecommu-
nication, Plumbing Union. Member, Reading Borough Council, 1954-72, leader of
Labour Group, 1964-71.

Mr Graham Young, solicitor. B Decem-
ber, 1935; ed Culford School, Bury St
Edmunds, and Trinity College, Cambridge.
Hon secretary, Swindon and North Wilts
NSPCC since 1965; chairman, Swindon
and North Wilts Cadet Tattoo; charter
member and former president, Swindon
Lions Club.

Mr Roger Hubbard, teacher. B September, 1941; ed Edmonton County Grammar School, University College, Cardiff.

Mrs Kate Blakeney, hospital worker.
Aged 30. Member, Central Committee of
the WRP. NUPE.

TAUNTON   minor

Electorate 63,131.   1970: 61,805

*du Cann, E. (C)	23,841
Keene, D. W. (Lab)	15,401
Mann, M. (L)	13,607
C majority	8,440

No change

	1970		1974	
Total Vote	48,852		52,849	
Turnout	78·9%		83·7%	
C	26,158	53·5%		45·1%
Lab	17,823	36·5%		29·1%
L	4,871	10·0%		25·7%
C maj	8,335	17·1%		16·0%
Swing		+5·1%		−0·5%

Mr Edward du Cann,
chairman of the 1922
Committee since 1972.
Founder Chairman of
the Select Committee
on Public Expendi-
ture; chairman of the
Conservative Party
Organization, 1965-67.
Was Minister of State,
Board of Trade, 1963-
64; Economic Secre-
tary to the Treasury

from July, 1962. Elected February, 1956;
contested Barrow-in-Furness, 1955, and
West Walthamstow, 1951. B May 28,

1924; ed Colet Court, Woodbridge School
and St John's College, Oxford. Banker.
Founder of the Unicorn Group of Unit
Trusts, formed in 1957. Chairman, Keyser
Ullmann Holdings Ltd, Investeco Overseas
Holdings and International Life Insurance.
Director, Barclays Bank Ltd (London
Board).

Mr David Keene, barrister. B April, 1941;
ed Hampton Grammar School and Oxford University. Member, Society of
Labour Lawyers and Fabian Society.

Mr Martin Mann, barrister. B September, 1943; ed Cranleigh School. Co-author
of Liberal policy for review of the Common Agricultural Policy.

TEESSIDE Middlesbrough   major

Electorate 60,011

*Bottomley, A. G. (Lab)	27,324
Dickens, G. K. (C)	13,915
Lab majority	13,409

	1974			1974
Total Vote	41,239	C		33·7%
Turnout	68·7%	Lab maj		32·5%
Lab	66·2%			

Mr Arthur Bottomley
was Minister of Over-
seas Development,
1966-67; Secretary of
State for Common-
wealth Relations,
1964-66. Returned at
a by-election in
March, 1962; repre-
sented Rochester and
Chatham, 1950-59,
and Chatham, 1945-
50. Secretary for

Overseas Trade, 1947-51; Under-Secretary
for the Dominions, 1946-47. B February,
1907; ed council school and extra-mural
university classes. Walthamstow Borough
Council, 1929-49 (Mayor, 1945-46). Chairman, Select Committee on Race Relations
and Immigration, 1968-70. Vice-chairman,
Commonwealth Parliamentary Association,
1968. Full-time official, National Union
of Public Employees, 1934-45, 1959-62.

Mr Geoffrey Dickens, training manager
(engineering). B August, 1931; ed Harrow and Acton Technical Colleges. Member, Hertfordshire County Council.

TEESSIDE Redcar   major

Electorate 62,192

*Tinn, J. (Lab)	28,252
Hall, R. (C)	18,998
Lab majority	9,254

	1974			1974
Total Vote	47,250	C		40·2%
Turnout	76·0%	Lab maj		19·6%
Lab	59·8%			

Mr James Tinn was MP for Cleveland, 1964-74. Teacher and former steelworker. B August, 1922; ed elementary school and Ruskin College and Jesus College, Oxford. Former chairman, trade union group of Labour MPs; member, Select Committee on Overseas Development; branch secretary, National Union of Blastfurnacemen.

Mr Ronald Hall, company director. B October, 1919; ed James Mackinlay School, Redcar. Contested Rother Valley, 1951, and Rotherham, 1959. Member, North Riding County Council, 1956-68, Teesside County Borough (Mayor, 1971-72) since 1967, Cleveland County Council, since 1973. Managing director, Ron Hall (Decorators) Limited, Redcar. Past President, Middlesbrough Master Painters.

TEESSIDE Stockton major

Electorate 85,276

*Rodgers, W. T. (Lab)	37,876
Sloan, Miss B. (C)	25,505
Jones, E. (Comm)	791
Lab majority	12,371

	1974			1974
Total Vote	64,172	C		39·7%
Turnout	75·2%	Comm		1·2%
Lab	59·0%	Lab maj		19·3%

Mr William Rodgers, economic consultant, was Opposition spokesman on aviation supply, 1970-72. Chairman, Trade and Industry sub-committee of Expenditure Committee. Minister of State, Treasury, 1969-70; Minister of State, Board of Trade, 1968-69; Under-Secretary, Foreign Office, 1967-68; Under-Secretary Economic Affairs, 1964-67. Returned at by-election, April, 1962; contested Bristol, West, by-election, March, 1957. B October, 1928; ed elementary and high schools in Liverpool, and Magdalen College, Oxford. General Secretary, Fabian Society, 1953-62; St Marylebone borough councillor, 1958-62. *Appointed Minister of State for Defence, March 1974.*

Miss Beryl Sloan, training office. B May, 1944; ed Eastcliffe Grammar School, Gosforth, Ruskin College, Oxford, and Hull University. Former inspector of taxes; member, Inland Revenue Staff Federation. For two years publicity officer for Newcastle Regional Hospital Board branch of NALGO.

Mr Ernest Jones contested the constituency in 1970 and 1966. Plumber. B September, 1935; ed Mill Lane Secondary School. EETU-PTU.

TEESSIDE Thornaby major

Electorate 62,131

Wrigglesworth, I. W. (Lab & Co-op)	21,503
*Sutcliffe, J. H. V. (C)	19,785
Tennant, R. (L)	7,827
Lab & Co-op majority	1,718

	1974		1974
Total Vote	49,115	L	15·9%
Turnout	79·0%	Lab & Co-op	
Lab & Co-op	43·8%	maj	3·5%
C	40·3%		

Mr Ian Wrigglesworth, press and public affairs manager of National Giro. B December, 1939; ed Stockton Grammar School, Stockton-Billingham Technical College, and College of St Mark and St John, Chelsea. Former director, South Suburban Co-operative Society Ltd, and former head of research and information department of Co-operative Party.

Mr John Sutcliffe, MP for Middlesbrough, West, 1970-74; contested Middlesbrough, West, 1966; Chorley in 1964 and Oldham West, in 1959. Company director and barrister (Inner Temple, 1956). B April, 1931; ed Winchester and New College, Oxford. Chairman, Teesside Youth Clubs Association. His father, Sir Harold Sutcliffe, was MP for Royton, 1931-50, and Heywood and Royton, 1950-55.

Mr Robert Tennant, chartered librarian. B August, 1936; ed Ripon Grammar School and Leeds School of Librarianship. Member, executive committees, North Riding and North Yorkshire, NALGO.

THANET East major

Electorate 47,746

Aitken, J. W. P. (C)	17,944
Bean, R. E. (Lab)	11,347
Cox, J. (L)	8,997
C majority	6,597

	1974			1974
Total Vote	38,288	Lab		29·6%
Turnout	80·2%	L		23·5%
C	46·9%	C maj		17·2%

Mr Jonathan Aitken contested Meriden in 1966. B August, 1942; ed Eton and Christ Church, Oxford. Managing director, Slater Walker (Middle East) Ltd 1973-74. Formerly special constable, East Suffolk County Police. Former journalist, and author of four books.

Mr Robert Bean contested Gillingham, 1970. Polytechnic lecturer. B September, 1935; ed Sir Joseph Williamson's Mathematical School, Rochester, and Medway College of Technology. Member, Chatham council since 1957. UCATT.

Mr John Cox, managing director. B September, 1930; ed Hurstpierpoint College, Sussex, and New College, Oxford. Member, Thanet District Council; Broadstairs UDC.

THANET West   major

Electorate 43,633

*Rees-Davies, W. R. (C)		16,880
Tiltman, I. (L)		9,220
Ramage, D. (Lab)		7,969
C majority		7,660

	1974			1974
Total Vote	34,069	L		27·1%
Turnout	78·1%	Lab		23·4%
C	49·5%	C maj		22·5%

Mr William Rees-Davies represented Isle of Thanet 1953-74. Contested Nottingham, South, in 1950 and 1951. Barrister (Inner Temple, 1939). B November, 1916; ed Eton and Trinity College, Cambridge; cricket blue. Chairman, all-party committee on tourism 1966-68; member, Select Committee on Anti Discrimination.

Mr Iain Tiltman, sub-postmaster. B April, 1945; ed T.S. Mercury, Hamble. Member, National Federation of Sub-Postmasters.

Mr David Ramage, bank official. B August, 1947; ed University College School, Barnet College of Further Education. NUBE.

THIRSK & MALTON   major

Electorate 63,717

*Spence, J. D. (C)		27,580
Brooks, M. J. L. (L)		13,172
Coupe, M. D. (Lab)		10,855
C majority		14,408

	1974			1974
Total Vote	51,607	L		25·5%
Turnout	81·0%	Lab		21·0%
C	53·4%	C maj		27·9%

Mr John Spence represented Sheffield, Heeley, 1970-74; contested the seat 1966 and Wakefield, 1964. Building and civil engineering contractor; director of companies associated with construction. B December, 1920; ed Queen's University, Belfast.

Former national president, United Commercial Travellers' Association. Secretary, Conservative Industry Committee, 1971-72; Secretary, Yorkshire group of Conservative MPs, 1972-74; joint secretary from March 1974. Joint secretary Conservative agriculture committee, from March 1974.

Mr Michael Brooks, farmer and inventor. B December, 1936; ed Charterhouse and Huddersfield Technical College. Holds patent on system of wind-driven electrical generation and storage.

Mr Malcolm Coupe, post office engineer. B May, 1937; ed York Technical School, Scottish School of Adult Education, Dalkeith, and Leeds University. POEU.

THURROCK   same

Electorate 88,607. 1970: 84,259

*Delargy, H. J. (Lab)		36,217
Bright, G. F. J. (C)		17,699
Fleetwood, Miss K. (L)		15,534
Lab majority		18,518

No change

	1974		1974
Total Vote	55,384		69,450
Turnout	65·7%		78·4%
Lab	30,874	55·7%	52·1%
C	19,486	35·2%	25·5%
L	5,024	9·1%	22·4%
Lab maj	11,388	20·6%	26·7%
Swing		+6·7%	−3·0%

Mr Hugh Delargy was elected in 1950; represented Platting division of Manchester, 1945-50. Former teacher, journalist, labourer and insurance official. B 1908; ed elementary and secondary schools and in Paris and Rome. Assistant Government whip, 1950-51; Opposition whip, 1951-52. Manchester City councillor, 1937-46. A vice-chairman, British Council, since 1969.

Mr Graham Bright contested the constituency, 1970. Director of a food supply firm. B 1942; ed Hassenbrook Secondary School and Thurrock Technical College. Member, Thurrock UDC and Essex County Council.

Miss Kaye Fleetwood contested the seat in 1970. Sales manager of scientific company. B January, 1942; ed Loughton County High School and West Ham College of Technology.

TIVERTON major

Electorate 69,320

*Maxwell-Hyslop, R. J. (C)	27,164
Suter, F. J. (L)	21,623
Hewetson, R. (Lab)	8,308
C majority	5,541

	1974		1974
Total Vote	57,095	L	37·9%
Turnout	82·4%	Lab	14·5%
C	47·6%	C maj	9·7%

Mr Robin Maxwell-Hyslop was elected in the 1960 by-election. Contested Derby, North, 1959. Engineer and former personal assistant to the director and general manager, sales and service, Rolls-Royce Aero Engine Division. B June, 1931; ed Stowe and Christ Church College, Oxford. Chairman Anglo-Brazilian Parliamentary group. Joint Secretary Conservative parliamentary aviation committee since 1972; member, trade and industry sub-committee of Public Expenditure Committee.

Mr Frank Suter, solicitor, contested the seat in 1970 and 1966. B 1921; ed Taunton School. Member, Devon County Council and Tiverton Borough Council.

Mr Roy Hewetson contested the seat in 1970. Solicitor. B 1939; ed Monmouth School.

TONBRIDGE & MALLING major

Electorate 65,104

Stanley, J. P. (C)	24,809
Vann, M. (L)	14,701
Straw, J. W. (Lab)	14,683
C majority	10,108

	1974		1974
Total Vote	54,193	L	27·1%
Turnout	83·2%	Lab	27·1%
C	45·8%	C maj	18·6%

Mr John Stanley, planning manager with Rio Tinto-Zinc Corporation Ltd. Contested Newton, 1970. B January, 1942; ed Repton School and Lincoln College, Oxford. Formerly with Conservative Research department.

Mr Michael Vann contested Marylebone in 1970 at the General Election and the subsequent by-election. Solicitor. B March, 1946; ed Marlborough College and Trinity College, Oxford.

Mr John Straw, barrister. B August, 1946; ed Brentwood School and Leeds University. Member, Islington Borough Council since 1971. ASTMS.

TORBAY major

Electorate 85,059

*Bennett, Sir F. M. (C)	33,163
Trethewy, Mrs B. (L)	20,755
Tench, J. R. W. (Lab)	14,389
C majority	12,408

	1974		1974
Total Vote	68,307	L	30·4%
Turnout	80·3%	Lab	21·1%
C	48·5%	C maj	18·2%

Sir Frederic Bennett was returned for Torquay at the by-election in 1955. Represented Reading, North, 1951-55; contested Birmingham, Ladywood, 1950, and Burslem, 1945. Barrister (Lincoln's Inn 1946, Southern Rhodesian Bar, 1947). B December, 1918; ed Westminster School, Lloyds underwriter, Director various financial and industrial institutions in United Kingdom and abroad. Former member, Select Committee on Overseas Aid; former joint vice-

chairman, Conservative Parliamentary, Foreign and Commonwealth Affairs committee.

Mrs Bridget Trethewy, a housewife, contested Honiton, 1970 and 1967 by-election. B February, 1938; ed privately. Chairman, Multiple Sclerosis Society.

Mr Jack Tench, bus driver. B June, 1937; ed Torquay Boys' Grammar School. Member, Torbay CBC since 1971.

TOTNES   major

Electorate 80,120

*Mawby, R. L. (C)	30,565
Rogers, A. H. (L)	20,922
Luscombe, H. M. (Lab)	13,249
Lewis, J. (Ind)	394
C majority	9,643

	1974			1974
Total Vote	65,130	Lab		20·3%
Turnout	81·3%	Ind		0·6%
C	46·9%	C maj		14·8%
L	32·1%			

Mr Ray Mawby was elected in 1955; Assistant Postmaster General, 1963-64. Former chairman, West Country group of Conservative MPs. B February 6, 1922; ed Long Lawford council school near Rugby. Director, Beaverbrook Western Newspapers. Electrician; former president, treasurer and shop steward, Rugby branch, EETPU. First president, Conservative trade unionists' national advisory committee; former executive member of the 1922 Committee. Member, Commons Expenditure Committee.

Mr Anthony Rogers, company director, hotelier and sales representative. B April, 1938; ed Kingsbridge Secondary Modern School. Chairman, Kingsbridge UDC; member, Kingsbridge RDC, South Hams District Council.

Mr Harold Luscombe contested Tavistock in 1970. Railway signalman. B July, 1939; ed Camels Head Secondary Modern School. Member, Plymouth City Council since 1964. NUR.

TOWER HAMLETS Bethnal Green & Bow   major

Electorate 53,442

*Mikardo, I. (Lab)	21,371
Gates, T. (L)	6,417
Murphy, C. P. (C)	4,787
Lab majority	14,954

	1974			1974
Total Vote	32,575	L		19·7%
Turnout	60·9%	C		14·7%
Lab	65·6%	Lab maj		45·9%

Mr Ian Mikardo, MP for Poplar 1964-74, represented Reading, 1945-50, Reading, South, 1950-55, and Reading, 1955-59. Commercial and industrial consultant. B July, 1908; ed Portsmouth Southern Secondary School and Portsmouth Municipal College. Chairman of Labour Party, 1970-71; Member, party national executive, 1950-59 and since 1960. Chairman, Select Committee on Nationalized Industries, 1966-70. President, Association of Scientific, Technical and Managerial Staffs; member, National Joint Council for Civil Air Transport. Elected Chairman of Parliamentary Labour Party, March 1974.

Mr Tudor Gates, novelist, film and television script writer. B January, 1930; ed King Edward VII Grammar School, King's Lynn; Raines Foundation Grammar School; Clark's College, Walthamstow. Contested Bethnal Green, 1964, 1966 and Isle of Thanet, 1970.

Mr Christopher Murphy, advertising agency executive. B April, 1947; ed Devonport High School and Queen's College, Oxford.

TOWER HAMLETS Stepney & Poplar   major

Electorate 60,069

*Shore, P. D. (Lab)	28,869
Greenway, H. (C)	5,539
Halpin, K. (Comm)	1,278
Lab majority	23,330

	1974			1974
Total Vote	35,686	C		15·5%
Turnout	59·4%	Comm		3·6%
Lab	80·9%	Lab maj		65·4%

Mr Peter Shore was elected to the Shadow Cabinet in 1971. From 1971-74 opposition spokesman on European affairs, with responsibilities for prices and consumer protection. He was Minister without Portfolio and Deputy Leader of the House, 1969-70; Secretary of State for Economic Affairs, 1967-69; Parliamentary Secretary, Ministry of Technology, 1966-67. Elected for Stepney in 1964; contested St Ives, 1950, and Halifax, 1959. Political economist and head of Labour Party research department, 1959-64. PPS to Mr Harold Wilson, 1965-66. B May, 1924; ed Quarry Bank High School, Liverpool, and King's College, Cambridge. *Appointed Secretary of State for Trade, March 1974.*

Mr Harry Greenway contested Stepney in 1970. Deputy headmaster and writer. B October, 1934; ed College of St Mark and St John, London, and Caen University. Member, Conservative National Advisory Committee on Education.

Mr Kevin Halpin a former Ford's shop steward now working at Acton Rails. Member, East London Dockland Action Committee; chairman, Liaison Committee for the Defence of Trade Unions.

TRURO   major

Electorate 71,439

*Dixon, P. (C)	23,493
Penhaligon, D. C. (L)	20,932
White, Rev M. W. (Lab)	12,945
Whetter, J. C. (Mebyon Kernow)	850
C majority	2,561

	1974		1974
Total Vote	58,220	Lab	22.2%
Turnout	81.5%	Meb Kernow	1.4%
C	40.3%	C maj	4.4%
L	35.9%		

Mr Piers Dixon was elected in 1970; contested Brixton, 1966. Investment adviser and stockbroker. B December, 1938; ed Eton, Magdalene College, Cambridge, Harvard Business School. Joint vice-chairman, Conservative parliamentary finance committee; chairman, West Europe Group, Conservative Foreign Affairs Committee.

Mr David Penhaligon, research and development engineer. B June, 1944; ed Truro School and Cornwall Technical College. Contested Totnes, 1970.

Rev Malcolm White, Methodist minister and teacher. B 1937; ed Ladysmith Elementary School, Exeter School. Member, World Methodist Council.

TYNEMOUTH   same

Electorate 77,081. 1970: 78,913

Trotter, N. G. (C)	26,824
Carlton, D. (Lab)	20,437
Turner, R. (L)	13,393
C majority	6,387

No change

	1970	1974
Total Vote	59,921	60,654
Turnout	75.9%	78.7%
C	30,773 51.3%	44.2%
Lab	23,927 39.9%	33.7%
L	5,221 8.7%	22.1%
C maj	6,846 11.4%	10.5%
Swing	+2.8%	-0.4%

Mr Neville Trotter, chartered accountant. Contested Consett, 1970. B January, 1932; ed Shrewsbury School, King's College, Durham University. Member, Newcastle City Council since 1963.

Mr David Carlton, polytechnic lecturer, contested Twickenham in 1966. B July, 1938; ed grammar school and London School of Economics.

Mr Rodney Turner, advertising manager. B March, 1945; ed John Talbot's Grammar School, Whitchurch, College of Law, London. Contested Tynemouth, 1970.

ULSTER, MID   same

Electorate 84,106. 1970: 77,143

Dunlop, J. (UUUC)	26,004
Cooper, I. A. (SDLP)	19,372
*McAliskey, Mrs B. (Ind Soc)	16,672
Thornton, N. (UU Pro Assembly)	4,633
UUUC majority	6,632

UUUC gain

	1970		1974
Total Vote	70,518		66,681
Turnout	91.4%		79.3%
Ind Unity	37,739	53.5%	—
UU	31,810	45.1%	—
Ind	771	1.1%	—
Nat Soc	198	0.3%	—
UUUC	—	—	39.0%
SDLP	—	—	29.0%
Ind Soc	—	—	25.0%
Pro Assem	—	—	6.9%
Ind Unity maj	5,929	8.4%	—
UUUC maj	—	—	9.9%

Mr John Dunlop is an hotel owner and lay preacher. Aged 52, he became a member of the Northern Ireland Assembly last year.

Mr Ivan Cooper, Minister of Community Relations in the Northern Ireland Executive was elected MP for Mid-Derry in the Stormont Parliament in 1969. Member, Northern Ireland Assembly. Aged 30. Former member of the Young Unionist Association.

Mrs Bernadette McAliskey, as Miss Devlin, was elected at a by-election in April, 1969, at the age of 21. At the time she was the youngest MP and made her maiden speech on the day she took her seat. B April, 1948; ed St Patrick's Academy, Dungannon, and Queen's University, Belfast, where she was a student when first elected.

Mr Neville Thornton was Ulster Unionist candidate for the constituency in 1970. Teacher. Aged 30; ed Portora Royal School and Stranmillis College, Belfast. Organizer and acting-secretary, Ulster Unionist Council for the past three years.

WAKEFIELD same

Electorate 65,930. 1970: 64,705

*Harrison, W. (Lab)	27,032
Koops, E. J. L. (C)	15,614
Fussey, A. (L)	10,009
Lab majority	11,418

No change

	1970		1974
Total Vote	47,091		52,655
Turnout	72·8%		79·9%
Lab	27,352	58·1%	51·3%
C	15,668	33·3%	29·6%
L	4,071	8·6%	19·0%
Lab maj	11,684	24·8%	21·7%
Swing		+3·0%	+1·5%

Mr Walter Harrison, Opposition deputy Chief Whip 1970-1974; a Lord Commissioner of the Treasury 1968-70, and assistant Government whip, 1966-68. Elected in 1964. Foreman electrician. B January, 1921; ed Dewsbury Technical College and School of Art. Member, West Riding County Council since 1958, and Castleford Borough Council since 1952 (Alderman, 1959). Vice-chairman, East and West Riding non-County Boroughs Association, AMC. *Appointed Treasurer of the Household and Government Deputy Chief Whip, March 1974.*

Mr Eric Koops is director and secretary of a European investment group. B March, 1945; ed Eastbourne College and Lancaster University.

Mr Antony Fussey is a town planning assistant. B July, 1950; ed Hymers College, Hull, and London School of Economics. Member, NALGO.

WALLASEY same

Electorate 69,352. 1970: 72,024

Chalker, Mrs L. (C)	22,428
Paterson, R. G. (Lab)	19,936
Tyrer, P. (L)	12,734
C majority	2,492

No change

	1970		1974
Total Vote	53,978		55,098
Turnout	74·9%		79·4%
C	24,283	45·0%	40·7%
Lab	21,172	39·2%	36·2%
L	5,577	10·3%	23·1%
Anti-CM	2,946	5·4%	
C maj	3,111	5·8%	4·5%
Swing		+2·3%	−0·6%

Mrs Lynda Chalker, statistician and market researcher. B April, 1942; ed Roedean School, Heidelberg University, Westfield College, London University and Central London Polytechnic. Director of international market research company. National Young Conservative vice-chairman, 1970-71. Member, National Union Executive Committee, Conservative Political Centre, National Advisory Committee, and Young Conservative National Advisory Committee. Governor, Roedean School and Battersea County School.

Mr Gordon Paterson, shop manager, contested Wirral, 1970. B November, 1916; ed Oldershaw Grammar School, Wallasey. Liverpool City Technical College and Battersea Polytechnic. Wallasey Borough councillor, 1966-69, 1971-74. Member, USDAW and chairman, Liverpool General branch.

Mr Peter Tyrer, assistant master. B February, 1947; ed Austin Friars School, Carlisle and De La Salle College of Education, Middleton. Elected Wallasey Borough Council, 1971. Member, NAS.

WALLSEND same

Electorate 89,475. 1970: 85,556

*Garrett, W. E. (Lab)	41,811
Chambers, Mrs F. (C)	24,564
Temple, D. (WRP)	1,108
Lab majority	17,247

No change

	1970		1974	
Total Vote	63,715		67,483	
Turnout	74·5%		75·4%	
Lab	39,065	61·3%		61·9%
C	24,650	38·7%		36·4%
WRP	—			1·6%
Lab maj	14,415	22·6%		25·5%
Swing		+3·9%		−1·4%

Mr Edward Garrett, member Select Committee on Agriculture, 1966-69. Elected 1964. Engineer. B March, 1920; ed elementary schools and London School of Economics. Contested Hexham, 1955; Doncaster, 1959. Union organizer at ICI, 1944-64. Member, Northumberland County Council, 1955-64; Prudhoe UDC, 1946-64. Sponsored by AUEW, engineering section.

Mrs Frances Chambers is a trade association executive. B 1944; ed Notre Dame High School, Sheffield; Bedford College, University of London; and the Open University.

Mr David Temple, face electrician at Murton Colliery, Durham. Expelled from Labour Party, 1964. Dual member, EEPTU and NUM.

WALSALL North major

Electorate 70,789

*Stonehouse, J. T. (Lab and Co-op)		32,458
Hodgson, R. G. (C)		17,754
Richards, J. (Comm)		819
Lab and Co-op majority		14,704

	1974		1974
Total Vote	51,031	Comm	1·6%
Turnout	72·1%	Lab & Co-op	
Lab & Co-op	63·6%	maj	28·8%
C	34·8%		

Mr John Stonehouse, who represented Wednesbury, 1957-74, was Minister for Posts and Telecommunications from 1969, when the Post Office became a public corporation, until June, 1970. Postmaster General, 1968-69; Minister of State, Technology, 1967-68; Minister of Aviation, January-February, 1967; Under Secretary for the Colonies, 1966-67; Parliamentary Secretary, Ministry of Aviation, 1964-66. Contested Burton, 1951 and Twickenham, 1950. Economist. B July, 1925; ed Taunton's Secondary Grammar

School, Southampton, and London School of Economics. Chairman, since 1970, of British Bangladesh Trust Ltd, Global Imex Ltd, and Export Promotion and Consultancy Services Ltd. Director, London Co-operative Society, 1956-62, and president, 1962-64.

Mr Robin Hodgson is a director, a London investment bank and a steel fabricating firm, Walsall. B April, 1942; ed Shrewsbury School, St Peter's College, Oxford, and University of Pennsylvania.

Mr Joseph Richards, secretary of Walsall branch of Communist Party. B 1939; ed Holyhead Road Secondary School. AUEW.

WALSALL South major

Electorate 58,775

George, B. T. (Lab)		20,775
Smith, H. (C)		19,195
Haines, D. (L)		6,038
Lab majority		1,580

	1974		1974
Total Vote	46,008	C	41·7%
Turnout	78·3%	L	13·1%
Lab	45·1%	Lab maj	3·4%

Mr Bruce George, polytechnic lecturer in Birmingham. Contested Southport 1970. B June, 1942; ed Mountain Ash Grammar School, University of Wales, Swansea and University of Warwick.

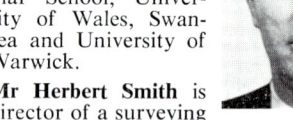

Mr Herbert Smith is director of a surveying firm and of the Walsall Mutual Building Society. B 1922; ed Willow House, Walsall. Member, Walsall Borough Council since 1949, leader of Conservative Group since 1953, Mayor of Walsall 1964-65. Member, Conservative advisory committee on local government since 1966.

Mr David Haines, superintendent in children's reception centre. B January, 1945. Full time social worker since 1968. Primary and secondary education.

WALTHAM FOREST Chingford
major

Electorate 56,537

*Tebbit, N. B. (C)		19,921
Gerrard, M. A. (Lab)		14,238
Nicholson, D. A. (L)		12,060
C majority		5,683

	1974			1974
Total Vote	46,219	Lab		30·8%
Turnout	81·7%	L		26·1%
C	43·1%	C maj		12·3%

Mr Norman Tebbit, journalist and former BOAC pilot, represented Epping, which he won for the Conservatives, 1970-74. B March, 1931; ed Edmonton County Grammar School. Member, Select Committee on Science and Technology; secretary, all-party new town Members' group; former vice-chairman, Conservative Party housing committee. Former officer, BALPA.

Mr Michael Gerrard, export manager. B August, 1935; ed Finchley Grammar School and Lincoln College, Oxford. Member, Harlow urban and new district councils.

Mr David Nicholson, lecturer in further education, contested the Cities of London and Westminster, 1970. B October, 1939; ed Liverpool College of Education and Oxford University.

WALTHAM FOREST Leyton   same

Electorate 63,887.   1970: 66,540

Magee, B. (Lab)	22,785
Dare, B. S. (C)	12,848
Brown, P. J. C. (L)	8,707
Bothwell, Mrs S. P. (Nat Front)	2,097
Lab majority	9,937

No change

	1970		1974
Total Vote	41,292		46,437
Turnout	62·0%		72·7%
Lab	23,386	56·6%	49·1%
C	17,906	43·4%	27·7%
L	—		18·7%
Nat Front	—		4·5%
Lab maj	5,480	13·3%	21·4%
Swing		+2·1%	−4·1%

Mr Bryan Magee, writer and broadcaster. B April, 1930; ed Christ's Hospital and Keble College, Oxford (President of Union, 1953). Appointed lecturer in philosophy, Balliol College, Oxford, 1970, and Visiting Fellow of All Souls, 1973. Contested Mid-Bedfordshire in 1959 and 1960 by-election.

Mr Barry Dare, chartered accountant, is director, investment company and chairman, market analysis company. B July, 1936; ed St Paul's School and University College, London. Twickenham councillor, 1961-65.

Mr Timothy Brown, newspaper executive with *The Economist.* B December, 1937; ed Kelly College, Devon, Royal Naval College, Dartmouth. Former regular Army officer in the Royal Northumberland Fusiliers.

WALTHAM FOREST Walthamstow
                                major

Electorate 51,907

*Deakins, E. P. (Lab)	19,726
Gill, P. S. (C)	10,992
O'Flanagan, M. P. (L)	8,157
Lab majority	8,734

	1974			1974
Total Vote	38,875	C		28·3%
Turnout	74·9%	L		21·0%
Lab	50·7%	Lab maj		22·5%

Mr Eric Deakins, who was MP for Walthamstow, West, 1970-74, was appointed a front bench spokesman on EEC in December, 1973. Commercial Consultant FMC (Meat) Ltd. Fought Walthamstow, West, 1957, Chigwell 1966 and Finchley 1959. B October, 1932; ed Tottenham Grammar School and London School of Economics. Member, Tottenham Borough Council, 1958-61 and 1962-63. Member, select committees on expenditure, and on EEC secondary legislation. wtgwu. *Appointed Under Secretary for Trade, March 1974.*

Mr Peter Gill, data processing manager, has been a Merton councillor since 1964, and Deputy Leader of its Conservative group, 1971-73. B July, 1932; ex Raynes Park and Woking county grammar schools. Vice-chairman Joint Advisory Committee on Local Government Purchasing, 1970-71.

Mr Peter O'Flanagan, co-director of building firm. B February, 1925; ed Downlands College, Toowoomba, Queensland and Rockhampton Polytechnic, Queensland.

WANDSWORTH Battersea North
major

Electorate 44,522

	1974		1974
*Jay, D. P. T. (Lab)	18,503		
Randall, S. (C)	8,080		
Savile, J. (L)	4,683		
Reakes, Mrs M. (Marx-Leninist)	208		
Lab majority	10,423		

	1974		1974
Total Vote	31,474	L	14·9%
Turnout	70·7%	Marx-Lenin	0·7%
Lab	58·8%	Lab maj	33·1%
C	25·7%		

Mr Douglas Jay has been chairman, Common Market Safeguards Campaign, since 1970 and London Motorway Action Group since 1968. President of the Board of Trade, 1964-67, Economic Secretary to the Treasury, 1947-50, and Financial Secretary, 1950-51. Elected in July, 1946. B March, 1907; ed Winchester and New College, Oxford; a Fellow of All Souls, 1937-37. Director, trades union unit trust, since 1967. After working as a journalist specializing in economics he entered the Ministry of Supply in 1941 and two years later went to the Board of Trade as a principal assistant secretary. Personal assistant to Mr Attlee as Prime Minister, 1945-46. Member, NUJ.

Mr Simon Randall, solicitor, is chairman of Bromley Housing Committee, and a councillor there for six years. B 1944; ed Westminster School. Author of pamphlets on housing and drugs.

Mr John Savile, promotion officer. B May, 1920.

WANDSWORTH Battersea South
major

Electorate 46,466

	1974
*Perry, E. G. (Lab)	14,431
Bradbury, A. V. (C)	12,778
Mulholland, G. (L)	5,919
Clifton, J. (Nat Front)	787
Lab majority	1,653

	1974		1974
Total Vote	33,915	L	17·4%
Turnout	73·0%	Nat Front	2·3%
Lab	42·5%	Lab maj	4·9%
C	37·7%		

Mr Ernest Perry, an Opposition whip, 1970-74, was Lord Commissioner of the Treasury, 1969-70 and assistant Government whip, 1968-69, was elected in 1964. Insurance contractor. B April, 1910; ed LCC schools. Member, Battersea Borough Council, 1934-65 (mayor, 1955-56) and Alderman, Wandsworth Corporation since 1965. President, Battersea Labour Party and Trades Council. Sponsored by NUGMW. *Appointed Assistant Government Whip, March 1974.*

Mr Anthony Bradbury, solicitor. B September, 1941; ed Kent College, Canterbury, and University of Birmingham. Fought Battersea, North, 1970. Member, Greater London Council and ILEA, 1967-70. Chairman, governors of Putney College for Further Education since 1968.

Mr Gerard Mulholland, travel consultant. B April, 1943; ed St Edward's College, Liverpool, St Joseph's College, Blackpool, University College, London, and Gray's Inn.

Mr John Clifton contested Uxbridge in the 1972 by-election. Technical assistant, kitchen engineer. B June, 1946; ed Wandsworth Comprehensive School.

WANDSWORTH Putney
major

Electorate 66,049

	1974
*Jenkins, H. G. (Lab)	21,680
Wade, G. (C)	20,241
Slade, A. (L)	10,629
Lab majority	1,439

	1974		1974
Total Vote	52,550	C	38·5%
Turnout	79·6%	L	20·2%
Lab	41·2%	Lab maj	2·7%

Mr Hugh Jenkins was Opposition spokesman on the arts 1973-74. Member, Advisory Committee on Theatres, 1974. Elected, 1964; contested Mitcham, 1955, and Enfield, West, 1950. Assistant general secretary, British Actors' Equity Association, 1957-64. B July, 1908; ed Enfield Grammar School. Served on LCC, 1958-64. Member, Arts Council, 1968-71. Joint chairman, all-party films committee. Former research and publicity officer, National Union Bank Employees, and editor, Bank Officer. Member, ASTMS. *Appointed Under Secretary for Education and Science with responsibilities for the arts, March 1974.*

Mr Gerry Wade, public affairs adviser, was chairman Greater London Young Conservatives, 1970-72, and national vice-chairman, 1972-73. Former national political director PEST. B July, 1942; ed St Enda's High School, Dublin, St James' RC School, London, and Victoria JC and T College, London. Westminster City councillor, 1966-71.

Mr Adrian Slade contested Putney in 1966. Advertising director. B May, 1936; ed Eton and Trinity College, Cambridge.

WANDSWORTH Tooting   major

Electorate 53,460

*Cox, T. M. (Lab)	18,795
Elliot, C. (C)	12,687
Heron, R. (L)	7,108
Lewis, L. (Comm)	337
Lab majority	6,108

	1974			1974
Total Vote	38,927	L		18·2%
Turnout	72·8%	Comm		0·9%
Lab	48·3%	Lab maj		15·7%
C	32·6%			

Mr Thomas Cox, an electrician, was MP, Wandsworth, Central, 1970-74; contested Stroud, 1966. B 1930; ed state schools and London School of Economics. Former alderman, Fulham Borough Council. EETPU. *Appointed Assistant Government Whip, March 1974.*

Mr Clive Elliot, publisher. B August, 1944; ed Epsom College; director of Elliot Right Wing Books.

Mr Richard Heron, computer systems consultant. B 1939; ed Clifton College and University College, Oxford.

Mr Lou Lewis, carpenter. B August, 1938. Show steward, UCATT.

WARLEY East   major

Electorate 57,061

*Faulds, A. M. W. (Lab)	24,780
Lewis-Smith, Miss S. (C)	17,209
Lab majority	7,571

	1974			1974
Total Vote	41,989	C		41·0%
Turnout	73·6%	Lab maj		18·0%
Lab	59·0%			

Mr Andrew Faulds was MP for Smethwick, 1966-74; Opposition spokesman on the arts, 1970-73. Contested Stratford, 1964 and 1963 by-election. Actor. B March, 1923; ed George Watson's and Daniel Stewart's schools, Edinburgh, Louth Grammar School, Stirling High School, and Glasgow University. Member, British Actors' Equity; Public Expenditure Committee.

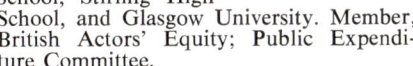

Miss Susan Lewis-Smith, management and training consultant with the Industrial Society. B January, 1936; ed Downs School, Seaford, Lausanne University. Contested Nuneaton, 1970.

WARLEY West   major

Electorate 60,756

*Archer, P. K. (Lab)	28,891
Soskin, A. (C)	14,267
Lab majority	14,624

	1974			1974
Total Vote	43,158	C		33·0%
Turnout	71·0%	Lab maj		33·9%
Lab	66·9%			

Mr Peter Archer, QC, represented Rowley Regis and Tipton, 1966-74; contested Brierley Hill, 1964 and Hendon, South, 1959. Barrister (Gray's Inn, 1952) and author. B November, 1926; ed Wednesbury High School, London School of Economics and University College, London. United Kingdom delegate to Council of Europe. Chairman, Parliamentary Group for World Government, Society of Labour Lawyers and Amnesty International (British section). *Appointed Solicitor General, March 1974.*

Mr Anthony Soskin, farmer and company director. B January, 1940; ed King Alfred School, London, University of Durham, and McGill University, Montreal. Member, Bedfordshire County Council since 1967; former member, Luton rural district council, 1966-70; chairman, South Bedfordshire Constituency Conservative Association, 1972-74.

WARRINGTON same

Electorate 46,251. 1970: 50,012

*Williams, W. T. (Lab & Co-op)	19,550
Hayton, J. W. (C)	8,444
Deakin, Dr F. J. (L)	6,187
Lab & Co-op majority	11,106

No change

	1970		1974	
Total Vote	32,617		34,181	
Turnout	65·2%		73·9%	
Lab & Co-op	20,970	64·3%		57·2%
C	11,647	35·7%		24·7%
L	—			18·1%
Lab & Co-op maj	9,323	28·6%		32·5%
Swing		+4·9%		−1·9%

Mr Thomas Williams, QC, was returned at a by-election in 1961; represented Baron's Court, 1955-50; and Hammersmith, South, 1949-55. Barrister (Lincoln's Inn), 1951; QC 1964. B September, 1915; ed at Aberdare Grammar School, University College, Cardiff, and St Catherine's College, Oxford. Recorder of Birkenhead, 1969-71; chairman Co-operative group of MPs, 1969-70; chairman, consumer group of Labour Party, 1966-70; member, Lord Chancellor's Committee on Public Records; chairman, Fray Valley Hospital Committee, 1967-70; member, SE Metropolitan Regional Hospital Board, 1965-71, and King's College Hospital governors since 1968.

Mr Joseph Hayton, company secretary. B 1937; ed Dalston Secondary School, Cumberland, and Northampton College of Technology. Hillingdon, 1968-71.

Dr Frederick Deakin is a general practitioner. B January, 1928; ed Boteler Grammar School, Warrington, and Liverpool University.

WARWICK & LEAMINGTON major

Electorate 77,904

*Smith, D. G. (C)	30,167
England, J. W. (Lab)	18,874
Jones, T. (L)	14,500
C majority	11,293

	1974			1974
Total Vote	63,541	Lab		29·7%
Turnout	81·6%	L		22·8%
C	47·5%	C maj		17·8%

Mr Dudley Smith, Under Secretary of Defence for the Army, 1974, and Under Secretary for Employment, 1970-74, was elected at a by-election in March, 1968. Won Brentford and Chiswick, 1959, held the seat in 1964, but was defeated in 1966. Opposition whip, 1964-66. Secretary, Conservative Parliamentary Labour Committee, 1962-65. Contested Peckham, 1955. Former divisional director and senior executive, Beecham Group Ltd, and journalist. B November, 1926; ed Chichester High School. Member, Middlesex County Council, 1958-63.

Mr Joseph England, university research worker. B April, 1933; ed Cyfartha Castle Grammar School, Merthyr Tydfil, Nottingham University. GMWU.

Mr Tim Jones, law student. B April, 1951; ed Christ's Hospital, Horsham, Jesus College, Cambridge, and London School of Economics.

WATFORD same

Electorate 55,564. 1970: 56,523

*Tuck, R. H. (Lab)	18,884
Clarke, D. W. (C)	16,089
Jacobs, A. (L)	11,035
Wotherspoon, J. (Nat Front)	651
Lab majority	2,795

No change

	1970		1974	
Total Vote	43,098		46,659	
Turnout	76·2%		84·0%	
Lab	19,698	45·7%		40·5%
C	19,622	45·5%		34·5%
L	3,778	8·8%		23·6%
Nat Front	—			1·4%
Lab maj	76	0·2%		6·0%
Swing		+4·3%		−2·9%

Mr Raphael Tuck won the seat in 1964. Barrister (Gray's Inn, 1951). B April 1910; ed St Paul's School, London, London School of Economics, Cambridge and Harvard Universities. Professor of Law, Saskatchewan University, Canada, 1941-45; professor of political science, McGill University, Montreal, 1945, and Tulane University, New Orleans, Louisiana, 1947-49. Constitutional adviser to Premier of Manitoba, 1943; special research, Department of Labour, Ottawa.

Mr David Clarke, contested the seat in 1970 and 1966, and Woolwich East, 1964. B November, 1931. Insurance broker. Ed Flays College, Uxbridge. Former leader of Conservative group, Hayes and Harlington Council. Co-opted member, Hertfordshire Education Committee.

Mr Anthony Jacobs, company director and chartered accountant; chairman, British School of Motoring Ltd and Tricoville Ltd. B November, 1931; ed Clifton College, Bristol, and University of London.

Mr Jeremy Wotherspoon, estate agent. B September, 1941; ed St Christopher School, Letchworth. ASDAW and TGWU. Parish councillor, Graveley, Hertfordshire.

WELLINGBOROUGH major

Electorate 84,562

*Fry, P. D. (C)	29,099
Mann, J. H. (Lab)	26.829
Jessel, Mrs P. (L)	15,049
James, D. T. (Ind C)	897
C majority	2,270

	1974		1974
Total Vote	71,874	L	20·9%
Turnout	85·0%	Ind C	1·2%
C	40·5%	C maj	3·1%
Lab	37·3%		

Mr Peter Fry won the seat at the by-election in 1969. Insurance broker. B May, 1931; ed Royal Grammar School, High Wycombe and Worcester College, Oxford. Contested Willesden, East, 1966 and Nottingham, North, 1964. Secretary, Conservative Transport Industries Committee; Forestry Group; and British Yugoslav Parliamentary Group. Treasurer, all-party group for responsible family planning. Vice-president and former hon sec Buckinghamshire County Rugby Football Union. Member, Buckinghamshire County Council, 1961-67.

Mr John Mann, lecturer, contested the seat at 1969 by-election and 1970. B March, 1940; ed Wellingborough Grammar School, London School of Economics.

Mrs Penelope Jessel, lecturer in social administration. B January, 1920; ed St Leonards School; St Andrews, Fife; Somerville College, Oxford; London School of Economics. Contested Birmingham, Hall Green, 1964 and April, 1965, by-election; Banbury, 1966; Petersfield, 1970. President, Women's Liberal Federation, 1970-72

WELLS minor

Electorate 68,041. 1970: 65,381

*Boscawen, R. T. (C)	25,430
Butt Philip, A. (L)	17,645
Pearce, D. K. (Lab)	14,399
C majority	7,785

No change

		1970	1974
Total Vote		50,615	57,474
Turnout		77·3%	84·5%
C	25,106	49·6%	44·2%
Lab	16,335	32·3%	25·0%
L	9,174	18·1%	30·7%
C maj	8,771	17·3%	13·5%
Swing		+4·9%	+0·9%

Mr Robert Boscawen, a former Lloyd's underwriter, was elected in 1970; contested Falmouth and Camborne, 1966 and 1964. B March, 1923; ed Eton and Trinity College, Cambridge. Member, Select Committee on Expenditure, Employment and Social Services sub-committee; vice-chairman Conservative Parliamentary Health and Social Security Committee and Conservative West Country Members' Committee. Member, London Executive Council, National Health Service, 1956-65.

Mr Alan Butt Philip, financial controller. B August, 1945; ed Eton; St John's College, Oxford; Nuffield College, Oxford. Former president, Oxford University Liberal Club.

Mr David Pearce, teacher. B August, 1950; ed Birmingham University. TGWU.

WELWYN & HATFIELD major

Electorate 66,451

*Balniel, Lord (C)	22,581
Sewell, C. W. (Lab & Co-op)	21,166
Robinson, P. (L)	12,923
C majority	1,415

	1974		1974
Total Vote	56,670	Lab & Co-op	37·3%
Turnout	85·3%	L	22·8%
C	39·8%	C maj	2·5%

Lord Balniel, Minister of State, Foreign and Commonwealth Office, 1972-74, and Minister of State for Defence, 1970-72, represented Hertford, 1955-74. B March, 1927; ed Eton and Trinity College, Cambridge. Principal Opposition spokesman on social security, 1967-70; a spokesman

on social security, 1967-70; a spokesman on foreign affairs, 1965-67. Chairman, National Association for Mental Health, 1963-70; president, Rural District Coun-1963-70; former president, Rural District Councils Association.

Mr Christopher Sewell, teacher, contested Ilford North 1970 and Harrogate, 1951. B 1927; ed Bedford School, Aberavon County School, and Jesus College, Oxford. Former journalist, marketing executive, purchasing manager and industrial forecaster. London borough councillor for 10 years.

Mr Paul Robinson, company representative, has been group leader, finance and housing committees' chairman on the Liberal-controlled Rickmansworth Urban District Council; member, Hertfordshire County Council and the new Three Rivers District Council. B 1938; ed Kings Norton Grammar School, Birmingham, and Peterborough Technical College.

WEST BROMWICH East   major

Electorate 53,169

Snape, P. C. (Lab)	21,895
Bell, D. W. (C)	16,686
Webster, M. (Nat Front)	2,907
Lab majority	5,209

	1974		1974
Total Vite	41,488	C	40·2%
Turnout	78·0%	Nat Front	7·0%
Lab	52·8%	Lab maj	12·5%

Mr Peter Snape, clerical officer with British Rail. B February, 1942 ed St Joseph's Roman Catholic Primary School, Stockport, and secondary modern school. NUM.

Mr David Bell, surveyor, contested Birmingham, Northfield,

1970. B 1926; ed Wesley College, Dublin. Member, Birmingham City Council.

Mr Martin Webster, journalist and political organizer. B May, 1943; ed Saint Columba's College, St Albans. Contested West Bromwich in a by-election in May, 1973.

WEST BROMWICH West   major

Electorate 57,938

*Boothroyd, Miss B. (Lab)	25,112
Smith, P. M. (C)	11,681
Bowen, G. (Nat Front)	3,107
Lab majority	13,431

	1974		1974
Total Vote	39,900	C	29·3%
Turnout	68·9%	Nat Front	7·8%
Lab	62·9%	Lab maj	33·7%

Miss Betty Boothroyd, member for West Bromwich since May, 1973 by-election. Contested Rossendale, 1970, Nelson and Colne by-election, June, 1968, Peterborough 1959, Leicester South-East by-election 1957. B October, 1929; ed Dews-

bury Technical College and School of Art. Hammersmith borough councillor, 1965-68; chairman parliamentary staffs trade unions, 1958-65; accompanied Labour Party delegations to Europlan conferences, Soviet Union, China and Vietnam.

Mr Peter Smith, public relations adviser, fought Rowley Regis and Tipton, 1970. B 1938; ed St George's College, Weybridge. Member, London Borough of Camden Council, 1968-71.

Mr George Bowen is a security officer. B July, 1925; ed St Michael's School, West Bromwich.

WESTBURY   minor

Electorate 72,999   1970: 67,454

*Walters, D. M. (C)	26,197
Court, A. W. G. (L)	17,778
Smith, A. J. (Lab)	16,453
Thynne, A. (Wessex Regionalist)	521
C majority	8,419

No change

	1970		1974
Total Vote	52,718		60,949
Turnout	77·0%		83·5%
C	26,524	50·3%	43·0%
Lab	17,413	33·0%	27·0%
L	8,781	16·6%	29·2%
Wessex Regnlst	—	—	0·8%
C maj	9,111	17·3%	13·8%
Swing		+5·7%	−0·6%

Mr Dennis Walters was elected in 1964; contested Blyth in 1959 and the 1960 by-election. Director of investment companies and travel company. Chairman, Asthma Research Council since 1969, and joint chairman, Council for Advancement of Arab-British Understanding since 1970. B November, 1928; ed Downside School and St Catharine's College, Cambridge. Founder member of the Bow Group. Chairman, Federation of University Conservative and Unionist Associations, 1949-50; joint secretary, Conservative Foreign Affairs Committee, 1965-71.

Mr Glyn Court is head of the language department, Taunton School. B May, 1924; ed Taunton School, University College, Exeter, and Paris, Grenoble and London Universities. Member, Ilfracombe UDC, 1965-68, and of Somerset County Council since 1973.

Mr Anthony Smith, producer of BBC outside broadcasts. B 1938; ed Lord Wandsworth College and University of Southampton. ABS.

Mr Alexander Thynne (Viscount Weymouth). B May, 1932; ed Eton and Christ Church, Oxford.

WESTERN ISLES same

Electorate 22,683   1970: 23,518

*Stewart, D. J. (Scot Nat)		10,079
Wilson, A. W. (Lab)		2,879
Mackay, J. J. (C)		1,042
Macmillan, M. K. (Utd Lab Pty)		1,031
Scot Nat majority		7,200

No change

	1970		1974
Total Vote	15,232		15,031
Turnout	64·8%		67·4%
Scot Nat	6,568	43·1%	67·0%
Lab	5,842	38·3%	19·1%
C	2,822	18·5%	6·9%
Utd Lab Pty	—	—	6·8%
Scot Nat maj	726	4·8%	47·9%
Swing		+10·5%	—

Mr Donald Stewart has represented the constituency since 1970. Provost of Stornoway, 1958-64 and 1968-70; Hon Sheriff Substitute, 1960. Sales director of Harris Tweed firm. B October, 1920; ed Nicolson Institute, Stornoway. Elected Leader, Scottish National Parliamentary Party, March 1974.

Mr Andrew Wilson, postal officer, aged 53. Member, Labour Party since 1948.

Mr John Mackay, teacher of mathematics, Oban High School. B November, 1938; ed in Argyll, and Glasgow University. Oban councillor and burgh treasurer. Vice-convener of the Argyll Conservative Association.

Mr Malcolm Macmillan was MP for Western Isles from 1935-70. Expelled from Labour Party in 1972 after disagreement on selection of candidate. Journalist. B August, 1913; ed Glasgow and Edinburgh University. Chairman, Scottish Parliamentary Labour Party 1945-51. Chairman, Government Advisory Panel on Highlands and Islands, 1947-54; Post Office advisory council, 1946-51, and Scottish advisory council on civil aviation, 1947-53.

WESTHOUGHTON minor

Electorate 71,416   1970: 69,564

*Stott, R. (Lab)	30,574
Tetlow, B. H. (C)	17,909
Hale, R. S. (L)	10,939
Lab majority	12,665

No change

	1970		1974
Total Vote	53,521		59,422
Turnout	76·8%		83·2%
Lab	29,674	55·4%	51·4%
C	23,847	44·5%	30·1%
L	—	—	18·4%
Lab maj	5,827	10·9%	21·3%
Swing		+9·5%	−5·2%

1973 by-election: Total vote 46,140 (63·5%—Lab 26,294 (57·0%), C 19,511 (42·3%), Dem Soc 335 (0·7%)—Lab maj 6,783 (6·5%)

Mr Roger Stott, a telephone engineer, won the by-election in 1973; contested Cheadle, 1970. B August, 1943; ed secondary school, Rochdale College and Ruskin College. Organizer, Rochdale branch, Post Office Engineering Union. Member, PLP shipping group. Served on Rochdale Council.

Mr Brian Tetlow, estate agent and insurance broker. B 1929; ed Xaverian College, Manchester. Former constituency Young Conservative chairman. Chairman, Bolton East Conservative Association. Member, Greater Manchester County Council since 1973.

Mr Richard Hale, company director. B July, 1933; ed Wigan Technical College. Member, West Lancashire District Council.

WEST LOTHIAN   same

Electorate 76,943   1970: 72,367

*Dalyell, T. (Lab)		28,112
Wolfe, W. (Scot Nat)		21,690
Pollock, A. (C)		11,804
Bett, C. (Comm)		438
Lab majority		6,422

No change

	1970		1974
Total Vote	55,487		62,044
Turnout	76·7%		80·6%
Lab	29,360	52·9%	45·3%
Scot Nat	15,620	28·1%	34·9%
C	10,048	18·1%	19·0%
Comm	459	0·8%	0·7%
Lab maj	13,740	24·8%	10·3%
Swing		+3·2%	+4·2%

Mr Tam Dalyell was elected at a by-election in June, 1962. Contested Roxburgh, Selkirk and Peebles, 1959. Teacher and political columnist, New Scientist. B August, 1932; ed Eton, Edinburgh Academy and King's College, Cambridge. Chairman, PLP sports group; vice-chairman, Scottish Labour Group of MPs, and of PLP foreign affairs and defence committee. Member, Select Committee on Science and Technology, 1967-69, and Public Accounts Committee, 1962-66.

Mr William Wolfe, chartered accountant. Contested the seat 1962, 1964, 1966 and 1970; North Edinburgh, 1973. B 1924; ed Bathgate Academy and George Watsons, Edinburgh.

Mr Alex Pollock, advocate; B. July, 1944; ed Glasgow Academy, Brasenose College, Oxford, and Edinburgh University. Called to the Bar, 1973.

Mr Christopher Bett, a boilerman. B 1934. Member, Communist Party NEC and Scottish Committee. Shop steward, BMC, Bathgate. AUEW.

WESTMORLAND   same

Electorate 55,599   1970: 53,365

*Jopling, T. M. (C)		22,036
Nixon, A. (L)		15,502
Hildrew, P. J. (Lab)		6,419
C majority		6,534

No change

	1970		1974
Total Vote	38,436		43,957
Turnout	72·0%		79·1%
C	21,253	55·3%	50·1%
L	9,426	24·5%	35·3%
Lab	7,757	20·2%	14·6%
C maj	11,827	30·8%	14·9%
Swing		+4·2%	+0·2%

Mr Michael Jopling, a Lord Commissioner of the Treasury, 1973-74, and Assistant Whip, 1972-73, was elected in 1964 contested Wakefield, 1959. Farmer and former partner in motor trade company. B December, 1930; ed Cheltenham College and King's College, Durham University. Former member, Select Committees on Science and Technology and on Agriculture. Joint Secretary, Conservative parliamentary agriculture committee, 1966-70. Vice-president, National Association of Parish Councils. Member, NFU Council, 1961-64; Thirsk RDC, 1958-64.

Mr Allen Nixon, stockbroker. B December, 1943; ed Beckenham and Penge Grammar School.

Mr Peter Hildrew, journalist and former BBC radio producer. B May, 1943; ed Windermere Grammar School and Christ's Hospital (Sussex). Master of Public Administration, Harvard, 1967. NUJ, Fabian Society.

WESTON-SUPER-MARE   same

Electorate 84,422   1970: 79,263

*Wiggin, A. W. (C)		33,838
Golding, P. A. (L)		20,237
Morris, R. E. (Lab & Co-op)		13,542
C majority		13,601

No change

	1970		1974
Total Vote	58,409		67,617
Turnout	73·7%		80·1%
C	33,816	57·9%	50·0%
Lab & Co-op	14,473	24·8%	20·0%
L	10,120	17·3%	29·9%
C maj	19,343	33·1%	20·1%
Swing		+4·9%	−1·5%

Mr Jerry Wiggin was returned at a by-election in March, 1969. Contested Montgomery, 1966 and 1964. Farmer and business consultant. B February, 1937; ed Eton and Trinity College, Cambridge. Joint Secretary, West Country Conservative MPs' Committee, 1969-70, vice-chairman, Worcestershire NFU, 1969.

Mr Philip Golding, architect, contested Beckenham in 1966 and 1970. B September, 1929; ed City of London School and South West Essex Technical College and School of Art. Member, Orpington UDC, 1960-65; member, Bromley Area Health Authority; governor, Bethlem Royal and Maudsley Hospital.

Mr Roy Morris, political secretary, Bristol and Bath Region, Cooperative Retail Services Ltd. B March, 1932; became full-time Labour Party agent. Member, Bristol City Council since 1963.

WHITEHAVEN same

Electorate 50,792   1970: 50,289

*Cunningham, J. A. (Lab)	23,229
Vose, P. B. (C)	15,867
Lab majority	7,362

No change

	1970		1974
Total Vote	39,392		39,096
Turnout	78·3%		77·0%
Lab	22,974	58·3%	59·4%
C	16,418	41·7%	40·6%
Lab maj	6,556	16·6%	18·8%
Swing		+3·7%	−1·1%

Mr John Cunningham, union organizer, was elected in 1970. Member, Select Committee on Science and Technology, since 1970. Full-time officer, NUGMW, 1969-70. B August, 1939; ed Jarrow Grammar School and Bede College, Durham University. Member, Duke

of Edinburgh's study groups for industry, and Chester-le-Street Urban Council since 1969 (chairman, finance committee).

Mr Peter Vose, consulting scientist. B 1928; ed Glasgow High School, Kilmarnock Academy and Glasgow University.

WIDNES same

Electorate 74,393   1970: 71,598

*Oakes, G. J. (Lab)	35,654
Maynard, A. H. K. (C)	19,155
Lab majority	16,499

No change

	1970		1974
Total Vote	49,225		54,809
Turnout	68·7%		73·7%
Lab	28,384	57·7%	65·0%
C	20,841	42·3%	34·9%
Lab maj	7,543	15·3%	30·1%
Swing		+3·0%	−7·3%

1971 by-election: Total Vote 33,099—Lab 22,880 (69·1%), C 10,219 (30·9%)—Lab maj 12,661 (38·2%).

Mr Gordon Oakes won the by-election in 1971. Environment and local government spokesman. Represented Bolton West, 1964-70. Member, Select Committee on Race Relations, 1969-70. Solicitor. B June, 1931; ed Wade Deacon School, Widnes, and Liverpool University.

Contested Bebington, 1959, and Moss Side, Manchester, in 1961 by-election. Sponsored by TGWU. Member, Executive, NW Region of Labour Party since 1971. Vice-president, Rural District Councils Association and Urban District Councils Association. Member, Widnes Borough Council, 1952-66; Mayor, 1964-65. *Appointed Under Secretary, Department of Environment, March 1974.*

Mr Ken Maynard, travel agent. B 1918; ed a London grammar school. Deputy-chairman, Walton Conservative Association, 1960-70; member, Liverpool City Council, 1960-70; Widnes town councillor since 1970; Cheshire county councillor since 1973.

WIGAN same

Electorate 56,390   1970: 57,616

*Fitch, E. A. (Lab)	30,485
Beard, P. (C)	12,283
Lab majority	18,202

No change

	1970		1974
Total Vote	41,656		42,768
Turnout	72·3%		75·8%
Lab	28,102	67·5%	71·3%
C	12,882	30·9%	28·7%
Comm	672	1·6%	—
Lab maj	15,220	36·5%	42·5%
Swing		+5·6%	−3·0%

R

Mr Alan Fitch, Opposition whip, 1970-71, was returned at a by-election in June, 1958. Appointed to Speaker's Panel of Chairmen, 1971. Vice-Chamberlain, HM Household, 1969-70, a Lord Commissioner of the Treasury, 1966-69; an assistant Government Whip, 1964-66.

Mineworker. B March, 1915; ed Kingswood School, Bath. Member Select Committee on Nationalized Industries, 1959-64. Chairman, North-West Regional Council of Labour Party.

Mr Paul Beard, barrister, and Recorder of Crown Courts since 1972, contested Oldham East, 1966 and Huddersfield East, 1959. B 1930; ed Sheffield City Grammar School and King's College, London.

WINCHESTER   major

Electorate 82,120

*Morgan-Giles, Rear-Adm M. C. (C)	
	30,843
Matthew, J. W. (L)	20,339
Allchin, Dr W. H. (Lab)	15,655
C majority	10,504

	1974			1974
Total Vote	66,837	L		30·4%
Turnout	81·4%	Lab		23·4%
C	46·1%	C maj		15·7%

Rear-Admiral Morgan-Giles was returned at a by-election in May, 1964. Vice-chairman, Conservative Defence Committee since 1965. Delegate, North Atlantic Assembly. Member, executive committee, Inter-Parliamentary Union. B June, 1914; ed Clifton College. Chief of

Naval Intelligence, Far East, 1955-56; Captain (D) Dartmouth training Squadron, 1957-58, and of HMS Belfast, Flagship of the Far East, 1961-62. Rear-Admiral, October, 1962. President, Royal Naval College, Greenwich, 1962-64, when he retired. Chairman, HMS Belfast Trust and King William IV Naval Foundation (Almshouses). Member, RNLI management committee. Liveryman, Shipwrights' Company.

Mr John Matthew, assistant bursar, Winchester College, fought the seat, 1970, and Basingstoke, 1966. B June, 1923; ed Winchester College, and Christ Church, Oxford. Winchester City councillor since 1969; Hampshire County councillor since 1973.

Dr Bill Allchin, consultant psychiatrist. B March, 1921; ed Westminster School, and Universities of Oxford and London. Member, Medical Practitioners' Union, ASTMS; specialist in care of the young.

WINDSOR & MAIDENHEAD   same

Electorate 79,065   1970: 77,743

*Glyn, Dr A. (C)	31,022
Kahan, G. H. (L)	16,027
Golder, M. (Lab)	15,413
Funnell, D. P. (Unofficial C)	1,041
C majority	14,995

No change

	1970		1974
Total Vote	54,821		63,503
Turnout	70·5%		80·3%
C	32,264	58·9%	48·8%
Lab	16,214	29·6%	24·3%
L	6,343	11·6%	25·2%
Unoff. C	—		1·6%
C maj	16,050	29·3%	23·6%
Swing		+6·5%	−2·3%

Dr Alan Glyn was elected in 1970; MP for Clapham from 1959-64. Barrister (Middle Temple, 1955) and medical practitioner. B September, 1918 ed Westminster School, Caius College, Cambridge, and St George's Hospital Member, Chelsea Borough Council,

1959-62. Member, Inner London Medical Committee from 1967. Freeman, Worshipful Society of the Art and Mystery of Apothecaries of the City of London, 1961. Member Greater London Central Valuation Panel.

Mr George Kahan, company director, contested Dorking 1966 and Esher 1970. B June, 1931; ed St Paul's School and Imperial College.

Mr Michael Golder is an investment manager.

WIRRAL   major

Electorate 92,123

*Lloyd, J. S. B. (the Speaker)	38,452
Whipp, A. J. (Lab)	22,605
Gayford, M. (L)	14,123
Speaker majority	15,847

	1974		1974
Total Vote	75,180	L	18·8%
Turnout	81·6%	Speaker maj	21·1%
The Speaker	51·1%	Swing	−1·2%
Lab	30·1%		

Mr Selwyn Lloyd, QC, was elected Speaker in January, 1971. He was Lord Privy Seal and Leader of the Commons, 1963-64; Chancellor of the Exchequer, July 1960 to July, 1962; Secretary of State for Foreign Affairs, December, 1955 to July, 1960; Minister of State, Foreign Office, 1951-54; Minister of Supply to April, 1955, and Minister of Defence for the next eight months. President, National Union of Conservative and Unionist Associations, 1966; Opposition spokesman on Commonwealth affairs, 1965-66. Elected for Wirral in 1945; contested Macclesfield as Liberal in 1929. B July, 1904; ed Fettes and Magdalene College, Cambridge; president of the Union, 1927. Called to the Bar (Gray's Inn) 1930; QC, 1947. Recorder of Wigan, 1948-51. Former company director and former member, Commons Services Committee and Committee of Privileges.

Mr Alan Whipp contested Crosby, 1966. Merseyside organizer, National Union of Bank Employees. B July, 1933; ed secondary school and Liverpool College of Art. Member, Crosby borough council for five years.

Mr Michael Gayford, managing director of a private group of companies (chemical merchants and building products). B May, 1931; ed Leas School, Hoylake; Stowe School; Lawrenceville School, New Jersey, Grenoble University. Member of Wilmslow DC, 1963-66.

WOKING   major

Electorate 67,214

*Onslow, C. G. D. (C)	25,243
Wade, P. (L)	17,660
Tattersall, J. W. (Lab)	11,583
C majority	7,583

	1974		1974
Total Vote	54,486	L	32·4%
Turnout	81·1%	Lab	21·2%
C	46·3%	C maj	13·9%

Mr Cranley Onslow, Under Secretary for Trade and Industry (Aerospace), 1972 to 1974, was elected in 1964. Journalist. B June, 1926; ed Harrow School, Oriel College, Oxford, and Geneva University. Member, Foreign Service 1951-60. Former member, executive of the 1922 Committee; vice-chairman, Conservative Aviation Committee, 1967-72. Member, Dartford Rural District Council, 1960-62, and Kent County Council, 1961-64. Member, English-Speaking Union, and associate of Royal Institute of International Affairs.

Mr Peter Wade, executive in technical publicity. B April, 1920; ed Woking County Grammar School. Member, Woking RDC, 1962-65. Contested the seat, 1970.

Mr John Tattersall, a senior British Airways pilot until retirement last November. B July, 1920; ed elementary and grammar school. Member, Wokingham Borough Council, 1963-69 and 1971 to present. Deputy Mayor of Wokingham, 1972-73.

WOKINGHAM   major

Electorate 72,938

*van Straubenzee, W. R. (C)	27,223
Cuff, S. M. M. (L)	16,791
Crew, R. W. (Lab)	16,269
C majority	10,432

	1974		1974
Total Vote	60,283	L	27·8%
Turnout	82·6%	Lab	27·0%
C	45·1%	C maj	17·3%

Mr William van Straubenzee, Minister of State, Northern Ireland, 1972-74, and Under Secretary for Education and Science, 1970-72, was elected in 1959; contested Clapham in 1955. Solicitor. B January, 1924; ed Westminster School. Member, executive committee of National Union of Conservative Association, 1949-59; national chairman of Young Conservatives, 1951-53. Member of Richmond (Surrey) Borough Council, 1955-58. A Church Commissioner. In 1965 elected to the House of Laity of the Church Assembly for the Diocese of Oxford. Opposition spokesman on education, 1969-70. Appointed to Shadow Cabinet as Opposition spokesman on education, March 1974.

Mr Max Cuff, editor of the *Richmond Herald*. B April, 1943; ed grammar school.

Mr Ronald Crew has been chairman of the constituency party for three years. B 1923; ed Brighton Intermediate School and RAF School, Halton. Member, national executive council, ASTMS. Secretary, Sandhurst Local Labour Party, 1966-73.

WOLVERHAMPTON North-East
major

Electorate 68,905

*Short, Mrs R. (Lab)	28,935
Hawksley, P. W. (C)	16,318
Webber, A. (Nat Front)	2,548
Jordan, C. (British Movement)	711
Lab majority	12,617

	1974		1974
Total Vote	48,512	Nat Front	5·2%
Turnout	70·4%	Brit Move	1·5%
Lab	59·6%	Lab maj	26·0%
C	33·6%		

Mrs Renée Short, elected in 1964, contested Watford in 1959 and St Albans in 1955. Freelance journalist. B April, 1919; ed Notts County Secondary School and Manchester University. Member, Estimates Committee, 1964-70; Expenditure Committee since 1970; chairman, Anglo-GDR parliamentary group; vice-chairman, all-party East-West trade group; secretary, Anglo-Soviet parliamentary group. Member, Labour Party NEC; Roundhouse Theatre Council; Hertfordshire County Council, 1951-66 and Watford Rural Council, 1951-64. Sponsored by TGWU and member of NUJ. National president, Nursery School Association, and Campaign for Nursery Education.

Mr Warren Hawksley, bank official. B March, 1943; ed Denstone College, Uttoxeter. Member, Salop County Council since 1970.

Mr Anthony Webber is an undergraduate at the City of London Polytechnic. B May, 1951; ed Elizabeth College, Guernsey.

WOLVERHAMPTON South-East
major

Electorate 54,963

*Edwards, R. (Lab & Co-op)	21,746
Heath, J. S. (C)	10,841
Bamford, T. (L)	5,511
Parker, J. (Nat Front)	1,546
Lab majority	10,905

	1974		1974
Total Vote	39,644	L	13·9%
Turnout	72·1%	Nat Front	3·9%
Lab & Co-op	54·8%	Lab & Co-op maj	27·5%
C	27·3%		

Mr Robert Edwards, MP for Bilston 1955-71, contested byelections Newport, 1945 and Stretford, 1939 and general election, Chorley, 1935. General Secretary, Chemical Workers' Union, 1947-71. Member, Estimates Committee. Former deputy leader, British delegation, Council of Europe, from 1968. B 1906; ed council school and technical college. Served in Spain with the Republicans during the civil war.

Mr Stanley Heath, solicitor, contested Stoke-on-Trent North, 1970. B March, 1918; ed Newcastle-under-Lyme High School and Manchester University. Councillor, Newcastle-under-Lyme (six years), Stoke-on-Trent (three years). BLA.

Mr Terence Bamford, assistant general secretary, British Association of Social Workers. B August, 1942; ed St Albans School; University College, Oxford and London School of Economics. Contested Chesterfield, 1966, 1970.

WOLVERHAMPTON South-West
major

Electorate 63,584

Budgen, N. (C)	23,123
Middleweek, Miss H. V. (Lab)	16,222
Wernick, J. (L)	9,691
Cooper, G. (Nat Front)	1,523
C majority	6,901

	1974		1974
Total Vote	50,559	L	19·2%
Turnout	79·5%	Nat Front	3·0%
C	45·7%	C maj	13·6%
Lab	32·1%		

Mr Nicholas Budgen, a barrister, fought Birmingham, Small Heath 1970. B November 1937; ed St Edward's School, Oxford and Corpus Christi College, Cambridge. Chairman, Birmingham Bow Group, 1967-68.

Miss Helen Middleweek, a social administrator. B March, 1949; ed Wolverhampton Girls' High School and Cambridge University. Member, TGWU, NALGO Labour Friends of Israel.

Mr Joseph Wernick, director in family business. B August, 1920; ed at Wolverhampton Grammar School and Wolverhampton and Staffs Technical College. JP in Wolverhampton.

WORCESTER same

Electorate 74,132   1970: 69,895

*Walker, P. E. (C)	27,377
Morgan, Rev. W. B. (Lab)	19,910
Smith, D. S. (L)	12,724
C majority	7,467

No change

	1970		1974
Total Vote	50,992		60,011
Turnout	72·9%		80·9%
C	29,717	58·3%	45·6%
Lab	21,275	41·7%	33·2%
L	—	—	21·2%
C maj	8,442	16·5%	12·4%
Swing		+4·8%	−2·1%

Mr Peter Walker, Secretary of State for Trade and Industry, November, 1972-74. Secretary of State for the Environment, 1970-72 Minister of Housing and Local Government, June to October, 1970. Elected at the by-election in March, 1961. Contested Dartford in 1959 and 1955. Former chairman, Lloyd's insurance brokers and chairman and director of other companies. B March, 1932; ed Latymer Upper School. Member of the party national executive until 1962; national chairman of Young Conservatives, 1958-60. Appointed to Shadow Cabinet as Opposition spokesman on industry, trade and consumer affairs, March 1974.

Rev William Morgan, clergyman. Formerly coalminer, social worker lecturer. B October, 1940; ed Bargoed Grammar School. TGWU.

Mr David Stuart Smith, surveyor/auctioneer. B November, 1947; ed Kings School, Worcester.

WORCESTERSHIRE, SOUTH minor

Electorate 73,014   1970: 70,375

Spicer, M. H. (C)	28,126
Birch, J. (L)	20,961
Pugsley, D. P. (Lab)	9,757
Hunt, G. (Ind C)	850
C majority	7,165

No change

	1970		1974
Total Vote	50,749		59,694
Turnout	72·1%		81·7%
C	30,648	60·4%	47·1%
Lab	12,839	25·3%	16·3%
L	7,262	14·3%	35·1%
Ind C			1·4%
C maj	17,809	35·1%	12·0%
Swing		+5·7%	−2·1%

Mr Michael Spicer, company director and former financial journalist, contested Easington, 1966 and 1970. Member, Conservative Research Department, 1966-68; director, Conservative Systems Research Centre, 1968-70. Joint managing director, Economic Models Ltd and Director, Policy Data Processing (Westminster) Ltd. B January, 1943; ed Wellington College and Emmanuel College, Cambridge.

Mr John Birch is a quantity surveyor. B December, 1947; ed Alcester Grammar School.

Mr David Pugsley is a barrister. B December, 1944; ed Shebbear College, North Devon, and Cambridge University.

WORKINGTON same

Electorate 52,792   1970: 52,280

*Peart, T. F. (Lab)	24,000
Page, R. L. (C)	16,230
Lab majority	7,770

No change

	1970		1974
Total Vote	40,507		40,230
Turnout	77·5%		76·2%
Lab	24,975	61·6%	59·6%
C	15,532	38·3%	40·3%
Lab maj	9,443	23·3%	19·3%
Swing		+1·6%	+2·0%

Mr Frederick Peart, Opposition spokesman on defence from 1972, agriculture, 1971-72, and House of Commons matters, 1970-71, was elected in 1945. Shadow Cabinet, 1970 unsuccessfully contested deputy leadership of PLP, July, 1970. Teacher. B April, 1914; ed Wolsingham Grammar, Henry Smith School, Hartlepool, Bede College, Durham University, and Inner Temple, Inns of Court. President, Durham University Union. Lord Privy Seal and Leader of House of Commons, April-October, 1968; Lord President of the Council and Leader of the House, 1968-70; Minister of Agriculture, 1964-68. Director, Fatstock Marketing Corporation, 1971. Chairman, Accommodation and Administration Sub-Committee, Commons Services Committee, 1970. *Appointed Minister of Agriculture, Fisheries and Food, March 1974.*

Mr Richard Page, director of vehicle distributing concern. B February, 1941; ed Hurstpierpoint College; Banstead urban councillor, 1967-70.

WORTHING same

Electorate 72,258 1970: 71,935

*Higgins, T. L. (C)	33,613
Foley, M. H. C. (L)	14,683
Neves, M. W. J. (Lab)	8,286
C majority	18,930

No change

	1970		1974
Total Vote	50,376		56,582
Turnout	70·0%		78·3%
C	33,051	65·6%	59·4%
Lab	8,989	17·8%	14·6%
L	8,336	16·5%	25·9%
C maj	24,062	47·8%	33·4%
Swing		+4·3%	−1·5%

Mr Terence Higgins, Financial Secretary to the Treasury 1972-74 and Minister of State, Treasury, 1970-72; was elected in 1964. Economist and an Associate of the Institute of Chartered Shipbrokers. B 1928; ed Alleyn's School, Dulwich, Gonville and Caius College, Cambridge (president of the Union, 1958) and Yale University, where he was lecturer in the Department of Economics. Opposition spokesman on Treasury and economic affairs, 1966-70; secretary, Conservative Pariamentary Finance Committee, 1965-

66; economist with Unilever, 1959-64. Former Olympic and Commonwealth Games athlete. An Opposition spokesman on Treasury and economic affairs from March 1974.

Mr Michael Foley, linguist. B January, 1936; ed Springfield Grange, Buckinghamshire, Bishop Otter College, Chichester and University of Surrey.

Mr Michael Neves. B September, 1933; ed Fawcett Secondary School, Brighton; Brighton Technical College, Garnett College of Education. Methodist local preacher. ATTI.

WREKIN, THE major

Electorate 81,955

Fowler, G. T. (Lab)	30,642
*Trafford, Dr J. A. P. (C)	24,121
Powney, I. (L)	11,487
Lab majority	6,521

	1974		1974
Total Vote	66,250	C	36·4%
Turnout	80·8%	L	17·3%
Lab	46·2%	Lab maj	9·8%

Mr Gerald Fowler was MP for the seat 1966-70 contested Banbury, 1964. Joint Parliamentary Secretary, Ministry of Technology, 1967-69; Minister of State, Department of Education and Science, 1969-70. B January, 1935; ed Northampton Grammar School, Lincoln College, Oxford and Frankfurt University. Leader of Wrekin District Council since 1973; Oxford City councillor, 1960-64. Branch secretary, ASTMS, 1960-63. *Appointed Minister of State for Education and Science, March 1974.*

Dr Anthony Trafford, consultant physician, won the seat for the Conservatives in 1970. B July, 1932; ed St Edmund's, Hindhead, Charterhouse, Lincoln's Inn, University of London and Guy's Hospital. Fulbright Scholar, United States, 1963. Director, Artificial Kidney Unit, Brighton, 1967. Director, private bank. Prior to 1970 election, director of farming company.

Mr Ian Powney, accountant. B November, 1950; ed Bishop Vesey's Grammar School, Sutton Coldfield, University of Kent. Elected, Sutton Coldfield Borough Council, 1972; West Midlands Metropolitan County Council April, 1973.

WREXHAM same

Electorate 75,494 1970: 72,744

*Ellis, R. T. (Lab)	27,384
Pritchard, J. L. (C)	14,301
Thomas, M. (L)	14,297
Roberts, H. W. (Pl Cymru)	2,624
Lab majority	13,083

No change

	1970		1974	
Total Vote	54,699		58,606	
Turnout	75·2%		77·6%	
Lab	31,089	56·8%	46·7%	
C	15,649	28·6%	24·4%	
L	5,067	9·3%	24·4%	
Pl Cymru	2,894	5·3%	4·5%	
Lab maj	15,440	28·2%	22·3%	
Swing		+2·9%	+2·9%	

Mr Tom Ellis contested West Flintshire, 1966. Mining engineer. B March, 1924; ed Ruabon Grammar School, University of Wales and University of Nottingham. Former president, Wrexham Fabian Society.

Mr John Pritchard, employed in housing management. B 1946; ed Haberdashers' Aske's School and St David's University College, Lampeter.

Mr Martin Thomas, barrister. B 1937; ed Grove Park School, Wrexham, Peterhouse, Cambridge. Contested West Flint, 1964, 1966 and 1970. Former chairman, Welsh Liberal Party.

Mr Hywel Roberts, teacher. B September, 1938; ed Blaenau Ffestiniog and University College of Wales, Aberystwyth. Head of management and business studies, Flintshire College of Technology, ATTI.

WYCOMBE major

Electorate 78,256

*Hall, Sir J. (C)	29,521
Back, W. F. (Lab)	18,822
James, M. (L)	15,512
C majority	10,699

	1974			1974
Total Vote	63,855	Lab		29·5%
Turnout	81·6%	L		24·3%
C	46·2%	C maj		16·7%

Sir John Hall, elected in a by-election in November, 1952. Chairman of Select Committee on Nationalized Industries since 1973. Contested Fulham, East, 1951, and Grimsby, 1950. Vice-chairman 1922 Committee. B September, 1911; ed privately. Chartered secretary

and chairman and managing director, Viscose Development Ltd, and director of brewery companies. Deputy president Inter-Parliamentary Union since 1970. Knighted June, 1973. Joint vice-chairman, Conservative finance committee, from March 1974.

Mr William Back, local government officer, contested Nottingham, South, in 1964. B September, 1919; ed Mountain Ash Grammar School. Cabinet-maker, sponsored by Furniture, Timber and Allied Trade Union.

Mr Maurice James, training equipment assistant. B September, 1935; ed Oriel College, Hanworth.

YARMOUTH major

Electorate 70,331

*Fell, A. (C)	24,711
Hollis, Mrs P. (Lab)	19,774
Coleby, P. (L)	12,524
C majority	4,937

	1974			1974
Total Vote	57,009	Lab		34·7%
Turnout	81·0%	L		22·0%
C	43·3%	C maj		8·7%

Mr Anthony Fell, an art dealer, regained the seat for the Conservatives in 1970. He won it from Labour in 1951, held it in 1955, 1959 and 1964, and lost it in 1966. Contested by-election at Brigg, 1948, and South Hammersmith, 1949, and 1950. B May, 1914; ed Bed-

ford School and Tauranga High School, New Zealand. Engineer; former member AEU.

Mrs Patricia Hollis, university lecturer. B 1941; ed Plympton Grammar School; Cambridge, Oxford, Berkeley and Columbia Universities, USA. Norwich City councillor since 1967 and chairman, housing committee. Member AUT.

Mr Peter Coleby is a chartered accountant and freelance script writer. B November, 1935; ed St James Grammar School, Isle of Wight. Member, Waveney District Council. Equity.

YEOVIL   minor

Electorate 74,575   1970: 70,178

*Peyton, J. W. W. (C)	25,955
Taylor, Dr G (L)	18,465
McVicar, M. T. (Lab)	17,362
Tippett, J. (Dem C)	720
C majority	7,490

No change

	1970	1974
Total Vote	55,728	62,502
Turnout	79·3%	83·8%
C	27,689 49·7%	41·5%
Lab	20,621 37·0%	27·8%
L	7,418 13·3%	29·5%
Dem C	—	1·1%
C maj	7,068 12·7%	12·0%
Swing	+4·3%	+0·5%

Mr John Peyton was Minister of Transport, June to October, 1970, and Minister for Transport Industries within the Department of the Environment 1970-74. Elected for Yeovil, 1951; contested Bristol, Central, in 1950. B February, 1919; ed Eton and Trinity College, Oxford. Barrister (Inner Temple, 1945). Chairman of an electrical and mechanical company, 1969-70.

Dr Geoffrey Taylor, consultant physician and farmer, contested Yeovil 1964, 1959 and 1954. B November, 1902; ed Merchant Taylors' School, London, Sidney Sussex College, Cambridge, and King's College Hospital. BMA and NFU.

Mr Malcolm McVicar, lecturer in business studies. B June, 1946; ed East Ham Boys' Grammar School, Exeter University. Member, TGWU.

YORK   minor

Electorate 76,509   1970: 74,769

*Lyon, A. W. (Lab)	25,674
Watson, J. G. B. (C)	24,843
Galloway, S. F. (L)	12,793
Lab majority	831

	1970		1974
Total Vote	57,041		63,310
Turnout	76·2%		82·7%
Lab	29,619	51·9%	40·5%
C	27,422	48·1%	39·2%
L	—		20·2%
Lab maj	2,197	3·8%	1·3%
Swing		+3·3%	+1·2%

Mr Alexander Lyon, was an Opposition spokesman on home affairs 1972-74 and on foreign and commonwealth affairs, 1970-72. He won the seat from the Conservatives in 1966; contested the constituency 1964. Barrister (Inner Temple, 1954). B October, 1931; ed West Leeds High School and University College, London. Member, Bar Council. Methodist local preacher and member, British Council of Churches. Member, Select Committee on overseas aid, 1970. Member, executive committee, Fabian Society and Society of Labour Lawyers. *Appointed Minister of State, Home Office, March 1974.*

Mr John Watson, personal assistant to Mr Heath in Bexley, 1970, is a non-practising solicitor and manager of the international division of John Waddington. B February, 1943; ed Bootham School, York, and College of Law, Guildford. National chairman Young Conservatives, 1971.

Mr Steve Galloway, tele-communications Superintendent with the Post Office. B July, 1948; ed St Mary's Grammar School, Darlington, and Harrogate College of Further Education. Elected to North Yorkshire County Council and to York District Council in 1973.

The following biographies of Labour candidates should be added to their respective constituencies:

BARNET Finchley
(Page 45)

Mr Martin O'Connor, insurance claims manager. B October, 1932; ed Finchley Catholic Grammar School.

BOLTON West
(Page 64)

Mrs Ann Taylor, part-time tutor, former infant school teacher. B July 1947; ed Bolton School, Bradford and Sheffield Universities. USDAW.

DEVON West
(Page 100)

Mr John Duffin, technical director. B February, 1936; ed secondary school. TGWU.

MPs' jobs, ages, schools

	C	Lab	L	Other
Barristers	54	29	4	3
Solicitors	11	11	—	3
Journalists	28	26	1	1
Publishers	3	1	—	—
Public Relations	1	1	—	—
Teachers, lecturers	5	69	2	2
Doctors, surgeons	3	6	1	—
Farmers, landowners	29	2	1	1
Company directors	77	5	2	3
Accountants	6	4	1	1
Underwriters and brokers	18	1	—	1
Managers, executives and administrative	17	27	1	2
Other business	23	23	3	4
Clerical and technical	—	6	—	—
Engineers	5	27	—	—
Trade union officials	—	22	—	1
Party officials	4	1	—	—
Mineworkers	—	16	—	—
Rail workers	—	5	—	—
Other manual workers	—	13	—	—

	Lab	C	L	Other
Oxford	54	96	5	1
Cambridge	24	75	2	1
Other universities	120	52	5	12
	197	223	12	14
Service Colleges	—	11	—	—
Technical Colleges and Colleges of Technology	39	8	—	1
	39	19	—	1
Eton	—	55	2	—
Harrow	—	9	—	—
Other Public Schools	25	108	7	5
Grammar	164	50	54	7
Secondary or Technical	24	8	—	2
*Elementary and Adult	9	2	—	—
Elementary	49	—	—	—

*Including Ruskin College and National Council of Labour Colleges.

Age	C	Lab	L	Other	Total
Over 70	—	5	—	—	5
66–70	9	10	—	1	20
61–65	18	40	—	—	58
56–60	40	39	1	1	81
51–55	49	46	2	4	101
46–50	52	55	4	4	115
41–45	63	56	2	3	124
36–40	38	21	1	4	64
31–35	22	25	3	5	55
Under 30	5	4	1	2	12
Total	296	301	14	24	635

The following abbreviations for trade unions and other bodies have been used:—

ABS—Associations of Broadcasting Staff; ACTT—Association of Cinematograph, Television and Allied Technicians; ALTU—Association of Liberal Trade Unionists; AMA—Assistant Masters' Association; APEX—Association of Professional, Executive, Clerical and Computer Staff; ASLEF—Associated Society of Locomotive Engineers and Firemen; ASTMS & AScW—Association of Scientific, Technical and Managerial Staffs, and the Association of Scientific Workers; ATCDE—Association of Teachers in Colleges and Departments of Education; ATTI—Association of Teachers in Technical Institutions; AUBTW—Amalgamated Union of Building Trade Workers; AUEW & DATA—Amalgamated Union of Engineering Workers and the Draughtsmen's and Allied Technicians' Association.

BALPA—British Air Line Pilots' Association; BLA—British Legal Association; BMA—British Medical Association; COHSE—Confederation of Health Service Employees; EETPU & ETU—Electrical, Electronic Telecommunications and Plumbing Union and the Electrical Trades Union; EIS—Education Institute of Scotland; EPEA—Electrical Power Engineers' Association; ETS—Electrodepositors' Technical Society; IBM—International Business Machines; IPCS—Institute of Professional Civil Servants; ISTC—Iron and Steel Trades Confederation; LSE—London School of Economics; MPU—Medical Practitioners' Union.

NACODS—National Association of Colliery Overmen, Deputies and Shotfirers; NALGO—National and Local Government Officers' Association; NAS—National Association of Schoolmasters; NATSOPA—National Society of Operative Printers, Graphical and Media Personnel; NATTKE—National Association of Theatrical, Television and Kine Employees; NFU—National Farmers' Union; NGA—National Graphical Association; NUAAW—National Union of Agricultural and Allied Workers; NUBE—National Union of Bank Employees; NUGMW or GMWU—National Union of General and Municipal Workers; NUJ—National Union of Journalists; NUM—National Union of Mineworkers; NUPE—National Union of Public Employees; NUR—National Union of Railwaymen; NUS—National Union of Students; NUT—National Union of Teachers.

PEST—Pressure for Economic and Social Toryism; PLP—Parliamentary Labour Party; POEU—Post Office Engineering Union; SLADE—Society of Lithographic Artists, Designers, Engravers and Process Workers; SMWU—Sheet Metal Workers' Union; TGWU—Transport and General Workers' Union; TSSA—Transport Salaried Staffs' Association; UCATT—Union of Construction, Allied Trades and Technicians; UNICEF—United Nations Children's Fund; UPOW—Union of Post Office Workers; USDAW—Union of Shop, Distributive and Allied Workers; WEA—Workers' Educational Association; WEU—Western European Union.

How the Nation Voted—February 1974

	Lab	Con	Lib	Scot. Nat. Pl Cymru	Comm	Others	Total
ENGLAND: Electorate							33,093,117
Votes	9,835,537	10,505,470	5,578,948	—	13,379	201,820	26,135,154
MPs	237	268*	9	—	—	2	516
% of vote/turnout	37·6	40·2	21·3	—	0·0	0·8	79·0
Candidates	516	516	452	—	23	167 inc. 54 Nat. Front	1,674
SCOTLAND: Electorate							3,666,325
Votes	1,058,159	950,901	229,099	632,032	15,069	1,393	2,886,653
MPs	40	21	3	7	—	—	71
% of vote/turnout	36·6	32·9	7·9	21·9	0·5	0·0	78·7
Candidates	71	71	34	70	15	4	265
WALES: Electorate							1,997,571
Votes	745,547	412,535	255,423	171,364	4,293	4,671	1,593,833
MPs	24	8	2	2	—	—	36
% of vote/turnout	46·8	25·9	16·0	10·7	0·3	0·3	79·8
Candidates	36	36	31	36	6	3	148
NORTHERN IRELAND: Electorate							1,041,886
Votes	15,483	94,301	—	—	—	607,802	717,586
MPs	—	—	—	—	—	12	12
% of vote/turnout	2·1	13·1	—	—	—	84·7	68·9
Candidates	4	7	—	—	—	37	48
UNITED KINGDOM: Electorate							39,798,899
Votes	11,654,726	11,963,207	6,063,470	803,396	32,741	815,686	31,333,226
MPs	301	297*	14	9	—	12	635
% of vote/turnout	37·2	38·2	19·3	2·6	0·1	2·6	78·7
Candidates	627	630	517	106	44	211	2,135

* including the Speaker

Votes shown as Conservative in Northern Ireland in 1974 relate to Unionist candidates who supported the Sunningdale Agreement.

The 1970 General Election

	M.P.s	Electorate	Total Votes and Turnout	Party Votes, Percentages, Members and Candidates					
				Lab	Con	Lib	Comm	Welsh Nat Scot Nat	Others
England	**511** *(1,403)*	32,737,025	23,360,896 71·4%	10,102,138 43·2% **216** *(510)*	11,282,524 48·3% **292** *(510)*	1,853,616 7·9% **2** *(282)*	20,103 0·1% — *(35)*	— — — —	102,515 0·4% **1** (The Speaker) *(66)*
Wales	**36** *(138)*	1,958,778	1,516,554 77·4%	781,941 51·6% **27** *(36)*	419,884 27·7% **7** *(36)*	103,747 6·8% **1** *(19)*	6,459 0·4% — *(8)*	175,016 11·5% — *(36)*	29,507 1·9% **1** *(3)*
Scotland	**71** *(256)*	3,629,017	2,688,235 74·1%	1,197,068 44·5% **44** *(71)*	1,020,674 38·0% **23** *(70)*	147,667 5·5% **3** *(27)*	11,408 0·4% — *(15)*	306,802 11·4% **1** *(65)*	4,616 0·2% — *(8)*
N. Ireland	**12** *(40)*	1,017,193	779,113 76·6%	98,194 12·6% — *(7)*	422,041 54·2% **8** *(12)*	12,005 1·5% — *(4)*	— — —	— — —	246,873 31·7% **4** *(17)*
United Kingdom ..	**630** *(1,837)*	39,342,013	28,344,798 72·0%	12,179,341 43·0% **287** *(624)*	13,145,123 46·4% **330** *(628)*	2,117,035 7·5% **6** *(332)*	37,970 0·1% — *(58)*	481,818 1·7% **1** *(101)*	383,511 1·3% **6** *(94)*

(The numbers of candidates are shown in italics.)

The Lost and Added Constituencies

by Professor Richard Rose
University of Strathclyde

The redistribution of parliamentary constituencies has not affected the total number of electors in the United Kingdom, nor has it changed the land to be apportioned into constituencies. But it has altered substantially the boundaries of hundreds of parliamentary constituencies, and created problems in relating seats in the House of Commons as it stood from 1955 to 1970 to that created by the 1974 General Election.

The simplest way to review the transition is to ask, first of all: where have the old constituencies gone? Of the total of 630 old constituencies, 599 form the core (that is, the largest single portion) of one or two new constituencies; 31 are lost constituencies, for they have been so dispersed (or were so small before redistribution) that they do not form the largest single portion of any new constituency.

The 31 seats lost by redistribution are listed below, with the party winning the seat in 1970 given in brackets.

Greater London
Brent: Wembley South (Con)
London & Westminster: Paddington North (Lab)
Ealing: South (Con)
Enfield: West (Con)
Hammersmith: Barons Court (Lab)
Hounslow: Brentford and Chiswick (Lab)
Kensington and Chelsea: South Kensington (Con)
Lambeth: Brixton (Lab)
Lewisham: Lewisham South (Lab)
Merton: Merton and Morden (Con)
Newham: East Ham South (Lab)
Southwark: Southwark (Lab)
Tower Hamlets: Poplar and Bow (Lab)
Waltham Forest: Walthamstow East (Con)

England
Devon: Torrington (Con)
Durham: Sedgefield (Lab)
Gloucestershire: Bristol Central (Lab)
Hampshire: Portsmouth West (Lab)
Lancashire: Liverpool Exchange (Lab)
    Manchester Exchange (Lab)

Leicestershire: Leicester South-West (Con)
Norfolk: Norfolk North (Con; the new seat by this name has old Norfolk Central as its core)
Nottinghamshire: Nottingham South (Con)
Staffordshire: Oldbury and Halesowen (Con)
    Wednesbury (Lab)
Warwick: Birmingham Aston (Lab)
    Birmingham Ladywood (Lab; the new seat by this name has All Saints as its core)
Yorkshire: Bradford East (Lab)

Wales
Glamorgan: Rhondda West (Lab)

Scotland
Lanark: Glasgow Central (Lab; the new seat by this name has Bridgton as its core)
Glasgow Kelvingrove (Lab; the new seat by this name has Woodside as its core)

Of the 31 old constituencies lost by redistribution, 11 had Conservative MPs in the previous House of Commons, and 20 Labour MPs.

In the course of creating the 635 constituencies in the new Parliament, the boundary commissioners found that 36 seats were so much above the average in size they old could provide the core of two seats after redistribution. In such circumstance, the constituency with the larger portion of an old seat can best claim to be its offspring. The second constituency created from the smaller portion of an old constituency is best regarded as an added seat.

The 36 seats thus added to the new House of Commons are given with the old constituency from which their core is taken included in parentheses (* indicates the old core in the added constituency is less than half of the new constituency's electorate):

Greater London
Bromley: Chislehurst (The bulk of old Chislehurst is now Sidcup)
Havering: Upminster (Hornchurch)
Waltham Forest: Chingford (Epping)

England
Bedfordshire: Luton West (Luton)
Berkshire: Reading South (Wokingham)
Buckinghamshire: Chesham and Amersham (South Bucks)
Cheshire: Cheadle (The bulk of old Cheadle is now Hazel Grove)
Devon: Plymouth Sutton (The bulk of old Plymouth Sutton is now Plymouth Drake)
Essex: Brentwood and Ongar (Billericay)
Maldon (The bulk of old Maldon is now Braintree)
Gloucs: Kingswood* (Bristol South-East)
Hampshire: Portsmouth North (Portsmouth Langstone)
Gosport (Gosport and Fareham)
Christchurch and Lymington (New Forest)
Hertfordshire: Hertford and Stevenage (Hitchin)
Hertfordshire South* (Barnet)
Kent: Thanet West (Thanet)
Tonbridge and Malling (Sevenoaks)

Leicestershire: Harborough (The bulk of old Harborough is now Blaby)
Northamptonshire : Northampton South (Northampton)
Nottinghamshire: Rushcliffe* (Carlton; the bulk of old Rushcliffe is now Beeston)
Oxon: Mid-Oxfordshire (Banbury)
Staffordshire: Dudley East (Dudley)
Staffordshire South-West (Cannock)
Walsall South (The bulk of old Walsall South is now Aldridge-Brownhills)
West Bromwich West* (Rowley Regis and Tipton)
Surrey: Chertsey and Walton (Esher)
Surrey East (Reigate; the bulk of old Surrey East is now Croydon South)
Sussex: Arundel (Chichester)
Mid-Sussex (East Grinstead)
Warwickshire: Birmingham Erdington* (Sutton Coldfield)
Coventry South East (Coventry East)
Yorkshire: Cleveland and Whitby (Cleveland)

Wales
Glamorgan: Cardiff North-West (Cardiff North)

Scotland
Dunbartonshire: Dunbartonshire Central (Dunbartonshire East)
Lanarkshire: East Kilbride (Lanark)

These 36 added seats were distributed as follows by the 1974 General Election: Cons 25, Lab 11.

(The core of each new Northern Ireland constituency is formed from the old constituency of the same name.)

CONSTITUENCY BOUNDARIES

The first revision of the parliamentary constituency boundaries since the General Election of 1955 meant that there were 635 seats contested at the February 1974 Election compared with 630 previously. The five additional seats were all in England.

The reports of the Boundary Commissions made major alterations in 322 of the 630 existing seats and minor alterations in a further 88. A few others had their name altered. Since the reports were published a few further minor revisions of boundary were approved by order in Parliament.

In their review the Boundary Commissions aimed to avoid constituencies with more than 80,000 or fewer than 40,000 electors and to achieve a concentration between 50,000 and 70,000 electors.

The statutory position is that for the next general review the Boundary Commissions must report between 1979 and 1983, although it is expected they will want to report as near to 1979 as possible. Inevitably that next general review will involve another major redistribution affecting almost every county and most constituencies. Their huge task is to adjust parliamentary boundaries to the new county and district boundaries which come into being on April 1, 1974.

Party Gains and Losses

	+	−
Labour	11	8
Conservative	3	19
Liberal	3	2
Others	12	—

LABOUR GAINS FROM CONSERVATIVE

	Lab	C	L	Others	Maj	Swing
	%	%	%	%	%	%
Bolton, East ..	41·3	37·9	18·2	2·6	3·3	−2·2
1970	49·5	50·5	—	—	1·0	+9·7
Brighouse and Spenborough	41·0	38·2	20·5	0·3	2·9	−1·4
1970 ..	46·1	46·2	7·6	—	0·1	+4·6
Chorley ..	40·3	39·6	20·0	—	0·6	−1·8
1970	44·3	47·2	7·9	0·6	3·0	+6·2
Gravesend ..	40·8	38·6	18·1	2·4	2·2	−2·0
1970	44·9	46·8	8·2	—	1·9	+4·9
Keighley ..	41·8	39·8	17·6	0·8	2·0	−1·7
1970	49·2	50·7	—	—	1·5	+5·7
Liverpool, Garston ..	42·3	41·2	16·4	—	1·1	−7·5
1970	43·0	56·9	—	—	13·9	+2·5
Middleton and Prestwich	39·8	39·0	21·2	—	0·8	−1·3
1970 ..	41·9	43·8	14·3	—	1·8	+4·5
Preston North	41·5	40·9	17·5	—	0·6	−4·0
1970	43·2	50·6	6·2	—	7·5	+6·7
Preston, South	42·5	37·9	19·5	—	4·6	−4·0
1970	48·3	51·7	—	—	3·3	+5·3
Redbridge, Ilford, South ..	40·1	37·4	22·5	—	2·7	−2·9
1970 ..	43·0	46·2	8·4	2·3	3·2	+4·5
Stockport, North ..	39·4	39·0	21·6	—	0·5	−1·3
1970 ..	46·0	43·8	10·2	—	2·2	+5·3

CONSERVATIVE GAIN FROM LABOUR

	Lab	C	L	Others	Maj	Swing
	%	%	%	%	%	%
Berwick and East Lothian	42·3	43·4	—	14·2	1·1	+1·2
1970 ..	45·6	44·2	—	10·2	1·4	+1·2

CONSERVATIVE GAINS FROM LIBERAL

	Lab	C	L	Others	Maj
	%	%	%	%	%
Ripon ..	10·9	49·6	39·4	—	10·2
1970 ..	26·2	60·7	13·1	—	34·5
1973 by-election	13·8	40·5	43·5	2·2	3·0
Sutton, Sutton and Cheam..	12·6	45·4	41·9	—	3·5
1970 ..	27·3	58·1	14·6	—	30·8
1972 by-election ..	8·6	31·8	53·5	5·7	21·7

LIBERAL GAIN FROM CONSERVATIVE

	Lab	C	L	Others	Maj
	%	%	%	%	%
Isle of Wight	10·8	39·0	50·2	—	11·2
1970 ..	22·6	52·4	22·2	2·8	29·8

LIBERAL GAINS FROM LABOUR

	Lab	C	L	Others	Maj
	%	%	%	%	%
Cardigan ..	33·2	13·3	40·2	13·3	6·9
1970	33·4	17·3	29·6	19·6	3·8
Colne Valley	38·9	20·8	40·3	—	1·4
1970 ..	39·9	22·0	38·1	—	1·8

PLAID CYMRU GAINS FROM LABOUR

	Lab	C	L	Plaid Cymru	Others	Maj
	%	%	%	%	%	%
Caernarvon ..	35·6	16·7	7·2	40·5	—	5·0
1970 ..	40·1	20·0	6·5	33·4	—	6·7
Merioneth	32·0	15·0	18·4	34·6	—	2·6
1970 ..	39·8	13·3	22·6	24·3	—	15·4

SCOTTISH NATIONAL PARTY GAINS FROM LABOUR

	Lab	C	L	SNP	Others	Maj
	%	%	%	%	%	%
Dundee, East	33·7	26·3	—	39·5	0·4	5·8
1970 ..	48·3	42·3	—	8·9	0·4	6·0
1973 by-election	32·7	25·2	8·3	30·2	3·6	2·5
Stirlingshire, East and Clackmannan	36·4	19·5	—	43·5	0·6	7·0
1970 ..	50·7	28·2	5·6	15·5	—	22·5

SCOTTISH NATIONAL PARTY GAINS FROM CONSERVATIVE

	Lab	C	L	SNP	Others	Maj
	%	%	%	%	%	%
Aberdeenshire, East ..	6·7	35·0	7·5	50·8	—	15·8
1970 ..	18·0	40·9	11·3	29·8	—	11·1
Argyll ..	12·6	38·6	—	48·8	—	10·3
1970 ..	25·3	44·8	—	29·9	—	14·8
Banffshire ..	6·4	34·5	13·0	46·1	—	11·6
1970 ..	17·4	38·7	21·0	22·9	—	15·8
Moray and Nairn ..	1·0	46·5	—	52·5	—	5·9
1970 ..	22·8	49·4	—	27·8	—	21·6

INDEPENDENT LABOUR GAIN FROM LABOUR

	Lab	C	L	Ind Lab	Others	Maj
	%	%	%	%	%	%
Blyth	28·5	15·1	17·4	39·0	—	10·4
1970	74·2	25·8	—	—	—	48·4

UNITED UNIONIST ULSTER COALITION GAINS FROM ULSTER UNIONIST

	UUUC	SDLP	Alliance	Repub Clubs	Unity	Maj
	%	%	%	%	%	%
Armagh	53·7	29·3	8·1	6·7	2·2	24·4

	UU	Nat Unity	NI Lab	Maj		
1970	55·3	31·8	12·9	23·5		

	UUUC	SDLP	Repub Clubs	Maj		
Down South	52·1	42·7	5·1	9·4		

	UU	Nat Unity	L	Maj		
1970	54·2	33·7	12·0	20·5		

	UUUC	SDLP	Repub and Clubs	Lab Trade Union	Maj	
Londonderry	52·6	37·7	7·8	1·8	14·9	

	UU	Nat Unity	Derry Lab	Maj		
1970	53·1	36·6	10·3	16·5		

UNITED UNIONIST ULSTER COALITION GAIN FROM INDEPENDENT UNITY

	UUUC	SDLP	Ind Soc	UU Pro Assembly	Maj	
	%	%	%	%	%	
Ulster, Mid	39·0	29·0	25·0	6·9	9·9	

	Ind Unity	UU	Ind	Nat Soc	Maj	
1970	53·5	45·1	1·1	0·3	8·4	

UNITED UNIONIST ULSTER COALITION GAIN FROM UNITY

	UUUC	Unity	SDLP	UU Pro Assembly	Maj
	%	%	%	%	%
Fermanagh and South Tyrone	43·6	26·3	25·0	5·1	17·2

	Unity	UU	Maj		
1970	51·1	48·9	2·2		

Women MPs

There were 23 women members elected in February 1974, three fewer than in 1970. There were six new women members, four Labour, one Conservative and one Scottish National Party. Mrs Barbara Castle (*Blackburn*) has returned to the Cabinet as Secretary of State for Social Services and Mrs Shirley Williams (*Hertford and Stevenage*) has been appointed Secretary of State for Prices and Consumer Protection. The full list is as follows (*denotes new member of this Parliament):

Labour
Miss Betty Boothroyd (*West Bromwich, West*); Mrs Joyce Butler (*Haringey, Wood Green*); Mrs Barbara Castle (*Blackburn*); *Mrs Maureen Colquhoun (*Northampton, North*); *Mrs Gwyneth Dunwoody (*Crewe*); Mrs Judith Hart (*Lanark*); Mrs Lena Jeger (*Camden, Holborn, St Pancras, South*); Miss Joan Lestor (*Eton and Slouth*); *Miss Josephine Richardson (*Barking, Barking*); Mrs Renee Short (*Wolverhampton, North-East*); Dr Shirley Summerskill (*Halifax*); Mrs Shirley Williams (*Hertford and Stevenage*); *Mrs Audrey Wise (*Coventry, South-West*).

Conservative
Miss Harvie Anderson (*Renfrewshire, East*); *Mrs Lynda Chalker (*Wallasey*); Mrs Peggy Fenner (*Rochester and Chatham*); Miss Janet Fookes (*Plymouth, Drake*); Mrs Elaine Kellett-Bowman (*Lancaster*); Mrs Jill Knight (*Birmingham, Edgbaston*); Mrs Sally Oppenheim (*Gloucester*); Miss Joan Quennell (*Petersfield*); Mrs Margaret Thatcher (*Barnet, Finchley*).

Scottish National
*Mrs Winifred Ewing (*Moray and Nairn*).

The Liberal Impact

The Liberal Party nominated 517 candidates—the largest number ever—but only secured 14 seats in the new Parliament despite polling six million votes.

The party held 11 seats at the dissolution and nominated 185 more candidates than in 1970. The Liberals lost two seats, Ripon and Sutton and Cheam, to the Conservatives, Both seats had been gained in by-elections. They won the Isle of Wight from the Conservatives and Cardigan and Colne Valley from Labour. They also won Bodmin and Hazel Grove. At the 1970 election they lost seven seats. Nine Liberals were returned in the 1964 General Election and 12 in 1966.

Liberals were second in 146 seats, of which 18 were Labour and 128 Conservative.

LABOUR SEATS

Constituency	% margin
Leeds, West	8·6
Caithness and Sutherland	9·9
Liverpool, Edge Hill	21·2
Harlow	24·0
Greenock and Port Glasgow ..	27·6
Leeds, South	30·7
Ogmore	32·6
Chester-le-Street	33·1
Birmingham, Small Heath ..	35·2
Barking	39·0
St Helens	39·3
Newham, North West	39·8
Pontypool	41·5
Tower Hamlets, Bethnal Green and Bow	45·9
Sheffield, Park	47·1
Newham, South	51·2
Ebbw Vale	52·7
Dearne Valley	53·2

CONSERVATIVE SEATS

Constituency	% margin
Newbury	2·1
Sutton, Sutton and Cheam ..	3·5
Aberdeenshire, West	3·7
Truro	4·4
Leominster	4·6
Skipton	4·7
Hillingdon, Uxbridge	4·9
Chippenham	5·6
Bromley, Orpington	6·5
Pudsey	6·8
Hereford	7·6
Southport	7·6
Richmond upon Thames, Richmond	8·7
Bedfordshire, South	8·8
Southend, West	9·6
Reading, South	9·7
Tiverton	9·7
Chelmsford	10·0
Bath	10·1
Ripon	10·2
Maidstone	10·8
Scarborough	11·1
Cheadle	11·2
Devon, West	11·2
Dorset, North	11·5
Gillingham	11·6
Cheltenham	11·7
Denbigh	11·8
Worcestershire, South	12·0
Yeovil	12·0
Eastbourne	12·2
Gainsborough	12·4
Farnham	12·5
Salisbury	12·5
Shrewsbury	13·0
St Ives	13·4
Wells	13·5
Westbury	13·8
Howden	13·8
Woking	13·9
Eye	14·2
Maldon	14·3
St Albans	14·4
Altrincham and Sale	14·6
Saffron Walden	14·6
Totnes	14·8
Poole	14·9
Westmorland	14·9
Huntingdonshire	15·3
Havant and Waterloo	15·4
Cirencester and Tewksbury ..	15·5
Winchester	15·7
Petersfield	16·0
Oswestry	16·1
Aldershot	16·4
Barnet, Hendon South	16·4
Fareham	16·8
Dorset, West	16·9
Folkestone and Hythe	17·1
Guildford	17·2
Kingston upon Thames, Surbiton	17·2
Wokingham	17·3
Louth	17·4
Horncastle	17·4
Surrey, East	17·4
Harwich	17·5
Shoreham	17·7
Henley	17·7
Ashford	17·9
Torbay	18·2
New Forest	18·2
Blackpool, South	18·3
Bristol, West	18·4
Tonbridge and Malling	18·4
Melton	18·8
Brentwood and Ongar	18·8
Haltemprice	18·9
East Grinstead	19·1

Constituency	% margin
Richmond upon Thames, Twickenham	19·3
Chesham and Amersham	19·5
Cambridgeshire	19·9
Royal Tunbridge Wells	20·0
Sudbury and Woodbridge	20·0
Weston super Mare	20·1
Aylesbury	20·4
Hove	20·5
Derbyshire, West	20·6
Ludlow	20·8
Bournemouth, East	20·9
Chichester	20·9
Beaconsfield	21·4
Dorking	21·4
Bromley, Beckenham	21·7
Kingston upon Thames	21·8
Bridlington	21·9
Sevenoaks	22·1
Blaby	22·3
Bromley, Ravensbourne	22·4
Thanet, West	22·5
Harborough	22·6
Stratford-on-Avon	22·7
Harrogate	22·9
Bournemouth, West	23·4
Reigate	23·4
Windsor and Maidenhead	23·6
Honiton	23·7
Sussex, Mid	24·1
Knutsford	24·6
Lewes	24·8
Canterbury	25·0
Harrow, West	25·5
Epsom and Ewell	25·8
Enfield, Southgate	26·7
Redbridge, Wanstead and Woodford	26·7
Solihull	27·0
Sutton Coldfield	27·2
Surrey, North West	27·3
Morecambe and Lonsdale	27·6
Esher	27·6
Rye	27·8
Thirsk and Malton	27·9
Arundel	30·2
Croydon, South	32·4
Christchurch and Lymington	32·8
Worthing	33·4
South Fylde	36·2
Richmond (Yorks)	38·7
Kensington and Chelsea, Chelsea	39·7

By-elections June 1970 to February 1974

The by-elections between the two general elections reflected the great upsurge in support for the Liberals who gained five seats—four from the Conservatives and the other from Labour.

The Scottish National Party also won a notable victory over Labour at Glasgow, Govan.

The by-elections with winning MPs were:

1970
October 22
St Marylebone—Mr Kenneth Baker — C
November 19
Enfield West—Mr Cecil Parkinson — C

1971
April 1
Arundel and Shoreham—Mr Richard Luce — C
Liverpool, Scotland—Mr Frank Marsden — Lab
May 27
Goole—Mr Edmund Marshall — Lab
Southampton, Itchen—Mr Richard Mitchell — Lab
Bromsgrove—Mr Terence Davis (Lab gain from C) — Lab
June 17
Hayes and Harlington—Mr Neville Sandelson — Lab
July 8
Greenwich—Mr Guy Barnett — Lab
September 16
Stirling and Falkirk—Mr Henry Ewing — Lab
September 23
Widnes—Mr Gordon Oakes — Lab
September 30
Macclesfield—Mr Nicholas Winterton — C

1972
April 13
Merthyr Tydfil—Mr Edward Rowlands — Lab
May 4
Kingston upon Thames—Mr Norman Lamont — C
Southwark—Mr Harry Lamborn — Lab
October 26
Rochdale—Mr Cyril Smith, (L gain from Lab) — L
December 7
Uxbridge—Mr Michael Shersby — C
December 7
Sutton and Cheam—Mr Graham Tope (L gain from C) — L

1973
March 1
Lincoln—Mr Dick Taverne (Dem Lab gain from Lab) — Dem Lab
Chester-le-Street—Mr Giles Radice — Lab
Dundee East—Mr George Machin — Lab
May 24
West Bromwich—Miss Betty Boothroyd — Lab
Westhoughton—Mr Roger Stott — Lab
June 27
Manchester Exchange—Mr Frank Hatton — Lab
July 26
Isle of Ely—Mr Clement Freud (L gain from C) — L
Ripon—Mr David Austick (L gain from C) — L
November 8
Berwick-upon-Tweed—Mr Alan Beith (L gain from C) — L
Hove—Mr Timothy Sainsbury — C
Edinburgh, North—Mr Elex Fletcher — C
Glasgow, Govan—Mrs Margo MacDonald (Scot Nat gain from Lab) — Scot Nat

S

273

The Narrowest Margins

Seventy-two candidates were elected with a majority under 2,000: 37 Labour, 28 Conservative, three Liberal, and four others. The smallest majority was at Carmarthen, whose MP, Mr Gwynoro Jones, held the seat for Labour by a mere three votes over Plaid Cymru.

In Bodmin, Mr Paul Tyler took the seat for the Liberals from Mr Robert Hicks (Conservative) by nine votes, while Sir Harmar Nicholls held Peterborough for the Conservatives by 22 votes. In 1966 he won it by only three votes and by 4,565 votes in 1970. Marginal seats with majorities of less than 2,000 votes are as follows:

LABOUR

	Votes	%
Jones, G., *Carmarthen*	3	0·0
Madden, M. O. F., *Sowerby*	115	0·3
Bennett, A. F., *Stockport, North*	203	0·5
Atkins, R. H., *Preston, North*	255	0·6
Judd, F. A., *Portsmouth, North*	320	0·6
Edge, G., *Aldridge-Brownhills*	366	0·7
Rodgers, G., *Chorley*	405	0·6
Owen, Dr D. A. L., *Plymouth, Devonport*	437	1·2
Wise, Mrs A., *Coventry, South West*	513	0·9
Callaghan, J., *Middleton and Prestwich*	517	0·8
Selby, H., *Glasgow, Govan*	543	2·3
Lomas, K., *Huddersfield, West*	630	1·4
Garrett, J. L., *Norwich, South*	652	1·7
Loyden, E., *Liverpool, Gartson*	681	1·1
Cronin, J. D., *Loughborough*	697	1·2
Murray, R. K., *Edinburgh, Leith*	621	2·3
Lyon, A. W., *York*	831	1·3
Latham, A. C., *City of London, Paddington*	842	2·1
Cryer, G. R., *Keighley*	878	2·0
Cook, R. F., *Edinburgh, Central*	961	3·2
Colquhoun, Mrs M. N., *Northampton, North*	1,033	2·6
Shaw, A. J., *Redbridge, Ilford, South*	1,143	2·7
Whitehead, P., *Derby, North*	1,293	2·0
Bradley, T. G., *Leicester, East*	1,413	2·9
Clemitson, I. M., *Luton, East*	1,425	3·3
Jenkin H. G., *Wandsworth, Putney*	1,439	2·7
Jackson, G. C., *Brighouse and Spenborough*	1,546	2·9
George, B. T., *Walsall, South*	1,580	3·4
Overnden, J. F., *Gravesend*	1,582	2·2
Young, D. W., *Bolton, East*	1,613	3·3
Lee, J. M. H., *Birmingham, Handsworth*	1,623	4·9
Loughlin, C. W., *Gloucestershire, West*	1,624	2·9
Walker, T. W., *Kingswood*	1,641	3·4
Perry, E. G., *Wandsworth, Battersea, South*	1,653	4·9
Wrigglesworth, I. W., *Teesside, Thornaby*	1,718	3·5
Thorne, S. G., *Preston, South*	1,887	4·6
Tierney, S., *Birmingham, Yardley*	1,947	4·3

CONSERVATIVE

	Votes	%
Nicholls, Sir H., *Peterborough*	22	0·0
Waddington, D. C., *Nelson and Colne*	177	0·4
Morris, M. W. L., *Northampton, South*	179	0·5
Allason, J. H., *Hemel Hempstead*	187	0·2
Money, E., *Ipswich*	259	0·3
Iremonger, T. L., *Redbridge, Ilford, North*	285	0·5
Fidler, M. M., *Bury and Radcliffe*	345	0·5
Ancram, M., *Berwick and East Lothian*	540	1·1
Redmond, R. S., *Bolton, West*	603	3·3
McLaren, M., *Bristol, North West*	650	1·2
Hayhoe, B. J., *Hounslow, Brentford and Isleworth*	726	1·3
Bray, R. W. T., *Rossendale*	797	1·9
Brocklebank-Fowler, *Norfolk, North West*	803	1·2
Woodhouse, C. M., *Oxford*	821	1·4
Fenner, Mrs P., *Rochester and Chatham*	843	1·3
Moore, J. E., *Croydon, Central*	1,314	2·5
Loveridge, J. W., *Havering, Upminster*	1,008	1·9
Hill, S. J. A., *Southampton, Test*	1,403	2·4
McNair-Wilson, M., *Newbury*	1,201	2·2
Balniel, Lord, *Welwyn and Hatfield*	1,415	2·5
Young, Sir G., *Ealing, Acton*	1,451	3·4
Edwards, R., *Pembroke*	1,479	2·5
Temple-Morris, P., *Leominster*	1,629	4·6
Fairgrieve, R., *Aberdeenshire, West*	1,640	3·7
Butler, A., *Bosworth*	1,687	1·7
Macfarlane, N., *Sutton, Sutton and Cheam*	1,719	3·5
Boardman, T. G., *Leicester, South*	1,766	3·2
d'Avigdor-Goldsmid, *Lichfield and Tamworth*	1,807	2·4

LIBERAL

	Votes	%
Tyler, P., *Bodmin*	9	0·0
Beith, A. J., *Berwick-upon-Tweed*	443	1·2
Wainwright, R. S., *Colne Valley*	719	1·4

OTHERS

	Votes	%
Thomas, D. E., *Merioneth* (Pl Cymru)	588	2·6
Taverne, D., *Lincoln* (Soc Dem)	1,293	3·1
Wigley, D., *Caernarvon* (Pl Cymru)	1,728	5·0
Ewing, Mrs W. M., *Moray and Nairn* (Scot Nat)	1,817	5·9B

LARGE MAJORITIES

The biggest majority, 35,644, was at Antrim South, where the United Ulster Unionist Coalition candidate, Mr James Molyneaux, polled 48,203. The biggest majority in England was that for Labour in Hemsworth 34,941.

Defeated Members

Mr Gordon Campbell, Secretary of State for Scotland, was the only senior minister in the former Parliament to lose his seat. He was dislodged from Moray and Nairn by Mrs Winifred Ewing, Scottish National Party, who won Hamilton from Labour in a by-election in 1967 and lost it to them in 1970. Altogether, 53 former MPs lost their seats.

Two junior ministers were defeated— Mr Kenneth Speed, Under-Secretary of State for the Environment since April, 1972, and Mr Nicholas Scott, who was promoted from the back benches to Under-Secretary of State for Employment less than two months before the Election.

Mrs Bernadette McAliskey, Independent Unity member for Mid Ulster, was beaten solidly both by the UUUC, which took the seat, and the SDLP.

Mr Selwyn Gummer, a Vice-Chairman of the Conservative Party, lost Lewisham West to Labour. A resounding Conservative defeat came in the Isle of Wight, where Mr Mark Woodnutt, who had a 17,000 majority over Labour in 1970, lost to the Liberals by 7,766 votes.

The full list of those who failed to be re-elected is:

CONSERVATIVES

Baker, W. H. K., *Banffshire*
Campbell, G. T. C., *Moray and Nairn*
Chapman, S. B., *Birmingham, Handsworth*
Cockeram, E. P., *Bebington and Ellesmere Port*
Coombs, D. M., *Birmingham, Yardley*
Cooper, A. E. , *Redbridge, Ilford, South*
Green, A., *Preston, South*
Gummer, J. S., *Lewisham, West*
Hall, Miss J., *Keighley*
Haslehurst, A. G. B., *Middleton and Prestwich*
Hicks, R., *Bodmin*
Holt, Miss M., *Preston, North*
Hornsby-Smith, Dame P., *Aldridge-Brownhills*
Kinsey, J. R., *Birmingham, Perry Bar*
Monks, Mrs C. M., *Chorley*
Montgomery, F., *Dudley, West*
Owen, I. W., *Stockport, North*
Proudfoot, G. W., *Brighouse and Spenborough*
Reed, L. D., *Bolton, East*
Scott, N. P., *City of London, Paddington*
Simeons, C. F. C., *Luton, East*
Soref, H. B., *Ormskirk*
Speed, H. K., *Meriden*
Stewart-Smith, D. G., *Belper*
Stuttaford, I. T., *Norwich, South*
Sutcliffe, J. H. V., *Teesside*
Taylor, F. H., *Manchester, Moss Side*
Trafford, J. A. P., *The Wrekin*
Trew, P. J. E., *Dartford*
Vickers, Dame, J. H., *Plymouth, Devonport*
White, R. L., *Gravesend*
Wilkinson, J. A. D., *Bradford, West*
Wolrige-Gordon, P., *Aberdeenshire, East*
Woodnutt, H. F. M., *Isle of Wight*

LABOUR

Barnes, M. C. J., *Hounslow, Brentford and Isleworth*
Clark, D. G., *Colne Valley*
Davis, T. A. G., *Bromsgrove and Redditch*
Douglas, R. G., *Stirlingshire, East, and Clackmannan*
Edwards, W. H., *Merioneth*
Machin, G., *Dundee, East*
Mackintosh, J. P., *Berwick and East Lothian*
Morgan, D. E., *Cardigan*
Richard, I. S., *Blyth*
Roberts, G. O., *Caernarvon*
Spearing, N. J., *Ealing, Acton*
Thomas, J., *Abertillery*

LIBERAL

Austick, D., *Ripon*
Tope, G. N., *Sutton, Sutton and Cheam*

OTHERS

McAliskey, Mrs B., *Ulster, Mid* (Ind Soc)
Macdonald, Mrs M., *Glasgow, Govan* (Scot Nat)
McManus, F., *Fermanagh and South Tyrone* (Unity)
McMaster, S. R., *Belfast, East* (UU Pro-Assembly)
Pounder, R. (UU Pro-Assembly)

Lost Deposits

The Election cost the Labour Party £4,200 in lost deposits—more than either of the other two main parties. The National Front lost their deposit in each of the 54 seats they contested and the Communists lost deposits in 43 of the 44 seats where they had candidates.

The numbers of candidates who forfeited their deposits and the cost to their parties was as follows: Labour 28 (£4,200); Conservative 10 (£1,500); Liberal 22 (£3,300); Scottish National 7 (£1,050); Plaid Cymru 26 (£3,900); National Front 54 (£8,100); Communist 43 (£6,450); Others 131 (£19,650). This makes a total of 321 (£48,150).

Retiring MPs

A total of 70 MPs—39 Conservative, 28 Labour, two Ulster Unionist, and one Alliance—did not seek re-election or were unable to secure nominations. This was 9 fewer than in 1970.

The most surprising departure was that of Mr Enoch Powell (Conservative), a former Minister of Health who was dismissed from Mr Heath's Shadow Cabinet in 1968 after a controversial immigration speech. Mr Powell, a fervent anti-Marketeer denounced the election as 'essentially fraudulent' on the day it was announced, and indicated that he did not intend to contest the Wolverhampton, South-West seat which he had held since 1950.

The 'Father' of the House, Sir Robin Turton, decided not to stand again as MP for Thirsk and Malton, the seat he had represented since 1929. Another Conservative who did not seek re-election was Dame Irene Ward (Tynemouth) who had been described as the 'Mother' of the House, and who first came to the Commons in 1931.

Another Conservative who retired was Sir Robert Grant-Ferris (Nantwich) who was Deputy Speaker from 1970 to 1974. A former Conservative Minister of Transport, Mr Ernest Marples, also decided not to stand. Mr Duncan Sandys (Streatham), Secretary of State for Commonwealth Relations and the Colonies 1962-64, and a former Minister for Aviation, Defence, Housing and Local Government, and Supply, left the Commons.

Labour MPs who did not seek election included Mr Richard Crossman (Coventry, East) who was Secretary of State for Social Services, 1968-70. He was a former Leader of the Commons, and Minister of Housing and Local Government.

Mr Patrick Gordon Walker, who was Foreign Secretary from 1964 until 1965 when he resigned after losing a Leyton by-election, did not seek election this time. After being returned for Leyton at the 1966 General Election, he held ministerial offices in the Labour Government. The full list is:

Conservative
Mr John Astor (Newbury), Mr Brian Batsford (Ealing, South), Sir Tufton Beamish (Lewes), Sir Clive Bossom (Leominster), Sir Tatton Brinton (Kidderminster), Sir Eric Bullus (Wembley, North), Sir Robert Cary (Manchester, Withington), Sir Frederick Corfield (Gloucestershire, South), Sir Henry d'Avigdor Goldsmid (Walsall, South), Mr Simon Wingfield Digby (West Dorset), Capt. Walter Elliott (Carshalton), Mr Tim Fortescue (Liverpool, Garston), Sir John Foster (Northwich), Sir Robert Grant-Ferris (Nantwich), Mr Brian Harrison (Maldon), Mr John Hay (Henley), Mr Joseph Hiley (Pudsey), Mr John Hill (Norfolk, South), Mr Richard Hornby (Tonbridge), Mr John Jennings (Burton), Mr Geoffrey Lloyd (Sutton Coldfield), Sir Gilbert Longden (South-West Hertfordshire), Sir Fitzroy Maclean (Bute and North Ayrshire), Mr Ernest Marples (Wallasey), Lt-Col Colin Mitchell (Aberdeen, West), Mr Michael Noble (Argyll), Miss Mervyn Pike (Melton), Sir John Peel (Leicester, South-East), Mr Enoch Powell (Wolverhampton, South-West), Mr James Ramsden (Harrogate), Sir Ronald Russell (Wembley, South), Mr Duncan Sandys (Streatham), Sir Charles Taylor (Eastbourne), Mr John Temple (City of Chester), Sir Richard Thompson (Croydon, South), Sir Robin Turton (Thirsk and Malton), Mr John Tilney (Liverpool, Wavertree), Dame Irene Ward (Tynemouth), Mr Norman Wylie (Edinburgh, Pentlands).

Labour
Mr Austen Albu (Edmonton), Mr Scholefield Allen (Crewe) Mr Alan Beaney (Hemsworth), Mr James Bennett (Glasgow, Bridgeton), Mrs Freda Corbet (Peckham), Mr Richard Crossman (Coventry, East), Mr George Darling (Sheffield, Hillsborough), Mr Elfed Davies (Rhondda, East), Mr Tom Driberg (Barking), Mrs Doris Fisher (Birmingham, Ladywood), Mr William Hannan (Glasgow, Maryhill), Mr William Hilton (Bethnal Green), Mr Douglas Houghton (Sowerby), Mr Fred Lee (Newton), Mr Carol Johnson (Lewisham, South), Mr Dick Leonard (Romford), Mr John Mackie (Enfield, East), Mr E. L. Mallalieu (Brigg), Mr Frank Marsden (Liverpool, Scotland), Mr Albert Oram (East Ham, South), Mr Thomas Oswald (Edinburgh, Central), Mr Reginald Paget (Northampton), Mr Charles Pannell (Leeds, West), Mr Arthur Probert (Aberdare), Mr David Reed (Sedgefield), Mr Patrick Gordon Walker (Leyton), Mr George Wallace (Norwich, North), Mr William Wells (Walsall, North).

Ulster Unionist
Mr Robin Chichester-Clark (Londonderry), Mr John Maginnis (Armagh).

Alliance
Mr Stratton Mills (Belfast, North).

Rise and fall of the Parties

The following table gives the state of the parties after each election since 1945; it also shows the size of the electorate and the percentage who voted.

	1945	1950	1951	1955	1959	1964	1966	1970	1974
Conservative ..	213	298	321	345	365	303	253	330	296
Labour ..	393	315	295	277	258	317	363	287	301
Liberal ..	12	9	6	6	6	9	12	6	14
Independent ..	14	—	—		—	1	—	—	—
Others ..	8	3	3	2	—	1 (the Speaker)	2*	7*	24*
Total ..	640	625	625	630	630	630	630	630	635
Electorate ..	32,836,419	34,269,764	34,622,891	34,852,179	35,397,304	35,894,054	35,957,245	39,384,364	39,798,899
Poll ..	24,978,949	28,769,477	28,602,323	26,759,729	27,862,652	27,657,148	27,264,747	28,264,807	31,333,226
Percentage ..	76·1	84	82·6	76·8	78·7	77·0	75·9	72·0	78·7

*Includes the Speaker.

In February 1974 election "Others" consist of the Speaker, United Ulster Unionist Coalition 11, Scottish National Party 7, Plaid Cymru 2, Social Democratic and Labour Party 1, Independent Labour Party 1, and Campaign for Social Democracy 1.

277

By-Elections

Constituency and date		Party

Constituency and date		Party

Constituency and date		Party

Constituency and date		Party

Constituency and date		Party

Constituency and date		Party

*The General Election Manifestos

The Conservative Party:

'Firm action for a fair Britain'

Today we face great dangers both from within our own country and from outside.

The problems are formidable, but there is no reason why they should overwhelm us.

The assets of the British people are great. Not simply our technical skills and our natural resources, but also, more important than these, the strength and stability of our institutions and the determination of our people in moments of crisis to ensure that good sense and moderation prevail.

If we are to make the best use of those assets it is essential that the affairs of this country are in the hands of a strong government, able to take firm measures in defence of the national interest.

This means a Conservative Government with a renewed mandate from the people and with a full five years in which to guide the nation safely through the difficult period that lies ahead.

That is why we need a General Election now.

Once the General Election is behind us then we must put aside our differences and join in a common determination to establish and maintain a secure, civilised, fair society.

The Danger from Outside

The world has changed dramatically since we last sought the support of the electorate.

In the last two years there has been a dramatic rise in the world price of almost all the essential raw materials and foods which we have to import from overseas.

Many of these prices have doubled in the past year alone, making it impossible to stem the rise in the cost of living.

Now on top of these increases comes the huge increase in oil prices, which in turn will affect the cost of almost everything that we produce or buy in this country.

Fortunately, as far as energy is concerned, Britain will in the long run be able to cope better than most. We have plentiful supplies of coal and natural gas. We are well advanced in the development of nuclear power. Above all, within five years from now we should be able to satisfy the greater part of our needs with our own oil from the seas around our shores, provided we make the determined effort that will be necessary.

But let no one suppose that as a nation we can deal with the immediate problem without hardship and sacrifice.

It will impose a greatly increased burden on our balance of payments, and for the time being will make us poorer as a nation than we would otherwise have been.

---

*The Conservative, Labour and Liberal manifestos are published in full, with extracts from the manifestos of the Scottish National Party, Plaid Cymru, Communist Party and National Front.

What we must continue to ensure is that any sacrifices are shared equitably and that hardship does not fall on those least able to bear it.

If the situation requires further action – whether it be in the field of public expenditure or of tax or monetary policies – we shall not hesitate to take it.

But the basis of our firm action will be fairness.

The Danger from Within

Events from overseas have held us back. They will not destroy us.

What could destroy, not just our present standard of living but all our hopes for the future, would be inflation we brought upon ourselves.

Despite the unprecedented sharp rise in world prices, price increases in the shops have, as a result of our counter-inflation policies, been much less than would otherwise have been the case.

We have also made sure that those worst hit by rising prices, in particular pensioners, are better protected than they have ever been before.

But we have also had to deal with the inflation which comes as a result of excessive wage increases here at home.

For more than two years we tried strenuously to deal with this problem by voluntary means. In particular we asked trade unions and employers to join us in working out a voluntary scheme to prevent one group of workers using its industrial strength to steal a march over those working in other industries.

Then other groups are inevitably provoked into leapfrogging. And so it goes on, with the old, the weak and those who do not or will not strike, suffering more at each turn of the inflationary screw.

In the end, after all our talks, although we agreed on objectives, the trade unions could not agree with us on a voluntary means of achieving them, and we had to ask Parliament for statutory powers over pay and prices to hold the line against inflation.

Stages 1 and 2 of that policy, which are now completed, proved more successful than our critics thought possible. The rise in prices due to internal causes was sharply reduced – to a greater extent, indeed, than in most other countries.

Now, in Stage 3 nearly six million workers have concluded wage agreements within the approved limits. The special position of the mineworkers has been recognised by an offer, within Stage 3, of a size which few other groups of workers can hope to achieve.

It is a tragedy that the miners' leaders should have turned down this offer.

The action taken by the National Union of Mineworkers has already caused great damage and threatens even greater damage for the future.

It must be the aim of any responsible Government to reach a settlement of this dispute at the earliest possible moment.

The choice before the Government, and now the choice before the country, is clear.

On the one hand it would be possible to accept the NUM's terms for a settlement.

The country must realise what the consequences of this would be.

It would mean accepting the abuse of industrial power to gain a privileged position.

It would undermine the position of moderate trade union leaders.

It would make it certain that similar strikes occurred at frequent intervals in the future.

It would destroy our chances of containing inflation.

The alternative is to reach a settlement with the NUM on terms which safeguard the nation's interests as well as the miners.

The basis of that settlement must be fairness.

The terms must be fair to the miners, but they must also be fair to the nearly six million workers who have now accepted settlements within the limits of our counter-inflation policy and the many others who are prepared to do so.

They must be fair to the even greater number of people who have no union to stand up for them and who rely on the elected government to look after their interests.

A Conservative Government with a new mandate and five years of certain authority ahead of it would be in a good position to reach such a settlement.

The present offer by the National Coal Board remains on the table. It can be accepted at any time.

We have accepted the principles of the Pay Board's report on relative rates of pay between one group of workers and another. We have already set up machinery for the examination of major claims about relative pay levels, based on the Pay Board.

As its first task, this new machinery will conduct a full examination of the miners' case within this framework. It will take due account of the relative claims of other groups, many of whom – such as nurses and teachers – gave evidence during the preparation of the Relativities Report. Moreover, we are prepared to undertake that whatever recommendation the new body makes on the miners' case can be backdated to the first of March.

It will be completely free to take evidence from any quarter and to decide upon its recommendations.

So it will be impartial and it will be thorough.

And it will be fair, not only to the miners, but to everyone else.

But whatever settlement is reached, the fact must be faced that, for a time, our nation's resources will be stretched to the limit, and those most in need of protection against inflation must have first claim on them.

This Conservative Government has already moved from a two-yearly to an annual review of pensions and all other benefits. We will now move to a six monthly up-rating of pensions and other long-term benefits.

This will have to be paid for by the community as a whole, out of higher contributions which must be shared fairly amongst *all* the people.

A fair and orderly policy for pay and prices, for pensions and benefits meets the economic needs of the country.

But at the same time, it must be matched by a fair and orderly way of dealing with our industrial relations.

The foundations for better relations in industry were laid in the Industrial Relations Act. We have never pretended that it would be easy to implement.

But other industrial countries have found that good industrial relations require a proper framework of law and we are sure that Britain is no exception.

We shall therefore maintain the essential structure of the Industrial Relations Act, but we shall amend it in the light of experience, and after consultation with both sides of industry, in order

to meet any valid criticisms
to make conciliation a pre-condition of court action
and to provide more effective control for the majority of union members by ensuring that they have the opportunity to elect the governing bodies and national leaders of their unions by a postal ballot.

We shall also seek to improve industrial relations by bringing in new legislation, following discussions with both sides of industry, designed to make large and medium-sized firms introduce a wider measure of employee-participation.

The best way of curbing the majority of extremists in the trade unions is for the moderate majority of union members to stand up and be counted.

But the fact remains that a small number of militant extremists can so manipulate and abuse the monopoly power of their unions as to cause incalculable damage to the country and to the fabric of our society itself.

Moreover, it is manifestly unfair that those who do not go on strike are, in effect, obliged to subsidise those who do.

It is no part of our policy to see the wives and children of men on strike suffering.

But it is only right that the unions themselves, and not the taxpayer, should accept their primary responsibility for the welfare of the families of men who choose to go on strike; and, after discussions with trade unions and employers, we will amend the social security system accordingly.

The General Election that is now upon us is a chance for the British people to show the world that at a time of crisis the overwhelming majority of us are determined not to tear ourselves apart, but to close ranks.

It is a chance, in other words, to demonstrate that we believe in ourselves as a nation.

This is our aim:

a Britain united in moderation, not divided by extremism
a society in which there is change without revolution

a Government that is strong in order to protect the weak

a people who enjoy freedom with responsibility

a morality of fairness without regimentation

a nation with faith in itself, and a people with self-respect.

We are a great nation, with a long and eventful history behind us.

We have survived grave perils in the past, and we can do so again now. But to do so, two things are needed, as they have always been: a united people, prepared to put aside our differences to fight the common threat; and a strong Government, able to do whatever is necessary to carry out the people's will.

In the pages that follow we set out our record over the four years since we were voted into office, our proposals for the future, and the nature of the choice now facing the nation.

Although we have not been able to do as much as we would have liked, and the problems which face us are immense, the record of the progress we have made so far, despite all the difficulties, both national and international, that have beset us, is important in two ways.

First, looking back, it provides a fair basis for a comparison with the record of our predecessors. Second, looking ahead, the achievements of the past four years provide the solid foundation for our further progress once the present difficulties are overcome.

Until the present crisis hit the country, the living standards of the British people, since we took office in 1970, had been rising more than twice as fast as they did during the period of the former Labour administration. One of the cruellest consequences of inflation is the unfair way in which it hits some groups in the community far harder than others. But despite the hardship caused by rising prices, for the great majority of the people of this country, the pronounced rise in living standards was a reality; and with the expansion of the nation's economy came a welcome restoration of Britain's strength in the world.

This prosperity has now, for the time being, been blighted by the effects of the three-day week, forced upon us by the need to ration electricity so as to prevent our power stations from running out of coal altogether as a consequence of the industrial action taken by the National Union of Mineworkers.

And even when the need for the three-day week is over, we must still, for some time to come, and in common with many other countries, expect a pause in the rise in our living standards; since, for the time being, all the extra national wealth created will be needed to pay for the higher cost of essential imports, notably oil, and will not, therefore, be available for increased prosperity at home.

This obviously has particular implications for those of our programmes and objectives which necessarily involve substantial Government expenditure, where everything is dependent on the economic resources available. Here the crisis makes it more essential than ever to avoid easy but irresponsible promises beyond what the country can at present afford. We have, therefore, undertaken a full and realistic review of all our policies in the light of the changed conditions faced by the Western world as a whole. As a result, in framing our specific proposals, we have concentrated on indicating what our priorities in the next Parliament will be; on outlining, in each field, those programmes that will be given first claim in present economic circumstances.

But while this means that the next year or two will inevitably be arduous and difficult, further ahead, provided we work together as one nation and stand firm against inflation, we can look forward to an economy more soundly based than we have known since the war, thanks to the increasing availability of North Sea oil. In addition to going a long way towards solving the energy crisis, this promises radically to transform our balance of payment position.

Meanwhile, during the difficult period that lies ahead, we shall continue to take special care to protect the pensioners, the lower paid, and those in need.

It may be that we are able to do more than is promised in this manifesto. That will depend, in part, on world economic forces beyond our control; but, more than anything else, it will depend on our ability to work together as one nation and on the extent of our success in winning the vitally important battle against inflation. Meanwhile, at this critical time in our nation's affairs, we believe it to be right to err on the side of caution; to promise too little rather than too much.

Beyond this, however, there is something that no crisis can change or slow down. That is our vision of the Britain in which we believe, the ideal which will inform all that we do.

A Britain united in moderation, not divided by extremism. A society in which there is change without revolution. A Government that is strong in order to protect the weak. A people who enjoy freedom with responsibility. A morality of fairness without regimentation. A nation with faith in itself, and a people with self-respect.

HOLDING THE LINE AGAINST INFLATION

Our consistent aim since taking office has been, and remains, to safeguard and enhance the well-being of the British people.

Throughout that period, and never more so than today, the gravest threat to our national well-being has been the menace of unrestrained inflation.

This was a legacy we inherited from our predecessors. In our 1970 Election Manifesto, we pledged that 'we will give overriding priority to bringing the present inflation under control', but warned that 'the Labour Government's policies have unleashed forces which no Government could hope to reverse overnight'.

We reduced Labour's rates of indirect taxation, which bore directly on prices. We made unprecedented efforts to obtain the co-operation of trade unions and employers in formulating an effective voluntary pay and prices policy. When agreement on this proved impossible, we sought and obtained the consent of Parliament to control pay, prices and profits by law.

But our warning that the battle against inflation would not be quickly or easily won has proved even truer than we feared at the time. For on top of all the problems we inherited, we have had to absorb an unprecedented rise in the world prices of almost all the essential foods and raw materials that we are obliged to import from overseas. It is this, and not membership of the Common Market, which has led to the substantial rise in the price of food in the shops.

When we took office nearly four years ago, prices were not merely rising alarmingly: the rate of increase was steadily accelerating. As a result of our policies so far, we have been able to reduce the rise in prices due to internal causes and, therefore, within our own control as a nation.

But the rate at which prices are rising is still dangerously high, and on top of everything else we now have to absorb a four-fold increase in the price of oil. This makes it all the more vital that we hold the line against inflation caused by excessive wage settlements at home.

We shall, therefore, press ahead with the pay and prices policy, if necessary stiffening it in the light of the developing economic situation.

We shall ensure that the Price Commission has the powers it needs to protect the consumer from unnecessary price rises, and we will examine further means of controlling the rise in prices of key items of food in the household budget.

We shall renew our offer to the TUC and CBI to join us in working out an effective voluntary pay and prices policy, ultimately to replace the existing statutory policy, in the management and evolution of which both sides of industry would jointly participate.

Meanwhile, however, it is manifestly unfair that those who do not go on strike are, in effect, obliged to subsidise those who do. It is no part of our policy to see the wives and children of men on strike suffering. But it is only right that the unions themselves, and not the taxpayer, should accept their primary responsibility for the welfare of the families of men who choose to go on strike; and after discussions with trade unions and employers, we will amend the social security system accordingly.

BEATING THE ENERGY CRISIS

Well before the current oil crisis emerged in the aftermath of the Arab-Israeli War of October 1973, we were developing, as a matter of urgency, a new and comprehensive energy policy.

288

Our objective was, first, to reduce our hitherto growing dependence on imported oil and, second, among home-produced sources of fuel and power, to plan for the proper balance between coal, North Sea oil, natural gas and nuclear power.

To this end we had already:

(a) Passed the Coal Industry Act, to provide massive funds for the industry's modernisation and substantial extra money for miners' pensions and other benefits; thus, for the first time in twenty years, providing the coal mining industry and those who work in it with a secure future;

(b) Accelerated the exploitation of the vast proven oil reserves in the British sector of the North Sea and set up the Scottish Petroleum Office under a Scottish Minister to co-ordinate all on-shore developments;

(c) Initiated negotiations to purchase the entire natural gas output of the Frigg field in the Norwegian sector of the North Sea;

(d) Merged Britain's nuclear power station capacity into a single new company, the National Nuclear Corporation, and agreed with the NNC and the Central Electricity Generating Board to build a new generation of atomic power stations.

In the light of the post-October 1973 energy crisis, and in particular the rocketing price of imported oil, still further steps were needed. Accordingly, we set up a Department of Energy under a Secretary of State, whose long term goal is to achieve national self-sufficiency in energy.

The first oil from the British sector of the North Sea is due to be landed this year and by 1980 the North Sea should be supplying the greater part of our national needs. In full co-operation with private enterprise, we will press ahead with the extraction and landing of North Sea oil, and prospecting for Celtic Sea oil, as fast as is technically and humanly possible. Labour's irrelevant and disastrous proposal to nationalise our offshore oil would needlessly deprive Britain of an invaluable source of capital, skills and experience, and would cause confusion and delay when the nation can least afford it.

Britain has pioneered nuclear power technology. Already we generate a higher proportion of our electricity in nuclear stations than any other European country, and we shall shortly be announcing the details of our new nuclear power station programme.

We are working out with the National Coal Board an expanded investment programme for coal. We shall press ahead with the rapid development of the newly discovered coalfield in Selby, Yorkshire – the largest and richest unworked seam in Europe.

The new Department of Energy is urgently examining every possibility for increasing our own national energy resources – including the use of methane gas, solar power and tidal power. However successful we are in developing the main sources of energy, the greater the range of available sources the less vulnerable we shall be.

The new Department is also working out the details of a major energy conservation programme, and will announce steps to ensure the maximum efficiency in the use of expensive fuel. We will give a strong lead on improving standards of building design so as to make the best use of fuel. We will encourage higher insulation standards in homes, offices and factories.

As a result of the measures already taken and those now proposed, we shall be better placed in terms of energy supplies than most other nations. However, while we should thus enjoy secure supplies of the fuels the nation needs, we cannot escape from the higher cost of those fuels. The days of cheap energy are gone for good.

Taken as a whole, our measures throughout the field of energy will set a secure pattern for the future. But the nation's position must also be safeguarded in the short term. We have already concluded an important agreement with Iran to procure a substantial quantity of oil in exchange for British exports.

We shall continue to work both within the framework of the European Economic Community and in the wider context of consumer/producer collaboration to ensure an adequate flow of oil from the major producing countries, so long as our dependence on overseas sources of supply remains.

T

INDUSTRY, AGRICULTURE, AND THE REGIONS

In present circumstances, energy policy must necessarily take pride of place in the Government's programme to provide the essential long-term framework for soundly based industrial and agricultural expansion.

But other aspects, to which we have rightly given priority in the past, will not be forgotten or neglected.

During the past four years we have introduced a wide range of new measures to bring new life to some of the older and decaying industrial regions of Britain, both for the benefit of the people of those regions and of the economic health of the nation as a whole.

Through the Industry Act, through free depreciation, and in other ways, we have provided more effective financial incentives for industrial expansion in these areas than they have ever previously enjoyed; and we have set up the Industrial Development Executive to ensure that these incentives give the greatest value for money.

We have greatly increased the programmes for improving housing and the social services in these regions, and for clearing away the scars of dereliction; and we have given them special priority in the provision of industrial training. We have also greatly improved their transport links.

An important source of new help for the regions over the years ahead should derive from our membership of the European Community. We attach importance to a substantial fund devoted to Community Regional Development, and a decision is to be taken early this year.

For the nation as a whole, we have introduced the Training Opportunities Scheme, to meet the needs of an economy in which rapid technological change and new patterns of demand shut down old jobs and open up new ones. We have nearly trebled the numbers being trained and retrained under Government auspices in Government Training Centres. Our Employment and Training Act has provided industry with help in increasing its own training, related to actual labour needs, through the newly established Manpower Services Commission.

We shall continue to expand the Training Opportunities Scheme, and continue to modernise the employment services.

We have announced new legislation to bring up to date the law dealing with the health and safety of people at work.

We have announced a massive ten-year expansion and modernisation programme for the steel industry.

After nearly four years of Conservative Government the British aircraft industry has the biggest order book in this century. In technology, in research and in production we have established skills and abilities which provide us with immense opportunities within Europe and throughout the world to see that this industry plays an important role in the future commercial success of Britain.

We are the first Government to have given special attention to small firms, appointing a Minister with special responsibility for them. We have implemented the majority of the Bolton Report recommendations, especially in the field of taxation. We do not believe that, in business, bigger is necessarily better.

Agriculture

We reaffirm our traditional Conservative support for British agriculture, which over the past four years, has enjoyed a marked resurgence of confidence.

The past year has seen some sections of our agriculture doing well, while others, such as the dairy industry, have been affected by the sharp rise in the price of feedingstuffs. The particular problem of milk producers is being dealt with in the Price Review to be announced very shortly.

The long-term prospects for the expansion of British agriculture have never been better. Membership of the European Economic Community, for the great majority of British farmers, is, and will continue to be, of enormous benefit, ensuring an enlarged market for farm produce, increased returns to efficient farmers and better protection from market fluctuations. Our current balance of payments problems make a healthy home agriculture more important than ever. Considerable opportunities for expansion exist, and our policies will continue to recognise this.

INDUSTRIAL RELATIONS

But the Achilles heel of the British economy has long been, and continues to be, industrial relations.

It is largely because of this that our economic progress since the war has consistently lagged behind that of most other industrial nations – and will continue to do so in the future, with grave consequences, unless a major improvement in industrial relations can be secured.

It is in large part because of this that we find ourselves in the present crisis, the gravest since the war.

By setting the pound free in the present unsettled situation, we have liberated the economy and the nation from the restrictions of being pegged to an unrealistic exchange rate. By drastically cutting taxation, we have liberated the economy and the nation from the stultifying imposts of Socialism.

But we have not yet been able to liberate the economy and the nation from the disruption, the inflation, and the inefficiency caused by bad industrial relations.

The need for action on this front was recognised by our predecessors, who first set up a Royal Commission to inquire into the subject and then prepared a major Bill to reform trade union law – only to withdraw it in an abject and humiliating surrender to trade union pressure. This disastrous incident has played a large part in creating the present situation.

In accordance both with our pre-election pledges and with the clear will of the majority of the British people, one of our first steps on taking office was to act where Labour had capitulated.

The Industrial Relations Act represents the first thorough-going reform of trade union law in modern times. Its purpose is to provide for an up-to-date and realistic legal framework for industrial relations, to strengthen responsible trade union leadership, to guarantee fundamental trade union rights, to provide remedies hitherto unavailable for the peaceful solution of disputes about negotiating rights, and to safeguard the individual from the abuse of power, whether by management or unions. Although it is a matter for national regret that its usefulness has been limited by the refusal, so far, of most trade unions to co-operate in its working, it is nevertheless already having some significant effects. More than 15,000 people have made use of remedies it provides to protect individual rights and the National Industrial Relations Court – although supposed to be banned by the unions – has dealt with almost 1,000 cases.

Other industrial countries have found that good industrial relations require a proper framework of law and we are sure that Britain is no exception.

We shall therefore maintain the essential structure of the Industrial Relations Act, but we shall amend it in the light of experience, and after consultation with both sides of industry, in order (a) to meet any valid criticisms; (b) to make conciliation a pre-condition of court action; and (c) to provide more effective control for the majority of union members by ensuring that they have the opportunity to elect the governing bodies and national leaders of their unions by a postal ballot.

We shall also seek to improve industrial relations by bringing in new legislation, following discussions with both sides of industry, designed to make large and medium-sized firms introduce a wider measure of employee-participation. We have set up a steering group drawn from the Government, the CBI and the TUC to study methods to improve job satisfaction.

TAXATION

In our 1970 Election Manifesto we promised both to reduce and reform taxation. Both these pledges have been carried out to the letter.

Whereas our predecessors, during their term of office, *increased* tax rates by £3,000 million a year, we have *cut* tax rates by an even greater amount.

Food has been relieved of tax altogether. The biggest cuts in income tax have been made by increases in the personal allowances, which give the largest relief, proportionately, to the less well-off taxpayer. Many people with small incomes have been relieved of income tax altogether. We have also reduced the rate of tax on the first slice of income from savings, which has helped those –

usually elderly – living on small fixed incomes, who have been particularly hard hit by rising prices.

In the field of tax reform, we have unified income tax and surtax in a single graduated system of personal tax, in a form that can be simply understood. We have reformed company taxation, so as to end Labour's discrimination against the ordinary shareholder. And we have replaced both Purchase Tax and SET by a 10 per cent Value Added Tax – the lowest standard VAT rate in Europe. No new tax is ever popular, and VAT is no exception. But it is fairer and less onerous than the taxes it replaced.

Our record on tax reduction and tax reform speaks for itself. Obviously in the present grave situation it would be irresponsible to make any commitments about tax rates. But what we can promise is that the burden of taxation on everyone in Britain will be far less than it would be under Labour, which is committed to a hugely expensive programme of state take-over, a massive expansion of public expenditure far beyond what the nation can afford, and to a belief in high taxation as an end in itself.

We shall continue our programme of tax reform with the Tax Credit Scheme. We will introduce legislation in the next Parliament in order to implement the scheme as soon as the economic situation allows.

The separation between the systems of taxation and social security has proved, in recent years, an increasingly difficult obstacle to the creation of a fair society. In particular, it has made it difficult to give sufficient help to those who, while not in acute poverty, are nonetheless struggling and hard pressed.

The Tax Credit Scheme will bring the two systems – of taxation and social security – together in a single coherent scheme, which will greatly alleviate this problem and bring immediate help to those now affected by it.

The introduction of the scheme will further simplify and modernise our tax system, and bring substantial savings in the cost of administration. For social security, it will represent the most important advance since the implementation of the Beveridge Report more than a generation ago.

The first step would be to pay tax credits for children, including the first child, for whom mothers at present receive no family allowance at all. These child credits, which will be paid to the mother, will be worth more than the existing income tax child allowances and family allowances which they will replace. Mothers will get cash each week through the Post Office, in exactly the same way as they cash the existing, but less valuable, family allowances.

When fully implemented the tax credit scheme:

will provide a positive social benefit in cash to millions of hard-pressed families with low incomes, especially where there are children;
will give credits as a right – automatically and without a means-test;
will relieve hundreds of thousands of pensioners from the need to claim supplementary benefit and give a significant increase in income to another 3 or 4 million pensioners.

HELPING THE PENSIONER

In the four years since we took office, we have:

(a) Increased pensions every year. Labour only increased pensions every other year.
(b) Paid, in each of the last two years, a Christmas bonus as well. Labour never did.
(c) Seen to it that, each year, the increase in the pension was greater than the increase in the cost of living; so that each time there has been a real increase in pensioners' living standards. During the last five years of Labour, the *real* purchasing power of the pension actually *fell*.
(d) Paid a pension to those over-80s to whom Labour denied one altogether.

In addition, we have raised the amount that pensioners may earn without having their pension reduced. We have improved the allowance which helps many of those on supplementary pensions with the cost of heating their homes.

We have lowered the age at which increases in public service and armed forces pensions become payable, and we have further improved the position of war pensioners and their widows. Public service pensions, armed forces pensions and supplementary pensions are all now reviewed every single year, together with the main national insurance benefits.

We have undertaken to give compensation to those public service pensioners who have been adversely affected by the provisions of the statutory pay and prices policy, and to allow similar steps to be taken by private occupational schemes.

We are acutely conscious of the hardship suffered by many pensioners as a result of inflation. That is why, for pensioners in particular, the most important section of our programme for the next Parliament is our pledge to hold the line against inflation.

Nevertheless, so far as the actual pension is concerned, we shall continue in the next Parliament the progress we have made so far.

We shall continue to give the pensioner first priority in the entire field of social service expenditure.

We have already moved from a two-yearly to an annual review of pensions and all other benefits. We will now move to a six monthly up-rating of pensions and other long-term benefits. We shall, of course, continue to ensure that pensions are increased by at least as much as the cost of living.

We shall continue to relax the earnings rule during the next Parliament. Our ultimate objective is to abolish it altogether.

What we shall not do is compete with the Labour Party in an auction of promises which we do not believe can be kept. We are confident that a dispassionate comparison of our record with that of our predecessors speaks for itself.

Finally, in addition to doing our best to fulfil the community's responsibility to those already retired or approaching retirement, we shall press ahead with our new pensions scheme, which will, in the long term, completely transform the financial prospects of those no longer at work. From next year, *everyone* in employment will be building up the right to a *second* pension, related to their earnings, on top of the basic State pension. For most people this will be provided through schemes run by the companies where they work; but there will be a reserve State scheme for those who cannot otherwise be properly covered.

The scheme for a second pension will include proper protection of pension rights on change of job, better provision for widows, and some safeguard against rising prices. It will ensure that, for future generations of the retired, there will no longer be such a big drop in income which is so often the biggest single problem for those ceasing to work today.

This new scheme will greatly improve the pension prospects for women in employment, for many of them will be able to earn a second pension for the first time and many, too, will get a second widow's pension also for the first time. Married women in employment will retain their right not to pay the full contribution to the basic State scheme.

MEETING SPECIAL NEED

A consistent feature of our social security policy since we first took office has been the bringing of new help to particular groups in society, hitherto insufficiently recognised by Governments, who have need of special help, whether in cash or in care.

Thus we have:

(a) Introduced, for the first time, a range of additional 'invalidity' benefits for wage-earners who cannot work because of long-term illness or incapacity;
(b) Introduced, for the first time, special tax-free attendance allowances for seriously disabled people who need a great deal of care and attention;
(c) Introduced, for the first time, a Family Income Supplement for low wage earning families with children;
(d) Introduced, for the first time, a widow's pension for women, without young children, who were widowed between the ages of 40 and 50.

We are, however, conscious of how very much remains to be done in meeting cases of special need, particularly so far as the disabled are concerned. We shall be carrying out by this autumn our statutory duty to report to Parliament on our proposals for improving the cash provision for the disabled, including the possibility of a disablement income.

We recognise the serious problem of acute family deprivation which exists in certain parts of the country – the inner city areas, some of our older industrial areas and, indeed, some of the new housing estates where there live families rehoused from the central parts of the cities. These areas often contain many of the various forms of deprivation – bad housing, the most out-dated school buildings, the oldest hospitals, lack of community facilities and a bad environment generally – coupled with an inability to cope amongst the families concerned, sometimes, but not always, caused by poverty.

We shall therefore start a new drive to bring more resources into these areas, both to improve living conditions and the environment generally, and to provide a wide range of advice and help to the families concerned. We will concentrate this help on the worst areas; and give more opportunity for local people to play a part in the affairs of their community.

In these and other deprived inner city areas we shall place special emphasis on housing needs and the setting up of comprehensive advice centres, in partnership with the significant contribution already being made by independent voluntary agencies.

In London, these problems are becoming intensified by a shortage of men and women to operate most public services and to teach in the schools. We have therefore referred the whole question of the London Allowance payable to teachers and other public servants to the Pay Board, and will act on the Board's report as soon as we receive it.

We shall provide family planning within the National Health Service.

We shall continue to improve the services for the old, the disabled, the mentally ill and the mentally handicapped at home, in the community and in hospital. We shall publish a White Paper on services for the mentally ill. We have increased greatly the numbers of home helps, district nurses and health visitors. We shall improve the services for children and legislate on adoption. We have set in hand help for the deaf and the arthritic and rheumatic. We shall act as necessary on the Finer Report on one-parent families when it is received.

We have much expanded the National Health Service. We have reformed its administration to improve services to the patient. We shall implement the principal recommendations of the Briggs Report on nursing, while preserving the identity of the health visitor. We will take any steps considered necessary to improve hospital complaint procedures in the light of the Davies Report.

Our hospital, health centre and social service building programmes are all much larger in real terms than those of our Labour predecessors. We plan to supplement the District General Hospital network by a network of community hospitals, basing them where practicable on some of the existing smaller local hospitals. We aim to continue reducing the waiting time for non-urgent surgery.

We reject Labour's proposal to abolish private practice and private provision in association with the National Health Service. This is unacceptable in principle and in practice would only reduce the skills available to patients as a whole.

Throughout the entire field of meeting special need, we are particularly conscious of the valuable work done by voluntary organisations, and we shall continue to help them without compromising their independence. To this end, we will review the legal framework within which charities operate.

HOUSING

The high level of interest rates in an inflationary world has inevitably put difficulties in the way of the expansion of home ownership to which we remain firmly committed. Nonetheless, since 1970, about a million families have become home-owners for the first time, bringing the total to more than half the families in Britain.

Over the first three full years since we took office, we have provided two million new or improved homes. This is 500,000 more than Labour provided in the previous three years, for which they were responsible.

The number of new home-owners would have been still larger had certain Councils not opposed the sale of Council houses to those Council tenants who were willing and able to buy them with the help offered by the Government.

Subject to a right of appeal by the local authority to the Secretary of State on clearly specified grounds, we shall ensure that, in future, established Council tenants are able, as of right, to buy on reasonable terms the house or flat in which they live.

We have made an agreement with the building societies which will ensure in the long term greater stability in the flow of funds for house purchase, and the building societies have agreed to introduce as soon as possible a scheme to enable first-time purchasers to pay less in the early years of their mortgage. We shall also seek other new ways to help young married couples to become home-owners earlier, including new ways of channelling the funds of leading financial institutions into the finance of house purchase.

We will provide new powers and more funds for the Housing Corporation and the voluntary housing movement. This will provide dwellings for both letting and co-ownership, and include new arrangements for people with special housing problems.

We shall provide more houses for renting in areas of housing need.

We will ensure that both the local authorities and nationalised industries release housing land for mixed schemes of public and private development.

We will continue with our slum clearance programme designed to clear the slums by 1982.

We will continue our programme to improve older houses and will give extra incentives for the selective improvement of areas of bad housing stress. Legislation will be carried through to give greater emphasis to the housing needs of inner urban areas.

We will strengthen action to cope with homelessness in areas of special need by co-operation with the local authorities in the efficient use of existing permanent and temporary accommodation and the provision of specially designed hostels.

We intend to pay particular attention to the housing needs of the elderly and the disabled who often need sheltered housing.

Our Housing Finance Act has, for the first time, brought fairness between one tenant and another by concentrating help with the rent on those areas and those families who most need it. Today, by law, and for the first time, every family in a rented home – whether council or private, unfurnished or furnished – can get such help if they need it.

This help has to be paid for. This has meant rent increases for the better off tenants who had hitherto often been enjoying bigger subsidies than many poorer families. But with nearly two million tenants already receiving rent rebates or allowances, a large number of families are now paying less rent than before the Act was passed.

At present, owner-occupiers with more rooms than they need are deterred from letting, unfurnished, any part of their houses. We will consider whether to remedy this by restoring to them the ability to regain possession. This would help provide more accommodation for renting.

We will keep security of tenure for all those who already have it.

We have announced the severest financial penalties ever on property profiteering, with special reference to empty office buildings.

Gains by individuals from the development value of property will now be subject to income tax, up to the top rate of 75 per cent, in place of the former flat rate of 30 per cent. As before, this will not apply to the principal home of an owner-occupier. Development gains by companies will be taxed as income at the full 40 per cent Corporation Tax rate, instead of 30 per cent. For the first time unrealised gains from property will be taxed by treating the first letting as a disposal for tax purposes.

We are also committed to taking new powers to deal with empty office premises. These will enable the Minister to take possession of, and manage, premises that have been unoccupied for more than two years. In addition, local authorities will be empowered to levy rates on unoccupied buildings at up to 100 per cent, and at a higher rate than this for certain empty commercial premises.

We wholly reject Labour's policy of preventing any further extension of freehold home-ownership by the nationalisation of every acre of land for new building.

IMPROVING THE ENVIRONMENT

Right at the start of the last Parliament we set up, for the first time, a Department of the Environment, which remains the only such ministry in the world with so wide a range of powers and resources. As a result, we are now acknowledged world leaders in environmental action in caring for towns, cities, villages, rivers and the countryside.

Conservative policy is to protect our environment where it is good, and to improve it where it is not good enough. We have already done much to achieve this. The Green Belt has been greatly extended. More than 100 new country parks have been opened since 1970. 'Operation Eyesore' has improved the local environment in thousands of towns and villages. Millions more trees have been planted. For every acre of derelict land cleared each year under Labour, we have cleared over three. We have set up a Nature Conservancy Council.

Clean air policy was at a standstill when Labour left office; we have more than doubled the number of Smoke Control Orders, bringing clean air and more sunlight to millions more people, especially in the North. Labour neglected the rivers – we have been improving their condition at an average rate of nearly three miles a week.

To reduce, still further, pollution of all kinds, we shall carry forward our legislation to cut down noise and establish quiet zones in urban areas; to accelerate the cleaning up of our rivers and estuaries; to curb fumes and smoke from vehicles; and to deal more efficiently with waste, especially toxic waste. We shall encourage the recycling of waste so as to conserve scarce resources and reduce imports.

We shall further extend and protect the Green Belt.

We shall strengthen the legislation necessary to protect and extend conservation areas, protect historic buildings and their gardens, control demolition, and preserve more carefully trees and archeological sites.

To supplement conservation areas in the towns and cities, we shall empower local authorities to designate environmental and amenity areas in all parts of the country.

We shall continue our drive to bring derelict land back into beneficial use.

We shall further strengthen the Countryside Commission.

Transport

Continued growth of traffic has brought with it problems as well as advantages; and has in particular made necessary an increasing reliance on public transport. We have recently announced a massive five-year programme for the railways to provide a modern network with a secure future and the opportunity to regain freight traffic from the roads.

We shall modify the bus licensing system so as to give greater freedom for new forms of local transport in country areas, while safeguarding existing services.

We are already working to establish a system of lorry routes to keep heavy vehicles out of towns and villages and away from narrow country lanes where they have no business to be. With this as our priority, we shall complete the major road network as soon as the economic situation allows.

We have given the new county authorities powers to enable them to fix their own transport strategies and priorities.

We will continue to take all possible steps to diminish noise and other nuisances caused by new roads and the traffic which uses them.

BETTER EDUCATION

Conservatives have accorded high priority in the national budget to the needs of education. Above all we are concerned to provide not merely more education but better education. Better education is not only a matter of resources. It is a matter of standards and of attitudes.

We have advanced in every sector of education but have attached special importance to primary schools, believing that it is the early years that so often determine a child's future progress. In the next Parliament we shall continue to give priority to the early years of education.

We shall gradually extend free nursery schooling throughout the country so that within ten years it should be available for all three- and four-year-old children whose parents wish them to have it. We shall encourage pre-school playgroups; their emphasis on involving the parent is particularly valuable.

Our second priority will continue to be special schools for the handicapped. We have substantially increased the building programme for new schools. Work will soon begin on the enquiry into special education which was announced at the end of 1973.

In secondary education we shall continue to judge local education authorities' proposals for changing the character of schools on their merits, paying special regard to the wishes of parents and the retention of parental choice. We believe it to be educationally unwise to impose a universal system of comprehensive education on the entire country. Local education authorities should allow genuine scope for parental choice, and we shall continue to use our powers to give as much choice as possible.

We will defend the fundamental right of parents to spend their money on their children's education should they wish to do so.

We shall continue to support the direct grant schools. They have helped to provide increased opportunities for able children irrespective of their parents' means.

We shall maintain the right of parents to choose denominational education for their children if they so wish.

The expansion of further and higher education will be less rapid than planned because of the reduced demand for places and the prevailing economic circumstances, but numbers will continue to increase. The review of students' grants is proceeding and we shall continue to improve the parental income scale so that parents on a given income will pay less towards the grant.

As soon as economic circumstances permit, we will improve the opportunities for adult education in the light of the Russell Report.

We believe that the aims of the Youth Service should be more clearly defined. We shall, therefore, be discussing its future development with the local authorities and voluntary bodies who mostly provide this service, and aim to ensure that decisions about the future of the Service take fully into account the views of the young people themselves. Given the right impetus, the Youth Service can do a great deal to widen the scope for young people to play a full and constructive part in local affairs and activities wherever they live and work.

Because of our concern over reading standards in schools we have set up an enquiry under Sir Alan Bullock to report on all aspects of the teaching of English, including the written and spoken word. The conclusions are expected later in the year.

A research study on mathematical standards is also in hand.

We share the public concern about indiscipline and truancy. Investigations are being conducted into these problems, and we shall examine their findings as a matter of urgency.

Higher standards of education can only be achieved through more and better trained teachers. There are now some 60,000 more teachers in the schools than there were three years ago; we are carrying out the objectives of the James Report, which was itself set up as a result of a promise in our last manifesto.

We wish to move the debate away from the kind of school which children attend and concentrate on the kind of education they receive.

The Arts, Broadcasting and Recreation

We shall continue to give the fullest support and encouragement to the arts, on which we are already spending £50 million a year, more in fact than any previous government. At a time when economic stringency is necessarily limiting our material objectives it is more important than ever to improve the quality of life.

The arts must be centred on the nation not on the capital. Generous grants have gone to the regions in the past. Major arts centres will be established in Cardiff and Edinburgh.

In accordance with the pledge in our 1970 election manifesto, we are introducing a network of independent local radio stations, under the general supervision of the Independent Broadcasting Authority, with local newspaper participation.

Four of these stations are already in operation. We will bring forward proposals for the allocation of a fourth TV channel when economic circumstances permit.

We shall give further impetus to the Sports Council, whose powers and funds we have already greatly expanded. Professional football clubs as well as amateur sports organisations will be encouraged to join with local authorities and voluntary bodies in the redevelopment of town centre grounds for multi-purpose recreational needs.

PROTECTING THE RIGHTS OF THE INDIVIDUAL

The rights of the individual citizen need to be protected both against the power of the State and against other large and powerful bodies – whether commercial undertakings, trade unions, or any other centre of power.

We have recognised this need in our measures so far, and will continue to do so in the next Parliament.

We have acted decisively to protect the individual consumer. We have passed the Fair Trading Act to increase the powers of the new Monopolies and Mergers Commission and set up a Director-General of Fair Trading, under the Act, to deal with unfair trading practices of all kinds. We have legislated to impose stricter standards on insurance companies. We have, for the first time, appointed a Cabinet Minister for Consumer Affairs, and have introduced new legislation to prevent the consumer from having his legal rights undermined by the small print of so-called 'guarantees'. We have also legislated against the abuse known as pyramid selling. We have made it easier for consumers to get cheap and speedy settlement of small claims in the County Courts.

In the next Parliament, we shall continue to act in defence of the consumer over a broad front. We will act to improve the effectiveness of the nationalised industry consumer councils, to prevent confusion over metrication by insisting on specific unit pricing of goods in the shops, and in a wide range of other fields. In particular, we shall bring forward the Consumer Credit Bill, which will require hire purchase agreements to show the true rate of interest, prevent the unsolicited mailing of credit cards, and, in general, comprehensively reform the law on consumer credit.

We shall carry through our proposals for new legislation to reform company law by requiring of companies a much fuller disclosure of information to the individual – whether shareholder, employee or a member of the general public. By this measure, we will make British free enterprise the most open in the world. We will have created a system of free enterprise more socially responsible to the public, and with the power of the consumer greatly enhanced.

We have appointed a Health Service Commissioner or 'ombudsman' to investigate individual complaints about the National Health Service. We will be introducing a similar system for complaints against local authorities.

Citizens' rights in Britain are far more extensive than most citizens' awareness of those rights. This is particularly serious in the deprived central areas of many of our large cities. In these and other 'stress' areas we shall set up comprehensive advice centres, readily accessible to those who need help.

We have substantially improved the arrangements for consulting the public in advance of major planning decisions, such as large redevelopment schemes and the route to be followed by road schemes.

We have greatly extended the scope of compensation payable to those whose property is adversely affected by developments such as road schemes. We have provided for special extra compensation payments where a home-owner or a tenant loses his home as a result of development.

We shall also reform the licensing laws in the light both of the Erroll Report and of public reaction to it.

We have legislated to remove discrimination against women over a wide range of the law.

We have introduced equal rights of guardianship for women.

We have taken special steps to ensure that movement towards equal pay for women is not held back by the provisions of our counter-inflation policy.

We have improved the enforcement of maintenance payments to divorced or deserted wives.

We will introduce major new legislation to end discrimination against women at work, and to set up an Equal Opportunities Commission to investigate other aspects of discrimination against women, and to recommend further action.

We have taken steps to bring about more effective co-ordination of the work of local authority social workers, doctors, teachers and all relevant professional staff in detecting and preventing the ill-treatment of small children. We will urgently study the report of the Committee of Enquiry into the death of Maria Colwell, to see what further measures may be needed.

We shall strengthen existing safeguards in relation to the adoption of children, following broadly the recommendations of the Houghton Report.

We shall introduce a reform of the abortion law, in the light of the forthcoming Lane Committee Report.

We will also, where necessary, act to ease restraints on publication under the present laws of contempt of court and defamation where these restraints do not infringe the rights of the individual. We will bring forward proposals to preserve the privacy of the citizen against unauthorised or unjustifiable intrusion, in the light of the Younger Report.

Other achievements and proposals concerned with the rights of the individual citizen appear elsewhere in this manifesto. Indeed the preservation and enhancement of individual freedom within a framework of responsibility is an underlying theme of all Conservative policy.

It is expressed in our determination to keep taxation as low as possible, so as to give the individual wage-earner greater freedom to spend or save what he earns as he thinks fit; in our Industrial Relations Act that gives new rights to individual trade unionists; in our proposals for giving employees a right of participation in the firms for which they work; in the importance we attach to parental choice in education; and in a housing policy that emphasises the freedom and independence that comes from home-ownership.

LOCAL GOVERNMENT

We have carried through the most important reforms of local government this century. We will continue those reforms by the appointment of local ombudsmen.

We will review the electoral provisions for London boroughs in the context of the arrangements for the rest of the country.

We favour a frank disclosure of local government finances to the people; for example, the publication by each local authority of a Balance Sheet, a Budget Statement, and annual spending programmes. Local government services have continued to expand during our term of office, but we have increased central Government's help to the ratepayers to meet the costs of that expansion. We have substantially increased rate relief to the householder. Three million ratepayers will benefit from the more generous rate rebate scheme we have introduced.

We will, if necessary, change the law and practice relating to the conduct of members and officers in local government wherever the possibility arises of a conflict between their official positions and their private interests.

We will strengthen and improve the regional offices of Government. Local authorities and the regional economic planning councils will be encouraged to work more closely together so that the views and needs of the regions can more effectively influence national decisions.

We are studying the Report of the Kilbrandon Commission.

We are publishing separate Manifestos for Scotland and Wales.

LAW AND ORDER

Protection of the law-abiding citizen is a prime duty of the State. We have given higher priority to the support of law and order and the reduction of crime than any Government for many years. The overall volume of crime in the country has been dropping for the first time for nearly 20 years, and although within this total, crimes of violence are still rising alarmingly there are some encouraging signs even in this field – for example, the marked drop in 1973 in the number of robberies and muggings.

We have increased and strengthened the police force. In real terms we are spending today over 15 per cent more on the police than in 1970. For the first time we have over 100,000 men and women in the Police Forces of England and Wales and they are backed up by an extra 7,000 civilians.

We have reviewed the powers available to the Courts. We have increased the maximum penalties for offences involving the use of firearms and for crimes of vandalism. We have widened and strengthened the powers of the Courts to order convicted criminals to compensate their victims. We have provided new non-custodial forms of punishment whereby offenders can be required to do useful work for the community.

We have substantially increased the size of the Probation Service and will continue to do so.

In the next Parliament we shall continue to give the highest priority to policies aimed at reducing crime and supporting freedom under the law. The further strengthening of the police will be of particular importance.

We shall maintain the impetus of our measures of law reform. We shall review the law against violent crime in the light of the Criminal Law Revision Committee's forthcoming report on offences against the person. We will further improve the legal aid and advisory services.

We will place the Criminal Injuries Compensation Scheme, first introduced by a Conservative Government, on a permanent statutory basis.

We shall provide for the introduction of an independent element in the procedure for complaints against the police.

The growing display of indecent material in public places gives offence to many people. Accordingly, we shall bring forward our Bill to prohibit this, and to tighten up the law against sending through the post unsolicited matter of an indecent nature.

We shall reform and liberalise the Official Secrets Acts, while retaining those provisions essential for the protection of national security.

Having reviewed the law on picketing, we have come to the conclusion that the present law as recently clarified by the Courts is adequate both to pro-tect the right of genuinely peaceful picketing and to penalise abuse. But we believe that the lawful limits to peaceful picketing need to be more clearly and widely known. We shall therefore publish a document setting out the law on this subject in the belief that this will be an assistance both to the observance and enforcement of the law.

We deplore the encouragement to politically-motivated law-breaking given by the Labour Party's pledge to remove, retrospectively, the penalties incurred by Clay Cross councillors for serious breaches of the Housing Finance Act. A Conservative Government will continue to uphold the rule of law.

As a people, we live in the freest democracy in the world, with a tradition of individual liberty within the law and of peaceful change. If that tradition is to be maintained, as we are determined that it shall be, it must not be abused. In particular, we reaffirm our conviction that a criminal act does not cease to be criminal by virtue of being committed ostensibly for political ends.

IMMIGRATION AND RACE RELATIONS

By passing the 1971 Immigration Act, against the combined opposition of the Labour and Liberal Parties, we have provided the country with the necessary means for preventing any further large scale permanent immigration and also with important new powers for preventing illegal immigration. The Act became fully operative in January 1973 and its effects in reinforcing all the other administrative action we have taken are already becoming evident. Thus the number of new immigrants admitted in 1973 was the lowest since control was first introduced by the previous Conservative Government more than a decade ago.

We intend that this decline shall continue. At the same time within this declining figure we are honouring our obligations to the categories of people in the Commonwealth for whom we have special responsibilities – namely the close dependent relatives of immigrants settled here lawfully before the new Act came into force and those people who, because of our imperial past, possess citizenship of this country and no other.

We have also set in hand a review of British nationality law, and dependent on its outcome, new legislation to replace present British Nationality Acts may be one of the measures required in the life of the next Parliament.

When we came to power in 1970, there were about $1\frac{1}{2}$ million coloured people lawfully and permanently settled in this country. The great majority are here to stay. Their children are being born and brought up here and Britain is the only country they know as their own. The harmony of our society in the future depends to an important extent on the white majority and the coloured minority living and working together on equal terms and with equal opportunities. We shall therefore pursue positive policies to promote good race relations.

The first need for this purpose was to reassure everyone that new immigration was being brought down to a small and inescapable minimum. But beyond that we shall take further action to improve conditions in the stress areas in the centres of many of our industrial towns and cities where immigrant communities frequently concentrate and where the local inhabitants have long had to endure poor housing and a deprived environment.

WORKING FOR PEACE IN NORTHERN IRELAND

For the best part of five years now, our British soldiers have carried out their duties superbly. Despite every kind of difficulty and provocation, they have succeeded, with exemplary restraint, in restoring and maintaining a substantial measure of law and order, in crushing the terrorist IRA leadership in Northern Ireland, and in creating the conditions that have made a political solution possible. No other army in the world could have achieved what they have done: no praise is too high for them.

In March 1972 conditions in Northern Ireland had reached the point where we were obliged temporarily to suspend the Province's Parliament and institute a period of direct rule from Westminster, appointing a Secretary of State for Northern Ireland. After almost two years of unceasing effort, the extremists were isolated and a reconciliation was brought about between the responsible political leaders of the Protestant and Catholic communities in the Province.

This eventually resulted in a successful agreement at the tripartite meeting at Sunningdale in December 1973.

In spite of the violence in Northern Ireland, industry there has shown a remarkable resilience. In 1973 unemployment dropped substantially, the number of industrial disputes was the lowest for a decade, and the rate of growth of industrial production was the highest in the United Kingdom. These achievements were made possible by a massive programme of Government aid and by the united determination of workers and management in the Province.

On January 1, 1974 the new Northern Ireland Executive took office. It is still a tender plant. But the fact remains that those who used to be political opponents are today working together on the new Executive in Northern Ireland to bring a better life to their strife-torn Province.

This has been possible, above all, as a result of firm but fair Government action which has succeeded, against all the odds, in mobilising the silent majority of moderate opinion in Northern Ireland to assert itself against extremists of all kinds.

In the next Parliament we shall continue, in the same spirit, to build on the progress we have already achieved.

BRITAIN, EUROPE AND THE WORLD

The prime objective of our foreign policy is to preserve peace and maintain the security and prosperity of the British nation. In order to achieve this we need friends and allies. In the last 4 years, sometimes in very difficult circumstances, Britain has made or consolidated friendships in the Far East, China, the Indian Sub-Continent, Africa and the American Continent. Progress has lately been made in re-establishing a proper relationship with the Soviet Union.

A successful Commonwealth Conference has recently been held in Ottawa.

Above all, by successfully negotiating British membership of the European Community, we achieved a major national objective which had eluded successive British Governments of both Parties for more than a decade.

We have now been a member of the Community for a little over a year. While it is therefore far too soon to attempt a complete assessment of the implications for Britain of this historic step forward, it is already clear that we are better able to secure our national interests both economic and political within the Community than would have been possible had we remained outside. Firms throughout the country have felt the benefit of British membership for their export trade.

Every aspect of world affairs underlines the need for a Europe which is united and can carry the maximum weight in the councils of the world. Whatever our internal differences, we must increasingly learn to speak strongly with one voice which can be heard among the greatest powers, and which can play its part in evolving mutually beneficial policies towards the rest of the world, including the developing countries. This is what membership of the Community is about. It means increasing economic strength for each member and above all the certainty that there will be partnership instead of rivalry and no more wars having their origin in Western Europe.

Meanwhile, by its very nature, the Community continues to develop and evolve. In particular, just as Britain has to adapt to the Community, so the Community has to adapt to Britain.

Since becoming a member, we have been a full and effective participant in the making of Community decisions. We have made it clear that we are not satisfied with every aspect of Community arrangements, and have sought – and will continue to seek – changes where these are desirable.

A Conservative Government will urge on our Community partners the need to extend the scope of Community action into industrial policy, technological collaboration and social and environmental questions. This is necessary if the full benefits of the larger market are to be reaped, and if we are to realise the full potential of the Community as an instrument for improving the life of the people.

We have already been instrumental in securing a decision in principle to set up a European Regional Development Fund, a considerable proportion of which will be devoted to helping the less prosperous regions of Britain. We have been pressing hard within the Community for a sizeable fund, and a decision is to be taken early this year.

The Community's Common Agricultural Policy provides British agriculture with very real opportunities for expansion. But in a number of ways the Common Agricultural Policy is now manifestly in need of reform; and we shall continue to work so that the necessary changes can be made.

The Conservative delegation to the European Assembly has already made a telling impact. We shall continue to work for ways in which the Community's institutions can be improved in order to make them more responsive to public opinion and to reinforce democratic control.

Meanwhile, we will ensure that Parliament at Westminster can play a full and effective part in the consideration of Community proposals in their formative stage.

Renegotiation of the Community in the sense of reforming its practice and redefining Britain's place in it, is a continuous process, which can only be conducted from within, and in which we are already playing a full part. Renegotiation in the sense of British withdrawal, which is what a section of the Labour Party seeks, would be a disaster for which future generations would never forgive us.

Community membership has been of major importance for our foreign and defence policy as a whole, providing us with a new dimension and a new voice in world affairs. We reaffirm our full support for the Atlantic Alliance within which we shall continue to seek still closer European co-operation in defence and procurement.

The problems presented to Europe and all the developed and developing countries by the increased price of oil need to be tackled both in Europe and through wider international consultation. A new understanding must be sought between consumers and producers in which plans for industrial development and investment to mutual advantage would play an important part.

We shall continue to play our full part in the United Nations. We shall continue to maintain close relations with our fellow-members of the Commonwealth, based on a common heritage and mutual independence. We shall seek to play our part in helping economic development in the poorer parts of the world. It is essential for Britain as a trading nation that the momentum of development in the Third World should not slacken.

We remain committed to try to reach a settlement in Rhodesia in accordance with the five principles. We trust that, meanwhile, Europeans and Africans in Rhodesia will make rapid progress towards agreement on constitutional changes which would enable independence to be granted by the British Parliament and sanctions to be lifted.

We shall seek to help the cause of peace in the Middle East. We reaffirm our belief that the integrity of the State of Israel must be maintained, and at the same time we will continue to give our support for withdrawal from occupied territories, in accordance with the relevant resolutions of the United Nations.

We will continue to play a full part in the negotiations over Mutual and Balanced Force Reductions and in the Conference on Security and Co-operation in Europe where we will insist on some movement in the field of an increased flow of information and ideas and people between East and West. While progress towards detente must be our purpose we note with concern the continuing expansion of all branches of the Soviet armed forces – especially its rocket forces and its navies on the high seas. We therefore need to maintain the NATO alliance and ensure that it is sufficiently strong to deter any breach of the peace.

We shall maintain the effectiveness of the British nuclear deterrent.

We shall continue to ensure that the morale and effectiveness of our armed forces are maintained at the highest possible level. This is vital if we are to retain our security, which is essential to all our aspirations.

THE ALTERNATIVE – AND THE CHOICE

We have set out in this manifesto our proposals both for dealing with the grave crisis now facing the nation and for building, once the crisis is overcome, on the solid progress made before it broke.

We believe that these proposals – firm but fair, based on realism and moderation – are what the British people desire and the situation demands.

They are also utterly different from those of the Labour Party.

The Labour Party today faces the nation committed to a left-wing programme more dangerous and more extreme than ever before in its history.

This commitment to extremism is no accident. In part, it has occurred as a reaction against the manifest failure of its policies of gimmickry and so-called pragmatism when it was last in office.

But, even more, it has occurred because the moderates within Labour's ranks have lost control, and the real power in the Labour Party has been taken over, for the first time ever, by its extreme Left wing. And this in turn has been made possible by the dominance of a small group of power-hungry trade union leaders, whose creature the Labour Party has now become.

The Labour Party today is committed to massive increases in taxation for all – rich and poor alike – not simply as a means to an end, but as an end in itself.

It is pledged to increase income tax, not just for the 'rich', but for millions of ordinary wage and salary earners.

It has threatened to increase VAT on a wide range of household goods and services, which would bring particular hardship to those less well off.

It has promised to levy heavier taxes on the self-employed.

Labour's policy for industry is one of massive nationalisation on an unprecedented scale.

In addition to taking over a number of named industries, Labour is pledged to nationalise key firms in other industries and threatens to take over any profitable firm throughout manufacturing industry.

In what would remain of private industry, it is explicitly committed to taking power to issue arbitrary State 'directives' to any company and, if it sees fit, to put in a Government 'trustee' to run the firm.

It has also talked glibly of nationalising banks, building societies and insurance companies – which would mean taking over the savings of the people.

Labour is committed to an irresponsible programme of public expenditure, costing on its own admission some £6,000 million a year, over and above the huge cost of its nationalisation plans. This was far in excess of what the national economy could afford even before the present crisis.

In education, it seeks doctrinaire uniformity throughout the State system, and would abolish the independent schools. It is similarly committed to abolishing freedom of choice in medical care.

It is committed to preventing any further extension of freehold home ownership, by taking over all the land on which future homes can be built.

It is also committed to indemnifying, at the taxpayers' and ratepayers' expense, those law-breakers of whom it politically approves. Never before in its history has the Labour Party shown such open contempt for the rule of law.

The total effect of Labour's present policies would be to wreck the economy, undermine the free society, and accelerate the present inflation beyond the point of no return.

It has no effective policy whatever for dealing with the crucial problem of wage inflation. It is committed to abandoning the legally-backed pay and prices policy; but all it has to put in its place are the outdated and divisive nostrums of class warfare.

It is not surprising that the moderates in Labour's ranks, who formerly held the balance of power in their bitterly divided Party, opposed each and every one of these extremist policies. But on each and every occasion, the moderates were defeated by the now ascendant Left wing, and these policies became firm official commitments.

However slick the public relations smokescreen, this is the reality of declared Labour Party policy – and they mean what they said.

In short, the return of a Labour Government at the present time would be nothing short of a major national disaster.

The choice before the nation today, as never before, is a clear choice between moderation and extremism.

We therefore appeal, at this critical time in our country's affairs, for the support of the great moderate majority of the British people, men and women of all Parties and no Party, who reject extremism in any shape or form.

For extremism divides, while moderation unites; and it is only on the basis of national unity that the present crisis can be overcome and a better Britain built.

The Labour Party:

'Let us work together'

Britain needs a new Government, and the Labour Party is ready with the policies essential to rescue the nation from the most serious political and economic crisis since 1945. We do not say that the dangers confronting us can be quickly dispelled; rising prices and housing costs and the new threat to our livelihood from the world-wide oil crisis canot be held in check at a stroke. We do say that the problems cut so deep that the solutions must cut deep also. The sooner Labour gets the chance to heal the savage wounds inflicted upon our society in recent years, and to turn the hopes and exertions of our people in a new direction, the better for the nation as a whole.

In this sense, we face not merely economic perils of a new dimension; we face a crowning test of our democracy – whether we can show the resilience, the ingenuity, the courage, the imagination, the sense of community necessary to meet the economic perils.

The Labour Party is proud of the contribution we made to the nation's salvation at critical times in our history, and it is in the same mood that we approach the interlocking crises of the 1970s.

Immediately, for the vast majority of families, the economic crisis takes the form of fear for their jobs, ever-rising prices, particularly food prices, and ever-rising housing costs, particularly council rents and high mortgage rates, coupled with the most drastic cuts in their income which our people have experienced since the 1930s – caused by the three-day working week introduced in panic by Government decree on January 1. For the nation the economic crisis involves an appalling balance of payments deficit, mounting debt and an ever sinking pound.

Apparently, the aim of the Prime Minister is to continue the scourge of the three-day week until he has secured a political victory over the miners. He scolds them as national enemies at the very moment when their services are more than ever indispensable to the nation. The folly of this style of politics passes description. But one day soon the Government will have to make a settlement with the miners; let us hope the clash has not by then become so bitter that the long-term prospect of sustaining an effective coal industry is fatally impaired.

The Tory Legacy

The longer the Conservative Government survives the more desperate the situation a Labour Government will inherit. The British people will understand if we are then compelled to give so absolute a priority to rebuilding the economic fabric of the nation that some of our expenditure will have to be delayed. The graver our economic situation the more important it will be to protect the poorer members of the community – such as the pensioners – by a drastic redistribution of wealth and income. However, the nature of the crisis will require that the structural changes we propose should be made even more urgently.

Whatever the circumstances in which we take office, we shall still have to meet the menaces of the mounting price of oil, of a £2,000 million deficit on the balance of payments, and of even more rapidly rising prices. How Labour will tackle that long-standing challenge of inflation naturally forms a central part of this document. But let us consider first the energy crisis.

The Energy Crisis

A huge addition is now being made to the price Britain must pay for oil from the Middle East and elsewhere, including heavy additional burdens on the balance of payments. Every available step must be taken to enforce the most efficient use of fuel and this must clearly be decided on a national scale. Government intervention in the allocation of precious energy resources would be willingly accepted by the community as a whole.

U

First, and with the utmost urgency, the coal industry must be given a new status, perspective, and security. In particular, the case which the National Union of Mineworkers has long presented is now more than ever seen to be in the national interest. A Labour Government will give the mining industry the backing it needs to revise its plans on a more ambitious scale. Immediately, the present Government should set up a Commission, composed of representatives of the NCB, the NUM, and the Government itself, to re-examine the industry's future, including distribution, in the light of the new necessities, and to report *within three months.*

Second, the new situation has greatly strengthened Labour's determination to ensure not only that the North Sea and Celtic Sea oil and gas resources are in full public ownership, but that the operation of getting and distributing them is under full Government control with majority public participation. We cannot accept that the allocation of available world output should continue to be made by multi-national oil companies and not by Governments. We will not permit Britain's own resources to be parcelled out in this way. It is public ownership and control that will enable the British people, through its Government, to fix the pace of exploitation of our oil, and the use to which it is put, so as to secure maximum public advantage from our own resources.

Third, a British Government should take the initiative to set up an International Energy Commission. Such a body, designed to establish a rational international allocation of available oil resources, together with research into new forms of fuel, should represent not only the industrialised nations but also the developing countries, which are bound to suffer most cruelly.

Fourth, the energy crisis has further profound implications for the way we conduct our whole transport system. If we are to conserve precious fuel we must do two things: one, move as much traffic as possible from road to rail; and two, develop public transport to make us less dependent on the private car. This will involve large scale investment in railways, tubes and buses and a fares policy which puts the needs of the travelling public first.

Fifth, the oil crisis is only one example of the problems which confront all nations in connection with the exploitation of the finite natural resources of raw materials of the earth. A Labour Government must co-operate internationally to use carefully the world's resources in the long-term public interest of both the developing and developed nations and to reject the present concepts of profiteering exploitation.

THE UNDERLYING CRISIS

Three years ago when Labour was in power, Britain had a big and growing surplus on the balance of payments. Mortgage rates stood at $8\frac{1}{2}$ per cent; Labour had built two million houses in six years; and the rise in the cost of living had been held down to less than 5 per cent a year. Today interest rates are at record high levels, and house building is at its lowest for more than ten years. The cost of living has gone up by 10 per cent a year and food prices have risen by no less than 18 per cent in *one year.*

The present Government came to office with promises of lower taxation, stable prices, reduced unemployment and increased financial strength. Three years later we have experienced a 20 per cent devaluation of the pound (or a 'float' downwards of that extent); unemployment has been over a million and is now rising again; prices have risen faster than at any time in living memory; and tax cuts for the rich have been paid for by price rises for the rest of us. We now have the lowest house building programme since 1963 combined with rampant inflation in rents and house prices. Wages are controlled whilst unearned incomes and capital values soar. The banks have doubled their profits through the record interest rates their customers have to pay. 1974 will certainly produce the biggest balance of payments deficit in our history.

The Common Market
Britain is a European nation, and a Labour Britain would always seek a wider co-operation between the European peoples. But a profound political mistake

made by the Heath Government was to accept the terms of entry to the Common Market, and to take us in without the consent of the British people. This has involved the imposition of food taxes on top of rising world prices, crippling fresh burdens on our balance of payments, and a draconian curtailment of the power of the British Parliament to settle questions affecting vital British interests. This is why a Labour Government will immediately seek a fundamental re-negotiation of the terms of entry.

We have spelled out in *Labour's Programme for Britain* our objectives in the new negotiations which must take place:

'The Labour Party *opposes* British membership of the European Communities on the terms negotiated by the Conservative Government.

'We have said that we are ready to re-negotiate.

'In preparing to re-negotiate the entry terms, our main objectives are these:

'Major changes in the COMMON AGRICULTURAL POLICY, so that it ceases to be a threat to world trade in food products, and so that low-cost producers outside Europe can continue to have access to the British food market.

'New and fairer methods of financing the COMMUNITY BUDGET. Neither the taxes that form the so-called "own resources" of the Communities, nor the purposes, mainly agricultural support, on which the funds are mainly to be spent, are acceptable to us. We would be ready to contribute to Community finances only such sums as were fair in relation to what is paid and what is received by other member countries.

'As stated earlier, we would reject any kind of international agreement which compelled us to accept increased unemployment for the sake of maintaining a fixed parity, as is required by current proposals for a European ECONOMIC AND MONETARY UNION. We believe that the monetary problems of the European countries can be resolved only in a world-wide framework.

'The retention by PARLIAMENT of those powers over the British economy needed to pursue effective regional, industrial and fiscal policies. Equally we need an agreement on capital movements which protects our balance of payments and full employment policies. The economic interests of the COMMONWEALTH and the DEVELOPING COUNTRIES must be better safeguarded. This involves securing continued access to the British market and, more generally, the adoption by an enlarged Community of trade and aid policies designed to benefit not just "associated overseas territories" in Africa, but developing countries throughout the world.

'No harmonisation of VALUE ADDED TAX which would require us to tax necessities.

'If re-negotiations are successful, it is the policy of the Labour Party that, in view of the unique importance of the decision, the people should have the right to decide the issue through a General Election or a Consultative Referendum. If these two tests are passed, a successful renegotiation and the expressed approval of the majority of the British people, then we shall be ready to play our full part in developing a new and wider Europe.

'If re-negotiations do not succeed, we shall not regard the Treaty obligations as binding upon us. We shall then put to the British people the reasons why we find the new terms unacceptable, and consult them on the advisability of negotiating our withdrawal from the Communities.'

An incoming Labour Government will immediately set in train the procedures designed to achieve an early result and whilst the negotiations proceed and until the British people have voted, we shall stop further processes of integration, particularly as they affect food taxes. The Government will be free to take decisions, subject to the authority of Parliament, in cases where decisions of the Common Market prejudge the negotiations. Thus, the right to decide the final issue of British entry into the Market will be restored to the British people.

Social Justice
Clearly, a fresh approach to the British crisis is required, and Labour insists that it must begin with an entirely new recognition of the claims of social justice.

To that end, urgent action is needed to tackle rising prices; to strike at the roots of the worst poverty; to make the country demonstrably a much

307

fairer place to live in. For these purposes, a new Labour Government, in its first period of office, will:

1   Bring immediate help to existing PENSIONERS, widows, the sick and the un-employed by increasing pensions and other benefits to £10 for the single person and £16 for the married couple, within the first Parliamentary session of our Government. Thereafter these figures will be increased annually in proportion to increases in average national earnings. We shall also follow this by replacing the Conservative Government's inadequate and unjust long-term pensions scheme by a comprehensive scheme designed to take future pensioners off the means test and give full equality of treatment to women.

2   Introduce a new scheme of help for the DISABLED.

3   Help the low paid and other families in poverty by introducing a new system of CHILD CASH ALLOWANCES for every child, including the first, payable to the mother.

4   Introduce strict PRICE CONTROL on key services and commodities. Bulk pur-chase and new marketing arrangements will help stabilise food prices, and selective use of subsidies will be applied to the items bearing most heavily on the family budget. We shall re-negotiate those elements of Common Market policy which deliberately impose food taxes on the people.

5   Repeal the HOUSING FINANCE ACT, and give back to local authorities the right to fix rents which do not make a profit out of their tenants. We shall extend protection from eviction to tenants of furnished accommodation; limit rent increases in unfurnished and furnished lettings; encourage the muni-cipalisation of privately rented property (except where an owner-occupier shares a house with a tenant); and take steps to secure a steady supply of mortgage funds at reasonable rates of interest to those wishing to buy their own homes; and abolish the agricultural tied cottage. We shall raise the total subsidy for local authority house building to that granted to owner-occupiers on their mortgage payments. This will be vital to reversing the serious fall in the housing programme under the present Government.
Land required for development will be taken into public ownership, so that land is freely and cheaply available for new houses, schools, hospitals and other purposes. Public ownership of land will stop land profiteering. It will emphatically *not* apply to owner-occupiers.

6   REDISTRIBUTE INCOME AND WEALTH. We shall introduce an annual Wealth Tax on the rich; bring in a new tax on major transfers of personal wealth; heavily tax speculation in property – including a new tax on property com-panies; and seek to eliminate tax dodging across the whole field.

Industrial Relations

These measures affecting prices and taxation policy will prove *by deeds* the determination of the new Labour Government to set Britain on the road towards a new social and economic equality. After so many failures in the field of incomes policy – under the Labour Government but even more seriously under the Tory Government's compulsory wage controls – only deeds can persuade. Only practical action by the Government to create a much fairer distribution of the national wealth can convince the worker and his family and his trade union that 'an incomes policy' is not some kind of trick to force him, particularly if he works in a public service or nationalised industry, to bear the brunt of the national burden. But as it is proved that the Government is ready to act – against high prices, rents and other impositions falling most heavily on the low paid and on pensioners – so we believe that the trade unions *voluntarily* (which is the only way it can be done for any period in a free society), will co-operate to make the whole policy successful. We believe that the action we propose on prices, together with an understanding with the TUC on the lines which we have already agreed, will create the right economic climate for money incomes to grow in line with production. That is the essence of the new social contract which the Labour Party has discussed at length and agreed with the TUC and which must take its place as a central feature of the new economic policy of a Labour Government.

A Labour Government will, therefore:

(i) Abolish the PAY BOARD apparatus set up by the Tories
(ii) Repeal the INDUSTRIAL RELATIONS ACT as a matter of extreme urgency and then bring in an Employment Protection Act and an Industrial Democracy Act, as agreed in our discussions with the TUC, to increase the control of industry by the people
(iii) Establish a standing ROYAL COMMISSION to advise on income distribution, both earned and unearned, with particular reference to differentials and job evaluation
(iv) Establish a non-governmental CONCILIATION AND ARBITRATION SERVICE, with the task of tackling industrial disputes at both national and local level.

Employment and Expansion

However, more will be needed if we are to create a new spirit in industry. The British people, both as workers and consumers, must have more control over the powerful private forces that at present dominate our economic life. To this end we shall:

7 Sustain and expand industrial development and exports and bring about the re-equipment necessary for this purpose through the powers we shall take in a new INDUSTRY ACT and through the Planning Agreement system which will allow Government to plan with industry more effectively.
Wherever we give direct aid to a company out of public funds we shall in return reserve the right to take a share of the ownership of the company.

8 In addition to our plans set out in point 5 above for taking into common ownership land required for development, we shall substantially extend PUBLIC ENTERPRISE by taking mineral rights. We shall also take shipbuilding, shiprepairing and marine engineering, ports, the manufacture of airframes and aeroengines into public ownership and control. But we shall not confine the extension of the public sector to the loss-making and subsidised industries. We shall also take over profitable sections or individual firms in those industries where a public holding is essential to enable the Government to control prices, stimulate investment, encourage exports, create employment, protect workers and consumers from the activities of irresponsible multi-national companies, and to plan the national economy in the national interest. We shall therefore include in this operation, sections of pharmaceuticals, road haulage, construction, machine tools, in addition to our proposals for North Sea and Celtic Sea oil and gas. Our decision in the field of banking, insurance and building societies is still under consideration. We shall return to public ownership assets and licences hived-off by the present government, and we shall create a powerful National Enterprise Board with the structure and functions set out in *Labour's Programme 1973*.

9 We intend to socialise existing nationalised industries. In consultation with the unions, we shall take steps to make the management of existing nationalised industries more responsible to the workers in the industry and more responsive to their consumers' needs.

10 Regional development will be further encouraged by new public enterprise, assistance to private industry on a selective basis, and new REGIONAL PLANNING MACHINERY, along the lines set out in *Labour's Programme 1973*. We will retain and improve the Regional Employment Premium. Revenues from North Sea oil will be used wherever possible to improve employment conditions in Scotland and the regions elsewhere in need of development.

11 We shall develop an active manpower policy with a powerful NATIONAL LABOUR BOARD. In the longer term, redundant workers must have an automatic right to retraining; redundancy should then lead not to unemployment, but to retraining and job changing.

Social Progress

These are our measures for transforming British industry into a responsible economic system. It is outrageous that, at a time when enormous private wealth is being accumulated, so little effort has been made to maintain and improve our public services. A Labour Government will:

12 Revise and expand the NATIONAL HEALTH SERVICE; abolish prescription charges; introduce free family planning; phase out private practice from the hospital service; and transform the area health authorities into democratic bodies.
We also intend to establish a disability benefit.

13 Expand the EDUCATION SERVICE by the introduction of a national scheme of Nursery Schools, including day care facilities, and by a big expansion of educational facilities for 16-18 year olds, by finally ending the 11+ and by providing additional resources for children in special need of help. We shall speed the development of a universal system of fully comprehensive secondary schools. All forms of tax-relief and charitable status for public schools will be withdrawn.

14 Pay special attention to the MANPOWER NEEDS of all public services now approaching breakdown, particularly in our inner urban areas. Our cities desperately need and must get better services, which are properly manned, and the resources to make this possible.

Not all of our proposals should be judged on economic tests. It is the duty of Socialists to protect the individual from discrimination on whatever grounds. Here several of our proposals have the advantage of bringing benefits at little economic cost.

15 WOMEN AND GIRLS must have an equal status in education, training, employment, social security, national insurance, taxation, property ownership, matrimonial and family law. Women at work, whether wives and mothers or those otherwise caring for dependent relatives, must receive more consideration from the community. We shall create the powerful legal machinery necessary to enforce our anti-discrimination laws.

16 Review the law of NATIONALITY so that our immigration policies are based on citizenship, and in particular to eliminate discrimination on grounds of colour.

17 Set up a NATIONAL CONSUMERS AUTHORITY with adequate finance to redress the balance between the consumer and the manufacturer and seller.

Peace and Justice in a Safer World

As in domestic policy the lesson of the last few years in Foreign Policy is that a narrow, selfish, inward looking approach to international problems is doomed to failure. We are, more than ever, one world and Labour's foreign policy will be dedicated to the strengthening of international institutions and global co-operation in response to the threats to the peace and prosperity of us all. To this end the foreign policy of a new Labour Government will be guided by four main principles.

One We shall seek to strengthen international organisations dedicated to the promotion of human rights, the rule of law, and the peaceful settlement of disputes. In particular, we shall re-dedicate Britain to the ideals of the United Nations and the Commonwealth, two organisations treated with scant regard by the present Government.

Two We shall commit Britain to a policy of equality at home and abroad which would involve radical changes in aid, trade and development policies. In particular, the next Labour Government will seek to implement the United Nations Development Target of 0.7 per cent of GNP official aid and will increase the aid programme to meet it, and will actively seek to re-establish a more generous and more liberal world trading pattern for the developing countries.

Three We shall oppose all forms of racial discrimination and colonialism. This will mean support for the liberation movements of Southern Africa and a disengagement from Britain's unhealthy involvement with Apartheid. We shall intensify the policy of sanctions against Rhodesia and agree to no settlement which does not have the whole-hearted consent of the African majority.

Four Whilst maintaining our support for NATO as an instrument of detente no less than of defence, we shall, in consultation with our Allies, progressively reduce the burden of Britain's defence spending to bring our costs into line with those carried by our main European allies. Such a realignment would, at present levels of defence spending, mean savings on defence expenditure by Britain of several hundred million pounds per annum over a period. At the same time we shall work for the success of detente. We shall participate in the multilateral disarmament negotiations and as a first step will seek the removal of American Polaris bases from Great Britain. The ultimate objective of the movement towards a more satisfactory relationship in Europe must be the mutual and concurrent phasing out of NATO and the Warsaw Pact.

Let the Nation Decide

The aims set out in this manifesto are Socialist aims, and we are proud of the word. It is only by setting our aims high, even amid the hazards of our present economic situation, that the idealism and high intelligence, especially of our young people, can be enlisted. It is indeed our intention to:

(a) Bring about a fundamental and irreversible shift in the balance of power and wealth in favour of working people and their families
(b) Eliminate poverty wherever it exists in Britain, and commit ourselves to a substantial increase in our contribution to fight poverty abroad
(c) Make power in industry genuinely accountable to the workers and the community at large
(d) Achieve far greater economic equality – in income, wealth and living standards
(e) Increase social equality by giving far greater importance to full employment, housing, education and social benefits
(f) Improve the environment in which our people live and work and spend their leisure.

Of course, as we insisted at the beginning, these aims, like the particular items in the programme, cannot all be fulfilled at once. We cannot do everything at once, and these are the priorities we have chosen. This preliminary manifesto, drawing upon the new policy statements which the Labour Party has discussed by its democratic process, over the past three years, sets out the specific numbered pledges which the next Labour Government will seek with all its strength to carry out in a single Parliament.

The task will not be easy. But we repudiate the despairing gospel preached in some quarters that the British people cannot govern themselves and that they have lost the art to act cohesively, through their various democratic institutions, as a civilised community.

That charge comes most insultingly from a Conservative Government which has adopted so many devices to corrode or destroy the power of those democratic institutions – local authorities, the trade unions, the House of Commons itself. These are the very instruments which Labour will use to restore and enhance the power of British democracy.

The Liberal Party:

'Change the face of Britain'

THE CRISIS OF GOVERNMENT

This country has seen two parties, Labour and Conservative, alternating in office during the last fifty years. For the last five years, both parties have had to deal with very similar problems; both have offered similar solutions; both, in Opposition have opposed the policies of their opponents and then adopted them on becoming the Government. In 1967 Labour in office introduced a compulsory policy of prices and incomes control which the Conservatives, in opposition, opposed vehemently. At the same time the Labour Party re-opened negotiations for Britain's entry into the Common Market and these negotiations concluded with the offer of terms of entry which were accepted by Labour in 1969. In 1969, the Labour Government also introduced its White Paper 'In Place of Strife' which advocated legislation to control Industrial Relations. The Conservative opposition opposed this measure. When the Conservatives returned to office in 1970 they immediately introduced the Industrial Relations Act which was bitterly opposed by Labour, despite the fact that many of the provisions for union registration and protection of employment had been in their own proposals. When the Conservative Government in early 1971 elected to join the Common Market on terms which Mr Roy Jenkins asserted were similar to those negotiated by the Labour Government, Labour opposed entry. Finally, having persistently opposed compulsory prices and incomes control, the Conservative Government did one more U-turn and introduced its own pay and price freeze in 1972 to be followed by Phase II and Phase III. Once more the Labour opposition stood on its head and opposed what had formerly been its own policy.

A Crisis of Confidence

Britain cannot be governed effectively when parties continuously change their policies and principles to make cheap political gains and without regard for their own principles or for public opinion. The crisis of inconsistent government has led to a crisis of public confidence in the two parties which have ruled this country for the last fifty years. Liberals refuse to accept that the present crisis is induced by any one political party, Tory or Labour. It is caused by the type of policies and politics which both parties espouse; policies which employ short term, instant cures, but which leave behind more problems than they solve; politics which are partisan, dividing and polarising the nation into confrontation between classes whether they be rich or poor, manager or worker, house owner or tenant. This country cannot be ruled from the extremes of right and left which set the people against each other – it must be run by a government whose neutrality is unquestioned, whose policies are fair-minded, and whose politics is not governed by vested interests.

A New Type of Politics

Politics has become sterile; the old two-party system has finally proved its inadequacy. Old political theories of unbridled free enterprise and undiluted socialism have been shown to be irrelevant. Even leading members of the Conservative and Labour Parties admit that their own administrations have failed to deal with our fundamental problems and yet they hang on limply to political power. Politics has gone away from the people and this, in a democracy, is the most dangerous development of recent years.

The Liberal Party's concern for the individual person expressed in our 'Community Politics' campaigns has been criticised by the old-fashioned politicians as the politics of the paving stone. Yet they forget that politics is fundamentally about people, and their problems – however trivial they may seem – should dominate the minds of all politicians. Liberals believe in the supremacy of the individual and that political institutions should serve, not enslave, the people. Fundamentally Community Politics is an attempt to involve people in the decisions that affect their daily lives at the time when the individual viewpoint can really be expressed effecively – not six months after the decision has been reached, through a futile protest or enquiry. Our policies to decentralise government; to democratise the vast bureaucracies which run our Education system, our Industrial Relations and our Health and Welfare services, are all designed to further the goal of 'people participation'.

A New Party

But a party which seeks to transform the politics and administration of Britain must itself be organised in such a way as to avoid the pitfalls of compromise partisanship and inconsistency which have befallen parties in the past. The Liberal Party is a party of no vested interest – financial or individual. Opinion Polls have consistently shown that we draw our support almost equally from all sections of the population, whichever way it is divided up, and that between 40 and 50 per cent of the people at any given time would vote for the Liberal Party if they thought that a Liberal Government would be elected. Our five by-election victories have indicated that many people feel that the time has come for a Liberal Government.

Unlike the other two parties we draw on no permanent source of financial support, while the Conservative Party consistently draws on at least a million pounds per year from the vested interests of big business, and Labour relies on the vested interests of the Trade Unions for over 90 per cent of its election funds. Is it any wonder that the country is polarised by Tory-Labour confrontation?

The Liberal Party is tied to no sectional interest. That is why we can justly claim that we approach the problems of our country with no doctrinaire prejudices, no class inhibitions and no sectional interests.

NEW POLICIES—A RADICAL PROGRAMME OF RECONSTRUCTION

Most of all, the present crisis demands fundamental changes in the policies which we adopt. The old values which have led to inequalities in wealth, property and power must go. Government must be seen to be acting fairly in the interests of all the people instead of the interests of the very few. We must set aside the sterile class conflicts, the debates about capitalism or socialism, and the policies that divide and weaken us as a nation. We must rigidly question any new initiative by asking the question: 'will it narrow the gulf between the classes; will it reduce conflict?' No policy will achieve any lasting progress without national acceptance. Until we achieve the ideal of national unity, any other policy aims to achieve economic growth or industrial efficiency, will be unattainable. What is therefore needed is a fearless programme of economic, social and industrial reconstruction and a clearout of the old values which have so dogged the progress of the nation.

Liberal Policy Aims

1 Establish the universal right to a *minimum income* balanced by a fairer *distribution of wealth*, through a credit income tax system and national minimum earnings guarantees.

2 Create an equal *partnership* between employers and employed in recognition of the equal importance of their contributions to the success of industry.

3 *Decentralise* government and bring political power to Scotland, Wales and the regions of England so as to ensure that decisions are taken as close to people as possible.

4 Involve people in exerting influence within their communities through *participation ;* and encourage proper consultation in the exercise of national responsibilities for Health, Education and General Welfare.

5 *Break-up* monopolistic concentrations of political and economic power so that individual initiative is not suppressed.

6 *Conserve and protect* finite resources for the lasting benefit of the whole community.

All these aims have one end; to serve the individual and to create the conditions in which he can develop his personality to the full.

THE LONG TERM CRISIS

Since the War, politicians, business leaders, trade unionists and journalists have all assumed that a high economic growth rate is desirable and have encouraged expectations that put a premium on the acquisition of more money to spend on material goods. But the pursuit of unlimited growth has been accompanied by soaring prices, high unemployment and high domestic demand which has led to recurring balance of payments crises. The usual remedy adopted by Tory and Labour Governments has been 'stop go' – boom followed by freeze and squeeze.

The Wilson and Heath Governments – have even acted similarly – and mistakenly – in either holding out against devaluation of the pound until world pressure forced an uncontrolled devaluation, or holding on to a mistaken belief in the importance of maintaining our balance of payments at the expense of rising unemployment, which finally reached the million mark in early 1972.

The result of these policies has been the frustration of targets unreached and the deception of unfulfilled promises, as the following examples illustrate:

Value of the Pound

Labour 1964-1970
'Devaluation does not mean of course that the £ here in Britain, in your pocket, or purse, or in your bank has been devalued.'
Harold Wilson TV Broadcast November 19, 1967
REALITY **In six years of Labour Government the £ lost nearly 20 per cent of its value.**

Conservative 1970-1974
'We have become resigned to the value of the £ in our pockets or purses falling by at least a shilling a year.'
REALITY **The £ of June 1970 dropped in value to 75p (or about 15/– in pre-decimal terms) in January 1974 (House of Commons Question/Answer), a drop of well over a shilling a year.**

Unemployment

Labour 1964-1970
'We see no reason why unemployment should rise at all, apart from seasonal increases.'
Harold Wilson (Labour Party Press Conference March 29, 1966)
REALITY **In six years of Labour Government Britain experienced the most prolonged period of high unemployment since 1940. For three-quarters of this period the number of unemployed was over half a million!**

Conservative 1970-1974
'If we could get back to Tory policies, the unemployment position would be a great deal better than it is today.'
Robert Carr, May 6, 1971
'We accept absolutely the responsibility for the level of unemployment.'
Robert Carr November 23, 1971
REALITY **During 1971 and 1972 unemployed was running at record war levels. Unemployment averaged 758,000 (3.3 per cent of working population) in 1971, and 84,000 (3.7 per cent of working population) in 1972.**

Cost of Living

Labour 1964-1970
'The continual rise in the cost of living can, must, and will be halted to give the housewife relief and her family a genuine rise in their standard of living.'
George Brown, Swadlingcote September 27, 1964
REALITY **In just over five years under the Labour government prices rose by 25 per cent.**

Conservative 1970-1974
'In implementing our policies we will give overriding priority to bringing the present inflation under control.'
Conservative Manifesto June 1970
REALITY   Retail prices have risen by over 33 per cent since the 1970 election. Food prices by nearly 50 per cent (Dept of Employment index of retail prices, December, 1973).

Statutory Wage Control

Labour 1964-1970
'As to the idea of freezing all wage claims, salary claims . . . I think this would be monstrously unfair . . . I do not think you can ever legislate for wage increases, and no party is setting out to do that.'
Harold Wilson BBC Election Forum March 10, 1966
REALITY   Four months later measures were taken to freeze wages and prices until the end of 1966, followed by 6 months of 'severe restraint'.

Conservative 1970-1974
'Labour's compulsory wage control was a failure and we will not repeat it.'
Conservative Manifesto June 1970
REALITY   A compulsory price and wage freeze was introduced by the Conservatives in November 1972, followed quickly by Phase II and culminating in the crisis of Phase III.

Housing

Labour 1964-1970
'We have embarked on a massive expansion of the housing programme . . . reaching by 1970 no less than 500,000 new dwellings. This is not a lightly given promise, it is a pledge.'
Harold Wilson (Election Speech) Bradford March 27, 1966
REALITY   It was abandoned in January – less than two years later. In 1970 less than 365,000 new houses were built, fewer than the 373,000 built in 1964.

Conservative 1970-1974
'It is scandalous that this year (1970), as last year, fewer houses will be completed than in 1964 when Labour took over. And far fewer are under construction.'
Conservative Manifesto June 1970
REALITY   This Government completed only 293,000 in 1973, the lowest number since 1959, and on current trends they will again fail to achieve 300,000 in 1974.

THE QUALITY OF LIFE

In addition, the damage to the fabric of society and the environment as a result of the pursuit of unlimited growth has been enormous. To the extent that growth has been achieved, it has not increased human happiness. Instead there has been evidence of increased social disintegration to which the growth in crime, mental illness, drug taking and divorce all testify. Furthermore, the destruction of whole communities in the interest of 'redevelopment', the scarring of the landscape by motorways and the shattering noise of jets over rooftops near major airports are a few of the more obvious symptoms of incompatibility between unlimited material growth and the good life.

The Liberal Strategy

Whether or not continued expansion is desirable, we now have to ask if it is indefinitely feasible. The Liberal Party believes that we now have to begin planning for an age of stability. The resources of this planet are limited and we shall not be able to go on increasing consumption of energy, raw materials and foodstuffs at current rates. The steep rises in world commodity prices and the restrictions imposed by the producer nations on oil supplies, are strong indications of a turning point in history, the significance of which has yet to be grasped by most politicians.

We must therefore act on two fronts to cut back on demand for our limited resources, firstly by effectively controlling domestic inflation which is causing intense pressure on our balance of payments and adding to the chaos of our industrial relations as well as preventing the development of long-term economic and social policies.

But secondly, we must now abandon the policy adopted by past Governments, based, almost entirely, on the crude maximisation of Gross National Product. GNP is not a measure of real benefit, including, as it does, outputs that are good, bad and indifferent, and to talk simply of unlimited increases in growth is to deprive people of the power to choose between the beneficial and the harmful.

Liberals advocate a policy of controlled economic growth, by which we mean the careful husbandry of resources and the limitation of private consumption by the few in favour of better public services for the majority of our citizens.

In terms of human resources a policy of controlled economic growth also recognises that the obligation to provide employment and a safe environment can no longer be sacrificed to the maximisation of industrial efficiency. People cannot be treated as 'lame ducks'.

INFLATION – THE PRESENT CRISIS

The major single problem facing the next Government will be that of inflation. Given the long-term crisis of resources which we face it is unlikely that inflation will ever be completely conquered but it can be controlled with determined and fair policies which have the support of the people. Conservatives and Labour Governments have pandered to vested interests to the detriment of the population as a whole. Both have been fearful of embarking on long-term policies to control the economy and attack inflation for fear of denting the profits of the big corporations and the wage packets of the strongest unions. Hence their timid attempts at controlling inflation have been undercut by promises of an ultimate return to a free for all.

Liberals would control inflation through a combination of industrial reconstruction and a permanent prices and incomes policy enforced by penalties on those whose actions cause inflation. We propose that prices, dividends and average earnings within a company should be limited to an agreed annual rate of increase. Any company which increased prices faster than that rate would suffer an extra surcharge on its Corporation Tax payments equivalent to the amount by which its prices had exceeded the agreed norm. Excessive dividends and profits pay-outs would also be penalised by a tax surcharge, on a sliding scale according to the amount by which such increases exceed the norm.

If average earnings per person (including fringe benefits) within a company rose faster than the agreed annual rate, then both the employer and the employees concerned would have to pay an extra surcharge on their graduated National Insurance Contributions, again on a sliding scale according to the amount by which earnings had exceeded the norm.

Of course, there would have to be provision for appeal and this would be best achieved by the compilation of *ad hoc* reports on earnings levels and pricing policies in particular industries along the lines of the old National Board for Prices and Incomes. Such reports would also cover changes in relativities and wage differentials, which will have to be narrowed considerably, and Parliamentary consent would have to be obtained before reports could be implemented.

Thus instead of countering inflation by increasing everybody's taxes, as Mr Powell and the Labour Party advocate, Liberals would tax only those who cause inflation and would control the supply of money into the economy without having to resort to the blunt instrument of brutal cuts in expenditure on social services which once again hit the poor hardest of all.

A great merit of this policy is that it would enable wage bargaining to take place without direct government intervention and inevitable accusations of partisanship. Yet it would still enable the Government to maintain overall control of the economy. But no policy can hope to succeed unless it is accepted and seen as fair by the great majority of people. Two major defects in past policies must be remedied if this policy is to succeed: the unfairness of the present wage bargaining system which favours those who shout loudest must be ended, and a fairer pricing policy must be evolved to ensure that price increases do not merely contribute to increased profits.

Fair Prices

Liberals would strengthen price controls by relating them to absolute rather than percentage margins. We would also insist that middle-sized companies were obliged to submit applications to increase prices, as are top companies. We would strengthen the powers of the Monopoly and Mergers Commission to investigate and regulate monopoly companies. The Government must stimulate competition where it can still be made to work, break up and control monopolies, prevent non-productive mergers and stamp out widespread restrictive practices. Nationalisation will not solve the problem of high prices or monopolies. As we have seen in so many nationalised industries, the public either has to suffer high prices or subsidise non-profit-making industries. Either way the consumer pays more.

But in the meantime, where there are rapid increases in prices which are beyond the Government's control, Liberals favour the incorporation of guaranteed wage increases into any agreed pay policy to allow compensation for any excessive rise in food prices which occurs. With food prices having risen by fifty per cent in three-and-a-half years such action is now required immediately.

A National Minimum Earnings Level

We must work to narrow the differentials between the highest and lowest paid in our economy. At a time when average earnings have reached over £40 a week, six million working people still earn less than half of this sum. A Liberal Government would introduce a statutory minimum earnings level for a normal working week and no employer would be allowed to pay less than this amount.

The importance of such legislation has been starkly illustrated by the three-day week. Those who suffered most in reduced wages and redundancies have been the poor – precisely those who do not have earnings guarantees.

But we must also reform the wage bargaining free-for-all in which the poorest inevitably come off worst. To do this effectively we must reconstruct our framework of industrial relations to spread the monopoly power now vested in a few very powerful Unions.

A NEW CHARTER FOR INDUSTRIAL RELATIONS

Britain lost more than 24 million working days last year – more than any other European country and almost double the amount lost in Italy, our nearest rival. Yet what have our opponents to offer as an antidote to industrial chaos? The Industrial Relations Act and the impotent Industrial Relations Court stand as monuments to attempted Tory repression, and a perpetual reminder to the Labour Party of its capitulation to Union pressure while in Government. Whatever the merits of the Act's provisions for contractual obligation and redundancy protection its practical effectiveness has foundered on Union opposition and Conservative folly. The dues which were expropriated from the AUEW political fund were drops in the ocean, but the action which confiscated money earmarked for the Government's opponents, was a devastating piece of party political warfare.

The Industrial Relations Act must be repealed and replaced by far-reaching legislation to introduce real democracy into industry. The Labour Party talks glibly about Industrial Democracy by which it means Union domination and the effective exclusion of over fifty per cent of our work force which does not belong to a union. The Liberal Party believes that *all* individuals should be involved in the industry in which they work and this has been the cornerstone of our policy for over fifty years. We believe that the two-party system in Britain based on a party of organised capital confronting a party of organised labour has helped to divide industry into two camps to the detriment of the community as a whole. We therefore advocate industrial partnership not merely as an aid in solving the economic problems of our country, but as a system which is right and just, and which will unite instead of dividing.

Liberal industrial policy has three objectives. Firstly, employees must become members of their companies just as shareholders are, with the same clearly defined rights. Secondly, it must be accepted that directors in public companies are equally responsible to shareholders and employees. Employees should be entitled to share in the election of the directors on equal terms with shareholders, and Works Councils representing all employees must be set up at plant level with wide powers to negotiate pay and conditions of work. Thirdly, employees should share in the profits of the company and the growth of its assets.

In the long term, the implementation of Liberal co-partnership policies will contribute to the solution of wage inflation, by ensuring that all employees benefit from wage increases and by including a measure of responsibility into wage bargaining. For in the day-to-day negotiations within each company employees would realise that there is little to be gained by wage increases in excess of productivity. Such increases would simply reduce the amount available in which the workers would share. In short our policies would achieve the identification of employees' interests with those of the firm by providing a visible link between the immediate limitation of wage demands and the future prosperity which will be generated for both employees and shareholders as a result. We cannot believe that any reasonable employer would prefer an industrial strike and the loss of millions of pounds to the hope of industrial harmony and responsible wage bargaining through industrial partnership. Similarly, no responsible employee would refuse the opportunity to become an equal partner in his firm with an equal share in its profits in favour of continued confrontation, inequality and insecurity.

THE ENERGY CRISIS

The short-term problems caused by the miners' industrial action and the interruption of Middle East oil supplies demanded immediate action to reduce consumption, and in the main the Liberals supported Government restrictions in the use of energy and the three-day week, both of which we were convinced were necessary to avoid even more serious disruption of economic life as stocks would otherwise have fallen below the danger level. However, we have been critical of the inflexibility of the Government's anti-inflation policy, which prevented the National Coal Board from entering into proper negotiation on the miners' claim. Instead of being recognised as the life blood of a nation now deprived of a large portion of its energy supplies, the miners were made the scapegoat for the Government's obstinacy in clinging to out-dated policies. Any settlement with the miners must be permanent and ensure continuing reward for their contribution to the alleviation of the Energy Crisis. We believe that a settlement could have been reached if, in addition to the increases offered under Phase III, the NCB could have undertaken to make further rises available as the industry expands.

All political parties, including the Liberals, must share the blame for the decline in coal output since the middle sixties. In order to reverse the decline, the NCB should be encouraged to press ahead with the development of new coal reserves in Yorkshire and the Midlands.

The Government's policy of exploiting North Sea Oil and Gas must be done at a rate determined by a National Energy Policy so as to allow indigenous industries to acquire the necessary expertise and equipment. The policy must also have regard to the longer-term future when imports of hydrocarbons are likely to be even more expensive and difficult to obtain. Royalties from the production of North Sea oil should be used in part to encourage the development of other industries in Scotland and the North East – and later, if exploration in the Celtic Sea is successful, in Wales. We are not satisfied that the revenues accruing to the nation from our own oil are fair in relation to the latest assessments of the size and value of the fields, and Liberals will ensure that huge windfall profits are not made by the licensees, many of whom are foreign concerns who have been given licences on exorbitantly advantageous terms.

The Liberal Party advocates continuity of work on British nuclear reactor systems. The first advanced gas-cooled reactors will come into operation during 1974, and it would be a grave mistake to switch horses now to the American pressurised water reactor system, as it is suggested we are likely to do. The evidence from the United States shows that they are less safe. But energy policy should not consist solely of adjusting supply to meet whatever demand is created by existing market forces. Governments can influence demand as well as supply by pricing policy, incentives and capital projects. At a time when public spending on education, housing and health is being cut, it is not acceptable to press on with the £3,000 million projected expenditure on Concorde, Maplin and the Channel Tunnel simultaneously, quite apart from energy and environmental considerations. Since, however, air travel will become far more expensive as jet fuel increases in cost, Maplin is no longer necessary, and the airlines will not buy Concorde, the former should be scrapped and the latter severely curtailed. Similarly, fewer people will be able to afford Continental motoring holidays with petrol at £1 a gallon, as predicted by Lord Stokes, and the Channel Tunnel should therefore be rail only, saving £240 million. These are all complex problems, and it cannot be denied that we have been caught unprepared by recent changes in the energy situation. The importance of the matter has been recognised implicitly by the Government, in the creation of a separate Department responsible for energy, but there is still no authoritative body to give impartial advice to both Government and Parliament. We need a permanent Royal Commission, serviced by adequate professional staff and with funds to commission research by industry, universities and government research establishments. This body would be required to publish reports at regular intervals, the first of which should be on the long-term proposals in the coal industry. Such reports should then be debated in Parliament.

Finally, the Government's long-term plan to reorganise the steel industry and close some steelmaking plants should be reviewed in the light of the changed situation. Liberals believe that concentration on bigger and fewer plants, on the scale adopted by the Japanese, of which we have no experience, may prove detrimental, particularly if uncertainties over fuel supplies continue. In addition, the economic and social dislocation within traditional steelmaking communities affected by such closures provides a very powerful argument for a complete rethink of strategy by both the Government and the European Coal and Steel Community.

SOCIAL RECONSTRUCTION

Underlying all our policies for social reconstruction are the twin themes of participation and individual freedom. Indeed the first is dependent on the second, for no person can play his full part in society unless he has the freedom to do so, and this must include freedom from discrimination, freedom from poverty and illness, the security of a roof over his head and the prospect of an equal start in life.

We are still a long way from achieving these goals even in 1974. Once again promises have been lightly made and cruelly broken because they have all been founded on assumptions of maximum production and economic growth. Only when we rid ourselves of the false logic that sees all social advancement as a product of economic efficiency will the well-being of society truly become a social service.

Health and Social Welfare

The reorganisation of the National Health Service has failed to unify the Health Service or to ensure adequate public participation in the decisions which affect them. Liberals would bring local authority welfare services into the main structure of a unified NHS by placing them under the financial and administrative control of the area Health Authorities. We also favour democratic election to Area Health Boards so as to ensure a strong voice for the community.

The Chronically Sick and Disabled Persons Act 1970, having been a Private Members Bill, has, in many areas, failed to give people the comprehensive services that were intended as it gives local authorities additional responsibilities without providing extra funds to discharge them. We would introduce a Bill encompassing the provisions of the 1970 Act, so that central finance can be made available for its implementation, and extending provision for the disabled to other fields such as education where urgent national provision is required in facilities and finance.

The Liberal Party opposed the increase in prescription charges, the abolition of free school milk in junior schools and increased school meal charges – all callously petty economies introduced by a Conservative Government and all hitting directly at the poor and needy in our society.

Security without Means Tests – A Credit Income Tax Scheme

Liberals have long advocated a system of credit income tax whereby social security payments would automatically be paid to those in need. The Government's tax credit scheme, however, falls well short of the Liberal ideal because it values administrative efficiency above adequate provision for social need, while the Labour Party still pins its faith in the paternalism and stigma of the old means tested welfare system.

The Liberal scheme represents a major onslaught on the Means Test Society and would replace most of the 44 means tests to which under-privileged and handicapped people are subjected.

The Liberal credit income tax scheme would sweep away existing tax allowances, family allowances, national insurance benefits, nearly all supplementary benefits, housing subsidies, rent and rate rebates, family income supplements and a wide variety of miscellaneous benefits. All income would be taxed according to a progressive scale from the very first pound, but *everyone* would be entitled to various 'credits' or allowances depending on circumstances. Where the liability to tax exceeded the value of credits there would be net tax to pay. Where the value of the credits exceeded the liability of tax the difference would be paid to the individual. automatically, through the tax system. Thus a redistribution of income could automatically be effected in favour of those needing help. There would be three types of credit – personal, housing and social. The most important would be the personal credit. This would be paid to every person and would be fixed at a level sufficient to guarantee a subsistence living to that individual. The credit for an adult would be greater than for a child. In the case of children under 16, the credit would be paid to the mother.

Then there would be a universal housing credit, paid regardless of whether the individual lived in rented or owner-occupied accommodation.

The third category of credits would correspond to national insurance benefits. There would be a credit for pensioners and for short- and long-term unemployment, sickness and disablement.

Whereas the Government scheme helps to tackle the poverty problem it has no intention of guaranteeing in every case that a family with no further help from the state would have enough to live on. The Liberal scheme does just this. It has estimated that a combined income and social security tax of 40 per cent (against the present 36 per cent) plus a recasting of VAT (but not on food) would be sufficient to operate the scheme. In the transitional period before the full introduction of our credit income tax scheme we propose that family allowances should be extended to the first child, and social security benefits proportionately increased with increases in average earnings. This is particularly urgent in the case of those such as widows whose circumstances can change so dramatically.

Provision for our Pensioners

Pensioners have had a bad deal from both Tory and Labour Governments. Amid extravagant claims that they have kept pace with increases in the cost of living, pensioners have actually been left behind in the great wage race. Under the Labour government pensions only rose marginally as a percentage of average earnings. The single pension represented 19 per cent of average earnings in 1964: and 21 per cent by the time Labour left office in 1970. Under the Conservatives the single pension has actually fallen back to 19 per cent of average earnings.

The Conservative Government's Occupational Pension Scheme incorporates a degree of compulsion which is anathema to Liberals in forcing everyone to contribute to a second pension scheme which will do nothing for today's pensioners. The last Labour Government had similar idealistic plans.

Liberals reaffirm the Beveridge commitment to introduce a basic pension which provides an adequate income irrespective of further financial provision. We would therefore increase the retirement pension in stages to 50 per cent of average earnings for a married couple and $33\frac{1}{3}$ per cent for a single person. Thus we would spread over a number of years a cost which if incurred immediately would amount to about £1,400 million. However, there would be a considerable saving in supplementary benefits which at present are claimed by a third of our 8 million pensioners, at a cost of £400 million.

This first phase of our pension plan would be a transitional stage, prior to the introduction of our full credit income tax scheme. Pensioners would be included in this scheme and would be entitled to a personal credit and housing credit as well as a pension credit resulting in an income of approximately two-thirds of average national earnings for a married couple. In addition we would reduce the retirement age for men to sixty. We would also abolish the earnings rule which penalises those who wish to go on doing a valuable job of work.

Education

Liberals have long recognised that resources for education are limited and across the board advance is impossible. We therefore took care to work out a ten-year development plan which would allocate clear priorities. In our view these should be:

1 The full implementation of the Plowden Committee's recommendations paying special attention to the need for pre-school education particularly in those areas of underprivilege and social deprivation, and the urgent reduction in the size of primary school classes to a maximum of 30 pupils.

2 The reorganisation of secondary school education on non-selective lines. There are more ways than one to organise a non-selective secondary school and we would allow local authorities maximum flexibility within minimum standards to adapt their system to local conditions.

3 A major reorganisation of curricula and school institutions to provide a more realistic last three years education for non-academic children.

4 The abolition of the binary system of further education and the closer integration of Universities, Polytechnics and Colleges of Education. In particular we would seek to establish Community Colleges open to all age groups, with the ultimate aim of providing further education to all who desire it. To this end an adequate student grant through our credit income tax scheme would be provided.

Homes for all

The Liberal Party opposes the present Government's housing priorities because it considers them socially divisive.

They have severely cut local authority house building at a time when rising house prices have hit those trying to buy their own home; rents have been raised under the Housing Finance Act while, at the same time, wages have been frozen and then reduced by the three-day week; finally, the Government has failed to reform the mortgage system and failed to act effectively to curb land hoarding and speculation.

Liberal policy would fundamentally change our system of housing finance and property taxation, providing help to householders and tenants on an equal basis and concentrating a two-pronged atack on the housing shortage by building more houses and preserving as many houses as are inhabitable. In particular, we would end the divisiveness and inefficiency in the national housing programme by encouraging more flexible and enterprising policies which will allow for greater co-operation between local authorities, particularly in respect of the homeless, and an enhanced role for self-build organisations, possibly through the establishment of Government-approved consortia.

These are our proposals:

1 Freeze all rents during the period of economic restraint.

2 Repeal the Housing Finance Act and replace it with a genuinely fair rents system geared to true housing costs and pay a single housing allowance to tenants and householders on an equal basis automatically through the tax credit system.

3 Make all new urban office building contingent on the grant of a certificate of social need and concentrate the resources of the building industry on the housing programme.

4 Institute a crash programme of house-building in both public and private sectors with full use being made of industrialised building techniques.

W

5 Concentrate on housing renovation and repairs wherever possible, rather than on wholesale demolition.

6 Oblige Building Societies to stabilise interest rates by drawing on their reserves. Introduce new types of mortgage for first home buyers with low level initial repayments which rise with increased incomes and the cost of living.

7 Withdraw tax concessions and improvement grants for second home purchasers.

8 Give greater financial encouragement and responsibility to Tenants' Co-operatives and Housing Associations.

9 Give local authorities power to acquire at cost price those properties which have stood unoccupied for three years.

PAYING FOR SECURITY – A RADICAL REDISTRIBUTION OF WEALTH

To finance all these proposals, there must be a radical redistribution of income and inherited wealth, the credit income tax proposals being the principal instrument for the former, and the Liberal proposal for a Gifts and Inheritance Tax, to replace Estate Duty and related in its incidence and rate to the gift or legacy and the wealth of the recipient, for the latter.

Site Value Rating

We must also ensure that a proper contribution is made by those who own property and land.

As a means of reforming the present rating system which penalises those who improve their property while subsidising those who let it decay, Liberals have long advocated that rates should be levied on the value of the site only, and not on the value of the site and buildings as now. This would enable much of the present burden of rates to be shifted from householders.

The rating of site values would also be levied on land which, after proper inquiry, had been zoned for development but which had not been developed within a reasonable period. This would be an effective punitive measure against land hoarders and speculators.

Site value rating also recognises the undisputed fact that today a major source of wealth resides in development land and property rather than in income. Over a period of years there is no doubt that the rating of land values could gradually replace income tax as a main source of revenue. It would also recover for the community a proportion of the increased value of land created by mere assignment of planning consent.

THE STATUS OF WOMEN

Liberals will put particular emphasis on securing equality of opportunity and equal treatment for women. As a nation we can no longer afford to ignore the talent and energies of half our population as we have done so often in the past. We would legislate to ensure equal opportunities for women in all spheres of activity particularly in regard to employment, remuneration and social interaction. In particular we advocate the establishment of an independent Sex Discrimination Board, establishment of the principle of equal pay for work of equal value, tougher legislation to outlaw restrictive and discriminatory practices in industry and equal social security benefits for men and women, with adequate provision for maternity leave. Our aim is to provide the opportunity for women who so wish freely to seek satisfying goals other than a lifetime of childbearing.

CIVIL LIBERTIES – A BILL OF RIGHTS

Every person is entitled to protection from arbitrary interference in his personal and private affairs. Liberals are concerned that in our increasingly complex and bureaucratic society, fundamental freedoms should not be impaired or the individual citizen put at a disadvantage in his dealings with authority. Hence we have long advocated that minority and individual liberties should be guaranteed through a Bill of Rights effective in all parts of the United Kingdom and at all levels of

Government and administration. Among protected guarantees should be the freedom of speech and assembly, the right to a fair trial, and protection against discrimination on the grounds of race, religion, sex or national or social origin. We would establish a small Claims Court where redress for minor injustices could be sought without recourse to the complexity and delay of the court circuit. Finally, we oppose any laws which penalise people retrospectively for actions done in the past, when through lapse of time they have become immune from prosecution or administrative action.

IMMIGRATION AND RACE RELATIONS

The Liberal Party regards freedom of movement as an important basic principle. However, since 1965 we have accepted that a densely-populated country such as ours cannot, at present, adequately cater for all those people who wish to come here. Accordingly we have supported a system of regulation whereby would-be immigrants are allowed to enter the United Kingdom only if they possess a work voucher showing that they have an actual job waiting for them or they possess particular skills which are needed in this country. While opposing illegal entry we strongly oppose the retrospective provisions of the 1971 Immigration Act and would take immediate action to remove these and other discriminatory clauses in that legislation.

We believe that we have a primary obligation to citizens of the United Kingdom and colonies, and also to Commonwealth citizens whose right to register as UK citizens after five years' residence in this country was removed by the 1971 Act and should be reinstated. We believe that a Royal Commission should urgently examine and clarify the rights of UK and Commonwealth citizens on the lines outlined above. In the meantime husbands and children from Uganda should be allowed to join refugees who have settled here. We are opposed to all forms of racial discrimination. The goal of integration is of critical importance and there should be a separate Minister for Community Relations and greater financial support for the Community Relations Commission.

THE FUTURE OF OUR COMMUNITY

The Environment

Liberals recognise the need for an urgent re-appraisal of the use man is making of his material environment. We are concerned that in the present economic crisis panic measures should not be taken for the sake of short-sighted expediency, that might cause irreversible damage.

The Liberal Party was the first to adopt a National Population Policy which includes free family planning advice as part of the NHS and a programme of education stressing the need for responsible parenthood in this era of scarce resources.

We insist on stringent controls on the use of all potential pollutants and in particular the establishment of a regionalised Pollution Inspectorate with investigatory and punitive powers over the use of noxious substances. In particular we are concerned that there should be the maximum recycling of all materials and that individuals and communities should have the legal means to resist, where necessary, threats to their environment from Government or commercial agencies.

The protection of our environment must be extended to the preservation of natural resources including our sources of energy, our landscape and our countryside. We strongly support the principles of nature conservation and assert that the co-ordination of policies in other fields such as agriculture and transport must be pursued urgently.

Finally, the global environment, of which Britain is only a small part, can only be permanently preserved through international co-operation and support for United Nations environmental agencies.

Transport

Transport is inextricably bound up with overall development and must be integrated with national, regional and town and country planning. Our main priority must be to provide for integrated policies which acknowledge the changed roles of our various modes of transport. Conservative and Labour Governments have consistently worked on a piece-meal basis, Liberals assert that it is time to work out an overall strategy. In particular we advocate the prohibition of any further closures of railways and waterways until a study group has reported on the possibilities of further transferring freight carriage to rail and water. A new attitude must be taken to our railways which takes into account social and environmental factors as well as capital expenditure.

Transport has become a social service in many cases, particularly the regions and rural areas. We believe that County Councils should collaborate with the Ministry of Transport in promoting research studies into rural transport needs and preparing schemes for meeting them. Liberals hold the view that there must be a limitation of access for private vehicles to designated areas of city and town centres. Adequate parking facilities on the outskirts must be complemented by free, reliable public transport within these areas. Liberals would also establish Regional Transport Authorities to determine priorities of investment in all forms of transport, co-ordinate long-term planning of main roads, ports, airports, railways and inland waterways. Immediate attention must be given to assess the impact of increased oil prices upon our transport infrastructure.

AGRICULTURE AND THE COMMON MARKET

Liberals are well aware of the grave difficulties being experienced at the present time in many sections of the agricultural community. The Government, so far, has been deaf to the Liberal warnings and appeals concerning the plight of the dairy farming and livestock sections of agriculture. This could result in an actual food shortage in this country, particularly with regard to fresh foods arising from the excessive slaughter of breeding animals by farmers who, overwhelmed by the high cost of feedingstuffs and the very high interest rates, believe that their future is extremely insecure.

Help should be given to these sections of agriculture immediately, for the sake of both the farmer and the consumer. To build up to a sufficient level of profitability for the farmer and maintain a decent basic price for the consumer can be achieved in a variety of ways. One way which is capable of instant implementation is to compensate the consumer by raising pensions, and increasing family allowances which should also be extended to the oldest child. In our view it is necessary to create a farm structure which will encourage young men to enter agriculture as a career, with a possibility of achieving management and ownership. In the immediate term an improved wage structure for the industry must be established. The Agricultural Credit Corporation must also be swiftly expanded into a Land Bank. Loans would be available at a fixed rate of interest for projects which might properly be regarded as medium-term, in particular for the purchase of livestock and for projects now covered by Government grants, but should not be available for the purchase of farms or of land. In the present climate, it is essential that United Kingdom Marketing Boards should be retained and voluntary co-operatives encouraged. The Annual Price Review should certainly be retained but be coupled with a five-year strategic review.

In order to help keep down the price of land and make farms more readily available to genuine farmers, agricultural losses should no longer, in any circumstances, be allowable against profits from other businesses. Furthermore, Estate Duty relief should be restricted to bona fide agriculturalists. This would help prevent the major transference at the present time of city assets into agricultural land. Agricultural land in productive use would be zero-rated under our policy for Site Value Rating.

The Common Agricultural Policy of the European Economic Community must represent a just balance between the interests of consumers, efficient producers and international trading. The widening of the Community has already resulted in a less protectionist attitude but Britain must make an all-out effort to broaden and deepen this attitude. In the UK we do not have the problem, which has existed in the Community, of uneconomic farming units and we accept the need for measures to reduce their number. Finally, Liberals believe that there should be a rapid expansion of domestic production and an energetic drive by this country to secure allies in the Common Market for a major modification of the Common Agricultural Policy, so as to secure reasonably-priced food for the consumer and an acceptable return for the farmer.

POWER, PEOPLE AND THE COMMUNITY

The Liberal Party believes in devolution, decentralisation and electoral reform. We favour the immediate implementation of the Kilbrandon recommendation to establish elected Parliaments in Scotland and Wales and to this effect a Bill has already been introduced into the House of Commons by Liberal MP, Jo Grimond.

In the long term we would establish a federal system of Government for the United Kingdom with power in domestic matters transferred to Parliaments in Scotland, Wales and Northern Ireland and Provincial Assemblies in England. The Westminster Parliament would then become a Federal Parliament with a reformed second chamber in which the majority of members would be elected on a regional basis. If Britain is to have effective and successful centres of commerce and finance outside London there must be a real devolution of political and economic power to the regions. Recent Local Government reform has removed decision-making even further from the people. We advocate the setting up of Neighbourhood Councils below the District Councils to act as efficient transmitters of protest and suggestion from the community.

Liberals would introduce proportional representation by the single transferable vote for all elections. The present electoral system buttresses the discredited 'two-party system' of confrontation. Electoral Reform, while giving fairer representation to different sections, will make co-operation between them easier. The success of proportional representation in Northern Ireland in uniting a divided community through a power-sharing executive is strong testimony for its introduction in Britain as a whole to heal the rifts in our society.

Parliament has lost touch with the country. It must be brought back to the people and its proceedings opened up to the broadcasting media. Its formality must not deter improvements in the organisation of business to make Parliament more efficient and effective, with really full-time members elected for fixed five-year periods.

Liberals urge the establishment of direct elections to a European Parliament which would give full democratic power of control over Community activities.

Maximum opportunity must be offered at all levels for involving citizens in the process of Government, through the fullest possible provision of information.

EUROPE AND THE WORLD

We must not allow our present national crisis to let us forget the immense problems of instability in the world, that have loomed and threatened in the last few months. The need for international co-operation and understanding has never been more pressing and the contribution of Britain to building a better world as well as our hopes of a better life in these islands depend on partnership with our democratic neighbours.

The European Economic Community

Liberals have always insisted on the duty of Britain to play a leading role in transforming Western Europe from warring rivalry into a united community, hence our consistent support for British membership of the Common Market. Furthermore, it is only as a full participant in the world's largest trading entity that we can hope to solve our chronic balance of payments problem and at the same time develop the political unity that will guarantee peace and free us from the spectre of domination by the super powers.

We deplore the delay in joining the Common Market for which Conservative and Labour Governments were equally to blame, but we are even more critical of the narrow-minded nationalism of many so-called 'internationalists' in the Labour Party who still shun their responsibility to represent their constituents in the European Parliament. We also condemn the Conservative Government for abdicating their great opportunity to develop the Community in a democratic and outward-looking manner in favour of meek compliance with the interests of the

French Government. The present Common Market structure is not what we voted for and the Liberal representatives in the European Parliament have lost no opportunity to point the way in which we feel the Community should develop. Liberals are thus effective but constructive critics of the policies of the Common Market. We want to reform its institutions to see real power exercised by an elected European Parliament. We want to see the progressive reduction of the protectionist aspects of the Common Agriculture Policy, an imaginative and effective regional policy and the harmonisation, not bureaucratisation, of economic and social policies, for the benefit of all members. Finally, we want to see the adoption of an outward-looking trade policy towards the rest of the world and particularly the developing countries. We believe that the great purposes of the Community can be achieved with far-sightedness and vision.

Foreign Affairs and Defence

Looking beyond the EEC we are in favour of the maintenance of NATO until such time as a new European security system based on mutual withdrawal and the mutual reduction of forces in the East and West has been successfully negotiated. Within this limit we support efforts at detente and in particular the Ostpolitik of the West German Government. We are opposed to the admission to the European Community of any country which has not a democratic form of government, and are unhappy about the association with NATO of countries like Portugal and Greece which are not democratic. The purpose of NATO should be to defend democracy.

But the maintenance of our traditional alliances is also of critical importance if we are to return stability to world commodity and money markets and absorb the massive disruption that has and will continue to be caused by the quadrupling of oil prices. Positive international agreements are vital to bring a new radical world monetary framework that could save the world from damaging economic recession and exacerbated racial tension. Finally, it is essential that through a new monetary framework Britain and the developed world recognise the plight of the third world and begin to grant realistic exchanges for raw materials and commodities that will raise the Third World from starvation and deprivation.

CONCLUSION

This is the Liberal Party's programme for national reconstruction. It is fundamental because we believe that the crisis which faces us as a nation is deep-seated and requires a fundamental response. It is ambitious because the multiple crisis that faces us offers the opportunity to put the past behind us and embark on a new era of reconstruction. Above all it is idealistic because we must raise our sights beyond selfish personal concerns, we must stop internal feuds which weaken and divide us and look to a future without class conflicts, partisan bitterness and excessive self-criticism.

The Scottish National Party

The Scottish National Party, in its manifesto, envisages ever-improving living standards for the people of Scotland based on North Sea oil revenue and a Scottish government. Oil and gas revenue would be used to finance what would otherwise be budgetary deficits. Ideally a Scottish government would restrict oil and gas production to prolong the life of reserves.

The manifesto asked: 'Do you wish to be rich Scots or poor British?' and added: 'The enormous wealth of the oil and gas fields off the Scottish coast, allied to our other vast resources, offers ever-improving living standards to the people of Scotland when they demand a Scottish government.'

The SNP would restore Scottish national sovereignty by establishing a democratic Scottish Parliament within the Commonwealth.

In the short term there would be a price freeze on essential food. An oil-rich Scotland could afford to look after its old folk. The SNP aimed at a retirement pension of £15.50 weekly for single persons and £25 for married couples. There would be a substantial family allowance for the first child, which currently secured no allowance.

Jurisdiction within Scotland would be exercised exclusively by Scottish courts, and the judiciary would be independent of the executive. There should be an end to hereditary and other titles.

'As an independent country we will have our own diplomatic missions abroad, and we will travel as Scots with Scottish passports. We will be represented at the United Nations and be a member of the Commonwealth. We firmly believe that a special relationship should be established among the countries of the British Isles.'

The SNP would not have nuclear weapons or bases on Scottish soil or in Scottish territorial waters. Existing nuclear bases were sited without the consent of the Scottish people.

There should be a referendum on whether Scotland remained in the EEC. A Scottish government would not necessarily be bound by agreements made on behalf of the people of Scotland by a British government.

On oil, the manifesto continued: 'All Scottish oil will normally be landed in Scotland and control over its ultimate destination will be vested in the National Assembly. The pace of oil developments will be related to Scottish needs (currently 11 million tons a year) together with such additional production as may be necessary to provide additional revenues for investment capital, having full regard to the need to conserve resources over generations rather than decades.

'The wealth represented by Scotland's oil is a capital asset and will in general be used to form other capital assets rather than to finance current expenditure, although in the early years, social expenditure will have special priority until the working population of Scotland enjoys an acceptable and equitable standard of living.

'Investment in the Scottish economy of revenues from Scotland's oil will be geared towards providing a strong economic base, capable of sustaining acceptable standards for all Scottish citizens, irrespective of further oil revenues. In other words the quality of life in Scotland will not be allowed to remain dependent on oil revenues.'

The Communist Party

Three aims need to be achieved in this Election: a Tory defeat, the winning of a Labour Government and the return of Communist MPs. Communist MPs and the big Communist vote are needed to strengthen the fight for the radical changes in policy essential to solve the crisis and defend and extend our democratic rights.

The Tories are the wreckers, the enemies of democracy, parading their Red bogey as a screen to hide their vicious attacks on democratic rights by such measures as the Industrial Relations Act, the abolition of collective bargaining and the imposition of Government-decreed wages.

There is a way out of the crisis, without decades of grim austerity. But it means changing the way this country is run, challenging big business, and shifting economic and political power decisively in favour of the people. This is what the Communist Party fights for. That is why it is singled out for attack by the lying anti-Red propaganda of the Tory Government.

There can be no solution to the crisis without radical changes in policy. This means a programme of action which puts the people first, challenges the power of big business, extends democratic rights, and advances living standards at the expense of profits. This is what Communists stand for.

Abolish Phase Three; introduce strict price controls and massive food subsidies; increase wages and pensions.

Emergency measures to tackle the balance of payments problem.

Tax the rich. A heavy wealth tax should be introduced immediately to raise £500m a year.

Defend and extend democratic rights.

Wanted—a nationally owned, integrated energy system covering coal, gas, oil, electricity and nuclear power.

Get out of the Common Market immediately and unconditionally.

These policies involve sweeping changes but they are long overdue. They would cope with today's problems and at the same time open the way to Socialism, which alone can provide a lasting solution to the crisis.

327

Plaid Cymru

Self government for Wales on the lines of the Kilbrandon proposals is the only hope for the future of the nation. Wales today is helpless and prostrate, tied to a bankrupt, out-of-date British state. The Wales of the future with a parliament of its own would be free to use its enormous potential wealth—coal, oil, water—and to build a prosperous and just country.

The Kilbrandon-style parliament falls short of the final aim, but as a first step it is vital. Wales is a rich country in natural resources, industrial skills and talent but there is no guarantee that Wales benefits. A Welsh coal board should develop modernised industry over the next 50 years, with wages matching conditions.

A Welsh Mineral Resources Board should own and control all oil, gas and mineral resources.

A National Development Authority should be responsible for developing 12 major growth areas. The medium sized 100-acre farm should be the basic unit of Welsh farming. A government-financed Land Development Bank should lend capital at low interest rates to help young farmers.

Equality for both languages must be ensured. A permanent language commission should be set up to encourage the teaching of Welsh and its use in broadcasting. Both languages should be used in administration.

There should be a national minimum wage tied to the cost of living, with free collective bargaining within income bands agreed by unions and governments, and a strict control of prices and unearned income.

There should be greater worker-participation in smaller companies and ownership of large companies to be in the hands of the employees. Vital industries should be nationalised with greater accountability to parliament.

National Front

The National Front is a fully constituted political party pledged to win power by the ballot box. It has no illusions that this will be achieved except by many years of hard struggle, and it straightaway is distinguished from other parties by offering its workers only toil and sacrifice. It is financed, neither by big business, as in the case of the Tories, nor by the unions, as in the case of Labour, but only by the subscriptions and voluntary contributions of ordinary British men and women.

The National Front is a party of British nationalism being pledged to work for the restoration of full national sovereignty for Britain in all affairs. It is a party of British nationalism as it stands strongly for the preservation of Britain's national identity with respect to the composition of her people, her culture and her traditional way of life. Finally it is a national party in so far as it seeks the full unity of the nation above divisions of class, faction, and vested interests. The National Front is a party of patriotism believing that the values of patriotism are essential in maintaining the cohesion and morale of the nation.

The National Front works for the withdrawal of Britain from the Common Market.

It believes that Britain's destiny lies with the British Commonwealth and resolves that every effort should be made to repair the damage done by recent Governments to Commonwealth unity. The present multi-racial conception of Commonwealth is unrealistic, and the Commonwealth should be reformed into a partnership of white countries.

The National Front advocates protection of the home market for most manufactured products as an essential basis for national industrial recovery and full employment.

The National Front upholds the wish of the majority of the British people for Britain to remain a white country and for this reason opposes all coloured immigration into Britain. It further advocates the repatriation, by the most humane means possible, of those coloured immigrants already here together with their descendants and dependants.

Index to Candidates

Those elected are shown in capital letters

Index to Constituencies

343

INDEX TO CONSTITUENCIES